•

The Losers

•

PAUL D. BETHEL

•

The Losers

•

The definitive report, by an eyewitness,

of the Communist Conquest of Cuba

and the Soviet Penetration in

Latin America

ARLINGTON HOUSE   *New Rochelle, New York*

SECOND PRINTING, JULY 1970

SBN 87000-053-5
Library of Congress Catalog Card Number 69-16944

MANUFACTURED IN THE UNITED STATES OF AMERICA

Contents

Dedicated to my children
DAVID *and* PAULETTE

Preface

The first edition of this book is being published exactly ten years following Fidel Castro's rise to power in Cuba. As Press Attache to the American Embassy in Havana, I was privileged to witness United States policy in action and to participate in many decisions which affected the course of the United States toward Cuba and, eventually, Latin America. This book is critical of U.S. policy wherever we need more protest, not less, for sound policy develops only from strong criticism. The price the United States has paid for the lodgment of Soviet power in the Caribbean has proved prohibitive; confusion and division in our State Department and the White House may last indefinitely, but the United States cannot tolerate Soviet invasion of this hemisphere indefinitely.

What I, the author, have attempted to do is to show to my countrymen how Cuba's plight relates to our own national fate. The Soviet military and political base in Cuba has the fixed purpose of continued aggression against, and subversion of, free governments the world over. The final target, without question, is the United States itself. How successful has been this onslaught may be seen in the ties that now exist between a Communist Cuba and anti-democratic militants in the United States—both black and white. The aim is total; this force of conquest will never stop of its own. It will be stopped only if there is mobilized a stronger resolve in the United States and the Americas to help Cuba become free and thereby keep our own domain free and inviolate. We cannot have the one without the other.

I want, especially, to thank Señor Raul Granja for his tireless research and his determination to help me make this book accurate in detail and compelling in thought. I also owe a debt of gratitude to José Antonio Lanuza, who was especially helpful in those sections of the book dealing with Chile and Guatemala. Last but not least, my gratitude to my wife, Diana, who not only typed the manuscript of "The Losers," but two other books written by me as well—"Cuba y los Estados Unidos," published by Editorial Juventud, Spain; and "O Trabalho Em Cuba," published by O Cruzeiro, Brazil.

Finally, I want to express my gratitude to the U.S. Citizens Committee for a Free Cuba and its President, Ambassador Spruille Braden, for appointing me Executive Director of the Committee and editor of its publications.

BOOK I

Retreat to Revolution

CHAPTER 1

•

Subversion Unlimited

•

IN JANUARY OF 1966, President Lyndon B. Johnson was busy with his "peace offensive," dispatching Administration aides to the far capitals of the world to discuss ways and means to settle the Vietnam war. That same month, Senator William Fulbright, Chairman of the Senate Foreign Relations Committee, initiated televised hearings which he and several of his colleagues, among them Senator Wayne Morse, hoped would bring public pressures to bear on the Administration and force Mr. Johnson to pull out of Vietnam.

Neither President Johnson nor Senator Fulbright needed to look any farther than Cuba, just ninety miles from Florida, to find out how serious the Communists were in meeting their overtures. A meeting of 600 Communists from 82 countries in Asia, Africa, and Latin America (called the Tricontinental Conference) was in progress in Havana, whose overriding purpose was not peace, but the expansion of the Vietnam conflict into a world-wide war of subversion and terror against the United States.[1]

Nor did President Johnson and Senator Fulbright need to look too hard to identify the real enemy. Russia was the chief planner, as well as omnipresent manager, of the Havana conference. On December 9, just a month before the delegates assembled in Havana, Soviet Foreign Minister Andrei A. Gromyko had made the fact plain. He rose in the chambers of the Supreme Soviet and briefed its members on the forthcoming Havana conference. "The Soviet Union," quoted *Tass*, "in taking part in the Havana conference . . . will do everything it can to help consolidate the front of the struggle against imperialist aggression." Gromyko described the participants as "an ample forum of representatives of anti-colonialist countries and anti-imperialist forces."

Head of the 40-man Soviet delegation to Havana was Sharaf R. Ra-

11

shidov. A candidate member of the Presidium of the Central Committee of the Communist Party of the Soviet Union and First Secretary of the Party Central Committee of Uzbekistan, Rashidov's position at the Havana conference carried the full weight of Soviet policy. That policy was not peaceful, but belligerent, reflecting the mood of the Soviet leaders, Alexei N. Kosygin and Leonid I. Brezhnev, who cabled a message to the Havana delegates which was openly hostile toward the United States.

The message said, in part: "Today, Havana attracts the attention of all fighters against the forces of imperialist aggression and colonialism, and for the national and social liberation of all peoples . . . U.S. imperialists are challenging all progressive forces." They zeroed in on this hemisphere, saying: "The imperialists act arbitrarily in relation to the Latin American peoples.

Rashidov took it from there. "Our purpose," he said to the world assembly of Communists in Havana, "is the formation of a united front against the common enemy." The common enemy, he said, "is international imperialism, headed by the United States." Delegate Rashidov spoke with a candor exceeded only by his impudence. "The Soviet Union," he said, "is responding to movements of national liberation." He then named Venezuela, Guatemala, Peru, the Dominican Republic, French, British, and Dutch Guiana, and even the U.S. island of Puerto Rico as targets for subversion by a Russian-directed Cuba.

The vital relationship between the Vietnam war and Soviet global designs is apparent in several other events recorded at the Havana conference. Among the first to speak at Havana was Nguyen Van Tien, the chief delegate of the Vietnamese National Liberation Front (Vietcong). He demanded world Communist support for "a war imposed on us by the Yankee imperialists and their lackeys." Tran Danh Tuyen, the North Vietnamese delegate, warned that victory in South Vietnam, or, alternatively, the neutralization of U.S. military forces there, was a prerequisite to the success of projected "wars of liberation" on other continents—the purpose for which the Havana conference was called. He couched that warning in terms "of the vital bearing of the Vietnam question on our three continents, and on the present situation of the entire world. . . ."

Hanoi's delegate to Havana laid down conditions for "peace" that could have no meaning other than the capitulation of the United States. One was that the United States recognize the Communist puppet, the National Liberation Front of South Vietnam (the political arm of the Vietcong), "as the only genuine representative of South Vietnam." With this precedent established, the Communist world will have achieved a key victory and the free world a stunning loss, for we would thus undercut ourselves in Latin America where the majority of countries have been battling National Liberation Fronts for years.

This fact was brought home with the establishment in Havana of a Tricontinental Committee to Aid Vietnam, and the willing adherence of Latin American Communists to its aims.* In a grisly episode, Pedro Medina, leader of the Venezuelan National Liberation Front (NLF) literally passed the hat to raise money for his Vietcong allies. The hat was the helmet of a U.S. pilot shot down over North Vietnam, and it was first ceremoniously given over in Havana by the National Liberation Front of Vietnam to Medina and his Venezuelan NLF. In a grandiose gesture of "solidarity" with the Vietcong brothers, Medina explained: "The Venezuelan NLF gives the helmet to the Tricontinental Committee to Aid Vietnam." He continued: "We will wage a campaign . . . on the island of Cuba and in Latin America, and we shall then carry it to each continent to give more importance and more brilliance to the week of solidarity with Vietnam. . . ."

Fidel Castro jubilantly accepted from Danh Thi Thanh a ring made of the wreckage of the plane. Danh Thi Thanh had been trumpeted by Radio Hanoi as the militiawoman who shot down the American aircraft. According to Radio Hanoi, "The Cuban Premier clasped and raised her hand, and, amid stormy applause, warmly praised the spirit of Vietnamese women."

The global scope of the subversive conference, and its bearing on the Vietnamese war, went almost unnoticed in American newspapers, and was virtually ignored by President Johnson and the Senate Foreign Relations Committee. This was true of another aspect of the conference, one much closer to home. For, higher on the agenda for the 600 conferees in Havana was the plan, repeated in scores of speeches and resolutions, to step up the pace of terror and subversion in Latin America. The means by which this is to be achieved was laid out by the Russian delegate for all to see—diplomatic friendship as a cover for class warfare.

"We believe," said Sharaf R. Rashidov, "that relations among sovereign states with different public systems should be based on peaceful coexistence." But he immediately added the important message: "It is clear that there is not, nor can there be, any peaceful coexistence between the oppressed peoples and their oppressors." In other words, to the Russians, "peaceful coexistence" represents formal relations at the diplomatic level with the very governments its agents are seeking to destroy internally through subversion and terror.

An important Soviet aim was achieved at the Havana conference. This

---

*It is significant that Cuba had established its own support for Vietnam one year before the Tricontinental Conference was convened. On April 7, 1965, Castro's *Prensa Latina* announced the formation in Havana of a "Latin American Commission to Aid Vietnam," with Hilda Gadea, the former wife of Cuba's guerrilla leader Major Ernesto "Che" Guevara, named as Secretary General. Emphasizing the hemispheric scope of the Commission, *Prensa Latina* reported other members of the Commission as representing Paraguay, Mexico, Bolivia, Dominican Republic, Argentina, and Panama.

was to give major direct support to guerrilla leaders, rather than to the established Communist parties of their countries, in appreciation of the tactics employed by Fidel Castro in 1957-58 in Cuba, and by the Vietcong in South Vietnam. "The real stars," according to the correspondent of the Paris newspaper, *Le Monde*, who had journeyed to Havana for the conference, "were the lean, bronzed men who arrived after so many detours, from the guerrilla camps of the four 'fighting fronts' of the hemisphere: Guatemala, Venezuela, Colombia, Peru. . . ."

The Communist paper, *Nepszabadsag*, of Budapest, also commented on the military nature of the delegations. It emphasized that the conference was not in the hands of "catastrophic politicians," but in the firm grip of Castro-type revolutionaries.

The conference was clearly aimed at all-out guerrilla war, rather than "politics." Russia's expectations for taking over Latin America, observed *Le Monde*, lie "in direct action, and more precisely in armed action. With the exception of those in Venezuela and Colombia, the orthodox Communist parties in Latin America have shown up to now no great enthusiasm for guerrilla wars."

The stage having been set, Sharaf R. Rashidov told the conference what was expected of it. "The Soviet delegation," he said, according to a *Tass* dispatch, "came to this conference to promote in every conceivable way the unity of anti-imperialist forces of the three continents, so as to unfold on a still greater scale our common struggle against imperialism, colonialism, and neo-colonialism."

Under Soviet guidance, various committees went to work on social, political, and economic affairs. These provided the temporary machinery for what was to emerge as the headquarters from which to wage Mr. Rashidov's "common struggle against imperialism." The headquarters, the Soviet delegate made clear, should be established in Havana.

Cuba, under complete Soviet control for years, was a natural choice as the operational headquarters for world-wide subversion and wars of "national liberation." Castro is fanatically anti-American and in the pocket of the Russians. Furthermore, Cuba had developed, under Soviet direction, an apparatus of subversion already active in the hemisphere. Following the Cuban missile crisis of October, 1962, those missile sites and camps which had been detected were converted into guerrilla training camps, and new camps have also been constructed, employing the most sophisticated means of instruction. The U.S. Senate Internal Security Subcommittee listed ten such camps as early as 1963.[2]

By the time President Johnson was concentrating heavily on the Vietnamese war in early 1966, these camps had grown to 43 in number, and trained as many as 10,000 activists each year—guerrillas, terrorists, propagandists, experts in sabotage and espionage, and specialists in radio equipment. At the time of the Havana Conference, Russian, Czech, Red Chinese and Vietcong "technicians" had been in Cuba for well over two years, working smoothly and thoroughly.

When the guerrilla candidate arrives in Havana by clandestine route, he is given a questionnaire on areas and personalities vulnerable to subversion techniques. He is asked, for example, about targets for sabotage and the terrain surrounding those targets, about homosexual tendencies among members of his hometown police force, army units, and politicians, and about tax irregularities condoned by local bureaucrats. This information, checked and rechecked by contacts in each country, provides a starting point for campaigns of subversion.

Venezuela, under almost constant attack for years by Cuban-supported guerrillas and terrorists, discovered in October, 1965, that the Communists had established an efficient underground arms factory near the capital city of Caracas. Venezuela's security police raided an innocent-looking, one-story farmhouse on the outskirts of the village of Lagunita, about 20 miles southwest of Caracas, to find beneath it a sizeable arms factory. Minister of the Interior Gonzalo Barrios said that it contained "enough explosives to blow up the entire city of Caracas." He added: "Specialists from Havana, Moscow, and Peking are trying to get into Venezuela to execute terrorist operations planned for 1966—what they called 'the year of explosives'."[3]

The full effects of that discovery had just about impinged itself on public consciousness when neighboring Colombia found that clandestine arms actually were being manufactured in the machine shops of its Ministry of Public Works. Nine Castroites were arrested. It is not known how many others got away. Castro-trained men had also infiltrated the notorious bandit gangs of Colombia, extorting more than a million dollars in ransom from relatives of 148 Colombians—mostly ranchers—who had been kidnapped during a period of one year. Alarmed, the Colombian National Association of Cattlemen took an unprecedented step. It agreed that each member would contribute five percent of his income to the government so as better to combat Castro-trained guerrillas.

In the remote valleys and mountains of Peru, Venezuela, Colombia, and Guatemala, minor government officials and pro-government peasants are found murdered—Vietcong style. The book of Castro's guerrilla chief, Major Ernesto "Che" Guevara, *Guerrilla Warfare,* is the handbook for Latin American rebel chiefs. It preaches the same tactics urged by the Havana conference, "to sow seeds of discord everywhere and keep the oligarchs busy putting out the fires."

How busy the law enforcement officers are being kept by those forces was indicated by Colombia's Director of Criminal Investigation. He found that, of 1,800 known nationals from Peru, Venezuela, and Colombia who had received terrorist training in Cuba over a six-month period, 750 came from Colombia. Castroite guerrillas have gone so far as to publish maps dividing Colombia into five "independent republics," demonstrating how far advanced they are politically. In one "republic," Marquetalia, the guerrillas managed to assert considerable pressure on the population. As in Vietnam, the populace lived, alternately, under government and guerrilla control.

The collaboration between Cuba and the Soviet-bloc embassies in Latin America subversion is exemplified by Ecuador, which broke off relations with Cuba, Czechoslovakia, and Poland back in April, 1962. After an uprising launched by youth organizations, which took their inspiration and directions from the Havana radio, a government investigation disclosed that the Czech legation had been handing over funds to the Ecuadorian Communist Party, funds obtained through the sale of Skoda trucks and other Communist-bloc products. Poland was also involved.

Bolivia broke relations with Czechoslovakia in October, 1964, when the Czech embassy in La Paz was shown to have delivered 500,000 Bolivian pesos to rebellious tin miners. The money was used to purchase weapons and to buy votes for Communist candidates in labor elections.

The Soviet Union has backed up its political "investment" in Cuba and Latin America by manipulating the United Nations. It has striven constantly to divert complaints against Cuban subversion lodged by members of the Organization of American States (the regional political grouping of 20 nations of the Western Hemisphere) from the OAS to the UN Security Council. For example, when in July, 1964, the OAS found Cuba guilty of subversive aggression against Venezuela, Soviet UN delegate P. Morozov immediately objected to the findings, claiming that only the UN Security Council is competent to define aggression. His hope, to bring the entire matter of Cuban aggression before the Security Council where the Soviet veto could block any punitive measures, failed because the United Nations charter recognizes the competence of regional organizations to deal with matters affecting their members. Nevertheless, the Soviet Union would have the world believe that Communist subversion, in the words directed to the UN Security Council by delegate Morozov, represents merely "the struggle which the peoples of Latin American countries are waging for national liberation."[4]

The Soviet Union has a direct as well as an indirect hand in subverting Latin America. According to a broadcast from Moscow, in August of 1965 Lumumba University (located in Moscow) is training thousands of Latin American students. Beamed to Latin America in the Quechua language of the Indians of Peru, Bolivia and Ecuador, the broadcast said that when these students return to their homelands, "they will teach their brothers the modern techniques they have learned. But they will do more than teach . . . they will fight alongside peasants and humble people to ensure that their countries have freedom."[5]

The Cuban training program is coordinated with international Communist subversion. Vietcong, Soviet, Red Chinese, and Spanish Communist instructors in Cuba teach not only Latin American recruits. They have a vigorous program for Africans, as well. Cuban Negro instructors have been used to train African guerrilla candidates in special camps established in the Provinces of Las Villas and Oriente. Defected Castro military officers stated, in 1966, that 200 Africans returned to the Dark Continent through Dar es Salaam, after eight months of "leadership training" in the Minas del Frío guerrilla camp in Cuba. This testimony came to light in an encounter on Lake Tanganyika on September 17, 1965, when a Congolese government patrol boat intercepted and sank a troop-and-supply boat which had been running Cuban-trained Congolese guerrillas from Tanzania into the eastern Congo. The same year, 27 Senegalese were tried in the African city of Dakar and, during the trial, they were found to have completed eight months of training in Cuba.

Castro's Soviet-financed fishing fleet is especially useful in bringing guerrilla troops to Cuba and reinfiltrating them to their homelands. This fleet has been sighted off the coast of Yucatán in Mexico, and Angola and Ghana in Africa. In searching for details concerning the use of Castro's fishing fleet for subversive purposes, this writer found them in an interview with a Cuban marine engineer who had defected from the Castro regime and was residing in Miami. The engineer, Celestino García Rojas, told me that "Cuban patrol boats and fishing vessels are continually introducing arms and men into Mexican territory." He added the important information: "Refrigerator compartments on Cuba's Lambda-class fishing boats have been enlarged to a depth of 25 feet and a width of 15 feet to provide more space for infiltrating guerrillas into other countries." García Rojas added: "I know, because I worked on the designs." Former Rebel Army Lieutenant Noel Salas Santos provided additional details regarding the military nature of Castro's fishing fleet. Salas, former commander of a guerrilla training camp at San Julián military base in Pinar del Río Province, broke with Castro, took asylum in the Brazilian Embassy in Havana, and came out of Cuba in the fall of 1963 in a mass release of political asylees. He said: "I personally accompanied one of the groups of Latin American guerrillas, trained under my command, to the fishing town of Arroyo de Mantua in Pinar del Río Province, and saw them off safely on the fishing boat . . ."

For all the foregoing reasons, Rashidov entered the Havana conference in January, 1966, with most of the aces up his sleeve. Russia had a proven record of success in Latin America, and success is what counts in the deadly game of world politics. Specifically, the Russians had given the lie to China's familiar attack against Moscow's "appeasement" of the United States.

Throughout the conference, the Chinese delegates kept up a drumfire of criticism of Russia's "peaceful coexistence." The criticism did not take hold, however. A special resolution on "Peaceful Coexistence" which came out of the Havana meeting stated: "Peaceful coexistence applies only to relations between states with different social and political systems. It cannot apply to relations between the social classes, between the exploited and the exploiters within separate countries, or between the oppressed peoples and their oppressors." The final Conference resolution merely parroted the words which Soviet delegate Rashidov had put forward only a few days earlier. The Russian line taken in Havana, backed by a proven record of guerrilla successes in Latin America, could hardly have been more militant.[6]

As a result of Soviet primacy in the debates, the Red Chinese sat down cheek-by-jowl on the central committee with the Russians, and together they plotted the demise of the free world. This committee, with the jaw-breaking name of the Committee of Assistance and Aid for the Peoples Fighting for Their Liberation, emerged as the central policy and strategy body for wars of subversion. In addition to Soviet and Chinese members, the Cubans were represented, along with representatives of nine other participating nations.

A General Secretariat was also established, which receives all information concerning the three continents, makes plans on the basis of the needs of each continent, and delivers its recommendations to the central committee over which the Russians and Red Chinese jointly exercise the power.

Havana was designated by the conference as headquarters for worldwide subversion until another meeting, scheduled to be held in Cairo, will establish the permanent site. Significantly, a Cuban, Captain Osmant Cienfuegos, designated Secretary General of the tricontinental organization of subversion

The vigor and sense of organization of the Communists in Latin America soon became apparent. The conference lasted from January 3 to January 15, 1966. Twenty-four hours after its adjournment, on January 16, the Latin American Solidarity Organization was set up—the first action group to come out of the conference. The 27 Latin American delegations met with Fidel Castro and Pedro Medina of Venezuela. The President of Cuba, Osvaldo Dorticós, the Cuban chiefs of staff of the three military services, and the principal Communist leaders of Cuba were also present. It was quickly decided that the organization would be permanently established in Cuba and that it would include Communist representatives from all the Latin American countries, as well as from Puerto Rico and Trinidad-Tobago.

Its operations soon commenced. On February 12, the Latin American Solidarity Organization backed a call to action by the Tricontinental Committee to Aid Vietnam. The appeal urged the recently departed delegates to launch "a wave of sabotage against Yankee interests throughout the world." It also called for "demonstrations, sit-ins, protest meetings, and denunciations in front of U.S. embassies all over the world." Sit-ins and demonstrations did, indeed, follow—not only in front of U.S. embassies, but also in front of the White House in Washington, and all over the United States, as dupes, left-wing extremists and Communist militants in this country welded together in obedience to the directions of a foreign power and a foreign ideology.

Largely ignored in this country was the direct threat made to American territory by the Viet-Cuba-Russian conclave in Havana. On February 8, Puerto Rican "freedom fighters" established a "Free Puerto Rico" embassy in Havana, and announced that a "pact of solidarity" had been signed earlier, on January 15, with the National Liberation Front of South Vietnam at its Havana headquarters. Aping Vietcong political tactics, the Puerto Rican Communists claimed that they were "recognized as the only legitimate representative of the Puerto Rican people." Shortly thereafter, 26 Latin American Communist delegations agreed to establish National Committees of Solidarity with Free Puerto Rico in their countries.

It is interesting to conjecture what reaction might have been forthcoming from Congress and the press if a "Free Iowa" or "Free Illinois" embassy had been established in Havana. Yet, Puerto Rico has commonwealth status and, as such, is no less under U.S. protection than Iowa or Illinois. But the Communist threats against Puerto Rico brought no outcry of public or official fury.

The situation in the U.S. island of Puerto Rico calls for the most serious attention. Latin American in culture and outlook, the Puerto Ricans, as Soviet delegate Sharaf R. Rashidov himself indicated, are slated for Communist penetration and terrorism.

The degree of Communist subversion in Puerto Rico is greater than is generally recognized. Some of the history was revealed by Norman Pietri, Puerto Rican delegate to the Havana conference. He said: "Armed struggle has taken place in Puerto Rico. The struggle for independence has continued in the streets, and is becoming stronger daily." Pietri continued: "The independence movement is continuously being organized among the Puerto Rican people so that we may unflinchingly confront U.S. imperialism. It is a fight waged from within the very heart of the monster. But as José Martí said, 'although we are living in the heart of the monster, we also possess David's sling.' The possibility of obtaining Puerto Rico's independence is clear and present, and we believe that, with the burgeoning of the mass movement now surfacing, Puerto Rico will also soon become a 'free territory of America.' "

On January 31, 1966, Radio Moscow broadcast what can be considered post-conference guidance concerning Puerto Rico. It is reproduced in part, below, to provide the flavor of Soviet designs on American territory:

"By using force the Yankees have dominated the island. They have turned it into their colony and, against the will of the Puerto Ricans, are using the territory of the Island for their criminal imperialistic goals. Puerto Rico has been turned into a base for the Navy, the Aviation and the North American Marines. Together with the Canal Zone of Panama, Puerto Rico is used by the Yankees to carry out their subversive activities against the Latin American countries. Its territory is also used to train Cuban counterrevolutionaries.

"Puerto Rico is an integral part of Latin America. The Puerto Ricans speak the same language. Their culture has the same origin as that of their sister countries in Latin America. Not only have they the same historic destiny but also a common enemy: Yankee imperialism.

"The Yankees have not succeeded—nor they will ever succeed—in severing Puerto Rico from Latin America and forcing the Puerto Ricans to permit that their country be used for imperialistic purposes.

"The end of the North American colonial yoke on Puerto Rico is very near. The Yankees will be forced out of the Island and Puerto Rico will occupy its rightful place in the fraternal family of the Latin American states with equal rights.

"This is Station Paz y Progreso. (Peace and Progress.) Listen to us, Puerto Rico! Listen, Puerto Rican patriots! In the name of Soviet public opinion we declare our support for your struggle to win the liberation and the independence of Puerto Rico. Listen and write to us to the following address: Radioemisora Paz y Progreso, Moscú, URSS."

Geographically, Cuba, Haiti, the Dominican Republic and Puerto Rico extend in that order in a straight line across the Caribbean from the tip of Florida to the Leeward Islands. Under Communist control, and appropriately equipped militarily, the latter three could effectively block sea and air approaches to northern South America and the Panama Canal. Cuba alone virtually commands the access routes to the Gulf of Mexico and Central America.

This is the political and strategic significance of Puerto Rico in the Communist master plan for the Western Hemisphere.

One of the most striking resolutions to come out of the Havana Conference underlined the course of subversion to be followed in this country. "In the uprisings in Watts, Los Angeles, and Chicago," the resolution stated, "the Afro-Americans openly declared that they were fighting against racism and U.S. imperialism in common cause with their Vietnamese brothers." Intruding ever deeper into the internal affairs of the United States, the Russian-managed conferees called for "the most powerful support to the Afro-Americans in their fight for human rights. . . ." The resolution described street marchers who carry Vietcong and Cuban flags in their processions in Washington, New York and elsewhere as "the progressive forces which defend this fight, and represent the American people's opposition to the dirty war waged by the Johnson administration in Vietnam." A call went out to Communists "on the three continents and throughout the world to give street marchers the most enthusiastic support."

Subversion was specifically encouraged in a follow-up broadcast from Havana. That broadcast urged American youths to dodge the draft and to "actively campaign against draft agencies" where, it said, "imperialism is forming international brigades of mercenaries in Vietnam." Even more direct appeals were made to dissidents in the United States. They should, said the communique, "boycott production and refuse to load ships, transport arms, or any kind of war materiel bound for North American troops."

Soviet preconference guidance had already been supplied in a *Pravda* editorial of December 27, 1965, just one week before the Havana Conference. Written in the peculiar Communist lingo which outlines future tactics through prose in the present tense, *Pravda* said:

"Crews jump ships and refuse to take arms and cargo to Vietnam, and meetings and demonstrations become even more massively attended. In the United States itself, tens of thousands of honest Americans express their indignation over the criminal policy of the White House."

The point is this: The overriding purpose of the Havana Conference was to organize, on a worldwide scale, subversion which is aimed finally against the United States. We are the target, it is clear, from the scores of high-pitched speeches and resolutions.

Why Fidel Castro? Why should the Soviet Union choose this wild revolutionary as a megaphone of Communist revolutions throughout the world?

Fidel Castro taught the Kremlin a valuable lesson. He taught the Russians that a local leader of a national-revolutionary movement may be more capable of achieving victory than the official Party appendages abroad.

In a careful analysis of national revolutionary movements, the Soviets concluded that such types as Fidel Castro, Douglas Bravo, and Sekou Touré are the natural leaders of national revolutions even though they fail to articulate clearcut political and economic goals.

Fidel Castro, for example, made his appeals to the Cubans in terms which were deliberately left unclear. Indeed, after the famous interview by Herbert Matthews, of the *New York Times*, with the bearded leader in the mountain redoubt in February, 1957, Matthews wrote: "The program is vague and couched in generalities, but it amounts to a new deal for Cuba. . . ."

That Castro had something entirely different in mind than a "new deal" for Cuba might have occurred to Matthews at the time. Evidence of Castro's anti-Americanism was available to objective analysts. And those who took the time to study Castro's arguments in his own defense at his trial, after the storming of Moncada Barracks, in Santiago, by a handful of his followers on July 26, 1953, could easily see that Castro was clearly of the *caudillo*, dictator, stamp, and as such no friend of democracy.

A great deal of nonsense has been written about Castro's speech in his own defense following the Moncada Barracks attack, a speech later issued in booklet form, *History Will Absolve Me*. Castro apologists say of that speech (as Matthews said of his own interview with Castro) that Castro promised free elections, free speech, and a free press, thus proving that he was a democrat at heart. Actually, the truth is almost the reverse of what Castro apologists would have us believe.

Addressing the Emergency Session of the Court of Santiago at his trial on October 16, 1953, Fidel Castro told the Cubans what would have been in store for them had his immediate thrust for power been successful. He planned, he said, to seize power in the name of the people and then to put into effect five "revolutionary laws." Castro's "First Revolutionary Law" could have had no purpose other than to undercut the very Constitution which Castro said he would uphold. "The revolutionary movement," said the embryo dictator, "as the momentous incarnation of this sovereignty [the Constitution] would have assumed all the faculties inherent to it . . . in other words, it would have assumed all the legislative, executive and judicial powers." With power in the hands of revolutionaries, the Constitution would then mean exactly what Castro wanted it to mean. This is apparent in his proposed "Fifth Revolutionary Law," which itself would have been unconstitutional in that it would have violated article 24 of the Cuban Constitution, which expressly forbids the confiscation of property. The judiciary would have been abolished, said Castro, and replaced by "special courts." Those courts were to have "full powers of access to all records of all corporations registered or operating in the country." A revolutionary witch hunt was envisaged by which Castro's "special courts" were to be empowered, he said, "to confiscate all holdings and ill-gotten gains of those who had committed frauds during the previous regimes." The revolutionary movement would determine what constituted frauds, said Castro, because "the judicial power would cease to exist and we would proceed to its immediate and total reform...." In other words, the judiciary was to have been molded after the revolutionary image. Part of that image comes through in the Castro statement that not only those found culpable of fraud by his revolutionary tribunals were to be punished, but "also the legatees and heirs."

Castro's remaining three "Revolutionary Laws," which, he said, "would have been proclaimed immediately," were also arbitrary and confiscatory. Most important, Castro said that the five measures which he would summarily force into law could not be changed by any future *democratically elected government.* "The first popularly elected government," he told the Santiago court in October, 1953, "would have to respect these laws, not only because of moral obligations to the nation. When people achieved something they have yearned for throughout generations, no force in the world is capable of taking it away again." Here is the clear voice of the dictator, whose power rests on one simple proposition: The leader and the people are one and indivisible.

Addressing himself to the very court which he intended to destroy because, he said, it had "placed itself against the Constitution and outside the Constitution," Fidel Castro falsely claimed that the Cuban people were the victims of capitalist exploitation. "The capitalists insist that the workers remain under a Claudian yoke," he said in comparing capitalists to the Roman emperor Claudius who so oppressed the plebians that they left Rome. He claimed, falsely on each count, that "we export hides to import shoes . . . 400,000 families live cramped into barracks and tenements . . . salaries of 400,000 industrial laborers pass from the hands of the boss to those of the usurer . . . 20,000 small businessmen are weighted down by debts, ruined by the crisis and harangued by a plague of filibusters and venal officials . . . 10,000 young professionals emerge from school and find themselves at a dead-end with all doors closed. . . ." Castro then specifically attacked U. S. business investments in Cuba which did so much to build up the economy and turn previously barren land into productive enterprises. He claimed that "more than half the best cultivated land belongs to foreigners," adding: "In Oriente, the largest province, the lands of the United Fruit Company and the West Indian Company join the north coast to the southern one. Yet, there are 200,000 peasant families who do not have a single acre of land to cultivate to provide food for their starving children. . . ."

How, it must be asked, could serious students of Cuban affairs believe that Fidel Castro was a democrat? How could they fail to understand what the young revolutionary had in mind when he spoke before the Emergency Session of the Court of Santiago on October 16, 1953? His five "Revolutionary Laws" alone were the very negation of the spirit of democracy. The manner in which Castro addressed the court, his distortions and his falsehoods, should have been enough to alert the observer to the fact that there stood a demagogue, not a democrat. It is also a fact that in January, 1959, Communist specifics were almost immediately added to Castro's blueprint to power, outlined in Santiago in October 1953. And that Mr. Matthews' "new deal" turned out to be quite something else needs no elaboration here. Castro's personal resentments against a neighboring United States, whose overwhelming power cast a shadow over his ambitions, his insatiable ego, and his drive for world prominence, found ready response in Communist philosophy and Soviet designs. In turn, Castro's mass appeal provided the all-important, perhaps the indispensable, cement for a Communist revolution in an emotional Latin American country. No dull Party functionary could have hoped to carry the Cubans along as Castro did. Fidel Castro provided the perfect answer, and he played his role perfectly. As long as he can hold the number one position in his country and not be overtly challenged by local Communist leaders, he will serve Russia well.

The strategy being followed by Russia, Red China and their satellites at the conclusion of the Havana conference of January, 1966, is to support discreetly so-called national revolutionary leaders in their quest for power. First, assist the local "Fidel Castro" to gain control of the country through a "nationalistic" war of liberation, then with his grateful assistance take over the country lock, stock, and barrel. Every effort is being made to avoid close identification of the local leader with international Communism, since such identification could damage the credibility of the movement. For, as Castro put it in December 2, 1961, if he had made it known publicly in 1953, 1957, or 1958 that he was a Communist, the Cuban people never would have let him emerge from the mountains. The propaganda by which Castro trapped so many dupes in our press and intellectual community back in 1957 and 1958—that his was a local, nationalistic struggle—the Communists obviously believe to be still effective today.

Consider for the moment some of the passages to come out of the final resolutions of the Havana Conference—passages which call for maximum guerrilla attacks by those "who are fighting with arms in their hands against the forces of domestic oligarchy which are at the service of the United States, as in Venezuela, Colombia, Peru, and Guatemala, or are being subjected to brutal persecution under military tyranny, as in Brazil, Ecuador, Bolivia, and other countries." In each of those countries, the leaders are guerrilla fighters.

The final resolution of that conference climbs to a chest-thumping peroration: "Faced with the criminal alliance of the reactionary forces, the people of the various countries in the three continents have reacted with active, vigorous and militant solidarity, and with their readiness to reply to every act of imperialist aggression by revolutionary action, carrying on this battle until the complete liquidation of all forms of imperialist, colonial, and neo-colonial oppression."

The Havana Conference was followed closely in Latin America and Europe. In Latin America, the conference caused profound dismay and was promptly denounced on February 2, 1966, by an extraordinary session of the Organization of American States. Ambassador Ilmar Penna Marinho of Brazil, Chairman of the OAS Council, said of the conference: "Except for the placing of nuclear weapons in Cuba in October, 1962, no event threatens more dangerously the territorial and political integrity of our continent."

What particularly alarmed Latin American governments was the conscious and conspicuous leadership of an official Soviet delegation in stepped-up plans to subvert the hemisphere. The only other governments to send official delegations were Red China, Ghana, the United Arab Republic and Guinea.

Those same Latin American governments were no less disturbed by the failure of the United States effectively to challenge open Soviet military intrusion into the South American continent and the Commonwealth of Puerto Rico. Irritation and disgust were also expressed privately by Latin American Ambassadors to the OAS at the distinctly low-key attitude of the United States alternate delegate at the OAS special session. Those ambassadors sounded their alarm over Soviet intentions in two hours of unbroken oratory. Yet, there was no attempt by the United States to turn this concern to advantage and take the leadership in some form of concrete action against a Russian-propelled Cuba—the very purpose for which the OAS meeting had been called.

The excitement displayed by Latin American ambassadors at the Special OAS session was a reflection of rising public concern at home, where the Havana conference was treated as the news sensation of the year. There was more than the mere suggestion that the United States was playing fast and loose with hemisphere security in return for an ephemeral accommodation with the Russians elsewhere in the world. In Panama, Radio Mia rumbled its displeasure. It reported that President Johnson had presented Congress with the highest budget in American history, a budget "prepared to wage war, make peace, and construct the Great Society in the coming year." Then the commentator editorialized: "While I was reading this report, I was thinking about the enormous quantity of money being spent in Vietnam to contain Communism there.

However, Communism exists right in front of Florida, and there they do nothing . . . it might be that they are afraid of it, or are keeping promises made to the Russians, while that insane bearded man Fidel Castro raves daily about invading Latin America."

The newspaper, *El Universo*, in Ecuador made uneasy comments about the possibility of a Soviet-American accomodation, saying that "while the Russians continue to seek agreements with the United States, they are not disposed to pay any price" to this end.

Peruvian Premier Daniel Becerra de la Flor said that the Soviet Union was involved in "tacit aggression," and that delegate Rashidov's statements in Havana now made Soviet activities in Peru official.

One by one, those countries in Latin America maintaining diplomatic relations with Russia which had been threatened by Sharaf R. Rashidov in Havana, called in the Soviet ambassadors and demanded an explanation. And it is here that we see most clearly Russia's double-track policy as it pursues "peaceful coexistence," as defined at the Havana Conference.

In Uruguay, a land on the verge of bankruptcy and beset with social problems as a result of a disastrously over-extended welfare state, the Soviets had found one of the weakest points in the hemisphere. The oversized Soviet embassy in Montevideo has long been the center of a clandestine network extending throughout Latin America. At the time of the Havana Conference, Uruguay was still suffering from the effects of a labor strike engineered by Russian agents. Russian Ambassador Igor Kowolsky was called on the carpet by Uruguayan Foreign Minister Luis Vidal Zaglio who demanded an explanation for the stand taken by Russia in Havana. After an embarrassed silence which lasted some days, Kowolsky lamely replied that Sharaf R. Rashidov was speaking "privately," not for the Soviet government. Moscow tried to improve matters by offering Uruguay a $30 million credit, payable over a period of five years. The clumsy move was taken in official Uruguayan circles as confirming Soviet guilt.

Provisional President Héctor García Godoy of the Dominican Republic also had cause for alarm. Talking with newsmen, García Godoy explained his fears by saying: "It is enough to read the statements made in Havana by one of the Dominican delegates."

But Latin American fears found little echo in the United States where the American public was left largely uninformed. While it was true that individual U.S. correspondents were not permitted to enter Cuba and cover the conference, they were not without information. The Associated Press, Reuters, the French press, and United Press International maintain offices in Havana and reported the events of the conference. Unfortunately, most of the U.S. comments, based on those informative

reports, described the Havana Conference as an event of little significance, except for the "signs" of a widening Sino-Soviet split. United
States and hemispheric security was not particularly involved, if one
were disposed to believe the journalistic and political pundits.

Actually, the Chinese found the conference to their liking. China had
no intention of giving up its place on the central committee established
in Havana any more than it was disposed to take a back seat to the Soviet
Union as a rival leader in the Communist camp. On January 19, after
the close of the conference, the New China News Agency put the conflicts in perspective with the report: "The Tricontinental Peoples'
Solidarity Movement ran into various difficulties at the outset. However,
in accordance with the will of the people of the three continents, the
movement is sweeping forward with irresistible momentum. . . ."

A classic example of a newspaper's falling, not only for the Sino-Soviet
split, but for the "peaceful coexistence" gambit as well, is contained in
the February 17, 1966 issue of the *New York Times*. Reporting over a
Washington dateline, it said that "Soviet officials are making quiet dis-
claimers of the aggressive calls for revolution in Latin America. . . ." The
story continued: "At the conference, the Soviet Union seems to have
been led by its desire to outflank the Chinese and by its obligations to
Cuba into *acquiescing* in aggressive statements about non-Communist
countries even though Moscow would prefer to maintain correct relations with some of them." (Italics supplied.)

The *New York Times* reporter needed only to have listened to one
comment, among many, made as late as January 13, by Soviet delegate
Sharaf R. Rashidov. He said that "for us, the Soviet people, common
interests in the struggle against imperialism, against the forces of reaction
and oppression, are above everything else." He then added the clincher:
"*Our people have helped,* and will go on helping the peoples of Asia,
Africa, Latin America to achieve national independence and to
defend them from the encroachment of imperialists. . . ." (Italics supplied.).

On February 2, 1966, the Organization of American States, in a rare
show of virtual unity, denounced the Havana conference. The vote was
18 to 0, with Mexico and Chile in their usual abstaining role. A protest
was taken to the United Nations. On April 2 and November 28 of the
same year, the OAS documented the Havana Conference and condemned international Communism as a "positive threat to the free peoples of the world." The OAS said that the conference represented the
gravest threat yet against the inter-American system, pointing out that
the Russians and the Red Chinese were collaborating in carrying out that
threat.[7]

Washington officials did not expect the OAS to take action adequate to the threat. They recalled Secretary of State Dean Rusk's futile attempt at an OAS conference in Río de Janeiro in the fall of 1965, to pull member states together into an organization for collective defense.

In Secretary Rusk's efforts in 1965 to establish a military organization for the collective defense of the hemisphere, he had named no names. The uproar in Latin America caused by the Tricontinental Conference of 1966, however, brought the enemy unmistakably into focus—a Soviet Russia which openly and officially sponsored that conference. For the United States to continue in 1966 what it had initiated in 1965 would have signified a willingness on the part of the Johnson administration to confront the Russians directly, something which it apparently was unwilling to do. In this sense, at least, the Soviets were remarkably successful in peddling their aggression in the appetizing package of "peaceful coexistence." The extent of that success (which was not for a moment lost on the Latins) can be measured by the fact that the U. S. didn't even respond to the direct Russian threats made against Puerto Rico.

Impatience with the United States among our Latin American allies rose to rather dangerous heights before the year 1966 had ended. In November, Panama's Ambassador to the OAS, Dr. Eduardo Ritter, inaugurated his one-year term as Chairman of the Council of the OAS with a speech in which he criticized the United States in unusually blunt language.

He said that members of the OAS "not only are the target of constant aggression by its enemies," but also "of the strong and dangerous aggression of silence by those who should be its allies." Sol M. Linowitz, U.S. Ambassador to the OAS, squirmed uncomfortably in his chair as Dr. Ritter added: "The objectives of American action should be the cessation of the purges and forced labor in Cuba, the gagging and persecution, the abuse and insult."

The best that Ambassador Linowitz could come up with was the registration of a complaint that Latin American countries were making "unnecessary" military expenditures.

The OAS Council Chairman also scored the U.S. news media for failure to report thoroughly on the constant efforts by Latin American countries to awaken the United States to the threat of a Soviet-propelled Cuba. For, slightly more than two weeks earlier, on November 1, 1966, a resolution of the legislature of the little Central American country of Costa Rica called the Tricontinental Conference "an act of war against the democratic institutions, the traditions, and the security and the liberty of our peoples." That important statement also calls for support for the Cuban people "in their revolutionary struggle against the Communist dictatorship, and recognizes their right, within the island and in exile, freely to fight for the restoration of their self-determination and their democracy." Yet, the resolution was virtually ignored by the U.S. press.

It was left to Colombia's Ambassador to the OAS, Alfredo Vazquez Carrioza, to put the issue squarely. In some exasperation, he told the OAS publicly to name names—meaning Russia. "If there is to be war and no peace," exclaimed the Colombian, "let it at least be known who declared it!"

CHAPTER 2

•

In the Beginning

•

How DID CUBA turn into a nest of subversion—bitterly anti-American and dedicatedly pro-Soviet? The answer is the rise to power of one man —Fidel Castro.

On reviewing conditions in Cuba in 1958, it seems remarkable that Castro came to power at all. He never would have made it if he had really followed the course attributed to him by Professor C. Wright Mills, Leo Huberman, and Paul Sweezy—namely, via a "peasant revolt." Nor would Castro have been any better off with Herbert Matthews' blueprint for victory. An editorial writer for the *New York Times*, Matthews has written that Castro's rise of power was due to ". . . a revolt against a small, corrupt, wealthy ruling class whom the United States had put into power." He adds one distortion to another, claiming that ". . . the Cuban peasants—say about 40 percent of the population—and many city dwellers, were living at not much better than a subsistence level before the revolution."[1]

These comments are typical of those made by a whole host of writers, many of whom made hurried trips to Cuba only after Castro came to power. They made up facts to fit their fancy. French writers Jean-Paul Sartre and Simone de Beauvoir, Britisher Paul Johnson, American editors and professors, such as Samuel Shapiro of Michigan State University, the late C. Wright Mills, *Monthly Review* editors Leo Huberman and Paul Sweezy, and, of course, Herbert Matthews, were among the early apologists for Castro.

The fierce support thrown behind Castro by American and foreign intellectuals and reporters was based, generally, on three propositions: 1) Cuba was an underdeveloped country, and therefore ripe for social revolution—a "peasant revolt"; 2) Cuba suffered the cruelest form of economic exploitation by the United States, and therefore was ready for an economic revolution; and 3) The excesses of dictator Fulgencio Batista justified the excesses of Fidel Castro. Combined, these factors presumably created an irresistible popular current which carried a reluctant (even protesting!) Castro into the Soviet camp.

None of these propositions is true. Nor is the conclusion. They represent the anti-capitalist attitudes of their authors, who, *wanting* a socialist triumph in Cuba, go to any extremes in justifying every totalitarian twist and turn made by Fidel Castro. They did so initially, during Castro's earliest thrust for power (and many still do so today), because of a fear that the demise of what they variously describe as "Castroism" or *"Fidelismo"* (never Communism) may mean the end of their own cherished hopes for Socialism, not only in Cuba, but in all Latin America, as well. The words of Diana Trilling, written back in 1951 to describe what motivated the appeasers then, are descriptive of Castro appeasers at the end of that same decade. A member of the anti-Communist Left, Diana Trilling wrote that "the idealist finds virtue only where he is not—in the nation which is not his nation, in the class which is not his class, in the races and religions which are not his race or religion."[2] Pro-Castro "idealists"—writers, leftist politicians, assorted professors and other academics, and way-out liberal functionaries in the State Department— cannot bring themselves to identify with their own capitalist society, and are quite willing to disown what they have in favor of another system and society. They are not in the least disturbed by their own intellectual dishonesty—a dishonesty which seeks to justify the triumph of Castro-Communism on the false grounds that capitalism failed in Cuba. Indeed, they rejoice in their pronouncements that capitalism is the loser in its clash with Castro's more "liberal" system. Wittingly, and in many cases unwittingly, these people are pro-Communist in effect. They are "losers."*

In reading the works of the "losers," one gets the impression, for example, that pre-Castro Cuba was literally seething with massive, uncontrollable revolt against the unbearable economic and social conditions brought on by capitalist exploitation. Heart-rending stories of the shoeless Cuban, allegedly bereft of the most elementary forms of medical attention, deftly overlook the truth. Professor C. Wright Mills, in his

---

*In the title and throughout the book, I use this term in reference to the coterie of Castro and Soviet apologists in the U. S. whose efforts have so greatly aided the Communist advances into free Latin America. In a manner of speaking, they could be called the "winners" (so far) in the conflict. But I refer to personal qualities (implied by Mrs. Trilling above) common to their breed—they are the misfiits, malcontents and "losers" of a free society, who, unable to achieve the status or power their "intellectual" gifts entitle them to, and frustrated in their efforts to "reform" their fellow men, retreat to safe havens such as the universities and the bureaucracy to air their sour resentment of democracy. It is worth noting that, lacking manliness, the "losers" are attracted like flies to those, like Castro or "Che" Guevara, of virile image. I trust the reader knows the breed.

fanciful book, *Listen Yankee!*, puts words into the mouths of Cubans which most probably were never uttered: "We speak Spanish, we are mainly rural, and we are poor."[3] He is accurate on the first point only, one that requires no value judgment. Mr. Matthews writes of the wonders of Castro's socialist state in these terms: "For the first time, proper attention is being paid to public health . . . providing shoes for poor children. . . ."[4]

What is especially disturbing about such statements is that they violate the readers' confidence; they prey on the ignorance of the public. People are impressed by the written word, and tend to accept the credentials of a writer, or of a given publication, at face value. The late C. Wright Mills was a professor at Columbia University, so it is not unreasonable for the reader to assume that he would perform as much research on his book as he would require of a college freshman student. It could also be assumed that an editorial writer for the *New York Times* would do what is required of a cub reporter—first dig out the facts, then write the story. But in the cases cited, and others too numerous to mention here, the simple element of truth is missing.

What, then, was the situation in Cuba in 1957 and 1958? Let us take the poor, diseased Cuban, as the first example. The University of Havana was foremost in Latin America in training doctors and dentists. Cuba had one doctor for each 998 inhabitants, surpassed only by Argentina with one doctor for each 764 inhabitants, and by Uruguay with one to each 860. It took seven years to get a medical degree in Cuba, compared to four and five years in some of the other countries.

Furthermore, every Cuban was entitled to free medical care in state hospitals. There were 69 such hospitals throughout the island providing free x-rays, medical checkups, laboratory tests, and free hospitalization. There were municipal first-aid clinics, also free, which employed 1,341 medical doctors.

One interesting development was that of the private cooperative clinic. One hundred sixty-eight of these dotted the island of Cuba where, for a monthly fee of between $2.00 and $3.00, Cubans received full hospitalization, free surgery, specialist consultation, and in-and-out treatment, which included medicines.

The Cubans were far from the filth-spattered *homo sapiens* squatting disconsolately and sullenly on flaccid shanks, as depicted by the "losers." As a whole, the Cubans were quite a healthy and robust people whose *guajiros* (peasants) would rather be caught dead than be seen at their favorite sport, a cock fight, on a Sunday without the clean, starched, *guayabera*—the traditional long dress shirt of Cuba.

Infant mortality in Cuba would also be a discouraging statistic for the "losers" to dig up, and they did not do so. In 1958, Cuba had the lowest infant mortality rate in all of Latin America, 37.6 per thousand, attesting to its medical care and to the abundance of relatively inexpensive medicines. When Castro came to power quite unexpectedly on January 1, 1959, Cuba's death rate was the lowest in Latin America.

The same enviable position was enjoyed by the Cubans as regards dental care. Here Cuba ranked third among her neighbors, surpassed only by Argentina and Uruguay. Incidentally, healthy Cuban teeth chewed up 75 pounds of meat per capita each year, again surpassed only by the molar activity of Uruguayans, Paraguayans, and Argentinians—all of them prodigious meat eaters. The calories consumed daily by the Cuban came to 2,870, compared to 3,100 for the U.S. citizen.

Let's take shoes. The truth is that the Cuban shoe industry was making 20 million pairs of excellent quality shoes in 1958, exporting a good portion of them. By 1962, shoes were rationed in Cuba; by 1964, Cuban shoe production had plunged to around 6 million pairs, many of which turned out to be two left or two right shoes in a pair, a situation that brought screams of "sabotage" from government management.

Pre-Castro economic advances were sound, and they were rapid. The fact is that Castro inherited a growing, not a declining, economy. And much of that growth is attributable to American investment and to the development of export markets for the Cuban economy.

Our Department of Agriculture worked closely with Cuban governments to cut down Cuba's need to import food. For example, an agricultural experimental station was set up in the Province of Camaguey to study ways to eradicate *hoja blanca*, a disease that decimated Cuba's rice crops. In 1950, Cuba produced only 106,000 meter tons of rice. By 1957, rice production had risen to 261,000 meter tons. This contrasts with what happened after Castro and the Communists seized private property. Production of rice for the year 1960-61 plummeted to 167,000 tons, 100,000 tons less than that produced three years earlier. The following year, according to a dismal report in the Communist newspaper, *Hoy*, production had again decreased..

In 1951, Cuba was importing about eleven million dozen eggs from the United States and elsewhere. With the development of new feeds, new incubation systems and disease preventives, egg imports in 1958 had been reduced to only 350,000 dozen. When Castro came to power, eggs were actually exported. By 1960, it took a detective, not a housewife, to find eggs in Havana, and, in 1964 and 1965, Castro had to resort to importing millions of eggs from Canada.

When Castro came to power, Cuba was exporting a quantity of meat. About 10,000 head of breeding cattle also were marketed abroad, due in large measure to the experimentation and investment in the cattle industry by such U.S. firms as the United Fruit Company, the King

Ranch, and several independent breeders and their Cuban colleagues. The herds have since been decimated by the Castro regime.

If the progress made by Cuba in cutting down its import of foodstuffs, for example, is representative of the cruel economic exploitation by U.S. interests, then that was indeed an exploitation devoutly to be desired. The fact is that the U.S. Government and U.S. business interests were foremost among those forces which helped diversify and strengthen Cuba's economy.

In 1939, American companies owned 66 of Cuba's 150 sugar mills. This was due, in part, to the reluctance of local capital to invest in its own country, a fear which one finds throughout Latin America. But, as government after government was elected at the polls from 1940 to 1952, and as Cuba was making advances toward democratic government and political stability, more and more investments were made by Cubans. During this period, 20 sugar mills were bought by Cubans, and, by 1958, U.S. interests controlled only 36 mills out of a total of 161, with the purchase of several more under negotiation when Castro came to power.

The Cuban Electric Company, a division of American and Foreign Power Company, Inc., brought electricity to all parts of the country. By 1958, Cuba had a per capita consumption rate of 396.7 kilowatt hours, which placed it fourth among the 20 Latin American countries. This is an admirable accomplishment when it is considered that Cuba does not have the water-power resources of mountainous South and Central America. Peru, an Andean country, with vast mountains, and snowcaps most of the year around, consumed only 195.0 kilowatt hours per capita, while Mexico's per capita consumption was 276.5 kilowatt hours—more than 100 kilowatt hours below that of Cuba.

The high rate of production and consumption in Cuba was due precisely to outside capital investment which the "losers" denigrate. And let us not forget that the American and Foreign Power Company, Inc., like International Telephone and Telegraph, the United Fruit Company, General Motors, Ford, are *people.* They are not the totalitarian economic giants depicted by so many American writers and intellectuals. They represent the savings of millions of little people—from bank clerks, to mechanics, to retired persons.

From 1948 to 1953, the Cuban Electric Company put some 30 million dollars of its investors' money into Cuba, expanding both service and production. From 1956 through 1960 (please note that the Castro years of 1959 and 1960 are included) another 195 million dollars of investment brought expanded electric service to Cuba's industries, to its city dwellers, and to its rural population. Additional electric plants were constructed in four of Cuba's six provinces, and by 1958 electric services were expanding by a healthy 12 percent each year.

What did the "revolution" do for its people in the field of electricity? On August 4,1960, the Cuban Electric Company was seized by the Castro government and converted into a state enterprise. Since the beginning of 1963, electricity has actually been rationed. Despite the rationing, today only 40 per cent of Cuba's population is receiving any service at all.

The deeper one probes into the pre-Castro situation in Cuba, the greater is his horror at the misrepresentations that have been foisted off on the American people. American capital investment, which played a constructive role in the economic life of Cuba, is denigrated. American oil companies, for example, showed great patience for a great expanse of time—to the point of supplying oil to Castro at considerable risk to their own American investors. When Castro seized U.S. oil holdings in Cuba in the summer of 1960, on the excuse that they refused to refine Russian oil, the Cuban government owed those companies over $60 million.

What is more, the books and articles which poured from the pens of the "losers" served to confuse the issues and to gain for the Communists the time they needed to consolidate their hold on Cuba. These books and articles, unfortunately, were not balanced by other works more searching in their analysis.

For example, in 1957 the Cuban industrial worker averaged $6.00 per 8-hour day. The Mexican got only $3.00 a day, the Japanese $2.54, and even the Australian received only $5.82 a day. Cuban dock workers at sugar ports earned $18.65 a day for Sunday work, a wage that would never be paid an "exploited" worker anywhere in the world. In 1958, Cuba had 29 telephones per thousand population as compared with only 15 for its "developed" Mexican neighbors. Cuba ranked third in newspaper circulation, and had an average of 32 cars per thousand population. Argentina had 35 cars per thousand, while Mexico and Brazil were so far down the list that they do not deserve mention here. Pre-Castro Cuba ranked third in the hemisphere in the number of radio sets, with 152 per thousand population, again surpassing every (Latin American)country except Argentina and Uruguay.

In fact, in determining the welfare of the pre-Castro Cuban citizen, one needs only to examine the *Statistical Abstract of Latin America* or other international reference works, to find that wherever a *high* rank indicates good standing (e.g. number of doctors per thousand, etc.) Cuba is usually among the first three or four countries in the hemisphere. Where a *low* rank indicates good standing (e.g. communicable diseases, infant mortality, etc.) Cuba is located among those countries having the lowest incidence.

Total income for 1957 was $2,319,900,000. Of this, wages and salaries amounted to $1,445,100,000, which represents 60.4 per cent of the total. The 1958 national income was $2,209,600,000, of which wages and salaries came to $1,407,500,000, or 63.8 per cent. What makes these figures all the more remarkable is that their source was not the Batista regime, but the revolutionary regime of Fidel Castro and his *Banco Nacional de Cuba*.[5]

There is another source, the International Labor Organization. Using a slightly different means of calculation, the ILO came up with 66.6 per cent of the national income paid out in wages and salaries. The ILO *Yearbook of Labor Statistics, 1960*, published in Geneva,[6] ranked pre-Castro Cuba fifth among all the nations in the world as concerns labor's share in the national income. The point is that the Cubans had gained for themselves the highest living standard of any tropical country—higher indeed, than in many European countries. And Cuban labor played its role in this area.

The origins of the Cuban labor movement can be traced back more than a century to the informal, fraternal associations of tobacco workers. In a little-known sidenote to Cuban history, we find that the tobacco workers were among the best educated of the working classes. While shaping the world's finest tobaccos into the world's most celebrated cigars, they found their minds were idle and bored. In response, they got together and paid readers to entertain them by reading aloud. They thus learned current events from the newspapers, the literary classics, the poetry of Cuba's apostle of freedom, José Martí.

It is noteworthy, as well, that Cuban workers have always been in the vanguard of the fight for liberty. Following an initiative of the tobacco workers, others gave a certain percentage of their income to finance Cuba's two wars of independence—the Ten Years' War lasting from 1868 to 1878, and that of 1895 to 1898. Fiercely independent, the Cubans fought against Spanish occupation with a determination that rivals that of our own Revolutionary War. Total casualties—dead and missing—came to around a quarter of a million people. This at a time when the population of the entire island was slightly over two million.

Whether for religious, philosophical, or other reasons, the Cubans have always shown their devotion to freedom. The slowly developing labor unions were no exception. The weak beginnings of the 1920s bore fruit in the early 1930s when the worldwide depression hit the sugar industry and gave unions a powerful thrust toward solidarity.

Economic troubles accentuated political dissatisfaction and unrest under dictator Gerardo Machado. Machado responded with repressive measures and the imposition of martial law that remained nearly three years. Machado's strong-arm gangs, *porristas*, carried out systematic campaigns of intimidation and brutality.

The downfall of Machado was precipitated by a bus-and-streetcar-workers' strike in August of 1933. It began spontaneously, but quickly spread and became a general strike. A few days later, the army commanders withdrew their support from Machado and the dictator fled the country. This was a history lesson in the power of organized labor well-learned by Fidel Castro. He tried to employ it by calling for a general strike in April of 1958, certain that the workers would support him. They ignored him, and he failed. But Castro knew what that power of labor could accomplish and in the fall of 1959 he destroyed the independence of the labor movement.

One reason Castro destroyed organized labor in 1959 is that the Cuban labor movement had turned its back on the European tradition where labor was largely subservient to a political party.

It can be surmised therefore, that Fidel Castro's call for a general strike in April of 1958 was generally interpreted in Cuban labor circles as a reversal of labor policy and history. What stirred the workers to revolt against Machado in 1933—economic misery and intimidation—had little currency in 1958. The workers had gained for themselves a place in Cuban society. Some prosperous unions even owned valuable properties in their own right. For example, the Restaurant Workers partly owned the new Havana Hilton hotel. Many unions owned excellent yacht clubs and operated them on a non-profit basis for a membership which paid dues of about $5.00 a month for the entire family.

In 1958, before Castro took power, the Cuban Confederation of Labor (CTC) had 33 national federations and 2,490 local unions. In 1958 there were 7,638 labor contracts in Havana Province alone. Profit-sharing systems were established in many industries. Minimum wage laws had been adopted, and workers received annually a Christmas bonus often amounting to a full month's salary. The law granted "all manual and non-manual workers the right to a one-month paid vacation for each eleven months worked during the natural year."[7]

Decree Number 798 of 1938, as amended in 1950, granted paid sick leave to all workers up to a maximum of nine days a year. By custom and contract it was a widespread practice to pay employees for those nine days even if not used. A 1945 law stipulated that office and retail store employees must receive an extra day of leisure each week, without loss of pay during the months of June, July, and August.[8]

Transport workers were on a six-hour day, but were paid for eight hours. A 36-hour week was observed in the Cuban Telephone Company (a subsidiary of the "exploiting" I T & T). Most Cubans wanted to work for American companies because of exceptionally good salaries, the opportunities to advance, and, not least, the chance to receive specialized training in the United States.

What the Cuban labor movement had gained from 1933 to 1958 was no less than a high degree of job security, good working conditions, moderate hours, and relatively high wages. In a tropical country, these working conditions represented a highly advanced labor situation.

It is clear that labor advances had been made over a period of decades under several different Presidents and dictators. Cuban labor was beholden to no particular ruler for its gains. It is a travesty on justice for the "losers" bitterly to complain that the Cuban workers did not go out on strike for Castro because, as one put it, "they and their leaders were in the pay of Batista." In fact, when Batista made his 1952 coup d'etat, CTC leader Eusebio Mujal opposed him but received no support elsewhere. The real point is that few Cubans in 1958 really knew what Castro stood for. Under these circumstances, who would risk the gains of half a century for the vague promises of a Messiah in the hills? The answer is: very few.

Two of Latin America's most eminent authorities on labor legislation, Professors Mario de la Cueva of Mexico and Guillermo Cabanellas of Argentina, describe Cuba's labor legislation and its Constitution of 1940 as "very advanced" and in many respects "the forerunner of progressive labor legislation in Latin America."[9]

Yet, many intellectuals and writers would have us believe otherwise. Mr. Matthews sums up this attitude, even today, with the startling pro-Castro statement that "even if the agrarian reform creates a Communist-type State system, the peasant did not have freedom and democracy before, does not know what they mean and cannot be expected to care. . . ."[10]

People *do* care about freedom and democracy, however. Here is the story of one, who cared so much for freedom that he, his wife, their four children and a godchild were among *21 peasants occupying a 19-foot boat* who fled Cuba. His name is José Blanco. He is 41 years of age, and worked for 21 years as a farm hand on Margarita ranch near La Palma in Pinar del Río Province. When found by the U.S. Coast Guard, the primitive boat was sinking in seven-foot waves. I interviewed him in Miami after he was released from medical care.

Among the 19 people rescued, only José Blanco had shoes, and they were patched with palm bark. "You would be amazed," he told me, "at the number of farmers who have no shoes to wear." This story was to be told over and over again by thousands who have braved the water of the Straits of Florida and opted for a freedom for which they supposedly ". . . cannot be expected to care."

More to the point was Sr. Blanco's views about pre-Castro Cuba. He said: "I used to earn 80 pesos a month working on the farm. In addition, I was given a good plot of land on which I could grow my own crops and raise my own livestock. Those government bandits confiscated the farm and took away from me the fruit of years of labor. I had four milk cows, 30 fattened pigs, 200 hens which laid eggs, and plots of yucca. From all of this I lived very well in peace and contentment. Then suddenly it was all taken away from me and I was paid nothing."

As to the State farm, always praised by the "losers," here is what Sr. Blanco had to say: "I was put to work as a State-farm employee, and was not permitted to earn more than $74 a month which, with all the withholding and deductions was brought down to $58 a month. I had to go to the black market to live." How he and the other peasants on the boat with him had managed to live, is little short of a miracle. Prices on the black market, which represents almost the sole means of obtaining adequate food, reduce one's real purchasing power by nearly 80%!

It is very clear that Cuban labor was not for Castro, neither before nor even after his assumption of power, as we shall see later. But, it is equally clear that Castro's support did not come from the peasantry, either. Claims by the "losers" that Castro's was a peasant revolt, made up of peasants and supported by them, collapse immediately when subjected to serious scrutiny.

Despite repeated calls to burn cane fields and sabotage the sugar industry, Cuba in 1958 produced a not unusual 5,610,600 tons of sugar. Sabotage by the public or the workers simply did not occur on any appreciable scale. Herbert Matthews' overdrawn reports in June, 1957, that the whole of Oriente Province was up in arms against Batista are not substantiated by any observable fact. While it may be that Mr. Matthews wished that the whole of Oriente Province were up in arms, and chose the journalist's method of prodding or encouraging the Orientales, through his reporting, to do just that, the truth is quite another matter.

Depending on which of the "losers" one reads, the number of Castro guerrillas in 1958 varied from 300 in Mills' account to the almost lyrical figure of 3,000 by Jean-Paul Sartre. But most were in agreement that the Castro forces were made up of *guajiros*. No matter how it is cut, 300 or 3,000, Castro's guerrillas could hardly be classified as a "peasant army," any more than they could be said to have been supported by other peasants with food, money and intelligence, or by rural sabotage against their "oppressors."

As one recalls Castro's landing on the coast of Oriente Province on December 2, 1956, one also remembers that only twelve of the original 82 escaped being shot to death by units of Batista's 33,000-man army. Castro received no substantial reinforcements until well into 1958. Take Castro's mournful lament, written on December 31, 1957, just one year before he was catapulted into power. He complained that he and his small band, augmented only once by some fresh recruits from Santiago, had been fighting for a year, ". . . bitterly forgotten by fellow-countrymen who, in spite of having all the ways and means, have systematically [even criminally] denied us their help."

Where was Mr. Matthews' great revolt in Oriente Province of 1957? Where was the Cuban "peasant army" of Messrs. Huberman and Sweezy, or the legions of the rural discontented of Professor Mills' mythology? The answer is fairly simple. The peasants were relatively comfortable. They bothered no one and no one bothered them. The horizons of plenty, which the *guajiro* of the "losers" should have been scanning, turned out to be nothing more than an intellectual fantasy by the authors.

Actually, U.S. Embassy intelligence came up with what is perhaps as good a guess as any as to the number of people in the mountains with Castro in mid-1958—442. Two "columns" sent out by Castro from Oriente to Las Villas Province in late summer of 1958—one headed by Major Ernesto "Che" Guevara, and the other by Major Camilo Cienfuegos—numbered only 202 men. Guevara's "column" came right through the U. S. agricultural experimental station in Camaguey.

Stopping at the station briefly, Guevara told manager Joe McGuire to have a man take a package to Batista's military commander in the city. He sent the package, containing $100,000 with a note, as a bribe to let his column pass. The column of ninety-nine men was described to McGuire as merely an "advance guard." In any event, Guevara's men moved on through the province almost within sight of uninterested government troops.

Another event, among many, suggests, in part, how Batista lost and how Castro won. In 1958, one of Batista's armored troop trains was "captured" following a fierce fight with rebel forces in the Province of Las Villas, according to reports at the time. What actually happened was that the train commander, an officer in Batista's army, *sold* the train to Castro. A few shots and bombs to make it look good, and the deal was consummated in a triumph of Castro propaganda.

A personal experience I had with the *guajiros* is revealing of their sentiments. In the summer of 1958, I traveled around the countryside in order to become more closely informed on the situation prevailing in the interior of Cuba. I had been repeatedly warned by leaders of the underground civic resistance movement in Havana that U.S. "support" for Batista had created great hatred against us among the people. In my capacity as Press Attache of our embassy in Havana, I commandeered the services of Gabriel Quintero, head of the audio-visual program of the United States Information Service, and set off on a week's trip. Since he and his crews were traveling constantly through the towns and villages of Cuba, Quintero was by all odds the most knowledgeable person in the Embassy regarding the attitudes of the country people.

We drove around the Provinces of Pinar del Rio and Havana, giving showings from the USIS truck, stocked as it was with documentary films. Early one evening we stopped at a village in the interior, and Quintero and I sauntered into a bodega, an open café-general store and local meeting house common in Latin American countries. Quintero called for the proprietor, told him we had some films to show to the country people, and asked where best they might be shown. The proprietor rolled his eyes, swabbing furiously at our table with a damp cloth, and warned us not to venture out at night. "The barbudos are all around," he said, and they had forbidden any auto traffic at night. The barbudos were Castro's "bearded ones," of course.

The proprietor left us in haste. Soon, we found ourselves being scrutinized by several men at the bar. One came over and asked Quintero if what the proprietor had told him about movies was true. If we had come all this distance, he said, a way must be found. "Don't worry about the barbudos," he said, smiling. Quintero took him out to the truck, chatted for awhile, then came back to the table.

"I've found out where to go," he said. "We are to go out of town to a place called four corners where there is a schoolhouse and a couple of bodegas. We will be met there."

We found the place at dusk. Quintero talked briefly with a nervous schoolteacher, introduced me, and the three of us went across the dusty street to the bodega where we sipped Cuban coffee. The teacher asked me countless questions about the United States, and about Japan where I had spent nearly five years. Before we knew it, the sounds of a gathering crowd penetrated the bodega.

I walked out and was frankly astonished at what I saw. It was as near to a picture of the old West as can be imagined. Men on horses rode in out of the dark, some carrying rifles, others with pistols shoved into their belts. What struck me most was the number of Negro and mulatto riders, moving in easy familiarity among the traditional *guajiro* types—the blue-eyed, bronzed farmers of Spanish descent. Having been brought up on a ranch in the American West it had never occurred to me to think of a Negro in the role of a cowboy. But in Cuba it was perfectly natural.

We soon discovered that the schoolhouse was much too small to hold the crowd of people which had gathered. Quintero overcame that problem by moving the film showing out of doors. The USIS panel truck was equipped with its own generator to provide electricity for the film projectors. We sat there, among the chirping crickets, slapping at mosquitoes and fanning away the bugs. For two hours, several hundred adults and children, many dressed in their best clothes for the occasion, saw motion pictures of the electoral process in the United States, scenes of the Rocky Mountains, and surfing in Hawaii and California. Films of President Eisenhower's inauguration ceremony in 1952 brought a round of applause.

The most impressive part of the evening, though, was the sight of the *guajiros* taking turns as sentries. Every so often, one would rise in the audience and, with rifle slung down, disappear into the darkness. The man he replaced would soon appear, lay his rifle down and watch the movie. The *guajiros* posted sentries against a chance foray by barbudos, and in defense of their right to watch an American movie.

When the films were over, they gave a cheer for the United States, and I was politely invited to the bodega for a drink of rum with one of the head men. The rest of the audience drifted off into the night, disappearing almost as silently as they had arrived.

To read some accounts, one is led to believe that the Negro and mulatto were emancipated by Fidel Castro. Putting this particular bit of nonsense into perspective takes us back into Spanish-Cuban history.

The independence rebellions of the Cubans against Spanish colonial rule were, in part, inspired by the abhorrence of the institution of slavery felt by native-born Cuban leaders. In fact, the father of Cuban independence, Carlos Manuel de Céspedes, set the example by freeing his own slaves on October 10, 1868, on the day that he sounded what is known as the "Grito de Yara," the call for the patriotic uprising, which led to the Ten Years' War. The emancipation of the Negroes was connected with Cuban independence of a century ago.

Negroes were prominent in all ranks of the patriotic forces in the two wars of independence. Negro soldiers formed the bulk of the patriot guerrilla troops in the eastern provinces and Negro leaders were conspicuous among the patriot officers of all ranks. Cuban history credits the final victory of independence, in which the United States shared, primarily to the military genius and example of two great generals—the white professional soldier from the Dominican Republic, Máximo Gómez, and the Cuban Negro guerrilla cavalry leader, Antonio Maceo.

The armistice agreement which terminated the Ten-Years' War in 1878 provided for a general amnesty and ratified the freedom given ten years earlier by de Céspedes and other Cuban leaders. The wartime mutual respect and comradeship of the Cuban patriots, both white and colored, carried over into peacetime relationships. While there is no Utopia in race relationships, nor is a Utopia likely to be achieved, there was a minimum of abrasion in White-Negro contacts in pre-Castro Cuba. In point of fact, Castro and his Communists aggravated the distinction between races, the better to create the class hatreds which served them so well.

Except in the realm of relatively genteel society, there was little racial discrimination, as we know it in the United States. Negroes and mulattoes rose to positions of leadership in the government, the military, the labor movement and in letters. Labor leader Lázaro Peña, although a Communist, made his mark in the pre-Castro era, just as the non-Communist Negro, Juan Almeida, made his mark as a comandante in the Castro period. In terms of Cuban experience, there is nothing remotely remarkable about a Negro comandante in Castro's armed forces, any more than it was remarkable that one of the leaders of the Bay of Pigs invasion force, Captain Erneido Oliva, was also a Negro.

The sports editor of the newspaper, *El Pais*, was Guillermo Portuondo Calá, a prominent Negro. Gastón Baquero, editor of Havana's most prominent conservative daily, *Diario de la Marina*, was recognized as one of Latin America's leading intellectuals. He was a mulatto. And a man of mixed blood was elected by popular vote to the highest office in Cuba, the President of the Republic, in 1940. His name? Fulgencio Batista.

"Losers" typically equate the Negro experience in the United States with that of other countries. When Castro began propagandizing the role of the Negro in his "new" society, conscious of the fact that in sociological terms integration is never fully achieved nor discrimination totally abolished, the "losers" fell like tenpins.[11]

Gripping stories which purport to contrast the sociological advance of the Negro under Cuban Communism with onerous class distinctions under democracy have no effect other than to justify Communism on false or overdrawn grounds. In doing so, the "losers" disagree with the Cuban Negro himself. Here is what some of them, who have fled to the United States, had to say on the subject in interviews with me.

Juan Cores Ibañez of Santiago said: "We Negroes were used as pawns in the Communist game. We were shamefully used for Communist propaganda." Negro newspaperman Orestes Secada, who escaped to the United States in a small boat, later would say: "Those who speak of the backwardness and ill-treatment of the Cuban Negro, who claim that they were exploited before Communism came to my country, are simply playing the Communist game. It is under Communism that we came to feel so inferior. Day after day the Negroes are indoctrinated by Communists to hate the white people, and everything possible is done to encourage race hatreds. The hatred is directed at the United States, of course, but the effect is the same in Cuba."

Negro escapees from Cuba testify that it is more difficult for Negroes to leave Cuba than it is for white people. This testimony is verified by defectors from the Cuban Ministry of Foreign Affairs. One, a functionary in its passport division, stated that upon finding that over 100,000 Negroes had applied to come to the United States, Castro personally ordered their passports cancelled. He was "enraged" that Cuban Negroes would opt to come to the United States in the face of ceaseless propaganda that U.S. Negroes still lived like slaves. A quip in Havana, made in reference to Communist claims that Cuban Negroes are now free while the American Negroes still are in the status of slaves goes like this: "Will anyone trade me off as a 'free' Cuban Negro so that I can go and become an American slave?"

Where did Fidel Castro get his money? Where did he get his political support? The plain truth is that initially Castro extorted money from Cuban businessmen, cattlemen, sugar cane growers, and the owners of sugar mills. If they did not contribute to the revolutionary cause, they were threatened with sabotage at the hands of militants in Castro's 26th of July Movement. Most of those threatened by Castro did contribute, delivering cash to Pastorita Núñez, a Castroite who accepted the money as she made her daily rounds as a conductor on one of Havana's bus lines. The voluntary contributions made by the working class in the last century to support Cuba's wars of independence were notably lacking in 1957 and 1958 to support what the "losers" claim was a popular revolt against alleged capitalist oppression.

Castro did not accompany his revolt against Batista with open charges of American oppression, or with the publicized aim of socializing the economy. In 1958, he took pains to hide the fact that land owners would be the first to feel his revolutionary justice, promising that "just compensation" would be made for land which might have to be expropriated so as to carry out his stated aim of an agrarian reform. The point made here is that the 1940 Constitution provided for a land reform, and the whole of Cuban society was represented in the formulation of that Constitution —including the land owners. Castro's "law" Number 3, which decreed an agrarian reform, drawn up in the Sierra Maestra by the relatively unknown Humberto Sorí Marín and broadcast and rebroadcast over Radio Rebelde in October, 1958, was based most meticulously on the 1940 Constitution.

Such was Castro's appeal to the basically democratic desires of the Cuban people. He had come a long way from that night in February, 1957, when he was interviewed in the Sierra Maestra by Herbert Matthews. Matthews wrote of Castro's program at the time that it was "vague and couched in generalities. . . ." But Matthews ceased being a reporter and became a sponsor with other statements about that program, such as ". . . it amounts to a new deal for Cuba, radical, democratic, and therefore anti-Communist." Castro was described in that celebrated interview as one who ". . . has strong ideas on liberty, democracy, social justice, the need to restore the Constitution, to hold elections. . . ."[12] How tragically wrong these judgments, based on just one interview, were, is obvious.

In his book, *The Cuban Story*, Matthews quotes Jaime Benítez, Chancellor of the University of Puerto Rico, as crediting him and the *New York Times* with making Castro respectable to doubtful Cubans. "'. . . be it said," Matthews quotes Benítez, "in fairness, of the *New York Times*, whose stories and editorials helped to make Castro and his movement acceptable to as yet undecided Cubans. . . ."[13] Such is the power of the press.

Castro never would have come to power if the Cubans had had the slightest notion of what was in store for them. Those who took Castro's statements at face value became powerful propaganda voices for his cause, a cause for which none of them would vouch authoritatively at the time. With Matthews' interview—which showed Fidel Castro to be alive while Batista and the United Press were claiming he was dead—Castro became a legitimate source of international news.

Most newsmen were unaware at the time that theirs was an encounter with an extraordinarily able propagandist—perhaps the cleverest manipulator of peoples in the history of the Western Hemisphere. There can be little doubt that Fidel Castro used the resources of world media to publicize programs which were cruelly opposite to those which he actually carried out. He simply outwitted some interrogators and made willing disciples of others.

Castro was no less effective with the Cuban people, of course. Having failed so miserably in April, 1958, to promote the general strike, and the popular uprising which was supposed to follow, he changed his tactics. Simply stated, those tactics were to provoke Batista to shoot Cuban civilians, and it was through these tactics that Castro obtained the political support necessary to his final victory.

Castro set urban terrorism in motion. In the cities, Castro's 26th of July Movement, together with other elements comprising the Civic Resistance Movement, struck at the civilian populace. For example, Sears was bombed in a daring attack, and several shoppers were injured. (The perpetrator of that bombing, Enrique Oltuski, was to become Castro's Minister of Communications at age 29.) A young woman at the Tropicana night club had her hand severed by a bomb placed in her evening bag by a terrorist. Noise bombs were set off in parking lots, trash cans, empty streets, and movie houses. By the summer of 1958, ushers at theaters politely inspected ladies' handbags and frisked their escorts before permitting them to enter.

Batista reacted according to Castro's plan. He met terrorism with counter-terrorism, in an ever-spiraling atmosphere of tension in the cities and towns of Cuba.

The youth of Cuba, particularly the students, took a leading part in the urban unrest that became a powerful factor in toppling Batista. More than one father was horrified to find his son in the garage making Molotov cocktails by filling Coca-Cola bottles with gasoline. There was reason for this, also. Leadership of the *Directorio Revolucionario Estudiantil* (DRE), the Cuban Student Directorate, had been virtually decimated in a bold attack on the Presidential Palace on March 13, 1957, aimed at assassinating Batista. The DRE had rejected Castro's demand, made at a meeting in Mexico in 1956, that he be put in charge of all anti-Batista activities. José Echeverría, the DRE leader, suspected that Castro was in liaison with the Communists, a suspicion of considerable merit as we shall see later in examining the famous 1964 trial of Marcos Rodríguez Alfonso, a Communist who informed on the DRE.

In any event, the crushing of the DRE in 1957 had the effect of riveting public attention on Fidel Castro and his small band of guerrillas as a major inspiration in the growing fight against Batista. While elements of the DRE did take to the mountains of Las Villas Province to carry on the battle from there, Castro had captured the center of the stage, where he was spotlighted as the military symbol of the people's opposition to Batista.

But from April of 1958 on, it was the civilian populace, not Castro and his men in the mountains of Oriente Province, that bore the brunt of the war against Batista. They, not Castro, were the real heroes of the revolt, as Batista called to his side as many political hoodlums as he could muster to do his dirty work. Batista's police struck, and they struck hard. They could not have committed all of the brutalities attributed to them by clever Castro propaganda, which, for example, put out the completely unsubstantiated claim that Batista had murdered some 20,000 Cubans. Here Batista blundered and Castro profited. The dictator forbade any mention of Castro or his military actions in the press, or over the radio. Cuban rumors, a thousandfold more potent than any factual account of civil strife, took over. With public opinion against Batista hardening day-by-day, the government's excesses were magnified, fanned by potent Castro propaganda beamed nightly from his mountain redoubt. The 20,-000 figure became fixed in the public mind as an index of Batista's cruelty. Castro's urban terrorists were justified in their excesses. After all, wasn't Batista an illegitimate President who had seized power by force in 1952? Such was the mood in Cuba the last six months of 1958.

Castro's propaganda actually reached the conference table of the American Embassy where some of it was accepted as fact. I recall one of Ambassador Earl E. T. Smith's daily staff meetings in the summer of 1958, at which an Embassy official repeated a report that several anti-Batista students had been chained to trees and telephone poles on First Avenue in the Miramar Section and machine-gunned by Batista's henchmen. After the "ohs" and "ahs" had died down, another officer reported that the "Tigers" of Rolando Masferrer, alternately an enemy and ally of Batista, were the killers. This information came to him from a "confidential source." My notes show that the conversation shifted to a discussion of Masferrer and to an indictment of some of the private gangs who had thrown in with Batista. The Ambassador then cut off the discussion.

The point is, however, that an unsubstantiated report of an atrocity moved swiftly from the status of rumor to that of "fact," even to the point of identifying the criminals. An unofficial investigation, carried out on the personal whim of an Embassy officer, turned up the truth. The story of this particular incident, like so many in rumor-ridden Cuba in 1958, originated harmlessly but burgeoned into a triumph of Castro propaganda. The original source was a maid who worked in a house across from a *sitio* (hide-away) belonging to a VIP of the Batista regime. The *sitio* was guarded by Masferrer's "Tigers," and they kept watch on the neighboring houses, taking whatever liberties they chose in doing so. The maid complained to her employer regarding the "freshness" of the hoodlums, who often came into the kitchen demanding coffee and food. She warned the already distraught housewife that her student son was known for his outspoken anti-Batista feelings, and that he might end up being shot right in front of the house. One night, the trigger-happy "Tigers" opened fire at shadows. That same night, the police overtook a speeding car filled with students, and jailed them on suspicion of terrorism. Somehow, the two stories became amalgamated into a "slaughter" of Cuban students by the "Tigers" of Rolando Masferrer. As the account made the rounds of Havana, the chains and the bodies were added by the always fertile Cuban imagination.

This example is not to suggest, by any means, that the American Embassy became a channel for Castro propaganda. What it does suggest is that some Embassy officers were caught up in the glamour of the anti-Batista cause, and had, in some cases, become unwitting accomplices of Castro's propaganda against Batista.

Pro-Castro and anti-Batista militants (they were not always identical) in the universities often *were* shot or imprisoned, however. But the public was caught between Castro's active propaganda, on the one hand, and Batista's sterile censorship, on the other. Inflated word-of-mouth accounts flew around Cuba and gave victory in the battle for the Cuban mind to Fidel Castro. The climate of rumor and fear which gripped Cuba's cities was skillfully played upon and exaggerated in nightly broadcasts from the mountains by Castro's Rebel Radio. The end result was massive desertion of Batista by Cuba's middle-class, and the acceptance of Fidel Castro only as the lesser of many evils. Castro's popularity in 1958 was by no means as widespread as his apologists would have us believe. That came later, as a result of final victory.

For well over six months in 1958 I interviewed, talked, ate, drank, and swam with hundreds of middle-class Cubans. They fiercely condemned Batista for having come to power by force on March 10, 1952, interrupting the slow progress being made toward constitutional democracy over the period of the previous twelve years. Yes, there was corruption. But, they felt, the way to curb that corruption was to build solid democratic institutions to replace the weak and ineffective bureaucracy inherited from Spanish colonial rule. They hoped that Fidel Castro would do so. This was the true voice of Cuba, not the Castro propaganda of Mills' *Listen, Yankee!*

Needless to say, this is not a view shared by the "losers." It cannot be, for they recognize no strong middle class in pre-Castro Cuba. Captured very early by the revolutionaries, they were released very late, if at all, from the romantic grip of Fidel Castro. But the truth of matter is that while in the mountains, Fidel Castro himself found it necessary to appeal to the instincts of the Cuban middle and upper-middle class with promises which reflected their hopes and aspirations. By aligning itself, even negatively, with Castro, the middle class succeeded in eventually destroying itself.

However, to carry on his insurrection, Castro needed not only to induce a massive revulsion against Batista and his methods within the bulk of the Cuban people, but also to get money beyond that obtained through extortion to arm his terrorists and to operate his propaganda machine. He declared a "tax" levy on every bag of sugar produced in Oriente Province. If the harrassed sugar mill owner did not come through with the tax, he was threatened once more. Most came through with the tax. Some corporations and businesses located in Cuba's cities quite callously paid off Castro's couriers so as to be on the winning side—just in case. Money from this source increased as the year 1958 wore on and it was becoming apparent to just about everybody that it was only a matter of time before Batista abdicated or his successor, Andrés Rivero Aguero, scheduled to take office in February of 1959, collapsed.

There was an active courier service collecting money in the United States, as well, and getting that money into Cuba.

In making out a check to an anti-Castro Cuban one day in 1964 at the National Press Club in Washington, a bureau chief for a large mid-Western daily turned to him, laughing. "I don't know if you remember this or not," he said, "but I stood right at this bar six years ago and made out a check to be used to support Castro." The particular Cuban courier for an exile anti-Castro action group was the same courier who had worked collecting money for Fidel Castro several years before!

One incident, in particular, stands out. In 1958, a plane from Miami en route to Varadero beach in Cuba was hijacked by two members of Castro's 26th of July Movement, and, at the end, crashed. According to the lone passenger survivor of the crash, one of the two hijackers held the occupants of the plane and the crew at gun-point while another removed some boxes containing money from aperatures in the floor of the aircraft. This indicated that the ground crew of the airline, based in the United States, working with the hijackers had concealed the boxes in advance of the flight. The two calmly donned 26th of July arm bands and, pistols in hand, ordered the pilot to fly toward the Sierra Maestra, about 400 miles off course, where he was instructed to circle as the hijackers looked in vain for a previously arranged landing area.

Running low on fuel, the pilot took the plane to Nipe Bay in Oriente Province. The plane apparently ran completely out of fuel as it was being landed at a small airfield, and it fell into the bay. The two hijackers managed to escape, while all but one of the passengers met their death. Following an investigation, Consul Hugh D. Kessler of the American Embassy turned in a report that the two hijackers had made their way to the nearby Cristal mountains where Raúl Castro and his forces of the "Second Front" operated.

Be that as it may, by the fall of 1958 Castro had both money, and active support, where it counted—among the Cuban middle and upper-middle class whose sons were the victims of Batista's reprisals, triggered by Castro's terroristic urban war. It cannot be stressed too often or too strongly that here lay the main strength of anti-Batista forces.

Cuba's orthodox Communist Party was among the late, late, comers to jump aboard Castro's bandwagon. Party members viewed Castro as a "putschist," and thought that the overthrow of Batista could only be accomplished through massive force.[14] Such was their surprise (and a commentary, incidentally, on Communist claims of knowing the temper of the people) at the success of Castro's urban guerrilla warfare that Carlos Rafael Rodríguez, considered to be one of the best brains in the Cuban Communist Party, was spurred to drag his middle-aged bones up the Sierra Maestra to pay homage to Fidel Castro. By some doubtful accounts, Rafael Rodríguez brought with him nearly a million dollars which he contributed to Castro's war chest. If true, the money arrived after the all-important psychological shift by Cuba's solid middle class from Batista to Castro.

The importance of that psychological shift in Castro's favor may be measured by the fact that Batista's forces were at all times numerically so superior to Castro's mountain guerrillas that only massive desertion from Batista can account for his downfall. Two incidents mentioned earlier—"Che" Guevara's bribe of the Camaguey garrison, and the selling of Batista's armored train—indicate that the morale of government troops had begun to sag, and that the sellout had begun. It is to be wondered, with 6,000 to 7,000 troops sealing Castro's forces off in the mountains, why it was so easy for brigades of reporters and a well-known functionary of the Communist Party to move in and out of the Sierra Maestra. One comes upon accounts of this traffic in many books written on Cuba. But few authors seem to see anything remarkable about it.

The revulsion of the middle class against Batista had also taken its toll of the allegiance of the military to their commander-in-chief. Many "losers" would have the reader believe that the Cuban military establishment was composed of members of the upper, or "ruling class," and performed largely as an instrument of that class. True, there was an era —from 1902 to 1933—when members of Cuba's best families served as officers in Cuba's army, navy, and its burgeoning air force. However, that era came to an end with the overthrow of President Gerardo Machado, back in 1933. In what became known as "the revolt of the sergeants," following Machado's overthrow, the elite Cuban officer corps was deliberately and systematically destroyed by the leader of that revolt, Sergeant Fulgencio Batista, who appointed sergeants and corporals to the rank of officers. The tradition (if it can be called a tradition) of maintaining a military establishment that was representative of the middle and lower classes, continued to the day that Castro took power. Largely middle-class itself, the Cuban Army officer corps was, in 1958, no less vulnerable to Castro's propaganda than anyone else. The will of the troops to remain vigilant in the mountains, where there was precious little fighting, was eroded by accounts reaching them of Batista's counter-terrorism in the cities where their families resided. Castro addressed this point in his famous interview with Herbert Matthews in 1957: "The soldiers are fighting badly; their morale is low. . . ."[15] And Theodore Draper accurately describes the situation in his book, *Castro's Revolution*, when he writes that "The heaviest losses were suffered by the largely middle-class urban resistance movement, which secreted the political and psychological acids that ate into Batista's fighting force."[16] One can add to Draper's formulation the fact that propaganda directed at the armed forces sowed the seeds of doom. The Army was told that Castro's victory was inevitable, that the Army was fighting for nothing. In short, the Army's will to resist was broken.

The almost farcical nature of the engagements between the two forces was portrayed to me by William Morgan, an American who was Comandante with the Second Front of the Escambray Mountains in Las Villas

Province. One alleged major encounter in which battle commands by radio were rebroadcast over short-wave to a goggle-eyed Cuban audience, was a "tremendous propaganda play," said Morgan. He related that Comandante Eloy Gutiérrez Menoyo, his immediate superior, "broadcast battle commands, directed fictitious troops here and there, and had a helluva time," while the "background noises" were supplied by Browning automatics, rifles, and pistols in the hands of Morgan and a few of his men. "We yelled a lot, too," Morgan added to me in great merriment.

From other reports, painstakingly gathered in the months immediately following the flight of Batista, it seems that Morgan's chronicle of battle is not as far-fetched as it may first appear. After Castro's rise to power on January 1, 1959, it slowly dawned on the Cubans that his rise was not at all the result of military triumphs which he had been trumpeting nightly.

Embassy intelligence carefully weighed the evidence, and came up with the ridiculous figure of 182 casualties on both sides, after two years of "revolution!" This figure did not, of course, include those victimized by urban guerrilla warfare. The conclusion reached was that Castro's was largely a triumph of propaganda and of carefully worked-out tactics which assured him and his men in the mountains of maximum results at minimum risk to themselves.

But victory is victory, no matter how it is won. One of Castro's greatest triumphs lay in his extraordinary ability to attract American intellectuals and writers as camp followers.* They saw Castro as they wanted to see him; they saw pre-Castro Cuba as they wanted to see it. In doing so they became little more than influence peddlers for one of the greatest and most disgraceful hoaxes ever perpetrated against the American people. Furthermore, they did so for a Fidel Castro who held them in contempt for their gullibility.

Castro, the Cuban revolutionary, most certainly made a lasting impression on American policy. To an extent little realized, the Alliance for Progress was created as an answer to economic and social conditions which, it was alleged, led to the rise of the Cuban dictator. Once the Alliance was created, the bureaucrats defended it. This is nowhere more apparent than in a report to the President by our Ambassador to the United Nations, the late Adlai Stevenson, in the summer of 1961, following a swing around Latin America. In the "governmentese" of the bureaucrat, Mr. Stevenson made a tortured defense of the Alliance on the false grounds typical of the "losers." His report reads, in part: "Negative postures—as drawing attention to the Sovietization of Cuba, the establishment there of a police state apparatus of terror, the perversion

*We can add to the apologists already referred to, the names of Raymond Hulsey, Kyle Haselden, Carleton Beales, Waldo Frank, Walter Lippmann, Arnold Toynbee.

of Castro's originally stated revolutionary objectives—are not likely to counterbalance among the underprivileged even the slimmest evidence that the Cuban peasant has acquired a place in the sun; that however little the *guajiro* may actually have gained materially, the gulf between him and the rich has been greatly narrowed by the elimination of the rich."

One of Castro's contributions to insurrectionary movements throughout the world was his proof that in a revolutionary age, psychologically the odds always favor the revolutionary. Fidel Castro's numerous apologists in the United States, again to borrow from Mr. Draper's formulation, "secreted the political and psychological acids" that corroded the thinking of our political leaders. This is perfectly expressed in the fatuous phrases of Mr. Stevenson.

At once a visionary and a demagogue, Fidel Castro seems to have made as deep an impression on Kremlin thinking as his propaganda ploy (that the Cuban people demanded a complete turnover of their economic, social, and political system) made on liberals in the United States. His victory of the few over the many was the result of unflagging faith in armed guerrilla struggle. His means of achieving that victory—urban action, indiscriminate bombings, political warfare, and all forms of paramilitary conflict—blazed the trail for other revolutionaries to follow.

Castro's contribution to Communist tactics of "liberation wars" appears to have been endorsed by none other than Nikita Khrushchev, who did so in his famous speech of January 6, 1961. Delivered to an assembly of party organizers and academicians in Moscow, Nikita Khrushchev pointed out that "liberation wars" provide the Communists with unlimited maneuverability. By the process of elimination he ruled world war out as a means by which the capitalist countries would respond to the Communist challenge. "Capitalism," he said, "would be wiped out." As for "local wars," said the wily Khrushchev, the Communists can control those as well by threatening that free world response to Communist aggression [as in Vietnam] "may grow into a world thermonuclear rocket war." In other words, with world wars and local wars brought under Communist control through nuclear blackmail, the field is left wide open to Communist paramilitary conflict by indigenous forces where they clearly possess the initiative.

In Communist terminology, Castro's was a "liberation war." In winning, Castro provided the Communists with a living example for "wars of national liberation,"—wars which allow them unprecedented elasticity in selecting the most suitable techniques of conflict and the most favorable battlegrounds. Themselves safe from massive retaliation, the Russians take care of their share of the bargain by rattling their missiles against the West, peddling the theme of "peaceful coexistence," while at the same time supplying the insurrectionaries with the tools of revolt on the grounds that those revolts reflect "the peoples' " legitimate right to resort to force against tyranny, in their search for social and economic justice.

It would be well for Castro's apologists in the United States, the "losers," to contemplate for a moment what they have done. The support thrown to Castro on the basis of the democratic direction he *said* he was taking, while tragically wrong, may be taken merely as a measure of their gullibility. But, to base that support on a distorted picture of the economic and social picture of pre-Castro Cuba, is quite another thing.* It gave the Communists the enormous psychological advantage, by which their Cuban "war of liberation" was carried out under a false banner, one which was first raised by none other than American intellectual leadership itself.

*To illustrate the point on Negroes in pre-Castro Cuba, the following Negroes occupied important positions in government and elsewhere: Martín Morúa Delgado (President of the Senate and later Minister of Agriculture), General Gregorio Querejeta (Chief of the Army under Batista), General Manuel de J. Delgado (also, Minister of Agriculture), Dr. Miguel Angel Céspedes (Minister of Justice), Juan Gualberto Gomez (Congressman and Senator), Aquilino Lombard (Senator), Priciliano Piedra (Congressman). There are many more. Furthermore, Juan Gualberto Gomez worked hand-in-hand with Jose Martí, Cuba's liberator, a fact that eliminated all sentiment of racism in Republican Cuba.

To the knowledge of most people, Juan Almeida is the only Negro in a prominent position in the Castro regime. Illiterate, and a former bricklayer, Almeida has demonstrated none of the intellectual talent of his illustrious Negro predecessors in government.

CHAPTER 3

•

The Embassy

•

DURING 1957 AND 1958, the American Embassy in Havana also played its role in the Cuban drama. This role was variously interpreted in the camp of the "losers." To some, the personnel of the Embassy were blissfully unaware of what was really going on in Cuba. To others, our Foreign Service officers were unquestionably pro-Batista and anti-Castro. To most, the alleged stupidities of our Ambassadors not only were responsible for Fidel Castro's anti-Americanism, but in fact drove him into the arms of the Communists. What lay behind these attacks was a determination by the "losers" quickly to undercut the American Embassy whenever it exhibited any sign of strength to deal with Castro.

Earl E. T. Smith became American Ambassador to Cuba in the summer of 1957, replacing Arthur Gardner. The views of the *New York Times* regarding the two American Ambassadors were revealed in dispatches written by Herbert Matthews. He wrote on June 16,1957, that "Ambassador Gardner left Cuba today with the relations of the Cuban people toward the United States gravely impaired." While Gardner, it is generally agreed, was excessively friendly to General Batista, it seems clear from Mr. Matthews' writings that no Ambassador could expect his (Matthews') support unless he were, on the other hand, excessively friendly to Fidel Castro.

In the same dispatch, Matthews condemned Mr. Smith and longed for the appointment of a career officer. He wrote of Smith's confirmation as Ambassador that "poor Cuba was getting still another businessman, a complete novice to Cuba and Latin America, whose only known qualification for the appointment was that he was finance chairman of the Republican Party. . . ." He also said of the appointment that "everyone at the State Department realized that if ever a post required an experienced career officer, Havana in 1957 was the place."

Yet, when career officer Philip Bonsal was indeed assigned as Ambassador in 1959, and failed to get anywhere with Castro, Mr. Matthews wrote: "It was a curious quirk of history that Bonsal should have been a direct descendant of Gouverneur Morris, who was United States envoy to Paris during the French Revolution. As it happened, this did not give Philip Bonsal the mentality or temperament to understand or sympathize with the sort of revolution Cuba was experiencing . . . Bonsal could see only the American point of view."[1]

In other words, American ambassadors were judged by the *New York Times* on the basis of how sympathetic they were to Mr. Matthews' views of Castro. In another section of this book I shall go into Ambassador Bonsal's relations with Castro and his government and disprove Mr. Matthews' sweeping statement. Matthews' comments on three American Ambassadors are quoted here merely to demonstrate his richly obvious bias in favor of Fidel Castro. And since it was Mr. Matthews who did more than perhaps any other writer to establish the fiction that it was the United States, through its anti-Castro and pro-Batista personnel in the Havana Embassy, that "drove Cuba into the arms of the Russians," it is well to examine some of his points.

"One of the first things the Ambassador [Smith] did," writes Matthews of the novice diplomat, "was to go to Santiago de Cuba, the only city where we had a consulate, and to our mining interests in Moa Bay, as well as to the Guantanamo Naval Base."[2] These unkind cuts were taken at Ambassador Smith for visiting a "non-Cuba," which was representative only of U.S. interests, I suppose.

Matthews continues: "In Santiago, a large group of middle-class women demonstrated against Batista and were brutally treated by the Cuban police. Smith was shocked and said publicly: 'Any sort of excessive police action is abhorrent to me.'" Matthews continues further: "This was the last gesture Smith made on behalf of the Cuban people and against the Batista regime."

These passages sum up the Leftist argument against American policy in Cuba. Wanting Castro to win, they expected the American Ambassadors to be openly "against the Batista regime." In Ambassador Smith's celebrated Santiago case, he (improperly) did what no career officer (who, Matthews insists, was needed at the time) should do—namely, made public statements which amounted to direct interference in the internal affairs of a friendly country. It amounted to a rejection of the very government to which he was accredited.

American Ambassadors *are* expected to speak out publicly in defense of the interests of the United States. But statements such as the one gratuitously made by Mr. Smith in Santiago, Cuba, simply are not condoned, either by the government to whom an Ambassador is accredited or by his chiefs in Washington. This is an accepted tenet of diplomacy.

While there is much that can be criticized about American policy, let it be said in all fairness that when Ambassador Smith arrived in Havana he found his staff overwhelmingly favorable to Castro and unfavorably disposed toward Batista. In fact, the temper of the personnel in the American Embassy was exactly the reverse of what has been advertised by too many "losers" for much too long a period.

In 1957 and 1958, non-diplomat American residents in Cuba were actively caught up in the anti-Batista fight. Upper-middle and upper-class for the most part, they belonged to clubs frequented by Cubans of the same social and economic strata, and joined their friends in attempts to oust Batista. American businessman hid anti-Batista activists in their offices and in their homes, and contributed money to buy arms and food for urban guerrillas. Important, also, was their exerting tremendous anti-Batista pressures on the American Embassy.

American women were in the forefront of the fight. Mrs. Mariada Arensberg, a Ruston Academy teacher, worked hard in the urban underground movement in company with such Cuban allies as Mrs. Elena Mederos, a civic leader, who later became Castro's first Minister of Social Welfare. Gilbert Smith and his wife Louise lived next to me in the Miramar section of Havana. Bravely, they made their home a place where the sons and daughters of their friends fighting in the underground were able to find food and a place to hide from Batista police. They later turned against Castro's Communist dictatorship. In a strange twist of history, in the summer of 1960, I accompanied Tad Szulc to a meeting at which Louise Smith and Elena Mederos briefed that emissary of the *New York Times* on the Communist take-over of the democratic revolution for which they had fought.

Resistance to Batista was so widespread that it took on an open, almost club-like character. This was so because in the main Batista permitted the Cubans to talk, so long as the talk was not accompanied by acts of armed resistance to his regime. The atmosphere of open dissension was impressed upon me when, one fall day in 1958, I lunched at the Centro Vasco restaurant with Gastón Baquero, the brilliant mulatto editor of the newspaper, *Diario de la Marina.* I made the appointment because of rumors circulating in Havana that Batista might flee the country. Baquero was a *Batistiano* (Batista supporter), and I hoped to obtain his assessment of those rumors.

I was surprised, first of all, at Baquero's assertion that his support for the wily Cuban dictator was based less on admiration for him that it was on a deep and abiding fear of Fidel Castro. Castro, Baquero said with considerable feeling, "is a political gangster." He quickly dismissed rumors that Batista might flee Cuba, and came back to Castro, obviously his favorite subject. Baquero told me about a gangster organization, the Insurrectional Revolutionary Union (UIR), and said that Fidel Castro had been a member. The UIR was the brainchild of an amazing Cuban, Emilio Tro. Tro, according to Baquero, had enlisted in the U.S. armed forces and had fought with distinction in World War II. After the war, he set about creating the UIR as a loosely knit organization to help Tro and his followers reach the top of the political ladder by physically eliminating their opponents. Tro gathered about him a group of political "outs," said Baquero, each of whom had his own particular ambitions. The individual member agreed to cooperate with other members of the UIR, in return for their assistance in eliminating his own particular road-block to power. The UIR, according to Baquero, was a sort of Mafia, with no visible ideological base to it. Fidel Castro joined the UIR, Baquero stated, for the purpose of getting rid of Manolo Castro (no relative), an enormously popular student leader who blocked Fidel's bid for power on the campus of Havana University. Fidel Castro did not personally murder the student leader, only because he was waiting in ambush for him at the wrong place. Other members of the UIR gang were in the right place, however, and Manolo Castro was assassinated by them. I later checked Baquero's account of Tro, the UIR, and Fidel Castro's association with the UIR, with knowledgeable Cubans and with the CIA, and found it to be accurate.[3] Tro was himself finally gunned down by Mario Salabarria, chief of the National Police under President Ramón Grau San Martín, and Orlando León Lemus, another political gangster who cooperated with the police. With Tro's demise, the UIR dissolved.

Turning to Castro's proposals for an agrarian reform, Baquero said prophetically: "An agrarian reform will bring hunger to Cuba." Just then, Enrique Losada joined Baquero and me at our table. A respected lawyer, Losada was publicly known for his anti-Batista attitude. Nevertheless, he sat down to discuss the political situation with *Batistiano* Gastón Baquero, and opened the discussion by confessing that he also had grave doubts about Fidel Castro. Castro's "unwholesome background" disturbed him, Losada admitted, pointing out that statements made by Castro at his defense trial back in 1953 "were indicative of a totalitarian mind." I asked Losada what he thought of Baquero's comments that Castro's proposals for an agrarian reform would bring hunger to the Cubans. Losada answered: "Castro seems to be propagandizing an agrarian reform, rather than applying himself to devising a workable reform." He then posed the rhetorical question: "Why should he do this? Every *guajiro* in the country knows that the Constitution provides for an agrarian reform. What all of us are asking is: what *kind* of an agrarian reform!" Baquero ventured the opinion that the country would be better off with the known quantity of Fulgencio Batista, or a successor chosen by Batista, than the unknown quantity of Fidel Castro. Losada exploded, arguing that the choice should "not be between one or the other of two obvious evils." The only solution visible, Losada continued, was "for Cubans to get behind a caretaker government." His words, almost verbatim, were: "A group of non-political civic leaders should be drafted, a group with the guts to tell Batista to get out of the country, and for Castro to come out of the hills and stop his terrorism in the cities and towns. These leaders should prepare the government for democratic elections, elections which would even include Fidel Castro as a candidate for the President. Such a solution is our only hope." I will go into Losada's "solution" later in this chapter, since it was exactly what much-maligned U. S. Ambassador Earl E. T. Smith had been proposing to the State Department for nearly a year. The point here, however, is that at several junctures in the arguments between Losada and Baquero, the two men waved their arms and raised their voices in typically unrestrained Latin manner. It was a graphic illustration of the remarkable openness in which political discussions took place between Cubans in 1958.

A display of anti-Batista sentiment took place one evening, when a group of friends and I went to the Bodeguita del Medio for dinner. Located in the centuries-old center of the city, it was largely the creation of Hungarian refugee artist, "Seppy" Drobrogny, who had his studios just across the market square. Filled with trinkets, several photographs of journalist Mario Kuchilán Sol, who had been beaten by Batista's police, and a cast taken from Seppy's leg, broken while skiing abroad in Switzerland, and aided by Seppy's promotional efforts, the Bodeguita del Medio had become a major tourist attraction specializing in typical Cuban food and music.

More to the point, in 1958, the Bodeguita del Medio had also become a rendevous for revolutionaries. Its guitarist, Carlos Puebla, was known to be a fellow-traveler, and was said to have been a recruiter for Castro. On the evening that I was there, the place was crowded almost beyond capacity. Suddenly, someone shouted a request for Castro's 26th of July Hymn. Puebla obliged, and everyone rose and sang it at the top of their lungs. My eyes, however, were on a Batista soldier lounging, rifle in hand, at the doorway. When the hymn started, he got up, looked around hesitantly for a moment, and with a wave of his hand at the proprietor sauntered out into the street and away from the restaurant. About one-third of the people in the Bodeguita del Medio were resident Americans in Cuba, and they sang as lustily as anyone else there.

Indeed, evidence of anti-Batista and pro-Castro sentiment among Americans was to be found throughout Cuba. CIA agent William Patterson was stationed in Santiago, where he had gained the confidence of

Castro's 26th of July underground movement. His purpose, of course, was to obtain as much information as possible about Castro's guerrilla band in the nearby Sierra Maestra. Patterson was a major contact through which U.S. and other foreign reporters were gotten into the mountains for interviews with Fidel Castro and leading members of his guerrilla group. Usually, Patterson's favors were extended to the reporters in return for their telling him, upon their return to Santiago, bits and pieces of information which he had requested of them prior to their leaving for the mountains. They thus frequently supplied valuable intelligence for the U.S. government. By word and deed, Patterson was known to Fidel Castro as a valuable contact who helped the bearded leader gain worldwide publicity. In the intelligence game, this was considered a fair trade.

Oscar Guerra, American Consul in Santiago, also was close to leaders of the 26th of July Movement. There was rather general belief among Cubans in that city that Guerra was personally very sympathetic to Castro. Again, it cannot be said to what extent Guerra maintained his contacts for official reasons, but there was no doubt that also by word and deed, he was considered by the Castroites to be helpful to their cause.

Richard Cushing, the Public Affairs Officer of the American Embassy in Havana, helped American reporters in their constant search for the sensational Castro story. He managed, he told me later, to get at least one reporter into the mountains of Oriente Province where he interviewed Castro. In doing so, Cushing dealt with the Castro underground. And in 1957, he actually hid Rufo López Fresquet, one of Castro's underground leaders, in his own house. López Fresquet, incidentally, was a confidant of Herbert Matthews and like Elena Mederos, became a Minister in Castro's cabinet.

The reason why the Embassy official gave sanctuary to the Castroite is related to an assassination attempt on the life of Batista—the attack on the Palace by the Student Directorate, on March 13, 1957. López Fresquet and others knew of the Palace assault in advance, and believed that if it failed Batista's police would round up anyone known to be opposed to his regime. He, his wife, and children, "visited" at the Embassy official's house for several days before, during, and following the Palace assault.

The Embassy obviously knew about the assault in advance. So did CIA, whose chief in Havana, William Caldwell, was a close personal friend of the Public Affairs Officer. Yet, despite claims by Matthews and others that the Embassy and its Ambassadors were pro-Batista, not one word of warning reached Batista through Embassy sources. Considering that the old dictator was about to be "rubbed-out," it seems remarkable that a "pro-Batista" American Embassy refused to alert him of his impending demise. This is not to suggest that American embassies should be informers. It does suggest the obvious—that claims of pro-Batista sentiment in the Embassy were grossly, if not criminally, exaggerated.[4]

The action taken by the Public Affairs Officer may be defended on humanitarian grounds, though reprehensible according to diplomatic tenets. But the contrast between our diplomats' opening of a home to protect a Castro agent on the one hand, and refusing to alert President Batista of a plot to kill him on the other, should be obvious enough for even the "losers" to draw some conclusions.

The American Embassy itself harbored an American pilot who was illegally flying supplies from the United States and dropping them to Castro in the Sierra Maestra. On his *twentieth* flight in the summer of 1958, pilot Charles Hormel either ran out of gas or experienced mechanical failure and crashed his plane in the Bay of Guantanamo. Pulled out by U.S. Naval personnel, Hormel was spirited to Havana, taken to the American Embassy where Batista's police could not get at him, and then illegally gotten out of Cuba.

I came upon this event quite by accident. A heavily bandaged man, obviously an American, was standing in front of my office in the lobby of the Embassy. I went out to ask him to come in and sit down. He thanked me, but said he was waiting for the Assistant Naval Attaché, who arrived at that very moment and took Hormel to his office. A few minutes later Jay Mallin of *Time* magazine came to my office and asked, "Where is the pilot?" Startled, I told him that I knew of no pilot.

Mallin used a phone in my office to call the Naval Attaché, and went upstairs to meet him. He later told me the story. Met in the office of the Naval Attaché by the Air and Army Attachés, Mallin was asked to help them get Hormel out of the country. An old Cuban hand, with contacts within the Batista government as well as among the 26th of July Movement which were the envy of our political office, Jay obliged. He used one of his old tourist cards, faked to indicate that Hormel had come to Havana as a tourist. At the request of the military attachés, Jay personally took Hormel to the airport where he "explained" Hormel's bandages to the SIM (Military Intelligence Service) as the result of an automobile collision—a perfectly plausible explanation to those who have driven in the traffic of pre-Castro Havana.

These, then, were the American "militarists" whose failure to withdraw the military mission from Cuba in protest to Batista is offered up as proof by the "losers" that their sympathies were with the Cuban dictator. The logic of the "losers" is simple. Batista is a military man. American officers are military men. Ergo, they think alike and act alike. Yet, American military officers knowingly spirited a *twenty-mission* Castro pilot out of the country at the risk of being declared *persona non grata,* and perhaps even cashiered out of the service by their superiors.[5]

There can be no question that Batista and his henchmen tried to use the military mission in Cuba as proof that his regime enjoyed American support. But there can also be little question that few Cubans, least of all the members of Castro's underground who were in friendly contact with the Embassy, believed it. The fact is that the United States cut off military aid to Batista in March of 1958 with the eruption of urban guerrilla warfare in Cuba's cities. Even so, our military aid program to the Batista regime had been nominal, at best.

Second, that aid was only one such program among many being extended to Latin American countries in mutual defense. From fiscal year 1946 through fiscal year 1959 (interrupted in March of 1958), the United States sent Cuba about $11 million. Uruguay, holding a far less strategic position, geographically, than Cuba, and with a population about one third that of Cuba, received double the aid sent to Batista—$23.2 million.[6] And in the fall of 1958 when Batista attempted to identify U.S. support for his regime with a military celebration which he held at Camp Columbia, the Chief of the American military mission to Havana told off the Cuban General Staff in no uncertain terms. Elements of the Embassy quickly relayed U.S. reaction to the crude Batista maneuver where it should have counted—to Castro's underground leaders in Havana.

These incidents are cited here, not only for the story they tell in themselves, but to provide some background to the trouble which Ambassador Smith experienced with his staff at the Embassy. For, as a result of the pro-Castro sentiment of the staff, Smith came to rely less and less on their judgment and more and more on his own.

Mr. Smith came to know only later what his staff knew at the time— that the Santiago demonstration was staged precisely to force the American Ambassador to take sides. The three staff members who were along at Santiago urged him to make what essentially was an anti-Batista statement. As career officers they must have known that it would have no other result than to give comfort to Castro (who said nothing favorable about Mr. Smith's declaration, by the way) and his allies, enrage Batista, and make Ambassador Smith out to be something of an idiot in the State Department. Ambassador Smith wondered aloud one day to Dan Braddock, his Deputy Chief of Mission, if the members of his entourage might not deliberately have tried to undercut him. Certainly, the tenor of Ambassador-staff relationships was established with the Santiago incident.

One thing is certain. Ambassador Smith became increasingly suspicious of the motives of his officers. On one occasion, he virtually accused the CIA chief of being a Communist for harboring views which did not coincide with his own. Here we find arguments missing each other. Smith had been working for months on an alternative to Castro *and* Batista by proposing to the State Department that the U.S. get behind a provisional government of prominent private citizens which would rule until popular elections could be held. He believed, and not without reason, that reports from his political section to the State Department predicting the imminent fall of Batista merely served to undercut him. Such reports created a crisis atmosphere in Washington which impeded orderly progress toward Smith's solution—or so Smith thought. When he tried to temper the reports of the Embassy's political section so they would conform to his policy, Smith was unfairly accused by them of having sold out to Batista. The inferences which the Ambassador drew from those accusations are not difficult to imagine.

In all fairness, Ambassador Smith was not without excellent outside sources of information. A wealthy man, Smith not only had valuable outside contacts among men of knowledge and influence, but he is generally conceded to have been several notches above his predecessor in ability and energy. Six feet six inches in height, brusque, uncompromising, and explosive, Smith was in the habit of giving orders. He did not accept uncritically what was served up to him by subordinates. He questioned every report, examined the sources of those reports, and rejected those that did not meet his standards. In short, he took charge. In doing so, personality conflicts broke out between him and members of his staff like a siege of small pox. Less than a year following his appointment as Ambassador, Mr. Smith and his staff were as far apart as the poles on their political analysis of Cuba.

Despite allegations to the contrary, except for the largely technical work of the Embassy, there was a minimum of contact with the Batista regime. Batista was so discredited—among Cubans, American residents in Cuba, and the career personnel at the Embassy—that the important job of liaison with his regime fell, almost by default, to Ambassador Smith. He pointedly noted on more than one occasion, in answer to criticism that he was too close to Batista, that Castro couriers seemed to have the ear of the political section of the Embassy.

In point of fact, there was nothing abnormal about the contacts of Ambassador Smith or the contacts of the political section. The big question being asked in Washington was, "What is Castro? What is his program, if any?" Career officers went to the source—namely to Castro's underground leaders whom they trusted. The fact that our officers were badly advised by many underground leaders whose own basic democratic convictions were preyed upon by Castro, is beside the point. And Ambassador Smith did, in fact, receive some accurate information from Fulgencio Batista himself and from Prime Minister Gonzalo Guell. He also received bad information from the same sources.

As noted earlier, one tragedy is that the Ambassador and his political section were so far apart that they could not bring themselves together to compare notes and come up with a consensus. The other, and greater, tragedy is that legitimate American interests got lost in the process. The Ambassador's daily staff meeting often became a forum for ludicrous debates in which career officers would argue that their information, based on contacts with Castro's underground, was more accurate than reports on the same subject which Ambassador Smith was getting from Cuban government sources. Smith believed that some of his subordinates, at least, had become transmission belts for Castro propaganda.

Perhaps the most important split in the Embassy came in the fall of 1958. Ambassador Smith apparently had reason to believe that Carlos Márquez Sterling, the eminent Cuban lawyer-historian and prime mover behind Cuba's magnificent 1940 Constitution, could win the Presidency in the November elections. An unpublished poll taken by the very modern polling services of CMQ radio-television organization (given to me confidentially) showed Márquez Sterling to be by all odds the favorite of the Cubans among those running for President. The darling of the liberals in the 1940's, and a candidate again in 1958, Ramón Grau San Martín had repaid his supporters by empty demagoguery and by stealing a reported $84 million during his four-year tenure, 1944-48. Andrés Rivero Aguero, the other major candidate, was a puppet of Fulgencio Batista. Few Cubans harbored any illusions that, if Rivero Aguero were elected, the reins of power would be wrested from the hands of Batista. All factors considered, Ambassador Smith had reason to believe that Márquez Sterling could win, and that he would be a good President. The big "if" was whether or not the elections would be conducted honestly.

Castro and his apologists in the United States and elsewhere, were opposed to elections. The 26th of July Movement militants intimidated the Cuban people and told them to boycott the polls. Candidates for the presidency were actually threatened with death. At the other extreme, Batista controlled the polls through his police and his intelligence services. In the end, Rivero Aguero was declared to be the winner of the November 1 elections by margins which, in some precincts, were in excess of the total number of registered voters. The political section of the Embassy argued, with ill-disguised satisfaction, that the rigged elections left no other avenue open but for the U.S. to accept Fidel Castro. Ambassador Smith refused to accept their thesis.

It was an open secret in Cuba that the Ambassador and his staff were in disagreement, and Castro sympathizers made the most of it. Despite the resounding rejection of Batista's rigged elections by the Cuban people, Mr. Smith believed that, as bad as those elections were, they still represented the only mid-point between Batista's dictatorship and what he termed "Castro-Communism." Those views merely widened the split within the Embassy, and gave Castro's underground movement considerable latitude to play on anti-Smith sentiments.

Castro informants complained to their Embassy contacts, albeit with slim pickings for proof, that confidential information which they had given those contacts were transmitted to Batista by Ambassador Smith. Career officers in the Embassy frankly observed to themselves and to U.S. residents in Cuba that such claims were within the realm of possibility. These observations reached the underground movement with the speed of a crown-fire. They also reached Ambassador Smith, raising his temperature by several degrees.

One of the most puzzling incidents (to me at least) involves the attitude of the Embassy toward Castro's confidant and number-two man, Ernesto "Che" Guevara. The incident took place at a staff meeting in the fall of 1958, called by Ambassador Smith to discuss the ramifications of Guevara's march through Camaguey Province. Mr. Smith asked the political officer to brief the six of us present on what he knew of Guevara's trek. There was a consensus that unless Guevara and his men were turned back or wiped out, Batista most probably was through. We knew that his "column" consisted of only about one hundred men, if that. If Guevara made it into the mountains of Las Villas he would have done so only because Batista's troops were not fighting. As it later turned out, Batista called General Eleuterio Pedraza back into military service to evaluate his chances of survival. Pedraza's verdict was that the dictator's army was virtually evaporating as a fighting force.

More immediately important to the American Ambassador was the background of "Che" Guevara. After the political officer had finished his briefing, Mr. Smith asked him: "Is Guevara a Communist?" The question was received as something quite irrelevant to the discussion.With rising anger Smith repeated the question and received the vague answer that there were "rumors" regarding "Che's" Communist connections, but that the political section had nothing concrete. The Ambassador turned to the Economic Counselor, Eugene Gilmore, and asked him what he knew. Nothing. Mr. Smith was particularly persistent in questioning the CIA chief. He was newly assigned, having just taken over, and pleaded unfamiliarity with the issue under discussion. He said he would check into it, and report back later.

Smith jumped up from his chair irritably, looked around at the officers, and said: "What the hell is this? Top career officers and not one of you can tell me whether Guevara is or is not a Communist." He strode over to his desk in the mammoth office, and picked up the intercom to call his confidential secretary. He turned and almost shouted: "Well, I know that Guevara is a Communist even if you don't. And I'll tell you what I'm going to do. I'm going to burn up the wires to Washington and tell them that the Communists are marching through Cuba like Sherman's march to the sea. Now, how the hell do you like that?" We were perfunctorily dismissed.

Why was the Embassy apparently so ignorant of the background of one of Castro's top aides? My own contribution to his background at the Ambassador's meeting was only second-hand. Andrew St. George, the ubiquitous free-lance photographer, had related an incident to me which seemed to me relevant to the discussion. Andy had spent considerable time with the Castro forces, writing stories and photographing them in the hills. On one occasion he came across Ramiro Valdés, who was later to become Castro's Secret Police chief, laboriously reading a book on Marxism. As Andy joked with him about it, "Che" came up. Slapping Valdés on the back, "Che," according to Andy, turned to him and said: "Don't make fun of this boy. He's going to become a first-rate Communist." Valdés nodded emphatically, Andy said.

The background of "Che" Guevara should not have been difficult for our political section to uncover. Born in Rosario, Argentina, in 1927, Guevara lived most of his early years in Buenos Aires. Though most writers refer to him as a medical doctor, the record shows that he had not finished medical school. He spent most of his time absorbing the works of Marx and Lenin, and took part in Leftist student demonstrations at the University of Buenos Aires. Called into the Argentine military service, he promptly deserted and slipped into Peru. He later married Hilda Gadea, a Peruvian radical, who in 1965 was named chief of the Latin American Committee to Aid Vietnam.

Even though "Che" had a daughter by Hilda Gadea, he abandoned them both. He travelled to Venezuela and later to Guatemala where he connected with revolutionary groups supporting Communist President Jacobo Arbenz. When Arbenz came to power, "Che" Guevara took a position in his Ministry of Agriculture as an inspector, then moved into a post in the agrarian reform. With the overthrow of Arbenz in 1954, Guevara took political asylum in the Argentine Embassy in Guatemala City, and then moved on to Mexico City. It was in Mexico that Guevara made contact with Fidel Castro through Pedro Miret and Raúl Castro, trained with them on the ranch of former Spanish Republican (Communist) General Alberto Bayo, and landed in Cuba with Castro and his men on December 2, 1956.

Ambassador Smith's "burning up of the wires to Washington" in the manner that he did was essentially correct. The political section should have heeded the expressed fears of the Ambassador, at least to the point of conducting an all-out investigation into the background of "Che" Guevara. Anyone with the slightest knowledge of Guevara had to conclude that he was a dangerous man. Even the mere rumor of Guevara's pro-Communist background should have elicited more than the calm detachment exhibited by the political officer. Or, as Ambassador Smith sometimes wondered, was information being withheld from him?

Nor does it matter, as Mr. Matthews has it, that Guevara's Communism turned out later to be somewhat different from that of the Russians. Indeed, if one is to believe the nonsense written by him on this subject of the "Cuban variant," Guevara and Castro emerge as "non-Communist" Communists.

My own view of the matter is that the Embassy staff had, at the very least, become emotionally invested in the anti-Batista fight. As such, they were blind to the consequences of a Castro takeover, as were the brave Cuban people who were cruelly deceived by him.

Although I saw no evidence of pro-Communism in the Embassy, I also saw no evidence of real concern that Communism might be a guiding force behind Castro. There was an exaggerated fear among the career staff of being branded "McCarthyites," a fear nurtured and exploited by Herbert Matthews and other Castro apologists. Having succumbed to this subtle blackmail, the staff did not consider the possibility that Castro's hatred for the United States could logically lead to a partnership with Soviet Russia. Some of this hatred became perfectly apparent when, in June of 1958, Castro kidnapped 45 Americans and 3 Canadians, held them in the Sierra Maestra, and forced the American Consul in Santiago to negotiate with him for their release. Incidentally, the ineffable Mr. Matthews writes of the victims of the kidnappings that ". . . some of them found it a stimulating adventure which aroused sympathy for the rebel cause."[7]

In view of all the background, it is unfair and invalid for Theodore Draper in his writings to pin the label of "extreme Right-wing" on those who had to come to some critical conclusions regarding the responsibility of individual Americans for American policy.[8] As we shall see later in this book, Senators James Eastland and Thomas J. Dodd, as well as author Nathaniel Weyl—three of those scored by Draper—have considerable grounds for their charges when these are applied to the years 1959-1960. The Havana Embassy in 1959 and 1960 was definitely "appeasement minded." I am limiting myself here to the pre-Castro takeover.

I also believe that it is not valid to argue, as Matthews does, that the United States would have been helpless to do anything about the Castro movement in 1958, even if we had been convinced that it was Communist-penetrated. Of course, to dig for that evidence would have meant that the searcher had to admit to himself the possibility that Communism might, indeed, exist in the Castro movement. But more immediately important is the fact that it was Matthews and his kind who rigidly resisted any sincere investigation of the Castro movement at a time when it might have counted, and who equated such an investigation with "McCarthyism." Mr. Matthews makes wide use of "McCarthyism" in his book, saying that "McCarthyism had the abnormality of a disease, just as its contemporary equivalent of John Birchism has."

Attempts to find and fix responsibility for our ignorance of Castro's political direction are blocked with Matthews' comment: "This is typical of McCarthyism that events like this bring out in the United States." Matthews, in his defense of Castro, writes: "It is not easy to be a dissenter in the United States in a highly emotional period like the present when McCarthyism has been reborn with its special emphasis on Cuba."[9] But it was Matthews who obviously wrote about Castro and his movement from emotionalism rather than from facts. And long after the revolutionary euphoria in Cuba has been replaced by massive public hatred of the Castro regime, Matthews remains committed to what can only be described as his wish for a Titoist Cuba.

There is no argument with the dissenter. And the fact is that Herbert Matthews has always had the enormous advantage of airing his dissensions in one of the most powerful newspapers in the world, while book publishing companies accept his myths and publish them. All that is asked of the dissenter in a free society is that the facts behind his dissension be proved. But when those facts are proved hollow, when the defense of an ideology dedicated to our burial becomes blatantly apparent, he resorts to branding his critics as "McCarthyites." It is very much open to question whether such antics qualify the writer as a serious student of Cuban affairs.

Reading the works of Herbert Matthews, Theodore Draper, Leo Hubermann, Paul Sweezey *et al.* One gets the impression that there was no alternative to Fidel Castro, and that no alternative paths had been explored which could have brought peace and constitutional government to Cuba in 1957 or 1958. But in fact Ambassador Smith worked long and hard at arriving at a peace settlement, enlisted the support of the Church, moderate civic groups, and even received wobbly but significant agreement from Batista himself.

The American Ambassador was quite right in his assessment, as early as February, 1958, that the failure of Castro to obtain significant numbers of recruits represented the best opportunity to take advantage of Castro's weakness, at the same time rid the country of Batista, and come up with an interim government of civic leaders. As Castro had indicated in his letter of December 31, 1957, a little over a month earlier, his position was desperate. What Smith wanted at this time was State Department support for an approach to Batista saying that this was the moment for him to leave Cuba and appoint in his stead a broadly based provisional government made up of civic leaders to govern for a period until elections could be held. He counted on the weakness of Castro's forces, on Castro's failure to obtain recruits, and on the sincere public desire for peace and an end to Batista's rule, to prevent Castro from coming to power by force of arms.

What is not generally known is that Castro made tentative overtures toward peace, tied with the idea that the Organization of American States would supervise the elections. Then in typical Castro fashion he added a proviso that made the plan unworkable. He insisted that all Batista troops get out of Oriente Province and leave their arms behind them. He would then have achieved by quasi-diplomatic means what he had been unable to achieve through force of arms—namely, complete control over Cuba's largest province, its sugar, cattle, and coffee industry, a Castroite "North Korea," or "North Vietnam."

I have seen the memoranda of notes of the exchange between Ambassador Smith and the Papal Nuncio, Signor Luigi Centoz, regarding Church support for a cease-fire and the support of the Church for a government of national unity. Mr. Smith has added to these notes his own personal account of what happened, not only in discussions with the representative of the Vatican, but with civic groups. According to him, the big question on the lips of all was: "Was the United States willing to throw its support behind such a plan?" The State Department answer to Smith invariably was no.

The Church was one of the key factors in State Department thinking. If the Church did go ahead with the plan, and if it were successful, the State Department would reconsider its position on non-intervention, and perhaps throw its support behind the plan. This left things very much up in the air until March 1, 1958, when the Catholic Church of Cuba joined with the Papal Nuncio in publicly calling for a cessation of hostilities and for establishing a widely-based provisional government of national unity. Batista, according to Ambassador Smith, followed on March 3 by accepting the plan, agreeing to elections supervised by United Nations' and OAS observers, and to an uncensored press. A commission was established consisting of two former Vice Presidents of Cuba, the President of the Bankers' Association, and a representative of the Church.

The plan looked good until it was torpedoed by the leading contenders —Castro and Batista. Batista said he would accept the interim commission to establish elections, revise his government and make it representative of national unity, and cooperate to bring about a climate conducive to elections. Then he threw in his proviso that regardless of this cooperation he would not step down until February 24, 1959; the date that a new President would normally take office. Batista was unruffled by the fact that as an illegal President he had no right to make such a demand.

Fidel Castro was no better. He refused to see the Commission, saying that he would not cooperate with Batista. He then added, as I learned later from Batista's Minister of the Interior, Santiago Rey, and from my contacts in the State Department, that since the United States was standing aloof from the proposition he gave it little chance for success. In view of Castro's unbroken record of deceit, it is not unlikely that he threw in the lack of U.S. support of the Commission for his own use, knowing that our policy of non-intervention held us virtually immobile. It can be supposed that, with equal facility, he would have attacked the United States for intervention in Cuba's internal affairs, had the United States thrown its support behind the plan. In view of the psychological climate in Cuba, however, it is questionable whether such an attack would have been popular.

Certainly, Miguel Angel Quevedo, publisher of the internationally influential magazine *Bohemia*, had no illusions about Castro, even though he was at times victimized by Batista and was considered in 1958 to be a Castro supporter. In the many luncheons we had each Wednesday in his penthouse at the magazine office, he made it clear that, in his opinion at least, the United States missed the boat with its equivocations in January and March of 1958. He went even further, saying that when Castro failed to bring off the general strike in April, the United States should have publicly and unequivocally thrown its support behind another call for a government of national unity. In his view, the people of Cuba were appalled by the terrorism which had broken out; and no less appalled, initially, that Castro's underground movement had taken advantage of a restoration of Constitutional guarantees by Batista to launch that terrorism, with the view toward forcing the dictator to reimpose martial law. The psychological moment turned, according to Quevedo, when Batista met terror with counter-terror.

This brief summary of events in 1958 shows that there was at least a possibility of bringing about a cessation of hostilities, perhaps of even bringing the country to the polls in free elections. But this summary also indicates that it was the United States, through its Department of State which failed to make the hard decisions that would release us from the strictures of non-intervention, when such non-intervention merely served as a screen behind which a revolutionary dictator, on the one hand, and a personal dictator, on the other, could play games with the public and with our own national interests at will.

Personnel in the American Embassy and influential writers in our press were defeatist in their attitude, saying that there simply was nothing that could have been done in 1958, even if we had wanted to. Mr. Matthews' fictitious "great revolt" against Batista in Oriente Province insinuates that there was no climate for a peace that did not mean a Castro-imposed peace. Mr. Draper correctly finds that Batista's army was evaporating in the face of public revulsion against the Cuban dictator, but concludes incorrectly that nothing could have been done to save the situation.

But what if the United States had been convinced that Castro and his movement were headed in a Communist direction? And given general agreement in the Embassy that unless something drastic were done, this Communist movement would inexorably come to power, would this not have had an effect on United States' policy in Cuba?

Just as Mr. Draper was later to claim that there was little or no evidence of Communist direction behind the Dominican revolt of April 24, 1965, so he dismisses evidence that Castro might have been a Communist. He states in his disagreement with Nathaniel Weyl that Weyl "for some reason" fails to mention that General C. P. Cabell, Deputy Director of the U.S. Central Intelligence Agency, testified in November, 1959, before the Senate Internal Security Subcommittee that "we believe that Castro is not a member of the Communist Party, and does not consider himself to be a Communist."[10]

But in selecting passages in the testimony to refute Mr. Weyl, Draper does not cite important passages which may be in disagreement with his own views. In discussing Castro, General Cabell added a *caveat* to the remark quoted above by Mr. Draper. Cabell said that two of those closest to Castro—"Che" Guevara and Raúl Castro "are both strong friends of the Communist Party . . . such persons have been appointed by Fidel on the basis of friendship, trust, and loyalty *established during the revolution, and he is committed to defend their policies.*"[11] (Italics added.)

The trappings by which an obvious Communist movement is identified were not apparent during the initial stages of Fidel Castro's thrust for power, thus prompting a cabal of liberals to proclaim that Castro and his close associates were not Communists at all. They try to squeeze the Castro regime into a doctrinaire Communist mold. When it doesn't fit that mold, they say: "See, it cannot possibly be Communist." Theodore Draper squeezes very hard, then comes up with the comment in his book, *Castro's Revolution*, that Castroism "belongs to a new type of system, neither capitalist nor socialist, *that emerges where capitalism has not succeeded*, and socialism cannot succeed."[12] (Italics added.) While Mr. Draper does concede that Cuba was one of the most middle-class countries in Latin America and that the living standard in pre-Castro Cuba was "comparatively high for Latin America . . . almost as high as Italy's and much higher than Japan's. . . ." he does not attribute this standard of living to Cuba's capitalistic system, nor draw obvious inferences from his own facts—namely that capitalism was, indeed, successful in Cuba. Mr. Draper most certainly is right in saying that "socialism cannot succeed." The Communist system which Castro clamped on Cuba is basically the same system that has failed in East Germany, Czechoslovakia, Russia, and elsewhere.

Draper's fence straddling on this important point regarding the Castro regime is interesting in that it introduces a political-economic philosophy that fits no known category except, perhaps, that which disillusioned Cubans call *Fidelismo sin Fidel* (Fidelism without Fidel), a spongy idea of socialist economic planning, shorn of the personality cult of Fidel Castro. The leading exponents of *Fidelismo sin Fidel* are the economic planners in Castro's first government—Minister of the Treasury Rufo López Fresquet, National Bank President Felipe Pazos, Agricultural and Industrial Bank President Justo Carrillo, and Minister of Public Works Manuel Ray. Non-Communist, but pro-Socialist, they broke with Castro only after the Communists had reduced their positions to mere titles without authority, or were fired by Castro when their reputation as liberals was no longer needed as window dressing for his Communist regime. Despite the total failure of those gentlemen to cope with Communism in Cuba, many "losers" insist today that what they represent is an intrinsic good in the Castro movement that must not only be protected, but actually promoted. "Oh, if the Cuban regime would only follow the path of 'Titoism'. Oh, if Cuba would sever its military and foreign policy ties with Russia!" Then, according to the dominant thesis of Herbert Matthews, Cuba could become the leader of a thoroughly respectable, liberal (meaning Socialist) "third force" in the Western Hemisphere. This is what *Fidelismo sin Fidel* really means—an anti-capitalist movement of "losers."[13]

It is worth noting a key exchange at the Senate hearings between the late Senator Olin D. Johnston and the Deputy Director of CIA. The Senator from South Carolina asked: "Is it not true that he [Castro] is more dangerous than if he would come out and let them know that he was a Communist?" Cabell answered: "I personally would agree that Castro would probably lose much, or even most of his popular support should this occur."[14] These words spoken on November 5, 1959, by General Cabell were repeated almost verbatim by Fidel Castro on December 2, 1961, when he proclaimed that he had been a Marxist from his student days, but could not admit to it earlier because he would have lost his appeal to the people and to his *Fidelista* collaborators of the Left. In short, the easy accommodation of apparently conflicting principles among the anti-capitalist "economic planners" in Castro's first government were, indeed, enormously important to Castro in advancing Communism in Cuba.

Fidel Castro may or may not have been an out-and-out Communist—more specifically, a Marxist—since his student days, as he claimed in

December of 1961. And if he was, as the evidence certainly indicates, Castro withheld this fact for the reasons claimed—that he would have lost all public support. What can be said, however, is that the debates which raged around the person of Fidel Castro and his political allegiances back in 1958, seemed to obscure the important questions of his background, the political allegiances of his supporters, and the meaning of those allegiances. Communists do not join movements unless they have solid reason to expect a pay-off for their support. In mid-1958, following the signing of the Pact of Las Mercedes, Communists went to the Sierras where they occupied important positions in the Castro forces.

Communist affiliation with Castro, even though that affiliation came very late in the game, paid off with the early appointment of Communists to key posts in the Castro government. Major Manuel Piñeiro Losada took command of Oriente Province, following the flight of Batista, and today is Director General of Intelligence, a post from which he directs the training of guerrilla recruits for the subversion of Latin America. José Abrahantes Hernández became one of Fidel Castro's bodyguards, and today is in charge of the Cuba's G-2 apparatus, occupying the post of Vice Minister of the Interior. Flavio Bravo, secretary to pre-Castro Communist Party chief Blas Roca, and leader of the Socialist Youth, has held several positions of importance in the Castro government. Joel Domenech Benitez was also a leader of the Socialist Youth. Today, he is Minister of Industries and a member of the Central Committee of Cuba's Communist Party.

Another Socialist Youth member, Abelardo Colome, actually joined Fidel Castro back in 1957. With Castro's victory in 1959, he took over as Chief of the Department of Investigation of the Rebel Army. Later, Colome went to Venezuela, where for two years he helped organize guerrilla forces. Colome also is a member of the Central Committee of Cuba's Communist Party. José Matar, one time Secretary of Finance of Havana Province for the Communist Party, in 1953 accompanied Raúl Castro to the Communist Youth Congress in Bucharest. Joining the Castro forces in the Sierra in 1958, Matar succeeded to the position of head of the Committees for the Defense of the Revolution—nefarious packs of neighborhood informers. Other Communists allied with Fidel Castro before he came to power include Antonio Núñez Jiménez, Oscar Fernández Mel, Manuel del Peso, Jorge Enrique Mendoza Reboredo, Félix Torres. Virtually every Communist who joined Castro prior to 1959, and many who had not, were given positions of key importance in the Revolutionary Government, from Rector of Havana University to Secretary General of the Cuban Confederation of Labor.

Still, the possibility of avoiding disaster remained, even late in 1958.

Had Dr. Carlos Márquez Sterling won the election of November, 1958, there was the definite possibility that the people would have rallied around him, that the Army would have taken heart and supported his administration, and that Castro would have been isolated in the mountains of Oriente.

In fact, Castro's greatest fear was that Carlos Márquez Sterling would indeed be elected and that the people, tired of urban terrorism and guerrilla outbursts, would support him. Márquez Sterling told the electorate that he wanted to serve but two years of the Presidential four-year term, during which he would clean up the government and then propose new elections. Castro supporters tried to undercut the popularity with which the proposal was met, sneering that the proposal meant that Márquez Sterling would steal twice the amount of money in half the time. It also became known to Castro that should Márquez Sterling be elected, most of the old military chiefs under Batista would be fired. But, as Sterling correctly stated to Ambassador Smith, Castro was opposed to those elections because a fair election would only have the effect of isolating him politically as power was passed from Batista's hands to those of a new President.[15]

Sterling's assessment was repeated by a high-level Castro aide in confidential conversations with an Embassy officer in 1959. The aide, Jorge Serguera, said: "Fidel never had such bad moments as he did prior to the 1958 elections. He was beside himself that Márquez Sterling might win and that he would be frozen out." Serguera was first appointed Assistant Adjutant General of the Rebel Army, was on the staff of Raúl Castro and was later appointed Ambassador to Algeria. He still is among the most trusted functionaries of the Cuban Government.

It seems clear enough from the evidence that Ambassador Smith "intervened" with his anti-Batista statement issued in Santiago and in sympathetic talks with the Papal Nuncio for the establishment of a government of national unity. It seems clear enough from later testimony given to the U.S. Senate that he also intervened in bringing pressures against Batista. In a nutshell, there was enough evidence to identify U.S. "intervention," but not enough determination in the State Department to see that intervention culminated in protecting our national interests —interests which certainly coincided with the desires of the Cuban people for a peaceful solution of their problem.

And so it came about that Fidel Castro rode to power on January 1, 1959, as easily, and with as little outright fighting resistance to his movement, as any revolutionary in the history of Latin America. As a result, no Cuban has ever been presented with a more magnificent opportunity to consolidate public opinion behind him and to devote primary attention to programs for the benefit of all the people. That he did not do so and how, instead, he brutalized his machinery of government and spread Communist terror throughout Latin America from his own terror-stricken isle, is the subject of the balance of this book.

•

CHAPTER 4

Batista Out—Castro In

•

MY OWN PERSONAL INTRODUCTION to two years of unbroken horror during the Communist takeover of Cuba came with a telephone call at about 3:00 a.m. on January 1, 1959. It was Nicolás Bravo, news director of the nation-wide CMQ radio-TV network. Nicolás was one of my most important news contacts in Cuba—solid, well-educated, and perceptive. We had also become close friends, a relationship which made for an easy and invaluable exchange of ideas on the Cuban drama.

I answered the phone to hear his voice almost whisper: "It appears that the big man has fled." In a rush of details, Nicolás told how General Fulgencio Batista had fled into political exile by plane from Camp Columbia, his military headquarters in the Miramar section of Havana.

The call was by way of confirming what we had already suspected. Earlier that evening, my wife and I had driven to the house of Cuban friends to celebrate the New Year. Our route took us past the house of the son of General Francisco Tabernilla Dolz, Chief of Staff of the Cuban Armed Forces. It was surrounded by cars from the Military Intelligence Service (SIM), and people were running around in considerable confusion. My first thought was that it was a New Year's Eve party. Then I noticed that children were being bustled into cars, along with what appeared to be baggage. I asked my friend Raúl Armand, who was driving, to stop so we could see what was going on. He, his wife, and Aurelio Hevia and his wife were with us. Aurelio was a relative of Carlos Hevia, a candidate for President in the 1952 elections which had been frustrated by Batista's *coup d'etat*.

Just as I called out for Raúl to stop, a SIM car careened in front of us, forcing us to the curb. Two officers got out, asked where we were going, looked intently at my Embassy *carnet*, which I produced for identification, and told us to move on. As soon as we reached the small finca where the party was held, I called Nicolás Bravo at CMQ.

With the fighting in Las Villas Province reaching a climax most people were on edge. Nicolás had for several days been sleeping in the penthouse of CMQ so as literally to be on top of the news. I told him what I had seen. He said he had just heard that Batista was having a party at Camp Columbia and he would go there and check.

It was from a pay phone outside the main gate of the Camp that Bravo made the call to me that Batista had fled by plane to Santo Domingo.

Almost as important as the flight of Batista himself was the fact that nearly all of his top level officials—civilian and military—had gone with him. The specter of sacking and looting was real.

I immediately telephoned Ambassador Smith, but the several phone numbers at the Embassy residence gave the busy signal. I then called Dan Braddock, the Deputy Chief of Mission, and told him what I knew. Startled at the news, he told me to notify the political officer. If he had not heard the news, said Braddock, I was to ask him to check. Braddock called Consul General James Brown and instructed him to be prepared to put into effect our emergency plan for the evacuation of U.S. nationals, and for the protection of American lives and property.

The political officer had not heard of Batista's flight and set about checking into it. Meanwhile, I managed to get through to the Ambassador. In the middle of my report, he interrupted and said: "Yes, I know. I've had all the lines tied up trying to reach Washington." I found out later that Prime Minister Gonzalo Guell had telephoned Ambassador Smith from Camp Columbia to say good-bye just before he got aboard the plane!

The press presented a sticky problem. There were several American reporters in Havana who should be notified. Ambassador Smith balked, wanting first to get through to Washington. While we were talking he was interrupted by someone saying that the line was open to the State Department in Washington. He hurriedly gave me the go-ahead. I had some difficulty getting through to the wire services—AP and UPI. The first correspondent I contacted was Dick Bate of CBS. With the news scoop of the year in its hands, CBS in New York, he told me, refused to use his taped telephone report until it had been confirmed by AP and UPI. Bate was fit to be tied.

The reason for CBS skepticism is related to a contrary dispatch it had received earlier from AP in Havana. The AP bureau chief, Larry Allen, had just sent in a long story quoting a release by the Cuban Armed Forces Headquarters to the effect that the army had scored a smashing victory over the rebels in Las Villas. Newspapers in the United States were headlining that story on January 1, as radio reports were simultaneously telling of the flight of Batista.

Irate editors from Oshkosh to Ottawa were to call me all day on

January 1 for official confirmation that Batista had fled the country. Castro and the more vicious elements in the 26th of July Movement had immediately charged that the AP boner not only was deliberate, but that American wire service reporters in Havana were in the pay of Batista.

As I drove to the American Embassy early in the morning, I was struck by the tranquility of the city. I passed a blue police car and received a lazy salute from the driver. It seemed incredible, but it also seemed true that the police were ignorant of the momentous events which had taken place in Camp Columbia. It all fitted the pattern of Batista's behavior. He knew his Cubans. Batista knew that any advance planning for his departure would be an open secret within hours. When he pulled off his *coup d'etat* back in March, 1952, he first assembled his henchmen at a meeting at Camp Columbia and outlined the plans. When someone asked when the coup was to take place, Batista answered: "Right now. Immediately!" and strode out of the office at the head of his officers. He relinquished power on January 1, 1959, as he had seized it over seven years earlier—quietly and precipitately.

There were only a few cars at the Embassy when I arrived. At the code room I found John Topping, the political officer, and the CIA chief working on messages to Washington. Some of the officers were vacationing in the United States. What really hurt, until we rounded them up, was the absence of American secretaries. Local employees, such as Cuban secretaries, are not permitted to handle secret or confidential information although I suspect that during the first few hours of the emergency more than one security regulation was broken.

Surrounded by phones, I was posted in the Ambassador's conference room in the Embassy penthouse to watch for evidence of mob demonstrations, looting, and the like. I kept one line open to Nicolás Bravo at CMQ and another to the Embassy residence where the Ambassador was besieged by American and Cuban civic leaders begging for information, and giving gratuitous advice. It was about 5:30 a.m. when my eyes fixed on a police car making its way in the direction of the Embassy on the beautiful Malecón seafront drive. Suddenly the car came to a screeching halt near the Maine Monument. Two policemen got out and stood, apparently in excited conversation. Another police car raced wildly into view and stopped by the first, disgorging a policeman on the run. They knotted up in a group for a moment, with arms waving. Then they jumped back into their cars and took off at high speed in different directions.

Far down the Malecón, near El Morro Castle, I could make out another car coming toward the Embassy. As it came into view I could see figures standing on the running board of an old Ford. Then I saw the red and black flag of Fidel Castro being waved in the air. At the frantic, jubilant, directions of one of the figures clinging to the hood, the car turned and careened back to a forty-foot wooden cutout of a smiling President-elect Andrés Rivero Aguero. The figures spilled out of the Ford and began to tear away at the cutout. Soon, other cars came up; someone got a rope and three automobiles pulled down the wooden cutout to the accompaniment of cheers.

From then on, the city came slowly to life. Our fears that Havana would immediately erupt into raging mobs of destruction happily were not realized. For the most part the populace, frightened at an unknown future, was relatively orderly, and indeed stayed indoors. The civic resistance movement—anti-Batista actionists—took charge of radio and television stations and broadcast news bulletins which were as much rumor as fact. Announcers pleaded with the people to remain calm. "Don't disgrace the revolution in its hour of triumph" was a highly effective slogan.

Crude bands bearing the words, 26 de Julio, sprouted on Cuban arms like buttercups in Kansas on a warm spring day, as newspaper boys, shoe-shine boys, bellhops, and street walkers tried to share in the triumph of a revolution which they had done nothing to support. Females turned out in red blouses and black skirts, haughtily directing traffic into a beautifully hopeless snarl of honking cars which legions of Boy Scouts tried vainly to unravel.

Fidel Castro added to the confusion by making a speech in Santiago, proclaiming it the capital of the revolution. In a state of euphoria, he made conflicting statements at every bend of the road as he and his handful of men marched all the way to Havana, monopolizing the press, radio, and television and keeping the eyes of the nation on him as Cuba's "Maximum Leader." He was neither prepared for his sudden victory, nor was he willing to enter Havana until he considered it safe to do so. But he certainly was better prepared than the other groups in opposition to Batista.

Camilo Cienfuegos and "Che" Guevara were ordered by Castro to rush to Havana and seize the key posts of Camp Columbia and La Cabaña fortress to keep them out of the hands of troops of the Second Front of the Escambray and of the Student Directorate, both of whom had been fighting Batista's troops in Las Villas Province. It was thus immediately apparent that Castro intended to seize absolute power for himself and to freeze out of government participation other groups which had also been warring with Batista in the mountains and whose student and youth cadres had supported Castro and his urban guerrilla warfare.

To read most accounts by American writers one is led to conclude that the only opposition to Batista came from Fidel Castro. While it is certainly true that Castro had by all odds the most effective propaganda machine, it is far from accurate to suppose from this that the resistance of other groups did not play an important role in Batista's downfall.

With the failure of the Palace assault on March 13, 1957, under the leadership of Eloy Gutiérrez Menoyo, the Student Directorate established guerrilla operations in the Escambray mountains in Las Villas Province. This was in November of 1957. On February 4, 1958, Faure Chomón, another Directorio leader, landed at Santa Rita Beach with Rolando Cubela, several men, supplies, arms and ammunition. Following a break with Gutiérrez Menoyo, they set up an independent command and took for themselves the name of the Revolutionary Student Directorate. Menoyo changed the name of his guerrilla band to the Second Front of the Sierra Escambray. So, by early 1958 there were two groups fighting in Las Villas Province, with "Che" Guevara establishing a third, late that year.

Menoyo and Chomón immediately clashed with Guevara. Even though Guevara was a latecomer to the fighting in the Escambray mountains he demanded complete control over all the other groups there, and was turned down. Menoyo took the position that the mountains were free to all independent groups fighting against Batista—with one exception. Menoyo repeatedly rejected requests from old-line Communist, Félix Torres, to bring his forces into the Escambray. Significantly, Torres later joined Castro's forces under the command of Camilo Cienfuegos. Faure Chomón descended from the hills and went to Havana to plot another assassination attempt against Batista, which never came off. He returned to the mountains and joined in the siege of the city of Trinidad, which was taken on December 30 by a combination of forces from the Second Front of the Escambray and Revolutionary Student Directorate.

This, then, was the political picture of Cuba on January 1, 1959. Castro made his way to Havana, accompanied by camp followers from the press, who had already built an image on the shifting sands of Castro propaganda, making the triumph of the bearded dictator a self-fulfilling prophecy. Legitimate claims by other fighters for representation in Castro's government were lost in the shadow of Castro's propaganda image. He was, truly, the "Maximum Leader" of Cuba, thanks to all that had gone on before. Elements which might have leavened his brittle rule were rejected and reviled by him. Unlike Castro, they had little public support, and precious little reporting by our press.

Though one would never know it from what has been written, the final days of the war in Las Villas Province, in December 1958, found the Castro forces of "Che" Guevara sharing their victory with those of Menoyo and Cubela. On December 23, Menoyo captured the tobacco town of Manicaragua as "Che" Guevara received the surrender of the town of Sancti Spíritus. Menoyo's forces also took Hoyos, La Moza, Guao, San Juan de los Yeras, and ended up on December 30 in Topes de Collantes with a large and important area of the Sierra Escambray under Second Front control. The American adventurer William Morgan, who, together with Menoyo was to make news in Cuba for some time to come, was ordered to move against the major city of Cienfuegos when the flight of Batista made further military ventures unnecessary.

Guevara shared the victory of Santa Clara city with Rolando Cubela, military leader of the Revolutionary Student Directorate. On December 30, Guevara's forces struck at the Leoncio Vidal regiment, as Cubela moved against the big military Camp Number Thirty-One. Sporadic resistance led to almost immediate collapse and the surrender of the city the following day.

From then on it was a race between Menoyo, Cubela, Guevara, and Cienfuegos to see who would get to the seat of power in Havana first. Castro's broadcast over Rebel Radio in which he had ordered his men to take over La Cabaña Fortress and Camp Columbia, left the scraps to be picked up by those he clearly considered his enemies, now that power was within his reach—unless, of course, these enemies chose to challenge Castro in armed combat and to precipitate civil war.

On January 2, Gutiérrez Menoyo entered Havana and quartered his troops in the Sevilla Biltmore, Nacional, and Capri hotels. Camilo Cienfuegos went directly to Camp Columbia the same day and seized the general headquarters, including the entire military communications systems, the military airport and the files. Guevara arrived the day following and went straight to La Cabaña fortress, the second most important military objective in Havana. Castro's 26th of July Movement had already seized El Morro Castle the moment that Batista fled.

We in the Embassy were busy evacuating U.S. nationals. Some curiosity seekers, however, wanted to stay around and fraternize with the picturesque *barbudos* (bearded ones). Most of the *barbudos* had Catholic medals conspicuously hanging outside their shirts. Some were almost bent over by the weight of six and seven medals on heavy chains, eliciting remarks of wonder from more than one American evacuee that the revolution *certainly* was religious. Some went so far as to characterize it as a sort of Knights Templar. (The *barbudos* had been told to wear the medals outside their shirts.)

Not all of our citizens in Cuba wanted to stay, of course. We were astonished at the number who were there. Castro had consistently carried on a campaign to keep tourists away from Cuba in an attempt to wreck its $60 million annual tourist income. Noise bombs in the cities were specifically designed to produce that effect, with the knowledge that "bombings" would be reported in American newspapers. The more deadly stuff was always blamed on Batista. After about 24 hours, we counted nearly 3,000 American tourists in the capital city alone, as reports came from interior towns of others stranded there.

Ambassador Smith arranged for the Havana-Key West ferry to make extra runs. Planes and surface transportation had been paralyzed because of a general strike declared by Castro. The first three or four days were nightmares to the consular section of the Embassy. Many of the American tourists were caught without money; the banks and express agencies were closed. Food was scarce and becoming scarcer. Ambassador Smith, Dan Braddock, and I joined Vice Consuls in trying to bring order out of chaos at the docks. American embassies and consulates do not keep cash on hand for stranded tourists and sailors. Various aid groups who normally handle this chore overseas were closed.

Many American nationals were also disturbed—a sentiment shared by many of us at the Embassy—by Castro's immediate expressions of hatred for the United States. He said of his victory in his speech on the first of January that "It will not be like 1895 when the Americans came and made themselves owners of the country, intervening at the last minute, and later not even letting General Calixto García, who had fought for 30 years, enter Santiago de Cuba. . . ." This was the first shot fired in Castro's salvos of hatred against the United States, salvos that have not ceased to this day.

In the midst of his fulminations, Castro installed Manuel Urrutia Lleó as "citizen President," and dispatched him from Santiago to Havana to make arrangements for his own triumphal entry into the capital. He was a humble man, a country judge with no claim to brilliance or greatness. Urrutia was chosen by Castro because, as one of the five judges who tried Castro in October, 1953, his was the lone dissenting voice among the majority vote that sentenced Castro to a three-year prison term. (Castro was released before serving out his term when Batista declared a political amnesty.) Urrutia based his dissent on Article 40 of the Constitution, which reads: "Legal or administrative provisions, or those of any other kind which regulate the exercise of the rights which this Constitution guarantees, shall be null if they diminish, restrict, or impair them." Article 40 continues: "Adequate resistance for the protection of the individual rights above guaranteed is legitimate." Judge Manuel Urrutia Lleó argued, in effect, that Article 40 made Castro's insurrection legal, and Castro repaid Urrutia by making him Cuba's so-called citizen President. Pockets of resistance unexpectedly appeared among the more desperate elements stranded by Batista's flight, and it is now widely believed that this was the real reason why Castro sent Urrutia to Havana in advance of his own arrival—to judge the temper of the city.

I was caught in the cross fire of a drive to clean out one of the pockets of resistance as I drove down town to look in on the offices of United Press International. Bureau chief Francis McCarthy was receiving threats against his life from pro-Castro militants almost hourly. This was due to an earlier story in which McCarthy had reported to the world that

Fidel Castro had been killed when his group landed in Oriente Province to start Castro's insurrection against Batista. McCarthy's original source is said to have been Colonel Alberto del Río Chaviano, commander of military forces in Oriente. Although the report, obviously, was in error, it was widely believed to be true at the time, and the Cuban people put Castro almost completely out of their minds until he was dramatically resurrected by Herbert Matthews a few months later. With the flight of Batista, the Castroites immediately charged that McCarthy had deliberately tried to bury Castro from public interest, and they opened a campaign of intimidation by which they hoped to drive him out of Cuba.

Were it not for Herbert Matthews' February, 1957, interview with Fidel Castro in the mountains, and his espousal of Castro's cause in the most influential newspaper in the United States, McCarthy's UPI dispatch might well have been accepted for months. Throughout 1957, Castro's military exploits were largely fictional; Herbert Matthews accepted them uncritically. It is highly unlikely that Castro and his group of survivors could have carried on without favorable publicity, as Castro himself told Herbert Matthews. Ruby Hart Phillips, for nearly 25 years the regular reporter for the *New York Times* in Havana, says of Matthews in her book, *The Cuban Dilemma:* ". . . it was his stories that revived the Castro revolution when it was in its death agony back in February, 1957."[1] It also is well to again recall Chancellor of the University of Puerto Rico Jaime Benítez's praise of the *New York Times* ". . . whose stories and editorials helped to make Castro and his movement acceptable to as yet undecided Cubans. . . ."

That Castro told Matthews only those things which suited his immediate purpose came to light in April, 1959. Speaking before about a thousand people at the Hotel Astor in New York, Fidel Castro boasted how he had bluffed Matthews into inflating the strength of his pitiful force of eighteen men into a formidable force which Matthews reported worked "in groups of 10 to 40." Matthews quoted Castro in the mountains as saying: "We are winning." In his own name, Matthews added the following comment in his famous February, 1957, interview with Castro: "One gets the feeling that he is now invincible . . . the Army men are fighting a thus-far losing battle."

During our scores of telephone conversations, Mac had told me about the threats to his wife and to himself, but he was not concerned. Yet, when UPI man Jack Skelly called and said that he was worried about Mac's safety, I decided to go downtown to see how he was getting along. Except for "emergency vehicles," cars were forbidden to be on the streets. Only doctors on emergency calls and, I assumed, diplomats, escaped the interdiction. I followed instructions for emergency driving, turning on my parking lights and the dome light inside the car.

Just as I crossed the bridge over the Almendares river next to the Línea tunnel, two nondescript-looking men bearing pistols waved me to the side of the street. They climbed wordlessly into the back seat, one ordering me with a wave of his pistol to proceed toward the center of the city, more specifically to the Focsa building, the largest apartment house in the Western Hemisphere. There wasn't another car in sight. Every so often we would hear the crackle of gunfire somewhere in the city, and would strain our ears to hear where it came from.

I had driven about three blocks, when another man jumped in front of the car. He was also armed with a pistol. The two gentlemen in the back seat crouched on the floor with their guns poked out the window, and asked the newcomer to identify himself. He did so, apparently to the satisfaction of my other two unwanted passengers, and he hopped in. At the corner of Línea street and the Avenue of the Presidents, I stopped the car, told them who I was, said I had urgent business at the Embassy, and therefore could not take them to the Focsa. They exchanged glances, then shrugged their shoulders, and left.

No sooner had they left the car than a tremendous burst of gunfire broke out. It came from a police car down the block which was directing its fire at the second floor windows of a house not too far from the Presidente Hotel. My passengers dodged behind a hedge and opened fire on the police car. The fire was returned with a vengeance, and I was caught in the middle. I dropped to the floorboards as bullets zinged over the asphalt. Suddenly the shooting stopped. The occupants of the police car seemed to be with the civic resistance (or, possibly posed as such to get in on the fight) and had seized the police cruiser when it was abandoned. I could make out from the shouts that they had been firing at what they said were the "Tigers" of pro-Batista Rolando Masferrer who had holed up in the building.

There was an immediate truce between my three hitchhickers and the group in the police car. They ran toward each other shouting greetings mixed with profanity, directions, instructions, and cursing the "Tigers." The cursing turned into yelps of pain and anger when the "Tigers" opened up on them. With howls of rage, they crammed themselves into the police car, drove it across the middle strip of the boulevard, and smashed into the entrance of the house, shooting as they went. I took off and made my way to the Embassy.

I called the UPI office and explained my delay. Mac said he had several other reporters with him and asked me to bring whatever I could find in the way of food and cigarettes. Leaving the side entrance of the Embassy I ran into Robert "Curly" Way who owned a bar and restaurant just across the street. A friend of Mac's, Curly dredged up some cigarettes, bread, cheese, and added a couple of bottles of rum to the lot. He said he would go with me to see Mac.

As we reached the small Maceo Park, ten armed men wearing 26th of July armbands stopped the car and coolly examined us over the sights of their rifles. I told them I was from the American Embassy, and they asked for identification. I was a study in slow motion reaching for it. Once we were identified (I said that Curly was my assistant), the group broke into wide grins, pounded me on the back, and shouted, "Viva los Estados Unidos! Viva la Revolución!" One then leaned over to me and in a confidential whisper gave me the unremarkable password which would, he said, assure our not being molested—"26th of July!" Suspecting that the Directorio underground might not appreciate that identification, I hoped we wouldn't have to use it.

We continued driving at a snail's pace as far as the entrance to the Prado boulevard when we again were stopped, this time by a much tougher looking group of ragged militiamen, also wearing 26th of July armbands. We identified ourselves. Far from the "Viva los Estados Unidos," we were greeted with stony silence and waved on up the boulevard. There was literally a man behind every huge poplar tree in the center of the boulevard and behind each column of the Spanish-style covered walks on each side.

We hissed our way along—"26th of July!" "26th of July!"—up one side of the boulevard and back down the other until we arrived at the arcade of the Sevilla Biltmore hotel. The entrance was barred by a huge iron grill. Behind it were four armed youths, looking for all the world like the Dead End Kids, standing against a backdrop of shattered windows and looted shops. I could see McCarthy's office. It was the only office left intact. Mac, who speaks *criollo* Spanish with the best of them, outbluffed and outswore would-be looters and "summoned" protection from the Student Directorate.

The youths pointed their guns at my car through the slits in the grill and ordered me to state my business. I did, identifying myself as an official of the American Embassy. I was mistaken for the Ambassador. Filled with self-importance, the young "militiamen" shouted down the arcade to their chiefs that the American Ambassador had arrived for, of all things, "a visit." The shouts were heard out on the Prado, where they echoed and re-echoed in the still night: "The American Ambassador is here!" bringing a rush of other "militiamen." Youths who had been lurking behind columns and trees in slit-eyed ferociousness came up to examine me in round-eyed juvenile wonder.

The young guards in the arcade made an attempt to look military, clicked their heels and came to something resembling attention. The leader gave an awkward salute, knocking off his cap in the process, and said: "At your orders!" I told him I had come to see Francis McCarthy of the UPI, and would he please let me in. He didn't have the key to the lock of the grill, he said, then asked me politely to go around to the side door. I did, and was met by a small guard of other youngsters who escorted Curly and me solemnly through the hotel lobby, down the arcade to the door of the UPI. I said thanks, was asked for cigarettes which I gave to them and then lighted, each in turn, and went into the office. We were all very polite and formal.

Four or five sweating correspondents for American papers were beating out their stories on typewriters. With telephone circuits to the United States uncertain and planes grounded, McCarthy had made his teletype machines available to them. One enterprising reporter had gotten together scraps and was making a malodorous stew over a can of sterno. The cheese, bread and crackers proffered by Curly and me were well received. The bottles of rum were grabbed from our hands.

Mac sat hollow-eyed in a tiny inner office with his shirt open, snarling in Spanish at someone on the phone. It was another threat. Across from him sat a civic resistance type with a machine pistol resting on the desk. He rose and politely introduced himself as student leader José Puente Blanco who had responded personally to Mac's summons for protection. Shortly thereafter he was appointed Provisional President of the University Student Federation. I learned from him that Rolando Cubela and his forces had just moved in and physically occupied the University of Havana and that Faure Chomón, Cubela's chief, commanded the troops in the Presidential Palace. Puente Blanco said that they intended to stay put unless Castro gave other anti-Batista groups well-earned representation in his cabinet, and a voice in the policies of the revolutionary government.

I asked the student leader for his views of the political situation now facing Cuba, mentioning in this connection the occupation of La Cabaña fortress by "Che" Guevara, scheduled for the following morning, and the seizure of Camp Columbia that day by Camilo Cienfuegos. He had a good opinion of the character of Cienfuegos, he said, but winced at the thought of Guevara in charge of La Cabaña fortress. "If that man isn't a Communist," he said reflectively, "he might as well be one." He spoke at some length about Castro's dependence on Guevara, Castro's obvious admiration for Guevara's administrative and organizational skill, and Castro's lack of talent in the latter two fields. The "Maximum Leader" had a minimum of the skills needed to run a country of six and a half million people, said Puente Blanco.

The student leader told me something else which apparently had been overlooked at the Embassy, namely that Osmani Cienfuegos, the brother of Camilo, was a known Communist. An architect, Osmani moved up quickly in the Communist hierarchy under Castro, from Minister of Public Works to President of Cuba's three-man Foreign Relations Commission, and then to the super-spot—Secretary General of the tricontinental organization of subversion.

I was grateful to Mac. He had not said a word, letting me get the information, together with the young man's value judgments, without interruption. Well connected with the principal figures in the anti-Batista ranks, he supplied valuable insight into the quirks of character of many of them. When I left, he shook hands and said that if Castro did not have some built-in restraints through the appointment of other resistance leaders to his government, it was likely that he would rely more and more on Guevara and his "friends." "And that," he added, "would be a disaster."

It was about 4:30 a.m. when I returned home. I had taken a shower and was about to go to bed when the phone rang. It was our neighbor, who occupied an apartment just below us, Señora "Beba" Preval. She said that in fifteen minutes two men would be up to see me, one of whom she had been hiding in her apartment for the past three months.

In much less time than that the doorbell rang. I opened the door on two men. One was a giant of a young man with bright red hair, wearing a field jacket with a Directorio Revolucionario armband, and carrying a carbine. The other was much smaller, relatively nondescript in appearance and bearing no arms. He said nothing during the entire interview. I invited them inside to sit down and excused myself to go into the kitchen to make us some strong Cuban coffee. I looked down from the side terrace where we usually had breakfast and saw four cars with heavily armed individuals in them. I looked out the back window and saw two more cars. I opened the rear door, by the maids quarter, just a crack and found a Student Directorate guard with an M-1 rifle grinning at me. I went to the living room, served the coffee, and sat down with the two visitors.

Julio García, the big fellow, did the talking. "I assume that you know of the difficulties the Directorio is having with Fidel Castro," he said. I nodded that I did. He then angrily went into the history of Castro's buildup in the American and foreign press, saying that Castro's Communist ties had been deliberately overlooked.

Didn't we know, asked García, that Jorge Enrique Mendoza Reboredo the announcer for Castro's Radio Rebelde, had been a member of the Socialist Youth in Camaguey Province? Didn't we also know that Universo Sánchez, one of the twelve survivors of Castro's expedition, had as a father one of Cuba's old-line Communists? Or that the Communists had entered La Cabaña fortress before "Che" Guevara had even arrived in the city of Havana?

I listened at some length. The burden of his conversation was a more heated version of what José Puente Blanco had told me. But García went further. He said that it was necessary for the United States to persuade, even force, Castro to broaden his cabinet to include members of the Directorate, the Second Front of the Escambray, and even members of Cuba's political parties who had fought against Batista. "Unless we have this kind of broad representation," said García, "we face another dictatorship—this time a Communist dictatorship—and Castro will be the dictator." To give Castro absolute power, said the agitated youth, "is to sell this country out to Communism."

I said I had been told that the Directorate and the Second Front of the Escambray planned to force Castro's hand, using their occupation of the university and the Presidential Palace as a bargaining point. What then? García shook his head and frankly admitted that this was a bluff. He also admitted that the opposition had no one with the oratorical ability or the appeal of Fidel Castro. In any test of popularity Castro would win hands down and in doing so would gain more popular strength. Such tests should be avoided, he said. He pointed out that Camilo Cienfuegos had already taken over Camp Columbia, and Guevara was scheduled to enter La Cabaña fortress within a matter of hours, meaning that Castro had full control of the key installations in Havana. He also said, however, that the Directorate planned to obtain arms "where we can." The "where" came out the next day when it became known that units of the Directorate had gone to the air base of Santiago de los Baños and stripped it of arms.

As can be imagined, I found the views of the gargantuan Comandante of considerable interest. I took a chance and called the CIA chief at his home and related parts of the conversation, suggesting that he send someone over to talk to the man. After a long moment of silence, he said: "I'll be right over." This was unusual since the station chiefs of the Agency almost invariably work through intermediaries in order to maintain a screen of anonymity. In this case, as he told me later, he believed it necessary personally to dig into early evidences of Castro's dictatorial tendencies to see what those tendencies might mean to the future of Cuba, and particularly to the possible rise of Communism in the country.

The CIA chief quickly fastened on García's charge that old-line Communists had moved into La Cabaña fortress even before "Che" Guevara arrived in Havana. He found it interesting, if not significant, that the Communists chose to move into the fortress scheduled to be occupied by Guevara, and not El Morro Castle where the 26th of July Movement had taken over. The Embassy was later to discover that Communist leader Carlos Rafael Rodríguez established his office in La Cabaña on January 5th, two days after Guevara had arrived in Havana and three days before Fidel Castro made his heroic entrance into the capital.

Among the old-line Communists identified as having opened up offices in the medieval Spanish fortress during the very first days of the flight of Batista were Juan Marinello, President of the Communist Party (PSP), Salvador García Aguero, and Luis Fajardo Escalona. The identification came from three independent sources—Raul Granja, former secretary to Ernesto de la Fe, Secretary General of an anti-Communist organization; Oscar García, a member of the democratic Auténtico Party of Cuba; and a member of the Embassy staff.

The interest shown by the CIA chief in Comandante García's estimate of Communism in the Castro movement is related to an event that had taken place a few weeks before. In October or November, the CIA had become convinced that Castro forces had been penetrated by the Communists and, as it was made known to me later, took steps to block his coming to power by the force of arms. Following high-level conferences in the White House, State Department and the CIA, a decision was made at that late date to get Batista to accept a formula not too far removed from that proposed by Ambassador Smith early in 1958. The formula was to replace Batista with a combined military-civilian *junta*.

On December 9, 1958, an emissary was dispatched to Havana where he engaged Batista in secret talks designed to persuade him to establish a junta, relinquish power to it and leave the island of Cuba altogether. It was hoped that a call for an immediate cessation of hostilities by the provisional *junta*, and a statement, backed by the United States, that the provisional government would remain in power only long enough to tide the country over to elections, would receive public backing. With that backing, it was hoped, Castro would be forced to enter the political arena as a candidate for election. If he won, as many anticipated, he would at least have come to power through elections, with constitutional safeguards provided by an elected Congress and guarded by the Supreme Court. He would be judged on the merits of his administration and subject to removal through the electoral process.

William Pawley, businessman and former Ambassador to Brazil, was the emissary designated to approach Batista. By this time, Ambassador Smith had just about worn out his welcome with Batista, and felt frustrated in his efforts to bring about a peaceful solution to Cuba's problems. Pawley's mission was considered in the nature of a fresh approach. As it turned out, however, Pawley was given no authority to make that approach meaningful. Rather elaborate precautions were taken to keep Ambassador Smith in the dark regarding the Pawley-Batista talks. He was called to Washington for consultation, with an explanation, given later, that the maneuver was designed to protect him in his position as Ambassador should the Pawley-Batista confrontation blow up. Whatever the reason for trying to keep Smith in the dark, the attempt failed. Smith had been made aware of the impending talks well in advance by none other than the prominent Cuban lawyer, Mario Lazo. Smith was furious. If Lazo knew about the meeting, he reasoned, it could also be assumed that other Cubans did, including Fidel Castro, whose spies were everywhere.* It was not unreasonable for Ambassador Smith to suspect that

*This is not to imply that Lazo would spread the report. An honorable man, he was

Batista might even have known the details of Pawley's proposal before the American emissary boarded his plane for Havana. The leak represented a breach in security of the utmost importance, and might well have contributed to the failure of Pawley's mission. Yet, those responsible for that leak still remain unknown.

In any event, Mr. Pawley later testified before a Senate committee that he had been engaged "to stop Fidel Castro from coming to power as a Communist." Taking into account the round-about nature of wording in an exchange before a Senate committee, it still is apparent that the decision to block Castro from coming to power by force of arms tells a great deal more about high-level fears of Castro and his Communist affiliations that do the few words quoted by Mr. Draper from General Cabell's testimony to reflect that the CIA did not believe Castro to be a Communist. The Cabell comment was a philosophical discourse, made at a delicate period when Castro was in power in 1959; the CIA's moves against Castro a year in advance of Cabell's testimony were the result of concrete decisions on the basis of operational knowledge of the Castro movement.

In Pawley's judgment, he failed to persuade Batista to step down because Assistant Secretary of State Roy Rubottom denied him the authority to say that the United States would support its own proposal.[2] In other words, a respected emissary was selected to make the U.S. proposal to President Fulgencio Batista that he give way to a civilian-military junta. Yet that emissary was not authorized to say that the proposal had U.S. support! Of course, results expected from the formation of the *junta* might have failed. But the fact remains that the proposition was shot down by the State Department as it barely left the ground. Why, it must be asked, was there the appearance of an effort to bring peace and stability to Cuba without the substance to make that effort meaningful? Could it be that the State Department acted reluctantly in advancing its proposition to Batista (and only under great pressure by the Central Intelligence Agency), then deliberately undercut the only remaining possibility of preventing Castro's forceful assumption of power?

One explanation is that, in the eyes of the State Department, the Pawley mission's goal was merely to determine the feasibility of the plan. Yet, it is recalled that similar proposals made by Ambassador Smith for nearly a year under vastly more propitious prospects for success were shot down by the State Department with the same unerring aim that exploded Mr. Pawley's trial balloon. A few days after the abortive Pawley mission, on December 14th, Ambassador Smith was ordered in for the kill by the State Department. In a talk with Batista, he virtually ordered

respected.

the dictator to leave the country but was not authorized to submit any alternatives.[3] Batista listened politely. Less than three weeks later he was in exile in the Dominican Republic and Castro was in the seat of power in Havana.

However wrong they may be, it is not unreasonable for Mr. Smith and Mr. Pawley to believe even today that career personnel in the State Department and the American Embassy did, indeed, want Castro to come to power by armed force. By December 9th, Batista had played out all his cards and had no bargaining position left. Instead of quibbling with his views, as it did, the State Department could have had its emissary tell Batista what our position was and that we intended to back it up. Under these circumstances, screams of intervention by the dictator could only have redounded to our credit.

In the light of the evidence, the burden of guilt for the debacle of Cuba falls on Washington, not on the two men who espoused an alternative course of action and openly identified themselves with it. Charitably, at best it could be said of the State Department that it had shown all the agility of a giant crushed by the weight of its own body.

With the retirement of any coherent American policy from the scene, the Cubans themselves played out the rest of the drama in a series of agreements, double crosses, and belated pleas for U.S. intervention, such as those made by Julio García and José Puente Blanco. On December 24, General Eulogio Cantillo had gone to Oriente Province where Castro's rebels were moving about, virtually without any armed opposition. He went to a sugar mill near the town of Palma Soriano, taking with him four bottles of Spanish brandy, a favorite drink of Fidel Castro. There the Batista general and the guerrilla leader met. Also present at the four-hour meeting were Castro's "girl Friday," Celia Sánchez, accompanied by Vilma Espín, who, within a few weeks, was to marry Raúl Castro. (Vilma Espín was a member of the Party's Socialist Youth organization in Santiago.) Catholic Father Pedro Guzmán took notes of the proceedings and agreements, while Raúl Chibas took photos commemorating the occasion.

Cantillo told Castro that the Cuban military leaders had been plotting the overthrow of Batista* and were prepared to cooperate with the rebels in his ouster. Castro demanded unconditional surrender. The agreement which finally worked out was that the military garrison of Santiago would lay own its arms, supply Castro forces with tanks and transportation, and

---

*How deep the plotting went is revealed in the booklet, "La Verdad," published in Miami in 1960 by Colonel Florentino E. Rosell. One plan was for a military *junta* to replace Batista, establish its headquarters in Las Villas Province, and continue the fight against Castro. The *junta* was to function under a government of National Integration consisting of Carlos Márquez Sterling, Ramón Grau San Martín, Carlos Prío Socarrás and Aureliano Sánchez Arango. Cantillo's deal with Castro, plus the military realities of the situation, torpedoed the plan.

deliver the city into the hands of the *barbudos*. Then the military would join the rebels in demanding the ouster of Batista and fraternize together. Ambassador Smith remarks on the initial good will between rebels and the military at Camp Columbia in Havana. He writes in his book, *The Fourth Floor*, that "upon entering Camp Columbia, I was amazed to find the officers of the Cuban Army mingling on a fraternal basis with the bearded officers."[4]

Following the agreement with Castro, Cantillo returned to Havana where he told Batista that all was lost and that the rebel forces (as he well knew) were expected to enter Santiago momentarily. With that, plus discouraging reports of the army's failure to fight in Las Villas Province, Batista left. Although every officer in the room at Camp Columbia that fateful morning of January 1, 1959, knew he could profit by arresting the dictator on the spot, none dared do so—a tribute to the strength of Batista's personality.

From the steps of the plane on which he was to fly to Santo Domingo, Fulgencio Batista calmly turned and wished General Eulogio Cantillo, whom he left in charge of the military, good luck in the peaceful transfer of constitutional authority brought about by his "resignation." He warned Cantillo to be wary of colonel Ramón Barquín. Barquín was at that moment in prison on the Isle of Pines for having plotted the assassination of Batista in 1956.

The transfer of authority was not so simple, however. Vice President Guas Inclán was not present at the meeting at Camp Columbia and could not be found. It was not known if he had fled, or might flee, into exile. As a result, the name of Carlos M. Piedra y Piedra, the eldest member of the Supreme Court, was put forward as the next in line for succession to the Presidency. The court refused to certify Piedra on the extra-legal but pragmatic ground that with Batista's flight from Cuba, power had passed into the hands of the rebels. At 2:00 p.m. on January 1, Piedra retired from the Presidential Palace.

Meanwhile, as Chief of the Armed Forces, General Cantillo had ordered a cease-fire. This order, plus the other evidence, indicates that Cantillo intended to surrender the government and the armed forces to Castro and go into retirement. According to Colonel Rosell, he and Cantillo had made a pact between them that with the overthrow of Batista both would retire from active duty. There is nothing in General Cantillos' background which suggests that he nurtured any political ambitions. As military chief of Oriente Province in 1958, he was fully aware that further armed resistance was hopeless. He ordered that none of the garrisons put up any further resistance. The commanders of the army, air, and naval forces in Santiago turned over the city, met and discussed the situation with Fidel Castro, and cooperated with him in every respect.

Nevertheless, before Cantillo could make a formal surrender of the armed forces, he was accused of treason by Castro. Speaking in Céspedes Park in Santiago on January 1, Fidel Castro made General Cantillo's cooperation out to be a *coup d'etat*, designed to freeze him out of power. A proclamation signed by him and read over the radio claimed that "the |coup d'etat" was intended to "stab the people, and their revolution . . . in the back." Castro said that treason had been committed by Cantillo for permitting Batista to leave the country.

On the face of it, Castro's charge is ridiculous. By the evening of January 1, 1959, the time that Castro delivered his speech, the country was to all intents and purposes in his hands. Yet, he met Cantillo's cease-fire order with this command to his rebels, broadcast over Rebel Radio: "Our forces must continue their operations against the enemy on all the battle fronts." He then put to death the very commanders in Santiago who had made his entrance into the city a bloodless triumph.

Batista's warning to Cantillo to be careful of Colonel Ramón Barquín was prophetic, indeed. Castro ordered Barquín's release from prison and commanded him to go immediately to Havana and place General Cantillo under arrest. Barquín did so and the General was immediately sentenced to be shot by firing squad. Only the timely pleas of the American and Brazilian Ambassadors saved his life. Comandante Camilo Cienfuegos agreed to a stay of execution. Later, General Cantillo was sentenced to fifteen years imprisonment. Even so, the lightning-like seizure of the General prevented him from publicly airing his side of the story

It is believed that Castro did not want to accept General Cantillo's surrender. If Cantillo peacefully turned over the reins of Cuba's civil government and its military forces it would amount to a public admission of the truth—that the military had refused to fight for the hated dictator, Batista, and had cooperated in his overthrow. This was not a picture which Castro would find very much to his liking. He had been preaching, and continues to preach until this day, that it was his rebels, his own personal fortitude, and gallantry in battle that had brought a vicious and powerful military machine to its knees.

Castro embarked at once on a campaign to denigrate the regular armed force, destroy its moral base, and create a militia. Systematic destruction of the military and police organization of Cuba began on the day Castro took power. "No honorable military man has to fear anything from the Revolution," Castro said in his very first speech in Santiago. Most of the military considered themselves honorable, indeed, and did not associate themselves with the lies which Castro told, on the other hand, about a military system which "killed innocent women and children." *Batistianos,* he said, had committed heinous military crimes against the rural

population, and they must go. But he added that "in this fight there are
no losers . . . we will be generous with everybody . . . there will be no
vengeance, no hatred. . . ." Castro's first speeches upon taking power
were typical—what he said was almost invariably the direct opposite of
what he did.

Castro spoke in Santa Clara on January 6 en route to a hero's welcome
in Havana where he called for ". . . a million men prepared to defend
liberty with arms in their hands." He said that "all citizens will receive
military instruction. . . ." This was the first reference to creation of a
militia.

Thus, two precedents of highest importance of the direction Cuba was
to take were established in the very first days of 1959—the destruction
of conventional military order and the creation of a "people's militia."
Classically Communist in concept, the precedent was established by
none other than Fidel Castro himself.

Castro's attacks on the military indicate that he had the famous show
trials of the military very much in mind from the moment he assumed
power. He was determined to strip the last vestige of decency from
thousands of military men as part of his strategy to destroy the regular
army. How determined Castro was came out after the trial of 43 pilots
and airmen. A Revolutionary Tribunal was appointed to try them under
the accusation of genocide, indiscriminate bombings of villages and brutality in general. The Tribunal failed to produce the names of even five
persons who had been killed through this "slaughter" from the air, and
absolved "each and every one of the accused" of the charges.

Castro's rage knew no bounds. In a wild appearance on CMQ radio
and television, he repudiated the findings of his own Revolutionary
Tribunal and ordered a retrial in the name of "the people." A new trial
commission was appointed on which Communist Manuel Piñeiro served.
Castro virtually directed the commission to come up with a verdict of
guilty. It did so.

The fierceness of Castro's attack, his absolute negation of justice and
his contempt for the rule of law should not have been airily dismissed,
as it was for the most part, as unimportant and irrelevant. Castro's actions
as in the case of the airmen and pilots were most important and quite
relevant to the course that Castro and his Revolution were following.
Specific examples of Communist power came almost immediately to light
where the most elementary standards of legality and human decency
were contemptuously violated and replaced by Communist violence.

The Bureau of Repression of Communist Activities (BRAC), and the
Movement of American Integration (MIDA) were attacked by Communists in cooperation with Castro's forces. Located almost directly in front
of the rebel-held Camp Columbia, BRAC had files containing thorough

information on Communist activities in Cuba, the workings of the Communist *apparat*, and more important, information on liaison between the Communist Party and Fidel Castro. The latter information was obtained in a raid on the house of Juan Marinello in September of 1958. Marinello was President of the Cuban Communist Party.

MIDA was an international anti-Communist organization, headed by a Brazilian, Carlos Penna Botto. It maintained offices in every Latin American country. The main files were in Havana where MIDA's Secretary General, Ernesto de la Fe, had his headquarters. De la Fe was named Minister of Information following Batista's *coup* in 1952. He held the position for two years, and was Minister without Portfolio for another year-and-a-half. Such are the complexities of Cuban politics that he broke with Batista in 1956 fearful that the dictator was again planning to appoint Communists to his cabinet as he had during his 1940-1944 term. Carlos Rafael Rodríguez had held the cabinet post of Minister without Portfolio, and Batista had also permitted another Communist, Lázaro Peña, to take over the Cuban Confederation of Labor. Under de la Fe, the MIDA developed voluminous files on Communist activities in Latin America—perhaps the most complete files in the hemisphere.

The Communists apparently thought so, too. For on January 4, 1959, Ernesto de la Fe was arrested in his offices at 30 Consulado Street in Havana and put under guard at the Ocean Hotel. His captor and that of his secretary, Raúl Granja, as mentioned earlier, was Communist Luis Fajardo Escalona who headed rebel troops put under his command by "Che" Guevara. MIDA files were taken to La Cabaña fortress, where old-line Communists had established their headquarters, and there burned. De La Fe was arrested on the pretext that he had been in Batista's cabinet. Ironically, it was Communist Carlos Rafael Rodríguez, who also served in Batista's cabinet, who supervised the burning of the files.

Still another anti-Communist was to feel the wrath of "revolutionary justice." Salvador Díaz Verson, publisher of the magazine, *Occidente*, also held the position of president of two important anti-Communist organizations—the Anti-Communist League of Cuba and the Inter-American Organization of Anti-Communist Journalists. His offices, located at 558 G Street in the Vedado section of Havana, were sacked and his files burned. A member of the FBI office in the American Embassy witnessed the event.

Díaz Verson claims that 250,000 names of Latin American Communists were burned, along with manuscripts of his unpublished book, *Red Czarism*. In a booklet, *History of an Archive*, Díaz Verson has subsequently related that "four military trucks from the Seventh Military District of La Cabaña, and several men dressed in rebel fatigue uniforms bearing machine guns entered the offices." His files were taken to La Cabaña fortress and, like those of BRAC and MIDA, burned.

The case of the Bureau of Repression of Communist Activities (BRAC) is an interesting study in Communist tactics. Captain José de Jesús Castaño, head of the Bureau at the time, resigned his commission on January 1. He did not flee the country as others had. Comandante Camilo Cienfuegos instructed his aide to tell Castaño to stay on the job. He did so, and it cost him his life.

The Captain was something of an intellectual, well educated, speaking four languages. Known as a non-activist in the sense that his interest in Communism was intellectual rather than political, Castaño was credited with knowing by heart the backgrounds of virtually every Communist in Cuba. He also was said to have performed the interesting task of tracing the careers of embryo Communists from their first contact with Communism, and studying their introduction into the Party, and examining their motives for joining the movement. He was, as the phrase goes, a serious student of Communism.

Within a few days of Castaño's receiving orders to stay on the job, a group of Communists assaulted BRAC offices, but not before its employees had burned the file of BRAC agents. The Communists were led by Melba Hernández, another "girl Friday" of Fidel Castro, who had participated in Castro's attack on Moncada Barracks on July 26, 1953, the date from which the 26th of July Movement derives its name. Today she is a member of the Central Committee of the Cuban Communist Party, and head of the Cuban Committee on Aid to Vietnam. Castaño was captured personally by Miss Hernández. None of the rebel troops who ran out from nearby Camp Columbia when the assault was launched, did anything to stop the violence. Melba Hernández was well-known to all as a confidante of Fidel Castro, and the rebels assumed that the sackings and the arrests had Castro's sanction.

The BRAC files were taken to the camp of the Corps of Engineers and there burned. Captain Castaño was, like anti-Communist Ernesto de la Fe, taken to La Cabaña fortress. A mock trial was held whose principal purpose was to denigrate the Captain. He was accused of rape by another Communist female, Alicia Agramonte. In this instance, however, the accusation backfired and all Cuba laughed. Alicia Agramonte easily qualifies as one of the ugliest women in Cuba. If the Captain had the power to hold a female prisoner and rape her, the last person he would choose would be Sra. Agramonte. Nevertheless, the execution of Captain José de Jesús Castaño was personally ordered by "Che" Guevara, and he was shot.

Faced with open Communist violence, openly or tacitly supported by the Revolution, the Student Directorate began to beat a hasty retreat.

They learned that Communists capable of cooperating with Batista were equally capable of cooperating with Castro. On January 5, Castro's "Citizen President" Manuel Urrutia Lleó arrived at Rancho Boyeros airport in Havana. He did not go to the Presidential Palace, occupied by the Directorio, but to Camp Columbia where he consulted with leading members of the 26th of July Movement. Three members of the Movement were then dispatched to the Palace to discuss the situation with Directorio leader Faure Chomón.

The three, Manuel Ray, Roberto Agramonte, and José Manuel Gutiérrez were cordially received by Directorio leaders Faure Chomón and Rolando Cubela. To the surprise of many, the student leaders agreed to let Castro's President occupy the Palace without further opposition. Forces of the Student Directorate retired to the stadium of the University of Havana and later disbanded.

On January 7, one day before his triumphal entry into Havana, Fidel Castro announced in Matanzas Province: "I love democracy." He also pledged: "The Provisional Government will not maintain relations with the Soviet Union or with Communist nations."[5]

With that declaration, Fidel Castro prepared to enter Havana.

•

CHAPTER 5

The Great Betrayal Begins

•

ON JANUARY 8, 1959, Fidel Castro entered the Cuban capital as few other Cuban heroes before him. Met at the outskirts of Havana by a contingent of his men from Camp Columbia, Castro got out of the car in which he had been traveling and joined Comandante Camilo Cienfuegos in a jeep. He was accompanied by a ragged group of revolutionaries—the bearded, and Johnny-come-latelies with an eight-day stubble on their chins. The shouting of literally hundreds of thousands of Cubans at Castro's triumphal entry was punctuated by a twenty-one gun salute from Cuban Navy ships, the frigates "José Martí," and the "Máximo Gómez."

The nation's television cameras revealed a young man, tall and not yet corpulent, who was drinking in the adulation of the crowds with unabashed joy. Women threw flowers, *barbudos* stuck blossoms in the muzzles of their rifles. It was a great day, a tumultuous day, as Fidel Castro arrived in mid-afternoon at the Presidential Palace and received the greetings of Provisional President Manuel Urrutia and his cabinet. Though Urrutia held the title of President, none doubted who held the real power.

Castro spoke briefly from the balcony of the Presidential Palace and did little to add prestige to its then occupant. He said that he had never liked the Presidential Palace, that it evoked in him "no particular emotion." The fact, however, was that the Presidential Palace stood as a monument to the Student Directorate, and their bold attempt to assassinate Fulgencio Batista in 1957. Castro wanted his own monument.

He preferred, he said, to be in the mountains. The fortress there had proved stronger and more durable than "the fortress of tyranny," he added. Castro then invited the people to come to Camp Columbia, "because Columbia now belongs to the people."

Castro traveled in an American-made tank, accompanied by his young son, Fidelito. Fidelito had been flown to Cuba from Long Island, where Castro's divorced wife, now remarried, had installed the youngster in school. The appearance of the Revolutionary father and his son (though Castro had shown little concern over the boy's welfare) riding together in triumph, made a tremendous impact in the emotion-charged atmosphere. Castro stopped briefly at his old school, Belén, dismounting to kiss its flag in a masterful display of showmanship. Only a few months later, the school was to close its doors because it refused to permit Communist indoctrination in its classrooms.

At the moment, however, none of the impending tragedy was apparent. Cuban women threw themselves in the path of his march, hoping to stop the column long enough so they could kiss Castro's hand or touch him. It took nearly five hours for Castro to make his way a few miles to the military camp, there to give many Cubans their first immersion in the fiery water of his deceit.

Arriving at Camp Columbia about nine-thirty that evening, Castro mounted an improvised speaker's box and asked of handsome cowboy-hatted Camilo Cienfuegos: "Am I doing well, Camilo?" Cienfuegos answered: "You are doing well, Fidel." This exchange soon became a revolutionary slogan.

Fidel Castro had long been considered an orator of consummate skill and his address at Camp Columbia on January 8, 1959, ranks among the most important speeches of his career. He wove a web of oratory that trapped his foes, gave wings to the hopes of undeserving mobs, and established direct communication between him and "the people." That night Castro, a master of the innuendo, showed himself king of the propagandists.

"The people are listening," he said in his speech and of his speech. "The Revolutionary combatants are listening," adding ominously, "and the army soldiers whose destiny is in our hands are listening." He went on: "The first thing we who have made this Revolution must ask ourselves is, why did we make it?" Fingering the microphone during a pregnant pause, a habit that was to persist through the years, he cautioned potential opposition: "If some of us are hiding some ambition, are pushing for command, this is not a noble proposition." Who won the war? Castro gave victory to "the people," the faceless, impersonal mobs who had done precious little to support him. The merit in his "appointment" is that mobs are incapable of organized opposition. They were a safe repository for his ambitions.

Castro ignored the significant role played by the middle class and upper-middle class in Batista's defeat. They were destined to be destroyed. "The people, the people, won the war!" he shouted. Hammering home the theme which was to identify the Revolution with the mobs, he continued: "This war was won by nobody else than the people. . . . !" And "the people" responded, shouting and chanting: "We are with you Fidel! We are with you!"

Answering a rhetorical question, Castro said that "the greatest crime that can be committed in Cuba today would be a crime against the peace. Anyone who threatens the tranquility and the happiness of millions of Cuban mothers is a criminal and a traitor!" He had not shown any particular concern for "Cuban mothers" during his two years in the mountains, during the urban guerrilla warfare that took the lives of innocent bystanders, or by his consistent refusal to accept an honorable compromise that would bring peace to Cuba. But that day, January 8, 1959, was different. His own power might be challenged momentarily by those who demanded a share in the victory. They were the "traitors."

Castro built his case carefully. "Cuban mothers . . . of the soldier, the Revolutionary, of the citizen . . . feel that their sons, finally, are out of danger," he said. Having identified "the people" with himself and with his Revolution, Castro identified their common enemy as the Student Directorate which had taken arms from the arsenal of San Antonio de los Baños and hidden them. "Arms for what?" asked Castro. "To fight against whom? Arms, for what? To blackmail the President of the Republic? To threaten the Government? To create organizations of gangsters?"

Castro then applied the crusher with his question-and-answer delivery. "If we have a Government of young and honorable men and if the country has faith in them, if we are going to have elections, why should arms be stored away?" The crowd shouted back: "Arms for what?" From that moment the Student Directorate was destroyed as a political force.

The following day, events of some importance took place. One was Castro's appearance on the nation-wide radio-TV program, "Meet the Press." He manipulated the panel of questioners and the moderator as he had the crowds the night before—as a propaganda tool. There was barely time for questions since Castro talked for hours. This particular night he made several promises. He said the political parties would again be organized within a period of "eight to ten months," with general elections to follow in "about eighteen months." To embroil the people in politics within "five months of liberation," he said would be "a crime." Again reverting to "the people," Castro said that "if the people [meaning Fidel Castro] asked" the U.S. Military Mission to leave Cuba, then they ought to go. They went.

That same day, January 9, the Communists were in the news. Old-line Communist labor leader Lázaro Peña returned to Cuba from exile in Europe, the Communist newspaper, *Hoy*, appeared openly on the newsstands, and Camilo Cienfuegos clarified the position of the Communist Party in Revolutionary Cuba.

Speaking to reporters at Camp Columbia, Cienfuegos said that "The

Communists . . . have the right to become legalized . . . if they observe the democratic patterns of life which reign in the country. . . ." In other words, the Communists would be accepted if they no longer were Communists, something which obviously would not happen, and, three days later, Communist poet Nicolás Guillén was proclaimed Poet Laureate of Cuba.

None of these events created much of a stir in Cuba. The Cubans remembered that Batista had worked actively with the Communists in the early 1940's. What they forgot was that he did so to gain votes for his 1940 election, and more important, that he controlled the Communists. They also overlooked the fact that on January 12, the Revolutionary Council, known as the Council of Ministers, revised articles 21, 24, and 25 of the Constitution. This revision permitted Castro summarily to execute his enemies and arbitrarily to confiscate properties. In another legal act of exceptional importance, Osvaldo Dorticós Torrado, and an old-line Communist from the city of Cienfuegos, was given enormous power to formulate "Revolutionary Laws." If the country was to be governed by the 1940 Constitution, as Castro had told the world, what was the need for "Revolutionary Laws"? Dorticós was chosen over a panel of well-known lawyers proffered by four members of the Council of Ministers.

In short, much of what Castro had said he would do when he spoke at his trial in October 1953 was not only being done in rapid-fire order in January, 1959, but it was being done with the obvious support of the Communists. And initial public rumbles against Castro's high-handedness, and outspoken criticism in the press over the appointment of Dorticós, were met with the by-now familiar Communist counter-charge that the complainers were *Batistianos*, or "McCarthyites," and the complaints abruptly stopped. Thus, the revision of key articles in the Constitution provided a vital factor in revolutionary intimidation. It was also apparent within four days of Castro's arrival in Havana that he was determined to eliminate all opposition—physically, if necessary.

It was during this hectic period that Earl E. T. Smith was recalled as American Ambassador to Cuba and a search for a career official ended in the selection of Philip W. Bonsal, Ambassador to Bolivia at the time of his appointment.

I received a call the night of January 10. It was Ambassador Smith asking me to come at once to the Embassy residence. There he told me he had been recalled as Ambassador, adding in a philosophical mood that his recall had been dictated by necessity. We sat down together to work out a press release to replace a first draft he had already prepared. We finally agreed on wording and he "cleared" the release with the duty officer at the State Department. One of the sticky points in the release was the question of when he and his wife were to leave, and by what means. The next day, we had another of the Ambassador's celebrated staff meetings at the Embassy. All of us were somewhat edgy, having slept very little over the past ten days. We were beginning to be concerned, as well, about the mobs. Castro's speech at Camp Columbia had virtually put the law of the land into their hands. Attempts by whatever authority happened to be around at the moment, to get people back to work, for example, more often than not were met with charges of *"Batistiano!"* Therefore, the departure of the American Ambassador took on an added significance.

With Mr. Smith's resignation and recall, Dan Braddock had been appointed as Chargé d'Affaires. Prior to the staff meeting, Dan had consulted carefully with the security people in the Embassy, and with each division chief, over the possibility of the mobs embarrassing the Smiths on their departure. This would not do, and most of us did believe that such a possibility existed. Dan opened the staff meeting on that note. Smith said: "Go on." Dan deferred to the Air Attaché, Colonel John Nichols. Nichols proposed that he use his old DC-3 plane and fly the Smiths directly to their home in Palm Beach.

Smith listened carefully, then said that he had made arrangements to go back to Palm Beach by ship. It was only an overnight trip, he said, adding that his wife and other members of the household would be much more comfortable leaving that way. Then the conversation went approximately as follows:

"We feel that there may be serious demonstrations at the docks, Mr. Ambassador, and that they should be avoided at all costs," said Braddock.

"What makes you think so?" Smith asked.

"Well, the reports of our security people. . . ." Braddock was interrupted.

"The hell with the reports. We've all been down at the docks trying to get tourists out, and I never had any trouble. Has anyone else had trouble?" Smith asked.

"Well, that's not exactly the point," said John Topping. "What we're trying to do is to avoid any embarrassment to you, to the United States, or to your family."

"All I can say," said Smith angrily, "is that you're suggesting that the American Ambassador sneak out of Cuba. That I refuse to do. I'm going to stay with my original plans, and, furthermore, my chauffeur is going to drive us to the docks with the American flags flying on the fenders of the Embassy Cadillac!"

He stood up, terminating further discussion. Then he broke into a laugh. "Don't let it bother you," he said looking around at the glum faces.

"I will be all right on this little journey, and so will the United States."
Then he went around the room shaking hands with each of his officers,
and was escorted out of the Embassy and to his car by a Marine guard
in full dress uniform. Dan Braddock accompanied him.

Mr. Smith was right. As it turned out, there was no difficulty at the
docks when he and his family left Cuba a few days later. When I arrived,
he was standing on the front deck receiving members of the diplomatic
corps who had come with their wives to see Mrs. Smith and him off. Less
than two years later, Dan Braddock and I were to stand on the deck of
the same ship and see off another American Ambassador who had been
reviled, humiliated, and scorned by the Castro regime. On that day we
saw organized demonstrations which were notably lacking when Amas-
sador Smith left the country. With the departure of Mr. Smith, the
American Embassy in Havana was without an Ambassador until the
middle of February.

The Revolution continued along its path, with each day making it more
apparent that the course was leading inexorably toward an institutionalized dictatorship in which individuals were contemptuously shorn of
their rights, and dissenters were met with charges of treasonable conduct,
counter-revolutionary activity, or worse. Immediately following the departure of Ambassador Smith, Raúl Castro ordered the execution of over
seventy army men. Given no trial, they were shot in front of an immense
excavation 120 feet long, and covered over into a mass grave by bulldozers.[1]

In a deal as cynical as was ever consummated by Fulgencio Batista,
Fidel Castro met with Student Directorate leader Rolando Cubela on the
steps of the University of Havana and there stripped Cuban students of
their autonomy. In return for Cubela's support, Castro made him President of the FEU, *Federacion Estudiantil Universitaria* (University Student Federation).

The appointment of pistol-packing Cubela, at the time a Comandante
in the Rebel Army, brought the university students under direct government control, destroying really free elections among the student
body even as courses were about to be renewed. From that moment,
every "student" leader has been a member of Castro's Communist government.

But the loss of student autonomy was sugar-coated. The Council of
Ministers passed Revolutionary Law Number 11 which invalidated all
degrees issued by private, specifically the Catholic, universities in Cuba
during the period that Havana University was closed by Batista because
of anti-Government riots and conspiracy. Degrees earned in the United
States during that time were also made 'subject to review." Thus, another
Revolutionary precedent was established—two wrongs make a right.

Castro did with the Universities what he was to do with other sectors of the country.

The passage of Revolutionary Law Number 11 coincided with a violent attack on Catholic universities through an editorial in Castro's official newspaper, *Revolucion*. Aping the exceptionally successful oratorical tactics of Castro at Camp Columbia in his "Arms for what?" speech, *Revolucion* titled its editorial "Roman Education For What?" Written by editor and *barbudo* Carlos Franqui, the editorial didn't confine itself to mere criticism of Catholic education, but expanded the theme into an attack on the Roman Catholic Church itself.

Almost immediately following passage of Revolutionary Law Number 11, the FEU seized the University of Havana and began purging professors and replacing them with "revolutionary" instructors. The seizure of the university and the expulsion of professors was justified by claiming that the professors did not comply with Laws 19 and 20 of the Educational Laws which were promulgated back in 1937, laws which state that professors must prove their capability as instructors by taking tests in their subjects every five years. To fill the gap in authority, the FEU appointed itself administrator. It is difficult to imagine how the student could determine the capabilities of the teacher, since he presumably knew little about the subject in which he enrolled at the university. The real reason for the takeover became immediately apparent when the governing council of the FEU announced on February 2 that it was proceeding with "the total political purification of professors, students, and employees." The subterfuge was all too apparent. The governing student council issued a blast at Fulgencio Batista for having closed the university, but did not say just how professors could take their tests in a closed institution. And Castro's Education Minister Armando Hart remained silent when a group of purged professors pointed out to him that Article 4 of the Educational Law specifically prohibited the kind of bullying to which they had been subjected by FEU hooligans. It reads: "The University of Havana will be governed by its professors, under their responsibility and by means of the faculty authorities and organisms which are determined by the Statutes. Under no circumstances may the professors delegate these faculties." Government complicity in what amounted to the ideological takeover of Cuba's top educational institution was so great as to be ostentatious.

Latin American embassies in Havana were crowded with political asylees. In direct violation of Article 31 of the Constitution, which expressly "offers and recognizes the right of asylum for political refugees," Castro refused to extend to these asylees "safe conduct" to the Havana airport, the gateway to leaving Cuba. The Latins were, of course, furious. Embassy after embassy had to rent additional buildings, build sleeping bunks in garages and basements, and even construct small shelters in embassy grounds, as thousands and thousands of terrified Cubans, their rights as citizens virtually eliminated by sweeping decrees, tried to get out of the country in order to save their lives. With his talent for twisting the facts to suit his deeper political objectives, Castro used the requests for "safe conduct" by Latin American Ambassadors as the occasion for an attack on the United States which does not even permit its embassies in Latin America to accept political asylees! To hide the fact that decent Cubans were fleeing for their lives, a fact that did not exactly redound to the credit of his "humanist" revolution, Castro simply classified them all as *"Batistianos,"* war criminals, and the like. Once they had taken asylum in Latin American embassies in Havana he said, "we can't do anything about it." Without once addressing himself to the complaints of Latin American diplomats, who were turned down in their "safe conduct" requests for their Cuban asylees,—legitimate complaints under international law—he viciously turned on the United States.

Part of his fury was due to the rising public criticism in this country of the slaughter taking place in Cuba. Despite Castro's claim that "the Revolution would take no revenge . . . that we will have no more blood . . ." his actions belied his words as farcical trials continued throughout the country with executions taking place daily. And despite the fact that asylees were in Latin American embassies, he charged that "the war criminals" were all destined to come to the United States anyway, a statement which must rank among the more extraordinary interpretations of international law. Clearly, Castro wasn't interested in law or justice. His interest lay in a propaganda campaign against a United States public which dared question the senseless killings that were taking place in Cuba, killings which Castro himself said had ceased. "What we are going to demand of the government of the United States, because the attacks come from there, is the return of the war criminals and the millions of pesos that have been robbed from our country," he shouted before a crowd in front of the Presidential Palace on January 16, 1959, eight days after arriving in Havana.

The United States Government immediately replied that it would return all those Cubans proved to be criminals by the Cuban Government. Obviously, certain norms in classification have had to be established over the decades. Were this not so, any dictator taking power could have members of the opposition extradited and then have them shot.

The shocking truth is that Castro wanted the "war criminals" to stay in the United States as a focal point of attacks against this country, to the point of running roughshod over Article 31 of Cuba's Constitution. It reads: "The Nation will not authorize extradition of those guilty of political crimes nor will it attempt to obtain extradition of Cubans guilty of those crimes who take refuge in foreign territory." Nor did the Castro regime make any effort to provide bills of particulars in cases where they demanded extradition.

Either unaware of Cuba's Constitutional guarantees, or believing that the Constitution really no longer had any meaning in Castroland, the American Embassy kept pressing the Foreign Ministry for the data needed to remove this constant source of friction. Legitimate requests from the Embassy were met with charges to the effect that everyone knew who the war criminals were, and that U.S. requests were designed merely to avoid turning over those criminals. On one occasion, the well-meaning but enormously inept Foreign Minister, Roberto Agramonte, tried to get his staff to come up with documented cases to submit to the Embassy, and *he* was attacked by his own subordinates for even suggesting the matter. Agramonte did not realize, as was the case with many in the American Embassy in Havana, that Fidel Castro and his Communist colleagues did not *want* anyone extradited from the United States. This suspicion was articulated one morning at the Ambassador's staff meeting by Naval Attaché, Captain Robert Clark. Chargé Dan Braddock, now in command, looked intently at Clark for a moment and said: "It's beginning to look that way, isn't it?"

The sincerity of Castro's claims that "war criminals" were taking millions of pesos out of the country needs to be examined from several angles. First, what the asylees took out of the country themselves was as nothing compared to what the staffs and Ambassadors in some Latin American embassies were extorting from them. Political asylum became a big business—perhaps the biggest business in Cuba—with potential asylees having to approach several embassies in Havana until one could be found whose demands fitted their pocketbooks. Some Latin American Ambassadors came to Cuba living on the inadequate pay of their governments, and left Havana as millionaires.

The fleecing of Cubans forced to bargain for their lives and the lives of their families was as well known in Havana as the fact that Fidel Castro wore a beard and that "Che" Guevara seldom took a bath and rarely changed his clothes. In 1961, I had a conversation about the subject at the Columbus Hotel in Miami with Castro's former Minister of the Treasury, Rufo López Fresquet. He, too, had fled the country. López Fresquet told me that it was impossible to come up with an accurate account of the money which Latin American embassies had extorted from Cubans, but his "guess" was that "it ran into several millions of dollars." He also said that the Ministry of the Treasury was aware of the extortion and that his own attempts to do something about it in 1959 fell on deaf ears.

What was the key issue for the Revolutionary Government? Was it merely that millions of dollars were leaving Cuba? Apparently not, for Castro never raised his voice in protest against the shake-down of Cuban citizens, even though he and his regime were charging almost daily that the treasury had been looted by *Batistianos* and that the country was broke. Let us look at those charges for a moment. The most obvious point to be made here is that so hasty was Batista's flight that none of those who left the country with him had time to return from the meeting at Camp Columbia to their homes and offices to pick up so much as a wrist watch. Batista was so fearful that his flight might become known that he prevented them from doing so. This is not to say that the Batista government was not graft-ridden. It was. But to say that there was graft was one thing. It was quite another for the Revolutionary Government to charge, as it consistently did, that because of it, the treasury was empty. And if it was, why wasn't a protest raised against the flight of money via the diplomatic pouches of Latin American embassies? This is a key point because such charges were used as an initial excuse not to indemnify Cubans and Americans for property which was later expropriated by the state.

Yet, on January 28, Castro's Minister of the Treasury, Rufo López Fresquet told members of the Association of Cuban Executives that monetary reserves were adequate to keep the peso on a par with the U.S. dollar. Fresquet then outlined a fiscal program which, he said, "very shortly" would end Cuba's immediate financial crisis. The week following Fresquet's rather optimistic address, National Bank President Felipe Pazos announced that "Cuba's present economic crisis will be temporary." Pazos listed five relatively mild belt-tightening measures then under consideration. Those to be adopted, said Pazos, would not last long "because of the uniquely transitory nature of the present crisis." Pazos stated that although Cuba's gold and dollar reserves had dropped $60 million below the legal limit established by the National Bank the peso was sound. "Given the fine prospects for our exports and the probable reduction of our imports, our balance of payments should quickly return to a position of balance," said Pazos, adding: "This will permit us to overcome the immediate crisis which we are facing."

On December 31, 1958, the Cuban monetary reserves alone stood at $124.2 million. In fact, the President of the National Bank of Cuba, Joaquín Martínez Saenz, did not take political asylum in an embassy nor flee the country by other means. So sure was he that the relative financial solvency of Cuba would be recognized by the Revolutionary regime that he stayed in his office at the bank where he was later arrested by members of the Rebel Army. It was the Revolutionary Government that plundered Cuba's assets when it came to power. By 1961, even after robbing both

Americans and Cubans of their private properties, the available monetary reserves of Revolutionary Cuba stood at exactly zero.

Castro's former Minister of the Treasury had an answer for the strange attitude of the Revolutionary Government toward the robbing of Cuba by the Latin Americans. As long as many Latin American Ambassadors and their staffs profited from the Revolution, he said, they would try to avoid a diplomatic break with Cuba. More than one Ambassador sent dispatches to his foreign ministry at home in which the realities of Cuba were doctored to suit his financial interest. And there was blackmail. The Cuban Foreign Ministry was known gently to encourage some of the Ambassadors to speak publicly, on appropriate occasions, in favor of the Revolution. The total result of this chicanery was that the Revolutionary Government of Cuba reaped political rewards on all sides. No explanations were asked of the Latins for their callous robberies. Instead, the fury of Fidel Castro was directed toward his main enemy, the United States, which he claimed was the final destination of those in asylum in Latin American embassies in Havana. Castro was essentially correct. None of the Latin American countries would open their doors to the flood of persecuted Cuban refugees, and it was left to the United States to provide a haven for them. It was not until years later that a few Latin countries permitted a trickle of Cubans, carefully selected for their skills, to enter as immigrants.

Castro launched an attack on the United States from yet another quarter—Communism. "I don't know why there are calumnies against our Revolution," he said one day, "that it is Communist or that it is infiltrated by Communism." The facts are that Castro had prostituted the truth so many times in the fewer than ten days of power that questions were, indeed, being asked. For example, the very day following his complaint, the Cuban Government recognized the Communist government of Czechoslovakia. Yet Castro had publicly announced little more than a week earlier that the Provisional Government of Cuba would not extend relations to the Soviet Union or to other Communist countries. True, as Castro apologists were quick to point out, the United States itself maintained diplomatic relations with the Prague regime. But this is not the point. The point is that the President of the United States did not emphatically and voluntarily reject diplomatic relations one week and inexplicably extend recognition the next.

It was also of some concern at the time that Spanish Republican (Communist) General Alberto Bayo arrived in Cuba. It was he who trained Fidel Castro and his men in guerrilla tactics on a Mexican ranch and prepared them for their insurrection against Batista. Bayo arrived in Havana in time to read an interview in the January 20 issue of *Revolucion* by one of his disciples—"Che" Guevara. When considered along with all that had gone on before, the nature of the interview makes clear that Cuban leaders, particularly Fidel Castro, were themselves largely responsible for making the issue of Communism of international importance. They did so through speeches of denial shouted from the balcony of the Presidential Palace, over radio and television, and in interviews such as the one published in *Revolucion.* Guevara's interview was a case of crying foul before a glove had even been laid on the combatant.

In his front-page interview, Guevara spoke with characteristic bluntness. He said that "Wall Street is dedicated to combat those people who are fighting for their liberty, and as with the case of the people of Guatemala, that same aggression is being planned against the people of Cuba."[2] Not only was the analogy imperfect, it was absurd. "Wall Street" was almost literally besieging the Presidential Palace, clamoring for the opportunity to invest in a country that had just been delivered into the control of Fidel Castro and his Revolutionary Government! The American Embassy was bending over backwards trying to ignore the insults and overlook the lies and deceit which were pouring forth from Fidel Castro and his principal aides. What aggression could the United States possibly be planning against Cuba on January 20, 1959?

"Psychologist" Herbert Matthews has it in his book, *The Cuban Story,* that "the psychology of Fidel Castro and the other young revolutionaries was such that the more they were attacked for being Communists or the dupes of Communists, the more difficult it became to oppose Communism if they wanted to." This statement is in error in many respects. Matthews sets the beginning of these attacks at May 3, 1959, when Stuart Novins of CBS launched, according to Matthews, "the first, and probably most damaging, major attack in the field. . . ," quoting Novins as stating that "this Cuban island is today a totalitarian dictatorship and is rapidly becoming a Communist beachhead in the Caribbean."[3]

Apart from the obvious—that Novins was correct in his analysis—how does Mr. Matthews explain Fidel Castro's denial in January of charges which, according to Castro's most eminent apologist at the time, were not made until May? And what about other completely unfounded and disgraceful charges made against the United States by "young revolutionaries," such as "Che" Guevara? Nor is another of Mr. Matthews' points well taken; namely, that from the outset, the course of social welfare set by the revolution was bound to collide with U.S. business interests, and that therefore the "young revolutionaries" girded themselves for that collision well in advance. It was none other than the grey eminence of the revolution, "Che" Guevara, who had put that collision in its true perspective when, in January, 1959, he virtually said that the Communist direction to be taken by the Revolution could count on a reaction from the United States. Let it be clearly understood that it was

Guevara who likened the Cuban Revolution to the Communist takeover in Guatemala and warned of U.S. reaction to a Communist takeover in Cuba.

Matthews continues with his analysis of the "young revolutionaries," writing of them that ". . . to turn against the Reds would have seemed like truckling to the United States, yielding to American attacks. . . ." This picture of moist-eyed, emotional, and petulant children who threw themselves into the arms of the Communists is far from the true portrait of the hard-eyed and hard-hearted men who could summarily order the execution (and at times personally administer the *coup de grace*), of hundreds of men and have their bodies dumped into common graves; or, as in Guevara's case, without a flicker of emotion, tell the colossal lie that the United States was "planning aggression against the people of Cuba." How do Mr. Matthews and other "losers" explain away the brutalization of government, the intimidation of the people, and the denial of every basic right to Castro's victims? There have been few bloodier chapters in the story of Latin American dictatorships, though in these early stages the Cubans were vastly more shocked than "losers" such as Matthews, who tended to think of the blood purge, and of unfounded attacks against the United States, as a requisite to liberal reform.

What did it all mean? To the thinking man it meant that the events of the first two weeks of Castro's coming to power established the basis for most of what was to follow. It indicated that there was both ideology and conscious direction behind Castro's revolution. Almost before the query of Communist infiltration could be raised, the Revolutionaries were there with a prepared counter-charge—*Batistiano!* That counter-charge was hurled early and continued late. Its purpose: to smear as "McCarthyism" the accusations that the Revolutionaries and particularly "Che" Guevara, knew were bound to be made. One needs only to consider the words of "Che" Guevara to see in them the chilling evidence of Communism to come.

Guevara's interview in *Revolucion* ended with the following sentence: "Finally, he said that all of the people ought to meet Wednesday, January 21, in front of the Presidential Palace, in order to destroy the campaign against the triumph of the Revolution."

There was no campaign against the Castro order. But Castro needed the mobs. Mob meetings became the forum before which leaders of the Cuban Revolution expounded the policies of the government. Whenever a note was received from the American Embassy that displeased its leaders, whenever an event occurred which needed propagandizing, mobs were called out to "ratify" the decisions of those leaders.

Experienced in the ways of dictatorships, the Cubans very early began to experience some doubts about the Castro regime, although that superb actor, the "Maximum Leader," was largely absolved of any direct blame for its excesses. Specifically, the bloodletting was being questioned. Executions by Castro's firing squads had, by January 21, run into the hundreds, the exact number being unknown. What made the Cubans uneasy is that they occurred whenever it seemed expedient to make an example of the dissenter. This is not to say that Castro's lies did not find currency in our press. They did, and came to be believed, in part, by the American public.

On January 21, 1959, the mobs were called out to "ratify" the shootings being carried out in all of Cuba's six provinces. The labor unions, headed by Castro-appointed labor leader David Salvador, filed into the spacious park in front of the Palace, along with thousands of other Cubans curious to see what new excitement was in store for them. Communists and extremists, among them hastily organized units of the Socialist Youth, bore placards and banners which read: "Death to the Collaborators of Batista!" "To the Shooting Wall with the War Criminals!" They were the cheer leaders for murder.

Fidel Castro presided over the mobs, exercising his "direct democracy." Your revolution, he said, is being unjustly attacked by its enemies. He flavored his potpourri of words with the sauce of humility, saying: "It is possible that our fighters are trembling today before this multitude as it never trembled before the bullets of the enemy." He exaggerated the size of the mob, the better to claim public support for his undemocratic behaviour. "We can say here, today," he shouted, "that there is no place large enough in all of Havana for a meeting of all the people who support the Revolution!" However, he said that the Assembly on that day was not to "celebrate a victory of arms, a victory of reason, but a victory of justice, a moral victory."

He held up a straw man—threats against his life: "I know who my enemies are; they can kill me whenever they want. . . ." But his brother Raúl, he said, would carry on. "And even if they kill Raúl," he added, "behind him will come another, and another, and another." Then he asked the mobs to give their assent to the executions, or, as he put it, to "justice taking place." "Those who agree with the justice being applied, those who are in accord with the shooting of the bullies, raise your hand!" They did, with shouts of "To the shooting wall!" The people had spoken. To the ignorant, to the superstitious *santero* and to the conspiratorial-minded, occult forces were planning to destroy the "people's revolution." The word came from the mouth of none other than the warrior and prophet of the revolution, Fidel himself, and it must be so.

Castro then turned to his astonished guests seated on the balcony of the Palace and said: "*Senores* representatives of the diplomatic corps, *senores* journalists of the continent, the court of a million Cubans of all ideas and all classes has voted!" this, then, was "Revolutionary justice." This was the final meaning of Castro's October, 1953, court address: "History Will Absolve Me."[4] The leader and the people are one and indivisible.

A week before Castro's demonstration of "direct democracy," a very tired Ira Wolfer came to my office. Wolfer had been an American resident in Cuba for over fifteen years, had married a Cuban, and both had been active in the 26th of July Movement. When Castro came to power, Ira did much of the official interpreting for major figures of the new regime, even for Fidel Castro himself. He told me that morning that he had been ordered by Castro, as a "gesture of good will," to arrange for reporters from the United States and from Latin America to come to Havana to see "revolutionary justice for themselves." All costs, including transportation and hotel accommodations would be paid by the Revolutionary Government.

Specifically, the reporters were being invited to attend the trial of a Major Jesús Sosa Blanco, to be held in public in the enormous Sports Palace on the outskirts of Havana. I was nonplussed, and asked Ira: "Don't you know that this is the very opposite of a good will gesture? For heaven's sake, among hundreds of American reporters you're going to find plenty who will clobber Castro for holding that kind of public exhibition of hate. Is this what Castro wants? What's he trying to do, anyway? Raise more problems between Cuba and the United States?"

I had seen portions of two trials and couldn't conceive of a worse example of "justice." The Revolutionary "judges" presiding were for the most part not qualified for their responsibilities, and in one trial it was obvious that they were under directions to come up with a verdict of guilty. The pro-Communist Defense Minister Comandante Augusto Martínez Sánchez openly told attorneys defending the military that their role "never was to argue that the government's charges were unfounded," but to confine themselves to "pleas for clemency." That, said the Defense Minister, was the role of the defense "in a Revolutionary society," and that is exactly what Castro had in mind back in 1953 when he said that he would "reform" the judiciary.

In any case, Wolfer said that he had direct orders from Fidel Castro to invite the reporters. He commented wryly that the trials were being called "Operación Verdad" (Operation Truth).

The trials were held in the appropriate atmosphere of the Coliseum-like structure of the Sports Palace, and were covered by perhaps the largest array of journalistic talent in Cuba's history. The red carpet had been rolled out for the press, television cameras were permitted on the floor of the arena, and Major Sosa Blanco was arraigned in the boxing ring before a group of bearded officers of the Rebel Army. The charges: that he was a war criminal, guilty of "crimes against the people." He denied the charges.

Mobs who had "voted" the night before at the Palace demonstration were invited to attend the trial, and they packed the 16,000-seat auditorium. The type of person attracted to the spectacle added little to the dignity of a trial where members of the Revolutionary Tribunal made their comments over a public address system, and the shouts of coffee and beer vendors moving amongst the crowd at times interrupted the testimony of the witnesses. Major Sosa Blanco aptly described the scene in saying, "I am in a Roman Colosseum."

As the trial progressed, it was apparent to millions of Cubans, as it should have been apparent to Castro's apologists, that the show unfolding before their eyes had all the earmarks of a hate-making machine. The one necessary ingredient, justice, was totally absent. Witnesses were folk from the back-country area in Oriente Province where Major Sosa Blanco had been stationed (incidentally, Comandante Augusto Martínez Sánchez went to Oriente and personally selected them). The farce was apparent from the very beginning when the witnesses were required formally to identify a defendant whose movements and facial expressions were recorded daily over television, with his picture flanking front page articles and editorials in Cuba's newspapers. The prosecution not only kept the witnesses together in the same room in the Sports Palace, but thoughtfully provided them with a television set.

The Revolutionary Tribunal kept the focus of attention on the past, sometimes with gratuitous dissertations on the alleged cruelty of Batista's army. There was a tense viciousness in the crowds as witness after witness was led forward to testify. Shouts of "to the Wall" (*Paredon*), were hurled at the defendant. To this confusion was added still another. After solemnly identifying the defendant, some witnesses referred to the perpetrator of certain specified crimes as "Major Merob Sosa." As it turned out, they were talking about an entirely different man, one who operated in the same general area of Oriente Province as Sosa Blanco, but was not Major Jesús Sosa Blanco at all. A cruel man and a mental case, Merob Sosa had been shipped off by the army to New York where he was undergoing treatment in a hospital at the time of the trial.

Embarrassment followed embarrassment. Under the close questioning of defense attorney Arístides D'Acosta, it turned out that few, if any, of the witnesses had actually seen the crimes attributed to the defendant. They recounted stories that had been told to them by friends and relatives. The false face of "revolutionary justice" was unwittingly exposed by the simple country people themselves. Their bald and naive truths under D'Acosta's questioning unbuttoned the trials and revealed them for what they were—a farce, and a thinly disguised threat to anyone who dared differ with the Revolution. Sosa Blanco himself, and the witnesses brought forward to condemn him, were incidental to this vastly greater purpose.

While the crimes charged to Major Jesús Sosa Blanco may have been committed by him, the government prosecutors were less than convincing in proving his guilt. This, plus open public revulsion at the spectacle, forced Fidel Castro to order the trial held behind closed doors. Sosa Blanco was, of course, condemned to death and shot.

The American working press was, for the most part, repelled by Revolutionary "justice." Many reporters said so in their dispatches, thus bringing down upon themselves the wrath of Herbert Matthews. He writes: "The American press in general has the shameful record that it printed almost nothing of . . . slaughter by the thousands by Batista while it has chronicled in the most lurid way the execution (without torture, incidentally) of hundreds by Fidel Castro—nearly all 'war criminals' in the first weeks of the revolution." What "slaughter by the thousands" by Batista? Where is Mr. Matthews' documentation for such a sweeping statement? His sources are precisely those that tricked him in 1957 into inflating Castro's pitifully small band of guerrillas into a formidable force —Castroite sources. Included among those sources for Matthews' report of "slaughter" are none other than Communist Vilma Espín de Castro, and pro-Communist Celia Sánchez, Castro's own "Girl Friday." For him to accept their judgments uncritically is as grave an error as that committed by those who accepted Batista's judgments at face value. What Mr. Matthews is saying is that American journalists should have refrained from reporting what they saw. It is difficult to see how our press could have made the executions and the Sosa Blanco farce more "lurid" than they really were. What those reporters were witnessing was the very negation of justice, and the deliberate debasement of the rule of law. It should be asked: Who invited the reporters to come to Cuba? And who defined the term, "war criminal"?

Representative Charles O. Porter of Oregon journeyed to Havana for a first-hand view of the situation. He attended one of our Embassy staff meetings where he lectured us on what does and does not constitute illegal trial proceedings. When he returned to Washington, Porter spoke before Congress and gave them the benefit of his views. On January 25, 1959, the Democratic Congressman said: "I do not believe there has been any 'blood bath' in Cuba nor do I believe that Castro and his 26th of July Movement are denying fair trial to accused war criminals, although I believe their procedures should be much improved." Surprisingly, Porter established himself as something of an expert on Cuban affairs by alleging: "My opinion is based on two years of observing the Cuban situation." He was well-informed, just as those who questioned the trials and shootings in Cuba were, in his words, "not fully informed, often through no fault of their own." They were not fully informed, he said, "because they don't realize the magnitude and high morality of the revolution. . . ." He accepted the definition "war criminal" as uncritically as Herbert Matthews, and flatly asserted that "cases against the accused war criminals were not hastily concocted on the say-so of some hysterical woman," adding: "All evidence was that the trials were just and had been done properly."[5]

As the Cuban military establishment was debased and crushed, "popular militia" units began to make their appearance. Initially, the units were made up of the type of mobster attracted to the mass demonstrations before the Presidential Palace and to the barbarities committed at public trials. Many were sheer opportunists hoping to get what they could out of the new regime, finding that their worth to the Revolution was judged by the intensity of their "anti-imperialist" and anti-American declamations. While some decent and respectable Cubans volunteered for an hour or two a day to learn how to march under the tutelage of instructors sent throughout the city each evening, the overall composition of the militia in its early stages of development was definitely lumpenproletarian. Cuba's first militia units were comprised of the social scum —the idlers, the anti-social elements, and those who were ferociously resentful of nearly anybody and everything. Given the class-conflict nature of the Cuban Revolution from the very beginning, it was not surprising that this should be so. And Communist influence was to be found there.

The creation of a militia, first announced by Fidel Castro on January 6, 1959, was important to the designs of the regime. Not only was the militia to replace the old military order; it was the bully-boy of the new order. Militia groupings were developed in key sectors of the country. Far from being organized to "repel aggression," the militia was the indispensable organ of internal control. Most important, the growth of the militia coincided with extension of the political controls by the regime. Organizationally, units were established in the labor unions throughout the country, with militia groups scattered among union locals in such a manner as to exercise widespread control of the construction workers, communications workers, the printers, etc. The goal was to be able to enforce demands of the regime whenever worker resistance was encountered.

Once having destroyed the military order, the groundwork was laid for Communist capture of the labor unions, and thereby the control of the communications media—newspapers, wire services, and radio-TV. Castro would then control the military, the unions, and the mass media —classically the targets of any Communist regime.

Another early target of Castro, as we have seen, was the United States. The Cuban military order was destroyed to the accompaniment of propaganda that described Batista's troops as "U.S.-trained," and bombardments as having been made by U.S.-built aircraft,"[6] thus making Castro's early anti-Americanism seem just and reasonable to those in the United States who were not well acquainted with the Cuban situation. Castro chose to ignore the fact that the "training" being conducted by the U.S. military mission to Cuba was minimal. For example, one typical task was instructing the Cubans on how to operate Army field kitchens.

Nor did Castro and his apologists mention that Batista had been turned down by the United States in his request to purchase military aircraft, and that he proceeded to buy British "Sea Furies" instead. Yet, the British remained remarkably free of attack. As to the U.S. military mission itself, Castro's almost verbatim comment was: "What can the U.S. military mission teach us, when we have already defeated those whom it trained?"

The U.S. military mission was set up in Cuba as the result of treaty commitments to hemispheric defense against outside aggression. Obviously, he who was to become the aggressor wanted no foes in his encampment. Castro wanted no American military men around when he formed a militia organized for internal intimidation, on the one hand, aggression against the hemisphere on the other, and for defense against what "Che" Guevara warned would eventually become a military reaction by the United States against a Communist base in this hemisphere. It was this thinking that made it absurd to believe that the Castro regime wanted anything to do with the United States or its institutions. Castro's purpose was to promote the cry of "McCarthyism" against the United States.

Some of this thinking came through just prior to the Sosa Blanco trial, and it involved the integrity of the American press. The day of that trial, Castro met with reporters in the Copa Room of the Havana Riviera hotel and virtually invited them to accuse the regime of being Communist. I attended that press conference to hear him say to nonplussed and goggle-eyed reporters: "I want to make it clear that I am not Communist because I am certain that what will be said of us is that we are Communist." Why so certain? Why did he protest so much? Indeed, in examining the statements and actions of the principal leaders of the Castro regime in the first few weeks of its coming to power, a case can be made that those leaders were embarked on a determined campaign against American newsmen and news services, and not the reverse, as Professor Samuel Shapiro, then of Michigan State University, and so many others would have it.

An incident in early February had already established the tenor of Castro's relations with the Cuban press. The weekly humorous publication, *Zig Zag*, enjoyed a reputation for letting the air out of gassy politicians and political hacks. Its full front page cartoons were brilliant, and though Fulgencio Batista was often the butt of *Zig Zag's* subtle and devastating humor, he let it pass. When, in February 1959, *Zig Zag's* cartoon tried to show that Castro's movement, like virtually every Cuban political movement before it, was being hitch-hiked by political hacks, Castro exploded. In this instance, the full-page cartoon showed Castro marching along, followed by a few of his *barbudos* and a multitude of civilians wearing derby hats. The derby is known in Spanish as a *bombin*, and the appelation is tagged onto those who are political turncoats, professional flatterers who follow every government in power. *Zig Zag* was trying to warn that Castro was being plagued by office-seekers and apple polishers who vastly outnumbered his own sparse contingent of *barbudos*. Castro chose to challenge *Zig Zag*, charging the management with saying that he had taken the *bombines* under his wing, something which *Zig Zag* never intended to portray and few, if any, Cubans so interpreted. Speaking before a large group of Shell Oil workers (Castro almost invariably made his pronouncements before "workers" and "peasants," by the way), Castro accused *Zig Zag* of employing "cowardly writers" who, he alleged, had pictured him as "consorting with *bombines!*" He ordered *Zig Zag:* "Don't ever portray me in the company of *bombines!*" Newsmen were astounded at the humorlessness of Fidel Castro. Privately, they began asking themselves: "Today, it's *bombines* he forbids us to draw. What may we expect tomorrow? Subjugation of the press?" If Castro chose to misinterpret a cartoon, he might well choose to misinterpret vastly more important things. And he did.

In one of his early speeches in Santiago, Fidel Castro had indeed laid the groundwork for the subjugation of the press. He denounced the "mal-intentioned" U.S. press which, he said, "is responsive only to vested interests," and he endorsed the idea of an international news service, "written in our own idiom" by Latin American reporters. Recruitment for such a service went forward almost immediately and by the beginning of March, 1959, a new news service called *Prensa Latina* was in operation.

Curiously, Castro's words and actions recall those of another dictator many years earlier. That dictator was Juan Perón of Argentina who established *Agencia Latina*, and with its establishment, had a news service which would faithfully carry on the propaganda work of his regime. The analogy became even more striking with the appointment of Jorge Ricardo Massetti as Director General of *Prensa Latina*. Massetti had been a prominent member of Perón's news agency and a visitor to Fidel Castro's hideout in the Sierra Maestra. His appointment was the first evidence of cooperation between the extremes: the Communists of Cuba and the Fascists of Argentina. History teaches that these two extremes will accommodate each other when it fits their common purpose. (This came more clearly to light in 1965 when it was revealed that Jorge Ricardo Massetti had returned to Argentina clandestinely to take command of guerrilla camps being established there to train Communists and Peronistas,* and when Peronista leader John William Cooke headed the seven-man Argentine Communist delegation to the Tricontinental Conference in Havana in January of 1966.)

An entire floor of the Edificio Médico in downtown Havana was rented by *Prensa Latina* and by early March it contained $168,000 in Westrex sending and receiving equipment, and $40,000 in cameras purchased in the United States. Most of the equipment came from Czechoslovakia, however, and was brought into Cuba duty-free at the instructions of Angel Tamayo, Director of the Radio Division of the government's Ministry of Communications. This in itself made a mockery of the contention, as expressed publicly by Jorge Ricardo Massetti, that *Prensa Latina* was "the creature of no government nor ideology." When the board of directors was announced, the mockery could no longer be ignored. "Che" Guevara was listed as an advisor on the editorial board, and another Communist, Baldomero Alvarez Ríos, was chairman of the board. Pretenses that the news service was representative of Latin America were feebly provided with the appointment of Mexican Guillermo Castro Ulloa as President and Argentinian Rodolfo J. Walsh as Chief of the Special Services Department. The former left Cuba shortly thereafter, reportedly absconding with $100,000 in his pockets; the latter was a Communist. What was proved very early was that *Prensa Latina* was associated with the Revolutionary Government of Cuba *and* was an instrument of that government's policy.

To justify the creation of the service, continuous attacks were launched by the regime and its supporters against American news services and their cables. Angel Boan of the *Diario Nacional*, the first independent newspaper taken over by Castro, specialized in slandering AP and the UPI in a daily column called *"Lo que no dicen los Cables"* (What the Cables do not Say). He was rewarded on April 24 by being assigned to Washington, D.C. as *Prensa Latina's* bureau chief.

A side-note to that appointment: When Boan applied for a visa to go to the United States, I was called by the consular section of the Embassy and my views were solicited. The Consul pointed out that a U.S. visa is a privilege extended to foreigners to go to the United States, not a right to be demanded. After reviewing Boan's file, he believed that the visa privilege should be withheld.

I concurred with the Consul on the basis of Boan's public written record of violent hostility to the United States and his espousal of every

* Massetti was killed by Argentine authorities in an army-guerrilla clash in 1965.

forward thrust of the Communists. Specifically, I did not believe Boan should, in effect, be rewarded. For one thing, Cubans were closely watching the attitude of the American Embassy and would most certainly arrive at negative conclusions regarding our policy should Boan be given a visa to go to our nation's capital and there continue his tirades against this country. Members of the Cuban Association of Reporters had called on me to express concern over Castro's attacks on the American press and to dissociate themselves from those attacks. They were equally concerned over the rapid development of *Prensa Latina* and expressed the hope that the American Embassy would make it difficult for Boan and others of his ilk to obtain visas to the United States. They believed that Cuban newspapers would soon be pressured by the government to stop publishing AP and UPI news and substitute the propaganda of *Prensa Latina*. Nevertheless, at the recommendation of newly arrived U.S. Ambassador Philip Bonsal, affirmative action was taken in Washington, and the visa issued without objection.

Prensa Latina was organized to the accompaniment of concerted and determined intimidation of the whole body of Cuban journalism. The fierceness of the attacks played on the guilt feelings of a press community which had for decades received government subsidies. However, the Revolutionary regime identified those subsidies with Batista, claiming that the Cuban press had been bought off by him. If the word "lurid" can be appropriately used anywhere at all, it can be used to describe the exposé of newspapers and individuals who had received money from a "Palace list." Published under banner headlines in *Revolucion*, the story of government subsidies took on a significance all out of proportion to the realities.

"Losers" in this country accepted the accusations of *Revolucion* uncritically. For example, in accommodating Castro's takeover of the news media, Professor Shapiro neglected to inform his readers that governments in many European and Asian countries also subsidize the press. Completely overlooked was that subsidization of the press in Cuba antedated the Batista regime by several decades. Batista did not invent the practice, lamentable though it might be. The fact is that Havana could not publish, as it did, fifteen daily newspapers without outside financial help, and that help traditionally came from a succession of Cuban governments.

In this regard, Mr. Shapiro walks into a neat self-constructed trap. He introduces a puzzling element to his accusations that Batista had "bought" the press by adding that Batista also "censored" the press.[7] It might have occurred to Professor Shapiro, as well as to other apologists on this subject, that, if Batista had indeed bought off Cuba's press, there would have been no need for censorship. And it might also have occurred to him to probe further and ascertain the reason for this contradiction. Had he done so, he would have discovered the obvious—that the traditional subsidies were not even remotely related to his charge that the Cuban press had sold out to Batista. Indeed, Batista's censorship indicates the exact opposite, which was that despite the subsidies, the newspaper community was violently anti-Batista. This is demonstrably true. When Ambassador Smith managed to pry the lid off Cuban censorship for two weeks in the spring of 1958, perspiring Prime Minister Gonzalo Guell got him out of bed to say that the Batista regime could not survive the press attacks launched against it during the two-week period. It is noteworthy that press subsidies continued despite the seriousness with which Batista viewed the attacks.

What is not generally known is the method by which many reporters were paid by the Cuban government. Government Ministries created jobs to which reporters were assigned, and they were paid for their work. Economic reporters were employed by the Ministry of the Treasury, National Bank or with one or another of Cuba's financial agencies; agricultural writers were found working in the Ministry of Agriculture, and so on. With few exceptions, they retained their positions regardless of changing administrations and were beholden to no politician nor any particular political party. Some became experts in their fields and came to be a sort of ex officio bureaucracy.

Indeed, Castro's first Minister of the Treasury, Rufo López Fresquet, continued to maintain reporters on the payroll and did so for two very good reasons. One was that without those employees, many of whom had been with the Ministry for decades, the Ministry would not have been able to function properly. The other was that more than one tax collector was discouraged from graft by the presence of newspaper reporters who could, and did, expose in their financial columns irregularities in collections. The point is not to justify the strange practices which prevail in many Latin American countries, but to try to understand them and the reasons for their existence, and not to arrive at the simplistic conclusions of those like Mr. Shapiro.

Reporters in Cuba received, on the average, only about $130 a month for their work on newspapers and magazines. This practice has its roots in Spanish colonial rule when, in a combination of corrupt administration and a desire to stimulate arts and letters in the colonies, Spanish Governors augmented salaries and created jobs in the private sector. Corrupt? In Anglo-Saxon terms, yes. But many of the Spanish practices in the New World were, by Anglo-Saxon standards, totally corrupt. The *Conquistadores* were exactly that—Spanish conquerors. They came to the Western Hemisphere, not to settle and live, but to steal and leave. Spain held on in Cuba well after other Latin American countries had wrested their freedom from the mother country, and the practice, of course, continued longer. Cuba was most important to Spain. It was the supply and refitting base from which Cortez, Pizarro and other *Conquistadores* launched their assaults on Mexico and the South American continent and Spain was determined to hold Cuba until the bitter end precisely because of its strategic location in the new world.

"Losers" have made much of the corruption of the press in Cuba and falsely accuse it of pro-Batista sentiments. Their prejudices prevent them from relating the consequences in all of this to Spanish occupation and blocks them from understanding how a bus driver-owner found satisfaction in pocketing an eight-cent fare which belonged to him in the first place! This, in microcosm, is the legacy of Spanish rule. If anything is to be concluded from this aspect of Cuba's history, it is the miracle that Cuba grew and prospered in so short a time following the Spanish-American War. *Botelleros* (reporters and others on government payrolls) in the end usually wound up with an income equalling what they should have received in a less surrealistic society. And this is due largely to another strange Spanish practice—take only according to your position and your worth. True, the practice was abused as are all practices, but the opposite proved to be the rule.

All of this was changing under the impact of modern business practice and the respect which United States democracy commanded among the people of the island. In historical terms Cuba, the last to be freed from Spanish rule,was well on its way to outstripping its sister republics in embracing the new enlightenment. Cubans thought that Fidel Castro was the child of their own enlightenment, but came to find that he was but the bastard son of an even newer tyranny–Communism.

This explains the innuendos as well as the outright attacks by Fidel Castro (whose family properties were not, by the way, confiscated by Batista even when he was in open revolt in the mountains of Oriente) against the Cuban press. .

We arrive here at the final truth, which is that the Revolutionary Government of Cuba was not even remotely concerned with "liberating" the press. Its concern was exactly the opposite, and its lies and distortions in achieving the goal of that concern exemplify perfectly the axiom, "the end justifies the means." Having created a climate of terror, Castro was soon to transform the Cuban press into a pliant mouthpiece for his regime.

By the end of January, 1959, the Revolutionary regime had become even more open in its adherence to Communist doctrine. The first week of February, "Che" Guevara made another announcement, saying, "We are indoctrinating the Revolutionary Army." He also gave out the vastly more important notice about that indoctrination to the effect that it would not be a simple literacy campaign. This army, he said, "will maintain constant contact with the civil population. . . ." Two hundred Catholic teachers went to Camp Columbia, renamed Camp Liberty, offered to teach the soldiers how to read and write, and were summarily turned down. Within a few days it was announced that Juan Marinello, President of the Cuban Communist Party, had been appointed as head of the Language and Literature department of the Havana Normal School. The date of his appointment was February 6, 1959. The day following, he left for Moscow on a special mission for the Revolutionary Government.

On February 13, 1959, Dr. José Miró Cardona resigned as Prime Minister of a government in which he was Prime Minister in name only. He later confessed to me that neither he, nor President Manuel Urrutia, nor any member of the Council of Ministers had the slightest control over the government. What Castro (who occupied the post of Commander in Chief of the Armed Forces) said on a Tuesday night before mobs at the Presidential Palace became law on Wednesday, and nobody cared much whether what he said was even ratified by the Council.

On February 16, Fidel Castro was sworn in as Cuba's Prime Minister. In his speech of acceptance he promised to drain the Zapata swamps and turn the land over to the *guajiros* (which of course never happened), and to lower the salaries of his cabinet (which did happen).

Other events were occurring in the international sphere, however, which received considerably less publicity. Francisco Carrasco, director of the Revolutionary Council of Nicaragua, an organization composed of Cubans and Nicaraguans, met at the Havana Hilton hotel and publicly called for the overthrow of the Nicaraguan Government. The first outward indication that General Alberto Bayo was organizing expeditions against Cuba's neighbors also came to light. He took charge of the meeting, assisted by no fewer than four members of the Cuban government, among them Castro's secretary Celia Sánchez, "Che" Guevara's former wife Hilda Gadea, Faure Chomón, who had made his peace with Castro, and Rebel Captain Omar Fernández. At the same time, directors of the Communist Popular Dominican Movement came together with the United Dominican Front and merged into the Revolutionary Unity Movement, which was to lead some months later to an invasion of the Dominican Republic.

Within a few days of these events, Ambassador Philip W. Bonsal and his wife arrived in Havana. It was a testimonial to American prestige that literally thousands of Cubans besieged the airport to welcome the emissary from the United States. But it was more than that. No one of any real stature in the Cuban Government was there to greet him. Only the protocol chief of the Cuban Foreign Ministry was present. And as the Ambassador made his way past the crowds, and said a few words to the television audience, the people ran up to whisper their anxieties about the course the Revolution was taking. Less than two months after Castro's arrival in Havana, it was apparent from the scene at the airport that the American Ambassador had stepped into a Cuba whose people were plainly troubled, but at a loss to know what to do.

The rain was cascading down that night, almost as an omen of the flood of problems and abuse that the overly patient and too accommodating American Ambassador would bear. The atmosphere surrounding his public reception in Havana, an atmosphere of foreboding, contrasted sharply and unpleasantly with the high hopes and emotional outbursts with which Fidel Castro had been greeted by the Cuban public a bare six weeks earlier.

CHAPTER 6

•

Destruction and Reform

•

AMBASSADOR PHILIP W. BONSAL presented his credentials to President Manuel Urrutia on March 4, two weeks after his arrival in Havana. Technically, until that formality had been dispensed with, Bonsal had no official position in Cuba. The conduct of the Embassy remained formally in the hands of Dan Braddock while Mr. Bonsal was catching up on what had been going on, and deciding upon a course of action to follow in the turbulence of revolutionary Cuba.

Mr. Bonsal found out very quickly that civic leaders on whom new Ambassadors normally rely for guidance and support had been undercut by Fidel Castro. The business community, and even heads of the civic resistance whose money and support had made victory possible, were under subtle and not-so-subtle attack. Mobs were being harangued daily by Castro and told that they had been exploited by the "moneyed class, the created interests," and that with the triumph of the Revolution this exploitation had come to an end. The United States was under attack from so many quarters that in some cases a dizzied Embassy staff half-believed some of the charges.

The elements Ambassador Bonsal encountered in Cuba, which, as a Foreign Service officer, he was expected to work with, were a democratic community of leaders without followers, investors whose investments were under direct attack by a popular leader, and a U.S. personnel painfully on the defensive. All were operating, for different reasons, under a cloud of guilt nurtured and cleverly exploited by the most skillful, evil, and indefatigable orator of our times.

Speaking night and day, Castro toyed with native opportunism of the masses from whom he had received so little active support. His constant orations taught the less sophisticated, the naive *guajiro* and urban lower class, that Cuba's magnificent Constitution of 1940 was really not essential to democracy. They learned to their astonishment how they had been exploited by the capitalists. They stared in wonder at the trappings of Havana hotel rooms, where the regime put up thousands of them free of charge, neglecting to tell them that the money which made those hotels possible came from U.S. investors, and from Cuban labor unions themselves.

The mobs gazed up at the balcony of the Presidential Palace in hypnotized fascination with the bearded figure there as he rewrote Cuban history. They numbly or wildly acclaimed revolutionary decrees in a "direct democracy" that little by little eroded the bedrocks of civilized society —the home, the church, the family, the economy—and forcibly replaced the wearing of Catholic medals, so much in evidence at first, with the strings of pagan beads on the part of members of the government militia.

Castro maintained his marathon pace of speech-making for a good reason. He knew that the Cuban temperament is not suited to sustain grudges for long. He knew that Cubans are quick to forget the past, particularly if they have been somehow made to feel guilty about it. He also knew that Cuban mobs have an amazing facility to go along with whatever dictator or President may be in power at the time. The faces that looked up at Castro in 1959 were, for the most part, the same faces that had hailed Fulgencio Batista at that same balcony.

But while Castro accepted the rush of Cubans to his political bandwagon, he made that acceptance contingent on a roaring displeasure with the past. The lower classes were force-fed a Castro diet of hatred, and made to understand that hatred was their staple, the very stuff of class warfare. Their stake in the future was related to the degree to which they supported the destruction of everything that had gone on before.

Once that message got through, the demands became more specific, the tone more strident, and the *humildes* (the humble ones) were finally and firmly placed in a strait jacket of their own character. Like the legendary backward-flying bird, mob-supported Cuba was flapping along in reverse, crazily and inanely, into the dark pit of Communism. This, then, is what Ambassador Philip W. Bonsal faced when he arrived in Cuba in 1959 and consulted with civic leaders.

Cuban and American business leaders were baffled and largely helpless in the face of Castro's onslaught. Employees who had been with firms for years, who had benefitted from Cuba's labor legislation, its medical plans, and annual bonuses were confused, caught as they were in the cross currents of Castro's oratory and his pie-in-the-sky programs on the one hand, and their loyalty to employers on the other. Almost without exception, however, the militia units which were being formed came from the bowels of the organizational structure of business and society. The least productive and the least capable were to be found there. Their contribution to society, just as their contribution to Batista's overthrow, was considerably less than that made in both areas by a middle and upper-middle class which by reason of education, culture, personal pride, and plain initiative outshown their less fortunate brethren. The lower classes in any society contain the seeds of resentment, and it was from these seeds that the bully boys of the Castro revolution initially sprung. And, as Castro had promised on January 6, 1959, guns had been placed in their hands.

Dressed in militia uniforms, authority dangling from the holsters on their hips, hotel bus boys, garbage collectors, taxi drivers and office clerks found that they could intimidate their superiors and receive the support of the revolutionary regime. An interesting point is that initially the militia appeared in public without arms, giving the popular impression that they were unarmed. However, when a bully job was called for, militia drew arms from police stations and militiary camps. As organization progressed, instructions began to flow through the ranks, instructions which had no other aim than to bring the whole of Cuban society under the control of the government. To this end, arms were issued openly.

Local labor unions began to lose their hold on laborers as militiamen usurped both power and position. Union officials were intimidated, harassed, and threatened outright. Any objection to the tyranny of organized mob rule branded the objector a McCarthyite, a *Batistiano*. Authority no longer accrued to the leader by reason of capacity, learning, or application. Authority was given those who were the most vocal in their support of the Revolution and the most zealous in carrying out its dictates.

More than one business leader was jolted when a group of militiamen-employees walked unannounced into his office and flatly told him how to conduct his business. Initially, the instructions of the employees were to demand their "fair share" of the profits as part of a systematic shake-down of the economy.

Overlooked by most writers was another major factor relating to internal control. Initially, local unions were intimidated by militiamen, and individuals were given the right to demand and even extort money from employers. But once the government had "intervened" or otherwise taken control of private business, those "rights" were dissolved in mass assemblies in which the poor, duped devils were forced to shout away their rights to raises in salaries. In many instances, they "volunteered" to reduce those salaries.

How, then, in Castro's revolutionary climate, amid the confusing writings of editorialists and intellectuals in our magazines and universities, was an American Ambassador to assess his role in Cuba? Ambassador Bonsal was a sensitive and intelligent man of great personal charm. He also was a liberal. The State Department leaned heavily on Bonsal's liberal record, including the episode in Colombia when he was declared *persona non grata* earlier in his career by dictator Gustavo Rojas Pinilla. In view of the additional fact that he was a career officer and not a wealthy political appointee, Mr. Bonsal's background led to expectations of a brilliant tour in Cuba.

After considering the revolutionary climate of Cuba, Mr. Bonsal arrived at a philosophy to guide him. He decided to demonstrate to the leaders of the new regime in Cuba that the United States, and particularly the American Ambassador, was as liberal as they supposedly wanted us to be. This was a mistake. Actually, Castro and his cohorts wanted no projection of a liberal United States. Bonsal chose the path trod by John F. Kennedy which took him to the House of Representatives, to the Senate, and, the year after Mr. Bonsal's appointment, to the White House —the path of imagery. A formidable specialist in public relations, Ambassador Bonsal went everywhere, shook everybody's hand, projecting the public image of a cultured, *simpatico*, United States of America.

Under less demanding conditions, Mr. Bonsal might have been successful. The combination of political infighting (which he was to leave to the State Department), and public relations gimmickry, was not without a certain appeal. But what Mr. Bonsal was doing in Castro's Cuba was precisely what Student Directorate leader Julio García had so correctly warned against earlier.

Next, there was just too much information flowing into the Embassy at the time to ignore the possibility, and indeed, the probability, that Cuba was being skillfully maneuvered behind the Iron Curtain. Nothing less than a direct confrontation with that probability was needed. But to do so would put the Ambassador directly in the ring with Fidel Castro, a place where a man of his pacific proclivities had no desire to be.

Another point seemingly in favor of "soft" tactics dealt with relations with Latin America. It was argued that if we were to take strong issue with Castro's already evident anti-Americanism, we might lose some friends south of our borders. Apparently, it did not occur to the State Department that Nicaragua and the Dominican Republic, Panama and Honduras, were much concerned over the creation in Cuba of what amounted to governments-in-exile representing Communists in their respective countries, and that those "governments" were overtly identified with members of Castro's own government. It was with a chill, the Honduran Ambassador told me, that he learned that General Bayo was associated with those groups.

The attitude of the State Department reflected a peculiar prickling— a guilt complex about Cuba. Considering that the Department of State had consistently refused to back Batista or to support Ambassador

Smith's plans which might have flushed Castro out of the hills and brought him in to the arena of free elections, peculiar is the only word to describe that feeling of guilt. Nevertheless, the State Department and the American Embassy in Havana took the view that to deal firmly with Castro meant that we were against his stated aims of reform, even though considerable doubts were being raised as to the seriousness of his intentions regarding those reforms.

It was therefore decided that a U.S. stance of patience and understanding would win us friends and strengthen our position *vis a vis* Latin American countries. Step one—support which we expected from South and Central America—presupposed that there was a step two. The second step would be a much tougher and considerably more realistic course of action to be taken in Cuba. The U.S. sugar quota, the mystique of the Monroe Doctrine, and the defense measures open to the hemisphere under the Pact of Rio de Janeiro were clubs which could be used unilaterally or collectively, as circumstances dictated. As it turned out, we took step one-and-a-half and fell on our faces.

The attitude of an Ambassador invariably establishes the tenor of operations in an Embassy and the morale of its officers. This was true during the tenure of Ambassador Smith, with sometimes unpleasant and self-defeating results. It was no less true of Ambassador Bonsal, with similar results, but for exactly opposite reasons. His unfortunate reliance on the magic of imagery left the figures in Castro's Revolutionary Government singularly unmoved, and his treatment by them was as disgraceful as few American Ambassadors have had the courage or the patience to endure. It was clear that Fidel Castro was clamping the Cuban people into a Communist state and there was worry and discomfort among us that this posed a real threat to the security of the United States. We were discomfited to see that the new Ambassador gave little concrete guidance to developing a policy that would somehow derail Castro's express train and bring to an end the hideous prospects of a Communist regime on our doorstep.

Ambassador Bonsal did not take a firm position in promoting U.S. interests because he was in basic disagreement with those interests. Bonsal was close to Castro's economic planners—for example the President of the National Bank, the Minister of the Treasury—and indeed endorsed their policies of liberal reform. More important, he did so because he agreed with them (though he conceded that Cuba had benefitted from U.S. investments) that American interests, both political and economic, were largely responsible for what he believed to be the stifling of something which he called "the rising sense of Cuban nationalism." Thus, Bonsal considered that Castro's efforts (but not his tactics) to eliminate U.S. influence in Cuba were made in pursuit of a just and reasonable national goal. Having conceded this point, it was inevitable that he would concede yet another—namely that Castro's violent anti-Americanism was representative of broadly based Cuban revulsion against the United States. In the end, Ambassador Bonsal had little heart for the hard decisions that went with his job. Treasury Minister Rufo López Fresquet knew it; National Bank President Felipe Pazos knew it; and it can be assumed that Fidel Castro knew it. Ambassador Philip W. Bonsal's equivocations made him a prime target of Castro's bullying tactics.

Perhaps unconsciously, Bonsal alternately ignored and minimized the effects of visible signs of increasing Communist control. The Ambassador would search for passages in an otherwise scurrilously worded note from the Cuban Foreign Ministry and pronounce those passages "encouraging." There was a dogged determination on his part to look for the bright side of life, far beyond what could be supported by any visible facts. In itself, this was little enough encouragement for the Embassy staff to seek out and analyze Communist advances. There was even less encouragement to ponder courses of diplomatic action, in the interest of both the Cuban and American people, to arrest those advances.

There could be little doubt that the Ambassador knew he was being deliberately held at arms length by the Revolutionary Government. Time after time, he tried to get an appointment with Fidel Castro and, time after time, he was rebuffed by the Foreign Minister, on one flimsy excuse or another. Somehow, this all seemed perfectly reasonable to Castro's apologists, though it was not considered reasonable in diplomatic circles. Castro declaimed time after time that he wanted the friendliest of relations with the United States, yet he refused to see an Ambassador who was hand-picked for the job. In fact, Ambassador Bonsal became so desperate that he called me to the office one day, saying he understood that I had the private phone numbers of Celia Sánchez and Teresa Casuso, the females guarding Castro's door. I said that I did not have the phone numbers, but could get them for him (which I did). But the very idea of an American Ambassador to Cuba being forced to stoop to such practices is a commentary on the state of relations with the Revolutionary Government. Bonsal's first interview of real importance with Fidel Castro did not materialize until September 5.[1]

Mr. Bonsal's acquiescence in that state of relations certainly should never have been permitted to continue. Because of the slow-moving nature of the bureaucracy of the State Department in Washington, its ambassadors overseas almost invariably are the ones to push Washington for decisions and action. Almost from the outset of Mr. Bonsal's tenure in Cuba, the reverse was true. State usually was pushing for the American Embassy, and particularly for the Ambassador, to come up with ideas and a vigor to match that of the Revolutionary Government. The same political officer who had been described as "left-leaning" by Ambassador Smith in 1958 was now warning Ambassador Bonsal that unless the United States and its Ambassador in Cuba, began not only to defend itself against Castro's tirades, but to seize the initiative and put the Cuban dictator on the defensive, we would lose all respect from the very Latin American nations whose support we were trying to cultivate. After one dinner with a group of Latin American ambassadors in Havana, political officer John Topping said at the staff meeting the following morning that he was treated as though he had "no guts." It needed little noting that Latins are extraordinarily impressed by virility, and that the worst insult that can be levelled at a person is to imply that he is not a "man."

Nevertheless, Embassy policy rocked along on the flimsy foundation of imagery, interrupted briefly and dramatically when José Figueres, the hero and ex-President of Costa Rica, came to Havana, took the side of the United States in the cold war and was personally and publicly cut down by Fidel Castro. He arrived on the very day that the government prosecutor in Camaguey Province, René Burguet Flores, reported that 48 members of the regular army had been condemned and shot.

Figueres' appearance on March 23, 1959, may have been planned by the Revolutionary Government for its own purposes. Figueres was widely known in Latin America as a genuine liberal and a fierce fighter for democracy in Costa Rica which was considered to be one of the strongest democracies in the hemisphere. The occasion of his appearance wasn't the happiest. He was asked to address a crowd which had been called to the Presidential Palace (by this time "summoned" would be more accurate) to "uphold" the Revolutionary Laws and "celebrate" government intervention in the Cuban Telephone Company. (The sugar coating was ever present). Only a few days before the meeting, the Council of Ministers had drastically cut rents throughout the country, and forbidden anyone to own more than one residence. The Palace meeting which was also to "uphold" this uneconomic and nonsensical decree, back-fired on Castro to a degree, though the importance of a back-fire was probably evaluated in the overall perspective of the revolution. Many Cubans, particularly those of recent Spanish descent, had traditionally put their money into property rather than in the bank, and the cut in rents as well as the restrictions placed on ownership hit a considerable number of people where it was least expected. For example, my cook owned three modest homes on the outskirts of Cuba. Two were lost to her by reason of the decree, which said that occupants could virtually seize the property and consider all previous rent as payment toward ownership. This deprived the owner of a choice as to the buyer (whether solvent or not), not to speak of the choice of selling or keeping the properties. The third house had its rent reduced to the point where it was uneconomical even to have anyone in it. This practice appears to have been premeditated confiscation.

However that may be, labor leader David Salvador opened the speech-making session at the Presidential Palace, introducing Figueres in typically florid fashion. Wearing his famous campaign hat and khaki uniform, Figueres spoke of his affection for the people of Cuba, his respect for the United States and said he was happy this was so. He said: "If an armed conflict between the United States and the Soviet Union should break out, Latin America will line up solidly at the side of the United States." Then came the incredible action of Salvador. Interrupting the Costa Rican statesman, he grabbed the microphone and shouted that this was not so. "The United States," roared Salvador, "only wants us to take its chestnuts out of the fire!" The audience was stunned for a long moment of silence. Then the revolutionary cheer leaders began to chant: "Fidel! Fidel!" Figueres continued his address with platitudes for an appropriate length of time and then sat down.

Fidel Castro took the stand and, in a dark mood, said: "I never thought that I would have to appear in one of my most difficult public appearances . . . for me it has never been as difficult as today when I have to disagree with the ideas expressed by our illustrious visitor, José Figueres." He went on: "All the reactionary oligarchy in the continent incite against the Cuban revolution. The press campaigns emanating from the [imperialist] monopolies of the international news agencies find an echo in the press of Latin America." He ended on a shuddering note of self-destruction saying: "Whoever tries to seize Cuba will find nothing but dust bathed in blood."

Exactly two days later, Manuel Mora, head of the Communist Party in Costa Rica, arrived in Havana at the formal invitation of the Revolutionary Government.

Fiercely independent Herminio Portell Vilá, one of Cuba's most respected and honorable historians, was horrified at the implications of Castro's speech. In his regular television show, he pointed out that by reason of geography, economics, culture, and inclination, Cuba could never turn its back on the Western Hemisphere. He followed this with a lengthy magazine article and from that moment forward was constantly attacked by *Revolucion, Hoy,* and the Castro-controlled radio networks of Cuba.

Castro had his reasons for taking issue with José Figueres. For the fact of the matter was that he had already turned his back on Cuba's international obligations, assumed under the Pact of Río de Janeiro. Moreover, he personally established another precedent—armed subversion of his neighbors.

Comandante Ricardo Lorié was dispatched by Fidel Castro personally to Belgium where he purchased $9 millions in arms. *This was in February of 1959.* On November 3, 1963, the Venezuela Government discovered a three-ton arms cache to sustain Cuban-trained and Castro-supported guerrilla units. They were the same arms purchased by Lorié back in 1959. He related how it happened:

Lorié signed a contract with the Belgian National Arms Factory which, he said, included the sale of "22,500 automatic FAL rifles, 50 million rounds of ammunition, 70,000 anti-personnel shells, anti-tank rifle grenades capable of penetrating 13 centimeters of steel, and 30,000 anti-tank grenades which could go through 30 centimeters of steel." Lorié testified that the rifles were numbered from 1 to 22,500, corresponding to the purchases made. They also had the Cuban coat of arms engraved on them. "When I returned and reported the terms of the contract," said Lorié, "Fidel was furious with me that the rifles had been numbered and engraved with our coat of arms. He also asked me why I hadn't purchased 50,000 rifles, and why arrangements hadn't been made for the immediate purchase of a complete arms factory. I replied that to make such a factory economically feasible, it would have to turn out nearly a million rounds of ammunition daily, requiring technicians and experts in the field of armaments not available in Cuba. He was unconvinced, saying: 'I know what I'm going to do with those arms.'"

The rifles found in the arms cache on a Venezuelan beach in November 1963, then, were purchased under the personal authorization of Fidel Castro in February, 1959, *less than two months after he came to power.* From the evidence, it seems to be beyond debate that Castro came to power with plans to subvert Latin America. These plans were not foisted off on him by old-line Communists lurking in the shadows of his rule, as some people would have it.

Lorié said: "Castro's reaction to the numbering on the arms indicated to me that he most certainly had something sinister in mind." How sinister, was later revealed by an OAS mission to Venezuela which identified the arms as those described by Lorié. Venezuelan authorities found that serial numbers and the Cuban coat of arms had been filed from the rifles, but both were raised through the application of acid, and identified.

The defected Comandante, who lives in Miami, says he now understands Fidel Castro's anger. "Fidel kept turning the conversation back to the numbering of the arms and the engraving of the shields, demanding that these details be eliminated from the contract. They could not be eliminated, I said, because it was international practice to give each rifle a serial number, and just to make such a request would certainly be questioned. Castro also was visibly annoyed and excited when I told him that the rifles could not be manufactured and delivered to Cuba by July, 1959, the month that he wanted delivery." Lorié completed his weapons-purchasing ordeal with Castro in April of 1959.

That same month, a private firm in the United States offered, through Dr. Salvador Lew, a Cuban lawyer, to sell Castro an unlimited amount of military equipment, from pistols and tanks to helicopters. The prospective clients authorized Lew to assure the Cuban government that they would handle all aspects of providing military arms for Castro. He also was told to assure the Cuban government that prices for the arms would be equal to or below those which it would pay in Europe.

This constituted a sharp reversal in American policy. For years, the United States had been restricting sales of arms to the volatile and strategically located Caribbean countries, as was clearly evident in its cancellation of Batista's orders for rifles and aircraft in 1958. Having learned of moves to purchase Belgian arms, it apparently was believed that Castro was determined to get them somewhere and the United States thought the purchases should be made within the framework of the Inter-American Defense Board. Unified defense presupposes standardization of arms and military organization. It is assumed that U.S. officials were aware of the offer, since federal authorization was needed to ship arms to another country.

As was feared, however, Dr. Lew's offer was rejected. He approached Carlos Olivares, the Civil Secretary to Raúl Castro who, after Fidel had assumed the office of Prime Minister, was appointed Minister of Defense. Following a conference with the younger Castro, Olivares gave the answer—no. The answer, however, was subject to review by Fidel Castro and his answer was a crashing no.

It was at this time that Castro announced that he would travel to Washington at the invitation of the American Newspaper Editors and Publishers Association. High hopes were held that Castro's trip, his visit with U.S. leaders, and an expected offer of economic assistance to Cuba would bring about a climate of good relations. Unknown to the general public, however, Fidel Castro torpedoed the trip before it got underway. He sternly instructed travelling companions Felipe Pazos, his President of the Cuban National Bank, and Rufo López Fresquet, his Minister of the Treasury, under no circumstances themselves to bring up financial assistance from the United States, and to reject any offers that were made along that line.[2] The rejection of a U.S. loan for arms, then, was followed by the advance rejection of any kind of financial deal with the United States. There was little left in the way of negotiations with Fidel Castro.

Castro's attitude toward the United States was not confined to mere public expressions of dislike. The very first trip he made to a foreign country came about on January 23, 1959, when he flew to Caracas to visit President-elect Rómulo Betancourt of Venezuela. Of that interview, Betancourt said: "We had exchanged a few words and Castro then put to me what he called 'the master plan against the gringos.' This consisted in the government of Venezuela lending $300 millions to the government of Cuba. I replied that this was impossible."[3]

Thus, it is established beyond reasonable doubt that before his visit to the United States, if Castro had indeed needed money, he could have gotten it. He was actually afraid he might get it, and instructed his financial experts to shun it. What is suggested by Castro's statements to his Minister of the Treasury and to the President of Cuba's National Bank, is that Fidel Castro wanted no part of the United States whatsoever. His statement to President Betancourt indicates that he was attempting to obtain allies in Latin America for his anti-American campaign *within two weeks after arriving in Havana.*

These simple but incontrovertible facts ought to put a term to the disgraceful nonsense written that Castro was "rejected" when he got to Washington,[4] and was browbeaten by an Ambassador Bonsal who, actually, didn't have it in him to deal harshly with anyone.

Anyone with the slightest acquaintance with the characters of Fidel Castro and of Ambassador Bonsal, must find the following passage by Mr. Matthews ludicrous.

Says the wide-eyed, innocent, Fidel Castro to Matthews in 1960: "You ought to have heard the conversations with Ambassador Bonsal from the beginning. He lectured me, criticized us and our Revolution, complained, threatened . . . I can assure you I felt humiliated as a Cuban at the way I, the Prime Minister of Cuba, was being talked to. . . ." With the bait thus set, Castro sprung the trap as he continued: "You ought, also, to hear how the Soviet representatives talk. They are friendly, respectful, sympathetic, understanding. They are not ordering us about, making demands. They make us feel like a sovereign country."[5]

Tough, uncompromising, vindictive Fidel Castro had been bullied by well-mannered, soft spoken Philip W. Bonsal. This is hardly a convincing picture.

I have made so many references to the writings of Herbert Matthews that perhaps one more can be assimilated by the reader. I do so simply because of the extraordinary pro-Castro position he has taken on virtually every facet of the revolution. For example, he says of Cuba's attacks on her neighbors:

"Of the so-called invasions from Cuba only one—the two small groups that entered the Dominican Republic in June, 1959—had Castro's official backing. The others were either the work of adventurers and mercenaries, like the landings in Panama in April and in Haiti in August, 1959, or groups that evaded Cuban vigilance. Washington made a great propaganda splash about Cuban 'expeditions' and keeps on doing so, but no evidence was ever brought out to prove that Fidel backed or even desired any invasion except the Dominican one."[6]

The innocence attributed to Fidel Castro again overlooks the truth. Through accounts published in the Cuban press it was clear that General Alberto Bayo and four members of Castro's government had been busy planning invasions of Cuba's neighbors in the Caribbean. Haitian exiles, Luis Dejoie and Daniel Fuguoli, transmitted calls for revolts in their country over radio stations in Cuba which had to be known, and indeed sanctioned, by the Cuban government. General Bayo had also opened a guerrilla training camp at the beach of Tarará, using extensive powers of the Cuban government to "intervene" certain areas, including buildings which were turned into barracks.

On April 22, 1959, just two days following an address by Castro at the United Nations in New York, Panama was invaded by a group of 87 Cubans and Panamanians, headed by the Cuban, Cesar Vega. On May 1, the group surrendered to the Panamanian National Guard and to members of an OAS team sent to investigate the invasion. True, Fidel Castro immediately dissociated himself from the attempt. What else was he to do? If it had been successful, the story would certainly have been different. Castro could not, however, dissociate himself from members of his government who were openly identified with the subversive groups in Havana; nor from the fact that the Cuban government was intimately involved in "intervening" areas in Tarará and that the intervention was published in Cuba's *Gaceta Oficial.* ." By the simple device of reading Cuban official publications, one can arrive at enough proof to satisfy the average individual.

But even if that were inadequate, on July 27, the OAS issued a formal report saying that members of a group which invaded Nicaragua had been trained in La Cabaña fortress by "Che" Guevara. Of the invasion of Haiti, it was revealed in OAS documents that not only had the group come from Cuba but that among those captured were members of Castro's Rebel Army, men on active duty with that army at the time of capture!

The American Embassy in Havana was particularly aware of what was going on with regard to the invasion of Nicaragua. On May 31, a group of Cubans landed in a plane in the hilly country of Nicaragua and were joined by another group of Havana-trained Nicaraguans who had first gone to Honduras, there to cross over the border into Nicaragua in order to link up with the airborne units. An American adventurer, Leslie Bradley, was involved in the exploit, but to his astonishment he was arrested by Guevara and held in La Cabaña fortress. We learned that Bradley was an "insurance policy" taken out by Guevara and Bayo. According to

Embassy investigators who talked with Bradley, the Castroites planned to use Bradley as their ace in the hole should the invasion fail (as it did) or, more important, should the United States decide to push the matter before the OAS and clamp down hard on Castro. In return for his life, Bradley would be forced to testify that the United States was behind these invasions (as Guevara later stated) in an attempt to implicate Cuba and "crush" a social revolution.

Unquestionably, Castro's bloodiest venture took place in the Dominican Republic. Military attaches at the Embassy had been watching preparations for the invasion for some months, and were aghast at the openness with which they were carried out. Agents carefully followed everything that was going on, to the point of reporting that Raúl Castro himself personally took charge of the departure of the group. There was enough factual evidence for the United States to at least consider a military blockade of Cuba, if it were so disposed. But nothing came of it other than a forwarding of detailed Embassy reports to Washington.

The details were that on June 14, 1959 fifty-six men boarded a plane bearing Dominican markings near Manzanillo in Oriente Province and headed for the Dominican Republic. The military commander of the group was one of Castro's Comandantes, Delio Gómez Ochoa, who, later captured, talked to his captors. Among other things said by Gómez Ochoa was that he had been named invasion head personally by Fidel Castro.

Landing at the airport of Costanza in the Dominican Republic, the force quickly overcame guards who had been duped by the Dominican markings on the plane. The group did not make it to the mountains, there to take refuge as Fidel Castro had in Cuba. They were weighted down with ammunition, and threw much of it away. Because of their olive green uniforms, with red and blue shoulder patches bearing the initials U.P.D. (Patriotic Dominican Union) on them, the invaders were fairly easy to identify. They were cut down, many of them by machete-wielding *guajiros.*

The other part of the invasion force consisted of two yachts, the "Carmen Elsa" and the "Tinita." Army Attaché Samuel Kail of the American Embassy was so well-informed of the events that he gave the Ambassador's morning staff meeting what amounted to a daily running account of the progress of the invasion force, which left from Nipe Bay in Oriente Province. The two invasion yachts actually flew American flags as they approached the coast of the Dominican Republic. And they were escorted, for some reason, by Cuban Navy frigates "José Martí," "Antonio Maceo," and "Máximo Gómez." One reason for the escort, it was surmised, was that the Cuban Navy vessels supplied the overburdened yachts with food and water on the way.

General Rafael Trujillo, Jr., son of the Dominican dictator, reported that the two vessels were sunk in combined action by the Air Force and Navy. The "Tinita" got close to shore when it was sunk. The "Carmen Elsa" was intercepted about a quarter of a mile off-shore. The venture from the sea was as disastrous as the one launched against the Dominican Republic by air.

While the invasion itself was a resounding failure, it provided the date, June 14th, and an ideology, Communist, that was to become Castro's weapon of internal subversion of that country. The June 14th Movement was to emerge as one of the major factors in the Dominican revolt of April 24, 1965.

Castro himself remained largely above the battle—in the case of the Cuban invasion of Panama literally so.

Flying from the United States to Buenos Aires after his trip to Washington and Canada, his plane passed over Havana. Dramatically, from 19,000 feet in the air, Castro addressed the people of Cuba via their radios saying that Cuba had nothing to do with the invasion of Panama. Such activities, he said, are "damaging to the prestige of the Cuban revolution."

What made Castro's public address of unusual interest is that it covered up what was going on at the very moment of delivery. The guerrilla training camp established at Tarará was being enlarged and refurbished, and El Cortijo school in Pinar del Río Province and the Minas del Frío school in Oriente Province had joined a growing complex of guerrilla establishments as far back as February 11. Certainly, "the public" deserved no scolding from the air for the invasion of Panama. It was not a public doing. What was required were orders from Fidel Castro to his henchmen—General Bayo, Camilo Cienfuegos, Vilma Espín de Castro, Omar Fernández, Celia Sánchez, "Che" Guevara, and his own brother Raúl—to stop "damaging the prestige of the Cuban revolution" by observing the very "principle of non-intervention" which Fidel Castro proclaimed from the rarefied atmosphere of 19,000 feet. Those orders, of course, were never given.

A scapegoat was found for the Panama invasion in the person of Rubén Miró, a loud-mouth who, in Havana, had been proclaiming the overthrow of Panamanian President Ernesto de la Guardia. He was picked up and whisked off to jail. When things calmed down, however, he was ordered released.

Cuba remained almost literally an open house for armed attacks on its neighbors. Political exiles came to revolutionary Cuba from all over the hemisphere, some with money, some without it, to plot the overthrow of their governments. That the climate, as well as the terrain, for subversion existed in Cuba in early 1959 can hardly be denied. Raúl Castro said:

"No one can export revolution," adding, "we morally support, nevertheless, any group which takes the path of insurrection in his country." He continued: "More than that, we recommend it." Those groups which were not directly controlled by the Revolutionary Government were usually rounded up, thus giving the government an appearance of doing something about the plotting. It was, but in an entirely different manner. Those groups controlled by Castro gradually were being brought into the embryo system of organized Communist subversion supplied through the guerrilla camps under construction in Cuba. Little was heard about that activity at the time.

The American adventurer, Comandante William Morgan, provided our Embassy with details regarding the early Communist takeover of the Cuban government. He resolved to do something about it, and, in company with Comandante Eloy Gutiérrez Menoyo, came straight to the Embassy, causing a minor sensation by walking fully armed to the desk of the Marine guard in the foyer of the building and asking to see me. Two rebel soldiers, armed right up to their luxuriant beards, accompanied Morgan and Menoyo. The Marine politely told them that they must check their pistols and rifles at the desk. The four reacted as though they had been asked to surrender. Fortunately, Jack Wyant happened along. A young Foreign Service trainee, Jack had been assigned to my office to gain experience before being assigned to a post on his own. As a child, he had been brought up in the interior of Brazil and spoke perfect Brazilian Portuguese. He also spoke Spanish with a Brazilian accent.

Friendly, lanky, and freckle-faced, Jack was the picture of the all-American boy—until he began to speak Spanish with his heavy Portuguese accent, a feat which he performed for the startled foursome arguing with the Marine. With easy humor he told them that it was not the practice of an American Embassy to have heavily armed types resembling Buffalo Bill walking around the premises. He assured them that checking their arms with the Marine did not mean that the pistols and rifles were being surrendered, and offered to take them to see me. Hesitantly, Menoyo and Morgan checked their shooting irons and accompanied him. The other two soldiers said they preferred to keep their arms and would wait outside the building. Jack brought Menoyo and Morgan to my office.

With the introduction, they were offered chairs. I seated myself and surveyed the two with what I am sure must have been ill-disguised curiosity. They were interesting characters, differing sharply in appearance and bearing. Menoyo was dark, and slender, Morgan was squat, blond, blue-eyed and tough. Lolling back on a tilted chair, with hands clasped behind his head, Morgan watched with tolerant arrogance the polite behaviour of his more cultured colleague. Morgan then said that

Menoyo was planning a good will tour to Miami, "or something like that," and needed some tips on how to handle the American press.

Wyant left the office and came back with a fistful of literature which American Embassies the world over use to orient visitors to the United States. I told Morgan that as an American, himself, he could be Menoyo's guide in the United States. "Naw, not for the kind of stuff he needs," Morgan replied. He added with a quick grin that he would like to go along, but said he was "kinda restricted." He was referring to the possibility that once he set foot on U.S. soil he ran the risk of being picked up by Federal agents and trotted off to face a court martial for desertion from the Army of the United States. "Besides, he'll be meeting with the Mayor of Miami and all kinds of high class people," Morgan added of Menoyo's trip.

When Jack Wyant gave some additional materials to Menoyo, Morgan broke in and suggested that Menoyo and Jack read it over while he and I went to another room "to kick a few things around a little." It was apparent that Morgan had more on his mind than Menoyo's interest in the *mores* of the United States. This conversation was to lead to a labyrinthian series of intrigues, plots and counterplots, and finally to an "invasion" of Cuba.

After Jack and Menoyo had disappeared, Morgan said that the Second Front was still intact, an entity apart from the Castro government. I was surprised to hear this, having understood that the Second Front of the Escambray had been disbanded, along with the forces of the Student Directorate. Morgan said the Second Front was building roads into previously inaccessible areas of the Sierra Escambray, but that he and Menoyo had ideas other than just public works.

It was important, said Morgan, to try to cut Castro's popularity, and that the Second Front, where Menoyo had many followers and friends, was being quietly organized into a political party "as that son-of-a-bitch Fidel promised." Morgan added that Castro "hasn't the slightest intention of holding elections." He then asked if the Embassy could provide him with heavily illustrated and easy to read pamphlets for the uneducated people in the mountains. "We want the material," he said, "to be anti-Communist." I focused on that comment in a hurry, since it was the first real indication that the Communists might be working with the *guajiros.* Using a few descriptive and unprintable adjectives to describe Félix Torres, the Communist leader who Menoyo had prevented from coming into the Escambray mountains in 1958, Morgan said of Torres that "he now has the full confidence of Fidel and Raúl and has moved Communists into the area to indoctrinate the *guajiros.*" Said Morgan: "You can imagine what the commies are saying about Menoyo and me after our run-ins with Torres and with Guevara." I could imagine.

I brought in an artist, got authorization to produce small, simply worded and simply illustrated six-page pamphlets. They were printed in comic book style. Few if any outsiders knew about it, but it was Morgan who gave me the ideas for some of the booklets and it was the Second Front that distributed hundreds of thousands of them throughout the Sierra Escambray.

Each of the little booklets had a theme—the life of José Martí in the United States, and similar topics. Skillfully laid out, simply captioned, and written by Gerardo Rodríguez Morejón, a wonderful, wizened old historian who specialized in children's educational books, the booklets could be understood even if the reader was illiterate. John Nepple of the Embassy's Point Four economic program, was fishing one week-end off the coast of the town of Trinidad near the Escambray. He came in for water and to buy some food, and a young boy who was tending boats came up to him saying that he knew a great deal about the United States, proudly producing three well-worn copies of the comic book series. He also told John that he had to be careful whom he showed them to "because there are some people who don't like us to read them." Those people, it may be supposed, were Félix Torres and his band of Communists, who, within two years' time were to bring terror and oppression to the poor farmers as resistance to Communism increased among them.

Returning to Menoyo's proposed good-will trip to the United States, Morgan said that it represented a venture into "foreign affairs" for the Second Front. It was hoped, said Menoyo, when he joined us later, that "a good reception by Miami officials will interest the press" and stimulate press feeds back into Cuba. Specifically, as it turned out later, Morgan and Menoyo hoped that the press pick-up through Cuba's newspapers and radio-TV stations would help build a public image of Menoyo within Cuba itself and gain some political backers among the rapidly growing number of influential Cubans who were thoroughly disillusioned with Fidel Castro.

What was important to the Embassy about all this was the appearance of what seemed to be the first organized opposition to Fidel Castro and his Communist adherents. I carefully reported to the political section what had been told to me by Morgan, was asked by John Topping to keep in contact with the Second Front and follow the progress of the daring young men, and report what happened.

One of the first things that was done by the Second Front was to hire an American press agent—Pat Valentine. This developed a few weeks later into a press conference at the Capri Hotel where Menoyo announced his intention to go to Miami, as I believe he put it, at the invitation of the Mayor of Miami, Robert King High. Menoyo's announcement was duly reported in the Cuban press, eliciting no explosion from Castro or from anyone else in the government. Yet, I was approached by a confused and perturbed Pat Valentine. On the one hand, he said, he was hired for a public relations buildup of Eloy Gutiérrez Menoyo. But on the other hand, said Valentine, he was surrounded by so many restrictions that it was hard to do any kind of a job. Obviously, Mr. Valentine did not have much of a grounding in Cuban politics. One thing he had learned which perturbed him considerably was that he was functioning more and more as a political campaign manager and less and less as a public relations consultant. It had become increasingly clear to Mr. Valentine that in building up Menoyo, he ran the risk of angering none other than the man on the white horse, Fidel Castro himself. In a masterpiece of understatement, he characterized his position as "delicate."

The delicacy of his position was driven home to Mr. Valentine the day of the departure of Menoyo for Miami. Several hours after the Menoyo entourage was to have departed, a very agitated Valentine called me from the military airport at Camp Columbia. Was there any reason I could think of, he asked, why Raúl Castro had pulled Menoyo off the plane and escorted to his chambers at military headquarters? I could think of at least a few but chose to say nothing over the phone. After a lengthy delay, Menoyo finally got away and arrived in Miami. The trip was successful, from the standpoint of press play given to Menoyo's visit to Miami in the Cuban press. But even then the newspapers were careful not to connect the Miami visit with any political ambitions of Menoyo.

Menoyo and Morgan dropped out of the limelight following the junket, and Mr. Valentine resigned, complaining bitterly that Morgan was absorbed in comic books most of the time. Also, said Valentine, Morgan kept company with a very unwholesome American who lived at the Capri Hotel, whom he described as a "gangster."

However, contact was again renewed by Morgan a few months later, when an attempt was made to implicate the American Embassy, through me, in a phony "invasion" of Cuba from the Dominican Republic—an attempt which we shall come to later.

Then came Castro's monstrous agrarian reform, and with it even more visible signs of public disenchantment with Castro and Communism than had already been supplied by Messrs. Menoyo and Morgan. The act was passed on May 18, 1959, amid high hopes that recognized inequities in the ownership of land would be corrected. The author of the agrarian reform, as originally formulated in the Sierra Maestra, was Major Humberto Sorí Marín. As Castro's first Minister of Agriculture he refused to sign the law as it was finally fashioned. He was pressured into doing so, and then resigned his post.

The reasons Sorí Marín resigned are not difficult to understand. He expected a genuine agrarian reform. What Castro proposed as reform was, in fact, an extension of government control over the country. Castro's personal attitude toward agrarian reform once he had come to power was quite the opposite of what he had been proclaiming when he was in the mountains. In January, 1959, the School of Law of the University of Oriente proposed a national forum to discuss the agrarian reform. Virtually all elements in Cuba were favorably disposed toward such a reform as had been incorporated in Cuba's Constitution, but never carried out. Professor Fermín Peinado of the University of Santiago writes of Castro's reaction to the plan in his booklet, *Beware Yankee:*

"When Mr. Castro came to the university in February, the Secretary, Dr. Echemendía, informed him of the project. Castro's comment was: 'What do they want to do, oppose me?' The alarmed Secretary apologized and explained to him the contents of the proposal, to which Castro replied: 'Good, but since what you want is what I want, the best thing to do is wait for me to enact the law and when it is published, you can comment on it.' "

When the law was passed, despair among Cuba's thinking class was deep. The law was frankly confiscatory, and to all intents and purposes it imprisoned the peasants in rural concentration camps. Buried in one of the paragraphs was wording to the effect that the sugar mills should be stripped of their canelands. The law was believed (incorrectly) to provide that 200,000 Cubans would receive this land. Little understood by the farming people were three provisions which made them mere state employees: 1) The land could not be sold or mortgaged; nor could the owner of the land parcel it out to his children; 2) The peasant had absolutely no control over what he wanted to grow on that land. The Agrarian Reform Institute would tell them what to grow; and 3) The Agrarian Reform Institute would set the price for the crops, with the peasants compelled to sell at those prices. What happened, of course, is that the peasant was simply changing bosses—from the private owner to the government.

Before enactment of the law, the peasant could bargain with private owners from whom he was renting, and could take full advantage of fluctuating market prices, as well. He soon learned that no such latitude was permitted when the government took control of the land. Indeed, witnesses watched peasants summarily shot for selling so much as a chicken or a pig to anyone other than the government.

Professor Peinado points out that as an agrarian reform, the act could only be taken seriously abroad, by those ignorant of Cuban conditions. But not only was it taken seriously: it was both defended and lauded. In San Juan, Puerto Rico, Professor Arnold Toynbee addressed a group of distinguished professors and statesmen on the subject of Cuba's agrarian reform. Among the distinguished personages present were Chief Justice of the United States Earl Warren and Puerto Rican Governor Luis Muñóz Marín. Also present was Herbert Matthews.

The February 8, 1962 edition of the *San Juan Star*, headlined and reported the lecture as follows:

"CUBAN LAND REFORM PRAISED: TOYNBEE SEES IT AS MODEL FOR REST OF LATIN AMERICA

"Cuba's controversial agrarian reform was praised last night by British historian Arnold J. Toynbee as an instrument for overthrow of the oligarchies which, he said, control vast expanses of land and block social and economic progress in Latin America. . . .

" 'As for Cuba,' said the white haired former London University professor, 'her land reform law of May 1959 is important in virtue of being one of those acts of the present Cuban revolution that have set a standard—and a pace—for reform in the rest of Latin America.' The revolutionary land situation was in the same crying need for reform in Cuba as it was and still is in many other Latin American countries. . .

"Perhaps it does need a revolutionary explosion of 50 megaton power to blow up the agrarian road block that has hitherto obstructed both economic and social progress in Latin America so grievously. The landlords have been successful in resisting, not only adequate land taxation. And their utilization of the vast areas of land under their control shows a poor performance. . . ."

Here again, a renowned professor had violated reader faith. He neither understood his subject nor did he apply himself to learning the facts before lending his formidable international reputation in support of an uneconomic and evil law, and proclaiming that the Communist advances in Cuba "have set a standard—and a pace—for reform in the rest of Latin America." Actually, Castro's agrarian reform triggered the most massive, and active, resistance known in the history of Cuba. The "liberated" *guajiro* flatly refused to cut sugar cane or to work in the fields, forcing Castro to empty offices and factories in the cities and make the urban workers go to the fields and do the work which the stubborn *guajiro* refused to perform.

The mistaken view of the theorist was reflected in the United Nations when the organization published its account of land reform in its "Third Report on the Progress of Land Reform." It presents an idyllic picture of rising food production and the romping happiness of *guajiros* whereas, in fact, the Cuban peasants on the states farms were desperately resisting collectivization. Even the Castro regime itself admitted that resistance, stating publicly that "many small farmers are allergic to the word 'cooperative.' "

The U.S. Department of Agriculture correctly assesses the Agrarian Reform in saying:

"Figures released by the INRA indicate that some two-fifths of the lands 'utilized for agriculture' have been organized into 'cooperatives' and 'peoples' farms. *Land of both is owned by the state.* The 630 'cooperatives' resemble to an extent Soviet collectives (Kolkhozes) and each is administered by an INRA official who obtains credit from the national organization, keeps records, and directs activities. Members of the 'cooperative' initially paid production costs and received a daily wage plus a share of the profits, *but today they are essentially wage earners receiving a daily wage and an occasional bonus. Some of the earnings are in the form of scrip, good only at the local 'people's store.'* " (Italics added.)[7]

How and why Cuba's agrarian reform was so blatantly prostituted is revealed in a memorandum by rebel Lieutenant Manuel Artime who attended one of the early sessions at the INRA offices. The substance of the memorandum was confirmed to me in the spring of 1965 by Orlando Cuervo, former Vice Minister of Commerce under Castro. If there is anything that tends to prove Castro's allegiance to Communism, and to suggest that he was one of the world's greatest actors in hiding that fact, it is the account of the INRA meeting.

It might be useful to point out, parenthetically, that when Artime was with Castro he was little mentioned in our press. When he defected and became civilian head of the Bay of Pigs invasion force, and later mounted armed expeditions against Castro from Central America, his efforts were referred to as "right-wing" in dispatches published in the *New York Times*. And, while the absolute accuracy of Artime's memorandum cannot be confirmed beyond what Orlando Cuervo has to say about it, it cannot be denied that subsequent events have served to confirm it. For, if Artime is dismissed as nothing more than a story-teller, Castro's apologists must admit that he was also an extraordinary prophet.

Here is what Manuel Artime had to say of the INRA meeting:

"Vice President of INRA, Núñez Jiménez, [Castro was President] opened the discussion. 'These meetings are private . . .' he said. 'Here we shall discuss the real aim of the revolution which the Cuban people cannot yet assimilate. You, the members, represent Cuba's real government. *INRA is the real Cuban state—all other government departments act only as a screen.* Each one of you has complete authority within his sphere but must act in accordance with what is said at these meetings."

What Núñez Jiménez said was, in fact, already being followed by the government. While initially Castro's cabinet consisted of thorough-going middle class elements, and the important posts of Minister of the Treasury, Minister of Public Works, and the sub-cabinet post of President of

144 • THE LOSERS

the National Bank of Cuba went to personalities who were Left-of-center, they served only as the shield behind which the Communists organized a government within a government. Accusations by Tad Szulc and others that the United States failed to work with.these "moderates"[8] does not take into account an extremely important factor. That factor is that way-out liberals and Left-of-Center liberals did not take a stand against Communism in Cuba. They went along with it until they, themselves, had been devoured, a tragedy that was almost repeated in Santo Domingo in 1965.

From the first days of 1959, Communist cadres under the militant protection of the Revolutionary Government, exercised control over youth, labor, and women's groups, as well as over the scores of local, neighborhood, and national associations that were created after the revolution. This gradually emerged as a single broadly based political organization which helped consolidate the revolution. And the Communists did the consolidating. Castro's 26th of July Movement was never built into a political organization to support the Maximum Leader. Why not, it may be asked? And why did Castro choose to turn to the Communists for organizational support when it would have been so easy to build his own powerful group, independent of both the Communists and of the Right-wing? That he consciously followed the path of Communism cannot be denied.

It was in the shadow cabinet that the shots were called on policy. The Ministries themselves merely carried out the orders of the Communist organization which lurked in shadows, and later emerged as the ORI (Integrated Revolutionary Organizations).

The man who created the shadow cabinet was Fabio Grobart, alias Abraham Simkovich, a rather mysterious Eastern European who functioned as a direct contact with the Soviets. He came to Cuba back in 1933 to purge the Cuban Communist Party when it failed to take full advantage of President Gerardo Machado's downfall, and assume control of the country. When Batista came to power in 1952 as an anti-Communist dictator, Grobart (Simkovich) left the country and circulated between countries in the Caribbean and the Soviet bloc. It was apparently clear to him, as it was to others, that Castro's magnificent role of an actor and the power of his oratory could not forever provide the glue to keep the revolution from coming unstuck by public reaction following bold Communist moves in so many areas.

This comes through very clearly in other passages of Artime's memorandum dealing with Castro's entrance into the INRA meeting, and the comments he made while there:

"Then, after the inevitable delay, Castro, the Prime Minister and official President of INRA, appeared. He began by criticizing measures which had been stupid or costly, although he emphasized that the question of cost was not all-important."

Then Artime quotes Castro as follows:

"It is true that there is not enough money. But when we do not have any money we shall take away the banks' money and put the entire economy under state control. . . . Soon those who want to invest money will have to be real geniuses to find some way of investing their money. Perhaps in houses? There is a rent law already in force and I have prepared another law which will come into force if the people show signs of dissatisfaction. This law will transform tenants into owners. . . . They will not invest it in industry—which they could only do over Ché Guevara's dead body. Thus the capitalists must waste their money or put it into banks because they cannot take it out of the country. . . . It is true that in the end all property owners, big, medium, and small, become enemies of the revolution, but it would be silly to make them all enemies at one go. . . . We must behave as we did during our war: first we shall capture the plain, then, attack the towns. On the plain the retailers are weakest and disorganized. We must begin with them. We must explain that the people's shops have been set up only in order to protect the peasants from high food prices. . . . Later we shall compete with urban traders and force them to lower their prices. . . . The land itself will belong to the state—but the peasants cannot be told this because it would make them furious."

The importance of Artime's memorandum, which was privately circulated in Havana at the time (with a copy reaching our Embassy), is that it reveals Fidel Castro in true perspective in the Cuban picture. But so confusing was the situation at the time that those in the Embassy reporting on the laws and the rapid-fire changes occurring in Cuba had little time, or at least took little time, to stop and to assess what it all meant. In fact, Ambassador Bonsal once told a Cuban newspaperman that his "role was merely that of a reporter," and that policy formulation was the responsibility of Washington. While the statement on policy formulation is undoubtedly true, in stating that truth the Ambassador correctly and perhaps inadvertently revealed the absence of value judgments which might be expected to have come from the Embassy in making its reports.

However that may be, old-line Communists immediately took control of INRA, the super-state. Along with INRA Vice President Captain Antonio Núñez Jiménez and "Che" Guevara were to be found Santos Rios, a Communist with 25 years' service to the Party, Oscar Pino Santos, who was to become Cuba's Ambassador to Red China, and Severo Aguirre who, a decade or two earlier, had tried to establish Communist cooperatives in Oriente Province. Communist economic planner and editor of *Hoy* Carlos Rafael Rodríguez later moved up to the superpost, the President of INRA, turning over his editorial chores to Blas Roca, Secretary General of the now openly designated Cuban Communist Party.

With the Communist capture of INRA came Communist propaganda. Rebel soldiers were photographed building houses for *guajiros*. Contrary to what the government was itself saying about peasant dissatisfaction with the agrarian reform, such people as Professor Shapiro magically found the peasants to be quite satisfied, if not ecstatic, with their lot. He also quite magically finds that the men in INRA were youths "without ideology," a comment which most probably amused the veteran ideologues directing INRA.[9] Shapiro might, at least, have suspected a hoax when INRA published a photograph of a six-year-old cow, claiming it to be the result of an agrarian reform, which itself was less than one year-old.

Though signed in May, Castro's Agrarian Reform Law would take effect only when published the following month in Cuba's *Gaceta Oficial*. During this period, resistance steadily grew, and the business community of Cuba tried in vain to effect changes in its more drastic provisions. First, the Cattlemen's Association of Camaguey Province drafted three suggestions for the consideration of the government, warning that unless action was taken to ameliorate some of its more drastic articles, "the Agrarian Reform Law could paralyze the economy and lead to widespread hunger and misery." The National Association of Cattlemen took up the matter with the Castro regime, pointing out that the provisions of the law with which they were in disagreement should not be misinterpreted as opposition to agrarian reform. What they did claim—and which indeed came to pass—was that as presently drafted, the Agrarian Reform Law would destroy private property and lead to a national economic crisis.

Castro's answer was: "The Agrarian Reform Law will not be deterred even if it rains railroad spikes," adding the more arresting statement: "This is a great battle in which the fate of the Revolution is deeply involved—perhaps the most important of its battles so far, including the Sierra Maestra." *Revolucion's* reaction was predictable. It attacked the National Cattlemen's Association in vitriolic terms. In an apparent slip, *Revolucion* said that the cattlemen had "no moral base to challenge an Agrarian Reform Law *dictated by the Cuban State.*" (Italics added). Using "the leader and his people are indivisible" argument, *Revolucion* charged that by questioning Castro, the cattlemen had proved that they were "against the most legitimate principles of democracy, attacking, directly, the Cuban people." *Revolucion* said it was "alerting the people against the maneuvers of these counterrevolutionary gentlemen," and did so by alleging that the cattlemen were "plotting" to cut off the supply of meat to Havana. "The cattlemen do not realize," thundered *Revolucion*, "that a radical social transformation has taken place in Cuba, and their opinions have no more value than the opinions of other groups of citizens!" This last phrase is revealing. If Cuba was destined to pursue a free-enterprise economy, the expert opinions of producers for that economy should certainly be of more value than those of "groups of citizens" in regard to something as technical as the Agrarian Reform Law. The attack of *Revolucion* also hinted at a fear that the cattlemen and, indeed, others, were beginning to understand the radical transformation taking place in Cuba, and suspected it of being Communist.

Not all criticism came from sugar mill owners, sugar cane planters and cattlemen, however. More than 700 tobacco growers in Pinar del Río Province published a declaration which said that they would "rise in arms and carry out our fight in the Sierra Maestra if the law is enacted as now written." They were joined by 1,000 small farmers whose spokesman, Félix Fernández Pérez, declared: "We will continue fighting to prevent the unheard-of robbery permitted by this law." Humberto Tarafa, a veteran of Castro's guerrilla forces in the Sierra Maestra also spoke out in response to attacks against critics of the Agrarian Reform Law. Speaking in his post-guerrilla capacity as a representative of small sugar cane growers for Vertientes sugar mill, Tarafa said: "Counterrevolutionary, *latifundista*, reactionary, oligarch, stool pigeon, *Batistiano*, myrmidon, war criminal, and other words are used by the government to describe those who raise their voices in defense of rights and principles that are not in accord with Marxist ideology." What made the Agrarian Reform Law especially repugnant to Tarafa was that it was preying on the ignorance of the *guajiro*, leading him to believe that he would be given land when that law actually held out to him only the prospect of a life of serfdom on a state farm. That is not what Tarafa had fought for in the Sierra Maestra. "Let us," he said, "unite all the brethren of anti-Communist sentiments, raise the banner of democracy, and march to the defense of the agrarian reform *and* the *guajiro* by seeing to it that the law does what it is supposed to do—provide land for the landless." Small farmer spokesman Fernández Pérez angrily (and accurately) pointed out that the Agrarian Reform Law was in violation of the Cuban Constitution itself. He observed: "The law fails to recognize the basic constitutional principles of respect for private property," adding: "We represent thousands of families that have lived on the land for generations, and the government wishes to evict us for one purpose—so the state can control it in all its aspects—including the persons who work the land."

Armed resistance to the Agrarian Reform Law broke out in three of Cuba's six provinces, and bombs again began to explode in Havana.

Castro answered by shaking up his cabinet, replacing Foreign Minister Roberto Agramonte with pro-Communist Raúl Roa, unceremoniously dumping Julio Martínez Paez, and Orlando Rodríguez, while forcing the resignation of Humberto Sorí Marín who had dared oppose the Agrarian Reform Law. Communist Ramiro Valdéz, head of the dreaded G-2, was elevated to the post of Minister of Interior and took charge of all internal police and spy activities in the country. Castro then ordered his Council of Ministers to decree, as they did, the death penalty for "seditious acts." Small farmer spokesman Félix Fernández Pérez was immediately arrested "on suspicion of treason," thus putting the tobacco growers and business leaders on notice to shut up or be locked up. Fidel Castro spelled it out in one of his interminable television appearances where he said: "We do not beat anyone, we do not torture anyone, and we do not murder anyone;" then added the important caveat: "but neither will we hesitate to shoot those who are guilty of acts against our government."

Revert, for a moment, to Tad Szulc's complaint that the United States had failed to work with the liberal reformers, the "moderates," in Castro's cabinet. It would seem that two of those moderates, heading Cuba's most important financial institutions—the Ministry of the Treasury and the Cuban National Bank—would be concerned over the warnings issued by the business community that the Agrarian Reform Law would 1) destroy private property, and, 2) create a national economic crisis. As economists, the heads of those two institutions had to realize that those allegations were based on sound readings of an Agrarian Reform Law which could have no purpose other than to kill off the very private investments which both government officials had publicly stated were critically needed if Cuba was to be kept afloat financially. Yet both those officials—Rufo López Fresquet and Felipe Pazos—lent their support and their names as "moderate liberals" to that law, and, indeed, to the one which made opposition to it "acts of sedition." For example, on June 4, Treasury Minister Rufo López Fresquet appeared on the television program "Meet the Press" where, dodging and weaving, he proved that for "moderate liberals" in Castro's cabinet the shortest distance between two points was a squiggly line.

Fresquet's tax reforms, for which he had reason to be proud, were discussed. Under circumstances which precluded a Communist takeover, Fresquet's revisions in the tax structure might well have turned out to be the most important fiscal measure in the history of Cuba. But the work of the Ministry of the Treasury did not involve just the collection of taxes, and in the course of the panel interview Fresquet was questioned at some length regarding the government's mass purchase of items which seemed to carry with it no fiscal accountability. How come? Speaking "sort of" on behalf of the Cuban National Bank as well as his own Ministry, Fresquet lamely said that neither the bank nor the Treasury was responsible for those purchases. How, then, came the question, could he speak of a rational fiscal reform when that reform seemed to be rather open-ended? As the questions continued, it became apparent to the television viewers that the "moderate liberals," represented in this instance by Fresquet, were working under the enormous shadow of the super-state INRA, the Institute of Agrarian Reform. It was also obvious that the Minister of the Treasury hadn't the slightest idea how many hundreds of millions of dollars were in the coffers of that super-state, how the money was accounted for, or to whom. Fresquet's otherwise admirable efforts at fiscal reform were revealed to be nothing more than the idle dreams of the economic planner, as, for example, his statement that he would grant a 25% tax reduction to private businesses if they would locate outside Havana Province and thus create job opportunities elsewhere in Cuba. Could Fresquet really believe that INRA, which was also taking over the responsibility for industrial development, would permit private investment of any size or importance to compete with the state? (The answer, for the public at least, came in December 1959, when Felipe Pazos was fired by Castro from his post as President of the Cuban National Bank and replaced by "Che" Guevara!)

It was within the context of the relationship of the INRA to Cuba's traditional government institutions that another panel member asked Fresquet if he, Pazos, or other liberals in Castro's government harbored any reservations about the Agrarian Reform Law. "Nothing could be farther from the truth," Fresquet started out briskly. Then he began hedging. "Why, the revolution fought to return the country to constitutional government," he said, adding: "The Cuban Constitution provides for agrarian reform, therefore I support the agrarian reform." Fresquet's evasiveness on this vital issue indicates that he indeed knew but did not say, just as imprisoned Félix Fernández Pérez knew and *did* say, not only that the Agrarian Reform Law was unconstitutional, but that it had as its purpose complete state control of the means of production and distribution, both classically Marxist in concept.

Cuba's business community was struck dumb by Fresquet's apparent evasiveness. Instead of having firm friends in the social reformers in Castro's court, as they had thought, they now knew that those liberals were neither disposed to fight the Communists themselves, nor were they willing to back up the business community in its anti-Communist posture. It appears that constant Communist probes for weakness hit their mark. Cuba's social reformers (like their counterparts in the United States) revealed a totalitarian quirk of mind, a "big brotherism," that evidenced itself in a passion to plan the lives of others. They eschewed the "boorishness" of the business world, and sought solace in the cocoon of government planning. Pazos, for example, was not successful in the practicalities of business, and his mature life was spent in "high-level" economic planning where funds were generally ample and the faceless-ness of bureaucracy made it difficult to fix responsibility for errors. As between Castro and the business world, people such as Pazos choose easily. They are anti-capitalist, and the Communists toyed with that weakness. The Communists put Pazos, Fresquet, and other non-Commu-nist, *but not anti-Communist,* liberals in a corner, much like a busy mother puts a child in a corner with Tinker Toys, to fritter their time away on projects which couldn't possibly affect the course of the Com-munist revolution. Once committed to projects, the Communists accu-rately figured, the bureaucratic mentality of the liberals would drive them to defend those projects. The real power, of course, was held firmly in the grip of Communists in the INRA. It is this sorry background of the Cuban liberals that earned for them the appellation, *Fidelismo sin Fidel.* *

The fact is that the Cuban people, whose destiny, it might have been imagined, would be the object of concern to liberal writers in this country and liberal functionaries in Cuba, found no concern among them at all. The Cuban people found that they had lost their self-appointed cham-pions because they did not accept Castro, and had shown the temerity to turn their backs on government planners who knew what was best for them. Cubans had committed the unpardonable crime of failing to oblige the predisposition of the theoreticians, and they soon discovered that their welfare was studiously ignored. Worse, it was lied about. Very early in the Castro takeover the average Cuban had been badly served, while, in contrast, Castro and the Communists had been well served, by those writers who displayed amazing tolerance to Communist advances and to the reimposition of a dictatorship which they so bitterly decried in the persons of Batista, Franco, Perón, and Trujillo. Writing in *The Re-porter* magazine, Eric Sevareid said of such liberals:

"They (the Communists) must love the large school of American liberals who assume that any given country, however barren and illiter-ate, however profound its background of violence and chieftainship, is capable not only of economic modernization but of parliamentary democracy. They must love these liberals with social worker mentalities who do not grasp that illiteracy, low wages, concentrated land ownership, and so on are not 'social problems' but integral parts of life and therefore enormously resistant to quick change by anything else than the 'totalitarian disciplines' the same liberals abhor."

*Curiously enough, Pazos, Fresquet, Justo Carrillo and other economic planners were given positions with the Alliance for Progress and other U.S. or U.S.-supported agencies.

In a nutshell, the theoreticians pursued the will-o-the-wisp Fidel Castro in whom so many became invested, interpreting anything and everything in Cuba in terms of "liberal reform." In doing so, they divorced themselves from the human race.*

*This is not to say that Cuban "liberals" who served Castro at the beginning of his reign were bad men. They do, how-ever, fit the searing description penned by Eric Sevareid.

CHAPTER 7

•

The End of Freedom of the Press

•

INVARIABLY, COMMUNIST DICTATORS AIM at complete control of the press. This is just as true of Marshall Tito, whose "independent" brand of Communism bemuses so many writers, as it was of Josef Stalin in his hey-day and Alexei N. Kosygin and Leonid I. Brezhnev in theirs. In common with their totalitarian brethren, many right-wing dictators often, but not invariably, censor the press. Even Mexico's vastly complicated and obscure type of dictatorship has its methods of censorship —ranging from withholding newsprint from papers which disagree with the policies of Mexico's uni-party system, the PRI, to quietly jailing editors who disagree with that system. All varieties of censorship are, of course, repugnant to Americans since censorship strikes at the very foundations of democracy by suppressing freedom of individual expression.

Leaving the Mexican variant of censorship aside, there is a vast and significant difference between censorship from the Right and censorship by the Communists. For example, from time to time, the Batista regime censored the news. Its censorship was punitive. Whenever the anti-Batista voice of Cuba's press became too shrill or too persistent it was censored. As opposition to Batista increased, censorship became more severe. By 1954, two years after Batista illegally seized power in Cuba, censorship was a commonplace. Written rules were laid down by which Cuba's news media were to be guided. Censored were those portions of news stories which related to guerrilla activity, public opposition to the regime and Batista's reprisals against that opposition. Generally, reporters and editors were not molested for having expressed views that could not get past the censor. The individual newspaperman was left alone. News from foreign countries was untouched, as was most other news that did not threaten the security of the dictator. In a word, Batista's censorship was entirely negative.

What are the unmistakable signs of a Communist takeover? One sign is that the press comes under physical control of the Communists, and the news media are threatened and intimidated into a posture of positive and indeed abject support of the Communist regime. What is written by reporters and editors is not merely censored and then forgotten, within the normal meaning of censorship. Those who disagree with the Communist dictator and his policies are subjected to all the degradation which can be heaped upon them by elements of the institutionalized dictatorship. The news media cannot remain passive, nor can they even find refuge in the lesser evil of submitting to negative censorship. Rather, they are required, more often than not through the application of physical force, to become parrots for the regime. They must be positively and abjectly *for* the Communist dictatorship, and must comport themselves accordingly. Reams of materials supporting Communism are expected from reporters. If they are not produced, hell-fire and damnation are poured upon both editor and reporter.

From the outset of Castro's actual assumption of power, all of these signs of repression were present, a warning that a Communist dictatorship was being lodged in power in Cuba. Earlier, the Cuban press believed the words of the actor, Fidel Castro. For example, they believed him when he said from his mountain hideout in 1958: "Censorship is the true mark of the dictator and we will sweep it away," adding, "there is no half-way point on this issue." They also believed him on January 22, 1959, when he said at a press conference: "Write what you want. We want the press to work freely. No more censorship like the one the tyranny [Batista] imposed upon you. Only a government which has something to hide needs censorship. . . ."

The initial belief that Castro himself was not Communist, but was surrounded by Communists who were penetrating his regime, prompted the Cuban press for the most part to try to awaken Castro to this penetration. This belief was a fundamental error, for through his deeds alone Castro showed that his goals had become identified with those of Communism. The result was predictable. Any questioning of Communist inroads into his regime automatically was treated as an attack on Castro himself. At first, such attacks were classified as "counterrevolutionary." Later, it was spelled out in *Revolucion* so that even the most feeble-minded could understand: "To be anti-Communist is to be counterrevolutionary."

The growing concern of Cuba's news media was related to their own imminent demise, and they knew what they were talking about. Not only were they coming under constant attack by Castro, through his own press and the radio, but also by the Communists. Supported by the intimidating presence of the militia, the Communists were taking control of various unions—printers, cartoonists, and the like. A major target was Havana's Journalist Guild. Just as businessmen had been intimidated by militiamen who told them how to run their concerns, newspaper publishers, editors, and reporters were intimidated by newspaper boys, mechanical workers, and opportunists of various stripes, garbed in the authority of the regime—militia uniforms.

As in Mexico, Japan, and many other countries where wood pulp must be imported, thus threatening a serious drain on foreign exchange, Cuban governments allocated the newsprint. But Cuban government heads prior to Castro had not used their control of newsprint for political purposes —not even Fulgencio Batista, the "evilest" of Cuban dictators. Castro did. Newsprint allocation became a weapon against dissenting newspapers just as threats of the reallocation of frequencies were used against Cuba's radio-TV industry. Combined with other tactics, this move had the purpose of clubbing the news media into submission.

In fact, the newspapers, *El Pais* and *Excelsior*, were attacked by Castro because one of their directors, Cristóbal Diaz, had devised a plan to alleviate the shortage of newsprint. Díaz had been trying to interest the Batista government in developing a suitable substitute for newsprint from the waste of sugar cane. He, and the two newspapers, were summarily charged with the "crime" of being in business with Batista. And, with no proof offered in evidence, the Ministry of Recovery of Misappropriated Property followed up the charge, hinting darkly that the owner of *El Pais* and *Excelsior*, Sr. Alfredo Hornedo y Suárez, had built two hotels and the Blancita theater on land which represented graft paid to the newspaper owner by Batista. Santiago Claret, owner of the newspaper, *Informacion*, was alleged to have spent $100,000 on a diplomatic mission for the Batista government. Then, government-inspired rumors were circulated that *Diario Nacional* was being purchased by a group of *Batistianos*. Shortly afterward, the public relations chief of Castro's Ministry of Agriculture was given $16,000 cash in a brown paper bag by Castro's confidential secretary, Celia Sánchez, and told to deliver it to the newspaper owners as "down payment" from the government. Backed by a contingent of armed barbudos, he physically took control of the newspaper.

Castro, on the other hand, began early by favoring *Revolucion*, a newspaper which was no less in his grip than was its predecessor, *Alerta*, in the grip of Fulgencio Batista. Batista, it should be noted, had not favored *Alerta* as Castro favored *Revolucion* with exclusive information on government decrees and on other stories of national importance, thus making the latter the official, subsidized organ of the state. Reporters from *Diario de la Marina, Excelsior, El Pais,* and other non-government newspapers got a cold reception from the Palace press office.

Many were the early mornings when I walked to the Presidential Palace with Carlos Franqui, *Revolucion's* editor, where he picked up the latest decrees for exclusive publication. And quite often *Prensa Latina,* which maintained an office in the Palace, would have important news dispatches written and on the wires before AP and UPI even found out that anything important was going on. In this way, the Castro regime reserved to its own organs of communication almost complete control over news content. Frozen out of the ministries, as well as the Palace, Cuban reporters had to take what was written in *Revolucion* as the source for intent as well as the fact of government decisions. In this sense, *Revolucion* was the real censor of Cuba. It became impossible for the free press to separate propaganda from truth, and when in silent protest against this indirect censorship the free newspapers printed less and less of what appeared in *Revolucion* they were attacked for "failing to orient the people." To these signs of intimidation was added still another. Reporters were required to pay one year's income tax at once. However, those who chose to join the militia found that they were not required to pay one *centavo.*

Conflicts between the Castro regime and those news media not under direct government control were exacerbated by Castro himself. Early in March, Castro made a slashing attack on *Prensa Libre.* Waving a copy of the newspaper in front of television cameras, Castro blasted publisher Sergio Carbó for criticizing the massive firing of government workers. The story was this: The Castro regime revealed that there were hundreds of government workers on the payroll who did not work at all but were receiving checks anyway. The Revolutionary Government received unstinting support from the Cubans when it set about eliminating the practice. But when this evil was turned into a much greater evil, the press rebelled. The regime used the malpractice of previous governments as the excuse to fire government workers by the thousands in the application of a "spoils system" which found Fidelistas and Communists taking over. *Prensa Libre* cried "enough!" and brought down upon itself the full fury of Fidel Castro.

Diario de la Marina also observed the infiltration of Communists and their hatchet-men into virtually every walk of life in Cuba and warned that ". . . the Communist never says that he is a Communist, but is a leftist, a revolutionary, a socialist, or a humanist. . . ." Castro was so enraged at one of *La Marina's* barbs at Communism that he went to El Encanto, one of Cuba's largest and swankiest department stores, and there, haranguing the crowds, he urged them not to buy *Diario de la Marina.*

More important, however, was the less spectacular and more deadly work of government minions. They called on businessmen and brusquely announced their "hope" that they would not read advertisements by those businesses in any of the "counterrevolutionary newspapers," or hear announcements over equally "counterrevolutionary radio stations." Intimidation reached a low point when I was awakened early one morning by shouts and screams and saw my servants rush to rescue a newspaper boy delivering *Diario de la Marina*. He was being beaten unmercifully by a gang of Young Rebels under the command of a thug in a Rebel Police uniform.

The intimidation continued with militia units springing up in all of Cuba's newspapers except one—*Diario de la Marina*. La Marina paid its workers well, and had a very progressive retirement plan. There was little fertile ground there for the Communists to work. Since it was a conservative Catholic daily, there was some hesitation to take it over too soon. To do so, Euclides Vázquez Candela, sub-director of *Revolucion*, candidly told me later, might "turn the spotlight on Communism in Cuba." He said: "You may be certain that the last newspaper to fall will be the *Diario de la Marina.*" Planned or not, that is almost exactly what later happened. *Diario de la Marina*, Cuba's oldest newspaper and one of the oldest in the entire hemisphere, was the next to the last newspaper to go under, preceded by *Prensa Libre* only six days earlier. In the spring of 1959, however, there was still much to happen before Cuba's newspaper and radio and television networks capitulated.

Within a month of Castro's coming to power, the management of CMQ radio-TV was faced with a demand for $60,000 from embryo militia units which were then organizing in the station. The excuse was that a handful of CMQ employees left the station in October of 1958 saying that they had joined rebel forces "fighting Batista." Backed by Castro militants, they now demanded full pay from the network to reimburse them for the time they had lost. The element of patriotism which presumably motivated these people (although it could never be determined whether they actually had gone into the mountains) was turned into an outright shakedown, instigated by the government. As it turned out, the money was ordered to be paid to the Ministry of Labor, not to the employees. They "patriotically" donated the funds to the up-coming agrarian reform.

As proof that you can never pay a blackmailer in full, the Ministry of Communications joined the Ministry of Labor in a war of nerves against Cuba's radio and television management. Carefully planted rumors and casual official statements from the Ministry of Communications that one of the new Revolutionary laws under consideration by the Council of Ministers dealt with the reallocation of frequencies made the rounds of the industry. As this was being discussed by Cuba's radio industry, Sr. Abel Mestre, head of the board of directors of CMQ, was summoned to the Ministry of Labor where the Minister told Mestre that the $60,000 figure was in error and that CMQ owed another $96,000. The total figure of $156,000 was preposterous, representing nearly the quarterly payroll for the entire organization. The actual figure which should have been asked in the first place for the few who left CMQ in 1958 came to less than $15,000. Mestre refused.

Later that same day, he received a document signed by the Labor Minister authorizing the Ministry to draw $96,000 on the account of the network. An x was drawn where Abel Mestre was to sign, and the Minister thoughtfully clipped to the paper a copy of a government memorandum empowering the reallocation of radio frequencies. As these shenanigans progressed, *Revolucion* endorsed the reallocation of frequencies and the Communist newspaper, *Hoy*, kept up a drumfire of demands that the Communist Party be given the Ten-Ten frequency, and the radio station along with it.

Radio station CMCY was forcibly taken over by rebel units and delivered over to the Castro regime represented by Raúl Quintana and Vilma Espín de Castro, Raúl Castro's bride, both high-level Communists. The Revolutionary Government then alleged that a large amount of stock in TV channel 12 was "found" to have been held by Andrés Domingo y Morales del Castillo, Presidential Secretary of Fulgencio Batista. The laws which permitted government confiscation under the loosest possible interpretation caused the station to fall to the government. No effort was made to reimburse its stockholders or to give them the option to sell Domingo's stock, give the money to the government, and continue operating privately. In this instance, Fidel Castro himself was responsible for the decisions which placed Channel 12 in Communist hands.

Castro appeared on Channel 12 in March, 1959, where the station's labor problems and general difficulties were discussed. Castro volunteered the view that he did not care for commercial advertising. The panelists looked at one another in astonishment for a moment, then one asked: "Commandante Castro, if there is no commercial advertising, how can television stations be expected to survive?" Castro waved his hand and gave a long, rambling dissertation, which included the verbatim phrase that Channel 12 "need not worry, because the Revolutionary Government is the richest establishment in Cuba." His intent could not have been clearer, and two days later the channel fell to the government. Management was turned over to Paco Alfonso, a well-known Communist director and producer of television and radio shows. The government paid all costs of operation. The year was 1959; the month was March, less than twelve weeks after Castro came to power.

However, Channel 12 was a local Havana station, not a nationwide network. It was possible for government spokesmen to reach the nation only through privately owned Telemundo (which also owned the newspaper *El Mundo*) and over the giant CMQ radio-TV network. With Channel 12 under Communist control, almost immediately the Party tried by force to connect it with Telemundo. Following physical battles between Communist-led goons demanding jobs and loyal employees in Telemundo, the Minister told Telemundo that the Revolutionary Government frowned on "any type of discrimination," and virtually ordered the station to hire them. The station did.

Gradually, over a period of a year, Telemundo was brought under Government control through relentless pressures, a technique used throughout the industry. The squeeze was put on management as more and more station employees were intimidated into joining the militia. The Director General of the station, José Pérez, was permitted to communicate with the staff through only one person. That person was a militiaman with no experience whatsoever in television. More important, he also was a member of the PSP (Communist Party). Switchboard operators were ordered to harass Pérez, by letting his calls wait until the other party hung up, saying that he was too busy to receive calls, and also by simply misdirecting the calls.

The set artist was told to submit sketches to his own staff to see if they fulfilled the norms of revolutionary thinking. As it turned out, Communist Paco Alonso had established those norms in a series of written instructions for the television industry. In some cases, sketches made for Telemundo turned up as sets in Paco Alonso's Channel 12, and Telemundo paid the bill!

Lights were cut off in Director General Pérez's office, forcing him to work by candle light, and his secretary was withdrawn from his office for long periods of time to attend "revolutionary instruction" classes during normal working hours. Finally, the entire station was overrun with Communist-directed militia who, like so many termites, voraciously ate away the fabric of private ownership and debased individual dignity before the altar of mob violence. Pérez stuck it out until one day an employee, obviously acting under instructions, falsely denounced him as having threatened his life. Pérez was escorted to a police station, also in the hands of revolutionaries, where police officers unhesitantly wrote out a warrant and arrested him.

The warrant was miraculously dropped when, accompanied by a lawyer, Pérez moved his offices out of the station and into the parent newspaper, *El Mundo*. Lawyers tried to get the government to mediate what the Labor Ministry itself had described as a labor dispute, and were refused. Following extended legal hassles, the government finally appointed an "intervontor," a euphemism for outright government control.

It should have been apparent to the really serious observer of revolutionary Cuba that the purpose of the government was to pit group against group, and class against class. Those who justified confiscatory Revolutionary laws on the grounds that they were eliminating past evils, overlooked the truth.[1] The truth was that rather than eliminate those past evils and restore the country to honest practice, the Castro regime merely used the evils themselves as the anvil against which freedoms were pounded and destroyed.

The office of *Recuperacion de Bienes Malversados,* (Recovery of Misappropriated Properties) in line with Karl Marx's slogan: "Expropriate the Expropriators," was little more than an extortionist for the government. The Ministry was vastly more zealous in its "exposure" of financial activities—real and alleged—of those associated with former Cuban governments, than it was in setting those activities straight and reimbursing those who had been allegedly robbed. The government was demonstrably less interested in eliminating malpractices than it was in identifying those malpractices with a democratic system of government. In short, the Revolutionary regime of Fidel Castro dedicated itself to a policy of systematic destruction of all freedoms—personal and governmental.

What is of striking importance is that throughout the takeover of Cuba's radio and TV stations almost always apparent was the twin thrust of Castro's oratorical "guidance" and a Communist clean-up based on that guidance, just as had obtained in the destruction of the military order and in the deliberate debasement of other legitimate business interests. Furthermore, as was perfectly expressed by the creation of *Prensa Latina* and its relationship to overseas propaganda in newspapering, so the takeover of the radio industry was related, not only to internal control of the medium, but to international propaganda broadcasts as well. What was happening in Havana with the government's taking over radio and television stations was also occurring in the provinces. Government control of radio stations—which is to say Communist control—empowered Unión Radio, Radio Mambí, CMCY, and Ten-Ten to do in the radio field what *Revolucion* and Communist *Hoy* had done in the newspaper field. They brought private stations and networks under direct fire, "exposing" them through overwhelming barrages of invective, after calling on *Bienes Malversados* to supply the details, or to fabricate when proof was lacking.

Very early in 1959, Unión Radio announced that an "Inter-American or Latin American network" was to be established, and that the Cuban radio industry would be asked to cooperate. This was sandwiched between "news" spots which referred to the imminent reallocation of radio frequencies by the Council of Ministers. What actually was envisaged was the creation of an internal, government-controlled network, with the capability of broadcasting overseas which, of course, happened. It was specifically mentioned by José A. Fernández Pérez of Unión Radio that branches would be established "in Mexico and Venezuela." The question as to why little Cuba, which its leaders were saying had been robbed blind by Batista's *esbirros* (bullies) should even contemplate such a strange and enormously expensive project, was never asked by Castro's apologists. Nor did they attach importance to General Alberto Bayo's Communist background, or to the fact that he had trained Castro and his followers in Mexico, or to his presence in Cuba, apparently readying a guerrilla attack on Nicaragua. Cuba's aggressive designs were so apparent that it took a conscious effort for a qualified observer to overlook evidences of those designs.

Soon, Cuban visitors began to arrive in Red China. They included the turncoat, Faure Chomón, later to be named Castro's Ambassador to Russia; Violeta Casals, a Communist and Secretary General of ACAT (Cuban Actors Guild); Nicolás Guillén, the Communist Poet Laureate of Cuba; William Gálvez, Inspector General of the Cuban Armed Forces; and Communist Oscar Pino Santos of INRA. During the tour of Red China by these highly placed Cuban functionaries, Red Chinese officials quietly came to Havana. They brought with them up-to-date Chinese type and reopened Cuba's old Chinese Communist newspaper, *Kwang Wah Po.*

As Communist activities progressed in the spring, summer, and fall of 1959, the Cuban government repeatedly stated that properties expropriated from Americans would be paid for in twenty-year bonds bearing 4½ per cent interest. Cuba had no money to pay now, it said. Castro got ahead of us again on the propaganda front, claiming that the Cuban idea of payment in bonds had been virtually copied from U.S. occupation policy in Japan where we had pushed through an agrarian reform. We could hardly object to extending the same courtesy to Cuba, our friend and ally in World War II.

Castro's claim was a brazen distortion of the truth. Japan's traditional hostility toward foreigners had made it impossible for U.S. citizens or other foreign nationals to invest in Japan. Therefore, the Japanese postwar land reform had nothing whatsoever to do with U.S. holdings. Having spent five years in Japan, as Vice Consul in the city of Nagoya, and as Press Officer at the American Embassy in Tokyo, I knew something about the Japanese land reform, and believed that Castro's lies should be challenged.

I discussed the situation with the Agricultural Attaché and the Counselor for Economic Affairs. Together, we agreed to research the Japanese agrarian reform, make a comparison with what the Cuban government was saying about it, and then release the findings to the press. The Ambassador was hesitant about the idea, saying that "bonds are a tricky business," further suggesting that if the findings did indeed turn out as expected, the issuance of a release on the subject "would just stir things up" and probably do little good. This was enough for my colleagues, and they decided to drop the project. Even though Ambassador Bonsal had not vetoed the idea, they believed that his obvious coolness was a broad enough hint that the project would never see the light of day. Nevertheless, it was agreed that I go ahead and try to get as much information from Washington as I could, which we could then sit down and go over. But both the State Department and the United States Information Agency were as cool to the idea as was Mr. Bonsal, and the data were never received.

It was at about this time that my friend Nicolás Bravo approached me for my reaction to a television appearance by Ambassador Philip Bonsal. Nicolás correctly observed that the United States was being unfairly accused of all manner of crimes by Fidel Castro, and suggested that a dignified appearance by the American Ambassador on the television program "Meet the Press" would be extremely useful in getting the U.S. position across to the Cuban public. Following several discussions with Nicolás, in which he went so far as to let our Embassy pick a panel of respected reporters to serve as the panel of questioners, I took up the matter with Dan Braddock. Dan said that under ordinary circumstances he would be opposed to such an appearance. Considering Ambassador Bonsal's excellent physical appearance and his faultless Spanish, however, along with the guarantees already offered by Nicolás, Dan enthusiastically endorsed the idea.

We went to see the Ambassador together. I led off by giving Mr. Bonsal the background to the idea, offering a brief summary of pros and cons, including the guarantees of an objective panel offered by CMQ, and endorsed the idea. Dan then told the Ambassador that whatever qualms he, Dan, would ordinarily harbor were overridden by his concern that the American position in Cuba was not generally understood. He said that in his opinion, Ambassador Bonsal was uniquely suited to the task, adding the Spanish phrase, "El que calla otorga"—he who remains silent is guilty.

Ambassador Bonsal was momentarily taken with the idea and put himself to the task of writing an opening statement, after which he would answer questions from the panel. The panel was the stopper to his enthusiasm. Calling me to the office a few days later, he asked: "What about the members of the panel? They could really embarrass the United States if they should be either unfriendly or ambitious." I answered that the person being questioned at a panel usually has the initiative. I privately had no doubts about Mr. Bonsal's ability to be evasive. In fact, many of us in the Embassy feared that he might be too weak, rather than too strong. CMQ head Abel Mestre called on Bonsal in order to reassure him on this point, saying that if the Ambassador wished to write out the questions, he would see to it that the panel members, all known to Mestre and trusted by him, would ask them. I wrote up a series of questions and submitted them to the Ambassador for approval. Days and weeks wore on and neither Dan, Mestre, nor I could get Mr. Bonsal to give a yes or no answer. Finally, the whole idea was abandoned by him as "too risky."

Negative attitudes didn't stop there, however. Our newly appointed Labor Attaché, Henry Hammond, came to my office, accompanied by reporter Leon Dennan. Hammond had been talking to Cuba's democratic labor leaders, obtaining from them the details of the Communist takeover of the Cuban Confederation of Labor (CTC). It was Dennan, incidentally, who helped bring them together. The labor leaders were worried about the outcome of national CTC elections, scheduled for the fall. A day or two later, Dennan, Hammond, and I had lunch with a group of these leaders at Rancho Luna, a rustic but excellent restaurant on the outskirts of Havana which specialized in roast chicken. We talked for a great part of the afternoon, learning, 1) that old-line Communist labor leader and former collaborator of Batista, Lázaro Peña, was spending a great deal of time with Raúl Castro, and with Fidel as well; 2) that he had been promised a leading position within the labor movement; and 3) that a Communist "shadow cabinet" was being organized.

How that cabinet actually operated and the principal figures comprising the government within a government was described much later in my article in *The Reporter* magazine, "Does Castro Still Rule Cuba?" published on February 15, 1962. But more immediately important is the fact that the essentials of what I submitted to *The Reporter* in manuscript form in December of 1961, had been accurately predicted by my informants way back in the summer of 1959. What I learned from the labor leaders that hot summer afternoon was that old-line Communist Blas Roca was putting together a powerful seven-man Communist shadow cabinet. Behind him, of course, was Fabio Grobart (alias Simkovich).

The embryo organization of the Integrated Revolutionary Organization (ORI), referred to earlier, contained the economic planner, Carlos Rafael Rodríguez, who, incidentally, was President Osvaldo Dorticós' chief adviser to the Punta del Este Conference in January of 1962. The organization secretary of the group, I was told by the labor leaders, was Aníbal Escalante, a skilled Communist dialectician. Four other major figures were Severo Aguirre, who was secretary of Cuba's agrarian reform; Leonel Soto, who was placed in charge of public education and indoctrination; Lázaro Peña, the Communist labor leader; and Blas Roca, Secretary General of the Communist Party. Collectively, these men, I was told, were some day to emerge in positions of open political power in Cuba. Indeed, Ruby Hart Phillips reports in her book, *The Cuban Dilemna*, that during an interview with Carlos Rafael Rodríguez in 1959, he told her: "We are not participating in the actual government but we are participating in the revolution of the people."[2]

It was, of course, necessary that Castro keep his "moderate" cabinet above criticism as a sheath for Cuba's basic Communist policies. What the ministries could not carry out openly in the way of Communist direction, the shadow cabinet did. The burgeoning "literacy campaign," a case in point, demonstrates how the shadow cabinet translated Communist doctrine into Cuban government policy. Under Soto's direction, students began to be recruited, quietly in late 1959 and 1960, and openly thereafter, to journey into the countryside to teach the *guajiros* and "eradicate illiteracy." The texts used were Marxist, anti-American, and, of course, "anti-imperialist." Thus, literacy equalled indoctrination.

Munching on their chicken at Rancho Luna, the labor leaders told us that Lázaro Peña was in charge of the Communist wing of Cuban labor. Even though in the summer of 1959 he held no accreditation to the Cuban Confederation of Labor (CTC), he was seen at labor meetings, accompanied by Raúl Castro. As Communist influence increased, the labor leaders warned, Peña would take over the CTC. He did. In November of 1961, the Communists took over the CTC simply by transferring Lázaro Peña from his position in ORI to the post of Secretary General of the CTC.

Leaving Rancho Luna, we had few, if any, doubts about the authenticity of what we had been told. The detailed revelations of Cuba's labor leaders fit most convincingly into the over-all plot of Fidel Castro, later revealed in Manuel Artime's memorandum on the agrarian reform. More immediately important was the fact that Cuban labor treated the Communist threat as imminent and that they were disposed to fight. They feared that, if nothing were done to expose Communist machinations during the summer of 1959, the CTC elections would, to all intents and purposes, usher the Communists into power. The labor unions wanted help and guidance, and came to the American Embassy hoping to receive it.

It was natural that the Labor Attaché and I work together, since labor and the press, two traditional targets of the Communists, were under powerful intimidation. So were anti-Communists in the government—including President Urrutia. What happened to him, taken along with the known infiltration of the press and labor, convinced us that something must be done. Apparently suspecting Urrutia of being not only non-Communist, but of the greater crime, of being anti-Communist, the Communist newspaper *Hoy* launched vicious attacks on him. Urrutia, it seems, had been told about Communist indoctrination in the armed forces, the opening of guerrilla schools for the subversion of Latin America, and had suggested an investigation of Communist inroads into the Revolution.

According to Daniel James, in his book *Cuba, the First Soviet Satellite in the Americas*, Urrutia was himself placed under investigation for his anti-Communism by Carlos Olivares, Raúl Castro's former civil secretary, and at the time of that investigation, Under Secretary for Foreign Affairs. James builds an impressive case, quoting high-level members of the government, one of whom was a confidant of Fidel Castro. The gist of it can be summed up in a quotation from Castro himself as told to Justo Carrillo, a top economist: "In view of the definite information of Urrutia's disloyalty, we have assigned someone to check him and listen to his phone conversations."[3]

Communism was more than an important issue in Cuba by July of 1959; very little else was being talked about. The defection of Castro's personal pilot and commander of the Cuban air force, Major Pedro Luís Díaz-Lanz, was a bombshell. What is more, his defection revealed that there was powerful opposition in Castro's own 26th of July Movement to Communist penetration of the government. Certainly, views of officers who had fought with rebel forces had a special meaning. Díaz-Lanz knew about the army indoctrination schools, had attended one of the classes and verified their Communist orientation. In a press release issued from air force headquarters, he blasted Communism, for which he was personally called on the carpet by Fidel Castro. He defected, arriving in the United States by a small boat from Varadero Beach, some eighty miles east of Havana. The defection of Díaz-Lanz was followed by that of Ricardo Lorié, the purchaser of arms for Fidel Castro. Following a similar confrontation over Communism with Castro, Lorié also came to the United States. Rebel captain Jorge Sotus, commanding an army unit in Oriente, questioned the Communist direction of the government, as did Leftist Minister of Public Works, Manuel Ray.

When Major Díaz-Lanz arrived in the United States he spoke freely to the Internal Security Subcommittee of the Senate.[4] Widely disseminated in Cuba, his testimony shocked the Rebel Army, and served to stiffen opposition within Castro's ranks. To crush this resistance, Castro decided to go to the top, to the Presidency itself, and fry Urrutia before the country's television audience, and before the howling mobs of Castro supporters. There could be no more forceful lesson to Castro's opposition than the toppling of Cuba's President.

Blissfully ignorant of what was going on, President Urrutia continued with his anti-Communist stance, while at the same time venting his displeasure at what he clearly thought was the traitorous behavior of Díaz-Lanz. It apparently never occurred to the naive country judge, now President of Cuba, that what Díaz-Lanz had said might be true—namely that it was Fidel Castro himself who was directing the Communist course of the revolution. He soon was to learn otherwise.

On July 13, Urrutia was interviewed at the Presidential Palace by radio-TV commentator Luis Conte Aguero. During the question and answer period, Urrutia expressed his apparent conviction that Díaz-Lanz had traitorously implied that the Cuban government was Communist. He also suggested "that U.S. immigration authorities would perform a good service through the extradition of Díaz-Lanz so that he could be tried in Cuba."

Rumors had been floating around the city of Havana at the time to the effect that Urrutia no longer enjoyed Fidel Castro's confidence. In the television interview, Urrutia commented on the rumors, dismissed them, and in doing so acknowledged his status as a puppet. He said: "I don't know who said that Fidel Castro and I are not on good terms," adding plaintively: "I have signed all Revolutionary laws approved by the government, and signed them on the same day despite the fact that I have ten days to sign or veto any law. . . . It proves beyond doubt that I am fully backing the Revolution."

The interviewer, Conte Aguero, then drew Urrutia into a comment on attacks made on the President of the Republic by the Communist newspaper *Hoy*. President Urrutia said about the latest attack in *Hoy:* "Well, I have preferred not to talk about it, but since you ask me I will answer." His answer provided the genesis of his own overthrow.

"It is my duty," said Urrutia to Conte Aguero, "not only as President of the Republic, but also as a Cuban, to answer you. I know perfectly well that I will be called disloyal by *Hoy*. If they are referring to disloyalty to Russia that is beside the point because I have not sworn fealty to Russia. But, if they are trying to imply that I have been disloyal to Cuba, it will be very difficult for them to prove. What is true, and I want to make myself clear, is that the Communists are hurting Cuba very much. *Hoy* is dedicated mainly to defend Russian interests. And I want to declare now, assuming full responsibility for my words, that the Communists in Cuba are trying to open a second front of the Revolution. This is criminal!" His next words probably were more responsible than anything else for his downfall: "That is why I have said many times that I do not want the backing of the Communists, *and it is my opinion that the real Cuban revolutionaries should repel that backing, as well.* "(Italics added).

The following day, *Hoy* accused Urrutia of having acquired a "luxurious" home in the Miramar section of Havana. Urrutia answered that he was purchasing a "modest house" with the salary paid him as President, and that to do so he had borrowed money from a mortgage company. On July 17, *Revolucion* issued an early morning edition with billboard letters in red: "Fidel Resigns!" Nothing more; no story; no anything. Cuba was in an uproar. CTC leader David Salvador immediately called a one-hour labor strike, announcing that its purpose was "to get Dr. Castro to reassume his post as Prime Minister as soon as possible!" With suspicious speed, printed posters magically appeared in Havana's busses, in markets, and in factories, reading: "With Fidel to the End!" "Resign? What For?," "Fidel! Cuba Needs You!," "Fidel! Clean the Government of those who Vacillate!," "Fidel or Death!"

It was left to the non-government newspaper *Prensa Libre* to arrive at the truth. In its afternoon edition, *Prensa Libre* attributed Castro's resignation to "differences between Dr. Castro and the President of the Republic." That night, Castro appeared on CMQ television, saying his resignation was occasioned by "a matter of internal order." There were "discrepancies" between him and President Urrutia, Castro said, which were "moral, civic, and ideological." They were so great, Castro continued, as to be considered "unsolvable." He claimed: "The attitude of the President toward the revolution is becoming more hostile every day, to the point where he actually is slowing up the passage of revolutionary laws and impeding the work of the Council of Ministers." Castro endorsed *Hoy*'s attack on Urrutia for purchasing a house, then said that it was "immoral" for Urrutia to continue "receiving the pay of Batista." This innuendo referred to the salary paid to the President of the Republic, amounting to $100,000 a year. "The rest of us in the Cabinet," Castro continued, "reduced *our* salaries." The real reason for Castro's attack on President Urrutia was blurted out when Castro accused him of "treason." He was guilty of treason, Castro raged, because "in a very suspicious manner, the President now emerges as the champion in the anti-Communist fight!"

For hours Castro continued heaping filth on Urrutia, who, although he crouched stunned and weeping before his television set in the Presidential Palace, did not resign. Castro sweated through his shirt, his hair was wet, and he wiped the sweat from his face with his hands. He was the picture of nervous tension, as he glanced at his watch from time to time, gulped Spanish brandy from coffee cups, and at one point shouted: "Our revolution is not red! It is olive green, the color of the uniforms of the Rebel Army that emerged triumphant from the Sierra Maestra!" Castro continued talking, with interruptions afforded when messages from various groups supporting him and demanding the resignation of President Urrutia were read over the television and radio. But Castro did not want to command Urrutia to resign; he wanted Urrutia to recant, wanted to humiliate him into resigning voluntarily. At one point he said: "You can ask for his resignation, but you can't demand it." Shortly after midnight, Urrutia caved in and resigned. Cubans considered it especially significant that the man who delivered Urrutia's resignation to Castro was Comandante Augusto Martínez Sánchez, the same man who personally dragooned witnesses for the military show trials. Castro literally gave a sigh of relief, and his face lighted up in triumph as the pro-Castro crowd in the studio went wild with the announcement of Urrutia's downfall.

Castro did not immediately resume his post as Prime Minister. He let the suspense build up through the following days, as one organization after another sent telegrams of unqualified support for his leadership, and as radio and television commentators vied with one another, pleading with Castro to again assume the post of Prime Minister. Finally, at a mammoth demonstration on the 26th of July, Castro announced: "I obey the will of the majority of the people of Cuba. . . . their demand that I reassume the post of Prime Minister." This was no surprise. What was a surprise to the Cubans, however, and a very unpleasant one, was the selection of Osvaldo Dorticós Torrado to be President of Cuba. A man of Communist antecedents, upon asuming office Dorticós straight-facedly told the press: "Communism is no threat to Cuba," adding the bald lie, "there is not a single Communist in the Government of Cuba."

It was in this atmosphere that the Labor Attaché and I went to work. We agreed that, if Cuban unions of significant size and importance wanted help in trying to do something to save the country from a Communist takeover, the Embassy should help them. The issue arose, of course, as to the degree to which the United States could become identified with whatever help was to be extended to the unions in that fight. It was clear that Cuba's press, and its radio and television industry, would succumb to the Communist avalanche along with the Cuban Confederation of Labor. It seemed that the two elements would in the nature of things be willing to make common cause.

Fortunately, contacts within the radio and television industry permitted me to speak with frankness and without fear that our conversations would reach the ears of the Communists, or those of Fidel Castro himself. The Labor Attaché also enjoyed the confidence of select members of several of Cuba's 33 unions. We found Sr. Abel Mestre more than ready to cooperate. This was important, because both Abel and his brother Goar enjoyed considerable prestige in Cuba and in the Inter-American Association of Broadcasters. The same kind of cooperation was pledged by José Pérez of Channel 2, against whom Communist pressures were at that moment beginning to be applied. Both parties agreed, as they put it, "to stand up and fight."

What was envisioned at the time was the development of a series of two television programs and one radio program. The purpose of one, to be aired over CMQ radio-TV, was to show the Communists to be the traitors that they were, and to identify them with Batista. This would not have been difficult, since their cooperation with Batista itself provided a very persuasive story line. To be written as a dramatic mystery-type show, and titled "The Shadow," the series, in the words of Sr. Mestre, "would be a sensation." No names would be mentioned, but the characterization of the principals would leave no doubt in the public mind that the characters shown represented real Communists such as Juan Marinello, Blas Roca, and Lázaro Peña. The title, "The Shadow," was meant to emphasize the fact that, wherever power lay, the Communists lurked in the shadows ready to seize that power.

I talked with our Minister Counselor Dan Braddock about the proposal. He expressed concern, believing it a dangerous venture. But he also agreed that the situation in Cuba in the summer of 1959 was of such a nature that perhaps we should give it a try. He said he would take it up with the Ambassador. I prepared a dispatch to be sent to the U.S. Information Agency, outlining the series, and requested comprehensive research on the background of the Communists to the end that scripts written in Cuba by trusted members of the CMQ staff would be accurate and devastating. Also requested was a budget to pay part of the costs of the series. CMQ had offered to defray some of the expenses.

The Channel 2 program was also written up. Taking into account the pressures being exerted on the network by the Communists, we all decided to make this particular program a "soft sell," and design it to tie in with the Embassy's cultural program. One of the major elements of that program was sending Cuban leaders from the press, the cultural community, the educational field, etc. for a several weeks visit to the United States to learn the whats and the whys of American practice in various fields.

Another purpose, of course, was to establish points of contact in Cuba when those leaders returned. The Channel 2 program was to consist of interviews with the returnees and give the Cubans a picture of the United States as it really existed, not the picture they were getting from Castro's ravings and from Cuba's increasingly controlled press. Castro's underground leader, Elena Mederos, had resigned from his cabinet, presumably because she was not suited for the pressures of government work under the Revolutionary regime. She was approached to serve as the moderator or interviewer. Middle-aged, Sra. Mederos said she believed that in the revolutionary climate of Cuba, it would be wiser to have a younger person, and recommended several.

Meanwhile, the Labor Attaché had performed a smashing feat. He found three labor unions who were willing to be identified with the programs, to the point of being listed as sponsors. They were the prestigious electrical workers union, the union of shoe manufacturers, and one other which I cannot recall. What we believed had been accomplished was that the prerequisites to meaningful programs had been established. Cuban leaders in two important fields—labor and communications—were willing to stand up and be identified in an anti-Communist fight for the survival of freedoms in their country.

To say that the Ambassador was less than enthusiastic would be an understatement. But, as in the case of the Japanese land reform proposal, he did not veto the idea outright. We surmised that Dan Braddock had performed considerable work in the way of persuasion before the Labor Attaché and I discussed the project with Ambassador Bonsal. "What," the Ambassador asked, "if it should be discovered that the United States was behind the Communist-exposure programs? What then?" The question was interesting, since the proposition behind it implied that for the United States to take an anti-Communist stance was the equivalent either to being "right-wing," anti-Castro, or both. Yet, the U.S. Information Agency had successfully sponsored programs in other countries not dissimilar to what was proposed for Cuba. The big difference was that those programs were carried out in countries whose democratic political institutions were undoubted. The thought behind the Ambassador's question dragged into the open something with which few were willing to grapple —namely: was Cuba indeed going Communist?

Also basic to the issue at hand was this query: Was the United States willing at the time to associate itself with a resistance that might, in fact, become strong enough to openly challenge Castro's regime itself? If Thomas Mann had been Under Secretary of State at that time, perhaps the answer would have been: Take the risk. The plain truth of the matter is that neither the American Ambassador, nor his political section, nor the Department of State were disposed to take issue with Communism in Cuba in the summer of 1959. Moreover there was little disposition in the State Department, just as there was little disposition among our editorial leaders and intellectual writers at the time, to *dig* for evidence of Communism, and then try to do something about it—a something which might have obviated the need for a Bay of Pigs invasion.

Surely, the State Department could not have been unaware of the importance of the Díaz-Lanz testimony before the Senate in early July of 1959. Since State tried, in fact, to get Senator James Eastland to call off his hearings, it is to be supposed that the State Department did not want the facts of Communist infiltration in Cuba widely known. The American Embassy also vigorously opposed the hearings, on the grounds that they would worsen relations with a Castro whom the American

Ambassador had not, up to that moment, been able to contact. But the American Embassy overlooked the obvious—Fidel Castro had no desire to discuss matters with the Ambassador, to establish friendly relations with the United States, or to call a halt to his plans for the subversion of Latin America. The most charitable thing that could be said of the State Department and the American Embassy in Havana is that the keen analysis of political trends which both are expected to make of a foreign country was not made. When asked by the Ambassador one day if Cuba was, indeed, going Communist, the CIA chief, visibly startled that the question should even be asked, answered: "Well, we can't go around with litmus paper and mark things and then call them blue. What can be said, and what is expressive of the political direction of Castro, is that we know that the jails of Cuba are filled with anti-Communists, and there is not one Communist behind bars." After the chorus of "uh-huhs" from the staff, the Ambassador cut off further discussion.

This is not to say that Ambassador Bonsal was not worried about Communism in Cuba. He was. For a week in the spring of 1959, we called on all of Havana's newspapers together. Often, as we drove through the streets of Havana he would exclaim: "God, supposing this country should go Communist!" or, more often, "I think the basic conservative, Catholic nature of the Cubans will bring this country to its senses." Mr. Bonsal was a deeply disturbed American Ambassador, but he also was unwilling to lay his feelings to rest by directing his staff to concentrate on obtaining documentary, or even non-documentary, proof that Cuba was going Communist or to recommend a policy to deal with it.

Himself an intellectual, Ambassador Bonsal hesitated so long that, when his mind finally was made up that Cuba was indeed lost to the free world, it was far, far too late. Like many intellectuals, Mr. Bonsal was not a fighter. And while it may be argued that the United States was formally correct in not taking issue with Communism in the summer of 1959, because it had no hard intelligence to support the belief that Cuba was Communist, this does not speak too well for our political analysts. And the fact of the matter is that, having failed to correctly analyze the direction of Castro's revolution and, equally important, to gauge the latent strength of opposition to Communism in the summer of 1959, we could no longer make a challenge when that strength had been dissipated.

As may be imagined, without a strong endorsement from the Ambassador, the U.S. Information Agency was not disposed to move on the television and radio programs. In fact, they sent a telegram to the Embassy to ascertain Bonsal's support for the project and received a very equivocal reply. As the weeks dragged on into September, with U.S. equivocation apparent, union leaders, CMQ, and Channel 2 became disillusioned and disgusted and said that by the time the programs would get on the air, it would be too late.

At stake in the veto against using aggressive programs in the face of the situation existing in Cuba is this: Are hard-hitting informational programs to be used only in countries where the strength and morale of democratic institutions will permit their use? Where there are no conflicts over Communism? If this is the case, then the utility of the U.S. Information Agency is placed in grave doubt. Unless we decide to fight where the enemy is, then there is no fight at all, is there? And unless we support our friends and allies when they are disposed to fight, then we will have no allies at all, will we?

There was one flurry of considerable importance to our project. That came when, in September, *Revolucion* published an editorial which blistered Cuba's old-line Communists. They were asked by what authority they spoke for a revolution which they had done nothing to support until the battle had been won. Written by Assistant Editor Euclides Vázquez Candela, the editorial was a major sensation. (Incidentally, Vázquez Candela was quietly removed from the task of writing policy pronouncements, and reportedly was killed in a jeep accident while touring Algeria with "Che" Guevara.) But what the editorial meant in September, 1959, was that highly-placed non-Communist militants in Castro's entourage were showing signs that they might be willing to challenge the power of the old-guard Communists. Inferentially, of course, the editorial provided powerful evidence that the Communists were indeed occupying many seats of power and were speaking for the Revolutionary Government. I sent a dispatch to Washington quoting the editorial and stating in rather strong terms that if the proposed radio-TV programs had been on the air at this time, they might have had some effect. For at that very moment, the anti-Communist voices in Cuba were rising, both in number and in stridency, and it was necessary for Fidel Castro himself to still those voices.

On September 25, Castro appeared on television and unleashed a vicious and sustained attack against critics of his administration. He accused Agustín Tamargo, a writer for *Bohemia* magazine, of being "a reactionary counter-revolutionary agent," a charge that didn't hold up to serious scrutiny. Tamargo had, in fact, been stalled in his application for a U.S. visa because of earlier ties with pro-Communist movements. He had broken those ties, however, and the Embassy was investigating his break. Tamargo answered Castro in a column published on September 29 in *Avance* newspaper. He hotly denied Castro's accusations, saying: "The Prime Minister of Cuba tried to destroy the reputation of a man who has committed no crime other than to think with his own head." He continued: "Our people follow the course of the revolution, but not with a blindfold over their eyes." Tamargo concluded his article writing, "I will not continue as a journalist because you, Comandante Castro, don't want journalists: you want phonograph records!"

Bernardo Viera Trejo and Pedro Leyva, two more journalists who had been viciously attacked by Castro, also answered back. Leyva sharply criticized Fidel Castro for "the greatest spectacle in the world," staged by the "exclusive club of the revolution the night that President Urrutia was character assassinated and deposed from the presidency." He likened Castro's tactics to those of Adolf Hitler. Viera Trejo was less outspoken than either Leyva or Tamargo, but still left the clear impression that Fidel Castro was comporting himself in the manner of a bully, not as a responsible head of state.

On September 30, *Diario de la Marina*, a major object of degradation by Castro, took up the fight. The newspaper printed the shocking news that a charge had been filed in court, accusing *La Marina* of attempting to overthrow Castro. *La Marina* stated its case with considerable strength. The editorial said that it "was always disagreeably surprised when solemn charges arise out of personal resentments, and was all the more surprised when such charges are made by the Maximum Leader of the Revolution." The newspaper admitted that its views of the direction being followed by the Revolutionary Government "may be wrong," adding, however, that "Dr. Castro must also admit that he can be wrong." The editorial rejected Castro's charges that the questioning of some of his policies arose out of greed, and that its differences with him meant that *La Marina* was "plotting the overthrow of the Revolutionary Government." In a signed companion piece to the editorial, *La Marina's* publisher, José Ignacio Rivero, wrote that Castro sees an enemy in every difference of opinion, and "calls it counterrevolutionary, placing the dissenting reporter in the position of being a 'secret agent,' the equivalent of being marked with the cross of terror, like the 'Mark of Zorro.' "

As plots, counter plots, and the subjugating of the press continued to dominate the Cuban scene in the summer of 1959, the Communist destiny of Cuba's labor movement was being decided—without any counteraction from the United States. Unbelievably, the Russians began to move into a country less than ninety miles from Florida.

Resistance from Cuba's labor unions matched, if it did not actually surpass, that of the business community and the news media. The first really big jolt to organized labor had already come early—back on April 6th. On that date, the opportunistic directors of the CTC suspended the right of strike for a period of six months. The excuse given was the by-now familiar allegation that the national economy was in grievous condition because of the corruption of the Batista regime. Following the CTC declaration, Russians began to make their appearance. A May Day celebration in Havana saw Raúl Castro formally calling for the creation of a militia, which was already being organized and, in many cases, in actual operation. Russians Timofie Eremeov and Ivan Arapov came to

Havana. They were members of the Central Council of Russia's government-controlled labor unions. The Russians apparently arrived in Havana to help arrest the growing anti-Communist sentiment of Cuba's CTC.

During May, alerted by the CTC's suspension of the right to strike, unions belonging to the national federation elected non-Communists to leadership in the powerful Federation of Sugar Workers, the Cuban Association of Artists, the Union of Musicians, the Industrial Federation, and the Electrical Workers' Union. In fact, had it not been for the militancy of the Communists, backed by Fidel Castro, the Communists would have been thrown completely out of the labor movement. Following their victory, the sugar workers denounced the Communists and their newspaper *Hoy* in terms that later were reflected in the statements of President Urrutia. *Hoy*, the sugar workers said, was guilty of "unfounded defamatory, and counterrevolutionary statements" against their newly-elected leader, Conrado Becquer. Becquer, it should be noted, won his post by running against the Communists on a 26th of July ticket, winning by the almost unbelievable margin of 885 to 13.

Victory over the Communists may well have been in response to a television appearance by Fidel Castro on May 21, where the Prime Minister gave labor a verbal spanking. Up to that time the darlings of the revolution, urged and indeed directed to make demands against management, the labor movement was subjected to the heaviest guns in Castro's oratorical arsenal. He accused unions of making greater and greater demands, charging that they were completely forgetting that "the unemployed should come first." He branded as demagogues and political hacks "obstructionist" labor leaders who had incited the workers with false promises, and urged them to make "impossible demands." It was Fidel Castro who fitted that description, but he turned criticism away, saying: "Certain suspicious trends are beginning to appear all over the country." He added the vastly more arresting charge: "They are threatening the government with demands, with parades, with petitions that could put the masses of the people against the government." In other words, it was all right for labor to milk free-enterprise management, but it was treason to make any demands of the government for labor legislation, one of the burning issues of the day. Castro continued his blackmail, charging: "The time to have made those demands against the government was in 1952, 1953, 1954. That would have been the courageous thing to do."

The labor ranks noted that Castro seemed to take issue with the Communists, as well, when he answered a panel interviewer as to whether Castro thought that the Communists were involved in those impossible demands." Castro thought for a moment, then said: "There could be a coincidence." He added, with a shout: "This is not a red revolution! It is an olive green revolution!" What concerned him, said Castro, "is that labor is perturbing the interests of the revolution of such an extent that it can lead to the destruction of the government's authority. And that I won't tolerate!" He had clearly warned the 26th of July Movement, and the Communists, not to challenge his dictatorial authority openly. He, and only he, would decide how the dice came up. How they would come up was suggested (and overlooked) when, on the same television appearance, Castro turned to the subject of labor and the Institute of Agrarian Reform (INRA). Though the major positions had already either been given to Communists or were earmarked for them, he blandly told the television audience that he would draw upon the ranks of the faculty of the School of Agronomy of Havana University for the skills needed to run the INRA. He, of course, never did, except later to make old-line Communist and professor at the university, Carlos Rafael Rodríguez, President of the INRA. Castro's open declarations, of course, hid from view the subterfuges open to him, and which he was utilizing at the very moment of his speech.

It may be taken as a measure of widespread fear of Communism that Castro's oblique attack on the Communists was hailed with relief, as well as with wishful thinking, in Cuba. Even Carlos Todd, one of the shrewdist political analysts in Cuba at the time, wrote in *The Times of Havana:* "Dr. Castro is very wisely beginning to ease Communists out of key positions in the government. It is a process that will take a little time and no small amount of legerdemain." Writing about the impact of Castro's May 21 reference to the Communists, Todd said that there now was hope in the land because "one man (Castro) declared the Communists guilty of trying to 'perturb' the revolution. . . ." The essential point is that Castro had the full and enthusiastic backing of Cuban labor when, momentarily, he appeared to be taking issue with the Communists. He could have built on that backing. He deliberately destroyed it instead.

And the Russians were not idle. For, while independent union leadership was being overwhelmingly assumed by militant anti-Communists, the Communists themselves were eating away at the innards of the union organization. An "interpreter" for the Soviet labor delegation turned out to be not Vadim Vadimovich Listov, as advertised, but Vadim Kotchergin, a member of the Soviet Secret police.[5] Kotchergin spent time with Castro's G-2 chief Ramiro Valdez, with Major Manuel Piñeiro, who was to take over the G-2 post after Valdez assumed the post as Minister of Interior, and with Red Chinese intelligence experts who arrived clandestinely in Havana toward the end of May. Apparently, the Russians had correctly assessed the disposition of organized labor to rebuff the Communists in union elections. One result was that, prior to the national elections, scheduled for November 18, Labor Minister, moderate Manuel Fernández García, was ousted and replaced by trouble-shooter Augusto Martínez Sánchez, a confidant of Raúl Castro.

Castro's G-2 apparatus was becoming a formidable, functioning body under the direction of the Russians and the Red Chinese. G-2 members were infiltrated into the locals, unsuspecting union members were inveigled into supporting "unity among labor" and lent themselves to subversion of labor. Then the charges began to erupt. In Santiago, the port workers were shocked to find that Santiago Casaco had been ousted because of his criticism of Communist G-2 infiltrators into the union. He was, according to the government's Santiago newspaper *Sierra Maestra*, "a counterrevolutionary." Meanwhile, Labor Minister Martínez Sánchez tried to postpone the national union elections until the beginning of 1960, in order to give the Communists time to bring the locals under control, but he was overwhelmingly rejected by the democratic labor leadership. Thus, the stage was being set for the elections of the national labor confederation, the CTC.

The significance of the national elections is that they found the 26th of July Movement and the Communists locking horns for labor leadership. No longer could Castro take the position that it was his movement *vs* the *Batistianos*, as he had so successfully maintained for so many months. The Batistianos were in jail, or dead, or had fled the country. The 26th of July labor movement was shocked and dismayed to find that their group was opposed by pro-Communist Jesús Soto, and backed by none other than Raúl Castro and the old-line Communist leader, Lázaro Peña. What was proposed was a "unity" slate. Unity thus equalled Communist domination. Cuban labor, however, had several decades of organization behind it, and had no intention of yielding to the Communists without a fight. Many delegates came to the meeting with watermelons, in obvious references to a joke making its rounds of Cuba at the time— that the revolution was green on the outside and red inside. Castro had repeatedly said that the "color of the revolution is olive green, not red."

The labor meeting was an uproar, as the Communists tried to shout down the 26th of July Movement slate of candidates. But the 26th of July gave as good as it took. It accused Jesús Soto of treason for not having delivered, as he was supposed to, a truck full of arms to the Student Directorate when members launched their attack on the Presidential Palace on March 13, 1957. Soto had gone into hiding instead, taking refuge in a small hotel on the corner of Ayestarán and Bruzón streets in Havana.

From a close reading of labor accounts of what happened, it seems clear that Soto was definitely friendly with Lázaro Peña and offered to help Peña in taking over the movement if Peña, in turn, would assure him of Raúl Castro's backing. That backing was given. Fidel's younger brother accepted the proposition, as he, Soto, Peña, and Martínez Sánchez backed their "unity" slate of candidates, which would permit Communists to be represented on the national executive board of the CTC.

The free labor representatives stuck to their guns. Despite the tongue-lashing administered to the unions by Castro back on May 21, the Sugar Workers Union had passed resolutions which were a compromise between what he obviously wanted and what they considered to be labor's fair share of the profits. While it went along with the government's stated desire to convert the sugar mills into industrial units, and to create agricultural cooperatives in all, the Sugar Workers Union did not want to give up the rights of the individual. The union demanded that the government live up to its own Law 260 which increased agricultural workers salaries, and to extend full workers' benefits to those employed in semi-agricultural categories. These demands, of course, ran counter to Castro's plan to control all means of production. The Sugar Workers and the other 32 unions in Cuba were destined to work for the state, as the Artime memorandum made clear, not for private enterprise. Thus, they were not being opposed as they supposed only by the old-line Communists, whom they had bested in earlier labor union elections, but by Prime Minister Castro *and* the old-line Communists. And this fatal error in judgment was soon brought home to labor.

Fights broke out between the delegates as the overwhelming majority of the laborers refused to hear the Communists speak for unity. Shouts for "unity" by some of the Communists were met with roars of "26th of July" by the majority. Finally, Fidel Castro himself had to come to the hall. Even he couldn't establish order, shouting that the scene reminded him of "a madhouse." After speaking for hours, he came out solidly for the Communist "unity" slate, employing his by then familiar tactics of blackmail. "Irresponsible voices that cannot be revolutionary," he said, "can ony be the echo of counterrevolutionary voices, originating, perhaps, from the chorus of war criminals." With that, the Communists had what they wanted—an open door to power.

The play-acting began. The names of the three Communists, included among the original thirteen nominees running for the Executive Committee of the CTC, were withdrawn, ostensibly as a concession to the anti-Communist 26th of July labor leaders. The new slate of candidates drawn up by Secretary General David Salvador on the personal orders of Fidel Castro included, instead, three way-out "liberals," including Jesús Soto, who were in fact pro-Communist. The Communist delegates, under the tutelage of crafty Lázaro Peña who had set up headquarters in the nearby

Hotel Gran America, then stormed out of the meeting in apparent protest against the exclusion of Party men, thus giving the impression that the "moderates" had won important consessions. Lightning-quick, the Lázaro Peña-Raúl Castro managed conference pushed through its new unity slate and reduced the Executive Committee from thirteen members to only six. With the three pro-Communists, plus Labor Minister Augusto Martínez Sánchez, the Communists took charge. They secured passage of measures withdrawing the CTC from the anti-Communist hemisphere federation, the ORIT, and called for the "purification" of the labor movement. President Osvaldo Dorticós, and Prime Minister Fidel Castro attended that meeting and openly supported the Executive Committee action.

It is interesting to consider the conclusions that came out of the Castro-propelled labor conference. Typically non-labor for the most part, they included such "goals" as "fight with all means available North American imperialism . . . assume responsibility in the anti-imperialist fight of the Soviet Union . . . send a greeting to the Twenty-Second Conference of the Soviet Communist Party. . . ." A very significant slogan was added, "revolutionary vigilance," which amounted to organized Communist terror.

In response to the CTC resolution, the Communist commander of Pinar del Río Province, Derminio Escalona, announced that Student Militia had been organized in the secondary schools of the Province, to carry out revolutionary vigilance. Escalona also organized a Revolutionary Teachers' Brigade and called upon the teachers to give military instructions in their classes. By this time, it was learned that 32 People's Stores had been established by the government in Camaguey Province, after it had falsely accused the company stores of the sugar mills and sugar cane planters of not supplying their workers with needed merchandise, and of overcharging them for all other merchandise sold them.

The demise of an independent labor movement was accompanied, over a period of eight months, by the death throes of Cuba's press. *Why* the demise was told to the Cuban press by the Minister of Education, Communist Armando Hart. The occasion was Reporters Day, October 24, 1959. "Objectivity," Hart intoned to Cuba's press representatives, "is a myth of civilization." The only true basis for objectivity, he continued, is to report and to reflect public opinion. And where is that public opinion to be found? It is to be found, Hart told his goggle-eyed audience, in the shouting mobs before the Presidential Palace where Fidel Castro, the warrior and prophet of the revolution, exercises direct democracy. Said Hart: "When Dr. Castro speaks, he speaks for the people and therefore expresses public opinion." Hart went on, "Those who ignore public opin-

ion [as expressed by Castro] defend the interests of the oligarchy."
Revolucion reported Hart's speech in full, publishing its now-famous
dictum: "To be anti-Communist is to be counterrevolutionary!"

Cuba's free press became weakened by a steady decrease in advertising
revenues because advertising outlays were cut by business firms which
had been confiscated by the regime. Advertising revenues were decreased further by other businesses switching their advertising to *Revolucion*, and by the deliberate cancellation of government newspaper
advertising. Cuba's harrassed press was filled with despair at Hart's open
threats. More than that, they were angry. Elections to the Havana Journalists' Guild were scheduled to be held a month after Education Minister Hart's helpful guidance, and reporters boycotted the elections—a
fatal mistake. The Communist Party, on the other hand, was openly
offering to pay one year's dues of those who agreed to vote for the slate
of candidates they put up. The Communists bragged that their "unity"
slate had the backing of Fidel Castro himself. Whether this is true or not,
it can be said that he never denounced the Communists for claiming they
had his endorsement. Judging from Castro's support for "unity" at the
labor union elections, it seems safe to assume that he did in fact support
the Communists in the journalists' elections. This belief is strengthened
by the fact that one of the Communist candidates for election to the
Guild, Baldomero Alvarez Ríos, had, with Castro's support, been arbitrarily installed earlier as head of the editorial board of *Prensa Latina.*

Known Communists, among them Jorge García Villar, Tirso Martínez,
and Gabriel Molina Franchossi, were on the unity slate. When the votes
were counted (less than 13 per cent of the Journalists' Guild voted),
Alvarez Ríos emerged as head of the Guild, with the posts of Treasurer
and Vice Treasurer going to Communists. Eight of fourteen directors also
were Communists. It might be well here to examine the antecedents of
Alvarez Ríos, the man who was now not only in virtual control of Cuba's
press, but also of *Prensa Latina*, Castro's voice to the world. He attended
the Sixth World Youth Festival in Moscow in 1957, led the Cuban
delegation to the Seventh World Youth Festival in Vienna in 1959 (the
year of his elevation to the post of Czar of Cuba's press), and was a guest
of the Iron Curtain countries following the Vienna trip. There he contacted Communist news agencies and tied them in with *Prensa Latina.*
It might also be well to emphasize that the year of the Communist
takeover of Cuba's press was 1959—not 1961 or 1962.

But even before Alvarez Ríos had made his 1959 journey to the Iron
Curtain countries, he had provided quarters in his office for Kung Mai
to open the Havana Bureau of the Communist New China News Agency.
An exchange of news and photographs was immediately effected, an
exchange in which *Prensa Latina* agreed to provide photos from Latin

America in exchange for news and photos provided by NCNA from Asia. In other words, what Asia was to learn of Latin America and Cuba via the NCNA would be seen from the position of Castro's official propaganda organ. It hardly seems likely that the Red Chinese would tie up with a government news agency which was not Communist. Regardless of what Castro's apologists were saying about "non-Communist Cuba" at the time, in April, 1959, the Red Chinese certainly considered Cuba to be Communist.

Immediately following the Communist capture of the Journalists' Guild, the *coletilla* (little tail) made its appearance. The Guild ruled that the mechanical workers union of the newspapers had the "right" to attack editorial policy. When a foreign wire story (AP, UPI, for example) was considered unfriendly to the government, the Soviet Union, or to Communism, and was published, a *coletilla* was appended by a committee of mechanical workers. The *coletilla* was standard: "Due to the practice of freedom of the press, the foregoing article was published. However, the center of work of this newspaper points out that the story in question does not live up to the most elementary standards of journalism or truth."

Battles developed almost at once between Cuba's newspaper publishers and officers of the Journalists Guild. The *coletillas* were devised by a committee consisting of Baldomero Alvarez Ríos, Pedro Souret of the Cuban Communist Party, and Tirso Martínez, a Communist and secretary of the Guild. They increased in size and, from November 1959 on, gradually emerged openly as instruments of government censorship. Operating behind the facade of the Guild, the government created chaos and turmoil in the press that led, in a few months, to the complete surrender of press freedoms in Cuba.

Saturday morning, January 16, 1960, *Informacion* editor Angel Fernández Varela, heard loud voices in the corridor outside his office. His door burst open, and five militiamen alleging that they represented "the workers" of the newspaper, strode in. In the hands of their leader, pro-Communist Jesús Pulido, were two dispatches, one each from UPI and AP, which dealt with statements by two U.S. Congressmen commenting on Communist infiltration in the Castro government.

"You can't publish these," he announced to Varela, waving the dispatches under the nose of the editor. Varela bristled, rose from his desk and confronted the delegation.

"Who says I can't publish them?" Varela demanded.

"We do!" the militiaman replied. "This material is a calumny against the glorious revolution of Prime Minister Fidel Castro!"

Varela took the dispatches and glanced over them briefly. He had, of course, seen them earlier, but in view of the ultimatum looked to see if they had been tampered with. They had not. The dispatches were factual reports. Varela remonstrated with the militiamen, saying that news was news, and pointing out that they were suggesting censorship, something which Fidel Castro himself said would never again be imposed on Cuba's press.

"This is *not* censorship!" the militiaman retorted. "We are acting in defense of the Patria."

By this time, several reporters had gathered in Varela's office. The arguments became more heated. The crowd grew in size, and spilled out into the corridor. Office doors popped open and typists, office clerks and copy boys joined the crowd. Frightened by the opposition, one of the militiaman disengaged himself from the milling crowd and ran down the stairs to the street, shouting: "Counterrevolutionaries! Counterrevolutionaries!" He returned with another contingent of militia.

Jesús Pulido, the militia leader of *Informacion*, had, meanwhile, told editor Varela and assistant editor José Villalta that "the workers" would print one of the dispatches and then append a *coletilla* to it. Varela refused this obvious intimidation of the press, saying that if the militia insisted on publishing the *coletilla*, the newspaper would leave the space above it blank.

Pulido exclaimed to a nonplussed Varela: "But that would be censorship!" He turned, and with his militia group tagging at his heels, went to the Fourth Police Precinct and swore out a warrant for the arrest of editor Angel Fernández Varela on the grounds that he was imposing censorship on his own newspaper! This, Pulido maintained in his warrant, "would give the enemies of the Revolutionary Government of Cuba the opportunity to charge that press censorship exists in Cuba."

Varela and his staff immediately filed a counter-charge against Pulido and his goons, charging them "with evident coaction and a manifest violation of freedom of the press." Jesús Pulido and "the workers" were said by Varela to have rejected the authority and responsibility of *Informacion*. Their actions, said the Varela warrant, "clearly were unlawful," and Varela demanded that the police eject Pulido and his small coterie of militia supporter from the premises of the newspaper. The demand was rejected.

El Crisol came to the defense of *Informacion*. Not yet completely controlled by the militia, *El Crisol's* mechanical workers permitted the publication of the Varela charges against press freedoms. In addition, *El Crisol* editorialized: "With this attitude and this distressing act, militia workers have broken the traditional responsibility of workers for management, and violated the free judgement and criterion of every newspaper to publish or not, according to its own trained journalistic lights, the material which it believes to be informative to the reader."

Revolucion viciously attacked editor Varela and *Informacion*, printing what it called "the protest of the workers of *Informacion* against the management of that newspaper." *Revolucion* virtually called for the take-over of Cuba's newspapers by organized militia units operating within them. The following day, militia appended *coletillas* to a *Diario de la Marina* editorial entitled: "Explaining the 'New Style' of Press Censorship." The militia did not come from *La Marina*, however. They were brought by the government from *Informacion*. Thus *La Marina's* management was able to add their own *coletilla* to that inserted to the editorial by the militia. *La Marina's* editorial was directed at the Journalists Guild, and said, in part: "*La Marina* will never be able to explain to the country how those who should be vigilant and attentive to the liberty of expression and information in the profession of journalism are turning into censors and appliers of the muzzle."

Avance was the first newspaper to surrender to physical violence. Following a series of fights and arguments between publisher Jorge Zayas and the government, *Revolucion*, and the Guild over the use of *coletillas* appended to Zayas' editorials, the newspaper fell to "the workers" (i.e. militia) on January 19, 1960. Zayas, Pedro Leyva. Augustín Tamargo, Pedro Viera and the editorial and managerial staff of the newspaper fled the country. Communist cadres in the Guild pounced on anti-Communist Antonio Prohías, and forced him to resign as President of the Association of Cuban Cartoonists. On March 15 and 16, *El Pais* and *Excelsior* were closed down and converted to a National Printing Office. Fidel Castro attended the meeting and presided over the closing of the two newspapers.

Diario de la Marina and *Prensa Libre* did not die so easily, however. For months, publisher José Ignacio Rivero of *La Marina* kept up the fight against the Communist takeover of his country. The government was alarmed to learn that the circulation of the newspaper had tripled within a period of less than four months, clearly indicating growing dissatisfaction with Castro and Communism. That dissatisfaction took on specific dimensions when, the first week of May, 1960, the mechanical workers of *La Marina* met and voted to support Rivero in his fight with the Communist government of Fidel Castro. A committee drafted a strong letter of support, and 300 workers signed their names to it. It was to have been published on May 10. Late at night on May 9, a group of armed and swaggering thugs, led by the secretary of the Journalists' Guild, Tirso Martínez, and by the Communist Secretary of the Arts and Graphics Union, forced their way into the newspaper. Holding the printers at gun-point, they destroyed plates containing the letter and signatures of *La Marina's* workers, and began to ransack the newspaper. *La Marina's* Treasurer, Pedro Hernández Lovio, frantically dispatched telegrams to the President, the Minister of the Interior, the Chief of Police, and the Supreme Court, demanding that protection be extended to the newspaper under the laws of the land. None of the telegrams were answered.

After dispatching the telegrams, Hernández Lovio went personally to the nearby Third Precinct Police Station and asked the Captain on duty to arrest the gang that was ransacking the newspaper. The Captain replied that the "disturbance" did not warrant "police interference." The Captain punched Hernández Lovio several times in the chest with his index finger to emphasize his words: "Show me one man who has been killed, and I will take action." By 2:00 a.m., May 10, 1960, the newspaper was fully occupied by militia, and the Rivero family went into hiding, taking refuge three days later in the Peruvian Embassy. The last issue of *Diario de la Marina*, Cuba's oldest and most prestigious newspaper, came out on May 12 with the headline: "A Day With the People After 128 Years at the Service of Reaction." It's content was the purest puree of Communist garbage.

The demise of *Diario de la Marina* also signalled the demise of *Prensa Libre*, Cuba's only mass-circulation newspaper. Assistant Editor Humberto Medrano had for months stood by *Diario de la Marina* in its fight against government censorship and mob intimidation. When it went under, Medrano published a box story, edged in black, carrying an account of the intimidation and capture of Cuba's newspapers by the Fidel Castro regime.[6] Following the first day's publication of Medrano's box story, the militia called on Medrano and warned him to cease publication of his "reactionary propaganda." Medrano refused to heed them and, at 3:00 p.m. May 16, 1960, the management was forced out of the building, and the Union of Graphic Arts and the National Newspaper Guild took over. Within months, *Revolucion* moved into the new, modern plant of *Prensa Libre*, and turned over its printing plant to the Communist newspaper *Hoy*.

Cuba's radio and television stations also fell to the government. And it was Fidel Castro who led the attack—this time against radio-TV commentator Luis Conte Aguero. For weeks in the spring of 1960 Conte Aguero was involved in a daily war of words with the Communists, and, like *Diario de la Marina*, he was receiving significant public support. Letters poured into the studies of CMQ and *Radio Progreso* from all parts of Cuba, congratulating Conte Aguero for his anti-Communist stand. He read some of those letters over the air, and in doing so widened his differences with Castro. A staunch Catholic, the radio-TV commentator was considered to have placed the issues squarely as "Catholicism or Communism." Fidel Castro, however, maintained that Conte Aguero's position merely created "divisionism."

The war of words got hotter until one night, on television, Fidel Castro said that Conte Aguero was "playing the game of the enemies of the revolution!" On March 25, Conte Aguero read an open letter to Fidel Castro over *Radio Progreso*, warning that the Communists were stealing his revolution and asking the Prime Minister to do something about it. Following his broadcast, Conte Aguero went to CMQ where he planned to again read the letter on his regularly scheduled television program there. He was met at the studios by squads of Communist toughs and civilian-clad members of the Rebel Army who, wearing brass knuckles and carrying clubs, barred his entrance into CMQ. They successfully fought off attempts by Catholic Action Groups to break through the cordon placed around the building, and Conte Aguero fled for his life.

On March 28, Fidel Castro appeared on radio and television and spent nearly four hours attacking Conte Aguero. Government jackals—among them José Pardo Llada, Tony Fernández, Raúl Quintana—and all government newspapers, including, of course, the Communist newspaper *Hoy*, immediately widened their own attacks on Conte Aguero in an overwhelming barrage of invective. Radio commentator Pardo Llada broadcast a demand for Conte Aguero's expulsion from the country within 24 hours. If he didn't go, said Pardo Llada, "he should be shot!"

On March 29, the militia entered CMQ, impounded its books and froze the personal accounts of the two brothers who owned the television chain—Goar and Abel Mestre. Miraculously, the Ministry for the Recovery of Misappropriated Property "found" that 35% of the stock in one of CMQ's channels (it had three) "belonged to Batista." The mere mention of Batista was considered sufficient grounds by the government to do whatever it wanted, in this case to take control of the news content of the CMQ radio-television network and put it at the service of Communism. Old-line Communist Luis Gómez Wanguemert ascended to the position of news director, and Communist programs immediately followed. All this, of course, was done in the name of "the people"—a people who no longer possessed the slightest means of expressing an opinion contrary to that of the Communists.

In the face of what was going on, Herbert Matthews writes that "Fidel, I believe, was instinctively and by conviction anti-Communist for a long time." He adds the extraordinary comment that "the main factor with him was that he did not care much what the Communists did. The business of keeping the Revolution and the country going was so fantastically burdensome that he at first put the Communist problem in a minor category." Does this statement hold up under serious scrutiny? It does not. To say that Castro did not care much what the Communists did, side-steps the irrefutable fact that Castro himself put Communists in power. And could it be said of Fidel Castro, who lied, raged, and ranted over the issue of Communism, that by that raging and ranting he had "put the Communist problem in a minor category?" Indeed, it was Castro who, on both counts, put Communism in a major category.

Mr. Matthews also chides the United States for judging what went on in Cuba by American standards. When questioned, this statement also evaporates as an intelligent argument. The alarms being set off in Cuba were set off by Cubans, not by Americans, who saw their country being turned into a Communist dictatorship. And who set off the alarms? Members of Castro's own 26th of July Movement in the Army, the labor unions, and his own cabinet. And Castro consciously destroyed that movement when its basic democratic, even leftist, convictions, placed the Movement in opposition to the Communists. Primarily, Castro placed himself in a position of open conflict with the democratic aspirations of his own people. If he had not done so, there would have been little reason to be in conflict with the United States. A democratic regime in Cuba would have honored its international commitments rather than destroy them; a democratic regime in Cuba would not have debased the concept of justice; it would not have lied to the people; it would not have systematically destroyed private initiative and the elementary democratic right to collective bargaining between labor and management; and it would not have suppressed freedom of speech and of the press. It was the conscious degradation of the most elementary concepts of democratic freedoms that brought Fidel Castro into open conflict, first with the Cuban people. It followed as night follows day that a United States which also believes in democratic freedoms would be no less an enemy to Castro than the Cuban people themselves. This is the inevitability of a Communist revolution, not the revolution of "social justice" advertised by Castro's apologists, for the simple reason that a Communist revolution is made by *anti-social* elements whose regard for justice is perfectly seen in Castro's show trials, the violent suppression of Cuba's press, and in the intimidation of the individual by organs of the Communist police state. And those anti-social elements were the very tool Fidel Castro used to clamp Cuba in the vise of a Communist police state.

CHAPTER 8

CHAPTER 8

Morgan, Matos and "Our Pearl Harbor"

•

MEANWHILE, ALMOST LITERALLY "back at the ranch" in the cattle country of Camaguey Province, Major Huber Matos was asking a few questions about Communism. Soft spoken Matos, a teacher, had been one of the true heroes of the revolution. Point Four technicians from the American Embassy found him to be cooperative and intelligent, though socialist in his thinking. (His July 26 speech in Camaguey was certainly unfriendly to the United States.) One U.S. technician met with Matos and a group of his administrators to work out details of U.S. help in the building of schools in Camaguey, the Province under Matos' control. Significantly, as it turned out, one of the members of the group was Captain Jorge Enrique Mendoza Reboredo. According to the U.S. technician, Mendoza Reboredo was vocally opposed to any kind of cooperation with the United States, but was brusquely overruled by Matos.

According to the best information, Castro knew that Díaz-Lanz and Matos had been discussing Communist infiltration in the government. It was public knowledge that Matos, along with his friend Comandante Camilo Cienfuegos, had little use for Raúl Castro and "Che" Guevara. According to Díaz-Lanz, Matos refused to believe in the summer of 1959 that it was Fidel Castro who was directing the Communist take over of the country, saying to him in Camaguey one day that "Raúl and 'Che' are the Communists, not Fidel." Matos was sufficiently alarmed about Communism and about Castro's open attacks against the anti-Communist press, to take up the matter with Fidel Castro himself. The opportunity arose when Castro stopped off in Camaguey on his way to Manzanillo by plane. Matos later told Díaz-Lanz that he had, indeed, discussed Communist penetration with Castro and expressed his pleasure on receiving Castro's promise that all Communists would be removed from positions of power, including his own brother Raúl, "Che," Núñez

Jiménez, and Alfredo Guevara. The last named Guevara, incidentally, is not related to "Che," but it is of some significance that he was acknowledged by Fidel Castro himself to be a Communist. Alfredo Guevara had accompanied Fidel Castro to Bogotá for the Communist uprising there in 1948 and was put in charge of Cuba's film industry, including newsreels, when Castro came to power.

Worries about Communist infiltration in Castro's regime were reflected in yet another, and considerably more militant, quarter.

In late June, William Morgan surfaced again. I came home one evening to find a note from the maid, Zaida, saying that the well-known American Comandante "Weelyam Morgan" had called and asked me to telephone him at once. I did so, but with great reservations. By this time the dictatorship had progressed to the point where so-called key members of the Embassy were warned by the security officer that their phones had been tapped and that they be guided accordingly. Since, as Press Attaché, it was necessary for me to make some twelve telephone calls each night to the Ambassador, to the Minister-Counselor, and to others, I was inclined not to call Morgan. But the message from Zaida also said that the Morgan call was one "of life and death," so I phoned, to hear him whisper intensely: "Come to my house early tomorrow morning."

Morgan's residence differed but little from the houses of the other revolutionaries. Located at the corner of 66th street and 7th avenue in the swanky Miramar section of Havana, his house was sumptuous—confiscated from a *Batistiano*—and Morgan lived there in the comfort of the "new class." My car, of course, had diplomatic plates, so I parked it several blocks away and walked. I rang the doorbell and waited. The door opened just a slit, and through the slit emerged the muzzle of a rifle. A voice behind it asked me to identify myself. I did. It closed again for a few seconds, then was swiftly jerked open and, protesting, I was almost literally pulled over the threshhold by two fierce-looking bearded gents. Then Morgan appeared.

Dressed in his Rebel Army uniform, bearing the one-star rank of Comandante, (the highest rank in Castro's army) Morgan waved the sentries aside, greeting me like a long-lost brother. We walked over and around fifteen snoring *barbudos* stretched out in the living room and the hall of the house to a small, dark study.

Seating himself behind a desk, Morgan lighted a cigarette, offered me one, and reached into one of the drawers. He drew out several cans of what appeared to be tape for a tape recorder. "Do you know what that is?" he asked. I replied that I couldn't be certain, but that it looked like tape.

"This," said Morgan slowly and importantly, "is anti-Castro propaganda. We are broadcasting it to the Cuban people every night. Now, what do you think about that?"

What I thought of the conversation was to turn my back on Morgan and without a word walk out into the hallway. I turned around to see him sitting at the desk with his mouth open, staring at me. He spread his arms, and said, "What's the matter, chico?" I beckoned him to come out in the hall. He grinned and followed me into the hall.

"Listen, Willie," I said angrily, "whatever you have to say to me, or me to you, will be said in the wide open spaces, not in an office equipped with a tape recorder."

"You thought I was going to record you, eh?" Morgan chuckled. "Naw, I'm not interested in that. But it's your decision. C'mon, I want to show you something."

We walked out toward the back of the house, passing through a huge walk-in meat refrigerator. In the anteroom to the refrigerator, a sort of utility room, he had banks of portable AMPEX tape recorders. The rest of the walls were covered with sophisticated radio panels.

"Here," said Morgan, "is where we send out our propaganda." I said not one word.

We walked outside and I turned to look for roof-top antenna, and spotted a large directional television antenna. Nothing else. The garden in which we found ourselves was impressive, about half the size of a football field, with a large pool, cabañas and a bar at the end of it. It was quite a lay-out. I was thinking as rapidly as I could. Obviously, Morgan was still on the payroll of the Cuban government, though he claimed to be making anti-Castro broadcasts. The first point was a fact; the second, that he was making anti-Castro broadcasts, lacked proof.

Suddenly Morgan turned to me and said: "I have five thousand men, willing and able to fight against Communism." He went on: "Sure, Menoyo is the leader, but the boys follow men. Menoyo is also with us, though."

I stood there, for a moment, transfixed, then said, "What did you say?"

Morgan repeated what he had said before, grinning a little at my disbelief. He also claimed that he had "several hundred men in La Cabaña fortress, ready to go." "Che" Guevara, of course, was the commander of La Cabaña, and I questioned Morgan on this point.

"Don't worry," he said, plucking leaves off of one of the trees, chewing on them and them spitting them out, "I know what I'm doing."

"Well, since you've gone this far, Willie, you might as well tell me—exactly what are you doing?"

"Castro is a Communist, see," he said, "and we don't like Communists. I told you about this before. Well, we've been working to get our people into strategic spots." He chuckled: "One of them is secretary to 'Che'."

He also said he was trying to convince the government to organize a rural guard in the Sierra Escambray and put him in command. I asked who he was dealing with in these discussions and he answered: "Fidel." What did Castro think of the idea? Morgan didn't know.

Morgan then spoke with quiet intenseness. Resistance to Communism was growing by leaps and bounds, he said, and ticked off several commandantes and captains who "are with us." I hadn't heard most of the names, but took notes on a small pad which I carried around with me. Then I asked him what he wanted the Americans to do about it. "Plenty" he answered, "if you don't want Communism here." He then made the astonishing but apparently sincere statement that his forces, with adequate arms and ammunition, could overthrow Fidel Castro "within three days." This was indeed an eyebrow-lifter, I said, but what about public opinion? I asked. Would public opinion support him?

Morgan had a twig in his hand, broke it in half, then said: "That much for public opinion. What in hell did public opinion do in the fight against Batista, anyway?" I told him I thought it added quite a bit to his final downfall. But Morgan was not impressed.

Then I asked him just what he wanted of the Americans, and why he should assume that the U.S. government was willing to get behind a move to oust Castro. He said he "had been told." I told him frankly that I found no evidence to support what he had been told. He waved my comments aside with a conspiratorial wink and a nudge in the ribs, implying that both of us were adults and shouldn't play games with each other.

Morgan then came even more to the point. He said that hostilities might break out at any time, that he would be in the middle of those hostilities, and that he wanted a visa "right away" for his pregnant wife, a Cuban citizen. It really was difficult for me to tell whether he was using all that he told me as a buildup to get a visa or if he was driving at something else. I did tell Morgan that if his wife should receive preferential treatment in obtaining a visa, this would hardly go unnoticed among the Cuban personnel working in the consular section for the Embassy. I did not tell him that several of our employees were at that very moment undergoing a quiet investigation by the Embassy, on the suspicion that they were spying for the Castro regime—in some instances, trying to pave the way for visas for Cubans with suspicious records of adherence to Communism. This again brings up a point worth noting. We were investigating Embassy personnel on the suspicion that they were working for a Castro-Communist regime which we had yet to acknowledge was actually Communist.

In any case, regarding the visa for his wife, I said I would take it up with the proper authorities, but suggested that the safest path for his wife to follow was to apply for a tourist visa like any other Cuban, and then talk the situation over with immigration authorities once she was safe in Miami. He became a little nervous, wondering whether he had been wise to divulge "all this information" to me. I assured him that Embassy officers had no obligation to become a source of intelligence for the Cuban government. I also reminded him that, in view of what he had told me, I had taken considerable risk in even seeing him. So the score was even. When I left, I said that this would be the last occasion that he would talk to me. What he had volunteered in the way of information, I said, far exceeded my authority to be a party to. I did tell Morgan that he most probably would be contacted by another person who would use my name in making that contact, and left the house through Morgan's garden.

I went immediately to the Embassy, wrote a long memorandum of the conversation and gave it to the deputy chief of the CIA. We had a long conversation, during which he said he was not disposed to make contact with Morgan "just yet."

We all had reason to recall these discussions when, a few weeks later, mysterious rumors began to circulate that something was afoot which involved the Dominican Republic. Then, *La Calle*, a newspaper owned by a Castro government stooge, Luis Orlando Rodríguez, headlined a story that a conspiracy headed by dictator Rafael Leónidas Trujillo had been uncovered. On the day that the story broke, Fidel Castro was at the National Planning Office speaking with José Luís Díaz de Villegas on the development of plans being made for the American Society of Travel Agents to hold their annual convention in Havana in October— an explosive week, as it turned out.

The phone rang in Díaz de Villegas' office. It was for Prime Minister Castro, the speaker said. After listening for a few moments, Castro slammed down the receiver and, turning to a portion of the crowd (crowds followed him around wherever he went) he said: "Luis Orlando Rodríguez is a jackass!" He then telephoned his brother Raúl and his secretary, Celia Sánchez, ordering each of them to "kill the story" in *La Calle*. He immediately turned to Díaz de Villegas, saying with great relish (according to Díaz de Villegas,) that "a conspiracy is afoot." Castro left that night for the city of Trinidad on the south coast of Las Villas Province, leaving in the wake rumors of impending national disaster.

Despite his earlier protestations about not coming to the United States, William Morgan had indeed come to Miami. The official version, published in the magazine, *Bohemia*, is that in July Morgan met "an agent of dictator Rafael Leónidas Trujillo at the Dupont Plaza Hotel in Miami, receiving $100,000 in return for assisting Trujillo to invade Cuba." Acting as double agents, Morgan and Menoyo went so far as to lure well-known Cuban leaders into a plot to do away with Castro and to set up a "cabinet," which was to take over the country when Castro was overthrown. Apparently, my earlier caution in dealing with Morgan was wise, for the story published also added the spine-tingling information that his house had been elaborately equipped as "a counterrevolutionary headquarters."

Working with Castro in the bizarre plot, said the story, Morgan and Menoyo lured the "counterrevolutionary cabinet" to Morgan's house there to be confronted by Fidel Castro. At 9:30 that evening of August 6th, the story went on, Fidel Castro walked in and introduced himself to Arturo Hernández Tellaheche (who, the government had it, had been tabbed by the counterrevolutionaries to be "President"), along with Armando Caíñas Milanés, Ramón Mestre, and others. All were immediately clapped into jail. It was following this confrontation that Menoyo reportedly preceded Castro to Trinidad and established radio contact with the "invasion force" in the Dominican Republic that was to have overthrown the revolutionary regime.

It is here that the credibility of the government version breaks down. According to that version, a transport plane was lured from the Dominican Republic to land at the airport of Trinidad with a dozen "counterrevolutionaries" aboard. This was the "invasion" force which Castro claimed was charged with overthrowing his regime. Called the "banyan tree invasion," because Fidel Castro calmly awaited the "invaders" seated under a banyan tree, the force would never have had a chance.

Looking as much like Jehovah as possible, the by now obese Prime Minister sat before the television cameras in a Havana studio on August 14th and "judged" the invaders. Among them were the son of the former Mayor of Havana, Luis Pozo, also Pedro Rivera, a Roberto Pérez, and a Spanish mercenary by the name of Alfredo Malibrán. Unimpressed by Castro, Malibrán gave as good as he took from the bearded Prime Minister, and was whisked away from the cameras.

Ambassador Bonsal sat in the Embassy penthouse, his eyes glued to the television set. When the rumors had begun to fly a week earlier that something was afoot, the CIA had apparently suspected Morgan as being involved in the "plot," and had told Mr. Bonsal about it. My contacts with Morgan were also revealed, and the memorandum I had written about my encounter with him was also brought into the discussion. What made the Ambassador very edgy about the performance unfolding on the television screen was that the star witnesses for Castro as he "judged" the "invaders" in the name of the Cuban people were none other than Eloy Gutiérrez Menoyo and William Morgan. From time to time, the cameras were turned on them. They had shaved off their beards and sat on the floor of the studio with their legs folded under them, looking pleased as punch when the "Maximum Leader" singled them out for praise in frustrating an invasion of *"nuestra patria."* They beamed when Castro also said that the two of them had been given a reward of $100,000 and had donated it to the agrarian reform.

Ambassador Bonsal was certain that Castro would attack the United States, saying that the United States, through its Press Attaché, had been implicated in the plot. The CIA chief differed. Such an accusation would be difficult, if not impossible, for Castro to prove. He also took the view that, in making such an accusation, Castro would invite a break in relations with the United States, and coolly observed that, in view of growing internal resistance, Castro must be aware that a break with the United States at that time might topple his regime. As it turned out, our CIA chief was right. Morgan and Menoyo apparently had said nothing about their contacts with the American Embassy for the simple reason that they had not stopped plotting against Castro. What happened is that Morgan learned that certain of his activities had come to the attention of Castro. In typical Castro fashion, the Prime Minister telephoned Morgan, asking him what was going on. On the basis of all the available evidence we at the Embassy concluded that Morgan flipped completely over, and told Castro that he was acting as a double agent. Appealing to Castro's flare for the dramatic, as well as to his injured pride following the humiliating Cuban failure to topple Trujillo, Morgan brought the Prime Minister in on the plot, saved his own hide and that of Gutiérrez Menoyo, and decided to fight another day. It is probable that nothing was said by Morgan about his Embassy contacts, for Castro never once mentioned anything about them in any of his subsequent tirades against the United States.

Several months after the "invasion," *Bohemia* magazine published a picture story of Morgan developing a frog farm. His plan, according to reports, was to develop various kinds of products from frog skins— wallets, cigarette cases, and the like. Morgan ran the farm with labor supplied by the National Institute of Agrarian Reform, and the Communist management of INRA infiltrated its spies into the labor force to keep an eye on the burly American. No lily-white character himself, Morgan nevertheless was appalled by the excesses of the Communists located in high places, including the torture and execution of some of the men who had fought with Menoyo and him in the Escambray mountains. He gathered about him a body guard of trusted followers and with them ran his frog farm with the discipline of a military camp. Some mornings he would line up the laborers in military formation and, according to his friend, Comandante Lázaro Asencio, would shout: "I hate all Communists! They work for Russia, not for Cuba. All of you who are Communists and work for Russia take one step forward!" None, of course, did.

But Morgan kept the Communists from taking over his state-run frog farm, a feat that should have been emulated in other sectors of the Cuban government.

It was about this time that Army Chief of Staff, Comandante Juan Almeida, was married. Called to attend a meeting at INRA, Morgan had a woman's bag made of frog skins as a wedding present for Almeida's wife, and took the gift to Almeida at his office there. He left his body guard at the frog farm. As Morgan entered Almeida's office, he was immediately seized, disarmed, and jailed. The following day, a very small notice appeared in *Revolucion*, announcing that "Comandante William Morgan had been using military trucks under his command illegally to transport food and ammunition into the Escambray mountains," and had been arrested and jailed for counterrevolutionary activities.

From all accounts, Morgan comported himself admirably in dreaded La Cabaña prison. A man of enormous physical strength, he refused to vegetate. Up at dawn, he would put himself through calisthenics, then march around the compound shouting commands at himself. One would never have guessed from Morgan's self-discipline in La Cabaña that he had spent most of his American military service as a prisoner in the Federal Reformatory at Chillicothe, Ohio, and rounded it out in the Federal Reformatory in Milan, Michigan, for escape, robbery and A. W. O. L. from the Army of the United States. The final months of Morgan's life in La Cabaña are vividly portrayed by fellow inmate John Martino in his book, *I Was Castro's Prisoner*.[1] The Martino-Morgan conversations throw considerable light on the personality and ambitions of William Morgan. In any event, William Morgan marched to his summary trial, singing: "As the Caissons go Rolling Along." At 2:30 a.m. one day in February, 1961, Fidel and Raúl Castro attended his execution by firing squad. As his hands were being tied behind his back, an unidentified voice in the shadows of the lights beamed on Morgan shouted: "Kneel and beg for your life!" Morgan shouted back: "I kneel for no man!" But, they used a sharp-shooter, not a firing squad, to kill him. First, a bullet was put through one knee, then one through the other. As Morgan crashed to the ground cursing the Communists, the same unidentified voice from the shadows exulted: "There! You see, we made you kneel!" The rifleman put another bullet through one of Morgan's shoulders. He took his time putting a bullet through the other, prolonging the agony of his victim. Then, a captain walked up to Morgan and emptied a clip from his Tommy gun into his chest. That is how William Morgan died.

To return to 1959—in October of that year, Castro weathered an explosion that nearly toppled him from power. A popular commander, Huber Matos, was waiting impatiently for Fidel Castro to make good on his promise to throw the Communists out of power. What he saw, instead, was that same Fidel Castro putting Communists in power. Matos also found that what Manuel Artime had reported in his remarkable memorandum had come true. The Agrarian Reform Institute was indeed a super-state, and it was being run by Communists in Matos' own province of Camaguey. He questioned the creation of "People's Stores," because he knew that the charges against private ownership which led to the establishment of those stores were not true. He concluded that the reasons given were simply another screen for Communist penetration. When Matos objected, however, he found that the INRA captain in Camaguey Province, Enrique Mendoza Reboredo, had more actual power than he, supposedly Mendoza's chief. On top of this revelation came another. Some of his officers were being pressed into attending the El Cortijo school for Communist indoctrination, and from there being shipped to camps for guerrilla training, in preparation to their later becoming instructors to Latin American recruits.

Anticipating the results of the CTC conference scheduled the next month, on October 21 Matos decided to resign. In a letter to Fidel Castro, he said, "No one can talk to you about the Communist issue," but added, "I do not want to become an obstacle to the Revolution, and believing that I must choose between adapting myself or going into a corner in order not to create damage, the honest and revolutionary thing to do is go. . . ." But Matos could not "go" so easily. As in the case of reporters who were forced to be completely and abjectly *for* the Revolution, Matos found that he could not just resign, any more than Communists can turn in their party cards and forget all about it. Having differed with the regime, and having differed with Castro and his Communist friends, Matos had to be destroyed. And again it was Fidel Castro who did the destroying.

Matos' timing could not have been worse. Hundreds of members of the American Society of Travel Agents were conventioning in Havana. And on the day of his resignation, Pedro Luis Díaz-Lanz flew from Florida to Havana, dropping leaflets to the Cuban people warning that the Communists were taking over the country. The Díaz-Lanz flight was made at a very low altitude, so low that Dwight Martin, the new bureau chief for *Time* magazine, and I were able to see the plane from the balcony of one of the "hospitality" suites of the Havana Hilton. We were on the twenty-second floor. Standing talking to some Latin Americans, Dwight and I watched a plane fly erratically at low altitude down Línea Street, then zoom up over the hotel. He laughed and said: "This conference is really organized. Rum and punch on the balcony, and tourist leaflets dropping overhead."

There were at least two and possibly three, Castro informers with us at the time. When the news broke about Huber Matos' resignation, such informers were immediately assigned the task of talking to the delegations and explaining the Huber Matos incident, thus doubling as propagandists. The line they took was that "we revolutionaries still have some elements of the old order in our midst, trying to steal money from the people, and Fidel of course has to see that they are brought to justice . . ." and similar tripe. The next day, of course, the story changed. They then "clarified" the arrest, saying it had been found that Matos had worked with Díaz-Lanz in the "bombing" of Havana the day before. They laid great stress on the fact that the aircraft had come from the United States, but had little to say when one or two spirited American travel agents pointed out that Castro himself had received his support by planes from the United States. Still later, they had an answer for that. Planes supporting Castro from the United States never "criminally bombed defenseless Cuban people." This last excuse was given to them by Castro himself, who had taken to television and the airwaves to make the accusation.

At the moment of the "bombing," however, Dwight and I were busy trying to grab one of the many leaflets which were floating in our direction. Dwight finally got one—dropping his rum and soda twenty-two stories in the overreach—and he put it in his pocket. We had noticed that some of the informers had managed to get copies and were stuffing them in their pockets; one female informer had her bag filled with them before we left. Dwight took his out of his pocket and I translated it for him quickly. He took notes. Just then, one of the informers came up and held out his hand.

"I'll take that please," he said.

"What for?" I asked, folding the leaflet and putting it in my pocket.

"I'm security officer of the hotel," he replied very unconvincingly. I knew, and he knew that I knew, that he was no such thing.

"Sorry, there's nothing in here that involves the security of the hotel," and I showed him my Foreign Office Identification Card. He looked disconcerted for a moment, and I thanked him quickly and made my way out of the suite to the elevator. As I did so, I could hear cannon fire, was of a notion to go back and see what was happening, but then decided to go.

I did so, arriving at the Embassy by cab. Cannon fire continued. Rolling his eyes, the frightened cab driver wheeled his car into the Embassy parking lot, and turned on the radio to get a second-hand rather than an eye-witness account of what was happening. The Ambassador was out, and I gave the leaflet to Dan Braddock, who immediately sent it to Washington by teletype.

The Díaz-Lanz flight was made-to-order for Castro and, incidentally, for Communist propagandists. In an unbelievable story, *Revolucion* ran pictures of Cubans running into the street, collecting the leaflets, and burning them "in spontaneous public indignation." Castro was enraged that anti-Communists could, with impunity, fly over Cuban soil, just as Fulgencio Batista was indignant when the United States was the principal base of supply for Fidel Castro. The difference was in the handling of the matter. Batista complained through diplomatic channels. Knowing from experience how effective that base was and enraged that anti-Castroism and anti-Communism had reached such daring proportions, Castro took the propaganda offensive. In doing so, the bearded dictator this time reached another point—the point of no return in relations with the United States. For, from that moment forward, anyone who had the slightest thought that the United States "could do business with Castro" truly needed to have his head examined.

Having tried to establish that those who fled Cuba were all "war criminals," and having been successful in selling this line to the "losers," Castro baldly classified Díaz-Lanz as a "war criminal," and then sought to produce evidence that would support his charge. "War criminals," Castro charged over television, "had bombed innocent Cuban citizens" in the "attack" on Havana. While it was true that many Cubans had been wounded when Díaz-Lanz flew over the city, the fact is that they had been wounded by Cuban anti-aircraft fire. Police chief Efigenio Ameijeiras knew this to be the case. To cover it up, he put out a statement from the police headquarters the same day, saying that people had been wounded by "terrorists who threw bombs from speeding cars."

This explanation did not, of course, satisfy Castro's needs. On television, Castro charged that Cuba had been "bombed." He simply overwhelmed the real issue—that Cuba's troubles stemmed from political instability brought about by his own regime, in which differences of opinion had no peaceful or parliamentary channels by which they might be aired and resolved. It was not remarkable that Castro's opponents, like his own supporters less than a year earlier, had based themselves in Florida. He said, however, that the United States was harboring "war criminals," just as it was harboring the "blood-sucking imperialists" who exploit the poor. The responsibility for the wounded was, therefore, that of his enemy, the United States. He called a mass assembly to be held on October 26.

Within days, the public relations department of the Ministry of Foreign Affairs issued a scurrilously worded pamphlet, claiming that the leaflet drop by Díaz-Lanz "is Our Pearl Harbor." It stated that two dead and 45 wounded Cubans "were felled by the shrapnel of the plane." Gruesome pictures of wounded men, women, and children, allegedly tortured and slain by Batista's henchmen, were displayed alongside pictures of those henchmen. Side-by-side with these pictures were photos of those receiving medical treatment following the Díaz-Lanz flight. The message was clear: Batista is a war criminal, his henchmen are war criminals, and here are pictures of what they did. War criminals have found asylum in the United States, and here is what Díaz-Lanz did. Ergo, the enemy of the Cuban people is the United States.

But, what is said about these turbulent events by Castro's apologists? In their book, *Cuba, Anatomy of a Revolution*, Messrs. Huberman and Sweezy accept the Castro-Communist propaganda, reporting "the bombing of the capital city by Florida-based planes."[2] Of Matos, they say that he "had been arrested, along with a number of other officers, for conspiring against the regime." Huberman and Sweezy smear Matos by saying, without any substantiating facts, that he was "reputed to have had large personal ambitions. The arguments which he and his fellow oppositionists advanced were based on the by-now familiar charge that Communists were gaining control of the government."

What conspiracy was Matos accused of? What type of conspiracy could it be that prompted him merely to hand in a letter of resignation, only to be destroyed for doing so. And what about the toppling by Castro of the President of the Republic precisely over the issue of "the by-now familiar charge" of Communism in the government? Had those gentlemen not heard about Mr. Urrutia, about the Journalists' Guild, about the CTC conference?

The State Department sent a very strong note of protest to the American Embassy in Havana refuting Castro's charges of "bombing," and ordered the Ambassador to deliver it *before* Castro spoke on October 26th. The note was intended to put the Cuban Prime Minister on notice that he would be well advised to look before he lied. For the first time since Castro came to power, Washington was disposed to take the initiative and showed every outward intention of holding it.

The note was blunt and to the point. It said that the plane which flew over Havana dropping leaflets, an old B-26, had been found at a Florida airstrip. Its bomb racks had been fitted with permanent luggage racks, and the bomb-bay doors of the plane were sealed. Old machine-gun ports had also been sealed, said the note, since the plane had apparently been used by one or another firm for flying commercial cargo. A careful examination of the areas in which people were wounded disclosed that the plane had not flown anywhere near there. What had happened was that anti-aircraft gunners at La Cabaña fortress, located on a promontory overlooking the city, had fired down at the low-flying aircraft, missed, and struck civilians in Havana. Though the note didn't say so in its original version, it strongly suggested that the dropping of leaflets over Havana was child's play compared to the delivery of arms and ammunition to Castro's forces from Florida less than a year earlier. Later, in fact, Castro's Consul in Miami confirmed that the plane used by Díaz-Lanz actually belonged to Fidel Castro. In 1958, the B-26 had been used to shuttle arms to Castro in the Sierra Maestra. Sheepishly, the Consul took possession of the plane in the name of its owner—the Revolutionary Government of Cuba.

In sending the note to the Embassy for delivery, the State Department wanted to put Castro on the defensive. His accusations at the time of the leaflet drop had caused considerable damage to American prestige abroad. To leave those charges unanswered *before* his blast, scheduled for October 26th, would, it was believed, represent tacit admission of U.S. guilt.

The point of no-return had been reached. Either Castro righted his course or we were prepared to do everything necessary to protect our interests and those of the hemisphere. In effect, delivery of the note before October 26th was to put Castro on notice that this was his last chance to live up to his propaganda cries of desiring to have good relations with the United States. If he proceeded with his monstrous charges on October 26th, the Rubicon would have been crossed. Presumably, we were prepared to use our sugar quotas, the defense Pact of Río de Janeiro, and anything else needed to protect the United States.[3]

But the noble stand taken by the State Department was undercut by the American Embassy in Havana where Ambassador Bonsal boggled at the thought of delivering such a strong and specific note to Castro. By doing so, he said, he would further infuriate an already infuriated Prime Minister. The Ambassador set about rewriting the note in an effort to tone it down. He also strongly recommended that the note be delivered *after* Castro spoke. For, his argument went, if Castro was not planning to attack the United States, the U.S. note would have given him the opportunity to do so. This surrealistic logic was received unhappily in Washington, but after precious days had been lost in the Washington-Embassy exchange, the State Department caved in.

Mr. Bonsal's recommendations cut the very guts out of the position which the State Department wanted to assume in the first place. Instead of delivering the note to the Cuban government in Havana, in a precipitate retreat all along the line, it was finally agreed that the note would be delivered by the State Department to the emissary of that government in Washington—the Cuban Ambassador. Ambassador Bonsal would merely follow-up in Havana, dropping off a copy as a courtesy to the government to whom he was accredited. Yet, in an attack as grave as that made by Castro on the United States, the answer should be made at the source of that attack—the Cuban government itself.

This, then, was the defeatist atmosphere in which seven of us met in the penthouse of the American Embassy on October 26th. With a portable television set on the conference table, and several translators from the political section prepared to send almost simultaneous transmission of Castro's speech to Washington by coded teletype messages, we sat and waited. I held the draft note in my hands—the only copy made. My staff of translators and mimeograph operators waited downstairs to get to work. They could not do so, of course, until the Ambassador had given the okay.

We watched in late afternoon as the mobs began to gather in front of the Presidential Palace—300,000 people. Leading figures in the government began to arrive on the balcony in twos and threes, including Communist Osvaldo Dorticós who had been elevated to the Presidency when Urrutia was demolished by Fidel Castro over the issue of Communism. Even Gutiérrez Menoyo and William Morgan were present, though they had not been seen since August. The crowds swelled, banners appeared, reading: "We Want Political Prisoners Shot!" "Fidel! Shoot the Traitors!", and similar holiday messages.

To the surprise of many, Camilo Cienfuegos arose and spoke harshly of the United States, thus breaking a long silence. He seldom spoke at public gatherings. He had been considered by most Cubans and Americans as friendly to the United States, and to have democratic convictions as well. However that may be, there was a practically unanimous agreement later that Cienfuegos spoke that day, in the manner that he did, in frank fear for his life.

Sent to arrest Huber Matos only a few days earlier, Cienfuegos had refused to accept an order from Raúl Castro to do so. Fidel finally had to give the order, and tracked him down at the Havana Riviera Hotel to do so. His refusal to obey Raúl also had in it a black hatred for the Prime Minister's younger brother. On one occasion, the two had come to blows. The incident, related by an officer who was present, came about when Raúl Castro entered the makeshift quarters of Cienfuegos, finding him sitting shirtless behind a desk. Raúl sneered, saying: "Why don't you take off your pants, too?" Cienfuegos struck the younger Castro, knocking him across the room. As Castro drew his pistol, Cienfuegos pounced on him. The two men were dragged apart by other Rebel Army officers.

In any event, when Cienfuegos went to arrest Matos, he stayed talking with him in Agramonte Barracks in the city of Camaguey for some time. Cienfuegos arrived there at 8:00 a. m. Fidel Castro himself arrived two hours later, it is believed at the suggestion of brother Raúl who considered the Matos incident to be serious, indeed, to the point of doubting whether Cienfuegos would even arrest Matos. The possibility of the defection of the popular cowboy-hatted Cienfuegos over the issue of Communism had been suggested by more than one foreign Embassy in Havana.*

When Castro arrived unexpectedly in Camaguey, he went to the Provincial office of the Agrarian Reform Institute, there to hear Captain Enrique Mendoza Reboredo accuse Matos of treason. Inciting the mobs to come out into the streets, Castro joined them in a scene carried over the nation's television cameras—a scene as ridiculous as it was frightening. He ran from one side of the street to the other, gesticulating like a madman and urging the people "to march on Agramonte Barracks, the edifice of the *Batistianos*," where Matos sat talking quietly with his captor. "The people will march on the barracks!" Castro shouted. At one point, Cienfuegos emerged from Agramonte Barracks and fought his way through the crowds to Castro. There he told the Prime Minister that Matos had surrendered, implying there was no need for a mob scene. Irritation showed plainly on his face when he faced the television cameras.

Castro went to the barracks where, alongside Captain Enrique Mendoza Reboredo, he launched a tirade against Matos. The specifics of the charges were lost in his oratory. He did say that Matos was self-serving and "in the pay of the imperialists." With that, Fidel Castro returned to Havana, there to be faced with another embarrassment—the over-flight of Pedro Díaz-Lanz.

Cienfuegos must have seen that even those closest to Fidel Castro could not count on his loyalty or friendship—Matos, Lorié, Sotus, Urrutia, Díaz-Lanz. Indeed, closeness made the individual even more vulnerable to attack from a Prime Minister who preferred the comfort of the faceless and nameless mobs from whom no meaningful challenge to his authority could be made.

In Havana, after the speeches by Cienfuegos, and other minor dignitaries, Fidel Castro approached the microphone amid the shouts of the multitude. In the Embassy penthouse, with the volume of the television set turned up, Ambassador Bonsal and the rest of us inched forward on our chairs, for the political judgment of the Embassy was at stake in what Castro would say. We did not have long to wait. Castro said: "American territory serves as the base for planes which drop leaflets and bombs on our contry." White-faced, Ambassador Bonsal softly muttered an oath. "Why," asked Castro impudently, "is there the tolerance of the Ameri-

---

*U.S. intelligence actually managed to plant a tape recorder in Matos' office through the cooperation of officers loyal to Matos. The quality of the taped conversation between Matos and Cienfuegos was so bad, however, that only unrevealing snatches of words could be heard. I listened to the tape and had my radio technicians try everything to amplify the conversation, to no avail.

can authorities" to the "bombings?" "Since there is no reason to accuse the Revolutionary Government of anything else," he said, "they accuse us of being Communists."

In the absence of any response from the United States, the man who accused the United States of "bombing" Cuba pushed us into a corner by saying that the American government had accused Cuba of being Communist! Castro's cynicism knew no bounds on October 26, 1959. Weaving his lies into a catchall web to entrap his enemies, he extended the attack against the United States to Cuba's press, specifically mentioning the *Diario de la Marina* and *Avance* as "equally culpable . . . as those [the United States] who drop bombs on us. . . ."

Castro also re-established the Revolutionary Tribunals whose "justice" had so alienated the thinking Cuban as to force their suspension. "Those who are in agreement with re-establishing Revolutionary Tribunals," Castro shouted, "raise their hands!" Hands were raised. "Those who raised their hands," roared Castro, "believe that those who invade our country deserve to be shot; those who raised their hands believe that those who fly planes over our territory deserve the death penalty; those who raised hands believe that traitors like Huber Matos deserve the death penalty. . . ." The law of terror was "ratified" that night through the extraordinary process of "direct democracy."

Also that night as Castro raved, another vote was being registered. Cuba's burgeoning resistance movement "voted" against his regime by hurling a bomb into the offices of *Revolucion*, wounding a Francisco Nunez in the left leg as he was about to enter. Two more bombs also were exploded in the Havana suburb of Marianao. Castro responded with his apparatus of terror. In less than one year, the Cuban dictator had trod the same path taken by Fulgencio Batista eight years earlier. The difference was that Castro had the protection of "professional liberals" in this country, a powerful propaganda machine, an organization of armed mobs, and the determination to use all of them ruthlessly.

For example, Castro made claims that he was converting military barracks into schools, and the amount of propaganda turned out on this fetching theme appeared in many accounts written in this country about the Revolution. But, quite the opposite was happening. Castro was turning the schools into barracks by arming students and calling them "student militia," and telling youngsters that their duty was to "bring the Revolution into your homes." At a ceremony which allegedly turned Camp Columbia into a school, Castro spoke to the youngsters as follows: "If those in your house speak badly of the revolution, it is your duty to speak well of the Revolution." This was the beginning of a school-taught campaign by which children not only "spoke well of the revolution," but also informed on their own parents when they spoke "badly" of that Revolution.

Castro was no less ruthless with dissenting members of the American press. Attempts were made to intimidate the late Jules Dubois, Latin American correspondent for the *Chicago Tribune*, and Chairman of the Freedom of the Press Committee of the Inter-American Press Association. Dubois had been leading the fight for press freedoms in Cuba. He was recognized by informers as he was leaving the telegraph office and was surrounded and insulted by street gangs. The Communist-controlled hotel workers' and waiters' unions refused to transport him by elevator to his room in the Havana Hilton, or to serve him food in the hotel restaurant. The Revolutionary Tribunals also suggested that he be harassed in every way possible, including the cutoff of his overseas phone calls.

Back at the Embassy penthouse, an angry and shaken Ambassador Bonsal gave the word for me to go ahead and prepare the note for him to deliver to the Foreign Ministry, and to release it to the press. I took my copy pencil and started to write "Note of Protest delivered . . ." and got no further. The Ambassador took the pencil from my hand, saying angrily, "I'm not protesting. You don't have this thing right!" There was silence among the two or three of us still in the penthouse as he continued: "What I am delivering is the *copy* of a note which, when I deliver it, has already been placed in the hands of the Cuban Ambassador in Washington." I said, "Yes, but it *is* a note of protest, Mr. Ambassador. We have to call it something!" The Ambassador then said: "Don't put anything on it in the way of a title. Just have it translated and prepared."

As it turned out, there was even further delay. Castro's speech made the draft note obsolete. Having studied the speech as it was transmitted simultaneously, the State Department went to work on another draft.[4] It was not completed and delivered by the State Department to the Cuban Ambassador for many days, for reasons having to do with the sudden disappearance of Camilo Cienfuegos and with many indications it might be murder.

The press office of the General Headquarters of the Army broadcast a brief announcement the night of October 28 that a plane, identified as bi-motor belonging to the Cuban air force, had disappeared with Camilo Cienfuegos aboard. With him were the pilot and a soldier. That day, Fidel Castro and President Dorticós were seen conspicuously riding around the city in, of all things, a public bus, followed by mobs of Castro admirers.

With the announcement of the disappearance of Cienfuegos, Castro himself took command of the search, in the midst of a public uproar that rivaled his most successful public addresses. Television cameras dwelt on the Prime Minister frantically flying to Camaguey and Oriente Provinces, dramatically calling off the regularly scheduled flights of the Cuban Aviation Company and pressing the planes into the search. Castro was everywhere, monopolizing the television cameras, the radio waves, and headlines of the newspapers. He was shown in the map room of Air Force headquarters, looking at overlays of the area where the missing plane was last seen. He brought the father and mother of Camilo into the search and posed for heroic pictures of the three of them, eyes shaded by their hands, looking upward into the skies.

Castro brought pilots together before television cameras in the studios of CMQ where, with map overlays tacked-up on the wall, and with pointer in hand, he quizzed each of them as to where they searched, often answering his own questions before the pilots had a chance to reply. He also led them to a conclusion which he put into their mouths. The conclusion was that the plane, with insufficient fuel aboard, had gone North over the ocean to escape clouds, got lost and crashed into the sea.

Few believed Castro. Pilots in the area, in particular one on the Pan American flight which went from Florida to Camaguey city, reported to Miami that there were no clouds. The sky was not overcast; on the contrary, there was virtually unlimited visibility. The newspaper, *El Mundo,* published a photo of Camilo Cienfuegos, without his beard, asking that if he was identified to notify Cuban Army headquarters. The photo had been issued by the army, specifically by a comrade of Cienfuegos, Comandante Cristino Naranjo Vázquez. There were mutters around Havana, and among the members of Cienfuegos' old command who had fought with him in the hills of Cuba for two years, that the Communists might have done away with him. This explained the release of the picture, and the caption asking that if he was identified, to notify Army headquarters.

Then, Comandante Naranjo Vázquez himself was killed in what *Revolucion* described as "an unfortunate accident." Cienfuegos' comrade was entering Camp Columbia by car when it was intercepted by another bearing captains Beaton* and Domingo Ramos. Revolución said that Comandante Naranjo Vázquez and his two companions were dressed in civilian clothes, and that they were stopped by Beaton and Ramos and asked to produce their identification cards. "Unfortunately," said the newspaper account, "Beaton and Ramos opened fire on them, causing the lamentable deaths of the three officials."

Dictatorships arise out of such "accidents." Further, it seems inconceivable that Comandante Naranjo Vázquez, who shared quarters with other Rebel officers at Camp Columbia, and who was well-known because he usually was with Camilo Cienfuegos, would not be recognized. It also is inconceivable that other officers would, without cause, open fire on all three occupants of the car. In closing the chapter on the disappear-

*Beaton, in fear for his life for what he knew, defected and went into the mountains of Oriente. Castro labelled him "counterrevolutionary" and had his troops track him down.

ance of Cienfuegos, Fidel Castro himself brought up differences between the popular comandante and his own, unpopular, brother Raúl, innocently asking on television: "Where did information about those differences come from, anyway?" No one chose, of course, to step forward and give a bill of particulars. Pointedly, however, Castro lost no time in appointing politically reliable comandante Juan Almeida as Army chief to replace Cienfuegos, and in pointedly lauding his "loyalty" at the time of appointment.

It was not until November 9 that Assistant Secretary of State Roy Rubottom delivered the U.S. note of protest to Cuban Ambassador Ernesto Dihigo in Washington. By that time, it had all the effect of an Alka Seltzer dropped in the middle of the Pacific Ocean. The note read, among other things, that the United States found charges that it was responsible for the alleged bombing and machine-gunning of Cuban citizens in Havana, "to be malicious, inexact, leading to erroneous conclusions." It did not hold the Cuban government responsible for the charges, with the warning that unless those charges were publicly withdrawn, the United States would take appropriate action.

The Cuban Foreign Ministry did not deign to answer the note until November 13, and even then Ambassador Bonsal was subjected to a fifteen minute lecture by an Under Secretary. The Foreign Minister did not consider the U.S. note important enough to bother himself with it!

Even the "moderates" in Castro's government were no longer needed as a screen for Communism. Democratic-Leftist Felipe Pazos was replaced as President of Cuba's National Bank by non-banker and non-economist "Che" Guevara, causing a virtual panic in the business community. A story made the rounds in Havana to the effect that Castro told a group of his confidants that those among them who were economists should raise their hands. "Che" raised his. "Good," Castro said, "you are now President of Cuba's National Bank, the economist in charge of the financial destiny of our country." "Che" looked blank for a moment, the story goes on, then answered: "Oh, I thought you said Communist, not economist!"

Properties were being seized on all sides, with the Castro regime hardly taking time to publish grounds for the seizures. Because of the general turmoil, it almost passed notice when INRA chief Antonio Núñez Jiménez announced on December 8 that the government had put into operation 485 cooperatives (which Fidel Castro had announced from the mountains a year before would never be created). Some 400 "people's stores" were established (which was also unthinkable barely six months earlier). Four fishing fleets, comprising 430 boats, which had been operating as fishing cooperatives under a truly cooperative arrangement, were seized and placed under the Institute of Agrarian Reform.

When resistance to the wholesale government stealing of houses and apartments was encountered, Castro answered charges of Communism with reverse-English charges of "McCarthyism." He said of resistance, sometimes fierce resistance indeed, that "everyone knows that owners say that the Agrarian Reform is the most Communist in the world. When we lowered rents, house and apartment owners said that this was Communism and commenced to desert the country . . . priests are deserting, and what do they charge? They accuse us of being Communist, and cannot be representatives of Christ, or the truth, but are representatives of crime." His was not a "radical revolution," said Castro, "but a social revolution." And when "Che" Guevara was named President of the National Bank, Castro said, he was "astonished to see people who had money take it out of the bank." That didn't really matter, he said, "because we are going to print new money." New money was printed, and Guevara debased it by signing the currency with the name "Che," something like having our bills signed "Chuck," or "Nellie" by our Treasurer. Said Castro: "He who calls Guevara a radical is a tremendous Communist himself." And so on. And his lies and distortions were enshrined in the prose of the American "losers."

Thus Mr. Matthews finds the appointment of Guevara as President of Cuba's National Bank quite reasonable. After all, argues Mr. Matthews, there are no "revolutionary bankers," so why not Guevara?[5] A Czech commission paid a call on President Dorticós and gave him some "revolutionary" advice, for which Dorticós gave them heartfelt thanks in return. Said Miluso Goppoldova to Cuba's President: "In our country we carried out an agrarian reform, but did so after we were liberated in 1948, as you were liberated this year. . . ."

To the surprise of practically no one, elections for the presidency of the medical association of Oriente Province resulted in the victory of a military man—Captain Oscar Fernández Mel, a Communist. The Commercial Employees Union met and voted in Havana, also putting into power a Castro militiaman. Castro himself spoke at the election meeting and warned the assembled union members not to read *Diario de la Marina*, marking it for destruction which was to follow, because, he said: "There are two types of people—those who read *Diario de la Marina*, and those who sincerely believe in the Revolution." He also gave them a lesson in revolutionary economics and justice: "Those who take money out of the bank, well, they overlook the fact that it is just paper, and we can make new paper money." He went on: "We have the phrase that the customer is always right. That is true except when the customer attacks the Revolution."

At that meeting of the Commercial Employees Union, held at the Blanquita Theater on December 21, 1959, Castro outlined his rule of "Revolutionary terror." He said: "Now, no one can go to Miami, can they? They cannot go because when they go to the National Bank for dollars we don't give it to them." Cubans were trapped in one huge vast concentration camp—Cuba. Those who want to live in Cuba, said Castro "have to keep an eye on suspicious automobiles, keep an eye on landowners, keep an eye on counter-revolutionaries." More important, he said, is that when anything "suspicious" is encountered "by any Cuban, then he must go to the nearest police station and denounce those acting suspiciously."

The government revealed that in one year it had expropriated property amounting to the staggering figure of $354 million—one of the great mass robberies in modern history. It is noteworthy that of the total—which the government said it had distributed to various sections of what was clearly a state economy—education received only a half-million dollars, compared with $30 million for "tourism" and $3 million for the movie industry. The "tourist" money went into guerrilla training camps through a shift to a "general purpose" budget in the Office of the Prime Minister. The "movie industry" was *Prensa Latina,* Castro's propaganda arm! Castro himself was given a personal checking account from the Institute of Agrarian Reform amounting to $20 million. "Revolutionary bankers" have little respect for public moneys, or so it would seem.

Indoctrination was given the highest priority. With Huber Matos out of the way, the San Suspiro farm in Camaguey Province was taken over and began to operate as the Communist indoctrination center for rebel soldiers in central Cuba. Another was established near the Susset farm in Pinar del Río Province, and the government blocked off large areas near the town of Remedios in Las Villas Province and the Caves of Purio in the center of the Province. In each of these areas, government officials and soldiers came and went without divulging to curious villagers anything beyond saying that their activities were related to "defense of the *patria.*"

Typical Communist diatribe came out of Cuba when Guatemala charged in the OAS that a guerrilla campaign was being prepared against her "supported by the Cuban government, and with the consent of Raúl Castro and Ernesto Guevara." Dorticós merely turned the story around, saying: "Our government is well aware of the activities being carried out by Cuban counter-revolutionaries on Guatemalan territory, without the Guatemalan government paying the slightest attention to those activities." He scorned Guatemala, saying that the Cuban people would not appeal to the OAS for protection against the alleged invasion of Cuba, and said that Cuba would protect itself.

Following a clamor in *Revolucion* and *Hoy,* the Cuban government "acceded to the will of the people" and agreed that the Russians, who had made the request, would hold an industrial exhibit in Cuba. The release to the press said that the exhibit would be open to the public in February." It was "thought" that Soviet Vice Minister Anastas Mikoyan would also come along for the opening.

That same month of December, Ambassador Bonsal and his wife went to Washington where Mr. Bonsal had a series of serious high-level conferences with the State Department and with members of the White House staff. The rush of events could not be ignored. Soviet personnel were coming to Cuba quite openly at the time, under various excuses. One excuse, of course, was to prepare for the Soviet industrial exhibit. There were others too numerous to mention.

One day our printer came to my office—he was, by the way, the famous Count de Marigny implicated in the murder of Sir Harry Oakes, Governor General of the Bahamas, and acquitted—and said the union forbade him to print any more literature for the American Embassy. A delegation of militiamen had called on Freddy, as he was known to friends, and said that unless he immediately ceased doing printing work for the Embassy, he would be denounced as a "counter-revolutionary."

On that note, I left for Mexico and arranged for our regional printing office for Latin America, located in Mexico City, to supply our needs in Cuba and ship via diplomatic pouch to Havana. Certainly, there is something wrong when an embassy in a foreign country is not permitted to use the private printing facilities of that country. And the means by which printing was discouraged—through outright intimidation—meant that a "dictatorship of the proletariat" had indeed been established.

I returned to Havana at virtually the same moment that Ambassador Bonsal arrived back from Washington. The entire press corps was there, and I was seen as I left the plane from Mexico—a somewhat unhappy encounter. It was not to be known that I had gone to Mexico, and my mission there certainly was not to be made known. I was immediately hailed by reporters who thought that I had accompanied the Ambassador. Mounting suspicions and fears in Cuba made the slightest deviation from normal a matter of great concern. The reporters assumed that I had accompanied the Ambassador and that perhaps he had returned to Havana via Mexico.

It was well known that the U.S. Ambassador to Mexico, Robert Hill, was greatly agitated over what he considered a weak course of American diplomacy in Cuba. He had quizzed me about that course, as a matter of fact, when I was in Mexico. In any event, Cuban reporters came to the sudden conclusion at the airport that my mission to Mexico meant that "tough guy" Hill was to replace "good guy" Bonsal. It took my strongest powers of persuasion to get them to call off that particular story. Within half an hour, however, Ambassador Bonsal arrived from the States, thus getting us all off that hook.

Ambassador Hill's conversation with me in Mexico, in which he advocated that the strongest possible action be taken to curb "Castro-Communism," was not paralleled in Mr. Bonsal's talks in Washington. Frankly, many of us at the Embassy expected our Ambassador to return to Cuba with specific instructions to get tough. This was not the case. In a meeting with President Eisenhower, Ambassador Bonsal apparently persuaded him to take a soft line. What Mr. Bonsal brought back with him was the message from the American President that he "loved the people of Cuba." The message was released, largely ignored, and the U.S. Information Agency shelled out quite a sum of money expanding the message into a pamphlet for distribution in the Spanish language.

The Matos affair was brought to a close on December 15 and 16, when he and 38 of his officers were tried in the gloomy confines of La Cabaña. Of the five members of the Revolutionary Tribunal who sat in judgment on Huber Matos, four of them were known Communists, including the military commander of Pinar del Río Province, Comandante Derminio Escalona. Fidel Castro turned his back on the prisoners, and spent three hours haranguing the crowd that attended the trial. Not once did he face the accused. After castigating Matos for allegedly "putting the integrity of the revolution in doubt," Castro ended, shouting: "If you absolve Comandante Huber Matos, history will condemn you!" Defense attorney Francisco Lorié Bertot riddled the formal accusations levelled against Matos. In the process, he was frequently abused and insulted aloud by Raúl Castro. The following day, Matos was asked if he had something to say before being sentenced. He replied: "They are condemning me, but one day my name will be cleared, as will the names of my companions. Above the justice of men is the justice of God."[6]

Matos was indeed, as Daniel James describes him in his book, "a Dostoyevskian character . . . apologetic about his own role, and almost ready to blame himself for what is happening." Obviously a high-minded liberal, Matos could think of little else to say except: "If this tribunal believes that it is necessary to condemn me to death so the revolution will triumph and Cuba will progress, I will accept that verdict," shouting: "Long live the Cuban revolution!" Silent for a long, stunned moment, the crowd broke into angry anti-Communist shouts and grumbles which extended throughout the reading of the sentences—20 years for Matos, and from two to seven years for his followers. Neither of the Castros—Fidel or Raúl—even stayed to hear the verdict.

CHAPTER 9

•

The Russians Move In

•

THE FINAL MONTHS OF 1959 spelled the absolute *finis* to Cuban hopes for democracy. Those months also bore alarming signs that Cuban subversion of Latin America was being carried out with increasing vigor and know-how. Venezuelan President Rómulo Betancourt had informed the American Embassy in Caracas that he was demanding the "immediate recall" of Cuban Ambassador Francisco Pividal. He did so, "for intervention in the internal affairs of Venezuela," i.e., subversion. Guatemala, Honduras, and Argentina also had expressed alarm over the extent of Communist Cuban subversion of their countries, and brought the evidence of that subversion to the attention of the United States.

Yet, the moral base from which the United States could respond to the threat by calling for collective action was being eroded by Castro's unfounded charges of "Yankee aggression." Castro militants jangled tin cans under the noses of diners in Havana's restaurants, demanding contributions for arms and airplanes to "repel the Yankee invader." At the very moment Castro was preparing his mammoth October 26th demonstration against "Yankee aggression," the wives of Raúl Castro and "Che" Guevara were in Chile attending a Communist Latin American Congress of Women. And Foreign Minister Raúl Roa's denial that trouble-shooting Anastas Mikoyan, the scourger of Budapest, had been invited to come to Cuba, was viewed with suspicion. A denial usually meant the opposite.

Cuba's guerrilla training camps now had Russian "technical advisers." Red Chinese officers also were spotted in the Minas del Frío camp, one of the most important camps in Cuba. Spanish Republicans also began to appear in Cuba in considerable number.

When the Spanish Communists were defeated by General Francisco

Franco, a picked number decamped for the Soviet Union. They spirited away several thousand Spanish children and had them transported to Russia where they were given preferential treatment in educational and military academies, such as Frunze. There they were groomed to be used in the "wars of liberation" which were to come. In November of 1959, a young man, dressed in Rebel Army uniform, called the home of a Mrs. Nelly Incháustegui in Havana. He spoke a strangely accented Spanish for, as it turned out, he had been taken from Spain to Russia where he was reared. Sent to Cuba by the Russians in the summer of 1959, he called on Sra. Incháustegui, he said, because he had learned from his mother (still in Russia) that they were related to each other. Sra. Incháustegui's father had, indeed, come from the same village in Spain from which the young soldier had been taken. All in all, General Alberto Bayo now had begun, slowly and cautiously to gather in Cuba cadres for the expansion of guerrilla training, and for experimenting in subversion in Latin America.

Though Ambassador Bonsal was fresh back in Havana following his December consultations with the State Department, he did not remain long there. Hardly had he settled into his office than he was again yanked back to Washington, this time over an incident which was as dramatic, as ludicrous, and as stupid as can be imagined. For months, Fidel Castro had been burning with rage over the damaging and revealing memorandum written by Manuel Artime regarding the meeting at the Agrarian Reform Institute. Not wanting to give the memorandum undue publicity, however, he had not said much about it. In January of 1960, Castro appeared on television and excoriated Artime, the Spanish Ambassador, and the American government, virtually all in one breath.

Castro alleged that one of Artime's relatives was found with a letter in her purse (just "happened" to have it) which "linked" the Spaniards to Artime's "counterrevolutionary" activities in Cuba. Allegedly, the letter had been taken from the purse of Artime's relative, and Castro took great relish in reading it over television to the nation. The Spaniards were culprits, he said, because they had been conspiring with Artime against the Revolutionary Government. The alleged letter also claimed that Artime had been gotten out of the country and to the United States via the U.S. Naval Base at Guantanamo, located at the Eastern end of Cuba. The United States was thus also implicated.

The Spanish Ambassador, stout, muscular Don Pablo Lojendio, had just put on his pyjamas at his residence, preparing to watch Castro's televised antics from the comfort of his bed. As Castro wound his familiar thread of accusations, linking the Spanish Embassy, the Spanish Government, and particularly the Spanish Ambassador to Manuel Artime and to plots against Cuba, Lojendio exploded. Pushing his protesting wife aside, he called the garage and told his chauffeur to bring the car around. He dressed quickly and drove to the television station.

The scene shifts to that seen by the television viewer. Fidel Castro sat, facing an audience of bearded stooges, members of his cabinet, and militiawomen, all applauding him roundly in his attack on Artime. Suddenly, the station manager, Alfredo Núñez Pascual, went over to the Prime Minister, tapped him on the shoulder and whispered in his ear. Castro reared back, startled, as frank fear showed in his face for a moment. He clutched briefly at his holster. Spaniards have a strong sense of honor, as Fidel Castro himself knew from his overbearing father, and violence was entirely possible.

The audience sat stunned for a moment as they heard the Spanish Ambassador from the rear of the studio stage shouting: "They have insulted me! They have insulted me! I demand the right to reply!" Then the studio erupted in a panic. Cameras were jostled as they recorded skirts, buttocks and beards in wild confusion. Some of the audience ran for the exits; body guards leaped to the stage; President Osvaldo Dorticós sat rigidly in the front row of the studio, unable to move.

When the cameras were righted, they picked up a white-faced, angry, Spanish Ambassador, saying: "You talk so much about freedoms in this country, then give me the opportunity to reply to these calumnies made by the Prime Minister! You cannot insult my government, nor my government's ambassador without the right to reply. And I demand that right of reply right now!"

Ambassador Lojendio was surrounded by Castro's bodyguard, trying to push him out of the studio. Núñez Pascual was literally sweating it out, wringing his hands, and gesturing toward Castro who was on the outer fringe of the group. Lojendio bellowed: "Don't ask him! You are in charge of this station. You can decide for yourself. . . . !" At that point, the Spanish Ambassador was physically ejected.

Castro returned to the table at which he had been sitting, visibly shaken from the ordeal. As he lighted a long cigar, his hands shook. He gulped down a cup of cognac. (The interminable cups of "coffee" that he drank during press interviews, in fact, contained cognac). When the situation had assumed some appearance of order, Castro said that Lojendio was given 24 hours to leave the country. Suddenly, he remembered, turned to Dorticós and said: "Subject, of course to ratification by the President of the Republic." Dorticós, of course, "ratified" Castro's decision. After a few thundering comments, Castro abruptly changed the subject and rambled on, without any visible interest in his subject, on the economic plans of Cuba.

But even before Castro finished speaking, the mobs turned out in demonstrations against the Spanish Embassy. Venal commentator José

Pardo Llada introduced his radio program with the sound of a donkey hee-hawing, saying that it was the voice of the Spanish Ambassador. Mobs climbed up on the portico of the Spanish Embassy, took down the Spanish flag and burned it. No effort was made by the police to prevent the spoliation of a foreign embassy.

Early the next day, the diplomatic corps paid a farewell call on Ambassador Lojendio, among them American Ambassador Philip Bonsal. Within hours, *Revolucion*, came out with a vicious attack on the diplomatic corps and particularly on Mr. Bonsal. His farewell visit to Lojendio, said *Revolucion*, proved that the United States was hand-in-glove with the "conspiracies against Cuba."[1]

Discussing the event at his morning staff meeting, the American Ambassador warmly praised Ambassador Lojendio, but took a dim view of his exercise of diplomacy. "Maybe that's one way to be an ambassador," he said smiling, "but I don't subscribe to the practice." Unsmiling, Assistant Naval Attaché Philip Klepak said: "As a matter of fact, Mr. Ambassador, when Lojendio appeared, we thought this was the preliminary bout." Bonsal looked at him uncomprehending, and Klepak continued: "We were waiting for you to come on as the main event." Strained chuckles made their way around the table, and a few sharp glances were shot in the direction of the Assistant Naval Attaché.

Later that day, Ambassador Bonsal received a telegram calling him back to Washington for "consultation." He had been back in Havana less than a week, so the meaning was abundantly clear. The United States objected to the accusations leveled at this country by Fidel Castro, and chose the diplomatic method of showing it. Furthermore, Bonsal was ordered to leave immediately, and he did. But this time there were only AP bureau chief Harold Milks, a staffer for United Press, and a stringer for the American Broadcasting Company to see him off. The questions were few, and the answers were none. Mr. Bonsal was thoroughly angry. Again Dan Braddock assumed charge of the Embassy as Chargé d'Affaires.

Following Mr. Bonsal's recall for consultation, the government-controlled press, hand-outs from the ministries, and speeches by major figures of the Cuban government beat the drums for the Soviet Trade Fair. We had witnessed few propaganda buildups in Cuba to rival the one which preceded the fair. Government propagandists discovered with "surprise and pride" that many of the advance Russian publicists spoke Spanish. This was hardly a surprise. In their cups at the Hotel Nacional one night, two of the Russians revealed that they were not Russians at all. They were Spanish Communists with Russian names. In fact, some conjectured that Castro's blast at Spain, coming when it did, was to get the jump on Spain, who, it was believed, was prepared to ask for the surrender of some of the Spanish Communists who were entering Cuba from Russia.

It was at this time that the Cuban press was formally tied in to world-wide subversion. *Prensa Latina* extended its radio arm to include broadcasts to Central and South American countries. Half-hour programs were being beamed to sixteen Latin American countries. The programs consisted of "revolutionary chats"—tapes of Castro's speeches and speeches by other members of the Cuban government. In analyzing the content of the programs, we found that the central theme was aimed at gaining maximum credence for Cuban charges of U.S. aggression. Another portion of the program consisted of a fictitious round-up of Latin American editorial and other comment regarding Cuba. Communist newspapers were quoted liberally in their support of the Castro regime—without, of course, any mention of the fact that the source of the comment was Communist. Cynically, that same program was then rebroadcast over the government-controlled Cuban network, FIEL, as representative of foreign comment.

More important, in January the Castro regime quite openly sponsored the trip to Cuba of a large delegation of newsmen from behind the Iron Curtain, plus Communist news representatives from Indonesia and Japan. The Cuban government, which was so poor that it couldn't pay for properties which it had confiscated, paid all expenses for the group. Attending the Havana meeting, said *Revolucion*, were Lumbomir Fischer from the official Czech news agency, *Czecheta;* Nikolai Chiguir from *Tass;* Luka Muajic from the official Yugoslav agency, *Tanjug;* Estela Bohor Avishai from the *Agence Telegraphique Bulgare*, also an official from Bulgaria; Sam Kerner from the *Polish Press Agency;* Koer wet Kartaadiredja and M. Hasjimrhman, Communists from the *Indonesian National Press;* Li Ping Chuang and Ten Kan from Red China's *New China News Agency;* and many others.

What is more, on January 16, the entire group of foreign journalists, headed by Jorge Ricardo Masetti, Director General of Castro's *Prensa Latina*, paid homage at the grave of Rubén Martínez Villena, one of Cuba's best-known Communist poets. Of some significance was the fact that the group also included René Depestre, a prominent Haitian Communist, who was at that time busy recruiting Haitians for guerrilla training.

Out of that meeting came an agreement, which was to be put into effect a few months later, elevating the Haitian, René Depestre, to the post of Director of Cuba's National Printing Office. Another agreement designated Guillermo Lorentzen, a Guatemalan Communist, to share honors with Cuba's Communist Poet Laureate, Nicolás Guillén, in compiling a

"Revolutionary Dictionary." The "Revolutionary Dictionary" was an important step in the writing of Cuban history which was to follow.

The National Printing Office, said *Hoy*, would print 100,000 volumes of books each year. A minimum of 5,200,000 pamphlets were scheduled yearly from the same National Printing Office, according to the *Hoy* interview with foreigner Depestre, to whom "sovereign" Cuba entrusted its entire national output of literature! Soon, translations of Russian books began to appear, and the curriculum of the public school system included those books as compulsory reading. "Che" Guevara's pamphlet, "Guerrilla Warfare,"* also was produced in translated versions in Portuguese (for Brazil), English (for the U.S. and British dependencies in the Caribbean) and French (for Algeria).

It was in this atmosphere of deepening crisis that the Soviet trade fair made its appearance in Havana. It opened in February with the explanation by the government that there was nothing extraordinary about its appearance in Cuba, in as much as the fair had been shown in neighboring Mexico. However, Mexico was not on a revolutionary path toward Communism. Cuba was. The Soviet trade fair was a long step toward pulling Cuba behind the Iron Curtain.

Anastas Mikoyan of course came to Cuba to open the fair. He traveled the countryside with his beaming host, Fidel Castro, who showered attention on the Soviet Vice Minister in direct contrast to the manner in which he shunned the American Ambassador and publicly cut down Costa Rican José Figueres. Castro even gathered together the top-level Communist echelon of his government and went personally to the airport to receive Mikoyan. Among those present were "Che" Guevara and Captain Antonio Núñez Jiménez of the Agrarian Reform Institute. Núñez Jiménez presented Mikoyan with the first copy of his book to come off the presses of the National Printing Office. The book, *The Geography of Cuba*, is full of major errors, such as showing that Cuba's central highway passes through a town called San Luis, something any bus driver knows is not so. But what made this particular copy of the book of unusual interest is the fact that it was printed in Russian and handed over to Mikoyan with great ceremony.

The fair was a flop. Presented to Cubans long accustomed to the abundance and superior quality of American consumer goods and industrial products, the fair showed how crude the Soviets were in modern industrial techniques. Their UD-6 and UD-9 trucks were clumsy imitations of General Motors' products designed twenty years earlier. Like-

---

*Experts in guerrilla warfare claim that Guevara's knowledge of the subject was learned from U.S. Army Field Manuals which he found in the military library of La Cabaña Fortress.

214 · THE LOSERS

wise, Russian D-8800 stationary equipment engines—used for air compressors—were copies of Caterpillar models turned out in the United States a quarter of a century earlier.*

Notebooks were placed in strategic positions for the public to write in their comments. The comments were so uncomplimentary to Russia and its backwardness, to Soviet leaders, to Communism, and to Fidel Castro, that within 24 hours of the fair's opening, the Cuban government was obliged to station its militia forces by the books to discourage further adverse comment. (I had an Embassy photographer surreptitiously photograph several pages of the notebooks.) Finally, the government made school teachers take their classes through the exhibit in an effort to swell the attendance figures.

The main performance was reserved for a speech by Mikoyan and his Cuban hosts from the balcony of the Presidential Palace. Just before the address, Mikoyan went to the park in front of the Palace where he laid a wreath of the hammer and sickle on the José Martí monument. Catholic Action groups learned of the plan. As Mikoyan approached with the wreath, hundreds of Cuban youths burst upon the scene, handing out leaflets to the crowd which protested the "sacrilege," and singing Cuba's national anthem. The honor guard panicked, some of the soldiers firing over the heads of the singing throng, and a near-riot developed. Mikoyan took to his heels with part of the bodyguard. His speech, given later, consisted of an attack on the United States and an offer to purchase 350,000 tons of Cuban sugar.

The point of the fair and the trip to Havana by Anastas Mikoyan came with the announcement that Russia would buy, not 350,000 tons, but an additional 650,000 tons of Cuban sugar on a barter arrangement. Thus, the original agreement soared to a total of one million tons. The barter deal, and the price which Russia would pay for the sugar, clearly marked the agreement as a political maneuver which had little to do with sound economic practice.

Signed on February 13, 1960, the five-year commercial treaty between Russia and Cuba said that the Soviets would take a yearly quota of one million tons of Cuban sugar. But it also said that Russia would pay only a percent in American dollars each year, the rest to be liquidated through a $100,000,000 "loan" by which Cuba would receive Russian industrial equipment as payment for its sugar. The "industrial equipment" turned out to be chiefly Soviet arms and military equipment.

The most striking point about the deal was the price Russia was willing to pay for Cuban sugar—only 2.78 cents a pound. We paid 5.11 cents. The world market price was 2.9 cents a pound, a thoroughly uneconomic

*A Soviet technician marvelled at the "modern" water pumping station in the city of Cienfuegos, only to be told by the Cuban Manager that it was 40 years old!

price, considering that the Cuban cost of production ran well above the selling price. To make up the deficit each year the United States paid a sugar premium to several hemisphere countries, particularly Cuba, which amounted to the cost of production by sugar farmers in the United States. In other words, if it cost the American farmer six cents to produce a pound of sugar, we paid six cents to Cuba, to the Dominican Republic, and to other countries for their sugar.

The differential between the world market price on the one hand, and what the United States paid Cuba on the other, amounted to $150 million yearly. This arrangement protected our domestic market, a protection which was considered necessary for defense purposes—the manufacture of industrial alcohol and other sugar by-products—should our off-shore sugar producers be cut off from us through a war or unfriendly foreign alliances. The wisdom of the policy has since been proved, as Cuba directed its sugar to Russia.

There is yet another point not to be overlooked. Before the U.S. quota system was instituted, Cuba's economy was at the mercy of the world sugar market. If there was disaster in other countries, the market would go up and Cuba would prosper. But, when there was a glut on the sugar market, Cuba suffered greatly. Thus, the price of 5.11 cents paid in 1960 by the United States for 3.5 million tons of Cuban sugar was by way of helping Cuba stabilize its economy.

Still another point. Under the quota arrangement, Cuba received freely convertible dollars, thus giving the Cubans the option to purchase from any country they wanted. For example, a truck in the United States cost "x" dollars and a truck in Great Britain cost "y" dollars. The Cubans had the right to choose their market on the most advantageous terms. No such latitude existed in the barter arrangement with Russia. A Communist state, Russia determines the price and quality of every item that it manufactures. It needed only to raise the price of its bartered items (which it did, bringing belated charges of "overcharging" against the Russians from none other than Industries Minister "Che" Guevara) to rob the Cuban people blind.

Thus, we had the spectacle of the Soviet Union paying 2.78 cents a pound for sugar which already was selling for 2.9 cent on the world market—a price which in turn was recognized as uneconomic for the producers. As the latter price was so recognized, could the payment of an even lower price by the Russians be considered economic? Obviously not. On the other hand, patient, understanding Uncle Sam was paying the extraordinarily high price of 5.11 cents a pound, and being denigrated by the Castro regime in the bargain! In fact, "Che" Guevara publicly stated that the United States paid its sugar premiums so that it could "enslave the Cuban people."

The announcement of the Cuban-Russian agreement was made in a special edition of *Revolucion* late on Saturday morning. Several days earlier, I had asked Dick Cushing, now Public Relations Director of the U.S. Information Agency in Washington, for a list of comparative sugar prices paid by the United States and by Russia over a period of several years. I took the newspaper into the Embassy to read and found a communication from Cushing in answer to my request. The information was so favorable to the United States and so unfavorable to Russia, that I called Dan Braddock at his home, suggesting that in view of the announcement in *Revolucion* we issue a release explaining the American position on the sugar quota, now under frontal attack. Clearly, we were the whipping boys, with Castro seeking to justify his totally uneconomic agreement with Russia. Dan told me to draft something and have it ready for him. He would be right down.

Dan arrived and I gave him a draft listing the prices paid by the United States for Cuban sugar over a period of ten years, contrasting these with the prices which Russia had paid. The release also laid out in clear language the mutual benefits which accrued to the U.S. and to Cuba through the quota arrangement, and the sugar premiums which we paid under the quota system. Thanks to Cushing, we had all the information needed to give the lie to the charges of the Castro regime. The American position was defensible, particularly in view of the fact that the wage of the sugar workers was adjusted upwards, since they were assured equitable participation in the difference between the price of sugar on which their wages were based and the final average price at which the entire sugar crop was sold. The higher price paid by the United States of course raised the final average price of the crop. This was a social instrument which speaks well for the concern of pre-Castro governments with the Cuban workers—a concern which obviously was not reflected by Castro when he made his deal with the Russians. Dr. José Illán, a noted economist and former Castro aide, has this to say about the Russian-Cuban deal: "As a result of the low price at which Cuba's sugar was sold to the Soviet Union and to Communist China (which not only was lower than the average price that the U.S. used to pay, but also lower than the average price of the world market), Castro's Communist regime sacrificed the sugar workers by cutting 45% of the wages under Resolution 419 of the Labor Ministry in 1961."[2]

Our release was front-paged in Cuba's non-government newspapers, and was made the subject of many eye-opening editorials. The information we released also widened the already unbridgeable split between the 26th of July Movement and the Communists, giving the former badly needed ammunition to direct at their opponents. In fact, I went to the Embassy Sunday morning, the day after the release, sat across the street in a *bodega* to read the newspapers, and listened as the Russian deal was hotly debated among the customers. A Communist agitator argued "Yankee imperialism." Suddenly, about ten men seized and ejected him from the premises, spitting at him and shouting "Communist!" He screamed for the militia, shouting "counterrevolutionaries!" at the top of his voice. He was answered by shouts of "26th of July," as everyone melted away from the *bodega*, and I sauntered across the street to the Embassy.

Two days later, following what must have been several high-level conferences, Castro's Minister of the Economy answered our statement. The premium paid by the U.S. for Cuban sugar, he said, was in response to numerous tariff advantages which gave American businessmen a monopoly of the Cuban market. The Ministry statement also pointed out that during one period the United States paid an amount below the world market price for sugar. However, the period to which he referred was during World War II. The index to which he referred was artificial, for the fact was that during World War II Cuba *had no world market* to which to export. It had no possibility of shipping sugar to Europe or Asia where its world market normally was to be found.

The United States took all of Cuba's sugar, at the risk of losing its own inadequate merchant marine in the German submarine-infested waters of the Caribbean. Cuba was an ally of the United States, and the two allies made a mutually beneficial agreement. Virtually isolated from allied shipping which was needed to carry on the war, Cuba had no merchant marine nor Naval escort vessels to deliver its sugar. Cuba also faced war-time speculation on food and capital goods which was vital for its people and for its industries. So the two allies—the United States and Cuba—arrived at an agreement. The U.S. took all of Cuba's sugar at a price which assured Cuban producers a fair profit and steady income. In return for Cuban sugar needed for defense purposes, sugar which could be transported to its allies in regular armed convoys from American ports, the United States put a ceiling price on all food and capital goods sent to Cuba. Thus, paper speculation on an artificial world price of sugar was avoided when Cuba passed Law Number 20 in 1941 which put the agreement into effect. War profiteering in both countries—sugar on the one hand, and food and capital goods on the other—was stopped.

What do we have from Herbert Matthews on this subject? He writes that "there has been a great deal of nonsense written about the United States sugar quota system and the 'generous' subsidy that we are supposed to have provided Cuba by paying about two cents a pound above the world price of sugar for our imports from Cuba. This higher price was a subsidy for the American domestic sugar producers in order to protect their internal markets." It would seem that Mr. Matthews uncritically accepted the Castro view almost verbatim. How uncritically he accepted it is revealed in another passage where he writes that, "It is true that Cuba benefited, of course, but as a counterpart the United States obtained substantial tariff advantages for its exports to Cuba. Moreover, the sugar policy in general saddled Cuba with a distorted one-commodity economy at the mercy of the American Congress." Matthews winds up with a Guevara-like statement that sugar ". . . was a symbol of their subjection to the United States and of American power over them."[3]

Can Mr. Matthews really be serious? First of all, the sugar industry in Cuba is centuries old. We didn't invent sugar. Second, Cuba is an agricultural country where sugar is its most lucrative crop. The Cubans made that discovery all by themselves. What industry existed in Cuba, it should also be mentioned, was largely brought in by American firms who, in doing so, cut themselves out of an export market. As our businessmen knew from years of experience, industrially Cuba could only support a light metals industry. It did not have the natural resources to develop an industrial economy. How many hundreds of millions of dollars Guevara and Castro took out of the pockets of the Cubans and squandered on trying to develop an industrial country probably will never be known. And it was Castro himself who finally turned back to the "distorted, one-crop economy" that the United States "saddled" Cuba with, saying that Cuba would produce ten million tons by 1970. And what would the proceeds from the ten million tons be used for? To support "wars of liberation in Latin America."

Regarding the Matthews-Castro economic fables concerning tariffs, the customs agreement antedated the sugar quota and pricing system. They were not related, as the Castro-Matthews thesis would have us believe. All Cuban products which entered this country also received a customs benefit—fruit, the growing vegetable industry, molasses, and other items. On sugar alone, the difference between the full duty and the preferential duty in the year 1959 alone exceeded $12 million. Without this privilege, Cuba would have had to pay the $7 million in duty to export its sugar to the United States. Cuba not only paid nothing, but received $150 million above the world market price in what amounted to a subsidy. The obvious point is that the sugar quota system and the customs agreement worked to mutual advantage, thus permitting Cuba to be numbered among the most affluent societies in Latin America.

And what about charges that the quota system implied Cuban "subjection to the United States and of American power over them" which seem to bemuse Mr. Matthews. Who objected to this "subjection?" Certainly not the Cuban people and Cuban presidents before Castro. What Mr. Matthews is saying is that Castro objected. This is quite another thing entirely, having to do with Castro's political affiliation with Communist nations and not with any concern for the welfare of the Cuban people.

The tariff "advantage" referred to by Matthews and the Castro government merely permitted the United States *and* Cuba to reduce tariffs by a small percent. Thus, with a tariff preferential of 20% (one-fifth), a 25% tariff is reduced by one-fifth of 25%, or 5%. A tariff of 30% is reduced by one-fifth, or 6%. So what is described in the context of a tariff preference is not at all what it is made to appear. Therefore, to say that the tariff advantages gave the United States a virtual monopoly in Cuba is no less than calumny. And it is a dangerous calumny considering that our adversary—communism—in Cuba at the time was a foe committed to bury us, one who was establishing guerrilla training facilities to hasten that burial. It required no particular genius to suspect that the Castro regime was maneuvering Cuba behind the Iron Curtain. It did, however, require some ideological compromises for any American to defend Castro's barter deal on the grounds that bartering sugar to Russia would somehow make the Cubans "independent," while advantageous sales to the United States "enslaved" the Cuban people.

The Embassy suggested to the State Department that it follow up with a series of diplomatic notes, to be handed over to the Cuban government and released to the press. The series, which might run as many as ten or more, would outline and expand on U.S. sugar policy, the mutual benefits which accrued through the customs arrangement, the mutual benefits which came out of U.S. investments in Cuba, and so on. If the Cuban government found any of these time-tested arrangements disagreeable, the American government would be willing, even glad, to discuss them.

The State Department did not want to become an "instrument of propaganda," which is to say to become diplomatically involved in propaganda. The project was given to the U.S. Information Agency. In turn, the Agency sent a writer and cartoonist to Havana for the slow business of issuing a series of pamphlets, without the slightest possibility of having them printed in Havana. Even if the pamphlets were printed in Washington or Mexico we lacked the remotest possibility of assuring their circulation within Cuba. The government, obviously, would pick them up and have them burned.[4]

Thus, the idea of a spirited exchange in defense of U.S. policy, bogged down in bureaucracy. We lost the impact of diplomatic presentation with attendant loss of press exploitation. In short, we did nothing. And faced with nothing, the flow of agents from Russia, from its satellites, and from Red China and its satellites, became an avalanche which, with the Bay of Pigs to come, was to sweep a proud United States virtually out of the Caribbean.

French professor Charles Bettleheim gave up his post at the Sorbonne for a period and came to Cuba to assist in locking the country more firmly behind the Iron Curtain. After a study of the Cuban economy, on September 19, 1960, Bettleheim submitted a memorandum to the Cuban government stating that it should give up its idea of industrialization. Rather, he wrote, Cuba should "concentrate on agriculture for the next five years, at least." In doing so, Bettleheim wrote, Cuba would complement the industrial economies of the Soviet-bloc, adding: "Above all, you must take into account commerce with Socialist countries." In order to do this, Bettleheim baldly asserted, "you must discriminate against wages, since wage increases would dissipate funds needed for investment." To suppress demands by labor, the Frenchman continued, "I recommend that arbitrary tribunals, like those employed by the Soviet Union, be established at once." He also recommended that workers be given "production norms" to meet. "Persons failing to meet those norms," Bettleheim warned, "must then be punished." Labor, he stated firmly, "must be indoctrinated."

The Frenchman emphasized that "the government must concentrate the major part of economic power in its hands, so as to be in a position to control any opposition." To do this, he said, "the banks and the majority of all commerce must be nationalized so that the profits go to the state, thus enabling the state to bring the rest of the economy under control." Take advantage of the opportunistic elements of society, the "doctrinally weak Leftists," Bettleheim stated, by bringing them into the government. "This method," he believed, "is the best method to silence them as a political opposition." The profits earned by high productivity cooperatives and state farms, Bettleheim postulated, "must be withdrawn and reinvested elsewhere," adding: "Under no circumstances must workers on these cooperatives, regardless of their superior work, be permitted to share in the increased profits."

Niurka Escalante, a relative of old-line Cuban Communist Aníbal Escalante, announced on the openly Communist TV program, "Cuba Avanza," that on July 26 Cuba would host three Communist youth meetings—the World Federation of Democratic Youth, the International Union of Students, and the World Youth Assembly. Its purpose, "supported by Soviet youth who are building a new Communist society," she said, is to "give battle against Yankee imperialism, its insolent threats, economic aggression, plans for an armed invasion, and efforts to destroy our glorious revolution." The revolution was, therefore, Communist, if one was disposed to believe the Cuban government. The Cuban people were disposed to believe their government, if intellectuals in this country were not.

If that were not enough to make an impression on our "losers," another broadcast by the government station, Radio Rebelde, should have had some effect. It said: "The despicable dogs in North America do not want to hear anything that concerns peace. The senile generals and admirals in the Pentagon are peeping out of the thousands of windows of the majestic United Nations building, each with a hunting rifle in his hand, waiting for the appearance of the dove of peace to shoot it down."

The broadcast told the Cuban people that the Soviets are peace-lovers. "In vain," said the broadcast, "have the USSR and the neutral countries cried for disarmament." The Cuban people knew about this "disarmament" from Castro's speeches, from the explosion of "Le Coubre," which was shortly to follow, and from traffic jams away from the public gaze—on roads leading from sugar ports where the Soviets were unloading tanks, cannon, and airplanes. In a prophetic tone, another broadcast said that "peace will come when the enslaved Negroes in North America will march in the streets and the people will wrest power from Wall Street warmongers who pace their offices, their cages of hatred. . . ."

The Communist, Jacobo Arbenz, former president of Guatemala, whose overthrow by the United States—specifically the CIA—several years earlier had disturbed "Che" Guevara and established what he feared was a precedent for the overthrow of "non-Communist" Fidel Castro, had taken refuge in Havana. He also spoke on the Cuban radio. "They claimed in Guatemala, little Guatemala," said Arbenz, "that there was a Soviet submarine base there, and now suggest that such bases may exist in Cuba." No such suggestion had been made by the United States, but we would have been well advised to look behind the words of Arbenz. Communists have a strange knack of telegraphing their punches. Just as "Che" Guevara predicted "another Guatemala" in January, 1959, because he knew that Cuba would pose another Guatemala situation for the United States, Jacobo Arbenz had taken that "situation" one step further. The "non-Communist" then ended his radio talk by saying, in effect, that Cuba would become a military base for the Soviet Union. "To those who say that we must fight Soviet imperialism, we answer that we know very well that Soviet imperialism is non-existent."

Incidentally, Professor Arnold Toynbee cloaks Jacobo Arbenz in the mantle of an innocent social reformer. He said of Arbenz: "The political body of the Arbenz revolution, the leftist regime headed by Colonel Jacobo Arbenz, may lie amouldering in its grave, but its soul goes marching on." Toynbee added: "Its soul, as I see it, is the demand for social justice." In reporting Toynbee's lectures at the University of Puerto Rico where these comments were made, Norman Gall wrote in the *San Juan Star* that Toynbee was "often criticized for ambiguity, turgidity and for adapting facts to his theoretical interests. . . ." Gall may have been referring to Toynbee's attack on the middle-class which, Toynbee said, ". . . tries to sit on the social safety-valve." Surprisingly, Professor Toynbee also said of the middle-class that it has made "no appreciable change for the better. . . ."

Cuban Foreign Minister Raúl Roa, sitting in public with his hands coiling and uncoiling like a bouquet of snakes, called President Arturo Frondizi of Argentina "an indescribable piece of excrement," President Alberto Lleras Camargo of Colombia "an imperialist lackey," and President Rómulo Betancourt of Venezuela "another lackey of imperialism in the pay of Muñoz Marín and the North Americans."

These were the voices of "social reform" in Cuba that the "losers" refused to hear; they were the voices of hatred and resentment against decency. They were not the voices of the Cuban people. More important, those voices were not coming to us via the airwaves from Soviet Russia, Red China, or Yugoslavia, they were located right in this hemisphere—more specifically, 90 miles from Florida.

CHAPTER 10

•

Remember Le Coubre

•

CASTRO COULD NOT REMAIN "independent," though many of his earliest apologists claimed he could. It should be clear by now that, from the outset, Fidel Castro was an enemy of the United States. But that, obviously, was not enough. He had to make the Cuban people believe that the United States was their enemy, as well. The alleged hostility of the United States to Cuba was, therefore, not only exaggerated, it was deliberately provoked in order to "reeducate the masses." Writing in *France-Soir*, Jean-Paul Sartre ceased being a Castro propagandist long enough to say that, if the United States did not exist, Castro most probably would have had to invent it.

One "aggression" after another was charged against the United States, as Castro created the myth of the "implacable" enemy, echoing the old Communist theme of "encirclement" of the Soviet Union by "hostile" neighbors. The reasons for pounding home this theme in Cuba are as old as the concept of totalitarian authority itself. Among the major considerations in Cuba was the absolute need to unite the country behind Castro, and by doing so through false cries of "aggression," to clamp the people more securely in the vise of the police state.

Second, the Communist direction into which Castro was propelling his state meant that the internal transformation could take place only with the support of Soviet Russia and its satellites. It was hardly likely that the United States would continue very long to underwrite the construction of a Communist state while that state was falsely accusing it of "aggression.". The fact is that Castro's foreign policy was inextricable from his domestic policy—both being Communist. Revolutionary Cuba needed foreign policy support, and even military support, from Russia, and it received both. Thus, it was hardly a surprise when, the second week of August, 1960, Sergei Mijailovich Kudriatsev was appointed

Soviet Ambassador to Cuba. Kudriatsev's background fitted his appointment. He had been expelled from Canada the year before for espionage activities.

Castro had indeed taken a lion by the tail. What happened internally in Cuba had to be reflected in its external policies. Castro's earliest ventures in invading his neighbors follows the Marxist-Leninist line as did his creation of guerrilla training camps within weeks of his assumption of power. From the Marxist-Leninist point of view, the Cuban revolution could succeed only to the extent that it could successfully encompass Latin America. And that, of course, was the ultimate goal of the Communists, perfectly expressed by Castro on July 26, 1960, when he bellowed that he would convert the Andes into the Sierra Maestra of the continent. It was but a short step from this for Lázaro Peña to refer to the Communist capture of Cuba as "only the first step in the liberation of Latin America," and for Blas Roca to say that, when guerrillas in Venezuela ". . . achieve victory, when it has wrested free from imperialism, when it is in control of its fabulous riches, of its oil fields, then America will be aflame . . . and we no longer will be the solitary island in the Caribbean. . . ."

Castro certainly needed a "hate America" campaign in early 1960. Signs multiplied in 1960 that he was in trouble with his own people and thus needed to "unite" the country. Those who massed at the Presidential Palace to hear him speak, gradually took on the complexion of regimented groups rather than that of spontaneous mob gatherings. Urban bombings were added to rural sabotage, and, at night, the streets of Havana began to take on the deserted look that they had during the last days of Batista. There was good reason for this.

Castro's highly publicized housing campaign did not extend much beyond his oratory. A housing development, which, for propaganda purposes, was prominently located in East Havana, was still not completed. Government surveyors and building contractors protested the site of the sky-scraping development, but were overruled by Castro's housing board, who refused to listen to the protests. As a result, the expensive edifice, or complex of edifices, was built without fundamental attention to the supply of water, sewage disposal, and electricity. Yet unsuspecting reporters from the United States were generally given tours of the premises as an example of Castro's concern for the underprivileged.

The highway from Havana's Rancho Boyeros airport had signs erected along the way, advertising here and there the site of "people's housing developments." However, as Cubans living in the area were quite willing to show any inquiring reporter who might ask, the iron skeleton beams were quite rusty, and the only construction that had taken place in a year's time was confined to the periodic painting of "housing development" signs. In fact, in many instances, the government merely put its signs on buildings which were under construction by private builders when Castro came to power.

To a very large extent, the much-publicized housing program simply did not exist. And the story is told in statistics which were much less dramatic than Castro's housing signs and his propaganda construction in East Havana.

Cuba needed some 20,000 new urban and 10,000 rural dwellings yearly, and attempts to meet that demand were provided by Cuba's modern building industry which, in 1958, was a $61 million business. By contrast, by June of 1960, the Cuban government, which now owned the industry, had invested only $10 million in housing. This was a remarkably low figure, considering that in addition to normal revenues taken in the previous year, the government had also expropriated $354 million. Where, the people were asking, did it all go? Much of it disappeared in fortifications, in propaganda, and in criminal waste.

In the countryside, INRA officials shot *guajiros* when they stubbornly insisted on being given lands, as they had been promised, and refusing to work on the burgeoning system of state farms. Immense dissatisfaction was registered among workers in the livestock and poultry industry, as they saw entire herds of cattle decimated, pigs marketed before they were ready, and egg-laying hens sold for food. A ranking militiaman who worked on a ranch or a farm often was made an INRA manager on the basis of "revolutionary loyalty." Not only did the newly appointed INRA official usually know nothing about management, but he also met suggestions from better qualified people with charges that they were "counterrevolutionaries." The land didn't belong to the manager and, typically in a Communist or "collectivist" state, his primary interest lay in defending his authority.

Also, as is typical in a Communist state, the free-spirited farmer and ranch worker began to resist collectivization. The cowboy in Camaguey Province, like this *guajiro* counterpart in Oriente Province, saw nothing but terror and economic disaster ahead. In the spring and summer of 1960, men began to disappear from the burgeoning system of collective farms and to reappear with rifles in Cuba's mountains.

AP bureau chief Harold Milks reported from Havana that while it was true that "only a few hundred desperate men are carrying on the counter-revolutionary struggle in the Sierra Maestra, the mountains where Castro launched his revolution, yet when Castro visited Santiago recently to address the newly armed people's militia, he never left the heavily guarded airport." And on September 22, 1960, the regime reported that a Comandante Sinesio Walsh had defected from Castro and was commanding anti-Castro guerrillas, composed of *guajiros* and other dissidents. Walsh operated in the Escambray mountains of central Cuba. At the time, government press reports said that seven guerrillas and a large amount of arms had been seized in Pinar del Río Province. The government also reported that nine guerrillas ambushed a truck carrying militiamen and made off with arms and ammunition. As a result of rising resistance, the regime announced that it had drafted women militia to free men for active duty to clean out anti-government forces operating in the mountains. It also came to light that the Russians had been supplying weapons to Castro for some months. In fact, driving to the Embassy very early one morning, I came across a traffic snarl caused by a convoy of 80-ton tanks and heavy artillery which, the convoy commander belatedly discovered, were too large to enter the tunnel under the Almendares river. The weapons had been unloaded during the night at the harbor of Mariel, some 30 miles east of Havana.

Castro intensified his efforts to cut off possible sources of supply to the dissidents. Hardly a week passed that he did not refer to the overflight of small planes "based in Florida." He caught the United States in a legal trap, and vigorously pursued an attack on the U.S. "failure" to enforce its neutrality laws. He shouted to the world that the United States continued, not only to "bomb" Cuba, but permitted "counterrevolutionary elements" to fly from Florida and burn cane fields with live phosphorus. As he knew from his own unproductive efforts, cane fields are notoriously difficult to burn unless there are literally hundreds of people involved in setting the fires, or clouds of planes to dump tons of live phosphorus on the fields. Cane *was* being burned in Cuba, however, and this supplied some dimension to organized resistance against Castro and his regime.

Castro of course held the United States "responsible" for the burnings, though of three known flights by small planes over Cuba, none had even the remotest capacity to burn cane on the scale claimed. But in propagandizing his claims, Castro diverted public attention from the intensity of growing resistance in Cuba, and at the same time dried up support to that resistance from Florida—support which had been so valuable to him in his insurrection against Fulgencio Batista.

In February, a Piper Comanche mysteriously exploded in mid-air over the España sugar mill in Las Villas Province. Government newspapers published pictures of wreckage of the plane, some of which, they claimed, nearly killed a five year-old girl "as she lay sleeping." Castro's militia massed and marched, "reserves" were called up, public buildings were placed under double guard, and the eyes of the people directed away from evidences of internal resistance, and toward the "Yankee aggressors." The wrecked plane was dragged into Havana and put on display at the Foreign Ministry, as the Cuban government fired salvo after salvo of diplomatic notes and televised accusations at the United States. Two dead Americans were pulled from the wreckage. The pilot was identified as Robert Ellis Frost, said *Revolucion*, which further claimed that Frost was connected with "the Pentagon." As usual, the United States responded by apologizing almost immediately to every Castro charge, with no prior examination into the charges themselves.

In March, a Piper plane flew over Cuba, and was shot down. But its crew of two men, Robert Shergalis and Harold Rundquist, escaped with their lives. Immediately, the government radio and press took off on another thunderous propaganda clap which stopped as suddenly as it had started.

The plane was damaged by rifle fire but managed to land on a small country road in Matanzas Province, not far from Havana. Tipped off by a telephone call, Consul Hugh Kessler, in charge of American Citizens' Affairs at the Embassy, drove immediately to the spot. He found the pilot and co-pilot shaken and angry. In interviewing the two men, Kessler found that they had flown the plane over Cuba after *having been paid to do so by Juan Orta of the Office of the Prime Minister.* Within minutes of recording their confessions, the men were whisked away at the telephoned orders of the Cuban G-2 in Havana. When Kessler asked whether they wished to be represented by the Embassy in their defense, the two asked him to discuss the matter later.

It was with the delivery of the two men to the G-2 in Havana that the propaganda clap was called off, amid the strongest indications that Robert Ellis Frost and others had also been paid to stoke Castro's fiery propaganda furnace, and were deliberately murdered. Dead men tell no tales.

Certainly, Shergalis and Rundquist were mercenaries of Fidel Castro. On this evidence alone, a strong case could be made that Robert Ellis Frost and his co-pilot were also his mercenaries who had been murdered in cold blood.

A highly agitated Kessler came into my office, and took out of his inside pocket a memorandum which he had written for the Ambassador containing what Shergalis and Rundquist had told him of their being commissioned by the Castro government to fly over Cuba. I called the Army Attache and the Political Officer, asking them to come down to the office. They did, and quickly saw the implications of Kessler's memorandum. As Kessler said: "We have the evidence to really put Castro on the defensive." It seemed to all of us that a sustained counter-campaign against Castro's lies and insinuations would not only thoroughly discredit the Cuban dictator before the world, which had been reading newspaper accounts of his unfounded charges against "Yankee aggression," but also would reveal him to his own people as a liar and a cheat.

We also were of the unanimous opinion that Robert Ellis Frost most probably had been murdered. Given Cuba's own propagandized charges that his flight over the España sugar mill was a "bombing mission," there had to be a bomb. It seemed highly doubtful that Castro agents would have put a time bomb on the aircraft before it left Florida, for the timing had to be perfect. We concluded that the bomb most probably had been booby-trapped before take-off. When Frost's co-pilot opened the door of the tiny plane to push it out, a hair-wire or some other device caused it to detonate.

Was the story about Frost and the statement by Shergalis and Rundquist credible? This could hardly be doubted at the time, and was indeed confirmed later by a court in Miami. What if the Castro regime forced the men to deny their story under the threat of death? This, we agreed, was a chance we would have to take. In that event, the United States would have to stick to its guns and have the FBI scour Florida, seeking to produce Castro's agents (which it actually did). The Embassy and the State Department would point to the suspicious nature of the propaganda clap and its even more suspicious suspension. In short, the United States would have to use all resources available to discredit Castro. The least that we could expect of our counter-blast was that it would cast considerable suspicion on Castro's motives in Latin America and elsewhere— particularly among the U.S. public, which was the major target of pro-Castro propaganda from the "losers."

Kessler and I went to see the Ambassador, and laid out our case. It was not accepted. For reasons which are best known to him, Mr. Bonsal said he believed that the matter should be considered, not by the United States which was under propaganda attack from Castro, but by the Organization of American States in Washington. Responsible in large measure for psychological warfare in the Embassy, I pressed the issue. The argument was clear. It was the United States which was under attack by a lying Castro; it was our prestige that was being undermined every time he opened his mouth. It was difficult to see how 21 ambassadors sitting in their ivory towers in Washington could be expected, in effect, to "protect" the United States from Castro's propaganda blasts. Peoples and governments in Latin America were equivocal in their views of Castro and his revolution. The fact was that Castro's propaganda, beamed daily to sixteen of those countries by radio and carried to newspapers via *Prensa Latina*, was in large measure responsible for their attitudes. With a justified case in its hands—tacitly admitted by the Cuban government as it called off its propaganda and held its breath—the American government had a powerful instrument with which to awaken the Latins, and, indeed, its own citizens, to the dangers of Castroism. The OAS Ambassadors needed ammunition, not responsibility for an issue which the United States itself declined to face.

The issue went by default. A few nights later, I happened to encounter Sr. Guillermo Cabrera Infante, editor of *Revolucion's* magazine, at a night club in the Cerro section. He had been drinking heavily, saw me, came over to the table and said: "We have your number, now. We are going to drive you clear out of Cuba." It was not difficult to understand what he meant. If the United States refused to take advantage of the Shergalis-Rundquist incident, the Communists concluded, it refused to be provoked by anything.

Meanwhile, the two principals, Harold Rundquist and Robert Shergalis, lived in regal splendor, provided by a grateful Cuban government at the G-2 prison. They refused to be represented by the Embassy, and were not released until the exchange of prisoners and American citizens took place following the missile crisis of 1962.

From then on, Castro and his regime simply beat our heads in with unjustified charges, intimidations, and even the expulsion of some of our Embassy officers, and the deliberate shooting of another.

At exactly 3:10 p.m. on March 4, 1960, Havana was rocked by a tremendous explosion. A French ship, "Le Coubre," blew up in Havana harbor, snuffing out the lives of 70 persons and injuring some 200 more. The ship was unloading 75 tons of arms and ammunition under conditions which violated both maritime rules and common sense. The ship was tied up at the docks when it should have been anchored far out in the harbor and unloaded by lighter; and it was unloaded by members of Cuba's armed forces rather than by stevedores experienced in handling explosives. The result was the most awful damage to port facilities and surrounding buildings, and, of course, the terrible loss of life.

The regime again took the offensive, and again the United States was the victim of the offensive. Amid insinuations of sabotage and dark-hued hints that the United States had engineered the explosion, the Castro regime organized a death march. CTC leader David Salvador worked out the details of a parade of coffins from the Civic Plaza to the Colón cemetery. The route of the parade did not suit Castro. He appeared just before it started, listened to Salvador lay out the plans, then changed those plans. Instead of a direct route to the cemetery, Castro had it changed to coil through the city streets.

Fidel Castro, President Osvaldo Dorticós and other top members of the government headed the funeral march. The eyes of the country, the world's press, and foreign embassies in Havana were fixed on the parade and on Castro's funeral address rather than on the implications of the explosion itself—an explosion indicating that the regime was arming at a speed consistent with secrecy.

Very few people turned out for Castro's funeral speech that grey, gloomy, and gusty day in March. The weather seemed to fit the despondency of a people who were meeting their fate almost with resignation. The city of Havana was a frightened city. Cubans felt from their past experience that tons of armaments could mean only one thing—the ascendance of the military and the debasement of civil authority. Castro's words spoken at the funeral symbolically, at least, buried the Cubans, as well as the victims of the explosion of "Le Coubre."

In his speech, Castro quickly ruled out any possibility of domestic sabotage, something which most believed and which he clearly feared. "We have conducted a full investigation," he said, "through minute investigation and detailed conversations with workers, stevedores, and others, and we have come to the conclusion that the sabotage was not carried out in Cuba." He conceded at the outset that the explosion was an act of sabotage. However, said Castro, in referring vaguely to some kind of "mechanism," the "mechanism that caused the explosion was not installed [after the ship docked] in Cuba." He "arrived at the conclusion that the sabotage had been prepared elsewhere. . . ."

Then Castro spoke of the explosion of the battleship "Maine," which was a cause of the U.S. entry into the Spanish-American War. "We remember the 'Maine,' " he said, "whose explosion has never been well explained to us." The "Maine," he said, had been used as an excuse by the United States ". . . acting on a simple supposition . . . they declared war on Spain." He went on: "Those who were not interested in seeing us receive these arms are the enemies of the revolution—those who do not want our country in a position to defend itself, those who do not want us to defend our sovereignty!" Who are they? "Well," said Castro, "it is an open secret that the British government declared that the North American government was opposed to us buying British planes. This was admitted by the North Americans whose own spokesmen said they were making efforts to impede the selling of arms to Cuba."

The importance of answering Castro's lies concerning "bombings" from the United States was immediately obvious, considering his next remarks. "We have been fighting against these pressures, against these obstacles, and against a country using its powerful international influence through international diplomacy . . . *to prevent a people . . . from defending themselves . . .* against . . . colonizers . . . criminals who want to return . . . and those who want to maintain us in a position of slavery." He then accused a "North American consul and a military attaché of the North American Embassy in Belgium. . . ." of having impeded the very sale of Belgian arms which Castro had purchased the year before and earmarked for the subversion of Venezuela.

That wasn't all, said Castro. "In the first place, what right has any government to interfere with another in the defense of its sovereignty?" He went on, attaching little angels' wings to his "social revolutionaries."

"What government are we interfering with in the purchase of arms? What obstacles are we placing in the way of any people to arm themselves?" The revolutionary government ". . . lives in peace, and its people live peacefully with other people. . . ." Therefore, "What right does a government which maintains friendly and diplomatic relations—or ought to be friendly—to prevent other people from having arms?" Castro's pretensions of wanting to be friends with the United States were being contradicted almost daily through his unfounded charges, and he again added to his contradictions with still another: "These are the truths: enemy planes, planes piloted by mercenary criminals, come from the United States, and the government of that country, bent on not letting us have arms, has been unable to prevent those flights!"

Castro wound up with a full-fledged attack. "Out with a 'democracy' that supports the criminals and helps the exploiters!" He brought up the Robert Ellis Frost incident (which we had refused to exploit). Castro claimed that hospitals "were filled with victims as a consequence of the incursion of Cuban air space. . . ." In view of the recent history of "aggression" from the United States, said Castro, "what is strange about dropping a bomb on a sugar mill in an area where there are children, and dropping a 100-pound bomb on the region?" Right here the Prime Minister laid himself open to question. The bomb of Robert Ellis Frost exploded in the air. Where did Fidel Castro come by the knowledge that it was a "100-pound bomb?" From his agents in Miami who boobytrapped the bomb, causing it to explode in the air and kill the occupants of the plane?

Castro brought up "economic aggression" by the United States. The background to this is that the United States had nine times proposed holding discussions on future U.S.-Cuban economic relations. Under previous agreements, U.S. vegetable and fruit control officials were stationed in Cuba to see that products exported to the United States would meet U.S. import standards. It was a beneficial arrangement to both parties.

Months before, with U.S. inspectors given the cold shoulder by the Agrarian Reform Institute, the United States asked if the Cuban government wished to continue with the arrangement. Request after request was submitted, but the Cuban government did not answer. The inspectors were then withdrawn and returned to the United States. It is believed that the deliberate refusal of the Cuban government to answer our requests was intended to force the United States to withdraw the men, to facilitate the charge of "economic aggression."

That belief become conviction when, on February 22, 1960, the Cuban government expressed its readiness to take part in discussions, but demanded that, during the negotiations (of unspecified duration), the

American government had to promise that neither it nor Congress would carry out any "hostile" measures against Cuba. The Castro regime realized of course that the Eisenhower Administration could not make such a guarantee, if only because Congress was meeting and considering the sugar quota at the time, and because we have a separation of powers which does not permit the Executive branch of the government to infringe on the powers of the Legislative branch. The Cuban public, of course, did not understand these legal points any more than it understood that Castro's maneuvering was designed to serve his anti-American purpose.

That purpose came out in his "funeral address." He excoriated the United States for "retiring its inspectors of fruit and vegetables which we export from our country." He attacked the United States, saying that "we are being threatened by the possibility that they will not buy our sugar." He went on: "And why? Why do we have a weak economy? Because this is the economy foisted off on us by our foreign masters, a mono-culture economy, an economy of large estates, an economy of an underdeveloped country; a weak economy as the consequence of the policy of foreign masters for the last fifty years." He sounded rather like a combination of Herbert Matthews, Huberman, Sweezy, Professor Shapiro, and Jean-Paul Sartre.

"What is this?" Castro asked. "It is nothing more than an economic Platt Amendment," adding that the whole sugar quota system, and payment of the premium, had no other design than, as he put it, ". . . to kill us through hunger."

Castro then switched to "U.S. military maneuvers in the Caribbean." That, also, was a "threat" directed against Cuba (although U.S. Marines had carried out maneuvers on the uninhabited U.S. island of Vieques in the Caribbean for decades). The world was having troubles elsewhere, he said, so why was it necessary that U.S. Marines disembark in the "peaceful Caribbean?" It was not so peaceful, and Castro had seen to that through five abortive invasions, one of which was directed by Rafael "Pichirilo" Mejía, the helmsman of Castro's own yacht "Granma," which had brought Castro and his guerrillas from Mexico to Cuba where they commenced their insurrection against Fulgencio Batista.

He made one interesting statement which was commented upon at the time. "Why," he asked, "did the Marines disembark against positions occupied by guerrillas?" What positions? What guerrillas? He then parlayed his comments regarding Marine landings at Vieques into future attacks against Cuba itself. "They speak of sending Marines here, among other possible things, as if the Cubans would stand with their arms crossed over their chests . . . as if the Cubans were not going to resist any disembarkation here, and our people would yield!"

Who spoke of sending Marines to Cuba? What disembarkations? The whole episode of the explosion of "Le Coubre" was blamed on a United States which he alleged "wished to bring the Cuban people to their knees." Waving two cannisters "of the type that killed our people," over his head, Castro shouted that they could not have been exploded on "Le Coubre" through any means other than deliberate sabotage. He knew, he said, because he had airplanes take some of the unexploded grenades "to heights of 400 and 600 feet, and they were thrown out." And here, he said waving the canisters again, "are those grenades . . . which didn't explode."

Two days later, an AP dispatch reported that an officer of the Rebel army had both arms blown off while carrying one of the grenades.

Then there was the incident in which two officers of the Embassy, William Friedeman and Robert Sweet were declared *persona non grata* amid another propaganda outburst claiming that the two FBI agents were interfering in Cuba's internal affairs. The major work of FBI agents overseas is cooperating with local police officials to stop international drug traffic, identify criminals wanted in several countries, etc. In this instance, the two FBI officers were investigating the Shergalis-Rundquist case. After a cloak-and-dagger ride through Havana on several buses, the two were picked up by the very men they thought they were working with, arrested, and recalled.[1]

Newsmen were given a hard time, largely because of their efforts to take news photos. The regime had military preparations to hide. Dick Valeriani, with AP at the time and later with NBC, was picked up by informers twice and put in jail at the G-2 headquarters. Each time that Harold Milks, his bureau chief, and I tried to see him at G-2 we were told that the government was holding no American citizens–a patent lie which we could do little or nothing about. Valeriani had pictures of the explosion of "Le Coubre" in the back of his car when followed and then apprehended by the government informers. Presumably, the government wanted to screen all photos to eliminate what they did not want printed. The regime did print some of the photos, however, together with Fidel Castro's speech, in a slick and expensive pamphlet called *Patria o Muerte*, (Fatherland or Death) and issued it throughout the world under the auspices of its Ministry of Foreign Affairs.

Bill Mosier of the *Miami News* and Al Gooding of *Life* were jailed. Following efforts to get them out of the G-2, the Embassy was advised that the men had been released and were at the Hotel Nacional. I went there with the intention of picking them up, installing them at my house overnight, and then taking them personally to the airport the next day. I arrived in time to see Andy St. George and Harvey Rosenhouse of *Time* being escorted to their cars to undergo a search for films. Just prior to that, Andy had taken pictures of Gooding and Mosier standing outside the hotel.

Tad Szulc of the *New York Times* had volunteered to keep an eye on Gooding and Mosier until I got there. Both of us knew from experience that the release of American citizens often was accompanied by another immediate and more serious arrest. I phoned Szulc from the lobby to hear him say: "The cops are picking me up." I rode to the eighth floor to find a scene of considerable confusion. Informers dressed in civilian clothes stood before six American reporters in the hall. Also standing there was Wayne Smith, duty officer from the Embassy. Wayne was a big man, an ex-Marine, and took little guff from them. He answered insults with steady answers which were effective in cutting the thugs down to size. One of the mobsters, by the way, had formerly been a Batista policeman at the Sixth Precinct station.

After considerable arguing, it developed that the militia on guard at the pool of the Hotel Nacional had seen Andy taking pictures of Gooding and Mosier. Taking Castro's advice to "report any suspicious activity," they called the G-2. The G-2 then dispatched their bully boys with instructions to arrest the Americans first and ask questions later. Andy broke into the conversation to say: "If it's films that you want, you already have the films I took of these two men," turned, and walked away. The thugs didn't quite know what to do, and let him leave. As he left the hotel, however, he was followed to his apartment and put under surveillance until he left the country.

As we had suspected, Gooding and Mosier were wanted again by the G-2, but the men sent out to get them were not given their names. Tad, for example, heard a hammering on his door, opened it on a sports-shirted G-2 agent standing with a pistol in his hand. "Are you a reporter"? he asked. Tad said yes. The man replied: "Good, you are under arrest." All but Gooding and Mosier were released almost immediately. I was notified by the G-2 the next morning that Gooding and Mosier had been expelled from the country and had just departed by plane for Miami from Rancho Boyeros Airport.

The Embassy was in a quandary. American citizens were being subjected to intimidation—even to the point of physical attack. Should we advise American residents to leave Cuba? If we did, the argument went, it would merely serve to confirm Castro's lies that the move was made to protect them from the consequences of a planned invasion of the island. In fact, Ambassador Bonsal was even more cautious than usual in dealing with the Cuban government, in this instance, on the grounds that "undue firmness" in dealing with the Cuban government would endanger the lives of American citizens in Cuba. Fears became intensified when, in the first week of July, the United States suspended Castro's sugar quota. We resolved the problem of American residents by "leaking" the information that it might be "wise" for them to leave.

Public reaction to the suspension of the sugar quota was, by the way, disappointing to the Cuban government. Suspension made the Castro regime even more unpopular, and that unpopularity was immediately apparent in the reluctance of the Cuban people to voluntarily present themselves at the Presidential Palace to "denounce" our "imperialist designs." Tad Szulc drove around the Palace and came back to my office, saying: "This is certainly no spontaneous and indignant outburst against the Yankee aggressor." He had found, he said, "only about fifty or sixty people" at the Palace. Packs of government militants soon swelled the crowd, stimulated by vicious broadcasts by government announcers.

The reason for the absence of throngs of volunteers before the palace was that Cubans were depressed, disgusted and afraid. So were most Americans, as, for example, Mrs. Bertha Price, a long time U.S. resident in Cuba. In July, 1960, Mrs. Price drove into Havana from the suburbs. Communist toughs had blocked the road on Fifth Avenue, where they had gathered in front of the Jesús de Miramar church to shout insults at the worshipers inside. Spotted as Americans by the toughs, Mrs. Price and her two sons were set upon and badly beaten. A magnificently sturdy woman, Mrs. Price managed to kick one of her assailants in the groin and beat off the others. She was immediately arrested for assault and battery, and taken to G-2 headquarters where her questioning was witnessed by Tad Szulc, who also had been arrested, and briefly detained, as he arrived at the airport to return to the United States.

According to Szulc, middle- and upper-class Cubans were brought into the G-2 offices and questioned for hours about their alleged "counter-revolutionary" thoughts. From time to time sleazy informers, belonging to the so-called Committees for the Defense of the Revolution, would arrive, whisper to the desk sergeant, and later would appear with one or more persons in tow. It was, as Tad explained, an act of "deliberate debasement."

Catholics were prime targets of Communist intimidation. In early August of 1960, the Catholic hierarchy of Cuba issued a pastoral letter condemning "the growing advance of Communism," calling it a matter of "extraordinary gravity." The Church was viciously attacked by *Revolucion* in an editorial. The pastoral letter, said *Revolucion*, "had been schemed up by those privileged interests hurt by the revolution." Nevertheless, the Catholics scheduled a National Catholic Congress, attended by about 600 delegates of the Church from all over Cuba. The Most Reverend Evelio Díaz, auxiliary bishop and the highest-ranking fighter in the Catholic hierarchy, asked for an appointment with President Dorticós to obtain assurances that the congress would not be disturbed by organized mobs. Dorticós refused to see him. Worshipers who attended the special mass for the Congress were besieged by a mob of 500 persons, organized and led by militia units. The mob slashed tires of cars parked in the vicinity, shouted anti-religious slogans, and threatened to break into the Congress and shoot the participants. Bishop Evelio Díaz called the police, to be told by them that the Catholics had provoked the demonstration. About midnight, a female militia member armed with a machine-gun, entered the mass and mounted the altar where she told the worshipers to leave the premises "in groups of not more than five at a time," and warned them they could expect to be protected from the mobs for only three blocks beyond the church.

The worst was yet to come. Late one Saturday night, I was sought out at the Hotel Nacional by a friend, Raúl Godoy. He excitedly burst upon a group of us while we were dining, and said: "The government has shot a Marine!" I had visions of Marines landing on the Malecón, and followed him out into the hallway where he said that a Marine guard at the Embassy had been shot in the stomach during an argument with a secret police official. The incident, he said, had occurred at the Club Twenty-One, across from the Hotel Capri. It was only two blocks away, so I quickly walked there.

The club was nearly empty when it normally would have been completely full at this time of night. I noticed that people were going in and out, apparently having heard of the incident and wanting to satisfy their curiosity. I asked the bartender what had happened, and he motioned with his head to the door where there was a large blood stain. While swabbing the bar, he rolled his eyes to the side of his head, indicating that there were others at the bar who were listening—government informers.

I went to the Embassy where Forest Geerken, the administrative officer, and George Gray, a special economic assistant to the Ambassador, were busy accumulating evidence and interviewing some courageous Cubans who had been present and had volunteered to tell what they knew. It was not a Marine who had been shot, but Wayne Henderson, one of the Embassy's code clerks who handled the classified messages. Gray, Geerken, and I were worried about this aspect. What did it mean?

The story, as told by Marine corporal William Tomkins, and verified by Cubans who had been sitting at the bar (and the next day by the bartender himself) was the following: Henderson, and Tomkins, the Marine dressed in civilian clothes (thank heaven), went to the Club Twenty-One to listen to a popular songstress. They ordered their drinks, drank them, and then asked for the check. The check came to $1.80 (one peso and eighty centavos). After searching their pockets, they found they had no Cuban money. (By the way, the Cuban peso had for decades been on a par with the U.S. dollar and was used interchangeably in Cuba until Castro broke Cuba's economy, and the U.S. dollar brought four pesos on the black market).

Henderson explained that they had lost their pesos at the roulette wheel of the cabaret in the Hotel Capri earlier, offered to go home and get some more, but also said he had a U.S. five-dollar bill. The bartender understood the situation, but replied that he could only give them back change in Cuban money, and went to the till to make change. A man sitting at the bar reached over and took the bill from the bartender, saying "I'll take that." He turned to Henderson and said in English: "Where did you get American money?" Henderson replied that the situation had already been explained to the bartender, and asked the man why he was interfering. The as yet unidentified man ignored the question and asked: "How much more American money do you have?" Henderson replied that it was none of his business, that he was an American and had the right to carry American money on his person.

The questioner took out his wallet, flicked the card of the Department of Investigation of the Rebel Army in front of Henderson's eyes, saying: "You want to go to jail?" Henderson replied, according to witnesses: "No, I just want to settle my bill and leave." The man, identified in *Revolucion* as an Sr. Alberto Blanco, placed both Henderson and Tomkins under arrest. The three of them—Henderson, Tomkins, and Blanco —moved toward the door. Blanco said that Yankees are "dirty. . . ." Henderson started to hit him, but had his arms pinned behind him by Tomkins.

At that moment, a man and woman got up from a nearby table. As Tomkins held Henderson's arms behind him to prevent him from striking Blanco for insulting the United States, the other man pulled a pistol from his pocket and, in front of the uncomprehending eyes of Tomkins, put it to Henderson's side, pulled the trigger and calmly walked away. It all seemed like slow motion to the witnesses when they spoke about it later.

Blanco, the secret service agent, panicked. He ran out into the street as Henderson collapsed like a bloody rag into the arms of Tomkins. There was a cab in front of the club, and Blanco, now with his own pistol in hand, ordered a youthful bystander to help Tomkins drag Henderson into the back seat. As they did so, the cab driver got out and ran away. Blanco then ordered the helpful youth to drive Henderson and Tomkins to the Naval hospital, and then turned and ran.

The frightened youth was a poor driver. Following a hair-raising drive through Havana's Saturday night traffic, he arrived at the hospital, crashing the car into one of the pillars fronting the building. Attendants rushed out, listened to the account given by the distraught boy, and quickly removed Henderson from the car and carried him inside. Tomkins took advantage of the confusion, hailed a cab and went to the Embassy where he reported the incident.

George Gray, the Ambassador's special assistant on economic affairs, was duty officer. After getting as much evidence as he could, he went to the hospital and stayed with Henderson through an operation which lasted for two hours. Later he was privy to a telephone conversation between Under Secretary of State Carlos Olivares and the surgeon. Olivares called to determine the condition of the patient. The surgeon later explained that Olivares then screamed: "That's what these Yankees get for trying to pass counterfeit money." There was, of course, no basis for Olivares to make such a charge. There was less reason for government official Alberto Blanco to refuse to accept responsibility for taking a man to the hospital whom he had officially placed under arrest. Most important, Blanco did not even try to apprehend the man who shot Henderson, a man whose intent was murder.

A check was later made on the man who had shot Henderson. His name was Sergio Robreno, a captain in the Rebel Army, said by his associates to take drugs. The latter information was given in answer to questions concerning his cold-blooded behavior.

The case was debated in cables between the Embassy, and the State Department. Finally, we sent the Ministry of Foreign Affairs a legally worded note, but did nothing further to press the case. After a long convalescence from his wounds, Wayne Henderson was sent back home.

Cubans saw such events taking place with little or no U. S. response. Furthermore, they were astonished and dismayed at the picture of Cuba that was being shown over American television. CBS offended their sensibilities and stretched credibility out of shape with programs which tended to paint the militia as heroic "defenders of Cuban soil." NBC was little better. One hour-long program was quite helpful to the Castro cause. This was unsurprising, since the principal adviser was June Cobb, an American citizen employed in the office of Prime Minister Castro. Reports of those programs reached Cuba, of course, adding to the already considerable despair of Cubans whose views of what was going on were in marked contrast to what Americans were seeing and hearing.

Behind the facade created by dominant segments of the American communications media, lay the sordid realities. Tremendous economic difficulties had befallen the nation as Cuban trade was redirected toward the Soviet bloc and Red China. The Communist nations were not really interested in Cuba's main product, sugar, since Czechoslovakia and Russia could supply all the sugar needed for bloc countries. Thus, the Communist powers were not at all dependent on Cuba in any economic sense.

The Cuban public knew that it was certainly politically important for the Communist countries to move into Cuba and make that country dependent on them. This explains, in part, why the Red Chinese gave Cuba an interest-free loan. In fact, when Guevara was prepared to make a statement to the effect that the aid forthcoming from Red China was "disinterested," he was brought up short by Chinese Foreign Minister Chou En-lai. "Our help," said Chou, "is by no means disinterested." He went on to explain that disinterest applied to "financial questions," implying, however, that the Chinese were very much interested in political questions.

Cuba's economy was geared to the American market. Because American suppliers were very close at hand, the Cubans did not have to spend money on warehousing facilities and could maintain a comparatively low inventory. These were but two of the many "invisible" economic advantages of trade with a friendly partner and close neighbor. Now, of course, everything had to spend weeks at sea, warehouses had to be erected in Cuba, with consideration even given to changing Cuba's railways from narrow to broad gauge. Guevara said of the changes that "it is an event unique in the annals of foreign trade that a whole community of countries should change its types of production to help a country like ours." He meant, of course, that the Communist bloc was tailoring some of its production to the special needs of the Cuban economy, including industrial designs and even weight measures. Thus, it was apparent that the Communist nations intended to make Cuba dependent on them, economically, politically and militarily.

It was no great surprise when Nikita Khrushchev rattled his rockets against the United States, on July 9, 1960, saying, "the time of the U.S. dictatorship has passed. The Soviet Union is raising its voice and extends its hand of assistance to the people of Cuba . . . the peoples of the socialist countries will help their brothers, the Cubans, to defend themselves so that the economic blockade now declared against Cuba by the U.S. will meet with failure. . . . It must not be forgotten that now the U.S. is not at such an unattainable distance from the Soviet Union as in the past. Figuratively speaking, Soviet artillerists, in the event it becomes necessary, can, with their missiles' power, support the Cuban people, if the aggressive forces in the Pentagon dare begin intervention in Cuba."

The "economic blockade" referred to by Khrushchev was the cut-off of the American sugar quota. While it is quite true that both Castro and Khrushchev wanted the United States to sever ties with Cuba, it does not follow from this, as some "losers" have it, that we would have gained by maintaining that quota or that its suspension "played into the hands" of the Russians. The "losers" are suggesting that the United States should have continued the quota and thus have assisted in financing a forward base of the Russians in this hemisphere.

Khrushchev felt emboldened to add to his rocket-rattling phrase the statement that "the Monroe Doctrine has died a natural death." A sharp response from President Eisenhower, rocked him back on his heels. Said the President: "I affirm in the most emphatic terms that the United States will not be deterred from its responsibilities by the threats Mr. Khrushchev is making. Nor will the United States, in conformity with its treaty obligations, permit the establishment of a regime dominated by international Communism in the Western Hemisphere."[2] Khrushchev then complained that his remarks had been "taken too literally."

The Eisenhower-Khrushchev exchange defined the battle line. The embassy staff was sharply reduced during the summer. In the months leading up to the break in diplomatic relations, which occurred in the first week of 1961, diplomacy was gradually retired from the field. In comformity with President Eisenhower's declarations, the Central Intelligence Agency began to prepare the Cuban underground for the overthrow of the Castro regime and the eradication of a Communist base in the hemisphere.

Basic to that decision, which of course also extended to the training of Cuban exiles in the United States, was the belief that Castro's meaningful support had dwindled and would evaporate. Resistance to his regime was also assessed—largely by negative yardsticks. By the end of 1960, the Embassy estimated that there were between 15,000 and 20,000 political prisoners in Cuba's jails, and that perhaps 2,000 had been executed by the Castro regime. We possessed literally hundreds of reports of torture and other forms of mistreatment. The police organs of the state were everywhere, representative of the regime's hard-headed assessment of internal unrest.

It was not surprising, either, that the totalitarian state of Fidel Castro, as the regime of Fulgencio Batista, relied more and more on criminal elements to maintain control. The information was pieced together from various bits of testimony. One example: a guard at the Principe Prison in Havana, Juan Gonzalez Fernandez, was revolted by the types of individuals who held the reins of police authority in Cuba and managed to get transferred. He said: "Though many decent but misguided individuals joined the Castro regime at the outset, many of them have become disgusted and want out. Criminals serving time for various crimes (rape, robbery, murder) were released on parole, and sworn into the militia." There were scores of such reports, including another which said: "When daughters, mothers, and wives go to visit their loved ones in prison, they are made to stand for hours in the sun or in the rain. While standing in the lines, they are insulted, abused, and exposed to coarse wooing by the guards. Often, after waiting for hours, the visits are deliberately cancelled. Before reaching the place where they can talk with their loved ones, they are subjected to searches of their bodies by female militia members, many of whom are sexual perverts. . . ."

The regime also did everything in its power to prevent the flight of Cubans to the United States. Every traveler was required to have police permission and forbidden to take money with him. Airline tickets had to be purchased in the United States with American dollars, and the purchases had to be round-trip. In the fall of 1960, the International Rescue Committee made a social analysis of the refugees coming to Miami, finding that sixty-one percent were blue- and white-collar workers.

Scenes at the airport, from May until January, were particularly revealing. While there were defections of very important people, the statistics of the International Rescue Committee indicated that the defections which hurt Castro were those of the working class whose skilled and semi-skilled members were sorely needed. Castro could not shrug off the flight of his labor force as he could the flight of those liberals in his cabinet who had lent respectability to his Communist regime—the "doctrinally weak Leftists" so contemptuously referred to by Professor Bettelheim in his memorandum.

Hundreds of Cubans lined up at the counters of Pan American Airways —small children, elderly people, and harassed young and middle-aged couples. Personal luggage included tricycles, blankets, virtually everything that was movable. They could not take automobiles, their table silver, anything of value. The government seized all that. The value of watches and wedding rings was assessed by G-2 agents at the airport, and often those agents would take those watches and rings on the spot. One may judge the "honesty" of the regime by these and other facts.

For example, packs of neighborhood informers entered houses, took furniture, paintings, linens, clocks, and watches and turned them over to the government. The government in turn furnished the houses of Russian and Communist-bloc personnel with those items.

Most will recall the newsreels of East European refugees from Communism—sad, broken and impoverished—trekking into West Europe by ox cart, riding bicycles, going by foot, or even hidden under coal in a railroad gondola. If there had been a ninety-mile bridge from Havana to Key West, instead of the 100,000 or more Cubans who had fled by the end of 1960, their number would have swelled to where Castro would have been left with nothing more than a corporal's guard. What Castro and his Communists had succeeded in doing was triggering the greatest mass migration in the history of the Western Hemisphere. Yet the "losers" would have us believe that only the rich were affected.

More important to the considerations of our intelligence people was the fact that the *guajiro* had turned against the regime. Highly propagandized for years as the principal support for, and beneficiary of, the Revolution, the *guajiro* was recognized by the Cuban government to be its chief enemy. From 1960 on, the independent-minded Cuban peasant became the chief focus of support for the resistance and the destroyer of the agrarian economy of Cuba. This was clearly recognized when, early in 1960, INRA functionary Oscar Pino Santos wrote in an article entitled "Raíz, Estructura y Ritmo de la Reforma Agraria Cubana," that "counter-revolutionary elements [struck against] the Agrarian Reform ... with sabotage [in the cane fields] ... which, if successful, would have caused serious difficulties. ..."

But the point was this: the success which resistance could be expected to achieve was tempered by two equations—the moral and material support which it received from outside the country, and the unpopularity of Communism within the island. Theodore Draper admits to the intensity of public resistance at the time, writing that "the situation in Cuba had been building up to some kind of popular explosion...."[3] Thus, there were few doubts about the unpopularity of the regime. But, it was virtually impossible for internal resistance movements to be supplied from the outside with the ease by which Castro had been supplied years earlier in carrying out his do-it-yourself revolt against Batista. Having seized the initiative, Castro never relinquished it, keeping the United States on the defensive and preventing meaningful support to his enemies. If for no other reason, it was necessary to establish a military force outside of Cuba. And it was established.

The creation in 1960 of the anti-Castro Democratic Revolutionary Front in Miami, and under it a force of trained Cuban exiles, was not merely a personal reaction of a Republican President of the United States who disliked Castro and loathed Communism. The *Frente*, as it was originally called, was established on the hard-headed assessment that a Communist Cuba threatened the hemisphere and was a direct threat, as well, to the security of the United States. For example, two code clerks from the super-secret U.S. National Security agency were revealed to have defected to Russia in September 1960, and to have made their way to Moscow via Cuba. The two defectors, Bernon F. Mitchell and William H. Martin, were picked up at a Cuban port by a Russian fishing trawler and taken to the Soviet Union.

A handful of Cuban exiles secured documents from Castro's Embassy in Lima, Peru, which were revealing as to the designs of the Russian-Cuban combine now in power in Havana. The documents disclosed that "destitute" Cuba had been spending on the average of $20,000 a month in Lima for nearly eighteen months to suborn political leaders, legislators, students, and the mass media. Castro's Ambassador to Peru, Luis Ricardo Alonso, was ordered by Acting Foreign Minister Carlos Olivares to play upon national disputes between Ecuador and Peru, and other countries. One of the letters to Olivares from Alonso spoke openly of ties with the Communists. He wrote: "to inform you of the international funds that were entrusted [to me] to be delivered to the Peruvian Communist Party, which reciprocated by giving me a report about the work it is carrying out in all of Peru in defense of the Cuban revolution."

Alonso provided some dimension to guerrilla activities: "In accordance with instructions received from the Minister of the Armed Forces, Comandante Raúl Castro, I have been busy with the organization of the insurrectional groups in conjunction with the Communist Party and the Rebel Apra. . . ." Alonso went on: "I was able to develop the plan that was drafted in Havana. According to this plan, Peru should be made the center of the anti-capitalist defense."

But the most eye-opening part of the captured letter from Castro's Ambassador dealt with the fact that Russians and Chinese had already penetrated the Cuban government for the purpose of subverting Latin America. He wrote: "I have been told that the technical advisers of the Soviet Union and People's Republic of China in . . . your Ministry have based great hopes in the work that is being carried out in Peru." He also spoke of "assuming the revolutionary direction of the student masses, workers and the peasants, resolutely linked to the Cuban Revolution."[4]

Also in 1960, Clark Galloway, Latin American correspondent for *U.S. News and World Report*, came to my office in the Embassy in Havana. He had been to Brazil where he got a confidential look at the inner workings of *Prensa Latina* from defector Paulo de Castro, head of the Rio de Janeiro branch of that news agency. He told Galloway that *Prensa Latina* had an *apparat* for espionage purposes. According to his interview, as given to Clark Galloway, two of the directors of *Prensa Latina*, came to Río the year before and told de Castro that the agency was established precisely to implement Fidel Castro's foreign policy. Herman Koncke, a Uruguayan employee of *Prensa Latina* and a member of the *apparat*, confessed to de Castro that the news agency "was engaged in espionage and subversion."

For all of these reasons the CIA in Cuba was working with the embryo Cuban underground in a manner consistent with its possibilities of being effective. Theodore Draper writes that this is not so. "There was," he writes, "of course, no guarantee that there would ever be a large-scale popular rebellion against Castro; the existing policy, however, had for many months not even encouraged one, politically or practically." He says that "The Eisenhower Administration had not given the underground priority."[5]

It is here that Mr. Draper goes awry. To him, the Cuban underground represented the "progressive," or democratic forces—López Fresquet,

Manuel Ray, Pazos, Matos. In short, all those who at one time occupied high places in the Castro government, but who did not meet the Communist challenge from those positions of power. The outside group of exiles under training were doomed from the start because, Draper writes, they included *Batistianos*. After making a case that since the force included *Batistianos*, and since their inclusion "would not sit as well with Cubans in Cuba as with some of those in exile," he then surprisingly, reverses himself later concerning their importance by saying that "nevertheless, the invasion force was broadly representative of the entire exile community."[6]

The facts are that a considerable amount of sabotage and psychological warfare were being carried out the latter half of 1960 and the first few months of 1961. It is also a fact that these acts were carried out by quite an efficient CIA organization in Cuba. What the CIA did was to furnish direction and cohesion to the underground and to supply ideas, cadres for training, and necessary ammunition and equipment. Targets of the CIA-directed underground were largely confined to properties which had been seized by the government. Thus three major department stores in downtown Havana—the Fin de Siglo, La Epoca, and, later, El Encanto —went up in smoke. A huge tobacco warehouse located directly in back of the capital building was burned, according to the Cuban government with the loss of over a million dollars. Sugar-mill machinery was being sabotaged, and the acid content in the sugar deliberately raised by sugar mill chemists to make it inedible. Sugar sacks were neatly torn.

In the country, *guajiros* soaked rags in kerosene, tied them to the tails of rats, set them afire and threw them into the cane fields where the rodents would run wildly about, extending the fires so that the militia could not extinguish them readily. The regime responded by creating "voluntary fire brigades" in every sugar mill and office building in Cuba. In the fall of 1960, thirty-one bombs were exploded throughout Havana as Castro spoke to militia students at the University of Havana. Ruby Hart Phillips of the *New York Times*, Bob Berrellez of AP, and I each kept count and compared notes.

By February 27, 1961 (we broke relations with Castro on January 3, 1961), the Cuban government admitted that it was encountering fierce anti-Communist resistance with the announcement that it had captured "up to 900 counterrevolutionaries" in the mountains of central Cuba. A more realistic report coming from local commanders in the area of Cienfuegos said, however, that the government had suffered about 150 casualties in capturing about 300 insurgents. As these conflicting claims were being made, the Ministry of Armed Forces announced the beginning of a one-month campaign in which 50,000 militia were thrown into the battle against anti-Communist forces holed-up in the mountains.

Yet, Draper claims that an internal uprising "was a fundamental tenet of the Left." If that is so, then we must conclude, from the fact that the CIA was engaged in underground activities in Cuba, that the Central Intelligence Agency was with the Left. Mr. Draper does not think so, however, since he apparently did not know, or perhaps did not want to find out, that incendiarism going on in Cuba was neither spontaneous combustion nor the result of the Left underground, working all by itself. Through some research, interested observers could have discovered the truth. The truth was that the Central Intelligence Agency worked with those willing to fight—the underground *and* the exiles. This should put the CIA just about in the middle of the political spectrum.

The Left-Right thesis is important. As Draper, Tad Szulc and Karl Meyer, Matthews, and others of their persuasion have it, the possibility of a successful invasion was greatly diminished by the alleged war raging among the exiles. It is important to understand that this was not actually of any critical importance to ultimate success, but in propagating this artificial conflict, they served President Kennedy well by later saddling the CIA with responsibility for a defeat which was caused by the President's own timidity in action. There were disagreements, yes. There was no "war among the exiles," as Mr. Draper characterized it. Says Draper: "Those with an underground orientation could not hope to be effective in Cuba with the same type of program and propaganda that might appeal to many exiles in the United States."[7] What program? What propaganda? He continues: "Many of the exiles had never had any faith in Castro to lose, and he was just as obnoxious to them before taking power as after."

Doesn't Mr. Draper know that much of the political and military leadership of the Bay of Pigs force was made up precisely of those who *did*, indeed, have faith in Castro to begin with? Doesn't he know that the United States insisted on such a leadership for the very reason that it would lend credibility to the invasion force? Doesn't Draper know that the political leader was Castro's first Prime Minister, José Miró Cardona? Or that Manuel Artime was the civilian head of the Bay of Pigs? Or that Under Secretary of Commerce under Castro, Orlando Cuervo, was a communications officer for the invasion force?

More important, doesn't Mr. Draper know that the CIA brought Comandante Sorí Marín out of Cuba, trained him in underground warfare and command functions, and then sent him back in to maintain liaison between Mr. Draper's theoretical Right in Miami and the Left in Cuba, who, according to Draper and Szulc, were the combatants in this Left-Right conflict? Not only was Sorí Marín with Fidel Castro in the Sierra Maestra, he was also his first Minister of Agriculture whose "faith" in Castro was lost with the deceit of his own agrarian reform! Indeed, these are remarkable statements for Mr. Draper to make.

It would seem that Messrs. Draper, Szulc, Meyer, and many, many more were taken in by the astute political agitation of Manuel Ray who, by their definition, embodied the underground "Left." Mr. Ray is Left-wing by his own admission. But Mr. Ray also took full credit for acts of sabotage carried out in Havana under the name of his Party, the MRP, which he could not have carried out if it were not for the CIA, with whom he was working. If there was a conflict, it was exacerbated by the same Mr. Ray when he blasted his benefactors after the Bay of Pigs for a failure that was caused by John F. Kennedy himself. The CIA is an inviting target for people's frustrations, since it cannot talk back.

Mr. Draper is correct, however, in one aspect of his understanding of the political direction of the Kennedy Administration. In view of the Cuban Revolutionary Council's replacing the old *Frente*, he writes that a distinct shift had been made to the left. With Manuel Ray pressured into joining the group, the political shift to the left was not surprising, and the declaration which came out of the Council reflected that shift. What Draper really means, then, is that the shift to the left was a reflection of the same leftward shift of the Kennedy Administration, which had assumed control of the government. Written in Washington, the declaration of the Council renounced "the previous regime, which had impoverished the whole country for the benefit of a minority lusting for gold and power. . . . Let there be no mistake. During the immediate post-revolutionary period some of the ideals of the people, which were part of the national goal, were achieved."

The above statements were foisted off on José Miró Cardona; they were not a true expression of the situation in "the immediate post-revolutionary period. . . ." at all. The statement was curiously like another statement, written by Arthur Schlesinger, Jr. in the White House. It appeared in a "White Paper," and created considerable doubt in the minds of many people as to just how much the new Administration knew about Cuba, and how much was progressive nonsense:

"The positive programs initiated in the first months of the Castro regime—the schools built, the medical clinics established, the new housing, the early projects of land reform, the opening up of beaches and resorts to the people, the elimination of graft in government—were impressive in their conception; no future Cuban government can expect to turn its back on such objectives. But so far as the expressed political aims of the revolution were concerned, the record of the Castro regime has been a record of the steady and consistent betrayal of Dr. Castro's pre-revolutionary promises; and the result has been to corrupt the social achievements and make them the means, not of liberation, but of bondage."

The policy implications in the White Paper statement created a panic in the Cuban exile community. There simply was little truth in the White Paper statements. Had, then, the exiles been wrong in their assessment of Fidel Castro, after all? It would seem so from the White Paper. To a great extent, this passage was nothing more than a repetition of what the "losers" in our press had been publishing for two years. More to the point at the time was a fear among exiles as to what the line taken in the White House would do to the resolution of Mr. Draper's "Left" underground in Cuba. They, and the literally hundreds of thousands of Cubans trying to get out of Cuba, knew that what had been written as a White Paper and broadcast by the Voice of America throughout Latin America and into Cuba was not true. What did it mean? In fact, the underground tried to find that out in advance of the Bay of Pigs invasion.

Cubans, and many Americans as well, had listened to the tough words of President Kennedy when he was campaigning for election. It was not readily apparent, however, that he had really no idea of what to do about Castro. The public apparently believed him when, while campaigning, he advocated precisely what was being carried out at the time of his address: "We must attempt to strengthen the non-Batista democratic anti-Castro forces in exile, and in Cuba itself, who offer eventual hope of overthrowing Castro." He then added the totally false sentence: "Thus far these fighters for freedom have had virtually no support from our government."

But what many forgot was that John F. Kennedy had expressed himself otherwise, and in a manner completely in keeping with the White Paper. He said: "Fidel Castro is part of the legacy of Simón Bolívar who led his men over the Andes Mountains, vowing 'war to the death' against Spanish rule. . . ." Fidel Castro was far from the great Latin American liberator, as should have been clear to a future President who, by his own earlier statements, knew that he would have to deal with Castro. Thus, despite his many tough statements against Castro during the election campaign, once inaugurated, President Kennedy drastically altered his line. In February, 1961, he suggested that if free elections were held in Cuba, he would be disposed to negotiate differences with Fidel Castro. Equivocation continued when Secretary of State Dean Rusk told Senator George Smathers that he was "not yet disposed . . . to favor a Cuban boycott."

Victor Lasky's book, *JFK: The Man and the Myth,* is very revealing as to Kennedy's views on Cuba. Kennedy is quoted to the effect that it was U.S. failure to give Cuba sufficient economic aid that turned the people against us. The Kennedy quotations are: 1) "We refused to help Cuba meet its desperate need for economic progress," and 2) "We used the influence of our government to advance the interests and increase the profits of the private American companies which dominate the island's economy." Thus, Lasky correctly concludes: "In effect, Kennedy had adopted the Castro line, which was that the United States had been robbing the Cuban people blind."[8]

Thus, of all people, John F. Kennedy was the one most uniquely unsuited to carrying out the liberation of Cuba. His equivocations which put him on both sides of the fence during the election campaign carried over in his handling of the Bay of Pigs. President Kennedy had adopted the argument of the "losers." Cubans who were worried about the White Paper were quite justified in their concern, for every step President Kennedy took, commencing with the White Paper, was designed to weaken chances of success.

CHAPTER **11**

•

The Cuban Operation

•

THERE IS LITTLE TO INDICATE that, as candidate and as President, John F. Kennedy fully grasped the meaning of a Soviet Cuba, or that he was resolved to deal with the threat that it posed. There is little to indicate, either, that President Kennedy's inexperienced staff, his "New Frontier," had given much thought to Cuba beyond satisfying the demands of the election campaign. As the *Washington Post* remarked about Kennedy and his utterances on Cuba made during the campaign: "Mr. Kennedy has been rather extravagant in his criticism and rather unsatisfying as to just what to do."[1]

With no clear idea as to what to do about Fidel Castro, the new President and his staff were to take over the planning which had been initiated by President Eisenhower. Recognizing that the conquest of nations no longer was necessarily brought about by vast armies streaming across national boundaries, Eisenhower decided to plug holes in our treaty obligations, the holes through which Communist subversion was spreading, unopposed, throughout the hemisphere. President Eisenhower had seen in Cuba the chilling example of how skilled Communists took over the press and labor unions, seized control of the government, and were turning the country over to the Soviet Union.

It was with these insights that, a full ten months before the elections of November 1960, President Dwight D. Eisenhower set about strengthening the legal basis for the overthrow of Castro and the eradication of Communism from the hemisphere. Diplomacy and political considerations of the moment had to give way to acceptable military and paramilitary operations. Addressing the presidents of Latin American countries at Rio de Janeiro, Brazil, in January 1960, Eisenhower stated that the traditional concepts of "aggression" had to be revised to include "subversion," and, in so saying, he updated the Monroe Doctrine. "We would consider it to be intervention in the internal affairs of an American state," said the President of the United States, "if any power [meaning Soviet Russia] whether by invasion, coercion, or subversion, succeeded in denying the freedom of choice [of the way of life and government] of any of our sister republics."

At that same meeting in Rio, Brazilian President Juscelino Kubitschek made a dramatic statement: "Every day I am becoming more and more convinced that the decisive and final struggle for domination of the world will be fought in this continent."[2] Thus, a quasi-legal argument had been advanced supporting the use of active measures to overthrow Castro and to put an end to Soviet ventures in the hemisphere. And, in the succeeding months, President Eisenhower gradually turned planning for military activities over to the proper agencies of the government—the Pentagon and the Central Intelligence Agency who created the Cuban Democratic Revolutionary Front. Comprised of Cuban leaders and politicians in exile in Miami, the Front was just that—a front. Under its political cover, U.S. military officers and intelligence officials carried out the real work.

The Administration received support for its decisions from a most unlikely source—the American Embassy in Havana—which had become alarmed at the speed with which the Russians were occupying Cuba. From July 1960 to the end of that year, evidences of Soviet penetration, not only of Cuba but of the hemisphere, had shaken U.S. officials in Havana.

In August, 1960, the Soviets sent 700 "technicians" to Santiago. With them came huge crates and boxes. The boxes contained MIG fighters, while the crates, it is now suspected, contained parts of missiles. Suspicious cargoes were also being unloaded at the northern Cuban ports of Matanzas, Bahía Honda, and Mariel. Of the cargo received in those ports, the huge boxes and crates were singled out for special attention. As *U.S. News and World Report* put it at the time: "Cuban longshoremen are not allowed to handle them (the crates and boxes). They are unloaded by Russian crews." Tons of Soviet armaments openly poured into Cuba.

Travelers from Santiago to Havana remarked that the Russians seemed uncomfortable in their cheap and ill-fitting civilian clothes. Most wore checked sport shirts—either green, red, or blue. It was suspected at the time that the Russians were military men in mufti. It was later discovered that the shirts corresponded to military units—red was for artillery, blue for missile technicians, and green for engineers. They moved into the exhibition halls of Santiago's fairgrounds where, with military efficiency, they turned the halls into barracks. Shepherded by interpreters and Russian "guides" who acted like drill sergeants, the visitors moved around Santiago in groups, never singly or in pairs, and refused to answer questions put to them by Cubans, astonished by their presence, as to why they were in Cuba.

Russians also came through Rancho Boyeros airport near Havana in increasing numbers throughout the summer of 1960. Customs inspection waived, the Muscovites were speeded on their way in official cars provided by the Cuban government. The same month of August that saw the influx of Russians, Hungarians, and Czechs into the cities, also found hundreds of Iron Curtain personnel touring the interior of the island. The Cuban government made claims that they were looking for iron ore deposits, oil, and the like, but the excuses were not taken seriously. American engineers had been over the island with a fine-tooth comb for nearly fifty years. Their findings on the absence of iron and the presence of little oil were already in the files of the Cuban government.

United States intelligence was disturbed by other reports which indicated that the Russians had plans for military construction. Accompanied by Cuban military officers, groups of Russians toured the area of the deep-water Bay of Nipe in Oriente Province. Russians also appeared in and around Cuba's vast underground cave complexes in Pinar del Río, Matanzas, and Oriente Provinces.

In actual fact, it was not known just how many Russians had come to Cuba in 1960. Reports flooded our Embassy in Havana and our Consulate in Santiago that the Russians had been seen in small towns and villages in the interior, where there was no apparent reason for them to be. The reports were difficult to check. One, however, was not. United States Naval authorities at the Guantanamo Naval Base said that the Russians were dressing Cubans in U.S. Navy uniforms, and, against the backdrop of our Navy installations, taking motion pictures of them "beating" Cuban women and children. The films, obviously, were destined for Communist propaganda outlets throughout the world.

There was also a significant Russian cultural penetration of Cuba going on. At the University of Oriente in Santiago, 60 professors out of a total teaching staff of 113 were summarily dismissed because, said Santiago's Communist newspaper, *Sierra Maestra*, "their thinking did not coincide with that of the people." They were replaced by Soviet and Iron Curtain professors whose thinking ostensibly did. There, at the University of Oriente, they lectured on Communist doctrine and economics to a rapidly shrinking student body.

A regular exchange of diplomatic dispatches had been arranged between our Embassy in Havana and other American Embassies throughout the hemisphere. In reading those dispatches, we found how the daily denigration of the United States by Cuban authorities in Havana was providing an example for the rest of Latin America. There, Castroite and Communist mobs were demonstrating increasingly against "Yankee aggression" and "Yankee imperialism" in Cuba and taking the opportunity to accuse their own governments of supporting that "aggression" and "imperialism." There could be no question that mob violence being reported from other Latin American countries was receiving its inspiration and support from Cuba.

It gives one pause to consider that the bloody Canal Zone riots of 1964 were spawned back in 1960 when Cuban Ambassador José Antonio Cabrera journeyed regularly to Chiriquí Province and exhorted the ignorant Indian populace to march on the Canal Zone. He met with Communist and nationalist students and supplied them with money and direction to launch a steady propaganda campaign against "Yankee occupation of national territory."

In Argentina, we found that Cuban Ambassador Américo Cruz Fernández had made common cause with the *Peronista* movement of deposed dictator Juan Perón, begun work on guerrilla camps, and disseminated Communist propaganda under the direction of *Peronista* John William Cooke (head of the Argentine delegation to Havana's tricontinental conference in 1966).

In La Paz, Bolivia, Cuban Ambassador José Tabares Real joined forces with Communist Juan Lechín, leader of Bolivia's powerful tin miners' union. Together they plotted the overthrow of the Bolivian government.

Brazil had become a danger spot. Retiring President Juscelino Kubitscheck was out, and erratic, unstable Janio Quadros was in. During the election campaign of 1960, Quadros visited Castro in Havana. When he took office, Quadros said he would pursue an "independent" foreign policy, and he proved it by permitting the Castroites and Communists to move about Brazil at will. Castroites opened offices and recruited Brazilian youths to go to Cuba for guerrilla training (called "scholarships"). The National Students' Union urged its members to "defend the Cuban revolution."

As Ambassador to Colombia, Castro named a former guerrilla fighter who served under him in the Sierra Maestra. The task of Ambassador Adolfo Rodríguez de la Vega was to convert the natural guerrilla structure of Colombia's bandits, who for decades had virtually ruled the back country, into instruments of Communist direction. He supplied money in Colombia and guerrilla training in Cuba to two bandit leaders—Pedro Marín and Juan de la Cruz—and promised them a stake in a "new revolutionary government," when they returned.

The Central American countries of El Salvador, Costa Rica, and Nicaragua were under heavy pressures from Communist Cuba, which provoked bloody riots and political disturbances of various kinds. In Guatemala, plans to assassinate President Miguel Ydígoras Fuentes were accompanied by radio broadcasts from Havana where Jacobo Arbenz said: "I will soon be back at the head of a new triumphant revolution."

Something of what U.S. envoys were seeing of increasing traffic between the Iron Curtain and Cuba was related by Ambassador Robert C.

Hill. "Agents coming from Moscow and some from China go back and forth between the Soviet Embassies in Mexico and Cuba," he told me in Mexico City. He warned that Mexico City was a potential headquarters for clandestine Communist travel. Castro's Ambassador to Mexico, José Antonio Portuondo Baldor, called on the Soviet Ambassador before he even extended his credentials to the Mexican government. Perhaps foreseeing the inevitability of breaks between Cuba and other Latin American countries, the Russians and the Cubans concentrated on obtaining acceptability for their actions from the peculiar Leftist and anti-American-tinged government party of Mexico. It is difficult not to conclude that there was considerable advance planning.

The American Embassy in Havana watched and reported to the intelligence community in Washington on the rapid development of Cuba into a Communist monster crouching on our doorstep. The response was to recall Ambassador Philip W. Bonsal. From that time forward, policy was in the hands of military intelligence and the Central Intelligence Agency. The Eisenhower Administration had, in effect, given diplomacy ample opportunity to defend U.S. and hemispheric interests. When failure in accomplishing that mission could no longer be questioned, diplomacy was retired from the field.

Dan Braddock had again assumed charge of the Embassy, and set about examining the chief tenet which had been guiding U.S. policy. During several long staff meetings, we pondered questions. "Had our efforts to get along with Castro been effective?" The answer was no. "Did we stand well with our Latin American colleagues?" The answer was yes and no. Up until Castro's performance on October 26, 1959, the American posture of restraint had proved to Latin America that the United States was no gross bully attempting to do in a seemingly hopeful change for the better in Cuba. Incredibly, by the summer of 1960, however, mighty Uncle Sam was viewed in Latin America as the victim of the Cuban bully, Fidel Castro—not a flattering picture. Further, Latin American Ambassadors in Havana could find no ready explanation to forward to their governments as to why the United States permitted Cuba, an off-shore island, to carry on the subversion of Latin America in actual violation of treaty commitments which made it mandatory that we do something about it.

The State Department and the intelligence community in Washington must have been shaken by the seriousness with which the Embassy now tackled the Cuban problem. With the unanimous concurrence of the major Embassy elements—CIA, U.S. Information Agency, Navy-Air Force-Army intelligence—Braddock recommended that action against Castro be speeded up. It seemed most unlikely that the necessarily slow course of internal anti-Castro subversion could possibly keep pace with

254 · THE LOSERS

the speed with which the Russians were arming Cuba. Actions which were advocated were: 1) enlarge the capabilities of exiles to launch an attack, or attacks, on Cuba; 2) provide massive support to the Cuban underground, currently being trained by CIA agents; 3) interdict Soviet shipping, following a diplomatic confrontation and a demand that Russian arms shipments to Cuba stop; 4) as a last resort, and in the absence of a positive response from Russia, declare an airtight blockade under the various treaty provisions available to us.

The recommendations presupposed a break in diplomatic relations with Cuba, and a break was urged. We believed that a diplomatic break was imperative to the success of one, or more, of the recommendations. The admittedly dangerous and delicate mission of the CIA in arming and organizing the Cuban underground was made even more risky because it was being carried out within the context of outwardly peaceful diplomatic relations. The operations, obviously, were inhibited. Despite Castro's large militia force, the CIA knew from experimentation that the militia was not sufficiently organized to patrol effectively Cuba's enormous coastline. With all wraps taken off by a diplomatic break, gunrunners and infiltrators could move into Cuba like clouds of mosquitoes. And they would be as difficult as mosquitoes to track down and crush.

There was another point to breaking relations. American citizens had to be gotten out of Cuba. As underground activities swelled in intensity and effectiveness, it was certain that reprisals would be visited on those Americans still residing in Cuba. The Price and Henderson atrocities provided a foretaste of what could be expected, yet American residents stayed in Cuba as long as we had an Embassy in Havana. They did so in a largely vain attempt to recoup, for many of them at least, their life savings and investments. The Cuban government had not, of course, issued a single bond in payment for the expropriation of properties, nor was there any visible sign that it ever intended to make good on its responsibilities under international law.

One important recommendation from the Embassy to Washington dealt with psychological warfare. We had to indicate to the embattled Cubans that the forces of democracy—the United States and Latin American nations, in particular—were as dedicated to restoring their liberty as the forces of Soviet Russia were bent on destroying that liberty. Cubans looked on in despair as Russian ships arrived almost daily at their ports openly discharging military cargoes which could have no purpose other than to turn Cuba into one vast concentration camp. United States identification with Cuban liberation would, it was believed, be worth hundreds of tons of arms and ammunition.

We in the Embassy were particularly impressed by President-elect Kennedy's skill as an orator, and recalled his urging a month earlier, that

". . . we use all available communications—radio, television, and the press—and the moral power of the American government, to let the forces of freedom in Cuba know that we are on their side." With such a gifted and aggressive propagandist at the helm, apparently willing to use his talents in the interest of freedom, Embassy elements believed that we could expect a skillful and aggressive campaign to resolve the Cuban issue.

Embassy estimates that Castro now had a militia force in excess of 300,000 men apparently jolted Washington. For, in November, the State Department released information that *Castro's armed might was ten times that of Batista and was growing.* Significantly, though obliquely, the State Department also recognized the possibility of there being missiles in Cuba by gratuitously denying published reports that they were there.

Coincident with the State Department's release in November concerning the numerical strength of Castro's forces, the decision was made *not* to place primary reliance on internal subversion, *which was never a fast and hard plan.* Instead, it was agreed by representatives of the CIA, the Pentagon, the White House and the State Department, that gears should be shifted into high, and that we should develop a plan envisioning a perimeter landing in Cuba of a force sufficient to hold ground and to protect a group of Cuban civilians who would represent a Provisional Government on Cuban soil. That same month, CIA Director Allen Dulles and his deputy in charge of the Cuban operation, Richard Bissell, fully briefed President-elect Kennedy on everything that was going on. Specifically, he was told of the change in emphasis from guerrilla warfare to a perimeter landing, and the reasons therefor.

There is nothing in the written record to indicate that Mr. Kennedy objected to the switch in plans, though Kennedy apologists seek to see in the switch the death knell of the Cuban operation. Haynes Johnson, in his book, *The Bay of Pigs,* finds the change "astonishing in view of the known strength of Castro's forces then."[3] Tad Szulc and Karl Meyer write in their book, *The Cuban Invasion,* that the shift was made because of "the CIA's distrust of the left-liberal underground forces, a distrust which prompted them to place their main reliance on aging Cuban politicians."[4] These writers, and others, miss the point. They miss it, perhaps, because they are in a mental strait jacket which will not permit them to admit that by 1960 the Russians had to all intents and purposes taken control of Cuba. They still pursued the will-o-the-wisp view that Castro was "independent" of Moscow and international Communism. And the fact is that "aging politicians" provided little more than a useful political cover for Cuban youths who fought at the Bay of Pigs.

Despite all that had been done to impress Mr. Kennedy with the seriousness of the Cuban situation, on April 4, 1961, after listening to Richard Bissell of the CIA outline the plan for the liberation of Cuba, the President limited his comments to saying: "Under no circumstances are American forces to be used."[5] General Eisenhower, the experienced commander of the Normandy invasion, briefed Kennedy on the international situation following inauguration. Specifically, he told the new President that, with Soviet arms pouring into Cuba, "there is no time to lose. You may have to send troops in."[6]

Bissell's briefing, checked and agreed to in principle by the Joint Chiefs of Staff,* laid out the strength and weaknesses of the enemy, and how the one was to be sapped and the other exploited. The assessment was enough to alarm the most phlegmatic of personalities. In less than two years' time, the Russians had supplied Castro not only with enough arms for an enormous militia force, but with quantities of heavy and light caliber artillery, tanks, and, it was suspected, MIG jet fighters. One of the prime reasons for speed in striking at Castro's forces was to do so before he got a force of Russian MIGs into the air. Once that happened, only a major operation could dislodge him.

Indeed, pro-Kennedy writers, Tad Szulc and Karl E. Meyer admit in their book, *The Cuban Invasion:* "It was known that Castro had Soviet MIG fighters in crates and that Cuban fliers were training in Czechoslovakia. This meant that Castro would soon be unbeatable by any outside force that relied on conventional aircraft."[7] While the judgment in their second sentence may be considered somewhat extreme, Szulc and Meyer do arrive at the essential truth—further dallying would mitigate powerfully against success of the operation as then planned. Theodore Draper, however, finds in his book, *Castro's Revolution*, that the motivating factor behind the speed with which the Cuban operation was launched was a mere "deadline fixation" amongst Cuban exiles in the United States.

The plan for the Bay of Pigs operation outlined by Bissell on April 4, 1961, was a substitute for another plan which President Kennedy had

---

*It no longer is a secret that President Kennedy harbored inside of him anti-military sentiments, and it is even less of a secret that for some reason or another he held his seasoned military advisers in low esteem. This led to a breakdown of communications between the military and intelligence chiefs on the one side, and the politicians on the other, and Mr. Kennedy never filled that void with Presidential leadership. First, he called for a briefing from the CIA, then asked the Joint Chiefs of Staff for an "appreciation" of the validity of the Cuban operation. But he never assumed positive control of the operation, and the focus of responsibility was permitted to waver between the Defense Department and the Central Intelligence Agency, and the political theorists in the State Department and the White House. It does seem clear that the political theorists had the final say in the matter, but because of Mr. Kennedy's vacillation, were able to duck a responsibility which had never clearly been fixed. See Charles J. V. Murphy, "Cuba: The Record Set Straight," *Fortune*, September, 1961, and Theodore C. Sorenson *Kennedy* (New York: Harper & Row, 1965.)

earlier rejected. The earlier plan consisted of landing near the south coast of the city of Trinidad. For Trinidad, its sister city Cienfuegos, and the surrounding mountains of the Escambray were a hotbed of anti-Castro sentiment and counterrevolutionary activity. Should expected military defections on a significant scale fail to materialize, members of the Brigade had sufficient power to fight their way to the mountains and join forces with the rebels. The second-effort aspects of the plan were appealing to the military men in charge of the operation.

The Trinidad operation, however, was not appealing to President Kennedy and his State Department advisers. An amphibious landing in such a populous area, they said, would have all the earmarks of a U.S.-mounted expedition, and U.S. involvement would be difficult to hide. Why a landing in the Trinidad area would be more revealing of U.S. involvement than the alternate site at the Bay of Pigs still awaits a satisfactory explanation, as does the hypothesis that hiding U.S. "involvement" should take precedence over the elements needed for victory. It is a commentary on the political considerations then being attached to a military operation that, at one point in the deliberations, the State Department suggested that the military aircraft of the Freedom Fighters should first touch their wheels on the ground before firing a shot or dropping a bomb. In that way, it was argued, the United States could make a legal claim that the air attacks originated from Cuban soil, rather than from exile air bases in Nicaragua.

Despite the preference of the military for the Trinidad operation, Bissell's briefing on the swamps of the Bay of Pigs site was a hopeful one. As to the plan itself, let it be noted that there never was any thought that the small Brigade 2506, composed of 1,500 Freedom Fighters then training in Guatemala, would defeat Castro's numerically superior forces and then fan out and "occupy" the island. Nor was there any expectation that the first exile foot set on Cuban soil would immediately trigger a popular rebellion.

What was planned, Bissell made clear, was an intricately woven pattern of military power and psychological warfare. The Brigade had to land intact with its food, ammunition, and radio equipment with which to broadcast to the Cuban people and to other countries in the hemisphere. Second, the Brigade had to hold a significant perimeter of Cuban territory on which to establish civilian members of a "Provisional Government." A combination of internal sabotage and air power, combined with broadcasts to the Cuban people and broadcasts to nations of the hemisphere for recognition and assistance, was the order of battle. Once these steps had been completed, Castro could be brought down through the combination of a wave of defections and direct support to the "Provisional Government" by the United States and its allies in Latin America.

In order to carry out steps one and two—land intact, and hold territory
—Brigade 2506 had to dominate the air. Castro had six T-33 jets, six fast
British Sea Fury fighter-bombers, and four U.S. B-26 aircraft. To oppose
them, the CIA had sixteen B-26s, four 4-engine C-54s, and five twin-
engined C-46s. The latter two types were for cargo and to transport
paratroopers. Based in Nicaragua, the planes faced a seven-hour round
trip flight with fuel permitting only 45 minutes of combat flying over
Cuba.

Therefore Bissell impressed on President Kennedy and the advisers
assembled at the White House on April 4 that, for the plan to be successful, *all of Castro's air force had to be knocked out while it was still on
the ground.* With this accomplished, the shuttle of arms to and from the
perimeter would be protected. The plan was to seize immediately an
airstrip at Girón and move the exile air base from Nicaragua to the
beachhead. Once based on Cuban soil, the B-26s of the Freedom Fighters
could provide close air support, knocking out Castro's Russian tanks and
heavy artillery, and bring Havana's power plant, telephone and radio
communications, railroads, bridges, and the three oil refineries under
attack. Further, the air force could control Cuba's ports and cut off
shipping. So detailed were the plans that one of the ships which transported the Brigade from Puerto Barrios in Guatemala to the landing at
the Bay of Pigs had orders to proceed from there to Key West for supplies
and return to Havana harbor.

The April 4 briefing also made it clear that political considerations
which necessitated a switch in plans from Trinidad to the Bay of Pigs
meant that *there could be no prolonged guerrilla war.* For, if anything
went wrong, the landing force could not flee the fifty miles or so through
Castro's forces to the Escambray mountains.

Presidential adviser Theodore Sorensen writes in his book, *Kennedy,*
that the President "had been assured" by seasoned military advisers that
the Bay of Pigs was good guerrilla terrain. Haynes Johnson writes the
same thing in his book, *The Bay of Pigs:* "After Trinidad had been
eliminated as the target, the President and other important officials were
repeatedly assured that the Bay of Pigs was good guerrilla country and
that the entire force could operate there."[8] What is not mentioned by
either writer is that guerrilla training for Cuban Brigade 2506 *had been
suspended a full five months before landing, and that the President had
been so advised by his military and intelligence advisers.* Another factor
which mitigates against the Sorensen-Johnson thesis is that the only
manner by which guerrilla units could operate in sea-water swamps was
through systematic and adequate resupply of food, water, and ammunition. Both factors — the alleged assertion by unidentified military advisers that sea-water swamps represented good guerrilla terrain, and the

corollary proposition that resupply was essential—depended on protective air cover.

Furthermore, military estimates were that Castro could have as many as 14,000 men encircling the perimeter force within a period of 24 to 36 hours. With Castro's air force already destroyed on the ground, there would be a better opportunity in the unpopulated swamps to use the exile air force in close-support missions than there would have been in the populous Trinidad-Cienfuegos area. If there are two words to describe the vital element needed for success, those two words are *air power*.

The crucial nature of air power was reflected in the plans of yet another operation—"Operation Marte." Planned in conjunction with the landing of Brigade 2506 at the Bay of Pigs, "Marte" represented a little-known but enormously important element in the overall plans for unhorsing Fidel Castro. And it was here that guerrilla warfare was to have played an important role.

For months, 160 Cuban exiles had been training in guerrilla warfare at Belle Chaise, Louisiana. Commanded by Nino Díaz, the group was to be introduced clandestinely into Oriente Province, hundreds of miles east of the Bay of Pigs, and from there to conduct some startling operations.

The plan of the CIA was to unite the tough outside force with resistance groups which they had been training inside Cuba, over which they had complete control. Once the two forces were joined, they would represent a formidable anti-Castro force. "Operation Marte" listed the "controlled" resistance movements as follows:

"Tico's Group: A group that has some 100 men (estimated), known as 'Tico,' under the leadership of Lieutenant Roberto Herrera and Tico, is located in the zone between the cities of Guantanamo and Baracoa, and Moa Bay. During March (1961) this group skirmished with Castro forces in Baitiquiri, Puriales, Los Indios, and Imias.

"Fonseca's Group: A group that has 100 men under the leadership of Captain Argimido Fonseca, which is located in the zone between the cities of Guantanamo and Sagua de Tánamo. In the middle of February, 1961, members of this group got into a fire-fight . . . and it is possible that Fonseca's group has been forced to divide into small units.

"Calvino's Group: 'Pancho' Calvino has a smaller group (20 men) in the Western Part of Oriente Province. His exact location is unknown, but believed to be in the area of the small town of Embrita, to the northeast of Soledad sugar mill.

"Guevara's Group: a group of undetermined size, under the leadership of Alfonso Guevara Fournier, is located in the zone of Mina Panchita (on the Boca River) to the west of Imias.

"Lujo's Group: Captain Octavio Lujo Padrón has a group of undeter-

mined size located in the vicinity of El Cobre at a place known as La Trinchera.

"Other Groups: Other groups are operating in the Cristal mountains in the vicinity of Delicias (in the coastal areas of Puerto Padre) and in the zone to the south of Estrada Palma. It also is known that resistance groups are strong in Holguín, Manzanillo and the city of Guantanamo. We have unconfirmed information that patriots have disembarked in the vicinity of Baracoa.

"In addition to the leaders mentioned above, we have been informed that the following individuals are with the insurgent forces: Lieutenant Ivan Anaya, Juan Pérez, Lieutenant Castro (first name not known), and José Peña."

The leadership of the resistance indicates that Castro had suffered a considerable number of defections from his officer ranks. They brought with them invaluable information on the location and strength of Castro's forces, which information had been carefully checked and detailed in map coordinates contained in the plans of "Operation Marte."

The operation consisted of two parts. One, listed as "The Preliminary Phase," dealt with amalgamating the activities of the internal resistance with those of the outside guerrilla force. Each member of the outside force was to carry an extra rifle and ammunition to be given to defectors to the anti-Castro camp.

More important, the exiles were to establish communications with "the rear echelon" (The Key West Naval Base), and arrange for the drop of arms and supplies by parachute. By radioing certain codes to Key West, the landing party could expect to receive ready-prepared drops of arms, ammunition, explosives, compasses, everything needed to equip each 100-man guerrilla unit. Planes were to make the drops "from an altitude of 1500 feet" (this necessitating, again, the absence of Castro air).

Chiefly as a means to protect this "preliminary" operation, the combined exile-resistance force was to carry on "small guerrilla operations," and to "commence ambushing, sabotage, etc."

The second part of "Operation Marte" was listed as "The Action Phase." This phase clearly indicates that the planners of "Marte" did not envision a long, drawn-out guerrilla war of attrition, any more than they did in drawing-up the Bay of Pigs operation. The initial objectives of "The Action Phase" were listed as these:

· "a. Initiate guerrilla and sabotage operations against telecommunications, railways, and highways, in order to isolate key cities, as for example, Victoria de las Tunas, Holguín, Bayamo, Palma Soriano, Santiago de Cuba and Guantanamo.

"b. Carry out activities aimed at creating defections among and subversion against Castro's security forces.

"c. Carry out operations with a view toward destroying and breaking down installations, control towers, motorized transport, armored vehicles, supplies of gasoline, oil, and lubricants."

As these orders were being carried out, a shift was to have been made toward a rapid roll-up. Forces of "Operation Marte" were, the directives read, "to seize and to maintain control of critical areas of government activities" (i.e. get control of local governments and agencies, prevent them from supporting Castro, and put them to work for the insurgents).

The most startling evidence of sharp escalation from guerrilla to conventional warfare indicates that the final objectives of "Operation Marte" was to prepare the way for a major landing of outside forces. The order reads:

"As soon as it is possible, you must be prepared to carry out coordinated operations to give support to landings of a friendly force at (points ranging from) the north of the Sierra Cristal to the south of the Sierra Maestra."

All Cuban exile forces had been committed to pre-selected objectives, so the "friendly force" was to be non-Cuban, and, would consist of troops from other countries of Latin America. It was understood at the time that Venezuela had committed itself to supply a mixed force of 5,000 Marines and Army troops. Nicaragua, Honduras, and Guatemala also were committed to the success of the liberation movement and were expected to provide small units to the operation. The United States forces would, of course, move in concert with those of its allies. They were to land in the vicinity of Nipe Bay and drive across the valley to Santiago, thus cutting the island in two.

However, the landing of "friendly forces" was contingent on success at the Bay of Pigs. It was expected that, with Castro's air force knocked out of the sky, Brigade 2506 would have been able to land and to protect a "Provisional Government." The "Provisional Government" would, in turn, have broadcast appeals for recognition and support from other nations of the hemisphere. And "Operation Marte" would have paved the way for landings made in response to the appeals.

For this reason, a reason of timing, "Operation Marte" was to have commenced, on April 14, *two-and-one-half days before the landing at the Bay of Pigs.* By the end of the day on April 17, it was believed, broadcasts from the "Provisional Government" would have been on the air, and the way already paved for the landing of a force, or forces, of one or more nations of the hemisphere in Oriente Province.

Three air strikes were therefore planned against Castro's airfields. Of those planned, however, only one-half of one strike was permitted. Strike one was to have been composed of all sixteen of the B-26s available to the Freedom Fighters, and was scheduled for April 15. The President ordered that the number to scaled down to eight, and only eight planes hit the airports of Havana's Camp Columbia, San Antonio de los Baños in Havana Province, and Santiago. In a clumsy attempt to hide U.S. "involvement," one B-26 from the Freedom-Fighter camp in Nicaragua flew straight to Miami Airport. The plane bore the insignia of Castro's air force and, said Miami Immigration chief Edward Ahrens, was piloted by a defector. The bombing of Cuba that morning, U.S. sources claimed, had been carried out by the pilot of the plane in Miami and three other defectors from Castro's own air force.

So badly hidden was the entire operation (including U.S. involvement) that Castro had already assigned his forces to various points around the island, and actually was at command headquarters at Camp Columbia when the bombers hit in their first and only strike. Likewise, Raúl Roa, Cuba's Foreign Minister was in New York awaiting word of the invasion so that he could accuse the United States of aggression. When news of the bombing did reach New York, Ambassador Adlai Stevenson, who for some reason or another had not been informed of the deception, rebutted Roa's charges that the United States had launched aggression against Cuba, repeating that the raiders were Castro's own pilots.

Roa exploded Stevenson's story, pointing out that the characteristics of the B-26 in Miami were distinctly different from those of Castro's air force. Indeed they were. The exile B-26s had no tail-gunners. Tail guns had been removed and gasoline tanks installed to permit the long flight to Cuba from Nicaragua. The confusion that followed an angry Stevenson's discovery that his own boss, President Kennedy, had used him as a patsy was monumental. Exactly what Ambassador Stevenson said to President Kennedy by phone has not, so far as can be determined, been made known. There is more than a suspicion, however, that he demanded that no further air strikes be made against Cuba, since they made his position in the United Nations vulnerable to attack, not only by the Soviet and Cuban Ambassadors, but also by the bloc of Afro-Asian "pacifists" nations which Mr. Stevenson had been wooing.

However that may be, the fact is that air strike number two, scheduled for Sunday, April 16, was cancelled entirely by Presidential order. The planes were, as the communication read, "to stand down." With this, the Joint Chiefs and the CIA privately expressed concern among them over the President's steady retreat—a concern that had cropped up earlier, when on April 12 Kennedy had, in effect, told the Cuban people that we were *not* on their side. He did so in a public statement, saying, "there will not under any conditions be an intervention in Cuba by the United States armed forces." This statement elicited expressions of concern not only in Washington, but in Cuba as well. Cuban underground leaders were alarmed by the President's words, radioed their contacts in Miami, pointing out that Mr. Kennedy seemed to be telegraphing his punches, and asking what it all meant. The President, apparently, had forgotten all about his campaign statement saying that he would throw the moral support of the government behind the Cuban people and let "the forces of freedom know that we are on their side."

With the cancellation of the second air strike, the CIA and the Joint Chiefs momentarily considered washing out the entire operation. They reconsidered their position after assurances had been given that the third air strike would take place, with all B-26s assigned to hit Castro's air fields in saturation attacks as Brigade 2506 went ashore. Protected from a Castro attack from the air, the Brigade could then move on and capture the Girón airstrip. Operating from Girón, the air arm of the Freedom Fighters would put Cuba under an umbrella of anti-Castro protection, and knock out Castro's Russian tanks and heavy artillery.

The Joint Chiefs and CIA breathed easier as Sunday, April 16, drew to a close. The time and date beyond which there could be no tampering with plans was set for noon of that day. Incredibly, however, at 7 p.m. that night, President Kennedy sent White House aide McGeorge Bundy to Richard Bissell ordering that the final air strike be cancelled entirely. It seems significant that, after delivering the order, Bundy then journeyed to New York to confer with Adlai Stevenson.

Thus, as members of Brigade 2506 saw the dim outlines of their country on the horizon, all chances for the success of the operation had been withdrawn. Castro's air force was not destroyed. Despite vicious air attacks, the Brigade fought well and achieved most of its objectives, including capture of the air strip at Girón. They did so despite the fact that two of their transports had been sunk by an air force which was supposed to have been knocked out before the landing had been made. The transports carried the radio equipment by which the Cuban people were to have been alerted, and recognition of the outside world solicited. They also contained rifles with which civilian defectors were to have been armed.

The B-26s of the Freedom Fighters were no match for Castro's jets and his more heavily armed B-26s. Stripped of tail guns, they were sitting ducks once a Castro plane got on their tails. Their vulnerability was another crucial reason why Castro's air force had to be knocked out while it was still on the ground. *Yet, out of 48 sorties proposed to carry out the destruction of Castro's air arm, the President permitted only eight to be flown.*

Like Brigade 2506, "Operation Marte" had also been overcome by adversity. Following instructions, the commander of the group put ten men ashore from the ship, "Santa Ana" (its code name was "Perca"), at the mouth of the Macambo River in Oriente Province. This was at 9:30 p.m. on April 14. They were to have been met by an eleven-man "reception committee" which had set out from the U.S. Navy Base at Guantanamo. The team did not make the rendezvous, and, at 3:00 a.m., the morning of April 15, the landing party returned to the "Santa Ana." The ship sailed out of sight over the horizon and stayed there until it was safe to again move in close to shore that night—April 15.

While waiting offshore, the men learned of the first air-strike against Cuban airfields that day. They also learned that it was not full strength, but still there was little concern registered among their leadership.

The night of April 15, ten men were again sent ashore. Again they waited, from 9:30 p.m. until 2:30 the next morning of April 16, and again they were not met. "Operation Marte's" orders read that, if contact was not made on April 14 or 15, "the 'Perca' ['Santa Ana'] will proceed to a predesignated position where the commander will communicate with the rear echelon [Key West Navy Base] and await further orders."

What was not known at the time was that the eleven-man "reception committee" which had set out from nearby Guantanamo Naval Base had met with disaster. In traversing the rough terrain in the dark, two of them fell, exploding detonators among plastic explosives they were carrying, killing and wounding several of the party.[9] Instructed to maintain radio silence at all costs, the survivors could not communicate with the Navy base and explain their plight.

Meanwhile, the commander of "Operation Marte" had learned that the air-strike, scheduled for Sunday, April 16, had been cancelled. For obvious reasons, there was considerable concern registered over the cancellation. The intelligence estimates contained in "Operation Marte" revealed that Castro had one T-33 jet, three B-26s, one C-45, and two Russian-built helicopters based at nearby Santiago. They were all operational as of April 16, and, if not destroyed, could wreak havoc with the intricately planned operation. Guerrilla units—from "Marte" and their resistance colleagues inside Cuba—had to depend on air drops from Key West for their supplies. Unopposed by Castro's planes, low-level drops stood a good chance of being undetected. But with Castro's planes in the air, they could trace guerrilla forces by watching the drops and, later, it was supposed, could knock down the light, unarmed planes.

There was an even greater concern registered over the fate of the final objective of "Operation Marte" should Castro's planes not be knocked out. Three B-26s and one T-33 jet fighter could spell doom to efforts to land conventional forces from friendly Latin American nations. And with two helicopters hovering out of range of anti-aircraft fire, they could act as artillery spotters, thus bringing the beachhead under direct fire from Castro's long-range heavy artillery. The United States could not permit friendly forces to land without assurances that those forces would be free from air attack. Rear echelon headquarters at Key West debated the situation, then ordered the "Santa Ana" "to proceed to Point B and await further instructions." Point B was another possible landing area to the North and West of the original point.

Although "Operation Marte" had suffered damaging delay due to the misfortune of the "reception committee," the delay need not have been fatal. It is uncertain whether, following cancellation of the second air strike by Presidential order, U.S. Naval authorities and the CIA decided to hold "Operation Marte" in abeyance until certain that the third and last air strike had been made and that it was successful. That strike was scheduled for 1:40 a.m. on April 17. Once it had been made, the 160-man guerrilla force was prepared to land.

One thing does seem certain, however, and that is that the sequence of the two operations—the Bay of Pigs and "Marte"—had been switched. "Marte" was now to follow the Bay of Pigs. Success of "Operation Marte" now hinged solely upon success at the Bay of Pigs. If Brigade 2506 landed under the cover of the third air strike, and its B-26 aircraft moved from Nicaragua to the Girón airstrip near the beachhead, the day would have been saved for both operations.

The *basic* reason for "Operation Marte," to prepare for a conventional landing of friendly forces in Oriente Province," was based precisely on the political considerations behind the Bay of Pigs landing. Those political considerations were that Brigade 2506 would land, secure its perimeter, and bring in a "Provisional Government" which would broadcast pleas for recognition and support from the countries of the Western Hemisphere. But, if these considerations were not met (and the cancelled air strikes had put them in some doubt), "Operation Marte" had little reason for being, since there would be no landing of conventional forces without the request for them to land.

The evening of April 16, the CIA and Joint Chiefs of Staff learned of the Presidential decision to call-off the third, and last, air strike. There was no possibility at that time to call off the Bay of Pigs operation, since the point of no return, set at noon that day, had already passed. Such an option to cancel "Operation Marte" did exist, and it apparently was exercised, for the "Santa Ana" received orders to rendezvous off the Bay of Pigs, there to await orders to pick up survivors of the disaster.

For a period of two to three hours, there was a debate in Key West and at the Guantanamo base over the possibility of resorting to another option. That option would be to send the 160-man group into Cuba to carry-on guerrilla warfare activities, and forget about plans for a conventional landing. But there was considerable doubt in the minds of military planners that the Kennedy Administration, which had failed to provide air insurance at the Bay of Pigs, would have stomach for a protracted guerrilla operation in Oriente Province and would be prepared to take the risk involved in supporting such an operation.

The "Santa Ana" was ordered to the Marine base at the island of Vieques.

The President himself took command of a military operation and successfully destroyed it by appending political considerations. This is a matter of history. And, in his apparent eagerness to stave off criticism from liberal pacifists in this country and abroad, he proscribed any action to retrieve the situation. Not only had he pledged on April 12 that U.S. forces would not be used at the Bay of Pigs, he also instructed Secretary of State Dean Rusk to repeat that pledge on April 17, the very day that Brigade 2506 landed.

Proposals put to the President to save the day went for naught. Admiral Arleigh A. Burke's plea for "just one destroyer, Mr. President, or two jet aircraft," constituted "U.S. involvement," and his request was denied. As reported by Mario Lazo in his excellent account in the September 1964 issue of *Reader's Digest*, Kennedy's cancellation of the third and last air strike brought about a confrontation with his seasoned Chief of Naval Operations that crackles with drama. Burke's answer, according to Lazo, was: "We are involved, sir. We trained and armed these Cubans. God-dammit, Mr. President, we can't let these boys be slaughtered there." Lazo continues with his account: "The outcome of that meeting was perhaps the most timid compromise of all: the President agreed that Navy fighter planes, with their U.S. markings painted out, could 'fly reconnaissance' over the beach-head, but *there should not be more than two planes, and they could fly for one hour only, from 6:30 to 7:30 a.m.!*"

Decisions and compromises being made in the timid atmosphere of official Washington were considerably at odds with what was happening on the beaches at the Bay of Pigs. What was planned, and came within air strikes of succeeding is related by Manuel Artime, civilian head of Brigade 2506 in an address to a Catholic association in Miami, Florida, after his release from Castro's prison:

"Our plan was marvellous. Strategically, it was perfect. We landed on a promontory, a sort of island, surrounded by swamps. There were only three access points to our positions. Tanks couldn't come at us because of the swamps. We could have stayed there shooting for a month without being dislodged. We could have brought in members of our 'Provisional Government' and asked for recognition. Most important, Castro could not have survived the internal pressures our continued presence meant for him."

If that were so, then what happened? What happened is also told by Artime:

267 · THE CUBAN OPERATION

"We were told: 'the air will be yours.' But in fact Fidelista aviation dominated the skies. Those planes sank our ships with the arms, ammunition, radio equipment to broadcast to the Cuban people—and we were stranded. Our aviation which we expected would clear the roads [of tanks and troops], knocked out the bridges, well it hadn't done it."

The civilian commander then outlined the importance of close air support. "Just imagine," he said, "the enemy was able to emplace 155-millimeter cannon at a distance that we couldn't hit with the limited range of our mortars, we were sitting ducks—and the aviation we counted on to take care of Castro's heavy artillery, well, we just didn't have it."*

Conversations I had with Orlando Cuervo, a communications officer of Brigade 2506, reveal the feelings of the men stranded on the beach: "Without close air support, we were dead. Soviet artillery just pounded us to a pulp. All Castro had to do was bring up thousands of his men and not even commit them to a fight—just—just encircle us, pound us with artillery, and wait for us to surrender. Imagine! By Wednesday, April 19, we were out of food, water, and ammunition, and the enemy even had small spotter planes flying over our positions directing artillery fire. Far above them, we could see American jet planes circling. We heard when we were captured that, when the matter of U.S. jets flying over our positions was brought up in Washington, an official statement said they were merely on reconnaissance. That explains why there weren't any of those Castro planes the first day or two and why they sent them up later to direct artillery fire. Castro knew that the jets wouldn't come to our aid. We knew that the Essex and the Boxer were just over the horizon loaded with planes, but they were told not to help us."[10]

The intelligence community expected that there would be desertions from Castro's militia force. The biggest buildup of the military occurred after August, 1960, when Cubans were press-ganged into joining the militia. Forcible recruitment following a mammoth conscription drive and conducted amidst overtones of intimidation on the one hand and offers of preferential treatment on the other, had failed to attract even 2% of those directly approached. It was not too much of a surprise, therefore, when, a few months before the Bay of Pigs, elements of a reinforced militia battalion had defected to units of anti-Castro rebels which the battalion had been sent to dig out of the Escambray mountains.

On the first day of the landing, Castroite Comandante Duque's forces captured five paratroopers of the invading force. Interrogated, they told Duque that the total number of men being committed to the invasion

*It should be mentioned that, after the Bay of Pigs and leading hit-run attacks on Cuba's coastline, Artime faded from sight. By 1965, he was no longer considered a leader among Cuba's exile community.

was 20,000. He took the men with him in a jeep draped with a white flag to the village of San Blas where the Brigade had a command post. There, he offered to surrender the forces under his command—1,200 men. There was some momentary panic among officers of the Brigade. Their first inclination was to have him bring his men over, turn them around and start them fighting on the side of the invaders. Pinned down as they were, however, by Castro's planes, low on ammunition, and outranged by Russian heavy artillery, Brigade officers believed that it would soon become apparent to the turncoats that the landing force had no support. Once this had been determined, they feared, they would be at the mercy of nearly as many men as there were in the entire Brigade. Comandante Duque was made prisoner, and the offer of the surrender of his force declined.

It was reported that tank units at Camp Columbia and Camp Managua refused to obey orders to go into action at the beachhead, again confirming in some measure the predictions of U.S. military instructors to the Brigade that Castro's military was on the verge of revolt.[11] Five hundred workers of a sugar complex nearby started out to join the landing forces, until frantic messages were sent telling them that, for the moment, arms and ammunition were unavailable. Castro's *Bohemia* magazine later published, in typical Communist fashion, pictures of a large column of civilians (these selfsame sugar workers), captioning the photos to the effect that the civilians were "volunteers" on their way to assist the militia fight at the Bay of Pigs.

In Miami, we followed as many of the developments as we could. In November, 1960, knowing that a break in relations was imminent, my radio operator at the Embassy memorized the radio frequencies of Castro's 150-station internal radio network. We called upon this knowledge to listen to conversations between the command post and field forces. We found Comandante Sergio del Valle and Captain Osmani Cienfuegos to be in charge. Seated in Havana, they revealed that Castro also was somewhere else than the Bay of Pigs that first day of the invasion.

Our monitors also picked up the following messages from the men on the beach to U.S. Navy forces at sea:

"2AW to Air Command: Brigade commander on Blue Beach says he must have jet support. He is under heavy attack by MIG's, jets and heavy tanks. Pepe.

"2AW to Air Command: Blue Beach under air attack by 4 jets and 2 Sea Furies. Where is our jet cover? Pepe.

"2AW to Air Command: First Battalion under heavy artillery attack. Also Blue Beach from East. Request air knockout artillery as soon as possible. Where is our jet cover? Pepe.

"To Air Command: Where is F-Five ones (F-51s—World War II-model fighter planes) and transport? Pepe.

"To Base: Barracuda, Marsopa and Lou (code names for invasion ships) cannot arrive Blue Beach, discharge and leave by daylight. Request jet cover for us in beachhead area.

"To Base: Marsopa proceeding Blue Beach with 3 Lou's (landing craft). If low jet cover is not furnished at first light, believe we will lose all ships. Request immediate reply. Blue Beach under attack by MIG's and T-33. Request immediately jet support or cannot hold. Pepe.

"To Base: Will Blue Beach have jet cover tonight and tomorrow? Request air cover stay lower down as enemy planes come in low. Did not receive help from air cover. Pepe.

"To Air Command: Tell Cuban pilots we are fighting last-ditch stand. Give them gasoline and ammunition. Road north to Covadonga is full of enemy and there is artillery east and west of Blue Beach.

"To Air Command: Can't you throw something into this vital point in the battle? Anything. Pepe.

"To Base: Do you people realize how desperate the situation is? Do you back us or quit? All we want is low jet cover and jet close support. Enemy has this support. I need it badly or cannot survive. Please don't desert us. Out of bazooka and tank ammo. Tanks will hit me at dawn.

"To Air Commander: Blue Beach under attack by B-26. Where is promised air cover? Pepe."

The cancellation of air strikes, and the later refusal to provide air support, was critical in yet another area. What is not generally known is that Humberto Sorí Marín, former Castro Minister, had been re-infiltrated into Cuba after having been trained in the United States in underground techniques and liaison. His mission was of critical importance to the success of the underground in that he had been charged with plans for the underground to coordinate activities at the time of the invasion.

Sorí Marín made a fatal mistake. He called the resistance leaders from Cuba's six provinces to Havana, where he met with them in a group. There are several versions of what then happened. One is that a gossipy female neighbor inadvertently walked in on the group as the men were deliberating and remarked about the curious meeting to another woman. The second woman, the story goes, turned out to be an informer. Another version is that the underground resistance movement itself had been penetrated by Castro's spies. What *is* important is that Castro's G-2 moved in on the group with surprising swiftness, capturing every last leader and shooting Sorí Marín in the buttocks as he disappeared through a window.

The military support expected of the underground resistance had been nipped in the bud. Realistically, the CIA had to assume two things: the resistance movement had been penetrated before Sorí Marín had returned to Cuba; some among those who had been captured would talk. In blunt terms, the resistance had been destroyed. This is what Allen Dulles meant when later he said that the underground was not alerted for reasons of security. With that destruction, the air power which was to knock out Castro's planes while they still were on the ground took on another vastly important task to the success of the landing. The three oil refineries, key bridges, the water reservoir in the Marianao suburb of Havana—all marked for destruction by the resistance—could only be destroyed by air attacks. These targets remained untouched—another consequence of Kennedy's decision to cancel the air strikes of April 16 and 17.

In one of many post mortems conducted publicly on the Cuban operation, CIA Director Allen Dulles appeared December 30, 1961, on the television program, "Meet the Press," where he said: "There is quite a popular misconception that it was felt that there would be spontaneous uprisings," adding: "We never contemplated that." He said he had worked during World War II with the French underground, and stressed: "The last thing that we wanted was spontaneous uprisings to get people slaughtered by Nazi troops. In the same way, we were not looking for spontaneous uprisings in Cuba, but for other developments." Those "other developments"—among them, guerrilla activities in Oriente, leading to a landing of conventional forces from other Latin American nations and from the United States itself—were, of course, arrested when President Kennedy cancelled the air strikes.

As it turned out, the Communists are very thorough in detecting their enemies. They merely have to look around them, for the most part, and arrest three out of four people in sight. And that is almost exactly what Fidel Castro did on April 17, 1961.

In Havana on Monday morning, April 17, 1961, the peace reigning in the house of a doctor friend in the resistance, whom I shall call L.D., was rudely shattered by Castro's G-2 (secret police agents). They entered and searched his modest but comfortable house from top to bottom. For, like most middle-class Cubans, the doctor was considered to be an "enemy of the people." But the militia found nothing "counterrevolutionary." With two men covering the doctor and his cook from the doorway with Czech-made machine-pistols, the group leader finally said:

"Doctor, you must come with us."

"But why? Am I under arrest?" he asked.

"Not under arrest, just detained while we go over a few papers," the man replied. Faced with Czech machine-pistols, L.D. went with them.

He was taken to the Sports Palace just outside Havana, scene of Castro's show trials in 1959. He recoiled in horror at the sight that met his eyes. A hundred or so of Castro's militia were in the bleachers. Thousands of prisoners were in the arena below. Every so often, the militiamen would cock their guns, nervously snapping the bolts from time to time.

L.D. was searched, then told to enter the arena. It was so crowded that people could not sit down. Packed in like sardines, they had been standing all day long and well into the next morning. A woman with a broken leg hobbled in on crutches. She was either an Argentine or a Cuban employee of the Argentine Embassy. Protesting bitterly, the woman was nevertheless rudely shoved into the mob. Shortly thereafter a very agitated man came in—L.D. believes he was an Argentine diplomat—and protested vigorously over her arrest and detention. A militiaman confronted the diplomat, with his gun in hand. The voice of the diplomat gradually claimed the attention of the prisoners. A few ventured to cheer him on. At that very tense moment, a fuse blew and the arena was plunged into complete darkness. The militia panicked.

Prisoners dived for the floor, toppling over one another and upon one another as shots rang out, directed into the crowd from the bleachers, amidst shouts and commands from the militia. L.D., and scores more who later escaped to the United States, estimated that about two hundred shots were fired, as the prisoners lay quivering, expecting bullets to chunk into their bodies. Five minutes later, the lights came back on, and the dead, wounded, and dying were removed. Next to L.D. was a Negro boy. He did not get up. L.D. reached over to shake him and drew his hands away covered with blood. Shot through the neck, the Negro had strangled on his own blood.

Soon after, buses and trucks arrived. Men were separated from their wives and children. They were redivided into smaller groups and removed to other places for detention. The Sports Palace, it seems, was the staging area for more arrests to come. L.D.'s group was taken to the prison of Príncipe. An old Spanish fortress, Príncipe is located in Havana on a promontory at the conjunction of the Avenue of the Presidents, Carlos III Street and Rancho Boyeros Road. It has several ancient tunnels in the old wall, into which L.D.'s group was thrust—3,800 persons. Dust on the earthen passageway was as fine as powder and swirled up into a choking cloud under the feet of the prisoners. The walls were approximately six feet thick, with a barred opening every ten feet or so, one foot across and four feet high. Prisoners fought for space near these apertures to suck precious air into their lungs. Many fell to the floor or were propped up by their companions. It was so crowded that the people stood with shoulders hunched, gasping for air.

Six people died of suffocation the first day. There was no food, no sanitary facilities, and very little water. At the urging of four or five doctors, including L.D., a small space was marked off in which to urinate and defecate. It was torturous to move around, however, and many prisoners chose to use the places where they stood. The medical men, L.D. and other doctors, knew the dangers of death by suffocation, the possibilities of heart attack, and the mental strain of people terrified over the unknown fate of their families. They were most immediately concerned over the possibility of epidemic.

L.D.'s fears were realized when several of the prisoners developed diarrhea. He made his way to the tunnel entrance and called the guard. The guard cocked his pistol, came in a few steps, then retreated. L.D. called after him, "We are Cubans, man! Come and look at the conditions! Five have diarrhea, an epidemic will break out and you will be condemned before the world. Please get me the Captain of the prison, I beg of you!"

Captain Juan Odoardo, of youthful appearance and arrogant mien, put in an appearance. Imperiously ordering the prisoners to stand back while his entrance was covered by the machine-pistols of six boys, aged 15 to 18 years, he said: "What's going on there, anyway?" He ventured a few more yards into the tunnel, then retreated at the sight of the coughing, retching mob.

"We need medicines, badly," said L.D. "Unless we get them, people are going to die." Look at this, Captain, just look around you. Cubans looking like this. For what, Captain? Why?" he asked, spreading his arms before him emotionally. There was not a sound in the tunnel as 3,800 pairs of eyes drilled into the Captain. "Captain, we need air. Could you stand this very long, Captain?," L.D. continued. "Unless these people get air, Captain, they are going to break out by sheer force of numbers, Captain, and you will be forced to slaughter 4,000 Cubans. For what, Captain?"

Captain Odoardo turned on his heel and left. His guards backed out slowly, their machine-pistols trained on the quietly advancing mob. One man broke. He picked up a rock from the floor of the tunnel, screaming, "Cowards! Sons of. . . . ! I'll fight you with a rock if I have to!" Writhing and struggling he was pinned against the wall by his companions. A squad of militiamen ran up to the entrance of the tunnel guns at the ready. L.D. quietly asked everyone to move back. He and a psychiatrist moved slowly toward the man still clutching the rock. "Get away from him," said the psychiatrist gently to two men holding the distraught man.

"Don't come near me," said the man, "or I'll break your skull! Let that son of a . . . come get it," referring to one of the guards.

"He doesn't need it," said the psychiatrist soothingly, advancing slowly, step by step. "Look, compañero, he has a machine-pistol. He doesn't need a rock."

The tension was so great that L.D. in his own nervousness tore the nail from his right index finger without realizing it. If the man broke completely, the mob would break, and the guards would slaughter them. Sweating, but calm, the psychiatrist finally reached him, and gently took the rock. The man collapsed to the floor, sobbing uncontrollably. "Where is my wife?" he whimpered. "Where is my wife?" The tension released like a spring as a sigh of relief came from 3,800 throats.

An hour later, medicines arrived. The first food given the prisoners came on Wednesday at 5 p.m. when it was clear that the United States had abandoned the Brigade. Food consisted of rotten rice, and peas "hard as bullets." It had to be scooped up and eaten by hand. Those who ate vomited immediately. Others couldn't stand the odor of the food and threw it away.

By Thursday, April 20th, 80 to 90 cardiac cases were permitted to sleep out of doors at night. But by this time, 15 inmates had gone insane and had to be removed. On Wednesday alone, 79 fainted from lack of oxygen and were given shots by the small group of haggard doctors— their own fellow prisoners. On Friday, April 21, when it was clear that Brigade 2506 had been overwhelmed, there was a relative easing of the plight of those imprisoned. They were permitted to come out for air at regular intervals. At no time, however, was the tunnel cleared of excrement and vomit.

Among this group, by L.D.'s account, were 238 taxi, bus, and truck drivers, and representatives of just about every strata of Cuban society. Negroes and whites, Spaniards and Puerto Ricans, even some Indian and South American visitors had been arrested. These, then, were the "imperialists" whose imprisonment the government later attempted to justify. One day, either Friday or Saturday of the first week, the prisoners were allowed out for air as a group. One man was so weakened by diarrhea that he was barely able to make his way painfully out of the tunnel. He looked up on the fortress wall where a 15-year-old *miliciano* stood with a machine-pistol covering the crowd. The boy spat on this human wreck.

"For the first time in Cuba we have dignity!" jeered the boy. "Dignity" was the word used to describe the position of the *miliciano* in Castro's Cuba.

The man below squinted up at the boy through the bright sun, looked around at the pitiful condition of the prisoners, raised one hand to eye level, watching it shake uncontrollably, looked down at the excrement dribbling from his trousers, and addressed the youth quietly at first, and then in a rising voice charged with indignation.

"You call this dignity? You represent dignity with your yellow Communist friends and yellower Fidel Castro? Go ahead and shoot me if you wish! Go ahead! I'd rather be shot here in my own excrement than live in a society where you represent dignity and we are the result of that dignity! Go ahead shoot! I dare you to!"

The thousands of prisoners gaped; they looked at the man as though he were God. The discomfited boy nervously fingered his machine-pistol for a moment, looked around to assure himself that other militiamen were near, then he spat again at the old man and turned away. He was the same youth who for days had been splattering bullets on the stone wall just above the entrance to the tunnel to frighten the prisoners. Twenty to thirty prisoners rushed over to help the old man, but they were ordered back into the tunnel.

Little by little, small groups and individuals were released. Some were still held beyond May Day. Five thousand were held in the Blanquita Theater, other thousands were imprisoned in hotels and makeshift concentration camps. Churches were filled and guarded. From the provinces came reports of 6,000 imprisoned in the tuberculosis sanitarium built by Batista on a hill above Trinidad in Las Villas, the Topes de Collantes. The story of arrests was always the same. An imperious knock on the door, a search, prison, and terror. A traveler stopping at a *bodega* for a refreshment in a tiny town in Camaguey Province witnessed an incident, which demonstrated how general the arrests were. He was advancing from his car to the *bodega* when he saw two militiamen walk in ahead of him. Three men were drinking beer at the counter.

"Aha!" "Celebrating the invasion, are you?," said one of the *milicianos*. "You are under arrest!" The bewildered men hadn't even heard the news, since the government kept the landing as secret as possible, and this was the first the traveler knew about it.

A very conservative count, taken from terrified escapees to Miami and from press reports, indicates that at least another 125,000 to 150,000 suffered the known fate of the 45,000 to 50,000 in Príncipe, Blanquita Theater, hotels, La Cabaña, El Morro Castle, Topes de Collantes, and at a concentration camp near Matanzas city. The total figure accepted today is between 250,000 and 300,000.

Lieutenant Lorenzo León Hernández, who defected from Castro's army following the round-up of thousands of suspects in Matanzas province, told me that about 8,000 persons were herded into this concentration camp in Matanzas. The camp was reminiscent of those in Europe during World War II—an open field surrounded by a fence of barbed wire, where sunburned and peeling prisoners roasted in the hot sun by day and suffered chills by night. From information he obtained from Army headquarters in the city of Matanzas, Hernández estimated that more than a quarter of a million persons were arrested in the mass roundup of anti-Communist suspects. He said that eight men died of the complications brought on by hunger in the camp, and that several hundred more became seriously ill from malnutrition, from diseases caused by the lack of sanitary facilities and from exposure. Hernández also said that one night when, in protest, the prisoners refused to sleep on the ground, the guards fired machine guns over their heads to make them lie down and at the same time warned that, if the "invasion" succeeded, "we will blast the life from you and not a single one will remain to tell the story." The same threat was repeated by militiamen at Principe, Blanquita, and Topes de Collantes.

For the first three days there was no food at all. The prisoners were allowed to have only a little water to drink; none for washing. On the fourth day the militia brought in small portions of meat, malanga (a starchy tuber), and sweet potatoes. Later a Catholic priest was thrust protestingly into the enclosure. He was resoundingly applauded by those inside the camp and by the thousands of sons and daughters, fathers and mothers, and husbands and wives of the inmates, who sat by day and by night on the highway, protesting against mass imprisonment and demanding the release of their loved ones. In reprisal for his popular reception, the militia stripped the priest of his cassock and left him in his underwear. After a few days of the rudest humiliation he became ill and was finally transferred to Havana's dreaded Castillo del Príncipe, and there he died.

Cuban women made enormous sacrifices to fight Communism, and like the men of Cuba, suffered horribly. One young woman, Clarita Gómez, paid dearly for the part she and her boy friend played in the anti-Castro underground. Couriers for the Movement to Recover the Revolution (MRR), they were apprehended by the police. The young man was accused of treason, but the state lacked sufficient evidence to condemn him. Clarita was grilled, and told that if she turned states' evidence she would be freed. Clarita refused, maintaining that she was a prostitute and that her lover meant no more to her than other men who paid for her body. To Clarita's horror, policemen and militiamen took the tragic creature at her word, and the girl was forced to submit to their advances until Clarita's lover (ignorant of her sacrifice) had been released from custody and fled to Miami to join the Bay of Pigs invasion force. When he was safely out of the country, Clarita turned on her tormentors with the fury of a demon. She was placed under observation, and a determined search of her apartment turned up a small arsenal of arms. Clarita was sent to the Womens' Prison of Guanabacoa, a few miles east of Havana.

On April 15, 1961, Clarita heard the thunder of gun-fire from Camp Columbia. The next day she and her cellmates learned from the surly and jumpy guards that three Castro pilots had defected and each, in his own plane, had bombed and strafed Camp Columbia and then flown to the United States. The excitement among the hundreds of women prisoners was immense. Clarita had faith that she would soon be freed by her lover when the invasion force triumphed at the Bay of Pigs. The impending invasion was so well-known in Cuba that the guards carried on boastful arguments with the women, shouting: "The invading worms will be crushed underfoot." This was before the April 15 bombing, however. Following that event, the attitude of the guards underwent a remarkable transformation. On Saturday, two days before the invasion at the Bay of Pigs, the inmates were told that they could have visitors the following day—an unheard-of kindness by a prison administration that wanted to be on the right side, just in case the invasion succeeded. Relatives who flocked to the prison were gay and jubilant, chattering that the end of Communism was indeed near. The guards remained quiet and subdued.

Then came *the day!* The fifty or more women crowded into Clarita's cell heard the news of the invasion as it was broadcast over Miami station WGBS. Huddled around a small transistor radio which one of the women had managed to smuggle into prison, the inmates listened to a running translation into Spanish by Mrs. Gertrudis Maeder, a Swiss citizen who had been falsely accused of membership in the anti-Castro movement, and jailed. One day went by, then the next. The women sensed that something had gone wrong. Their militia guards, so quiet and subdued for two days, began, on Wednesday, April 20, to swagger around. They shouted out to the women that the United States had withdrawn its support from Cuban exile Brigade 2506, and had refused to use its planes against Castro's forces. The women had listened clandestinely on their radio to President Kennedy's April 20 denunciation of Russia and his clearly announced threat to send U.S. forces to Cuba to see the matter through to ultimate victory. "No! This cannot be! This is a lie!" the women shouted. "You are wrong," the militia answered, shouting: "The big ships of the United States took the brigade to shore, then turned around and abandoned it!" The women began to wail and pound the walls of their cells. Groups sat together in corners, counting their Rosary beads and praying to the Lord for help, praying to the Lord to let them know that it was not so. From cell block Number Four came a piercing scream: "Treason!" Soon the entire prison erupted into the rhythmic chant "Treason!" as the women grabbed spoons, pots, anything metallic, and pounded on the cell bars. The sound was deafening.

The desperation, the grief, the anger of Cuba's women political prisoners had a very special meaning. They learned that the back of the underground had been broken, that hundreds of thousands of people had been arrested—among them their husbands, friends, and even children. Other women prisoners, like Clarita, knew that their men were with Brigade 2506 and had either been killed or captured. Would all of these captives be shot? For nights on end, the women of Guanabacoa stayed on their knees until dawn, praying for the lives of their loved ones. An avalanche of women political prisoners arrested during the wholesale roundup, poured into Guanabacoa over the next several days. From them it was learned that the male prisoners in La Cabaña were subjected to systematic torture—stripped of their clothes in the middle of the night and made to stand at attention in the courtyard while ice water was sloshed over them. Those that made so much as a move were pistol-whipped. Others were lined up at the *paredon* where sharp-shooters barely missed them with bullets; or, at the *paredon*, given last rites, to hear: "Ready! Aim! Fire!" only to find that the squad had blank cartridges in their rifles! So the women of Guanabacoa prayed and prayed.

The administrator of the prison was removed, together with all of his militia. They were considered "politically unreliable" for their vacillating behaviour when it was believed that the invaders would be successful. The administrator was sent to La Cabaña as a prisoner; the militia were sent to a huge concentration camp at Guanahacabibes, there to undergo "rehabilitation." The new administrator was an ignorant and resentful former taxi driver who had been unable to make his way in the world prior to Castro, but now had found his niche in life as one of Castro's bullies. He walked past the cells, sneered at the women, called them prostitutes, and displaying the red kerchief around his neck, said he had been chosen to go to Havana to celebrate the "peoples' victory over Yankee imperialism." The women jeered him roundly, throwing debris through the bars of their cells. Not wanting to put in an appearance in Havana with a soiled uniform, the prison administrator beat a hasty retreat, shouting obscenities as he ran.

Clarita and her cellmates were especially fearful of being shipped from Guanabacoa to another women's prison located at Guanajay. Guanajay was a death house—and worse—so the women made a solemn vow among themselves to protect each other from being shipped there by all the slender means available to them. No sooner had they made their vows than rumors made their rounds that the more intransigent of the women were to be transferred to Guanajay. And indeed it was ordered that those whose names were called were to step forward. The commander went through the alphabet from a to z without a single response. Arrests had been made in Cuba on such a wholesale scale, that the prison had no reliable means by which to identify the prisoners! The commander blustered and shouted to no avail. Not one woman budged. He sent them all back to their cells, withheld mail, cut their pitifully inadequate water rations in half, and fed them only once a day—milk and bread in the morning.

One week later, the prison commander tried again. And again the women refused to step forward when their names were called. Harassment was added to slow starvation. Lightning-like raids were made on the cells, women were beaten and stripped of anything of value they might have on them—scissors, thread, needles, rings, anything. The women established sentries who spent two hours on duty and four off, military fashion, to give advance warning against forays by the militia. One girl in Cell Number Four, nick-named *Pulguita* ("little flea") because she was so tiny, was hoisted by means of a slender rope tied about her waist up the fifteen feet or so to the one small, barred, window where she maintained her vigil on what was going on beyond the prison walls. (The rope came from materials which women political prisoners wove into handbags, to be sold by the government.)

On Mothers' Day, May 14, the women were told that they would be permitted to receive guests. This privilege set the prison agog with excitement. The women shared what little lipstick they had among them, and, babbling excitedly together, they waited for the prison gates to open. The sound of a gathering crowd outside added to that excitement, and the guards went toward the prison gate to open it. *Pulguita* called down: "They're beginning to come!" She was silent for a long moment, then added: "Something is wrong. There are cars and some people outside, but most of them are not the ones coming to see us." She peered through the bars more intently, then said apprehensively: "There are many G-2 cars ouside, and I can see a few prison trucks!" Her cellmates were struck dumb. Yet, in a few minutes, the names of ten women were called out by a prison guard who said that their relatives were waiting to see them. First, however, there was a fast huddle in Cell Number Four, where an agreement was made among the women that should this turn out to be a ruse to lure them below and then ship then to Guanajay, the ten women would shout up to the others and alert them. Whispered from cell-to-cell, the agreement was accepted by all prisoners. Accordingly, the ten apprehensively made their way below. There was no sound, and in about an hour they returned to their cells, happy and chattering about their reunion with loved ones. The guard read off the names of 20 more, unlocked them and let them come down into the courtyard. Gertrudis Maeder and Clarita noticed, however, that among them were several who had just returned from seeing their families, and they wondered about this.

Suddenly, screams and cries for help came from below. To the amazement of Gertrudis, a husky girl lifted a flagstone from the cell floor and produced a small sledge hammer. At the woman's command, Gertrudis held the padlock and chain while her cellmate pounded away. The screams for help from below grew louder, interspersed with the sounds of scuffling and banging. "In less than a minute," Gertrudis told me in Miami in 1963 after the Swiss consul had managed to obtain her freedom, "the padlock broke and we all rushed crazily down the stairs and into the courtyard. Those from our cell quickly ran around the other cells, with this enormous woman breaking the padlocks with her sledge hammer." Gertrudis continued: "The courtyard was filled with screaming and shouting women." The guards beat a hasty retreat, barracading themselves in the prison office. "The women retaliated," Gertrudis related, "throwing empty cans, rocks, anything heavy, at the barred doors." The guards dared not shoot into the mass of women. Instead, they placed ladders against the walls outside the prison, and attempted to enter the open courtyard by coming over the roof. The women were not so easily fooled, however. They rushed to the top passageway, flanked with cells on the outside, and the courtyard on the inside. From there, they clambered to the roof, where they pushed the ladders away.

Frustrated, the prison commander called up a battalion of militia from a nearby camp. The militia tried to hold the ladders in place and were met with showers of garbage, dirt, and stones. Finally, a fire truck was brought to the prison. Guards rushed into the courtyard with the hose on full pressure. Women were bowled over. One named Rachel, many months pregnant, got the full force of the stream in her stomach, and fainted. This served further to enrage the women. They charged the guards and, through sheer force of numbers, wrested the hose away and turned it against their tormentors. The guards returned with yet another hose. Prisoners who had been busy pushing away ladders from the outside, turned and threw garbage and stones on the guards holding the hose in the courtyard. One old lady prisoner stood, her eyes starting for her head, issuing a high, piercing, scream for a half minute, then collapsed from exhaustion.

The prisoners managed to capture the second fire hose. It, too, was turned against the guards until the firemen on the truck cut off the water. Fearful that the racket would bring townspeople running to help the prisoners, the prison commander called for quiet. From the safety of his barred office, he promised that if the women would return to their cells he would not attempt to ship them off to Guanajay. Those whom the other prisoners had rushed down to help had already been shipped to Guanajay, he said, and there was nothing he could do about it. The women collapsed from fatigue, sitting and lying in the courtyard, some moaning, others screaming defiance at their captors. One prisoner was particularly distraught, for among those taken away to Guanajay was her sister-in-law whose husband had been executed two days earlier by a firing squad. At that moment, a guard approached the prison commander and whispered that one woman had managed to get away during the melee and had been found hiding in the kitchen. The prisoners sent a delegation with the guard and found the sister-in-law of the grieving woman hiding, bruised and swollen, behind some cupboards. It was through her that they learned what had happened.

As soon as the unsuspecting women had entered the office to see their families, she said, they were set upon by guards, who attempted to force them to enter prison trucks to be transported to Guanajay. The women fought tooth-and-nail, but, outnumbered by the guards, they were beaten unmercifully and thrust into the trucks. The families who had gathered outside the prison intervened in the ensuing melee and were themselves beaten. The nine-year-old son of one woman unsuccessfully fought and bit the guard who was forcing his mother into the prison truck, and went into a state of nervous shock when she was taken away. Some husbands and fathers managed to cling to the trucks as they drove away, and were shoved off the speeding vehicles on the highway.

Each panel truck, equipped with heavy wire windows, had an armed guard stationed in back with the prisoners. In two cases, the women overwhelmed the guard, got the doors open and jumped out. One, by the name of Bebita, jumped from the truck in the Havana suburb of Marianao. Bloody and barefoot, she ran into a *bodega* screaming: "They are going to kill me. They are going to murder me!" People quickly spirited the poor creature out the back door and to temporary safety. Bebita later was found, and those who gave her shelter sentenced to 20 years in prison. Another prisoner named Luisa jumped from the back of one of the trucks, but got her belt caught and was deliberately dragged for blocks. When the trucks arrived at Guanajay, women and guards had to be hospitalized.

Back at Guanabacoa, the women took stock of their partial victory. Although 20 had been spirited away, the guards had been frustrated in their efforts to send the entire 300 inmates to Guanajay. The prison commander again cut food and water rations. The next morning, little Pulguita was hoisted to her perch by the window to investigate the sounds of trucks and cars coming from outside. This time she was astonished at what she saw. "There are hundreds of soldiers and Negro women militia outside," she called down excitedly, hissing: "The soldiers are putting bayonets on their rifles."

At noon, the doors to the courtyard burst open, and there stood 500 soldiers and Negro women militia, all with fixed bayonets on their rifles. "It looked," Gertrudis recalled to me, "like a Roman circus, except that we were in the stands and they were in the ring." The women looked up, to see the roof lined with more soldiers. They looked down. There simply was no hope.

"How brave you are," Gertrudis called out to a Negro girl in uniform, "standing there with a rifle and bayonet. It takes 500 of you cowards to handle unarmed women. Shame on you!" The girl giggled nervously, but said nothing. Gertrudis was especially saddened to see how the Negroes had been made the butchers for the Communists. "Can't you see that you are the mere tools of this Communsit regime?" she pleaded with the girl. "Ask yourselves," she continued, "why is it that only Negro women militia were sent here! They are trying to soil you with the dirt of the revolution, the dirt of the Communists!"

The comandante in charge of the troops seemed to be a decent man. He remonstrated with the prisoners, saying that it was his unfortunate duty to send them to Guanajay. His oratory, like that of so many revolutionaries, was copied from Fidel Castro. He spoke of the benefits of the revolution, and of the opportunity which a "generous revolution" offered to those who wished to become "rehabilitated." And he was interrupted by jeers from the prisoners.

"Come now," Gertrudis shouted down at him, "what is generous about a revolution that treats people like pigs. How generous can a revolution be when virtually every Cuban, including Negroes, want to get out of this hell? Just look up and around you at these women," Gertrudis told him in a choked voice. "Is this any way to treat human beings just because they hate Communism and oppose it? Is it, comandante?"

The comandante did indeed look up and around him, and was visibly shaken at the sight of bruised and bleeding women, some with broken limbs, all with their clothes torn virtually to shreds. Yet they were defiant in the face of armed authority. He said that he would take it upon himself to apologize for the treatment which they had received. Struck by an idea, he then told them that they could expect to receive much better treatment at the Guanajay prison. Certainly, he continued, it could not be worse, now could it?

In the end, and in the face of overwhelming force, the women capitulated. They were sent to Guanajay. Many committed suicide, some went mad, others were executed, and still others are still there. Gertrudis was lucky. The Swiss Ambassador got her out, and she lived to tell the story.

What was happening in Washington was in sickening contrast to the persecution of the Cuban people by a bloody and barbarous regime. There, where a faltering will must be held largely responsible for that persecution, the Kennedy Administration was occupied with keeping its image untarnished. But in doing so, it certainly tarnished the integrity of the United States for many decades to come.

Theodore Sorensen virtually admits that the cancellation of the air strikes doomed the Cuban operation. Yet, he excuses President Kennedy's decision to cancel those strikes because, he alleges: "Our Latin-American friends were outraged" by the "overt, unprovoked attack by the United States on a tiny neighbor." Mr. Sorensen provides no facts to substantiate his claim.[12] And the facts are quite different. Aside from those Central American and Caribbean countries ready to participate in "Operation Marte," and thereby committed to the overthrow of Communism in Cuba, other nations in the hemisphere and around the world lauded U.S. action. Our deep involvement in hemispheric security was almost universally recognized. Thus the London *Daily Express*, more often than not anti-American in its editorial views, headlined: "British people give their support to Kennedy." In Rio de Janeiro, *O Jornal* expressed its opposition to the Communist takeover in Cuba: "This invasion is the beginning of the movement to restore to democracy the Cuban revolution, betrayed by Fidel Castro and his Communist gang." A high-ranking Venezuelan official confided to a correspondent of *Time:* "Kennedy is not crazy or stupid. Every country has the right to give its sympathy to whomever it wishes." Even in Canada and India there was recognition of the rightness of the U.S. action in Cuba. Wrote the *Calgary Herald:* "The United States has shown the utmost forbearance toward that unfortunate country ever since it fell into the hands of the Castro gang." And an Indian Cabinet minister reflected to a U.S. newsman: "We realize that you have to take certain actions for your own security, but we hope that you hurry up and get it over with."

It was the failure of the United States to follow-through that caused sympathy to turn to alarm, and, as *Time* reported, "to disgust." The London *Daily Mail* found the U.S. withdrawal of support "a shocking blow to American prestige." A Colombian official, asking to remain unidentified, was shocked, saying: "The United States should never have allowed the invasion to proceed unless it was to have been successfully carried out."

The final debate on the Cuban tragedy took place at the White House from late Tuesday night until 2:00 a.m. the following morning, April 19, during which Kennedy was told that unless U.S. airpower was committed to the battle, the men on the beach were doomed. It was at this meeting that Mr. Kennedy made his timid commitment of overflights by not more than two planes for one hour. Thus, he was fully aware that the invasion was doomed a full 24 hours prior to April 20. *Yet on that day, when President Kennedy knew that the Bay of Pigs battle was over and he had refused all pleas for aid which might have won the battle*, he spoke to the American Society of Newspaper Editors in defiant tones—heard in the depths of Cuba's jails—which indicated that he was prepared to commit U.S. troops to the battle. "We do not intend to abandon Cuba," he said, and he warned Russia that "we do not intend to be lectured on 'intervention' by those whose character was stamped for all times on the bloody streets of Budapest."

But this was not to happen. The speech must have been by way of a maneuver to keep the President above criticism at a time when the country was patriotically aroused and clearly on the side of the Cuban exile force. Taken together with Kennedy's well-televised walks and talks with General Eisenhower and widely-publicized meetings with General

Douglas MacArthur while the country waited breathlessly for the next move, the Kennedy speech planted in the public mind a false impression of firmness and action which would do until his liberal supporters could come to his rescue. It is also noteworthy that soon after Kennedy's meeting with Eisenhower at Camp David, Secretary of the Interior Stewart Udall volunteered the view that the fault really lay with the Eisenhower Administration for having decided to overthrow Castro in the first place.[13]

As Victor Lasky writes in *JFK: The Man and the Myth*, one of the "most extraordinary aspects of the Cuban tragedy seems to be the fact that President Kennedy managed to escape political consequences and emerged an even more popular figure—if the public opinion polls are to be credited."[14] Evidently, the American people attributed the defeat (which still was not properly assessed as concerns the gravity of the set-back) to Kennedy's being a "young and inexperienced President."

Behind the scenes, however, there was considerable activity aimed at shifting responsibility to the CIA and the military. The day that Kennedy spoke to the newsmen in Washington, April 20, he called Richard Nixon to the White House for a discussion of the tragedy. Nixon quotes Kennedy's words on the Bay of Pigs fiasco: "I was assured by everyone I checked with—all the military experts and the CIA—that the plan would succeed." Nixon continues in his own words: "Over and over again he reiterated the fact that these assurances had been given to him." Nixon then gets to the nub of the matter in his article in the *Reader's Digest* of November, 1964, writing: "He did not mention the fatal advice—given him by some of his liberal State Department and White House advisers —to cancel the two air strikes—and in effect, destroy the plan."

It is not at all inconceivable that what President Kennedy was saying privately, while accepting responsibility publicly, managed to reach the ears of Walter Lippmann. It is no secret that Lippmann was considered among Washington "insiders" as a journalistic spokesman for Kennedy in his most difficult moments. (For example, at the time of the Cuban missile crisis in 1962, the Russians read a proposal by pacifist Lippmann as an expression of President Kennedy's wishes at the time.)[15]

Whatever may be the truth of the matter, Lippmann urged the President to fix responsibility among his Administration aides, without making it clear whether responsibility was to be fixed for mounting the expedition or for making it fail. He wrote that ". . . confidence can be restored only by the resignation of the key figures who had the primary responsibility." Unknowingly, what Lippmann was suggesting was that the President resign. Lippmann had proscribed that obviously unthinkable view, however, by fitting all the principal figures into neat categories —"the Old Hands, Bissell and Dulles of the CIA, Lemnitzer [Army

General Lyman Lemnitzer] and Burke of the Joint Chiefs of Staff, and Berle [Adolf A. Berle] of the Department of State," and the "New Hands." He criticized the latter on the grounds that McGeorge Bundy, Walt Rostow, Arthur Schlesinger Jr., and Dean Rusk "had not protected" the President from the "Old Hands."[16]

Perhaps the most interesting part of the "protection" of President Kennedy deals with the point that "U.S. involvement" be hidden. Of such importance was this point that the President, allegedly, withheld air attacks because of it. Even this excuse, offered by many analysts, seems to be open to challenge. Tad Szulc and Karl Meyer, Haynes Johnson, and just about every writer on the Bay-of-Pigs fiasco readily admit that U.S. involvement in Cuba was an open secret, and that it was impossible to hide what was already known.

Tad Szulc should know. Stationed in Miami following the break in relations with Cuba on January 3, 1961, I received a telephone call from Szulc from Bogota. He said that reports of impending plans for the U.S. overthrow of Castro had reached him all the way down in Colombia, and asked that I meet him when he arrived by plane in Miami. I had no sooner hung up the phone than Stuart Novins of CBS called from Mexico, repeating that he also knew about the impending invasion. They both came to Miami and, within hours of talking with Cuban exiles, were in possession of the elements of the plan, minus the date on which it was to be carried out. They confided in me, and I asked that their stories be withheld, telling them that I felt compelled for security reasons to report our conversation to Washington. Both newsmen left for New York to consult with their respective editors, returned, and busied themselves with gathering background information.

Actually, as early as October 30, 1960, *La Hora*, a newspaper in Guatemala, had printed a story about the Cuban exile training camps there. The story was relayed around the world by the wire services. Paul Kennedy of the *New York Times* also reported on those camps over a Guatemala dateline. In fact, on the very day that President Kennedy was announcing that U.S. forces would not be used in Cuba, the *New York Herald Tribune* reported that there was dissension within the Administration over how far the United States should commit itself to supporting the impending invasion of Cuba.

Perhaps President Kennedy was not reading the newspapers and was therefore unaware that his attempts to "hide" U.S. involvement were fruitless. This is not a credible proposition, however. The President was known to be a voracious reader of the papers.[17] And, knowing what was being reported, the President had to assume that foreign ambassadors in Washington knew about U.S. involvement.

It is for these reasons that most writers concede that U.S. involvement in the Cuban operation was an open secret. Having conceded this, how-ever, many accept the paradoxical proposition that the President was determined to hide a U.S. involvement which, by their own admission, was widely known. They try to have it both ways.

An examination of what has been written and said about the more than a dozen meetings in which the Cuban problem was discussed suggests a partial answer. The examination reveals President Kennedy as more a spectator, who disliked association withthe plans, than a vigorous par-ticipant, and as more a cautious administrator than as a bold planner. On the one hand, Kennedy told the CIA to continue with preparations. On the other, he warned that he might call off the entire operation.

Commenting on the distaste with which Kennedy's White House staff viewed action against Cuba, Karl Meyer and Tad Szulc write in *The Cuban Invasion* that CIA Director Allen Dulles and his deputy Richard Bissell "sold" the Cuban operation to the Administration.[18] It seems remarkable that the President and his staff, who aspired to leadership of the Free World, would have to be "sold" on asserting that leadership in their own backyard.

The evidence suggests that Mr. Kennedy and his New Frontier shunned the hard decisions needed to conduct foreign affairs in an ag-gressive cold war climate. With no apparent talent for developing their own policy towards Cuba, they had nothing but carping criticism for the offerings of the intelligence community and the military establishment. And the word "professional" became a term of opprobvium in their mouths when used to describe men who were vastly more seasoned than they.[19]

The thinking of the New Frontier seems to have been guided by the kind of "progressive" nonsense revealed in portions of Arthur Schlesin-ger's "White Paper" on Cuba.* Refusal to substitute the hard realities of Soviet intrusion into the hemisphere for their own preconceptions did more than anything else to establish the philosophy of failure underlying the Bay of Pigs operation. Having no plan of its own, the New Frontier was quite willing to tinker and tamper with that of their seniors until they brought about the most unnecessary defeat in the history of the United States. It can hardly be denied that they did so knowingly. What remains to be answered is this: Did the New Frontier actually want a victory? The assessment by Nikita Khrushchev was that Americans are too liberal to fight—over Berlin, Cuba, or anywhere else. Another view is given by Hugo Bell Huertas, a Cuban diplomat who defected from his post at the Cuban Embassy in Baghdad following the Cuban missile crisis. In an

*One suspects that the New Frontier withheld from seriously challenging Communism for the fundamental reason that its overthrow would also do away with Socialist economic planning which was endorsed by that same New Frontier.

interview with me in Miami he said: "We knew from dispatches sent to us by the Cuban and Russian missions to the United Nations that the call-off of the air strikes was the work of President Kennedy and Adlai Stevenson. We had a sort of party in the Foreign Ministry and elevated Stevenson to 'General of the Army," and President Kennedy to 'Field Marshal.' "

Suppose, however, that Castro's planes had been knocked out on the ground and his airports destroyed according to plan. Suppose that the valiant men of the beach had not had their supplies cut off and their positions placed under direct attack by artillery which they themselves could not knock out. Suppose that they had had their radio equipment intact to broadcast to the Cuban people that a "Provisional Government" had been established on Cuban soil. Suppose that Castro's air force had been knocked out and that Freedom Fighters' planes had swiftly and systematically destroyed Castro's communications and oil refineries, and had attacked tank and militia forces at the beach. Is it reasonable to assume that under a severe pounding Castro's ill-trained and untested militia organization would have any more heart for the fray than Batista's almost non-combatant professional army?

With hundreds of thousands of Cubans crammed into jails and make-shift prisons all over the island, with no sanitation facilities and little food —with other hundreds of thousands of their families angered by the brutality of the regime—how long could Castro have kept the lid on the boiling country?

To ask these questions is to answer them. The shaky regime of Fidel Castro could not have lasted. The country would have exploded, and, with the explosion, Castro and Communism would have been propelled completely out of the hemisphere. In short, the plan as originally conceived, would have been successful.

BOOK II

Disaster

CHAPTER 12

Invitation to Disaster

THE FAILURE OF THE CUBAN operation brought about a complete break between the earlier Cuban policies of the Eisenhower Administration and those which were to be developed under President Kennedy. Discarded were the bitter lessons and traumatic experiences of 1959 and 1960. Apparently, the New Frontier was not impressed by what had been learned by others—at such a costly price—since it decided to walk the road of appeasement all over again. In the process, history was to repeat itself irrevocably, with the result that another crisis in Cuba became inevitable, and with that crisis, came the entrenchment of Soviet power in this Hemisphere. One can liken the forward thrust of Communism to a bayonet charge: If you strike steel, pull back; if you strike mush, keep going. And there was considerable mush in the emerging policies of the Kennedy Administration.

As columnist William S. White was later to remark about the aura of defeatism in our press, among our intellectuals, and, it is to be supposed from ensuing events, in the New Frontier itself: ". . . the mere fact of its [Bay of Pigs] failure strengthened those wistfully attached to the notion that we could somehow talk Castro's Cuba out of being a part of the Soviet apparatus. They had a field day of I-told-you-sos. They had always been against 'military solutions,' they said. Well, look what happened when a military solution was tried. The argument amounted to saying that because inadequate military measures was tried, any and all possible military measures would, therefore, be both wrong and inadequate. All the same, it had some effect; for nothing succeeds for the appeasement line like the failure of any line of action."[1]

What Mr. White was writing about was certainly true. Those of us working in the U.S. Information Agency's Miami office grinding out materials such as the Príncipe prison story were irritated, shocked and frankly dismayed to find that those reports made absolutely no impact on Washington policy makers. Cubans were beginning to seep out of the captive island, and what they reported to our staff upon arrival in Miami were human interest stories packing a potent political and propaganda wallop. We suggested that the U.S. Information Agency and the State Department urge President Kennedy to refer to these stories during his nationally televised press conferences and to condemn Communist brutality before the New Frontier's carefully cultivated court of world opinion. We recommended, as well, that the Secretary of State denounce those brutalities in the strongest possible terms. The very least we expected was that Adlai Stevenson, the towering figure of liberalism, would deliver a crushing address to the United Nations and couple his speech with a demand that the Human Rights Commission immediately convene, investigate, and condemn the Communist barbarities committed against the people of Cuba.

The word "liberal," however, has many different meanings to many different people. Official Washington remained singularly unmoved both by the atrocities being committed in Cuba, and by the propaganda advantages to be gained by an exposé of those atrocities. So did the liberal press.

One evening while dining with a small group of reporters in Miami, I tried to interest them in reporting, on television and through newspapers, a purely factual account of what was going on in Cuba. Literally scores of Cubans awaited the opportunity to tell their stories of Communist oppression in Cuba—rivalling those of Nazi persecution. But I was to discover that, like his official Washington counterpart, the "liberal" reporter had suddenly changed to the "man of vision," whose *Weltanschauung* could not be affected by the misfortunes of individuals. One reporter found Castro's barbarities not so shocking. "After all," he said, "we put Japanese Nisei in camps during World War II, didn't we?" Another reporter was disposed "to look ahead, not back." In plain fact, they were not interested in the fate of the Cuban people. Their interest lay in bludgeoning the CIA, chiefly because they had concluded, with characteristic lack of objectivity, that the intelligence community had deliberately destroyed the underground organization of the "democratic Left."

The new policy being developed in Washington by the White House staff took shape in the reaction of President Kennedy to the Bay of Pigs —immediately to back away from Cuba, his pre-invasion indecision giving way to a rush of post-invasion jitters and vulnerability to blackmail. And those same "liberal" reporters accommodated and supported Kennedy's withdrawal from a meaningful Cuban policy. A part of Kennedy's remarkably candid conversations with Richard Nixon on April 20, 1961, clearly addresses the President's withdrawal.

The President asked Nixon: "What would you do now in Cuba?" Nixon's reply follows: "I would find proper legal cover and go in,' I answered. I suggested three possible legal justifications for taking such action: 1. A new definition of aggression, based on the premise that Soviet-bloc equipment was used by the Castro forces, and that we had an obligation to see that the Freedom Forces were at least equally supplied. 2. Send American forces in under our treaty right because of the potential threat to Guantanamo. 3. Send American forces in to protect the lives and rights of American citizens still living in Cuba. I emphasized that I felt we must do whatever was necessary to rid Cuba of Castro and Communism."

The President, however, backed away, apparently blackmailed against taking any further action against Cuba for fear of a Russian move against West Berlin. Nixon reports Kennedy's reaction to his reply as follows: "Kennedy heard me out without comment, and then replied, 'Both Walter Lippmann [who had recently had an interview with Khrushchev] and Chip Bohlen [who had been our ambassador to Moscow] have reported that Khrushchev is in a very cocky mood at this time. If their appraisal is correct, he may believe this is the time to move against us and he might seize upon any action on our part in Cuba as an excuse for doing so. This means that there is a good chance that, if we move on Cuba, Khrushchev will move on Berlin. I just don't think we can take the risk in the event their appraisal is correct.' "

Nixon continues the account of his exchange with Kennedy: "Our conversation then turned briefly to Laos, where American support of a neutralist regime seemed to be leading to an eventual communist take-over. I told President Kennedy I thought that in both Laos and Cuba the important thing was to take some affirmative action, including, if necessary, at least a commitment of airpower."

"The President," Nixon writes, said: " 'I just don't think we ought to get involved in Laos, particularly where we might find ourselves fighting millions of Chinese troops in the jungles.' His next remark underlined that the failure to come to grips with communism in one part of the world has weakened our position in every other part of the world. 'In any event,' he said, 'I don't see how we can make any move in Laos, which is 5,000 miles away, if we don't make a move in Cuba which is only 90 miles away.' "[2]

While what President Kennedy was saying to Richard Nixon might have been true, by saying it he had proscribed action in Cuba, with the clear implication that the United States was not to take any vigorous actions against Communist encroachment anywhere in the world.

It was only a few weeks later, in May, that Kennedy's views, as expressed to Nixon on April 20, began to take on recognizable form. In a UPI story from Washington, "top officials," reportedly said that "The

Kennedy administration is expected to pursue in the future a new Cuba policy aimed at quarantining the Fidel Castro regime, and strengthening democratic governments in the rest of Latin America." "High administration officials," the UPI dispatch continued, said that "President Kennedy was more convinced than ever" that "the most positive policy would be to redouble *support for Latin America's battle against poverty and illiteracy which create conditions that allow Castroism or Communism to develop"* (Italics supplied).[3]

That statement of Administration policy was important in at least three respects: One was that the hazy notion of a quarantine gave the appearance of action against Castro without any true substance. The second was that the Administration defined "Castroism" as distinct from "Communism." The third, and possibly most important, was that John F. Kennedy's little-remembered campaign statement, made in 1960, to the effect that the United States had refused to help Cuba "meet its desperate need for economic progress," had now blossomed into the official Administration view.

The Kennedy view of Cuba and Latin America was, therefore, based on the false concepts of the "losers." Indeed, most of the policies now emerging from the New Frontier were virtually indistinguishable from those recommended for years by the "losers," upon whom the President was to rely for future support.

Under Secretary of State Chester Bowles, recognized spokesman for the ultraliberal line in the Administration, added some dimensions to Kennedy's policies when he followed up with a statement that the real danger was not Cuba at all, but hunger in Latin America. After all, said Bowles, the basic trouble in Cuba stemmed from the fact that the United States had treated "the Batista government very kindly," and that the Cuban people had been "exploited and treated unjustly" by us. Now, said the liberal Under Secretary, we must do away with economic conditions in Latin America that lead to more Castros.[4]

Military action against Cuba was ruled out in a later address by Bowles. He said: "It would be very wrong if we get trapped into a fight between the United States with its 180,000,000 people, and Mr. Castro and his beard and whatever number of Cuban people want to follow him. I really think that isn't the struggle. The struggle is against conditions in Latin America that created Castro in Cuba and could create more Castros if they are not met: poverty and injustice and the insecurity of a people who just feel that there is not much to live for."

Apparently the Bowlesian theories extended to helping Castro's Cuba, for, shortly after the declaration in Washington, the wire services revealed that the United States policy had contributed $463,000 of a million-dollar project for Communist Cuba through the United Nations

Technical Assistance Fund. This but added to congressional ire that had already been raised earlier when it was discovered that Cuba still enjoyed a $70 million business with the United States through the sale of tobacco, canned fish, fresh fruit, and molasses. But the storm of protests on both counts—the UN grant and Cuban trade—was countered by Administration spokesmen.

Deputy Assistant Secretary of State Richard Gardner said that the ground rules of the UN Fund prohibited "political considerations" from entering into decisions on dispensing the money to Cuba. He added a peculiar twist of accommodation for the Soviet Union, saying "I should like to point out that the Soviet Union has had to stand by and see special funds go to Taiwan. . . ."[5]

While this might have been true, Mr. Gardner's implied defense of the Soviet Union was irrelevant to the central issue which was that Russia, through a combination of force and intrigue, had invaded this hemisphere in violation of the Monroe Doctrine and of defense treaties devised to prevent that invasion. In addition, the amount of money reaching Taiwan through the UN Fund was but a drop in the bucket when compared to the billions the United States was sending unilaterally to that bastion of anti-Communism in the Pacific.[6] The reverse was true with regard to Russia. The Soviets are not noted for their openhanded aid to satellite nations. Convertible dollars were badly needed for Cuba, and the UN Fund money represented a significant breach in a "quarantine" which the Kennedy Administration had but recently characterized as its principal weapon against Cuba. Secretary of State Dean Rusk believed, however, that the cut-off of U.S. trade with Cuba should be effected only in concert with a cut-off of Cuban trade on the part of our allies.

Congress differed with the Administration. It wanted prompt action taken against Cuba. Representative Armistead I. Selden, an Alabama Democrat, slashed out at the "tentative and mincing steps" being taken by the Kennedy Administration to deal with the Cuban threat to our security. In May, an aroused House of Representatives passed a resolution branding Cuba a "clear and present danger," and urged the Organization of American States and the Administration to do something about it. The Resolution passed by a roll-call vote of 401 to 2.

Yet, on April 28, barely ten days following the Bay of Pigs, the wire services carried a cover-up story by "a U.S. diplomat philosophizing that we might as well face it, Castro himself is no immediate threat to us." And a State Department spokesman said: "Just because a lot of Cubans are against Castro does not mean that they are for us."

The cover-up was professionally managed. Columnist Charles Bartlett, (a confidant of the Kennedys, incidentally) wrote: "In order to avoid the possibility of a Congressional or public demand that it [the story of the Bay of Pigs disaster] be published," President Kennedy appointed his own body to look into the Bay of Pigs failure and report to him."[7] Significantly, members of the investigating group included the very people who were being blamed by the Liberal Establishment for the fiasco. They included CIA Director Allen Dulles, Chief of Naval Operations and Vice Chairman of the Joint Chiefs of Staff Admiral, Arleigh A. Burke, soon-to-be appointed Chairman of the Joint Chiefs, General Maxwell Taylor, and the watchdog, Attorney General Robert Kennedy. By making those appointments, the President had sealed the lips of the men closest to the Cuban operation, including the incoming Chairman of the Joint Chiefs, and he assigned his brother to the group to make sure that they remained sealed. Inferentially, of course, blame was directed away from the White House and toward the military and the intelligence services.

As the New Frontier had anticipated, the chorus of criticism came right on schedule following the Bay of Pigs. But the Liberal Establishment was most vocal in absolving Kennedy from blame, casting it, instead, on the CIA and the military.

Issues of morality flowed from the pens of such foreign policy experts as Walter Lippmann who, as noted previously, felt that the President had not been "protected" from Burke, Dulles, Bissell, and Berle. Almost within hours of the failure, intellectuals, writers, TV commentators, and politicians struck out at a role played by the CIA and the military establishment which could have been known only superficially at the time. None could have been completely informed of the vital facts, much less of the decisive role the President himself later was revealed to have played.

Political pundits of the Liberal Establishment told the American people not to take the defeat too hard. They argued that if we are operating in the periphery of the Soviet Union and Red China, we must expect those countries to operate in ours—namely Cuba. This a false analogy, for the United States does not operate in the periphery of the Soviet Union and Red China. The United States has not, for example, subverted the Communist regime of Czechoslovakia, taken over its economy lock, stock and barrel, and forced the Czechs to support our foreign policy. This particular "loser" airily concedes that peripheral areas of the Free World are legitimate political and military terrain in which predatory Communism may roam. Indeed, the struggle between Communism and democracy is not being fought on the same terms on both sides. As Cuba proved, the site of that struggle is always in the West—in countries outside the Communist orbit.

The judgment of those directing our policies in Latin America was summed up in 1961 by Eric Sevareid. Writing from Rio de Janeiro, he said: "I feel impatient about the crippling confusion still being sowed by so many of our respected voices, who write off the peripheral nations so easily, who believe that cloak and daggering or the use of force is beneath our virtue, and who seem to believe that any given land of human wretchedness can be saved by our money, technicians, more exemplary conduct at home, in our racial policies, for example, and by ceasing to support the local dictator. I believed that this over-all recipe would work. I wish to heaven that it would. But I know now that in many critical countries it won't. . . ."

But the voices of the "losers" were powerful and persistent. Little more than a month after the Bay of Pigs, the Columbia Broadcasting System added to the "crippling confusion." It presented on television a film which, said the moderator, had been taken during the Bay of Pigs by West German photographers.

The importance of the televised offering, said CBS, was that the photographers had been able to move about Cuba for eighteen days, and to speak with anyone they chose, without hindrance.

Among the scenes were views of Castro's forces at the Bay of Pigs. Fidel Castro himself was shown directing fire at a ship which had been sunk eighteen hours before he had even arrived at the beachhead. It was a very heroic presentation.

Other views of Cuba presented on the telecast did not coincide even with statements being published in Cuba's Communist newspapers at the time—statements that could not help exposing shortages of food and clothing. The West German photographers, however, presented films of a trade fair in which food being produced under the Communist regime appeared to be plentiful. And, of course, there were films of the skyscraping public-housing development in Havana del Este.

The West German reporters found a sort of gay, animated, spirit in Cuba in which "nobody took Communism seriously." Several hundred thousand prisoners rounded up during the Bay of Pigs landing took it seriously, however, as had hundreds of others who were summarily shot. Calculating on a conservative basis of a family average of five in Cuba, more than a million Cubans had been personally and bitterly affected by the massive arrests at the very time the reporters were there. Notably absent from the film was any evidence of the police brutality that characterized the swift reprisals of the government against its people as indicated, for example, in the fact of thousands of relatives lined up before the prisons of Príncipe and La Cabaña fortress waiting for word of the fate of their loved ones.

Suffice it to say that it was only a few months after this idyllic presentation of the Revolutionary horn of plenty and of the gay, animated Cubans that the Cuban government rationed food for the first time in the history of the country. *The ration was below what the Spanish government in 1842 had decreed be provided for Negro slaves.*

The news department of CBS should have known that it was not possible for newsmen to wander around Cuba during the Bay-of-Pigs invasion and its aftermath and talk freely to people and take pictures. The news department of CBS should also have known that, even in relatively normal times, a reporter seeking to move around the country required the specific approval of numerous government organizations. One of these is called the Committee for the Friendship of Peoples, a pistol-packing organization which is a direct copy of the prototype organization developed in Russia. Its purpose is precisely to control what the foreigner sees, hears, and reports.

While it is understandable that CBS would be interested in the sensational aspects of a brand-new film out of Cuba, it should have made all the foregoing facts very clear to the viewer. For, without a strong clarifying note, the film added to what Sevareid correctly assessed to be "the crippling confusion" in this country about Latin America—and more particularly, about Cuba.

It was but shortly after the failure of the Cuban operation that 132 lawyers saw fit to belabor the Bay-of-Pigs venture. In a petition to the White House, carried as a news story around the country and overseas, they found that the Bay of Pigs operation violated any number of treaties. The apparent organizer of the petition, Arthur Larson, wrote in a letter to the President that "I am afraid there is danger of the world rule of law beginning to look like a facade." Mr. Larson in his letter, and his colleagues in the petition, failed to mention that the Monroe Doctrine and the solemn treaty commitments made by the U.S. government for the mutual defense of this Hemisphere had already been violated by the Soviet presence in Cuba.

It was mystifying, confusing, and perhaps irritating for Americans to read the many newspaper advertisements by pressure groups condemning the Bay of Pigs venture. For example, on May 10, 1961, the *New York Times* published such an advertisement, signed by some seventy American professors. It stated, among other things, that "The major premise of U.S.-Cuban policy for at least a year has been that we must crush Castro." The purpose of this particular advertisement seemed to be an attempt by its organizers to strengthen the hand of the "losers." Among them were such experts in foreign affairs as a professor of astronomy, a lecturer on clinical psychology, a number of professors of English and foreign languages, and quite a scattering of mathematicians and architects.

Arthur Krock of the *New York Times* seriously questioned the objec-

tivity of the signers of the advertisement. In answer to one complaint
that the United States had "rebuffed and snubbed" Castro, Krock pointed
out that by actual count the United States had made a total of 25 offers
to discuss differences with Castro over a space of two years. He found
that the petitioners had chosen to commence the history of U.S.-Castro
relations in the middle, not at the beginning. He also found in his mail
an unusual number of remarkably uniform dissents—an organized mail
campaign.

In July of 1961, Havana announced that Cuba had completed the
takeover of all remaining U.S. business enterprises in Cuba. The same
month, however, the U.S. Treasury lifted a seven-month ban on sending
Federal benefit checks to Cuba. The money involved came to $700,000
a year, amounting to a subsidy of convertible dollars to the Castro regime.[8] With the U.S. contribution of $463,000 to Castro through the
United Nations Fund and the $70 million yearly trade with Cuba which,
said Secretary of State Dean Rusk, the United States was "not now
considering cutting off," Castro had been given approval by the Kennedy
Administration to obtain $71,163,000 a year from American sources.
This was, in the stated opinion of Florida Democratic Congressman Paul
Rogers, "a most peculiar manner in which to carry out a 'quarantine' of
Communist Cuba."

The hijacking at the end of July and the beginning of August of two
U.S. airliners by Cubans, and Castro's refusal to return an Eastern Airlines turbo-prop Electra to the United States, brought about a tremendous uproar on Capitol Hill. Senator Claire Engle of California said that
if it were determined (as it later was) that Castro agents had hijacked
a plane belonging to Continental Airlines, "then this would constitute
an act of war and should be dealt with accordingly." Senator Everett
Dirksen said he felt that the Kennedy Administration had "overlooked
a bet." He said this represented "a beautiful opportunity to serve notice
on Castro that the time for kidding and nibbling has come to an end and
that we mean business."[9]

The story behind the hijackings was the familiar one involving Castro's
tactics of blackmail. Several of Castro's own planes had been hijacked
by Cubans, desperate to get out of the country, and flown to the United
States. Once here, the planes were attached by legal process by persons
and firms who had been robbed of their properties in Cuba. They planned
to sell the aircraft for partial reimbursement of their legitimate claims.
Castro's reaction was immediate. He assigned some of his agents and
sympathizers in the United State to book passage on American commercial aircraft, hijack them, and force the pilots to fly the planes to Cuba.
Castro then offered to return the Eastern Airlines turbo-prop if the U.S.
returned all of his planes.

Not only did the Kennedy Administration succumb to this blackmail; it told Castro how he could recover his planes. An AP story out of Washington reported on August 3: "The United States told other nations Wednesday that there are normal legal processes by which Cuba could head off seizure of hijacked Cuban aircraft under U.S. court orders." We "told other nations," presumably because, with the break in diplomatic relations, the United States carried on no direct dialogue with the Cuban government. An outraged Congress, concerned with obtaining at least some compensation for robberies committed against American citizens in Cuba, boiled as the State Department suggested that Cuba claim immunity for its planes, adding that "if a timely request is made through diplomatic channels for recognition of the immunity of the aircraft," the court would dismiss legal attachment claims and the aircraft would be returned to Cuba.

What few realized at the time is that the New Frontier *had made up its mind not to raise issues with Castro.* I found this out during a trip to Washington, where many colleagues from the Embassy then stationed there said that "the word is out that the reason for the failure of the Bay of Pigs was because of Castro's popularity." Their disgust was of epic proportions. The word also was passed around to other departments and agencies that the less said about Cuba the better, with the additional admonition that while new policies were being worked out, it would be very unwise for personnel to comment on Cuba. The lid was on so tight that the most innocuous questions from reporters were pondered at the highest levels before an answer was given.

The picture now comes more clearly into focus. It was little wonder that the President, the Secretary of State, and the U.S. Ambassador to the United Nations remained silent about Castro's atrocities. Considering the mood of Congress at the time, such statements would pile fuel on a fire which the New Frontier was busily trying to extinguish. The fire was quite hot. In fact, Republican Senator Kenneth B. Keating of New York was burned up. He said that "if we don't put a stop to the steady flow of arms to the wild man of the Caribbean, we will soon find Communist missiles and bases staring us right in the face from Cuba."[10] Speaking on the matter of Cuba's lucrative trade with the United States, the New York Senator seemed to voice the sentiments of many of his colleagues when he said that "it is ridiculous that this trade has not been cut off before now."

Pre-Castro Cuba was an example of the constructive role of private enterprise in Latin America. For there, private American and Cuban investors (with negligible investment from the American government) had brought about a standard of living which was the envy of Cuba's sister republics. Yet, for the Kennedy Administration the real enemy was not predatory Communism which had robbed the Cuban people of both their freedom and that enviable standard of living. Rather than recognize that pre-Castro Cuba was an example of economic progress, and that the composite of Cuban freedoms must be restored, the New Frontier had resorted to the false clichés of the "losers."

Indeed, the rearguard action which the Kennedy Administration was fighting with Congress and the American people in order *not* to be pressured into rescuing Cuba hid from view the underlying policies of the New Frontier. Those policies were to encourage Latin American countries to endorse rather vaguely defined socialistic systems of government—systems which agreed with the political "philosophy" of the Administration. But, to put its policies across, the Administration *needed* a Communist Cuba—to hold up as a bogey man to reluctant leaders on the continent (while extending the carrot of $20 billion in U.S. moneys over a ten-year period), and to sell those programs to the American tax-payer. The idea was that alleged economic conditions in pre-Castro Cuba caused a popular revolt against Batista and that economic conditions in Latin America would, justifiably, create revolts there also. The point is that the U.S. posture did not recognize that Communists were at the root of the trouble. Indeed, the stance of the Kennedy administration seemed, almost, to justify Communist excesses in Cuba and elsewhere.

Denigration of U.S. private investments overseas and an implied lack of faith by *our* government in the U.S. capitalistic system, inevitably took its toll. With Castro's rise to power in 1960 and the statements of policy by the Kennedy Adminstration in 1961, a total of about $2 billion of private capital fled Latin America—more than Alliance for Progress moneys could hope to replace in a comparable length of time. In 1959, the regular yearly flow of American capital investments to Latin America had amounted to $218 million. In 1960, facing the threat of a Communist Cuba and watching the inability of the United States to cope with it, capital investments dropped to $90 million, and decreased further in 1961.[11] The New Frontier was not dismayed by this state of affairs— presumably because in pushing for Left-of-center leadership in Latin America (as, for example, in Peru, Colombia, and Chile), the Administration contemplated that that leadership would want increasing government control of investments, as they indeed have. Government-to-government loans and grants were very much to the liking of the New Frontier.

The propaganda of the U.S. Information Agency being devised for Latin America was brought into line with Administration policy. For example, its Miami office was instructed to minimize its reports on the political excesses of Communism in Cuba. Such reports, said the Assistant Director for Latin America, "are negative." In a policy speech delivered at a meeting of top-level officials of the Agency in Washington, he said that the Communist take-over of Cuba had certain advantages, such as putting the spotlight on Latin American countries which might fall prey to the kind of Right-wing economic exploitation that had brought about Castro. The Agency should, he said, push the "positive" programs of the Alliance for Progress in the propaganda output being pumped into Latin America, and contrast those programs with reports of economic failures of Communism in Cuba.

From this point forward, all hope of a militant policy that would eradicate the Communist base in Cuba was lost. It was alleged in Washington that the Soviet Union planned to create an image of Communist plenty in Cuba as a lure to the Latin American peoples. To counter that challenge, Washington image-makers turned to the Alliance for Progress which, they alleged, would demonstrate the superiority of free societies over Communist societies. Thus, the matter of Communist Cuba became one big public relations game as the New Frontiermen set enthusiastically about the business of destroying an "image" of "Communist plenty" in Cuba which never for an instant played a role in the political and military strategy of the Russians. In fact, the Russians were plundering the Cuban economy, not building it up. A complete cream cheese factory was removed from Las Villas and shipped to Russia, along with the bottling plant and brewery of the Polar beer company. Machinery was taken from shoe factories and shoe repair shops and sent to Bulgaria. A chicken dressing plant, three sugar mills, and two rum distilleries were dismantled and sent to the Soviet Union. These are but a few examples of the massive robbery of Cuba by the Soviet Union and its satellites.

News leaks are used extensively by various administrations in Washington to test public reaction to policies under consideration, or actually in force. In such a leak, Tad Szulc wrote from Washington again that in August of 1961: "The United States has begun to feel strong pressures for friendly coexistence from a number of Latin American republics and from Havana itself." The story went on to say that "an inclination to accept the Castro regime as a member in relatively good standing of the inter-American community is seen as developing in the Western Hemisphere." These "pressures," Szulc reported, made it quite unlikely that the inter-American conference scheduled to be held in January of 1962 —some five months later—would result in very strong action being taken against Cuba. Szulc also wrote: "There are strong indications, according to diplomatic sources here, that the Soviet Union is most interested in an accommodation between the United States and Cuba."[12]

Szulc's analysis, made in Washington, contrasted sharply with a poll of Latin American countries taken by the Associated Press through its correspondents in ten key Latin American countries. By a coincidence, the poll findings appeared on the same day as the *New York Times* article —August 15, 1961. The AP found that while there was considerable disenchantment with Castro among the people of Latin America, the issue went far beyond a popularity contest. "Most pro-U.S. government leaders in Latin America," said the AP poll, "regard it [Castroism] as a threat and in several cases have acted to check its advance." The AP poll was more explicit with regard to Panama where, it said, Castro's decline in popularity had been largely the result of the government's "strong moves to curb pro-Castro activity."

The marked differences in the two analyses—the *New York Times* in Washington and the AP poll in Latin America—may possibly have come from the fact that Szulc was known to be close to White House aides Richard Goodwin and Arthur Schlesinger, Jr., the prime movers of the Alliance for Progress. Thus, the *Times* article from Washington was more likely a reflection of what the New Frontier *wanted to do* than a routine report on unnamed "pressures." Schlesinger and Goodwin, it may be surmised, did not want the inter-American conference to be preoccupied with such "negative" business as taking a hard line with Castro. To do so would relegate their social revolutionary theories to a place of secondary importance on the agenda.

The results of the Punta del Este conference, in January, 1962, was virtually foreordained. There, Secretary of State Dean Rusk called for a Latin American counter-attack against Cuba. After weaving back and forth through the web of Latin American diplomacy, Rusk watered down his proposals to where his main points merely called for curbs on trade with Cuba and the ouster of the Red regime from the Organization of American States.

Those points arose out of the approach of historian Arthur Schlesinger, Jr., economist Walt Rostow, and Kennedy speech-writer-turned Latin American specialist, Richard N. Goodwin, three of the top White House advisers. Social experimenters and government planners, the trio tackled the problem of Communist subversion in Latin America with the mentality of social workers. A few quotes from Schlesinger's books identify the author, as, for example, his comment that "Keynes, not Marx, is the prophet of the new radicalism." He also wrote: "The non-Communist left has brought what measure of hope there is in our political life today."[13] If at all accurate his description may be applied to European socialism, not the Latin American variant. If Schlesinger, Goodwin, and Rostow had known Latin America better, (or at all, for that matter) they would have known that while Latin American socialists are non-Communist, they do not share the history of anti-Communism which sets the early European socialists distinctly apart from their Latin colleagues.

While Secretary of State Dean Rusk spoke for the United States, the trio of New Frontiersmen spoke for the President, and they made it quite clear to Latin diplomats that they favored going easy on Castro, and urged the Latins to turn to the economics of the Alliance for Progress as the surest means to counter Communist subversion.[14]

All that the United States got out of the 20 billion dollar "bait" was a narrow vote to expel Cuba from the Organization of American States, approval of the Alliance for Progress, and a call to nations in the Western Hemisphere to "maintain all vigilance necessary" against Communism. The most peculiar part of the meeting was that the nations of the Western Hemisphere were called upon to place "an arms embargo" on Cuba, with instructions to the OAS council "to consider extending the ban to strategic materials." The embargo resolution was forced through despite the fact that it was not the countries of Latin America, but Russia, which was sending arms to Cuba.

In Washington, President Kennedy seemed pleased with the results of the conference, making the empty statement that for "the first time in history the independent American States have declared with one voice that the concept of Marxism-Leninism is incompatible with the inter-American system." And, in an apparent effort to make certain that the world understood that he was pleased with the Punta del Este conference, President Kennedy personally received Rusk in Washington in what was described in press accounts as "a special welcome." Rusk then told a news conference that "trade with Cuba supplies Castro with dollars to help finance the Communist program of infiltration and subversion in the hemisphere," but apparently he did not find that fact too alarming, adding merely that the United States would "consider halting its purchases from Cuba." Boiled down, Punta del Este meant that the major implement of American foreign policy in Latin America consisted of the economics of the Alliance for Progress.

Apart from the fact that the Alliance for Progress was based on a false premise—an "exploited" pre-Castro Cuba—it was applied in the wrong place. When the United States provided aid to Europe under the Marshall Plan, it did so in the right place. The American criterion providing economic resources to a culturally and economically advanced community of nations made sense. Philosophically, to accept the premise that what worked in Europe would work in Latin America under the Alliance for Progress was all wrong. Whereas Europe was politically developed, with relatively strong institutions, Latin America was politically underdeveloped, with weak institutions.

The New Frontier gave exaggerated importance to the economic aspect of the struggle against Communism and underemphasized the basic fact that the "cold war" is fundamentally a war of ideas, effective propaganda and organization. Latin America was perhaps more in need of trained cadres of democrats, schooled in the techniques of dialogue, to work in the social spheres where ideas are generated—universities, high schools, political parties, labor unions—to meet and defeat the Communists at their own game. It seemed for a while that the Peace Corps would be the answer to this need. But even this fresh idea was weakened when the Peace Corps was prevented from dealing in political subjects and was thus made into a far less effective instrument of social welfare. It was weakened even more when the security clearance for potential members was lowered to permit even the wildest Socialist to enter its ranks.

But there was more than just the economic theories of the New Frontier that gave the observer pause. There was, for example, the matter of the prisoners from Brigade 2506 who had been captured by Castro. Indeed, no analysis of Cuban policy can be considered complete without examining the extraordinary role the prisoners played in President Kennedy's thinking. The one goal that Kennedy had set for himself was the release of those prisoners, and he pursued it with a tenacity that was notably lacking elsewhere. How the President felt about the prisoner issue was revealed in his remarkably candid conversations with Richard Nixon on April 20, 1961.

President Kennedy opened the conversations with Nixon by broaching the prisoner issue. He said, according to Nixon: " 'I have just come from a meeting with the members of the Cuban Revolutionary Council. Several of those who were there had lost their sons, brothers and other close relatives or friends in this action.' " (Dr. José Miró Cardona, President of the Council said of the meeting that Kennedy took the imprisonment of the Cubans as a personal blow, reacting, as though his own son were in a Cuban prison). Kennedy's sense of personal responsibility and tragedy is revealed, as well, in the President's next sentence to Nixon. " 'Talking to them and seeing the tragic expressions on their faces was the worst experience of my life.' "[15] This, and subsequent events, may or may not indicate that the President felt personally responsible for their imprisonment because he had cancelled the air strikes. However that may be, his anguish was undoubtedly real.

In this regard, certain comments made by Victor Lasky take on some significance. Commenting on Robert Kennedy's explosion immediately following the Bay of Pigs fiasco, Lasky says, "The outburst was remarkable for what it demonstrated about the Kennedys. The Cuban tragedy—one of the greatest defeats ever suffered by the United States—was viewed primarily as a personal affront."[16] If Lasky is correct in his analysis, it explains in considerable measure why the release of the Bay of Pigs prisoners was to play such an important part in Kennedy's attitude toward Cuba. For, what Lasky is saying would fit the situation almost

perfectly—John F. Kennedy felt *personally reponsible* for their imprisonment, and was quite prepared to accept any solution, including blackmail,
for their release. In doing so, Kennedy went directly against his own
political impulses in that the Congress and just about every segment of
American society except the "losers" were outraged over the implications in ransoming the Cubans. To publicly buck that sentiment was
politically unwise.

In an attempt by the Kennedy Administration to fill a policy vacuum
with public relations gimmickry, a Tractors for Freedom Committee was
formed in May, 1961. It appears that the inspiration to trade tractors for
the Bay of Pigs prisoners came from White House aide Richard Goodwin
and was supported by his colleague, the ubiquitous Arthur Schlesinger,
Jr. It originated in an offer by Fidel Castro to trade the 1,214 prisoners
captured at the Bay of Pigs for 500 tractors.

On May 24, Kennedy had gone so far as to say that export licenses
for the tractors would be granted "routinely" by the State Department.
Apparently to spur contributions by private citizens to the committee
which was to raise funds for the purchase of the tractors, a White House
spokesman said "it was quite likely" that President Kennedy himself
would make a "personal contribution" to the campaign.

Kennedy was astride two horses. On the one hand, he lent the prestige
of the President to the deal in a statement saying that ". . . I hope that
all citizens will contribute what they can. If they were our brothers in
a totalitarian prison, every American would want to help. I happen to
feel deeply that all who fight for freedom—particularly in our hemisphere
—then they are our brothers." He backed away from formal government
endorsement, saying, "the government is . . . putting forward neither
obstacles nor assistance to this wholly private effort. . . ." His caution,
apparently, was the result of a ground swell of public opposition to the
project.

Hostile Congressional opinion became even more hardened against the
ransom deal when Assistant White House Press Secretary Andrew
Hatcher replied, "no comment," to queries as to whether the President's
endorsement of ransoming the Bay of Pigs prisoners also indicated that
he would look with favor on using the same sort of barter system for
gaining the release of Americans held by Cuba and other Communist-
bloc countries.

Administration spokesmen rallied behind the tractors-for-prisoners
deal, saying that it was an invaluable aid to Kennedy's foreign policy
objectives. Congressional support followed when Senate Whip Hubert
Humphrey lent his voice in support of Kennedy. He said that Americans
should not be so concerned about ransoming the Bay of Pigs prisoners.
"A great nation demonstrates its strength, not its weakness," he said, by

saving human lives. Unanswered in this deluge of Administration support for the tractor-prisoner trade was how payment of the ransom would weaken Castro materially, the chief reason for President Kennedy's announced but unrealized "quarantine." Obviously, the shipment of millions of dollars (estimated at the time as $13 million) would have the opposite effect. Also left unanswered by Administration spokesmen was what effect succumbing to this blackmail would have on U.S. prestige (Humphrey thought he had addressed this proposition in his remarks) and how seriously other nations would take Kennedy's "quarantine," in consideration of the fact that it had already been breached by Mr. Kennedy through the UN Fund, Cuban trade, and the mailing to Cuba of Federal benefit checks.

To the careful observer none of this made sense. But there were few careful observers around with enough factual information seriously to challenge the various agencies of the executive branch in whom responsibility for the conduct of foreign affairs resided. Encouraged, Castro began to propose conditions. For example, Castro proposed trading prisoner Manuel Artime for "The Hook" Molina, a Castroite imprisoned in the United States for fatally shooting a nine-year-old Venezuelan girl in a New York restaurant. Administration spokesmen said that the tractor swap would help the climate of a good-will tour of Latin America then being planned by Adlai Stevenson—a trip during which the former Presidential candidate was in the rather absurd and degrading position of standing, figuratively, on the outer fringes of the Latin American crowd with his ear cocked to hear what was being said of us. Predictably, Stevenson returned from his trip and cautioned the American people "to be patient, orderly, and persuasive about the Red regime of Fidel Castro in Cuba."

Dr. Milton Eisenhower, in his book, *The Wine is Bitter: The United States and Latin America* (Doubleday, 1962), tells how the whole tractors-for-prisoners deal got underway in the first place, and how President Kennedy put him out on a limb. President Kennedy telephoned him on May 19, 1961, and said that Castro was sending ten prisoners of Brigade 2506 to the United States to negotiate for the release of the others. Writes Milton Eisenhower: "The President wanted to establish a committee of private citizens for the sole purpose of raising funds to buy the tractors," and said he would "explain the matter to the American people the next day."

But the promised Presidential statement never came. Instead, Castro suddenly began insisting that the trade be called indemnification for the invasion. At this point, writes Eisenhower, "the whole affair began to take on ominous overtones." He points out that Castro demanded supertractors, of little use to farmers and of likely military use, although originally he had implied that he would be content with farm tractors."

On May 23, Dr. Eisenhower relates, the President asked the American people to contribute to the fund but said the U.S. government "has not and cannot be a party to these negotiations." It was apparent to others, however, from State Department comments that licenses would be issued and, from the soundings being made around the Treasury Department for tax deductibility, that what the President was saying was something less than the truth. The committee of citizens was involved in subterfuge. Whatever those implications, Dr. Eisenhower writes of the Presidential statement on May 23 that, "Now I had the awful truth. Though President Kennedy had personally asked me to help, though I had understood this fact would be proclaimed to the public, *I now realized in chilling clarity that the President intended to maintain the fiction that all aspects of the case were private.*" (Italics added).

Meanwhile, Castro had upped the ante to $28 million and reduced the number of prisoners which he would release for that amount of money in tractors. Eisenhower wanted to call the whole thing off. That it was not called off, and the importance the ransom deal was to have on U.S. policy during and following the missile crisis provide one of the more intriguing stories of the Kennedy brothers—President and Attorney General. What can be said here is that a President determined to release prisoners from jail in Cuba through endorsing the public solicitation of ransom money was not likely to pursue a very firm course to overthrow Castro and thereby place the lives of those prisoners in jeopardy.

For a period, however, it appeared that the United States would react to the Communist challenge by meeting infiltration and subversion with a campaign of counter-warfare in those Communist countries responsible for subversion. The overwhelming Congressional vote to get tough with Castro seemed to mean that the American people, frustrated and angry at seeing a Communist regime established right next to their own homeland, were eager for a radical solution. Even President Kennedy made utterances that the United States should rely more on undercover "paramilitary" techniques of warfare.

There was some reason for the belief in April and May of 1961 that a great metamorphosis in national policy was underway. Upon assuming office, President Kennedy found that the United States had a military establishment which was largely unresponsive to the challenge of "inching wars" of Communist subversion. He set about rebuilding ground forces which had been too long neglected because of the false notion that they had been made obsolete by the modern concept of "push button warfare." Taken together with his inexplicable withdrawal of support at the Bay of Pigs, the only route open to him to gain the initiative, it was debated in Washington, was through covert operations.

Men of power and influence in Washington recalled Kennedy's speech on April 20, in which he vowed passionately, "We do not intend to abandon Cuba." They watched his meetings with some of the Republican leadership at which the doctrine of paramilitary operations was discussed and they concluded that all signs pointed to a facing-up to the Communist menace. The debate being conducted hotly in Washington was whether to expand or contract the sub-surface strategy of carrying out an undeclared war against Castro. Explode Castro's political base through support to guerrilla units and resistance forces, the argument went at the time, and Cuba would be made untenable to the Russians as a military base by which to threaten all of Latin America—even mainland United States. (This was a real fear haunting our military leaders.)

Gradually, the emerging school of thought which resulted in rare bi-partisan acceptance, was that the Cuban affair had been mismanaged, not that it was doomed to failure as the New Frontiersmen insisted. This line of reasoning held that the United States should do more of the same, stripped of the public relations considerations which, it was now believed, were responsible for defeat at the Bay of Pigs. What paramilitary operations would demand in Cuba, for example, were the personal attention and the political support of the President himself. For, an offensive of this type would place it largely beyond public scrutiny, requiring the President to work closely with Congressional committees to make certain that the normal system of checks and balances was not violated. There was good reason to believe that the Congress was in a mood to work closely with President Kennedy in developing ways and means of gaining the initiative in the Cold War.

However, within weeks after the sub-surface debates began raging hotly in Washington, President Kennedy himself spiked those debates. US military doctrine began to step down. Nuclear warfare, he declared, was "unthinkable," and the idea blossomed that, for most purposes, the United States must rely on conventional weapons. This was all right in itself, and had the support of a large portion of the military establishment. In fact, Kennedy prepared revisions for the 1962 Federal budget based largely on a shift to a more conventional military force. It was what he intended to do with that force, however, that kept the debaters guessing.

But before Congress was even asked to vote the funds, President Kennedy publicly seemed to put "conventional" war in the same "unthinkable" category as nuclear weapons. Even with the existence of an enlarged conventional military force, he was unwilling to use it. He put it this way: "The armies are there, and in large number. The nuclear weapons are there. But they serve primarily as the shield behind which Communist subversion, infiltration, and a host of other tactics steadily advance picking off vulnerable areas one by one in situations which do not permit our own armed intervention."

What the President of the United States was broadcasting to the world was that the United States would not engage in nuclear war; but neither would it pursue conventional war. However, he added that "we dare not fail to grasp the new tools," and he vowed "to re-examine and reorient . . . our tactics and institutions" to compete with this lower level of successful Red aggression around the world. The military breathed more easily, since it appeared that Mr. Kennedy had, in effect, argued himself into a position where, given his ruling out of any other means of combat, he had finally recognized that the only meaningful response to Communist aggression lay in hitting where the enemy is, not where he aims, with large dosages of unconventional (guerrilla) warfare. Cuba was very much in everyone's mind. Located right offshore, Cuba had a large, virtually uncontrollable coastline, a rebellious population, a nucleus of organized resistance, and a people who had enormous faith in the United States. In plain fact, while proponents of the use of conventional force made public statements defending the use of that force, it was generally agreed that unconventional warfare in Cuba was likely to be more effective. All of the opponents and proponents of the two types of reaction to Communist aggression agreed that some sort of war there must be or the Communists would sweep the world.

There were practical considerations of considerable dimensions, adding to an intellectual chill in which the debate was channelled. A cold assessment revealed that the proper course for the United States to pursue (always in consideration of President Kennedy's horror of both conventional, and nuclear war) was to strengthen its will and its capacity to throw its weight openly behind guerrilla-type operations in Cuba—and for the President to achieve world acceptance that countering Red aggression in this manner is preferable to other effective means open to us. Thus events in Cuba were watched carefully by intelligence people in Washington. The Cuban people were in impressive rebellion, and pressures mounted to get President Kennedy to put enough resources of the United States behind that rebellion to overthrow Castro.

By the summer of 1961, the Cuban resistance movement had revived, and the backbone of that resistance was the *guajiro*, the peasant. News that Communist indoctrinator, Manuel Ascunce, and militiaman, Pedro Latigua, had been caught and hanged by anti-Communist rebels in the Escambray mountains in Las Villas Province ignited Castro. He was equally enraged over the sabotage being carried out against his collective farms. Reports of the hangings reached him, together with news that saboteurs had burned a chicken-breeding farm with a loss of 40,000 chickens.

Castro summoned militants to a demonstration before the Presidential Palace. There, on November 30, 1961, he spoke of the spreading resistance and roared that anyone involved "in the increasing wave of sabotage" would be shot. He railed at acts of sabotage that were "destroying our sugar economy." In a frenzy of anger, Castro said that fighters in the hills and those responsible for terroristic activities in the cities would be caught, given summary justice, and shot within 48 hours.

Castro indirectly admitted that the guerrilla bands and urban terrorists were being supported by the Cuban people when he said that "anyone caught giving one mouthful of food to a counterrevolutionary" would be executed. He vent his wrath on the *guajiro*, and said that those living in areas where guerrilla bands were operating, who did not report the existence of those bands, "will feel the full measure of revolutionary justice." The extent of armed anti-Castro activity was admitted formally with the passage of Revolutionary Decree 988, amounting to an open declaration of war by the regime against its people.

On December 14, 1961, Communist Major Félix Torres, now military commander of Las Villas Province, presided over the opening of 16 newly constructed villages to which *guajiros* were then being transferred en masse and placed under round-the-clock surveillance. These measures were, of course, wrapped in the mantle of economic and social development. But Communist teeth showed when Torres said that "unlike 1960 when we had not a single revolutionary organization in these mountains, today there are 6,000 Young Rebels, 1,000 Vigilance Committees, and 1,420 'militants' of the Integrated Revolutionary Organizations watching the *guajiros.*"

Further clues regarding the intensity of anti-Castro activities were gratuitously provided by the regime when, a week following the transfer of the *guajiros* to state villages, *Revolución* announced that militia groups in Santa Clara (the capital of Las Villas Province) were given a farewell as "they left the city on their way to totally wipe out the counterrevolutionary worms in the mountainous region of the Escambray." The plan, obviously, was to hold the *guajiro* in check on the one hand, while the regime attempted to administer a fatal blow to organized resistance with the other.

The *guajiros* were no pliant instrument of government policy, however. They promptly set fire to their villages, cut telephone wires, and burned tobacco warehouses in the area. Instead of fighting the organized guerrilla units, as planned, Castro's militia were forced to occupy the villages and attempt to keep order among the *guajiros*. Raúl Castro took personal charge of military operations, and, between December, 1961, and March, 1962, had poured 50,000 militiamen into the area. Across the narrow waist of the island, in the small town of Remedios, he ordered the public execution of 16 *guajiro* youths for "having provided the counterrevolutionary elements with intelligence and supplies." The victims were forced to carry their own coffins to the outskirts of the town, there to be summarily shot by a firing squad.

One of the amazing exploits of the MRP underground movement (which, incidentally, had expelled Manuel Ray as its chief) occurred in Havana in the early fall of 1961. It involved five members of the Revolutionary Movement of the People (MRP). Its leader, Reynol González, had been captured, tortured, and forced to talk. As a result, within hours, many of its leaders were also captured, among them the MRP Coordinator General Carlos Bandín.

Bandín was taken to a residence in the Coronela section of Havana where G-2 agents began their interrogation and applied psychological and physical torture to their victim. Bandín was given the "hot and cold treatment." This consisted of turning on air conditioners until the room reached a frigid temperature. Abruptly, they would be turned off and conduits would blow hot air on him until he nearly suffocated. Then, frigid temperatures, again followed by hot air.

When Bandín first entered the room, it was well furnished. Good food was served to him three times the first day. But as he refused to talk, each day articles were removed from the room, one by one. The bathroom was locked and Bandín was forced to attend to his necessities in what was very soon a bare room without water. Instead of food, rotting garbage was proferred.

Finally, the Coordinator General of the MRP was taken from Coronela and placed in jail at G-2 headquarters. He was told that because of his failure to "cooperate," he had been condemned to be shot at La Cabaña fortress. Bandín was placed in a crowded cell of other condemned men, among them a member of the MRP underground. Inexplicably, the man was released, and notified other members of the MRP of the incarceration and impending execution of Bandín. The rest of the story sounds like a 007 adventure film.

At about 2:00 a.m. the following morning, two official military cars drove up to the G-2 offices—one at the 14th Street entrance, the other at the 5th Avenue entrance. The occupants of the cars were seven men dressed as officers in the Castro Rebel Army. All were armed. At a signal from a large Negro "lieutenant," three of the men in the car at the 14th Street entrance got out and took up stations to cover the entrance of the Negro. He walked in, telling the desk sergeant that he had orders to take Bandín to La Cabaña where he was to be executed at dawn. The sleepy sergeant told the "lieutenant" that he would have to go around to the side of the building and obtain a written release from the duty officer. The "lieutenant" departed, walked around the building, and waited for a time to elapse equivalent to what it would take him to obtain a discharge slip for Bandín.

He strode back into the jail, waving a slip of paper at the desk sergeant and entered the cell area shouting in loud tones for "that criminal, Bandín!" He did this so that Bandín would recognize his voice. The jailer in the courtyard unlocked the cell. The Negro "lieutenant" walked in, grabbed Bandín, and pummeling and cursing him, pushed him past the desk sergeant and into the car. The car sped off to the coast of Matanzas Province, where Bandín was put aboard a motor boat that took him to safety in Florida.

It was the same brave Negro underground leader who tried to assassinate Communist INRA chief, Carlos Rafaél Rodriguez, and met his death in the attempt. Rodríguez was travelling by car from Matanzas back to Havana late one night. The MRP underground fighter waited for him on the highway, machine-gunned the car as it passed, caused it to careen to a stop. He ran toward the car with a grenade, tripped and fell on it, and was blown to bits.

Underground reports shed considerable light on popular sentiment toward the Communist regime of Fidel Castro, and the attempts by the underground to shape the anti-Castro mood of the Cubans into a meaningful instrument to overthrow the regime.

In a report to an outside contact in January, 1962, an underground leader with the code name of "Victor" wrote:

"Since my arrival, I have not ceased to be busy. I made a reconnaissance trip the length of the island from Pinar del Río to Santiago, and have selected the companions who will work with me. I have found that Jorge in Matanzas and Manolo had received no material support from Mana [the United States]. After digesting this disheartening news, I had them come with me. We returned to our base, gathering information along the way. They will be in Oriente the month of March to complete the first part of their mission. I have instructed Salvador and Manuel to make reports independently of mine, although for the most part we work on them together. The hunger and discontent is growing rapidly among the people, and it is accompanied by a corresponding increase in repression and terror. There is a terrible atmosphere of hatred in the land. Indoctrination is being enforced and there is brutal repression. Everywhere shootings continue in accordance with Decree 988, with an almost anarchic 'justice' meted out, mostly in secret. For example, there were 2 shot in Florida, 17 in Sancti Spíritus in January, and 7 in Candelaria in Pinar del Río.

"Guerrilla patriots 'Cara Linda' and 'Machetero' are operating valiantly in Pinar del Río. Osvaldo Ramírez continues with his fighting in the mountains of Escambray. Around the middle of January, as near as

I can tell from the *guajiros* in the area, a sharp skirmish was fought close to Jatibonico in which at least 6 militia were killed, but the people in the area say that the figure is more likely to reach 15. Because the fighting started from an ambush by patriots, our people lost only two. It seems that these patriots continue fighting completely without aid from the outside.

"You probably know this, but many boats which try to flee Cuba are machine-gunned by government planes. I know of two cases where everyone in the family was wiped out by machine-gun fire when trying to leave by boat from Barlovento.

"When I was in Matanzas, I personally watched Soviet ships being unloaded. The cargo was arms and ammunition. I saw seven trucks, each loaded with huge peculiar metal boxes, and seven others transporting tanks. We wanted to follow to see where they went, but discovered that we ourselves were being watched suspiciously so we left in another direction. However, our companion later reported that he saw them going to Pinar del Río.

"There is an enormous and barbarous concentration camp in Guanahacabibes in Pinar del Río. It is filled to overflowing with political prisoners.

"Six Russian MIG aircraft are located at the airport in Santa Clara protected by concrete embankments. Four others are in Camaguey covered with berry bushes, located to the South of the runway. I will try to obtain more concrete plans. In the South of the Province of Camaguey the Fincas San Cayetano and San José have tunnels and fortifications under construction.

"Organized once again, we can now continue with our work."

A report from "Manuel" to "Victor" suggested as early as February, 1962, that missiles were being installed in Cuba. He wrote:

"After having been alerted, I spent several days in and around Cienfuegos. Some strange type of fortification is going up. They are for the discharge of heavy artillery, judging from the construction, but the lack of any type of ammunition trains makes me suspect that they are for missiles. Another strange thing is that a large number of men were sent to an offshore key from Cienfuegos, but only a few returned. According to exhausted returnees with whom I shared a cigarette or two, the men are working day and night. No one volunteered what was going on. When it turned out that I was not from Cienfuegos, they ceased talking and I thought it wise not to ask too many questions. I hope to go somehow to the Key and see for myself.

"Manuel" did go to the key, according to a short notice received by "Victor," and he was never heard from again.

"A report from "Salvador" during the month of January indicated that he thought the people were ripe for active participation in a fight to overthrow the Communist regime.

"The situation with the people is the same as it has been for the past year or more. They are totally against the government, and becoming more openly defiant. I find this particularly true in the cities of Havana and Matanzas. Something must be done to capitalize on their sentiments. We must assist them somehow. They are becoming a little reckless. Perhaps this is good. Perhaps this is bad. It is good because they no longer are giving in to the threats of the Communist and militia. They talk back. This would not happen if they were not sure that the great number of people are with them. On the other hand, if the militia should panic and shoot them we might have a blood bath. We must be organized to take care of the situation following the overthrow of the regime. I have been in contact with the patriots in the area of Jovellanos, know about Thorndyke, the work of 'Cara Linda,' and 'Machetero.'' It seems uncertain that they were caught and executed by the regime. Perhaps so, but *guajiros* doubt it. There is a worry. Can these groups maintain order when the tyrants fall? We must organize the cities and towns for this. But do we have time? Hatred is so great.

"Guerrillas are operating again in Jovellanos. One fellow who is not considered an infiltrator from the regime is 'Pichi.' He was an Army man, and has been carefully watched for loyalty. I am satisfied. The men follow him, and he has much sympathy among the population of the area. 'Pichi' says the forays he makes indicate that the regime is desperate in getting *guajiros* to cut cane. There is no clothing to speak of, and even less to eat. In this same area I have found other guerrilla chiefs. One is called Carlos Rojas. The other is known as Bringas. Bringas is also an ex-Army man. Bringas recently had to move out of his area, after three of his men were caught. They were imprisoned and shot at the Baseball stadium within 12 hours. The citizens were outraged and vocal against the militia. Although they were not known extremely well by the people of the area, they were respected for being against the regime. Two were white, the other a mestizo."

Urban resistance matched that of the guajiros in Cuba's countryside. April of 1962 was a very busy month for Castro's spies and his militia units. On April 25, arsonists burned thirteen stories of the unfinished National Bank of Cuba. Burning like a huge Christmas tree, the bank building illuminated the entire city of Havana and the glow was seen by ship passengers fifteen miles at sea.

The fire soon attracted thousands of people. A group started clapping hands in rhythm. It was taken up by others, then by more, and more, as the crowds took advantage of the fire to express their resistance to the Castro regime. Militia units were brought up, and the order given

314 · THE LOSERS

for the crowd to stop clapping. The order was ignored. Frustrated and afraid to shoot for fear volleys would trigger a mob reaction, the militia stayed back and did nothing.

Within 48 hours of the burning of the National Bank building, saboteurs struck again, blowing up the government fertilizer plant at El Cotorro, ten miles east of Havana, and causing it to burst into a raging blaze. Another huge blaze was set by saboteurs near the former British-owned Shell refinery. Just one day later, a school of Communist indoctrination was burned to the ground, followed by the burning of three more within the week.

From all parts of Cuba, in the spring of 1962, came reports of demonstrations, sabotage, and armed conflict between the ill-equipped rebels and Castro's forces. Travellers to Havana reported that traffic along the Central Highway, which cuts the island from end-to-end, was often impeded by local fire-fighting equipment used to battle blazes in villages along the way. Castro raged and ranted, saying in one speech that "All the people must join in revolutionary vigilance to close in on the enemies of the revolution." Radio Progreso said that "the counterrevolutionary worms who did not dare to fight our militia and our army . . . are now using live phosphorous and Yankee dynamite in criminal attacks against women and children. . . ."

On April 28, at the corner of Galiano and San Rafael Streets in Havana, a ruckus broke out just as shops were being closed for the evening. The people were sullen and nervous following the destruction of the bank building, the burning of the fertilizer plant, and the other acts of sabotage which had hit Havana over the previous few days. Suddenly, a group of women dressed in the uniform of the Cuban Confederation of Women appeared on the street corner to hold what the Communists term their "flash meetings." Passers-by, in no mood for Communist harangues, began to heckle the orators.

Suddenly, a group of women dressed in black appeared, pushed their way into the center of the crowd shouting anti-government slogans while they unfurled and waved small Cuban flags which they had hidden in their purses. The crowd quickly grew and cheered the anti-government demonstrators; leaders of the Women's Federation screamed insults in return. The situation was rapidly getting out of hand, when regular army units appeared, broke up the demonstration and arrested several of the crowd. The balance of the mob gradually dispersed, grumbling, cursing, and ominous.

That night another demonstration took place in a movie house in the town of Tarará, east of Havana. The movie was cut short, the lights went on, and a unit of the Federation of Cuban Women marched on stage where they began to harangue the audience to turn out for May Day festivities. The audience exploded. A woman took off her right shoe and threw it at the stage. The orator on stage said that the woman who threw the shoe would be found and arrested. Women in the audience responded by taking off their right shoes and throwing them at the orator. The crowd rushed the stage, and the Federation women fled through the back entrance.

The government was particularly on guard in the city of Cienfuegos, whose population, it was suspected, kept the rebels in the surrounding Escambray Mountains supplied with what food and military supplies they could steal or scrape together. In an attempt to soften the anti-religious campaign, which had been met by massive resistance by the populace, the regime permitted a religious movie to be shown during Easter week. In an attempt to dissuade the public from attending, Communist goon squads were sent marching into the theater shouting, "Viva Fidel Castro Ruz!" The audience responded by shouting "Viva Christ the King!" Fights broke out as the audience sang the religious hymn, "You will Reign." Squads of militia entered with machine guns and arrested 100 of the audience. As those arrested were paraded out of the theater, a crowd gathered outside and cheered.

Easter week of 1962 was also a period of great anti-Communist activity in the small town of Punta Brava in Havana Province. In one day alone, *guajiros* and townspeople burned 5 million arrobas of cane (which would have produced 62,500 tons of ground sugar). The government identified the farms where the cane was burned as El Mayor, Niña Bonita, Bauta, Zarate, El Carmen, and La Jacobita.

The local militia arrived, and the townspeople shut themselves in their houses, locking their window shutters and doors.

The following morning, select militia units were sent from Havana to Punta Brava. They employed sound trucks to exhort the public to come out of their houses and cut the burned cane which, if ground within a few days after burning, might have most of its sugar content saved. The population refused to come out. The militia taunted them: "We are the ones who triumphed at the Bay of Pigs! We are the ones who uphold our revolution, supported by our friends from the socialist countries!" Castro's military made telling use of the failure of the United States even to recognize the state of rebellion in Cuba, shouting: "You have no one —no one! Who are your friends? The Yankee aggressors? Where are they? The Yankees won't fight for you! Come out of your houses and cut cane, or you will die!"

The people of Punta Brava still refused to come out of their houses, and the militia went in. They broke in, and with Czech machine guns killed some. Others were dragged into the streets. One hundred men, women, and children were herded into the cane fields and, under the threat of Soviet weapons in the hands of the militia, forced to cut cane for 17 hours without rest, food, or water. Unused to handling the awkward machetes, some of the women suffered severe cuts; one severed her arm, another cut through her thigh; others bore less severe, but painful, cuts.

Outraged by the barbarities committed against the people of Punta Brava, the townspeople of nearby Cayo de la Rosa set fire to the idle textile plant of Ariguanabo. The militia were able to extinguish the blaze only after considerable damage had been done.

Scores of reports told of burnings, sabotage, and armed conflict in other areas of the island in the spring of 1962. *Guajiros* burned three more huge sugar plantations in Camaguey Province. Following the sabotage, the government took the unheard-of-step of completely closing down all commercial activity in the capital city of Camaguey (Cuba's third largest city) and herding the entire population into the fields to cut sugar cane. The same reprisals were later taken against people in the cities of Holguín and Palma Soriano in Oriente Province.

In Las Villas Province, three large chicken collectives fell before the torches of the people. In Pinar del Río Province, the *guajiros* burned five tobacco warehouses. Sabotage cut the tobacco industry's exports from $54 million in 1958 to less than $6 million in the 1962-63 season.

An interesting contrast in sociology and Communist tactics involved the Negro population of Santiago. Most of the middle-and upper-middle income classes of Cubans had either been shot or jailed, or had fled the country, leaving their homes vacant and at the disposal of the regime. Communist authorities then attempted to entice the Negro population in the Los Hoyos section of the city to move and take over those homes.

By this time, an increasing number of Negroes had seen through the designs of the Communists and refused to make the move. For, once having taken over the better sections of the city, they would be identified with the Communists, something which most of them were not prepared to accept. The plain fact was that the Communists had used the Negroes to create race and class distinctions which heretofore had not been a major social problem. Originally, Negro youths had been recruited extensively into the "Young Rebels," but the organization's loudly propagandized role of constructing a new society had turned out to be largely in the way of destroying the old. Negroes began to resent the regime's brazen use of race conflict for that destruction.

The Negro was also hungrier under the Communists than he had ever been before. In mid-April of 1962, about 100 Negro women of the los Hoyos section of Santiago decided to do something about it. They formed a conga line in the streets and, beating on pots and pans with large wooden spoons, began to snake dance through the streets of los Hoyos. As their numbers increased, they moved into the main business section of Santiago chanting as they danced: "We want food!" "We are hungry!" Some were heard to shout with the rhythm, "Down with Fidel!"

The militia were called in to keep the demonstration from congesting streets. This was a mistake. The Negroes accused the militia of trying to keep them in their own section of the city. Negro men took off their belts. Taunting the militia, they waved the buckles at them menacingly. Others took out knives and formed a guard for the conga line. The militia commander had second thoughts about the ugly implications of a clash with Negroes, and retired his men from the scene. The conga line, now swollen to several hundred women, continued its dance through the streets unopposed. The military commander of Santiago commandeered rations from Moncada Barracks and rushed them to los Hoyos.

The regime's reaction to its opposition was not always as conciliatory as that experienced by the Negroes in Santiago. In most cases, the Cuban government's reprisals are swift and in the form of intimidation by public trials and executions. A former clerk of the Camaguey Municipal Court described to the writer the trial of 47 *guajiros* in northern Camaguey Province. The accused were tried on the allegation that they had been supplying food to guerrilla leader "Arnaldo" who was operating in the hills of Cubitas.

"The trial took place in the Alcazar Theater," recalls clerk Manuel Angel Espada. "The front seats were occupied by *resentidos* [the resentful ones] who belonged to the various Communist organizations such as the Young Communists, the Federation of Cuban Women. Behind them sat the families of the accused peasants who came from the small towns of Florencia, Morón, Chambas, Lombillo, and Cubitas."

A great deal of effort was put into attracting public attention to the trial. Sr. Espada states: "A Communist announcer with a loudspeaker stood at the entrance to the movie theater, inviting and haranguing passers-by to come in and 'see justice done to the lackeys of imperialism.'"

"There was no justice," says Sr. Espada. "The two defense attorneys were actually members of the militia and widely known to be militants of the Communist Party of Camaguey. As for the prosecuting attorney, he had sent scores of Cubans to be shot by firing squad on little more than hearsay evidence."

During the five-day public trial the accused sat with their hands tied behind their backs. Sr. Espada states that "within an hour after the proceedings had ended, five were shot in the firing range of the old

Agramonte Barracks in Camaguey city. Appeals were summarily dismissed on the spot. Twelve of the prisoners were given 30-year prison sentences, and the balance of the 47 sentenced to prison terms ranging from five to twenty years."

Wholesale roundups were commonplace in 1962. With law relegated to caprice, it was standard practice for the government to resort to a blanket charge—"enemies of the state"—a term that covers every infraction from refusing to teach school or "volunteer" to cut sugar cane, to the more serious crime of speaking out against the Communist regime. In the latter case, the victims often are summarily charged and shot on the spot.

Escapee Reinaldo Guerra from Matanzas Province relates the circumstances surrounding one such trial and shooting. Twelve young people were arrested as "enemies of the state." The day of the trial, said Guerra, "a hearse delivered four caskets at the place where the trial was to be held. With so much opposition to the Communists, trials are conducted, as an object lesson, at the spot where the crime allegedly took place. It could be on a main thoroughfare, a classroom, or in the house of the victim."

In this particular case, Guerra relates, the trial was held on a dusty street corner in the town of Jovellanos in Matanzas Province. "Predictably," he adds, "the trial took only a few minutes, a firing squad was summoned, and four of the twelve were executed on the spot. The other eight drew 30-year prison sentences."

Perhaps the ultimate in Castro extermination techniques are the "mobile military tribunals" which first made their appearance in 1962. Old cars and panel trucks travel around the countryside and conduct on-the-spot trials. Three to five members of a summary military court go to an area where a disturbance has been reported. In many cases, the "judges" also serve as the firing squad.

In 1961, and 1962, the regime of Fidel Castro had been fully instructed in the various means the Communists employ to extract confessions from their enemies. Two of those means are the "cabins," and "the pool," and what happens in those torture chambers is told by Rogelio Rodríguez Pérez. In 1958 and 1959, Rodríguez Pérez was an ardent Fidelista. He had fought with the rebels and rose to the rank of captain. When he could no longer doubt the Communist direction taken by the revolution, Rodríguez Pérez defected and joined the anti-Communist underground. G-2 agents finally caught up with him in 1962, and the balance of his story relates what happens to those captured by the Communists:

"When I was captured in Matanzas on charges of counterrevolutionary activity, I was placed in a completely dark room where I remained for 30 days. Finally, G-2 agents came and interrogated me. I was so glad to see someone after so long a time, that for a moment I almost embraced them as friends.

"After days of interrogation during which I told them nothing, the chief interrogator laughed unpleasantly and said: 'We're not in a hurry. You will talk soon enough.' I was taken to what they call 'the pool.' It is a watertight cell in which water is discharged in pipes from the ceiling, and permitted to rise, and then to fall through a drain. I was thrown in fully clothed, and spent 32 days there. Sometimes I would sleep sitting down, then the water would rise up to my face and wake me up. When I stood, sometimes, they would let the water go above my head for awhile to frighten me. It was a frightful ordeal."

Rodríguez Pérez said that food was given to him at infrequent intervals, and that it would be thrown on top of the water from a hatch in the ceiling. "The worst part of it," he recalls, "is that I had to perform my bodily functions in the water. When they took me out of there after 32 days, I couldn't walk. My legs were swollen like I had a bad disease."

Then Castro's G-2 dragged the underground fighter to "the oven." He says of the oven: "It is a tiny place where you cannot stand and cannot sit properly. Once inside you cannot move more than a few inches in any direction. In front of your eyes is a 500-watt electric light bulb which is kept burning day and night. After three or four hours three more bulbs are turned on, one at a time. The heat scorches the skin and the light burns the eyes. I spent five days in 'the oven.' When I left there, my eyes bled and I was nearly blind."

Rodríguez Pérez states that "I left there, finally, a totally destroyed man. They let me go so that my family and friends could see what happens to those who defy the regime. My underground group, the anti-Communist Liberation Front, helped me to escape by boat to the United States."

It is truly remarkable how, in the face of the awful repressions of the regime, organized Cuban resistance and what became known as "popular sabotage" continued to increase throughout 1962.

Basculadoras (weighing cranes) by which the cane is transferred from ox carts in the field to flat-bed railway cars were sabotaged, cable on winches were sliced, and electric motors let run without lubrication. By the summer of 1962, the time taken to travel by rail from Havana to Santiago had doubled; railway ties and whole sections of tracks were removed by anti-Castro saboteurs. Train wrecks became commonplace. In truth, the Cuban people had become impossible thorns in the sides of their Communist masters.

On June 16, 1962, a nearly full-sized rebellion broke out in the northern port city of Cárdenas, requiring the Castro regime to deploy tanks and troops in massive retaliation against the people. President Osvaldo

Dorticós himself rode into the city in a tank. The Associated Press office in Havana, staffed by non-Americans, was permitted by Castro censors to pass the following revealing dispatch concerning that rebellion:

"The Castro regime sent troops and tanks to the Cuban city of Cárdenas Saturday in a display of force ordered after a counterrevolutionary demonstration.

"After the televised military parade through the streets of the city, 70 miles east of Havana, the government radio said the show of strength was prompted by 'little groups of counterrevolutionaries, parasites, and lazy ones who came into the streets waving counterrevolutionary signs.' The demonstrators were described on the broadcast as bandits, thieves, and dope fiends.

"President Osvaldo Dorticós addressed a gathering of Cárdenas citizens after the military parade, 'to warn our enemies we have staged this modest demonstration of the military force of a people in arms.'

"The Cárdenas show of force was televised to the nation and watched by monitors here."

The AP dispatch intimated that the people had not been cowed by the military show, adding: "However, the throng earlier failed to respond to repeated appeals to display 'revolutionary discipline' and to clear the way for the tanks to pass."

One of the Communist measures leading to such outbreaks was indoctrination of the children. Parents were bitter over the regime's reprisals against their opposition to Communism, opposition leading to the outwardly benign granting of "scholarships" to Cuban children which took them away from their homes to keep them in prison-like confinement in Havana. As *guajiro* resistance rose in 1962, the regime spirited away their children to Havana, telling them that they would receive there an education and a trade. By the end of the year, the number of children in state schools numbered upwards of 100,000. Interviews with those who escaped and made their way to the United States reveal that "education" was Communist indoctrination and a "trade" consisted of sewing uniforms for Castro's militia.

Minister of Education Armando Hart revealed that in 1962, 2,000 Cuban youngsters had been sent to Russia, 500 to Communist China, 1,000 to Czechoslovakia, and about 300 to Rumania. He did not mention that fourteen deserted ship and were given asylum in France and that another three jumped ship in Tangier.

Parents were given what amounted to a bribe for letting their children go to Soviet-bloc countries—$70 a month for each child. Most refused. And when some of those children who were shipped away tried to get back by writing to their parents about the conditions under which they lived aboard, the Ministry of Education was besieged by irate fathers and mothers demanding that their children be returned to them. Some of the more recalcitrant were returned to Cuba with the face-saving comment by the Ministry that they were home "for vacations." The regime retaliated against the parents, publishing their names and addresses in *Revolución*, and labeling them "enemies of the people."

It is certain that Nikita Khrushchev watched the state of rebellion in Cuba and the lack of response in Washington with more than mere detachment. He must have known from his own support of "wars of liberation" that all of the ingredients for the successful overthrow of Fidel Castro were there in overwhelming quantity in 1961 and 1962 had the President of the United States chosen to set about supporting the Cuban resistance by word and by deed.

In the spring of 1962, President Kennedy acceded to the wishes of a prominent newspaperman—a Kennedy supporter—to discuss the state of internal rebellion in Cuba. The newspaperman, who asks that his identity be withheld, was an authority on Latin America, a supporter of Manuel Ray and the "Left Underground" thesis, and had been watching the rising current of rebellion in Cuba very carefully. He produced a detailed rundown of the internal situation for the President, urging him to put the resources of the United States behind the people of Cuba. If the United States were openly to recognize that state of rebellion, to say further that this country was in sympathy with the struggle of the Cuban people for independence and to give a thinly veiled warning to the Russians to stay out of a domestic conflict in this hemisphere, he said, then the Cubans would indeed wrest themselves loose from Castro and Communism. The President listened, then made "the astonishing statement" that 'the CIA tells me that it can't be done,' and, waving his hand irritably, dismissed further talk on the subject."

Khrushchev must also have watched and listened in wonder as the New Frontier adopted the line of the "losers" to explain away the inaction of the Kennedy Administration in the face of the clear threat that a Soviet base in Cuba posed to the security of the United States. Khrushchev knew that statements from the New Frontier to the effect that Cuba had been the victim of economic exploitation were not true. The Communists were perfectly aware of the facts—the facts being that Castro came to power in the midst of a prospering Cuba, and that he was able to do so only by saying one thing while doing quite another. Nikita Khrushchev must have seen from all of this that the New Frontier was sparsely manned with men of will and the courage to make the hard decisions, that the Frontier could be breached. And he breached it.

There is even more reason to believe that Khrushchev had estimated much earlier that the new President of the United States actually had no real stomach for the Cuban fray. He had taken Kennedy's measure at a meeting in Vienna in June of 1961, and apparently had come to the conclusion that Kennedy would shrink from hard decisions. Khrushchev tested him further by building the Berlin wall, and there was no response. Everything taken together, there is little to suggest that Khrushchev ever questioned the power of the United States. What he did question was President Kennedy's nerve to use it. Surely Castro could have been ousted at the Bay of Pigs with the use of only a fraction of American power, and he could have been overthrown during 1961 and 1962 with minimal American support.

It is useful to consider what Khrushchev saw in President Kennedy at the Vienna meetings in June of 1961 which contributed to unrelenting Communist pressures, culminating in the missile crisis. At that meeting, Khrushchev kept probing Kennedy about the Bay of Pigs, a visibly sore subject for the President. Finally, in some desperation, Kennedy rather waspishly countered with: "Don't you ever make mistakes in your country. Mr. Chairman?" To the tough Communist leader, this statement amounted to an apology, and he never let Kennedy forget it during the balance of their meetings in Vienna.

On November 15, 1964, James Reston came out in the *New York Times* with his own analysis of what happened between Khrushchev and Kennedy at Vienna. Here is what Reston, who saw Kennedy within minutes of the final meeting with Khrushchev at Vienna, remembers: "The President came into a dim room in the American Embassy shaken and angry. He had tried, as always, to be calm and rational with Khrushchev, to get him to define what the Soviet Union would and would not do, and Khrushchev had bullied him and threatened him with war over Berlin.

"We will have to know much more about that confrontation between Kennedy and Khrushchev, one now deprived of life and the other of power, before we can be sure, but Kennedy said just enough in that room in the embassy to convince me of the following:

"Khrushchev had studied the events of the Bay of Pigs; he would have understood if Kennedy had either left Castro alone, or destroyed him; but when Kennedy was rash enough to strike at Cuba, but not bold enough to finish the job, Khrushchev decided he was dealing with an inexperienced young leader who could be intimidated and blackmailed. The Communist decision to put offensive missiles into Cuba was the final gamble of this assumption."

Time magazine also commented on the Vienna conference: "Flying back to the United States the next night, John Kennedy sat in his shorts, surrounded by his key aides. He was dead tired: his eyes were red and watery: he throbbed with the ache of a back injury that the nation did not yet know about but that had forced him to endure agonies on his European trip. Several times he stared down at his feet, shook his head and muttered how unbending Khrushchev had been. He hugged his bare legs and wondered what would come next."[17]

Victor Lasky writes about the aftermath of the Vienna conference in his book, saying: "Almost as soon as he returned to the White House, on June 5, Kennedy called for an estimate of the number of Americans likely to be killed in a nuclear war; the number was seventy million. The next day Kennedy used one word to describe the outlook for the United States. That word was 'somber.'"

Lasky reports further: "That same day Nikita Khrushchev cavorted and clowned at a diplomatic party in Moscow. UPI correspondent Henry Shapiro reported that the dictator looked more exuberant and relaxed than he had seen him in years. The Soviet boss acted like a winner."[18]

There now is rather general agreement that President John F. Kennedy had been cowed by Khrushchev at their meeting in Vienna. For example, at the opposite side of the political spectrum from Victor Lasky, Elie Abel writes in his book *The Missile Crisis*, (Lippincott, 1966) that at Vienna, "Khrushchev had bullied Kennedy over the Bay of Pigs defeat. Kennedy called it a mistake." He adds that CIA Director John McCone believed that the United States had led the Russians into the frame of mind to put missiles in Cuba by "creating a climate of inaction."

Abel also elaborates on Kennedy's susceptibility to nuclear blackmail. He writes: "The President returned from Vienna, by way of London, brooding about one defeat after another, and extraordinarily sensitive to any unnecessary talk about nuclear war. . . . The Western Allies, notably the Germans, seemed to require reassurances that they would not be left to fend for themselves. In a news conference held on the day the President returned from London, Roswell Gilpatric (Under Secretary of Defense) gave a public undertaking that if Europe was about to be overwhelmed by Soviet power, the United States would not flinch from the use of nuclear weapons. This was no revelation but a timely restatement of long established policy. Nevertheless, the President angrily telephoned Gilpatric that night to reproach him for talking too much."[19]

From Abel's comments, it would appear that our Allies in Europe also thought that President Kennedy had not been able to stand up to Khrushchev at the Vienna meeting. As also reported by Abel, Kennedy telephoned Gilpatric the next morning and apologized. "Kennedy," writes Abel, "explained that the Vienna encounter had left him tired and irritable."

Abel does not mention the silence within the Administration about the state of rebellion in Cuba, nor does he conjecture what it might have meant to Khrushchev. This, I believe, may have been a crucial factor for

Khrushchev in making his decision to put missiles offshore of the United States. For, the lack of support for the rebellious Cuban people, even to the point of remaining completely silent about that rebellion, may have meant to Khrushchev that Kennedy not only was afraid to challenge Russia (as he saw at Vienna), but was demonstrably afraid to challenge the Russian base in this hemisphere, Cuba. However that may be, President Kennedy had invited disaster through inaction, and disaster was to follow.

CHAPTER 13

•

Disaster

•

PRESIDENT KENNEDY'S CLIMATE of inaction extended far beyond the forgotten problem of Cuba. Indeed, the stationing of missiles off-shore of the United States in 1962 was preceded by such a precipitous U.S. retreat throughout the world before Russia's aggressive probes, that Nikita Khrushchev may have been persuaded that Washington was in the hands of near-pacifists. Certainly he had been provided with ample evidence for him to venture such a conclusion. Khrushchev rattled his rockets, threatened President Kennedy with nuclear war over Berlin, and refused to agree to a test-ban treaty on atomic explosions. The response of the New Frontier to Khrushchev's bullying tactics was typical of its responses elsewhere. High-lighted by a May 25 address to Congress in which the President called for the building of A-bomb shelters as "survival" insurance, throughout the balance of 1961 and well into 1962, the New Frontier put on public display its bone-chilled fear of armed conflict. Virtual panic hit the country, and, for a period, A-bomb shelter manufacturers were swamped with orders.

The practical effect of Administration-stimulated fear of nuclear war (defended, of course, by the New Frontier as the "responsible" behaviour of its statesman-president) was to limit the U.S. response to rising Soviet belligerency to repeated appeals to the Russians to sit down at the conference table and negotiate "differences." President Kennedy wanted negotiations because he was embarked on a determined bid for a *rapprochement* with the Soviet Union. He had much earlier confided his fears of a third world war to Ambassador Emilio Nunez Portuondo, two times president of the UN Security Council. A senator at the time, Mr. Kennedy told Ambassador Nunez Portuondo that should he ever become President of the United States, he would dedicate himself to establishing a *rapprochement* with Soviet leaders, and thereby avoid a third, and perhaps final, world war. He told the distinguished Cuban statesman: "We cannot retreat from the talking stage to the military stage."[1] That this indeed was President Kennedy's policy is revealed in the writings of New Frontiersman Theodore Sorensen. According to Sorensen, President Kennedy's policy was based on the conviction that "failure on the diplomatic front meant a return to the military front."[2] He rejected the tougher line advanced by mature men of wisdom and experience, as, for example, former Secretary of State Dean Acheson. An advocate of diplomacy backed by force, Acheson warned the President that Khrushchev's belligerency would not diminish until the Soviet leader was convinced that the United States was prepared to fight, if necessary, to uphold our treaty rights in Berlin and elsewhere, adding that obviously Khrushchev did not believe this to be the case.

Certainly, President Kennedy was aware of the critical need to rebuild Allied confidence in the United States following his dismal showing at the Bay of Pigs. Yet, not only did he pursue his conciliatory policy toward the Russians in the face of Khrushchev's threats of war over Berlin, but did so over the heads of Allied leaders. Germany's Chancellor Konrad Adenauer and France's President Charles de Gaulle were furious when the President initiated talks on Berlin with the Russians on terms which gave Khrushchev an enormous advantage. The President waived the vital issue of German integration on the grounds that Western concern was primarily one of protecting its access rights to Berlin. And, much like Ambassador Philip W. Bonsal who, a few years earlier, searched for passages in the otherwise scurrilously worded Cuban notes which he pronounced "encouraging," President Kennedy wheedled, cajoled, and, in the words of his biographer, Sorensen, "always managed to find some passage with which he could associate himself to keep the Chairman's [Khrushchev's] hopes alive."[3] Throughout this period, Khrushchev probed and tested the will of his adversary. Then, on August 13, 1961, the Russians had their East German puppets erect the Berlin wall. Instead of a strong response, the New Frontier rationalized inaction, saying that the East Germans had for years possessed the capability of sealing off West Berlin, and it limited itself to pronouncements that the wall was immoral, illegal, and inhumane, but certainly not worth the risk of war to remove.

Behind the negotiations over the German question, Khrushchev, the man with a face like a clenched fist, was playing a much deadlier game, nuclear poker, with his young adversary. And he was winning. Khrushchev told President Kennedy at their meeting in Vienna that the moratorium existing at that time on atom-bomb tests would continue unless the United States recommended testing first. Throughout the spring and summer of 1961, Russian representatives blocked negotiations underway in Geneva for a lasting treaty on A-tests, raising absurd objections to the U.S. position, and making demands which could have no purpose other than to humiliate the United States and gain time for the Russians. Each time the United States made concessions, the Russians raised the ante. President Kennedy was pressured on all sides to resume testing. It was obvious, scientists and military men argued in a rare show of unity, that the Russians had demonstrated at Geneva their disdain for a meaningful test ban treaty. The Joint Chiefs of Staff were more specific, warning the President that the United States could continue to delay its own testing only at the risk of seriously weakening our own defense posture. The President also was advised that the Russians most probably had been secretly conducting underground tests.

Certainly, no Communists skilled in the art of psychological warfare would overlook the apparent susceptibility of President Kennedy and his New Frontier to atomic blackmail. And they did not. Throughout the sterile Geneva negotiations, pronouncements from Moscow, Peking, Geneva, and Havana warned of the terrible consequences of a nuclear war. Then, on August 30 the Russians announced their resumption of nuclear tests in the atmosphere. Rather than call Khrushchev's bluff by immediately responding with U.S. tests in the atmosphere, President Kennedy showed signs of indecision and vacillation. It seemed clear that the Russians had been preparing for their explosions well in advance of the Vienna meeting and throughout the Geneva conference. Yet, Kennedy would go no further than to authorize the resumption of underground tests. He refused to resume tests in the atmosphere, and, characteristically, searched for a decision by consulting as many people as possible. White House Aide Arthur Schlesinger actually suggested that the United States should make no test in the atmosphere unless the Russians commenced a second series of their own! The crucial advice came, however, from British Labour (Socialist) Party leader Hugh Gaitskell, an old friend of the President, who asked him not to begin tests *before a new disarmament conference* with the Russians, scheduled for May 14, 1962, had been convened. The President delayed until pressures in Washington forced his hand. The United States finally recommenced atmospheric testing on April 25, 1962, a full eight months after the Russians had broken the moratorium. The period of the President's hesitation was marked by Nikita Khrushchev's boast that the Soviets, through their testing, had developed a monstrous 100 megaton bomb. Playing on President Kennedy's oft-repeated fears of atomic war, Russia's Army newspaper *Red Star* boasted that the United States couldn't build shelters deep enough to save this country from complete annihilation. Meanwhile, the President questioned the need for the United States to conduct more tests, pondered how much radioactive fall-out was contained in a bucket of rain water, and reasoned with surrealistic logic that a renewal of U.S. tests in the atmosphere would close the door on future negotiations with the Russians.

One point seems certain. Following the Bay of Pigs, initiative in the cold war had fallen into the hands of the Soviet Union. By skillfully maneuvering that initiative, Khrushchev kept the New Frontier concentrating on one area while he proceeded unopposed in others. There seems to have been little concern in Washington that the Russians might make any significant moves in Cuba. Perhaps this was due to the social welfare concepts of Messrs. Goodwin and Schlesinger which had successfully directed public attention away from the danger posed by a Russian satellite in this hemisphere and toward Latin America and the economic battles being waged there through the Alliance for Progress. Perhaps it was President Kennedy's own mental block occasioned by his failure at the Bay of Pigs and further aggravated by Khrushchev's bullying at Vienna. Whatever the reason, U.S. policy toward Cuba remained passive. Yet, as early as May 4, 1962, Cuba's *Bohemia* magazine raised eyebrows among Miami's Cuban exile community when it published a photograph of two huge Soviet missiles parading in Moscow with the arresting caption: "Here Are The Brakes," meaning the threat of a nuclear response from the U.S.S.R. should the United States invade Cuba. *However, an examination of the photos revealed them to be short-range missiles.*

An accompanying article entitled "Popular Defense" bore clear indications that something ominous was stirring. Claiming that the United States was preparing to invade Cuba, *Bohemia's* Communist editors accompanied the article with photographs of underground bomb shelters being rushed to completion, first-aid stations in operation, and hordes of unhappy looking "volunteers" being turned out for "popular defense." The May 4 issue of *Bohemia* made it unmistakably clear that Cuba was being placed on a war footing, including the erection of dummy coastal defenses "manned" by manikins attired in military uniforms. Cuba's war fervor flew in the face of any evidence of provocation. By word and deed the Kennedy Administration had turned away from any course of action which could be construed, even remotely, as presaging an invasion of Cuba. Yet, charges that the United States was planning to invade Cuba poured out of Havana and Moscow. To "Cubanologists," these charges bore a disturbing similarity to those made by "Che" Guevara back in January 1959 that the United States was planning to overthrow Castro and turn the country into "another Guatemala." There was no basis for accusations then, except in Guevara's knowledge that the Communist course being pursued by the Revolutionary Government would eventually provoke a response from the United States. And there was no basis for the accusations of aggression being made by Cuba in 1962, except within the context of mysterious policies which, the Castro regime feared, would provoke another U.S. response.

Then came the surprise announcement out of Havana that Minister of Armed Forces Raúl Castro had journeyed to Moscow. From July 2 to July 18, the younger Castro had several rounds of conversations with high-ranking members of the Soviet Communist hierarchy, with military leaders, and with Premier Nikita Khrushchev. Only then did U.S. interest in Cuba show a perceptible awakening. There could be little doubt that Cuba was deeply disturbed that U.S. intelligence might uncover something which they were trying to hide. By the end of July, Cuban objections to increasing surveillance by units of the U.S. Navy and Air Force had become strident screams. On August 3, Radio Havana claimed that U.S. planes had "violated" Cuban air space 27 times within 72 hours, and followed with the charge that the United States was using its Guantanamo Naval Base for the purpose of "spying." These accusations were accompanied by an announcement out of Moscow that Cuba and Russia had signed an agreement by which Russia sent a fleet of five ships to Havana "to carry out fishing explorations." Observers noted, however, that the photographs published in *Revolución* showed those ships to be heavily armed.

Seldom in history has a great nation like the United States been gratuitously provided with so many clues regarding the offensive posture of a neighbor. And the United States certainly did not lack sources of intelligence. For example, in addition to the physical surveillance maintained by its fleet and air arm, the United States had an elaborate system by which all refugees pouring into this country from Cuba were carefully screened. The United States also had the valuable services of the Cuban Student Directorate (DRE) which, with financial support from the CIA, had established headquarters in Miami and drew upon its extensive underground apparatus in Cuba to provide valuable intelligence. Some DRE intelligence reports were sent out via the diplomatic pouches of friendly embassies in Havana. Others were radioed to Miami in code. As early as the end of July, these reports revealed that the deep water port of Mariel had virtually been converted into a Russian city. Cubans living near the docks were evacuated, and Russians moved into their houses. Russian sentries stood guard while other Russians unloaded military cargoes from supposedly commercial vessels.

The first account of uniformed Russian troops in Cuba was provided on August 7 when Salvador Lew, a prominent and respected Cuban exile, made a detailed report on their arrival over Miami's Spanish-language station, WMIE. Reports from refugees pouring out of Cuba confirmed in considerable depth the accuracy of Lew's underground informants. The DRE leadership then told me that Russian soldiers attired in brownish-gray uniforms had been spotted in Matanzas Province moving inland in truck convoys. The convoys, I was told, included mobile generators, heavy artillery, and vast amounts of electrical equipment. More important, according to Lew's informant, every third truck towed a long missile, and nozzles on the bases of those weapons were clearly visible. Reports that the movement of men and weapons took place at night confirmed my suspicion that the Russians were attempting to avoid U.S. aerial surveillance which the Cubans were so stridently denouncing at that very moment.

Evidence mounted that the Russians were moving into Cuba in considerable force. The DRE revealed that between July 21 and August 1, approximately 5,500 Russian troops landed at Mariel in Cuba's westernmost Pinar del Río Province. The report was rich in detail, including the names of Russian ships—"Latvia" and "Muritzky." DRE intelligence sources inside Cuba radioed its Miami headquarters that on July 26 the "Maria Ulanova" had disgorged 1,500 Russian soldiers at Havana harbor while the "Khabarovsk" landed 2,500 troops and vast amounts of Soviet military hardware at the small sugar port of Bahia Honda in Pinar del Río Province. A few days later, a virtual armada of sixteen ships disembarked another 4,000 troops at that same port, along with tons of weapons, electrical equipment, surface-to-air missiles, trucks, and food. A composite of refugee accounts and more precise DRE reports indicated that another 5,000 Russian soldiers had been landed in the central and eastern provinces of Las Villas and Oriente. All told, approximately 20,000 Russian military personnel had entered Cuba in little more than three weeks' time. All but 5,000 had been put ashore at Havana and at ports *to the West of Havana closest to U.S. shores*—a fact, as we shall come to later, that figured prominently in the hesitations of the New Frontier.

For the most part, President Kennedy stayed aloof from the rising public and Congressional clamor for action. On August 22, he was briefed by CIA chief John McCone *and told that surface-to-air (SAM) missiles were being installed in Cuba*. McCone also told the President that he doubted the value of the placement of SAMs on the island except for the purpose of protecting long-range ballistic missiles, a judgment which now appears to have been incorrect. Two days later, Roger Hilsman, Director of the Office of Intelligence and Research of the State Department, held a background briefing for reporters, which seems to have been designed to let steam out of what was becoming an explosive story. He said that between July 26 and August 8, eight Soviet and Soviet-bloc ships had arrived in Cuba, thus confirming, in part, more precise information which had been made public by Cuban refugees, by the DRE, and by José Miró Cardona, President of the U.S.-supported

Cuban Revolutionary Council. Hilsman also said that another dozen Soviet ships had docked at Cuba's ports between August 9 and 24, but he put the damper on reports of largescale landings of Soviet troops, scaled the number down to between 3,000 and 5,000, and merely classified them as "technicians." The notion that the Russians were installing offensive missiles in Cuba (brought to the attention of Congress by New York Republican Senator Kenneth B. Keating), was deflated by Hilsman. While admitting that the large amounts of electronics equipment and radar vans unloaded in Cuba indicated that this equipment might be missile guidance systems, Hilsman suggested obliquely that it was for coastal defense. He admitted that some of the cargoes might include SAMs, but quickly added that this was nothing to be alarmed about, noting that the Russians had supplied SAMs to Iraq and Indonesia.*

Hilsman's comfortable view of the situation was not reflected in Congress, nor did it serve to lull the curiosity of the U.S. press. At a press conference on August 29, President Kennedy undertook the task of soothing rising public opinion. That same day, a U-2 flight over Cuba had taken photographs which showed two SAM sites in position, ready to fire. While it is uncertain whether this specific information was available to the President at the time of the press conference, it is certain that he had received virtually the same information a full week earlier from CIA chief John McCone. Yet he denied to reporters that the Soviets had installed SAMs in Cuba, saying, "We have no information yet." He also denied reports that Russian troops were in Cuba, and added, "I am not invading Cuba at this time." To make certain that it was fully understood that he had no intention of invading Cuba under *any* circumstances, the President admonished the press corps that no "secondary meaning" should be attached to his use of the words "at this time." Asked by a puzzled reporter how his position was to be interpreted within the context of the Monroe Doctrine, the President said: "We would oppose a foreign power extending its power to the Western Hemisphere," adding blandly, "and that is why we are opposed to what is happening in Cuba today."

President Kennedy's slippery behavior at his August 29 press conference did not please an aroused Congress nor placate the press, any more than did his September 4 public statement in which the President zeroed-in on the one thing to which he might react—the installation in Cuba of "offensive" missiles. There was no. proof that they were in Cuba, he said, and added: "Were it to be otherwise, the gravest issues would arise." Negative press reaction to President Kennedy's inexplicable behaviour rumbled across the country. The *Cedar Rapids Gazette* commented on

*Officials in the State Department and the Voice of America now believe that Hilsman ordered the assassination of South Vietnam's President Diem.

September 18: "What the Russians are doing there [Cuba] is clearly the type of thing the Monroe Doctrine was designed to prevent." Publisher John Knight of the *Miami Herald* had stated earlier, on September 2: "Kennedy must face the fact: Only force can oust Castro." Columnist Roscoe Drummond scored the President's reference to the deteriorating internal situation facing Castro as evidence of meaningful U.S. policy, saying: "What confronts the United States today is not a deteriorating Castro dictatorship but a powerfully armed Soviet satellite which the Kremlin can now use, in its own way, at its own will, for its own purposes." He called on the Administration to "liquidate Soviet penetration of the Western Hemisphere."

What had aroused the nation was the clear implication from the President's statements that unless the United States itself was placed under threat of immediate attack, Kennedy would stand by idly while Russian troops poured into Cuba and made a shambles of the Monroe Doctrine, the Defense Treaty of Rio de Janeiro, and the Pact of Bogota—all pillars of hemispheric defense. His views—those of the liberal isolationist— drew an almost immediate response from Moscow. In answer to President Kennedy's persistent use of the word "defensive" to describe Russian intervention in Cuba, the Kremlin announced that it would provide Cuba with "arms deliveries" to help meet "threats of aggressive imperialist elements." The total effect of President Kennedy's loose definition of "defensive" armaments meant, of course, that an "aggressor" had to be lurking somewhere. Certainly not he, for, as a State Department release responded to the Russian announcement almost on cue: "The announcement doesn't seem to represent anything new," adding smoothly: "We've been saying right along that the Soviet Union has been sending military equipment and technicians to Cuba." The dialogue on this vital subject of arms to Cuba between the White House and the State Department on the one side, and the Kremlin and the Soviet Foreign Ministry on the other, was disturbingly smooth. Furthermore, it served to identify "imperialist elements" as the common enemy of both Premier Khrushchev and President Kennedy. These were, in the words of one of President Kennedy's political speeches at the time, "self-appointed generals and admirals who want to send someone else's son to war."

That President Kennedy was determined to follow a policy of very limited U.S. reaction to the Soviet build-up in Cuba is apparent in his nationally broadcast news conference on September 13. In it, he carefully outlined to the Russians once again what he considered to be important:

> If at any time the Communist build-up in Cuba were to endanger or interfere with our security in any way, including our base at Guantanamo, our passage to the Panama Canal, our

missile and space activities at Cape Canaveral or the lives of American citizens in this country, or if Cuba should ever attempt to export its aggressive purposes against any nation in this hemisphere, or become an offensive military base of significant capacity for the Soviet Union, then this country will do whatever must be done to protect its own security and that of its allies.

Thus the Russians were provided with a clear picture, not so much regarding what the President would do about Cuba, but more important, what he would not do. The President did not object to the movement of Soviet forces into Cuba with which to occupy the country. He went one step further, repeating what he had said before: "Unilateral military intervention on the part of the United States cannot currently be either required or justified." And when Congress was prepared to pass a Joint Resolution calling for tough action against Cuba, President Kennedy stepped in and saw to it that the language was toned down. In fact, just before the President's September 13 press conference, an agreement was reached between Republican and Democratic leaders in the Senate to put aside for the moment other, tougher, resolutions. The Joint Resolution, signed by President Kennedy on October 3, reads:

Resolved by the Senate and House of Representatives of the United States of America in Congress assembled, that the United States is determined—
(a) To prevent by whatever means may be necessary, including the use of arms, the Marxist-Leninist regime in Cuba from extending, by force or threat of force, its aggressive activities to any part of this hemisphere.
(b) To prevent in Cuba the creation or use of externally supported military capability endangering the security of the United States; and
(c) To work with the Organization of American States and with freedom-loving Cubans to support the aspirations of the Cuban people for self-determination.

The joint Resolution failed to state that the movement of Soviet combat forces into Cuba would be met with appropriate counterforce as it constituted a clear violation of the Monroe Doctrine, the Pact of Bogota and the Rio Defense Treaty.

Important steps were taken by President Kennedy to maintain full control of the situation. One was to establish a close watch over government information to the press, and, in turn, to glean from the press what it knew about Cuba. Arthur Sylvester, Assistant Secretary of Defense for Public Affairs, had a representative of his office present at each interview between a reporter and a Pentagon official. And this went for everyone, regardless of rank. This policy was later modified to permit officials to report to Sylvester and give him the substance of the talk at the end of the day. The State Department also instituted a similar practice, but, in the face of pressures from publishers, modified its rules somewhat. Sylvester brought upon him the wrath of the press community when, following the missile crisis, he said that it was an inherent right of the government to lie (which it apparently did) to save itself in a nuclear war situation.

Another and vastly more important measure taken by President Kennedy was his insistence that each U-2 flight over Cuba required his personal authorization. He exercised this authority through McGeorge Bundy, Presidential Adviser on National Security Affairs, and the Committee on Overhead Reconnaissance (COMOR). For some reason which still awaits a satisfactory explanation, the committee had made a policy decision *limiting overflights of Cuba to that portion of Cuba lying east of Havana. This decision was made despite overwhelming intelligence that the bulk of suspicious cargoes and Soviet troops were being discharged at Havana and at ports west of Havana.* For almost a month and a half —from September 5 to October 14—Russia unloaded military and human cargo with no apparent attempt made by the New Frontier to scrutinize those activities through the prying eyes of high-flying U-2 planes.

It was only after CIA chief John McCone returned to the United States after a short honeymoon in France that this colossal "oversight" was discovered. McCone immediately set about trying to find out why no U-2 flights had been made over Pinar del Rio, and recommended that flights be made at once.* He received COMOR's lame excuse that the shooting down of a Chinese Nationalist U-2 over Red China on September 9 had dictated extraordinary caution in the further use of U-2s over Cuba. A U-2 flight over Pinar del Rio Province on September 5 had shown that missile deployment in that area was proceeding at a rapid pace. Instead of increasing the surveillance, as might have been anticipated, COMOR decided to reduce flights over that area! The most that can be said for that argument is that COMOR was more concerned with the security of the U-2 than it was with the security of this country. But that was not all. For days, President Kennedy and his advisers pondered just how intelligence could be obtained on Soviet missile construction in Pinar del Rio without risking the loss of a U-2, then finally

*The Senate Committee on Armed Services found no photography gap during this period, and points to two U-2 flights on August 29 and October 7 as evidence. It *does not*, however, explain the administration's failure to concentrate on Pinar del Rio Province. If frequent flights had been made over that area, Soviet MRBM's might have been detected much earlier than October 14. Obviously, they did not appear, together with tent cities, revetments, etc., overnight.

came to a conclusion which they should have reached four weeks earlier
—that the U-2 had to be used.

It was not until October 9, however, that COMOR finally approved
flight plans for U-2 surveillance of Pinar del Rio. Then, for some reason
which also awaits a satisfactory explanation, the U-2 flights were taken
away from the CIA and shifted to the control of the Defense Department. One practical effect of the shift was to remove the films from the
scrutiny of the CIA, whose proper business was intelligence, and place
them in the hands of the Defense Department and Defense Secretary
Robert McNamara.* Air Force Majors Rudolph Anderson, Jr., and
Richard S. Heyser, had to be trained to fly the CIA-built planes. Finally,
after being warned to expect SAM fire, on October 14 the two officers
made sweeps over Pinar del Rio.

Upon returning to their base in Florida, the two U-2s had their film
magazines rushed to Washington by jet aircraft, where photo interpreters
immediately went to work. Defense Under Secretary Roswell I. Gilpatric
was the first important official to learn the contents of those films. The
Russians, which the DRE and Cuban refugees had reported were in Pinar
del Rio Province, were indeed there. In droves. A tent city was springing
up near the town of San Cristobal. More important, the films disclosed
missile erectors and other paraphernalia associated with missiles. It
should be noted, however, that ground intelligence reports, particularly
those extracted by CIA interviewers in Miami through exhaustive interrogation of Cuban refugees, had already produced enough vital evidence
to have prodded the Administration to send U-2s over Pinar del Rio
several weeks earlier. *In fact, the DRE reported on August 31, six weeks
before the U-2 flights of Majors Anderson and Heyser, that missiles in
Pinar del Rio were expected to be operational within 60 days.* And even
though the DRE was an instrument of official U.S. intelligence, its report
was ignored by the Administration. In any case, the critical nature of
the October 14 photographs lay in their bearing evidence that "offensive"
missiles might be in Cuba, evidence which President Kennedy could no
longer ignore. He was forced to do something when presented with the
facts by his own staff, specifically by McGeorge Bundy between 8:30 and
9:00 a.m. on October 16, as he sat in his pyjamas and robe in his bedroom
at the White House reading the morning papers.

Acting on Kennedy's instructions, Bundy called a meeting of high-
level government officials for 11:45 that morning. They were: Secretary
of State Dean Rusk, Secretary of Defense Robert McNamara, the President's brother, Robert, Defense Intelligence Agency Chief General Jo-

*The Senate Committee on Armed Services denies that the shift was made because of an
alleged conflict between the CIA and the military. But it does not explain just why the
shift was made at all.

seph Carroll, Chief of the Joint Chiefs General Maxwell Taylor, Under Secretary of Defense Roswell Gilpatric, Under Secretary of State George W. Ball, Assistant Secretary of State for Inter-American Affairs Edwin Martin, Treasury Secretary Douglas Dillon, Ambassador Charles Bohlen, Sorensen, Bundy, and the President. Appointments Secretary Kenneth O'Donnell was added to keep up appearances that the meeting was routine. Non-government people, Dean Acheson, for example, and former Secretary of Defense Robert Lovett, also sat in on the meetings. Others, such as Adlai Stevenson, participated from time to time. But basically, the group named above came to be known as the Executive Committee of the National Security Council, and debated what was to be done in the face of the Soviet strike in the West. The Secretary of State did not attend.

Throughout the meetings, many of which were not attended by the President, Attorney General Robert Kennedy acted as Assistant President. He set the tone by blocking consideration of a lightning air strike to wipe out the missiles, saying quite irrelevantly: "My brother is not going to be the Tojo of the 1960s."[4] Sixty-nine-year-old Dean Acheson, veteran of many critical decisions, including the fateful rescue of South Korea in 1950, sharply disagreed with the 37-year-old novice in foreign affairs. He disdainfully pointed out that Japan's expansionist designs in the 1930s and 1940s, leading up to an attack on Pearl Harbor, could hardly be compared with U.S. policy in the 1960s. The fact was, Acheson argued, that the Russians were the aggressors in Cuba, that the President himself had warned on September 4 and again on September 13 that the United States would be forced to react if the Russians installed "offensive" missiles in Cuba. He recommended military action to remove them. Nevertheless, Robert Kennedy's views were those of the President, and they prevailed.

Why had the Russians decided to move intermediate and medium range missiles into Cuba? The Executive Committee debated this embarrassing question at some length, and turned to a consideration of an intelligence estimate, prepared back on September 19, by the Board of National Estimates. The estimate did not rule out the possibility that the Russians might move missiles into Cuba, but suggested that such a move would be for psychological reasons, to intimidate Latin America, and threaten the United States with nuclear blackmail. Why the Russians put them into Cuba was succinctly put by Dean Acheson when he undertook, at the President's insistence, to travel to France and persuade Charles de Gaulle to support Kennedy's stand on October 22. When asked by De Gaulle why he thought the Soviets had moved missiles into Cuba, Acheson bluntly replied that they did so because they believed they could get away with it—not exactly a flattering comment on President

Kennedy. President de Gaulle agreed. It is within the context of Acheson's answer to the French President that another part of the September 19 intelligence estimate needs to be examined. The estimate held that it was highly unlikely that the Russians would install missiles in Cuba because it would undoubtedly provoke a violent reaction on the part of the United States. But what might have been true during the preparation of the report in late August and early September had no currency during the deliberations of the Executive Committee in October. For President Kennedy had publicly indicated to the Russians that he was not going to be goaded into taking military action. Instead of deterring the Russians by issuing prompt and concise warnings in August and September that the United States would brook no nonsense in Cuba, he had for several weeks virtually invited them to come in.

The practical effect of President Kennedy's policy pronouncements, extending back over several weeks, was to limit the terms of reference under which the Executive Committee undertook its deliberations. And the President carefully boxed the political compass. On October 16, he briefed UN Ambassador Adlai Stevenson about the missile situation in Cuba, casually remarking that he might be forced to go in and wipe out the missile sites with air strikes. Stevenson reacted as might have been expected with expressions of horror at the thought, and immediately set about bolstering the position of Administration "doves." And on the same day that he spoke to Stevenson, the President, contrary to expectations under the circumstances, availed himself of an opportunity to speak with 500 editorial writers, reporters, and radio-television commentators who were attending a foreign policy briefing at the State Department. Though his comments were off-the-record, they were used, attributed only to "high officials" in Washington. It would be naive to believe that newsman from Communist countries would long remain in the dark regarding what the President said. And what he said, in effect, was that he was a liberal isolationist. "Our major problem over all," the President ruminated to his attentive audience, "is the survival of our country without triggering the third and perhaps last war." He hazarded the opinion that "The United States—the world—is now passing through one of its most critical periods."

As the President made campaign appearances around the country, Assistant President Bobby Kennedy kept the Executive Committee in line until a list of options was produced. The first was to do nothing. The second was to make a diplomatic approach to Khrushchev and ask him to remove the missiles. The third was to undertake a secret approach to Castro and split him off from Russia. The fourth was a blockade. The fifth was the by-now discarded air strike. The last was an invasion of

Cuba. Let it be noted that the first and second alternatives were seriously considered (with Dean Acheson objecting eloquently), making nonsense of the intelligence estimate of a "violent U.S. reaction." After some debate, the "do nothing" option was discarded, and a diplomatic approach to Khrushchev substituted. This received considerable support (again, with Acheson objecting), and was nearly adopted. Throughout the deliberations, President Kennedy and the New Frontier justified a low-key response on the grounds that Khrushchev might strike at Berlin (and Berlin had to be saved at all costs). It also was maintained that Khrushchev must first be warned before *any* action was taken. For a long period, while debating another possibility, a secret approach to Castro, the idea of a blockade kept coming up. This was repeatedly rejected on the grounds that if the Soviet ships did not stop, we would have to shoot *first* and risk provoking Russian action elsewhere in the world. Again, fear was expressed over the possibility of Russian retaliation against Berlin. In fact, an outsider might have concluded that the deliberations were not about Cuba, but Berlin. Above all, the New Frontier argued, whatever the course agreed upon, it had to provide a face-saving retreat for Khrushchev. This proviso reveals the mirror image which the New Frontier had of itself, and the stark ignorance of Communism on the part of those in whose hands the destiny of this nation had been entrusted.

It is practically a religion among Communists not to punish those of their leaders who withdraw in the face of superior force. Quite the opposite. Pursuance of a belligerent course under adverse conditions carries with it the unpardonable risk of threatening the Communist enterprise. Insistence among the New Frontiersmen that the United States had to offer Khrushchev a means of saving his own face has no basis in fact. What might have occurred to the "losers" is the reverse side of the coin. Never will a Communist leader be forgiven for failing to exploit the weakness of an adversary. Apparently the New Frontier of "losers" found no relationship between their President's weakness and the rising belligerency of Nikita Khrushchev which resulted in the building of the Berlin wall, the resumption of atomic tests in the atmosphere, and the lodgement of Soviet power in Cuba.

Finally, the blockade of Cuba, dressed up in the finery of a "quarantine," was accepted by the Executive Committee (Dean Acheson walked out in disgust) and recommended to President Kennedy. As advanced by Sorensen in his book, the blockade "offered a more limited, low-key military action than the air strike. It offered Khrushchev the choice of avoiding a direct military clash by keeping his ships away. It could serve as an unmistakable but not sudden or humiliating warning to Khrushchev of what we expect of him."[5]

Even the "quarantine" plan was weakened. Missiles destined for Cuba were to be stopped on the high seas, but that was about all there was to the embargo, since the U.S. response was to be as peaceable as possible. Earlier rejection of air strikes was based largely on the notion that it would kill Cuban civilians (although the missile sites were located far beyond populations centers) and even a Russian or two. To make certain that the air strikes took out every missile site, the New Frontiersmen argued, would mean extending the strikes to airfields and supply depots. The inevitable result would be the collapse of the Castro regime and the need to "occupy" the island, something which the New Frontier heatedly refused to consider. Furthermore, the "losers" maintained, a blockade of petroleum might trigger a bellicose response, so they would have none of it. They said that if Castro thought that a blockade was effectively cutting him off, he might even attack our ships, Guantanamo Naval Base, or Florida!

Despite repeated public assurances from Secretary of State Rusk that the United States would make no horse trades over Cuba, the President was doing just that. The second or third week of August, when Russian moves in Cuba were an open secret, he ordered the removal of our Jupiter missiles from Turkey and Italy. The Turkish Ambassador to Washington said that the removal of the missiles would be taken by his government as a serious retreat from our treaty commitments, and flatly refused to consider the matter. Under Secretary George Ball carried the Presidential message to the Turks, and, upon receiving such a specific negative response, decided to drop the proposal. Upon learning in October that his August order had not been heeded, the President was furious. He considered the Jupiters to be "provocative" to the Soviet Union.[6] And that the New Frontier had a Cuba-West Berlin trade very much in mind is amply evident in the debates of the Executive Committee. It seems curious that the President's principal preoccupation lay, not with Cuba, where the Russians clearly were establishing a military presence, but with West Berlin, where they were not. In fact, President Kennedy had Berlin, not Cuba, in mind when he obtained a Congressional renewal of authority to call up military reservists. He told Theodore Sorensen, in confidence: "If we solve the Berlin problem without war, then Cuba will look pretty small."[7] Thus, two widely separated trouble spots of the world, Cuba and Berlin, were firmly linked together—not by the Russians, but by the New Frontier.

Just when it appeared that the Executive Committee had been brought into line to follow the President's devious policy, some members became uneasy and balked at the weak U.S. response being proposed by the New Frontier. On Friday, October 19, three days before President Kennedy was to make his speech to the nation, Dean Acheson launched a formidable argument against the idea of blockade which ended in his withdrawal from further deliberations of the Committee. He advocated a strike against the missile sites, in the belief that unless the Russians were driven out of Cuba, the United States and the entire free world stood in peril of further Communist aggression. And again Assistant President Robert Kennedy disagreed with Acheson, this time on moral grounds, and effectively shut off further discussion of armed action by saying that his brother simply would never authorize an air strike, so the Committee had better forget it. General Maxwell Taylor, considered by many military men to be a "political" general, agreed with the younger Kennedy. One participant recalled: "Max is a moral man, and proved it by recommending that we give the Cubans twenty-four hours advance notice—then strike the missile bases."[8] This was a political judgment, having little or nothing to do with the sound military practice never to warn the enemy in advance.

Early morning that same day, the Joint Chiefs of Staff delayed the President for a half hour as he was about to leave for election campaigning in the hustings. They urged him not to resort to the blockade, arguing that it would hardly settle the long, drawn-out issue of getting the Russians out of Cuba. The night before, Secretary of State Rusk had suddenly taken a hard turn, recommending that if construction on the missile sites had not ceased by October 24, the U.S. Air Force should strike fast and hard, and a public ultimatum be issued simultaneously to Khrushchev that any counteraction would set off a war. Even McGeorge Bundy was having second thoughts about the effectiveness of a Naval blockade. The President set off for his campaign trip on October 19 a troubled and worried man. He told Sorensen and his brother that he was relying on them to pull everyone back into line. Saturday afternoon the President returned, to find that Sorensen and brother Bobby had delivered the goods. A draft speech by Sorensen announcing a "quarantine" of Cuba was ready, and everything was set for its delivery Monday at 7:00 p.m.

Earlier in the week, Adlai Stevenson had at once stimulated and depressed the President with a note suggesting a course of action. It is mentioned here because of its later importance. President Kennedy was depressed with Stevenson's reminder that the United States could not negotiate with a gun (more specifically a missile) pressed to its head. He was stimulated with Stevenson's other suggestion—that we give up the Guantanamo Naval Base, and more important, extend iron clad assurances that Cuba would never be invaded. Sorensen's comments on Stevenson's proposal to withdraw from Guantanamo and guarantee the survival of the Castro regime are worth quoting: "There was not a hint of 'appeasing the aggressor' in these plans, as some would charge, only an effort to propose a negotiating position preferable to war and acceptable to the world."[9] Stevenson even proposed leaving the missiles there, and calling in the United Nations to investigate, not only the missiles in Cuba, but also possible U.S. bases for attacking Cuba. This too drew admiration from Sorensen. Fortunately, however, the idea of abandoning Guantanamo was vetoed by the President. Instead, U.S. forces there were beefed-up considerably. As late as Sunday, President Kennedy again queried General Walter C. Sweeney, commander of U.S. Tactical Air Forces, whether one clean strike against the missile sites would guarantee putting them out of commission. General Sweeney answered to the effect that no commander could give 100% assurances that only one strike would be needed, but did offer an amazing 90% assurance of success. But the President turned down the air strike on the grounds that it might kill Cubans and, possibly, Russians, and result in the overthrow of Fidel Castro. He did tell the military that the air-strike option was not dead, and that he might resort to it if the blockade failed. By then, of course, the element of surprise would have been dissipated and the probability of causing larger numbers of casualties among Cubans and Russians would have increased considerably.

Indecision was apparent on the diplomatic front, and it was not until Saturday, the day before the final veto of the air-strike, that the issue was given serious attention. Again, the Stevenson proposal to guarantee the territorial integrity of Cuba came up for discussion, and was shot down by the majority of the participants. But the President, Sorensen, and Bobby Kennedy tucked the idea away for future reference. There was more urgent business to be taken care of. The Administration needed the support of our Allies in Europe and Latin America, and there was only one day left in which to get it. President Kennedy wanted to deliver his address on Sunday. But many Latin American ambassadors would normally be out of Washington for the weekend, so the speech was finally scheduled for delivery on Monday at 7:00 p.m. Letters were sent out to heads of state, and members of the Organization of American States (OAS) were asked to attend a meeting to be held on Monday. It also was agreed that Stevenson would take the U.S. case to the UN Security Council.

The mechanics of the U.S. Naval "quarantine" came under discussion, amidst indications that the President was adamant that no Soviet ships be sunk, even if they ran the Naval blockade. Chief of Naval Operations, Admiral George W. Anderson, Jr. said that Soviet vessels which refused to stop for boarding and inspection would have a shot fired across their bow, followed by a crippling shot into their rudders, if needed, to stop them. The President questioned the Admiral at some length to make certain that a shot into a ship's rudder did not risk hitting it elsewhere. Later, he was to tell McNamara to limit even this response, causing a dramatic confrontation between the Secretary of Defense and the Chief of Naval Operations.

An interesting, and perhaps significant, debate took place on Sunday regarding the release of photos of missiles and missile sites. The President surprised the Executive Committee by opposing their release to the public. He argued that the public would not be able to discern too much from the photos, and that their very release might create panic. The President was determined to control every phase of the operation, and to prevent any public reaction which might force him into a more militant position. He sketched into his speech sentences which said that the missiles in Cuba could reach Canada and Latin America, but rejected suggestions that he include the devastating capabilities of such nuclear weapons. And again, there was considerable talk among members of the Executive Committee that the Russian move into Cuba was to create a bargaining position in Berlin. The President himself frequently interjected this note into the debates, and his speech seemed to invite the Soviets to make such a move by saying that the blockade of Cuba would not deprive the people of the necessities of life such as the Soviets tried to do in their blockade of Berlin in 1948. He struck out of the speech what he considered to be the slightest hint that the United States might remove Castro, limiting himself to extending the pious hope that Cuba would one day be free.

The President had met with Soviet Foreign Minister Andrei Gromyko on Thursday, October 18, and listened to Gromyko's assurances that no offensive missiles were in Cuba, claims which were duly noted and remarked upon in his speech. He also drew the final tooth left in the head of a militant U.S. response, pledging to Gromyko that the United States had no intention of invading Cuba. It is not possible to really know what happened during the Kennedy-Gromyko meeting, since no one else was present. Therefore, a comment made by the President to Secretary Rusk and Ambassador Llewellyn Thompson immediately following the meeting may have some significance. He asked them if he had made a mistake in not telling Gromyko that he knew the truth about missiles in Cuba. They said no.

When President Kennedy met with leaders of Congress, he did so in very dramatic circumstances. Many were campaigning for re-election and were flown back to Washington in military jet aircraft. The President saw them at the White House barely two hours before his speech. He watched as Secretaries Rusk and McNamara, and CIA chief McCone briefed the Congressional leaders on the crisis, and was disappointed at their reaction. In the words of Elie Abel, the President "left the room, having spent more than an hour with Congressional leaders, in a smouldering rage."[10] He was particularly angry with Senator J. William Fulbright, an eminent appeaser at the time of the Bay of Pigs. Senator Richard B. Russell, the Georgia Democrat, demanded an invasion to eradicate the Cuban threat once and for all. To the President's surprise and anger,

Senator Fulbright supported Russell. Yet, Fulbright was still reacting with the reflexes of the liberal isolationist. At the time of the Bay of Pigs he believed it immoral for the United States to try to overturn a Communist regime. The situation as he saw it was quite different in October 1962. In this instance, the United States itself was being threatened, requiring an immediate military response.

At 6:20 p.m., Under Secretary of State George Ball began briefing 47 allied ambassadors and *chargés d'affairs* in the State Department's international conference room. The briefing began as Soviet Ambassador Anatoliy Dobrynin left the Department following a separate briefing by Secretary Rusk. At 7:00 p.m. sharp President Kennedy began his address to the nation.

> Good evening my fellow citizens.
> The Government, as promised, has maintained the closest surveillance of the Soviet military buildup on the island of Cuba. Within the past week, unmistakable evidence has established the fact that a series of offensive missile sites is now in preparation on that imprisoned island. The purpose of these bases can be none other than to provide a nuclear strike capability against the Western Hemisphere. . . .
> Several of them include medium-range ballistic missiles, capable of carrying a nuclear warhead for a distance of more than 1,000 nautical miles. Each of these missiles, in short, is capable of striking Washington, D.C., the Panama Canal, Cape Canaveral, Mexico City, or any other city in the Southeastern part of the United States, in Central America or in the Caribbean area. Additional sites, not yet completed, appear to be designed for intermediate-range ballistic missiles—capable of striking most of the major cities in the Western Hemisphere, ranging as far north as Hudson's Bay, Canada, and as far south as Lima, Peru. In addition, jet bombers, capable of carrying nuclear weapons, are now being uncrated and assembled in Cuba, while the necessary air bases are being prepared. . . .[11]

He also said: "It shall be the policy of this nation to regard any nuclear missile launched from Cuba against any nation in the Western Hemisphere as an attack by the Soviet Union, requiring a full retaliatory response upon the Soviet Union."

He pointed to Soviet deceptions, including Khrushchev's boast that he didn't need to station missiles outside the Soviet Union because his weapons were sufficiently long-range to permit the Russians to hit the United States by Soviet-based missiles. He also recalled the more recent meetings with Gromyko in which the Soviet Foreign Minister said that long-range missiles were not being installed in Cuba. As he ticked off the evidence of Soviet deceit, he punctuated each with: "That statement was false." The President outlined the "quarantine" at that very moment being instituted against Cuba, established that the United States would continue with aerial surveillance, and said he was taking the matter to the Security Council the next day.

Little noticed in the drama-charged atmosphere of President Kennedy's speech was that it amounted to very little more than an invitation to the Soviets to remove their missiles from Cuba. His deeper intent, to continue on the road to *rapprochement* with Russia, is reflected in the following passage:

> I call upon Chairman Khrushchev to halt and eliminate this clandestine, reckless and provocative threat to world peace and to stable relations between our two nations. I call upon him further to abandon this course of world domination, and to join in an historic effort to end the perilous arms race and to transform the history of man. He has an opportunity now to move the world back from the abyss of destruction—by returning to his government's own words that it had no need to station missiles outside its own territory, and withdrawing these weapons from Cuba. . . ."

Secretary McNamara briefed reporters immediately following the address, saying that the Navy would brook no nonsense, that it was prepared to sink Soviet ships if they did not heed the blockade. Secretary Rusk met with ambassadors of the so-called neutral nations to obtain their support, which he didn't, and Assistant Secretary Martin met with Latin American Ambassadors to get their approval, which he did. A side-note here. For some reason, both Theodore Sorensen and Assistant Secretary of State Edwin Martin believed that there was only a remote chance that members of the OAS would come up with the two-thirds vote needed to invoke articles 6 and 8 of the defense Treaty of Rio de Janeiro on which the blockade, or "quarantine," was to be based. This judgment was made despite the fact that Latins, as their history amply indicates, are notoriously impressed with force and determination. And, with only Uruguay abstaining, the Latin reacted as Latins, voting 19 to 0 in favor of the blockade. Public and political opinion in Latin America was so aroused that even anti-American and Red-supported President Joao Goulart of Brazil went along, as did "neutralist" Mexico. President Kennedy signed the OAS declaration the day following his speech.

But the blockade was not really a blockade at all, in the normal meaning of the term. The proclamation carried a very small list of contraband. While listing surface-to-air missiles among the items, no effort whatsoever was made to remove them. The contraband included the following items:

> Surface-to-air missiles; bomber aircraft; bombs, air-to-surface rockets and guided missiles; warheads for any of the above weapons; mechanical or electronic equipment to support or operate the above items; and any other class of material hereafter designated by the Secretary of Defense for the purpose of effectuating this proclamation.

Nothing was said about the removal of what amounted to a virtual Russian occupation force; there was no warning against turning Cuba into a submarine base; nothing was said to close the many loopholes available to Russia and its Cuban satellite. And this limited response was diluted even further. With a flotilla of 25 Soviet ships still moving toward Cuba, and no sign that they would turn about, Defense Secretary McNamara walked into the Navy Flag Plot in the Pentagon on October 24 (where the blockade operations were being directed) and asked Admiral Anderson what he would do if a Soviet ship tried to run the blockade. Admiral Anderson was schooled in his subject. The U.S. Manual of Naval Regulations had it all spelled out, and Anderson told McNamara so in blunt language. McNamara then took the rapidly purpling Admiral aside and counselled him that the blockade was not designed to shoot Russians, nor to humiliate Nikita Khrushchev. Its purpose was to put political pressure on the Russian leader so that he would respond to the limited demands of President Kennedy. Following several encounters between the unhappy Admiral and the Secretary of Defense, McNamara was virtually ordered out of the Flag Plot and curtly told that the Navy would run the blockade. Admiral Anderson was not reappointed Chief of Naval Operations. When his term was up the following June, he was given the post as U.S. Ambassador to Portugal, and then forgotten.

On October 25, that aging pacifist, Walter Lippmann, interjected his solution to the matter. He sounded so much like President Kennedy that some wags in the press corps suggested that the story was written in the White House. Apparently the Russians thought so, too. Soviet Ambassador Dobrynin considered it to be a trial balloon sent up by the White House. In his column Lippmann had written that there were three ways to get rid of the missiles in Cuba. One was to invade Cuba. Unthinkable. The second was to institute a total blockade. Also unthinkable. Instead, he suggested a trade. The Soviets would retire their missiles from Cuba, and we would take the Jupiter missiles out of Turkey.[12] Meanwhile, the Soviet tanker "Bucharest" and the East German passenger ship "Voelkerfreund" ran the blockade, and, at the President's order, had not been boarded to determine whether either ship carried any contraband. These events—Lippmann's Kennedy-think article, and the breaking of the blockade—may have suggested something to the Russians. Twelve of the flotilla of 25 Soviet ships enroute to Cuba broke away and turned back, and remained stationary until they received orders. The freighter "Marucla" was sent ahead to test the blockade. The ship was of Lebanese registry, and the President decided that it, not a Soviet vessel, would be the first ship to be boarded. It was. By coincidence, the interception was made by the U.S. destroyer "Joseph P. Kennedy, Jr." which found no contraband aboard, and let it continue.

Meanwhile, work continued—in fact, greatly accelerated—on the missile sites in Cuba, and the press and Congress began asking how much longer the President intended to wait. Although the public received no answer, the Russians did. Bobby Kennedy told Ambassador Dobrynin that the President would hold off another two days. UN Secretary General U Thant finally got into the act following the earlier confrontation in the Security Council between Adlai Stevenson and Soviet Ambassador Valerian Zorin in which the former accused the Russians of placing long-range missiles in Cuba, and the latter denied it. That took care of the United Nations action, until the U Thant message to President Kennedy and Premier Khrushchev. He asked the former to suspend the quarantine, and the latter to suspend arms shipments to Cuba so that negotiations might go forward. Both refused.

Behind the scenes the Russians were at work. Alexsandr S. Fomin, a Counselor of the Soviet Embassy and a high-ranking member of the KGB, sought out John Scali of the American Broadcasting Company. The intelligence agent suggested almost precisely what Adlai Stevenson had suggested to the President, and what Walter Lippmann had come out with a day earlier—a trade. The missile sites would be dismantled and sent back to Russia; Fidel Castro would receive no offensive weapons in the future; the United States would pledge not to invade Cuba. Scali took the proposal to Secretary Rusk, who pronounced it encouraging, and told Scali to tell the Russians that it was his, Scali's, impression that the United States was interested in the proposal. An answer came from another quarter, Nikita Khrushchev, who that same day apparently sounded President Kennedy out on his attitude toward Soviet troops in Cuba. The message said that missiles were nothing but a means of immediate extermination, and were useless unless backed up by Soviet troops in Cuba (which, as Khrushchev well knew, numbered not less than 20,000 at that very moment). He then laid down the surrender terms. The United States was to give assurances not only that it would not attack Cuba, but would see to it that others would not do so, and withdraw its quarantine of Cuba. It was a long message and the one persistent demand, repeated several times, was that the United States guarantee the territorial integrity of Cuba. This, clearly, was Khrushchev's aim and main concern and it suggested that perhaps his principal reason for placing missiles in Cuba in the first place was to occupy Cuba.

However that may be, the New Frontier erupted with cries of joy. There was light at the end of the tunnel, they said. Dean Acheson, who had stifled his pique, was again one of the principal consultants. He wasn't buying the optimism, said that the Administration was much too eager to liquidate the matter, and thought that the thumbscrew on Khrushchev should be tightened a little more every day. His point was that the Russians had no business in Cuba in the first place, therefore this vital point should not be an item to negotiate. His feeling that the New Frontier was much too eager to acquiesce in the Russian offer was borne out by a Hilsman suggestion that the approach by Fomin to Scali, and the Khrushchev note, be seen together because perhaps that is what the Kremlin intended! Predictably, in the face of Rusk's quick and affirmative response to Fomin, the Russians raised the ante, sending another teletype message that was considerably tougher in language.

This is quite a coincidence. Every one of the demands made by the Soviets had already been considered and pigeonholed for the moment by top members of the New Frontier, and aired by the President's friend Walter Lippmann. There was a glittering symmetry here. *The fact was that no formal proposal had been made to the United States.* What the Khrushchev messages and clandestine activities of Fomin amounted to was a feeling-out of just how far President Kennedy was willing to retreat. They soon found out. The U.S. press, the Congress, and even members of the Executive Committee, were clamoring for a decision from the President, and the advocates of an invasion were becoming more insistent by the hour. Apparently, domestic pressures for militant action brought exactly the reverse response. Bobby Kennedy had been pressing for an agreement which would incorporate the demands put out in the feelers from the Kremlin. He took Sorensen with him, and within an hour the two returned with a letter incorporating exactly those demands which the Kremlin wanted and which had been advocated by Adlai Stevenson, endorsed by Sorensen, and tucked away in the President's memory ten days earlier.

The letter of capitulation was signed by the President and dispatched to Moscow on October 27, just before the deadline set by Bobby Kennedy to Ambassador Dobrynin.

Published in the November 2, 1962, issue of Castro's *Bohemia* magazine, the letter reads as follows:

Washington (Prensa Latina)—President John F. Kennedy responded to a letter sent yesterday by the Prime Minister of the Soviet Union. . . . In his letter, Kennedy pointed out: 1. You would agree to remove these weapons systems from Cuba under appropriate United Nations observation and supervision; and undertake, with suitable safeguards, to halt the further introduction of such weapons systems into Cuba. 2. We, on our part, would agree—upon the establishment of adequate arrangements through the United Nations to ensure the carrying out and continuation of these commitments—(a) to remove promptly the quarantine measures now in effect, and (b) to give assurances against an invasion of Cuba. I am confident that other nations of the Western Hemisphere would be prepared to do likewise.

Another part of the letter indicates that President Kennedy was consciously trading Cuba off to the Russians in return for a *rapprochement:*

I would like to say again that the United States is very interested in reducing tensions and halting the arms race; and if your letter signifies that you are prepared to discuss a detente affecting the NATO and Warsaw Pact, we are quite prepared to consider with our allies any useful proposals.[13]

To make certain that all avenues were open to the Russians to receive the letter, Robert Kennedy personally delivered a copy to Ambassador Dobrynin at the Soviet Embassy, telling him that time was running out because the hard-liners in the government, and public opinion, were calling for some kind of definite action to kick the Russians and their missiles into the Caribbean Sea. Still, the President and his immediate staff had not made up their mind what the next step was to be—to tighten the blockade to keep Soviet oil from Cuba, or proceed with an air-strike to wipe out the missile sites. A meeting was set for the next morning, Sunday, October 28, to consider these two alternatives. At shortly before 9:00 a.m., Moscow Radio started reading the Khrushchev reply to President Kennedy (incidentally, one of ten letters exchanged between them), accepting the U.S. terms. It reads:

I regard with respect and trust the statement you made in your message of 27 October, 1962, that there would be no attack, no invasion of Cuba, and not only on the part of the United States, but also of other nations of the Western Hemisphere, as you said in your message. Then the motives which induced us to render assistance of such a kind to Cuba disappear. *It is for this reason that we instructed our officers*—these means, as I had already informed you earlier, are in the hands of Soviet officers—to take appropriate measures to discontinue construction of the *aforementioned facilities,* to dismantle them, and to return them to the Soviet Union. (Italics added).[14]

Khrushchev had what he wanted—an ironclad guarantee of Cuba.* His letter, formally received later, was completely different from earlier informal feelers to see how far he could go. It was a polished document, fully intended to be legally binding on the United States. The letter also agreed to on-site inspection by the United Nations. So eager was President Kennedy to accept what amounted to the U.S. surrender of Cuba that he decided not to wait for the formal letter to be received. He drafted a quick statement accepting Khrushchev's conditions and had it sent out immediately to Moscow via the Voice of America.

There was great jubilation among members of the New Frontier, who sought to see in the trade a great victory for the United States. In fact, in meeting with reporters that same day, October 28, Secretary Rusk cautioned them not to rub Russia's nose in its defeat! The enemy now was Fidel Castro. Inferentially, the Soviet Union was a *de facto* ally. Castro's strident demands at that time followed the pattern of Communist logic by supporting the double-track policy of the Soviets, making them the "good guys in the white hats." He later demanded (1) a cessation of economic pressures; (2) an end to attacks by Cuban exile actionists; (3) an end to any type of harassment of his regime by Cuban exiles; (4) a cessation of overflights of his territory; (5) immediate U.S. withdrawal from our Guantanamo Naval Base.

However, the President turned away from Cuba for the moment long enough to continue his pursuit of a *rapprochement* with the Soviets. He immediately drafted another more formal reply to Khrushchev's letter that Sunday morning.

> Mr. Chairman, both of our countries have great unfinished tasks and I know that your people as well as those of the United States can ask for nothing better than to pursue them free from the threat of war.[15]

The President also "agreed" with Khrushchev that a disarmament treaty should be negotiated, saying, "Perhaps now, as we step back from danger, we can together make real progress in this vital field." He suggested that "priority" be given to negotiations on nuclear weapons.

The formidable public relations machine of the New Frontier went immediately to work. At the final meeting of the Executive Committee that Sunday, someone is reported to have chortled: "What is Castro saying now?"[16] The President personally supervised all press releases.

*Significantly, as we shall see, Khrushchev never actually admitted that Soviet IRBM missiles were in Cuba.

He later gave each of the members of the Committee a solid silver calendar of the month of October, with the days of October 16 through October 28 more deeply engraved that the others. Gone was the President's reluctance to show photos of Soviet missiles. The press was flooded with photographs of Soviet vessels with 42 huge missiles on their decks, covered with tarpaulins, making their way back to Russia. To be sure, none of the Soviet ships were boarded for an inspection of the missiles, drawing some criticism from the press. But the critics were overwhelmed by claims of victory from the Administration. And there was a conscious effort by the Administration to turn criticism away from the Soviet Union and to focus wrath on Fidel Castro who, it was claimed, was now the chief culprit because he balked at settlement terms. At first Russia refused to withdraw its Ilyushin bombers, saying that they had been given to Castro. Finally, the Russians agreed to take the Ilyushins out of Cuba amidst more innuendos from the New Frontier which sought to contrast the "reasonable" attitude of the Soviets with the "intractable" behaviour of Fidel Castro. One very important effect of the missile crisis, of course, was that President Kennedy appeared to be ten feet tall in the eyes of the world. And the Democrats, who had looked gloomily toward certain Congressional defeat at the polls in November, emerged winners on the victorious image of President John Fitzgerald Kennedy.

After the first flush of victory, Congress, the press, and the American public began to have second thoughts about the missile crisis. On February 6, 1963, Defense Secretary McNamara held an elaborate press conference whose purpose was to convince the doubting Thomases that all "offensive" missiles had been removed from Cuba.

The Special Assistant to Lt. General Joseph F. Carroll, head of the Defense Intelligence Agency (DIA), told reporters: "By late October 1962, the Soviets had in place operational medium range ballistic missiles, non-operational intermediate range ballistic missiles* with launch facilities under rapid construction, seven assembled IL-28 bombers and 35 other in various stages of assembly."[17] On October 28, he said, all medium range missiles had reached full operational facilities, while facilities for intermediate range missiles would have been reached by December 15. Secretary McNamara pointed to a photograph showing one missile base under construction in October, then exhibited another photograph of the same base taken on January 27, 1963 which indicated that the launching site had been dismantled. Press reaction was mixed, but the general feeling was that the Administration was not completely successful in making its point. Left unanswered, for example, was why

*A big contradiction here. Later on in the briefing Secretary McNamara said that no IRBM's had been located in Cuba.

the U-2 flights over Pinar del Rio had been suspended from September 5 to October 14. However, the Administration insisted over the ensuing weeks that the threat from Cuba had been totally eradicated, pursued a policy of see no Cuba, speak no Cuba, hear no Cuba, and public interest gradually subsided.

Nevertheless, there is much about the Cuban missile crisis that remains cloaked in mystery. To remove that cloak, it is necessary to examine the following contentions which guided the policies of the New Frontier during the crisis:

(1) *The Soviet Union had never placed missiles outside its own frontiers, so the placement of missiles in Cuba came as a complete, and understandable, surprise to the New Frontier.*

Not only is this premise false, there is every reason to believe that the New Frontier knew that it was false. From April 1961 through August 1962, the West was provided with high-priority information on some of the innermost political and military secrets of the Soviet Union. Soviet Colonel Oleg Penkovskiy, certainly one of the most valuable secret agents in the history of the cold war, sent reports out of the Soviet Union to the West. He held the position of Senior Officer in the Chief Intelligence Directorate of the Soviet General Staff. Here is what Penkovskiy reported regarding the stationing of missiles in Soviet satellites:

> At the end of 1961 a firm directive was issued to equip the satellite countries with missile weapons. This was by a special decision of the Central Committee, Communist Party of the Soviet Union.* *The first country to receive missiles from the U.S.S.R. was East Germany, in 1960*[18]. (Italics added.)

Moreover, Penkovskiy reported back in 1961 that Cuba was the focus of Khrushchev's "adventurism," thus clearly warning the United States to be on guard in the Western Hemisphere.

(2) *The Soviet Union possessed a large arsenal of intercontinental ballistics missiles which could easily reach the United States from bases*

*Yet, Arthur Schlesinger, Jr. writes: "The Soviet Union had never before placed nuclear missiles in any other country—neither in the communist nations of Eastern Europe, nor, even in the season of their friendship, in Red China. Why should it now send nuclear missiles to a country thousands of miles away, lying within the zone of vital interest of the main adversary, a land, moreover, headed by a willful leader of, from the Russian viewpoint, somewhat less than total reliability?" *A Thousand Days* (New York: Houghton Mifflin Company, 1965), pp. 727-728. Is it possible that Sorensen and Schlesinger were actually ignorant of the critically important intelligence reports reaching Washington from Colonel Oleg Penkovskiy? Is it possible that President Kennedy kept those reports entirely to himself?

in Russia. In view of this, there was no need for the Russians to place missiles in Cuba.

This statement also is false. Back on May 30, 1960, U-2 flights over Russia showed that the Russians possessed very few ICBMs. Therefore, the New Frontier knew that Khrushchev's boasts that his ICBMs could bring a shower of missiles upon the United States were empty threats. Indeed, Colonel Penkovskiy had updated and added to that knowledge with his reports, one of which reads:

> Khrushchev is blabbing that we are ready, we have every-thing. This is just so much idle talk. He himself probably does not see the whole picture. He talks about the Soviet Union's capability to send missiles to every corner of the world, but he has not done anything about it because he knows that we are actually not ready. . . . As far as launching a planned missile attack to destroy definite targets is concerned, we are not yet capable of doing it. We simply do not have the missiles that are accurate enough. . . . *Many of our big missiles are still on the drawing boards, in the prototype stage, or are still undergoing tests. There are altogether not more than a few dozen of these, instead of the 'shower' of missiles with which Khrushchev has been threatening the West.* (Italics added.)[19]

Even the guidance systems on Russia's missiles, including the surface-to-air weapons (SAMs), were crude and faulty. Colonel Penkovskiy reported that test firings often resulted in civilian casualties:

> There have been many cases during the test launchings of missiles when they have hit inhabited areas, railroad tracks, etc., instead of the designated targets, after deviating several hundred kilometers from their prescribed course. . . . *Right now we have a certain number of missiles with nuclear war-heads capable of reaching the United States or South America; but these are single missiles, not in mass production, and they are far from accurate.*[20] (Italics added.)

Penkovskiy also analyzed Khrushchev's strategy during the sterile disarmament negotiations underway at the Geneva conference in the following terms: "Khrushchev will fire anyone who mentions complete suspension of nuclear tests. He will sign an agreement only after he becomes convinced that the U.S.S.R. is ahead of the U.S. in the use of nuclear energy for military purposes."[21]

(3) *The United States could overthrow Fidel Castro only at the risk of angering our Latin American allies.*

This is false. The fact, conclusively demonstrated in the 19-0 vote by the OAS to blockade Cuba, is that Latin American leaders were calling for action against Cuba. Guatemala's President Miguel Ydigoras Fuentes said about the Bay of Pigs: "President Kennedy has the responsibility for a sequel." And, just a few weeks before the missile crisis, President of the Dominican Republic Rafael Bonnelly had formally charged Cuba with subversion of his country, while Colombian President Guillermo León Valencia told reporters at the Overseas Press Club in New York: "Fidel Castro is responsible for spreading the cold war throughout Latin America." At the same time, Newspaper Enterprise Association reporter Leon Dennen conducted his own poll of the attitudes of Latin Americans, and wrote: "The Administration's passive acquiescence in the Russian arms build-up in Cuba has dealt a serious blow to U.S. prestige in Latin America." Dennen quoted what he described as "one outstanding pro-Western Latin American leader: 'Perhaps Mao Tse-tung was right after all that the United States is only a paper tiger.'"

(4) *Fidel Castro was infuriated over Russia's withdrawal of missiles, and, in the words of the chronicler of the New Frontier, Theodore Sorensen, "harangued and harassed the UN's U Thant when the Secretary General arrived to work out details."*

This, too, is an absolutely false version of what actually happened between U Thant and Fidel Castro. More disturbing still, as the Sorensen quote indicates, is that this version is propagated officially by the New Frontier. The facts are quite otherwise. *U Thant travelled to Havana on October 30, 1962, and virtually told Fidel Castro to refuse on-site inspection.* He did so, apparently, because of the association of his country, Burma, with 45 "neutral" African and Asian nations. Meeting with Fidel Castro and Cuban President Osvaldo Dorticós in the Presidential Palace at 3:10 p.m. on October 30, U Thant told them:

> As is well known, the Cuban problem was raised at the Security Council last week as meetings were being held by the 45 neutralist countries, principallly those that had attended the Bandung and Belgrade conferences. They held two meetings, and they sent representatives to confer with me, *since I also belong to a neutralist country.* . . . They asked me to take the initiative. . . . On October 24 I decided to take this initiative. (Italics added.)

It seems abundantly evident, therefore, that the Acting Secretary General was not representing the United Nations. He went to Cuba on behalf of the same Asian-African bloc of nations who, back in 1961, had refused to censure the Soviet Union for recommencing its tests in the atmosphere *in the middle of the same Belgrade conference* to which U Thant referred in his talks with Castro. Instead, the "neutral" nations dispatched Indian Prime Minister Jawaharlal Nehru to Moscow to talk things over with Nikita Khrushchev. To make certain that they were completely "neutral," they also sent swaggering Indonesian President Sukarno to Washington to plead with President Kennedy not to respond with U.S. tests. Cuba was a participant in that conference and, as U Thant well knew, its delegate roundly attacked the United States. Thus, the Acting Secretary General of the United Nations was hardly an impartial negotiator in his talks with Castro, and quickly set out to demonstrate that fact in the balance of his talks with the bearded dictator.

> Some press reports said last night and this morning before I left on my trip that I was coming to arrange for the presence of the United Nations in Cuba. *This is totally in error, for it would constitute an infringement on the sovereignty of the Republic of Cuba.* . . . I have no competence to associate myself with any of the proposals. (Italics added.)

U Thant scored the U.S. blockade, saying, "this blockade has been an extremely unusual thing, a very unusual act, except in times of war." He tossed Castro a cue: "This point of view is shared by the 45 governments which met, and who now direct me to make this query of you." He continued: "Two countries of these 45, the United Arab Republic and Ghana, made declarations to this effect," adding: "Other countries among the 45, *especially those who participated at the Belgrade conference*, will make similar statements if they are just given the chance." (Italics added.)

I translated the conversations between U Thant and Castro. They appear in my testimony, given before the U.S. Senate on March 7, 1967. Those conversations contain nearly a dozen statements by U Thant that a UN inspection team would "violate the sovereignty of Cuba." This was so, said the Secretary General, because the United States had made this demand unilaterally. Russia, which had already agreed to UN inspection, was not particularly involved insofar as U Thant was concerned. And when Castro demanded to know if the U.S. blockade had any basis in international law, U Thant murmured in reply: "That is exactly my point of view. It has no legal basis."[22]

Having encouraged Castro to reject on-site inspection, the UN Secretary General then told him that the Russians had backed off from their original promise to President Kennedy that they would work with the United Nations to see that all missiles had been removed. It was up to Cuba, said U Thant, to say yes or no to on-site inspection because: "The Soviet Government's reply is that this is a matter which pertains to

Cuban sovereignty." The Secretary General encouraged Castro to believe that the United States would pledge that it would not invade Cuba, eliciting a response from Castro which describes his togetherness with U Thant: "I now see that the Secretary General is centering his efforts on getting the United States to make a public declaration before the United Nations that it will not invade Cuba."

(5) *That the Soviet Union, in the person of Vice Premier Anastas Mikoyan, tried valiantly but futilely to get Fidel Castro to accept the withdrawal of missiles and to agree to on-site inspection.* One needs only to reach back into newspaper reports during this period to discover, not only that this story was officially nurtured, but that it remains today as the "true" version of Castro's rebuff of Mikoyan.

The story is absolutely false. Yet, for example, it is repeated as true by Elie Abel in his otherwise excellent book. He writes:

> Khrushchev found himself in a tight box of his own construction. Castro was sulking, Kennedy threatening, and the Red Chinese were crowing over his 'capitulation' to the imperialists. In Havana, posters proclaiming Cuba's eternal friendship for the Soviet Union were ripped from the walls. . . .[23]

Abel also accepts the inverse interpretation of Communist doctrine, writing: "It was sheer 'adventurism' Peking said, to have put missiles into Cuba in the first place—a judgment millions in other countries could accept; but to take them out under American pressures amounted to simple 'capitulation.' " Yet, Abel does not ask this question: What did the Red Chinese do by word or deed to discourage Russia's "adventurism" while it was occurring? The answer: Nothing. And why? Because the Russians were pouring troops into Cuba with the purpose of converting that island more completely into a base of subversion. And the Red Chinese had their own guerrilla instructors in Cuba's training camps at that very moment. It was very much to the common interest of Communist countries to have a sanctuary in which to promote worldwide subversion against the free world.* Not only had Khrushchev secured such a sanctuary; he had secured it less than 90 miles from the United States, a tremendous psychological victory for the Communists.

Yet, Abel writes (apparently from New Frontier sources):

---

*Indeed, Premier Khrushchev was in touch with Mao Tse-tung all during the missile crisis. The *New York Times* of June 27, 1967, quoted Khrushchev to the effect that Mao offered him China's fullest support: "Comrade Khrushchev, you have only to provoke the Americans to military action and I will give you as many people as you wish—100 divisions, 200 divisions, 1,000."

On November 2, after a brief stopover in New York, the wily Mikoyan flew to Havana. His unquestioned talents as Moscow's great persuader were of no effect in Cuba. He pleaded, argued, threatened, but Castro would not be moved. For days on end, Castro simply ignored his distinguished visitor. 'Mikoyan discovered that Castro was the first satellite he couldn't dominate,' said one American who kept in close touch with UN negotiations. 'When he returned to New York, he told us all about the beautiful beaches and the wonderful agricultural stations he had seen in Cuba. But it was quite obvious that he failed with Castro.'[24]

More important are the words written by Theodore Sorensen on the subject of the Castro-Mikoyan talks. Claiming that Castro was infuriated with Russia over the withdrawal of missiles from Cuba, Sorensen writes with the authority of the New Frontier:

> The Soviet negotiators, fearful that taunts from Red China would impair their standing in the eyes of other non-European Communists, were concerned with their relations with Cuba. *Fidel Castro*—who had earlier snarled that 'whoever tries to inspect Cuba must come in battle array'—*was stunned by Khrushchev's reversal, to which he obviously had not consented.* . . . Castro complained to him that Cuba had been betrayed, tried to give the impression that the Chinese were moving in, argued fruitlessly for a week, totally ignored him for ten days, and finally resumed discussions only when Mikoyan prepared to fly back to Moscow. . . .[25] (Italics added.)

These two accounts—one representing the official views of the New Frontier, and the other most probably given the author by sources within the New Frontier—*are totally false.* Havana's morning newspapers of November 1, 1962, reported that Mikoyan had been given a warm send-off in Moscow by Cuban Ambassador Carlos Olivares. Cuba's *Bohemia* magazine, a spokesman for its Communist regime, greeted Mikoyan's forthcoming visit as "living testimony to the unshakeable solidarity of that great sister nation." And *Bohemia* recorded all aspects of Mikoyan's trip to Cuba in meticulous detail, reporting that Mikoyan stopped off in New York for a visit with UN Secretary General U Thant, described by the Russian as "very fruitful, indeed." And we have seen from U Thant's interview with Castro what *he* considered to be "fruitful." *Bohemia* also reported that that same evening, November 1, Mikoyan had dinner in New York with Adlai Stevenson and special assistant John J. McCloy, after which no statements were made nor releases issued to the press. And we know, as well, what Stevenson thought of on-site inspection. More important is *Bohemia's* report on Mikoyan's arrival in Havana, a report which mires the New Frontier even more deeply in its own deceit, simply because it seems highly unlikely that intelligence which purported to detect long-range missile sites from an altitude of fourteen miles could overlook from a few inches what was written in *Bohemia.* That it was consciously overlooked seems probable, since the article eloquently refutes the contentions of the New Frontier:

> On Friday, November 2, at 6:03 p.m., as twilight covered José Martí airport, there stood on the runway the Ilyushin-18 that carried the Soviet Vice Premier. The reception committee consists of dual representatives—the Government, and the ORI [Integrated Revolutionary Organizations]. From the landing ramp of the aircraft, at the edge of the ritual pre-scribed by protocol, Mikoyan clapped his hands in a warm salute. Fidel! he was heard to shout.
> *Fidel and his visitor clasp each other in an embrace so close that they are indistinguishable one from the other. There they are, meeting more as friends than as officials, Vice Prime Minister Raúl Castro, Major Guevara, Foreign Minister Roa, Captain Aragones and other figures of our national life.*[26] (Italics added.)

The next day, November 3, the Communist newspaper *Hoy* quoted Mikoyan: "We are by your side, full of scorn for your enemies, and by your side we will fight. . . ." That same day the Soviet Vice Premier learned of the death of his wife in Moscow. He remained in Cuba to talk to Castro, sending his son back to Russia for the funeral. These next few lines printed on page 65 of the November 9, 1962 issue of *Bohemia,* destroy completely the myth that Mikoyan was "snubbed" and left to cool his heels by an angry Fidel Castro:

> The talks between the Vice Prime Minister of the USSR and the Cuban leadership should have begun on Saturday, November 3. But (due to the death of Mikoyan's wife) the meeting was postponed for 24 hours. On Sunday, the 4th, the conference began in the Cabinet Room of the Presidential Palace. Representing the USSR were Mikoyan and Ambassa-dor Alejandro Alexeyev. The Cuban representation consists of Fidel, Dorticós, Raúl, Guevara, Carlos Rafael Rodríguez, and Aragonés.

Mikoyan's reception upon arriving in Havana, and the circumstances surrounding a 24-hour postponement of the meeting occasioned by the death of Mikoyan's wife, hardly add up to the fiction on that subject propagated by the wily Mikoyan and endorsed by the New Frontier.

In fact, during negotiations with the Soviet Vice Premier, Castro took to television precisely to defend the Russians. He said: "There will be no breaches between Cuba and the Soviet Union. . . . because we are friends of the Soviet Union." The bearded dictator also revealed for the first time in that television address that the Russians had written off Cuba indebtedness for armaments sent from Russia and the Soviet-bloc nations, saying: "I want to say that several months ago, the Soviet Union decided to cancel all debts we owe for armaments."[27]

Castro actually scored those who might be inclined to grumble over the removal of missiles. Certainly, he had no objection to their removal, he said, because: *"The strategic arms are not the property of Cuba. When the Soviet Union decided to withdraw these arms we abided by their decision."* (Italics added.) He defended the Soviet decision, adding: "I explain this to you so that you can better understand the reasons which led the Soviet Government to withdraw them." He emphasized that he approved of the Soviet action and said that "confusion on this point will disappear, little by little." Castro lauded the Soviet and Soviet-bloc troops and called them "symbols of all the generosity, all the nobility, and all the friendship which the Soviets have shown us."[28] Castro, of course, knew that Soviet troops in Cuba were considerably more than "symbols;" they comprised a virtual army of occupation to help prop up his shaky regime.

Throughout the immediate post-crisis period, the New Frontier kept insisting that Soviet troops in Cuba were not organized military units, but a mere handful of "technicians." By doing so, the Administration provided a valuable screen behind which Vice Premier Mikoyan was able to carry out his mission to Cuba. That mission was to work out command responsibilities between Soviet generals and the Cuban armed forces. Among the Russian military commanders in Cuba were Colonel General C. O. Slazenko, commander of anti-aircraft units; Major General S. B. Dankevitch, chief of missile and rocket forces; and Major General I. Gussev, commander of Soviet Air Force units in Cuba. This, then, is why Mikoyan remained in Cuba, not that he was kept cooling his heels by a sulking Castro. Yet, it was not until Secretary McNamara's famous briefing on February 6, 1963, that the New Frontier admitted a partial truth with the statement that Soviet armed forces in Cuba numbered about 22,000, including four crack battalions of the Red Army.

(6) *That 42 Soviet missiles, with ranges of more than 1,000 miles, were in Cuba and later were withdrawn as a result of the Kennedy-Khrushchev agreements.*

On the evidence, the admittedly startling answer is no. The active phrase is "on the evidence," for the analyst can arrive at conclusions only on what has been made known. And admittedly there is a great deal about the missile crisis that remains unknown. But to begin with facts.

Much of what has been written about offensive missiles in Cuba is largely in the way of conjecture. In *The Invisible Government*, the authors have this to say about a single component of what *might* have been a 1,000-mile-plus missile: "In retrospect, the CIA decided the missile part had arrived in a shipment of Soviet cargo on September 8."[29] Theodore Sorensen writes of the first gathering of the Executive Committee: "At this meeting, I saw for the first time the crucial evidence. Barely discernible scratches turned out to be motor pools, erector launchers and missile transporters, some with missiles on them."[30] In a point apart, Sorensen writes that General Carter told the meeting that Soviet medium-range missiles could reach 1100 miles, but he does *not* say that the "erectors, some with missiles on them," were those same missiles described in the Sorensen account. Presumably they were not, for the simple reason that the positioning of MRBM's on erectors, as described by Sorensen, would indicate that they were prepared to fire, something which the Executive Committee had been formed *precisely to prevent.*

At Secretary McNamara's briefing on February 6, 1963, briefing officer John Hughes identified the aerial photograph of a "standard Soviet MRBM" in Cuba, gave it a range of 1100 nautical miles and said that the identification had come from observations of that missile made "earlier in the Moscow parade." Throughout the crisis, and the briefing session on February 6, the New Frontier referred to Soviet missiles only as MRBM and IRBM, not by the more precise code names given them by the NATO.

Mr. McNamara was asked by a reporter about the longer range IRBM's which President Kennedy said in his speech would reach even farther than the MRBM's, and he became decidedly evasive, replying: "We have photographs of IRBM's, *not on the island of Cuba*, but taken elsewhere." In other words, IRBM sites had been discovered, but not the IRBM's themselves. So the entire issue of "long-range" missiles actually in Cuba, the 42 that were taken out by the Soviets, revolves around what the briefing session referred to as the "standard Soviet MRBM."

By far the most arresting information regarding the "standard Soviet MRBM" was not disclosed at the briefing session or by any member of the New Frontier in writing about the missile crisis. It is provided by an authoritative reference work, the prestigious *Janes All The World's Aircraft.* Pages 422 and 423 of its 1963-64 edition carry pictures and descriptions of the "standard Soviet MRBM," identified by the NATO code name *Shyster.* The missile shown in *Janes* is the same missile that appeared in the May 4, 1962 edition of Cuba's *Bohemia*. To remove any doubt that the missile referred to by briefer John Hughes and *Janes* is the same, I refer you to the following *Janes* caption:

> "Weapons of this type were deployed in Cuba in the Autumn of 1962, but were withdrawn as a result of American/Soviet negotiations." The range is listed as a mere *"220 nautical miles"!*

Janes also states that a later version of this missile, known as *Sandal*, has a higher performance than the *Shyster*. But there is no indication that the *Sandal* was configured for more than the 220 mile range. It is, basically, the same weapon. On the contrary, it is a near-impossibility that its guidance and other intricate systems could have been changed to increase its range five-fold, and that stresses could have been altered to permit it to shoot so much higher and farther. For one thing, there was no need to do so. The Soviet Union had already developed another missile, the T-2, which had a range approximating that given in President Kennedy's speech—1,300 miles. And Secretary McNamara made it clear in his briefing that no missiles of that description had been seen in Cuba. So, the actual missiles under discussion during the missile crisis are those jointly identified by Hughes, members of the New Frontier and *Janes*. There can be little doubt that the 42 missiles withdrawn from Cuba were either of the *Shyster* or improved *Sandal* class—low-performance weapons that could barely reach the city of Miami, Florida.

However, Mr. Hughes also stated that IRBM sites were "under construction by late October 1962 . . . at Guanajay . . . Remedios . . . San Cristobal. . . ." All of these locations are near vast natural caves which the Soviets had been reinforcing since late 1960. During the question period of the briefing, Paul Scott of the Allen-Scott report referred to Navy sources, which, he said, indicated that a great amount of equipment for missiles remained in Cuba, including rings, generators and erectors. The report was flatly denied by Mr. McNamara.

This brings up the article written in the April 26, 1968 issue of *Life* magazine by Philippe Thyraud de Vosjoli, intelligence officer in the French Embassy in Washington. France also maintained diplomatic relations with Cuba and Vosjoli directed the French intelligence operation there. He writes (pp. 35, 36) that he was in personal contact with CIA Director John McCone and, on August 1, went to Havana to check rumors that Soviet missiles had been introduced into Cuba. Vosjoli's contact in Cuba, identified by him only as a former non-commissioned officer in the French army, said that he had personally seen "multi-wheeled tractors" towing huge Soviet missiles and told Vosjoli that they were bigger than anything the United States possessed. The French intelligence agent said that his contact was competent to tell the difference between long-and short-range missiles, reported them to Washington and promptly got himself into trouble.

Following the missile crisis, Vosjoli writes, his superiors in Paris accused him of misleading President de Gaulle into supporting the United States by his spurious claims that Soviet long-range missiles were in Cuba. Reporting a plot within a plot, Vosjoli claims that the French government had been infiltrated at a very high level by Soviet agents. It was they, he believes, who forced him to divulge the name of his contact (who was then promptly arrested in Havana) and to order him to spy on the United States. Constant denials by Vosjoli's superiors that long-range missiles were in Cuba at the time of the missile crisis may well have been an attempt by those Soviet agents to discredit his reports and to forestall questions as to what exactly happened to them, when, as those Soviet agents well knew, only *short-range missile had been withdrawn from Cuba.*

There are three important points here. One is that the New Frontier was advised by an allied intelligence officer that long-range (most probably of IRBM) range missiles were in Cuba. That advice came as early as the beginning of August, making even more inscrutable the denials of the New Frontier that they knew nothing worthwhile until nearly ten weeks later. The second point is that despite what must be considered a credible report from a credible source, U-2 flights over western Cuba were suspended, not intensified. The third point is this: What happened to the Vosjoli missiles? If his report was spurious, and considered as such by the New Frontier, why was it not reported as having been considered, along with other reports, and the reason given for having dismissed it? The books by Schlesinger, Sorensen and Abel came out considerably after Vosjoli resigned his position, so a mention of his report could not have compromised the Frenchman.

Assuming that Vosjoli's report was sound, what happened to those missiles? Robert Kennedy's "Thirteen Days" says that IRBMs were in Cuba and were expected to be operational by December 15. This brings up speculation raised by Hugo Bell Huertas, the former Castro diplomat to whom I have referred in connection with the Bay of Pigs: "Why should Khrushchev, almost ostentatiously, reveal his missile launchers, sites and supporting equipment with little or no attempt at camouflage?" (Secretary McNamara's briefing underscores the sparseness of Soviet camouflage.) Bell Huertas goes on, "He had to assume from his own experience with the U-2 back in May, 1962, that U-2 flights would be mounted over

Cuba and his installations spotted. Most of us in the Cuban diplomatic service believe that he anticipated this possibility just as a matter of course. What this indicates, then, is that he showed nothing above ground until he was well-prepared underground with something bigger and better."

If these big missiles had been introduced into Cuba, how did they get there? Bell Huertas thought they they had been brought to the island in the vast wells of Soviet oil tankers. One, the *Peking*, was at the time one of the largest such vessels in the world. "It would be a simple matter," Bell Huertas continued, "to cut hatches in oil tankers, which are unencumbered by winches and deck paraphernalia, and place missiles in the wells." He acknowledged that the construction of the wells of oil tankers made the operation more difficult than might appear, but said that a determination to do so by the Communist bosses of Russia on something as important as concealment of nuclear weapons would mean that the job would be done, period. One reason why tankers most probably were selected for this delicate task was, because, said Bell Huertas, "they are among the most innocent-appearing vessels on the ocean. No one expects them to carry anything but oil, whereas freighters are under constant watch."* This statement recalls that "Che" Guevara did considerable experimenting with Soviet oil tankers, and also recalls that these "innocent-appearing" vessels were equipped with counter-mine electronic devices (Cuban exile frogmen made five attempts to attach mines to them, while they rode anchor in Cuban harbors, and found this out). More interesting still, two of the five attempts were made on tankers in the harbor of Bahia Honda in Pinar del Rio where no refineries or oil storage facilities explained their presence.

Furthermore, said Bell Huertas, Soviet oil tankers were the one class of ships declared to be off-limits to Cuban personnel, no matter what their rank.

Next, we turn to Cuba's vast cave complexes and the discovery that IRBM sites were being erected in their vicinity. Back in the Fall of 1960, the able AP reporter Robert Berrellez told me that foreign intelligence sources had spotted Soviet engineers and Cuban personnel working in caves in various parts of the island—specifically at Soroa and Tapaste. Cuba's caves are fantastic for their spaciousness, one extending laterally underground for several miles. I drove out to the Soroa caves one Sunday to discover the truth of what Berrellez had turned up. Those caves, in Pinar del Rio to the west of Havana, were cordoned off by the army, and bore signs saying that the tourist facilities were being improved by the INIT, the National Institute of Tourism. But it did not escape notice that

*Recall that President Kennedy permitted the Soviet tanker, "Bucharest," to pass unchallenged through the blockade.

army troops enforced the order, and that the captain in charge looked upon me with deep suspicion and had a jeep follow my car until I had turned onto the main highway to Havana.

In 1961, a group of speleologists from Poland arrived in Cuba. They pitched tents at the caves of Bellamar, Yumuri, Los Portales, Amistad, las Curas and Purio. Indeed, a supplement in *Revolución* published pictures of the "tourist delights" encountered by the Poles. Headed by a man identified as Maciej Kuczynski, members of the expedition wore military dress and were escorted by Cuban Army major Eladio Elso Alonso. (Elso Alonso later became a staff member of the Cuban Nuclear Group). I questioned Bell Huertas about this, since he was stationed in the Cuban Foreign Ministry in Havana at the time, and could speak with some authority on their missions. He said that the Poles "were used as a screen, since the Poles are more 'respectable' Communists than the Russians." Behind this facade, Bell Huertas said, the Russians were pulling the strings and arranging for military construction to follow the explorations of the Poles. He then added an arresting comment: "A fundamental tenet in our teaching is always to show one thing openly to distract attention from what we are doing covertly. In other words, show something above ground to preoccupy the enemy while we proceed with the important work underground. Those caves could easily provide natural bomb-proof shelters for scores of missiles."

It may be of some significance that President Kennedy stated, the day following the McNamara briefing: "We cannot prove that there is not a missile in a cave or that the Soviet Union is not going to ship next week." And a CIA report on missiles and inspection is pertinent: "Absolute assurance on these matters could only come from continuing, penetrating on-site inspection." When asked about this by reporters, Mr. McNamara said: "I believe that the aerial reconnaissance we are carrying out shall serve as the basis for estimating the Soviet movements of equipment into Cuba." Taken together with the New Frontier cover-up of the U-Thant and Mikoyan missions, it is not difficult to suspect that Mr. McNamara's dazzling display of photo reconnaissance was designed as much to down-grade on-site inspection as for any other purpose. Certainly, he widened the credibility gap between the New Frontier and the public. He admitted that 22,000 Soviet troops were in Cuba, saying that 5,000 were moving out. When questioned why this had been repeatedly denied by the New Frontier during the pre-crisis period, he straight-facedly replied: "I think that you can see from the evidence we have presented today that there were no organized combat units in Cuba," a statement which was flatly challenged by the Senate Preparedness Sub-Committee, which said: "There is no evidence that any of the combat ground troops associated with the four mobile armored groups have been withdrawn," and said about Cuba's caves: "There are literally thousands of caves and underground caverns in the island of Cuba and many of these are suitable for the storage and concealment of strategic missiles and other offensive weapons."

Other flat statements by Secretary McNamara, the man-at-arms for the New Frontier during the missile crisis, were challenged at the time and have since proved to be hollow echoes of political expediency sounded from the White House. Among those is this one: "I have no evidence that Cuba is being used as a base for subversion against other Latin American countries. The President has stated that it is the policy of the government to prevent the use of Cuba as a base for subversion or overt aggression against the nations of the Hemisphere, and we have contingency plans to deal with it." Two weeks later, CIA Director McCone told the House Committee on Foreign Affairs that 1,000 to 1,500 persons came to Cuba from all over Latin America and participated in courses on "guerrilla warfare training and ideological indoctrination." He warned that the number in 1963, at the time of his testimony (February 19), was already even greater. So much for Mr. McNamara's credibility.

Then there was the curious number of trips made by James B. Donovan to Cuba throughout the missile crisis, a time when such trips would not ordinarily have occurred—"while the world teetered on the brink of nuclear war." Donovan was negotiating for the release of the Bay of Pigs prisoners, and a story as late as October 15, written by Benjamin L. West of AP, told of Donovan's increased interest in releasing the prisoners. Instead of cutting down his trips, the President actually encouraged him to continue at an accelerated rate. Donovan dealt directly with Fidel Castro, a fact that raises speculation that he was concerned with something more than mere prisoners and may, indeed, have been given a secret mission by the White House. In any event, the Cuban dictator told admirer Lee Lockwood in 1966: "I can tell you that even more agreements exist, about which not a word was ever said. . . . One day, perhaps it will be known that the United States made some other concessions in relation to the October crisis besides those which were made public."[31]

We must also account for the intrusion of Berlin into the deliberations of the New Frontier during the missile crisis, and also for Nikita Khrushchev's intrusion into the internal affairs of this country. Nikita Khrushchev played politics with the Kennedys—openly, crudely and contemptuously—suggesting that he considered the New Frontier to be made up of political animals rather than statesmen. On September 4, Soviet Ambassador Dobrynin called on Robert Kennedy and gave him a personal message from Khrushchev that Russia would stir up no trouble during the elections. Two days later, the Soviet Ambassador met with

Sorensen and delivered him the same message, with greater emphasis. Then on October 16, when everyone knew the fat was in the fire, Khrushchev called in U.S. Ambassador Foy Kohler and told him that he understood that the earlier announcement that the Soviets were sending a "fishing" fleet to Cuba had embarrassed President Kennedy, and this was the last thing he wanted to do. But rather than blister Khrushchev for his insolence, Sorensen and Bobby Kennedy merely complained to the Soviet Ambassador that Khrushchev's moves in Cuba had already added to the political problems of the President.

We may now examine the behavior of President Kennedy during the missile crisis. At all times, the President seemed completely in control of himself and took charge of every minute detail of operations. There was little hint during the missile crisis of the panic that marked his performance at the Bay of Pigs, except to evoke fear and panic among members of his Executive Committee and to de-escalate rapidly from one position to another. Yet, for an event in which "the world teetered on the brink of nuclear war," to use a favorite cliché of New Frontier chroniclers, President Kennedy's behavior is at once uncharacteristic and much too casual to be explained away with the comment that secrecy had to be guarded, and, for example, that the President's election campaign schedule had to be maintained. This is not a credible proposition.

More likely the President's aplomb during the difficult days of October evolved from a sense of security engendered by the Penkovskiy reports of Soviet deficiencies in the nuclear weapons field, plus his own knowledge of what the United States possessed. At the time, the United States had 600 intercontinental bombers, and many more medium bombers which could reach Soviet targets by refueling in flight. In addition, the United States had at least 100 intercontinental ballistic missiles and six nuclear submarines at sea, each equipped with 16 Polaris missiles. The strength of U.S. conventional forces in its own back yard, including Navy and Tactical Air Command aircraft, is so obvious that it needs no further elaboration. Against this array of might, the Soviets had, according to the Penkovskiy reports, "single missiles, not in mass production, and they are far from accurate." This knowledge, then, helps account for President Kennedy's calm delivery of his October 22 speech, a calm which was not necessarily related to keeping the Soviet Union in the dark that he knew what it was doing in Cuba.

Why, then, did the President constantly tell his advisers that nuclear war might erupt any moment? Certainly, he used the threat often enough to rationalize his own failure to act. In reading Robert F. Kennedy's memoirs (edited by Theodore Sorensen) which appeared in the November 1968 issue of *McCall's* magazine, one gets the disturbing feeling that the New Frontier deliberately engaged in nuclear blackmail to force the

American public, the Congress and Latin America to accept its policies. Those policies were to obfuscate what clearly was a resounding defeat for the United States. For example, in "Thirteen Days," Robert Kennedy says of the President in turning down a more determined but non-nuclear course to be followed in the crisis: "He reminded them that, once an attack began, our adversaries could respond with a missile barrage from which many millions of Americans would be killed."

What missile barrage? From where? With what? Did the President of the United States actually believe that the leaders of the Soviet Union would, in effect, commit national suicide by starting a nuclear war with their small arsenal of weapons? The President well knew that the Soviet Union had neither the intercontinental ballistic missiles nor inter-continental bombers in sufficient numbers to be decisive in an atomic war against the might of the United States. He also advertised that the missiles in Cuba were not positioned for an attack from that quarter. So why this exaggerated view of the situation? Communist leaders are pragmatic leaders not given to suicidal impulses. What did the Soviets have to gain by starting a nuclear war in which they risked total self-destruction over a sliver of an island many thousands of miles away?

It is known that President Kennedy was reluctant to order McNamara to give the February 6, 1963 postmortem briefing, and blamed rumors and speculation for having compelled him to do so. The CIA was not apprised of the briefing in advance and, on March 25, 1963, the President for the first time ordered a third person to be present when he talked to CIA Director John McCone. There is little doubt that the third person, McGeorge Bundy, was there to monitor the conversation, indicating, perhaps, that the President may have been concerned over just how much the CIA knew about the missile crisis. He had refused during the crisis to release photos of the missile sites in Cuba, and permitted McNamara to show only a few photos of the MRBM missiles, most of them covered.

In any event, the Sorensen-edited "Thirteen Days," dictated by Robert F. Kennedy a year before he was assassinated, admits officially that Sorensen and Kennedy drafted the letter acceding to Khrushchev's demands that Cuba not be invaded, or Castro overthrown in other ways, and the Kremlin had what it wanted—a sanctuary which has turned Cuba into the "North Vietnam" of the Western Hemisphere. This, it may easily be supposed, is what Khrushchev wanted all along and one of the reasons he placed missiles in Cuba in the first place—as nuclear blackmail against the New Frontier. Robert Kennedy's memoirs moralize and preach against war, but they also present a totally false or overdrawn picture of the imminence of nuclear war during the missile crisis. Yet he displays no tortured conscience about having deliberately and cold-bloodedly delivered nearly seven million people into the hands of a Communist regime which they had been sabotaging out of business. In short, the Sorensen-Kennedy-Schlesinger-McNamara presentation of the missile crisis is on the evidence one of the great deceptions of the modern world. Nowhere can they lay the slightest claim to credibility on the fundamental issues involved. Even the firm declaration that Cuba would be prevented from becoming a base for world-wide subversion has failed of accomplishment. And whether or not the New Frontier also traded Cuba to the Soviet Union in return for a cessation of threats of war over Berlin, as the evidence most strongly suggests, it seems clear that the Bay of Pigs prisoners and many other issues involving the personalities of the New Frontiersmen took precedence over the security of the United States and the free world.

Who won? Khrushchev spelled it all out in an address before the Sixth Congress of the Socialist Unity Party of East Germany on January 16, 1963, saying that the U.S.S.R. had not installed missiles in Cuba to change the balance of power or to prepare for a nuclear war, as the New Frontier claimed. "The only reason we installed our rockets in Cuba was to stop the U.S. imperialist aggression [non-existent, as we know] against Cuba . . . not to mount a nuclear attack upon the United States and thereby begin a world nuclear war." Khrushchev jubilantly shouted: "The U.S. President . . . gave his pledge before the world that the United States would not invade Cuba and would stop its allies from doing so!" This is quite a statement when compared to the moralizing of the New Frontier. And Khrushchev made it his first reaction to news that President Kennedy had been assassinated, saying that his successor must abide by the no-invasion pledge. He said later that President Johnson had agreed.

However that may be, the facts seem to be these: 1) the range of missiles withdrawn from Cuba deflates the doomsday interpretation placed upon this event by the New Frontier; 2) Khrushchev abruptly stopped threatening President Kennedy with war over West Berlin; 3) the Democrats won the 1962 elections; 4) President Kennedy removed Jupiter missiles from Turkey and Italy; 5) President Kennedy achieved a dubious claim to courage and leadership of the free world and set about intensifying *rapprochement* with an enemy who had just defeated him; 6) the Bay of Pigs prisoners were released, but the people of Cuba were cynically consigned to the straight-jacket of a Communist state; 7) Cuba today is Communism's most important base for subversion outside the Soviet Union; 8) IRBM's may still be in Cuba, siloed and ready. If this point was indeed known to President Kennedy, it alone explains the other seven.

Finally, we came to the falsehoods written by the New Frontier regarding the U-Thant and Mikoyan Missions to Cuba. When added to McNamara's claim that on-site inspection was not needed, that overhead reconnaissance was enough, we arrive at the final truth. This is that the New Frontier *wanted to abort on-site inspection* because an inspection team might, 1)discover that Khrushchev had out-bluffed the President or, much worse, 2) find that the two nuclear powers had cooperated in an unbelievably cynical deception. More important, all the aces of blackmail were in Khrushchev's hand.*

Colonel Oleg Penkovskiy was arrested in the middle of the missile crisis, sentenced and shot to death in the spring of 1963. A report written by him in 1961 reaches us as a voice from beyond the grave: "I always wonder. Why does the West trust Khrushchev? It is difficult to understand. We in the GRU sit around, talk, and laugh; what fools, they believed us again!" He warned us: "Do not retreat a single step from a firm policy."[32] Yet, for a man who gave the supreme sacrifice for democracy and decency, none of the three chroniclers of the New Frontier— R. F. Kennedy, Sorensen, Schlesinger—commits to his memory so much as half a line.

*Dean Acheson has since given his impression of the missile crisis. Writing in the January 19, 1969 edition of the *Washington Post*, he characterizes Robert Kennedy's behaviour as "emotional or intuitive." He also states that he favored destroying the missiles to ensure that they were definitely eradicated from the island, for a blockade "was a method of keeping things out, not getting things out . . ." The "blockade," he states, "left our opponents in control of events."¶Acheson justifies his recommendations for an attack, saying; "A sudden air attack by us on nonpopulated areas of Cuba would have been an attack not on the Soviet Union but on something--not people--in Cuba," adding; "his would hardly have called for a reflex attack on the United States at the expense of reciprocal destruction of the Soviet Union."¶He sums up; "One cannot escape the conclusion that . . . the chief advice reaching the President . . . came from his brother . . . out of a leaderless, uninhibited group with little knowledge in the military or diplomatic field."

CHAPTER 14

•

The Fighters

•

ASSURED THAT THE UNITED STATES, by stopping all external attacks against Cuba's Communist regime, was carrying out to the letter the cynical agreement made between President Kennedy and Premier Khrushchev, Fidel Castro and his Russian occupation force moved swiftly to break the back of internal resistance. There was need to move swiftly. For example, Cuban freedom fighters were sabotaging the rolling stock of Castro's sugar industry. From the end of December 1962 to the middle of March 1963, monitors of Cuba's official internal radio network revealed that sabotage accounted for five major train wrecks. This was so, according to one radio intercept reporting a train disaster, "because the people who are most against the Revolution are those working in the sugar industry." Sabotage of Cuba's vital railways was not confined to field hands, however. On March 9 and again on March 20, radio intercepts in Miami revealed that mechanics had sabotaged the valves on locomotives. A radio operator at the Josefita sugar mill told National Institute of Agrarian Reform (INRA) headquarters in Havana that only one locomotive was in operation because the other had been "derailed through sabotage." That the derailing of locomotives was indeed the work of saboteurs came from an official source, *Radio Rebelde*, when it issued a news report on March 20 that "anti-government groups spread the rails of lines at the Francisco sugar mill, causing the derailment of two trains," and warned that the guilty parties would be found and shot.

Cane fields were being burned in 1963 on a scale far larger than that of the previous year. That this was indeed so was revealed in another radio intercept from Carmita sugar mill to INRA in Havana. On March 13, the militia commander of Carmita radioed the following message to Havana: "We are working urgently trying to save burned cane from the Alberto Rodríguez, Basilia Fernández, and Israel Díaz farms. Please send

369

help." Cuba's hardy and stubborn *guajiros* not only refused to harvest cane; they also burned the fields. The situation became so grave that city-based committees of informers were called out en masse, according to an announcement over CMQ radio, "to stand guard over the cane fields day and night so that our third sugar harvest of the people will not be endangered." Shortly thereafter, the government announced that "247 members of a guerrilla band operating in the area of Cubitas, Camaguey Province, have been captured." However, escapees from the area told me in Miami that the "guerrillas" were *guajiros* who had refused to work for the Communist regime. Some were imprisoned, others shot, while still others were put to work on state farms under the surveillance of armed guards. And, on March 28, the Provincial government of Las Villas Province cracked down hard on the bureaucrats who were struggling without success to get the *guajiros* to work. A radio intercept on that day carried a message to the Escambray, Resulta, Balboa, La Vega, Resolución, Narcisa, and Natividad sugar mills, giving administrators "until the end of the day" to explain why a long list of *guajiros* "have refused to work in the sugar harvest this year." Two days later, Rigoberto Fernández, head of Cuba's so-called Volunteer Labor Force, admitted that even the "volunteers" from the cities were sabotaging the sugar harvest. In a speech to his bosses in INRA, Fernández said he was forced to "rotate" some of the volunteers. "They will be replaced," Fernández continued, "by those who do not resist cutting cane," adding: "We will *not* tolerate those who put our revolution in danger."

Felipe Torres, Communist Party Secretary for Camaguey Province, followed Fernández in condemning the "volunteers" for not working. And just how "volunteer" was Cuba's work force was revealed in yet another radio intercept. A conversation monitored in Miami between one of the "volunteers" in Camaguey Province and his wife in Havana revealed that the regime was shanghaiing people from the streets of Havana. The "volunteer" was permitted to communicate with his wife by official radio because he had been away from his job and his home in Havana for 13 days without having been given the chance to tell his employer or his distraught wife that he was even leaving town or where he was going.

By the middle of April, it was abundantly evident that Cuba's economy was suffering from massive desertions from its labor force. On April 30, Major Ernesto "Che" Guevara told INRA management with heavy sarcasm: "You must look carefully and find where the cane cutters have disappeared to." More revealing of the state of internal rebellion in Cuba was the May Day speech of Armed Forces Minister Raúl Castro. He said: "Today we face an economic problem of the gravest nature. The Revolution mobilized 50,000 people from their jobs in urban areas—

factories, offices, and stores—and made them *permanent* volunteer cane cutters." Despite these dragooning measures, however, the Minister said he had been forced to send troops to the fields to cut cane. "Despite everything," Raúl Castro thundered, and "despite the fact that volunteers worked on Saturdays and Sundays, we have not been able to guarantee normal daily grinding which would permit us to finish the harvest on time." And, speaking in the city of Matanzas eleven days later, Economic Czar Carlos Rafael Rodríguez said quite frankly that the people were sabotaging the Revolution "because of the enormous internal tensions." He added that the number one task of the regime was to "prevent the burning of cane."

Sabotage of Cuba's sugar industry extended beyond the sugar mills and cane fields. Speaking in Havana on June 8, Antonio Aguero, head of INRA's Agricultural and Production Directorate, said that the deficit from machinery destroyed through sabotage, plus the normal requirements of annual replacement, amounted to the staggering figure of $46 million. As a result of massive sabotage in Camaguey Province, Radio Rebelde announced, three quarters of the mills were being placed under the supervision of "the organization of the masses [mass terror], and other departments of the government."

Andrés Ortuno, auditor in Guevara's Ministry of Industries, skipped out of Cuba in May 1963 and accurately summed up the state of rebellion. He told me: "The *guajiros* refuse to go into the fields and cut cane, and are ingenious in making up excuses for their behaviour. As a result, the regime is trying desperately to develop a type of mechanical cane cutter that can do the job. Sugar mills which, prior to Castro, worked 24 hours a day without letup during the sugar grinding season, today grind on the average of about 16 days a month. For example, the Carolina mill in pre-Communist Cuba ground on the average of 76,000 tons in a forty day period, but ground only 43,000 tons for the same period of time in 1963. The year 1963 will see the lowest sugar harvest in the history of modern Cuba, because the Cuban *guajiro* has no use for Communism and has refused to work for his Communist masters."

The effect of popular sabotage on Cuba's sugar industry in 1963 may be measured by some comparative figures. In 1958, Cuba produced 5,-610,000 tons of sugar. The 1963 harvest plummeted to 3,800,000 tons, prompting Fidel Castro to take to the airwaves on June 4 where he ranted and raved against the "enemies of the Revolution" and accused them of being responsible "for an unfavorable balance of trade of nearly $200 million." Castro warned: "Workers will do well to remember that the Revolution is powerful enough to wipe them all out, to confiscate all that they own, in one day."

Undaunted by Castro's threats, members of Cuba's armed resistance movement fought with the courage born of desperation. They knew that the Kennedy-Khrushchev agreement, cutting off the outside supply of arms, ammunition, plastic explosives for sabotage, food, and intelligence, would in a very short time make their position untenable. They also knew that Russian military officers would, in time, turn Castro's motley array of militiamen and informers into a relatively efficient counter-insurgency force. Indeed, the Russians immediately began training select militants of the regime in counter-insurgency techniques, infiltrating some into the rebel bands still operating in the Escambray mountains. In a report smuggled out of Cuba, 21 year-old guerrilla chief Pedro Ramírez said he was surprised at the number of "defectors" from the Castro ranks, investigated, and discovered many of them to be graduates of Russian training schools.

Despite all the handicaps Cuban resistance groups fought like tigers. And they had the support of the populace and even of some elements of the militia. In June, Russian soldiers were brought in truck convoys to the Matahambre copper mines in Pinar del Río Province. There they relieved Castro's militia units of their automatic weapons, leaving them with only side-arms. In Matanzas Province, which, together with Pinar del Río Province flanks the Province of Havana, fighting broke out. There were major skirmishes between rebels and Castro's militia right on the outskirts of Cárdenas, Matanzas Province's second city. The regime immediately clamped on a curfew for the entire Province, by which the people had to be in their houses by 9:00 p.m. Cuban militia units commanded by Russian officers employed flame throwers to burn more than 100 palm-thatched cottages on the edge of the Zapata swamps near where the ill-fated Bay of Pigs force had landed two years earlier. *Guajiro* occupants of the cottages were accused by the regime of "feeding and giving comfort to counterrevolutionaries."

On May 22, Havana's Radio Progreso announced that government forces had been forced to "occupy" the small town of Jaguey Grande in Matanzas Province. Said Radio Progreso: "Complying with measures dictated by the Revolutionary Government, Jaguey Grande had 64 business establishments and a number of vehicles confiscated because the proprietors were continuing their cooperation with counterrevolutionary elements." And, in a June 18 speech, Fidel Castro added another town, El Cano in Havana Province, to the crushing of Jaguey Grande.

Castro said: "They can find out for themselves—in El Cano and Jaguey Grande—how the Revolution has quick methods, magnificent methods, to wipe out counterrevolutionaries as a class."

Open resistance and support given to guerrillas by the people of those two towns led to a repression as terrible as that of the crushing of Hungary by the Russians in 1956. People were slaughtered, houses were systematically robbed of silverware, table linens, curtains, and furniture by marauding militiamen as reprisals against public opposition to Communism.

One eye-witness to the El Cano repression vividly summed up the recollections of nine escapees from the town. I interviewed him in July 1963, shortly after the group had made its way to Key West by boat by the help of friendly fishermen. He said: "Two citizens of El Cano were shot down on the street by agents of Public Order (G-2). The public responded by closing down all businesses, retreating to their homes, and hanging black cloth from their windows in protest. Angered by the resistance, Castro ordered his troops to confiscate houses, businesses, farms, livestock, personal possessions, and furniture. Two youths were arrested for allegedly encouraging the people to resist this tyranny. They were thrown into a small brick structure equipped with powerful fans. Sand was shovelled onto the floor, and the fans put on full force. One died of suffocation; the other nearly died."

Castro's retaliation against the townspeople of Jaguey Grande and El Cano is eloquent testimony to the depth of popular resistance to Communism. Matanzas is mostly flat, with virtually no jungle or forested areas. The effectiveness of organized guerrilla activities which, by Castro's own admission, had pinned down 26,000 militia and troops, had to be due in large measure to the active cooperation of the civilian populace.

Said Castro on June 18: "The counterrevolutionary bands have been swept from this Province."

If what Castro said was indeed true, it had taken two months to accomplish the task, for, according to the bearded Prime Minister: "In eight weeks, our battle-hardened battalions liquidated 14 bands of counterrevolutionaries." Whatever the truth of his boast to have cleaned out anti-Communist elements in Matanzas, he admitted that 40% of them still remained in neighboring Las Villas when he said: "Sixty percent of the counterrevolutionaries in Las Villas Province also have been crushed."

Castro was in trouble. Carlos Hernández and Marcelo Marcos, escapees from Cuba, told me about the sabotage being carried out in Camaguey Province. The La Gaviota fish canning factory and its warehouse facilities in Santa Cruz del Sur were burned, according to Hernández. Marcos told of sabotage in these terms: "Chicken farms are being burned and electric facilities are sabotaged. The discontent is so great that those impressed into slave labor on state farms are refusing to work more than half a day." Admitting to the discontent, the regime countered by declaring an "emulation plan" for the labor force. This consists of assigning fixed production quotas, a well-known Communist innovation. "Those who do not meet those quotas," warned CTC leader Lázaro Peña, "are subject to direct disciplinary measures." The Communists went even further, requiring all able bodied men and women to carry a government labor permit. The permit spelled out that the bearer was required to work at any job designated by the state at a salary also fixed by the state. Workers who refused to comply had their food and clothing ration cards taken away from them. Then they were shipped off to state farms in cattle cars, there to work for the starvation wage of six pesos a month.

Those who managed to avoid detection were forced to live like hunted animals. Alfredo Aguilera Sánchez, who operated a small electrical repair business in Havana, escaped to the United States where, in the summer of 1963, he told me some of the details of the animal-like existence of those who refused to comply with the dictates of the Castro regime. Said Sánchez: "Throughout Cuba a man-hunt is constantly in progress. Militia groups will suddenly charge into groups of people strolling in a park, stop busses, and knock on the doors of houses demanding that they be shown labor cards. Those who do not have them are first interrogated by the G-2 to determine whether they are members of the armed resistance. If they are, their throats are cut. If they are not, they are hauled off to state farms."

Cuban resistance and Communist repression was met with official silence in Washington. Indeed, reporters covering the State Department and the White House were told nothing of the desperate civil war being waged in Cuba, with the result that the U.S. public and our allies knew little about the state of affairs on that embattled island. It was little wonder, therefore, that there was a significant rise in free world shipping to Cuba. Few members of the free world believed that the Government of the United States was any more serious in its announced policy of a boycott than was President Kennedy in his announced policy of returning Cubans to a liberated homeland. He proclaimed on the one hand that Cuba would be free, but on the other saw to it that no support was given to those fighting for freedom.

The result was not surprising. In November 1962, three British and three Greek ships put in at Cuban ports as our allies tested the U.S. boycott. Only faint squeaks of protest came out of the State Department, and the number of free world vessels calling at Cuban ports grew from a paltry six per month in 1962 to 70 in April 1963. More disturbing still, some of the ships supplied Castro with his most vital necessity: oil. The importance of oil to Castro's economy was reflected in a June 1 announcement out of Havana, placing Cuba on daylight-saving time for the first time since World War II. In making the announcement, the regime said that it was due to "the necessity to reduce fuel consumption in power plants," an announcement which set off demonstrations among Santiago's dock workers and brought immediate reprisals from Castro's police apparatus.

Taking no chances that the fifth anniversary of his rise to power would lack the necessary quota of cheering Cubans, Castro ordered that crowds be "imported" into the city of Havana for his 26th of July celebration. An official decree, dated July 9, declared:

"The people will be mobilized in the Provinces of Pinar del Río, Havana, and Matanzas for the festivities of July 26. The main event, which will commence at four in the afternoon, must count on the presence of the peasants and the workers."

The decree set Red action groups into motion. Units of the Young Communists and the Federation of Cuban Women held meetings where they discussed "the means by which the people will be turned out for the celebration." The means were simple. Action groups rounded up large numbers of workers and peasants, and gave them identity cards. They were taken to Havana in cattle cars, trucks, and busses and dumped in the Civic Plaza where they reported to designated squad leaders. The squad leaders stamped the identity cards to indicate that their owners had indeed showed up at the Plaza. And woe to the worker or peasant who reported back to work following the celebration without the stamp.

The suspicion with which the regime looked upon the Cubans was well founded. Hard hit by sabotage, the Interior Ministry's police apparatus was assigned yet another task, spelled out in Resolution 218 dated July 12, creating an "Office of Protection of Production." The salient features are worth quoting, since they reveal the depth of popular sabotage against the regime: "An Office of Protection of Production is hereby created. It is designed to protect industrial, farm, and livestock centers against sabotage and accidents. This office, created by Resolution 218 of the Ministry of the Interior, will prepare all plans to prevent sabotage and accidents . . . it will check all electrical installations, water, cleanliness, storage of raw and finished materials, and any inflammable gas or liquid."

The Russians bailed Castro out of his economic troubles through the purchase of a half-billion dollars of grain from Canada, a large quantity of which was shipped to Cuba. Severe shortages in Cuba not only of grain but nearly all staple foods made it urgent for Khrushchev to include Castro in the grain deal to avoid an increase in internal resistance. In a report in July, President of the INRA Carlos Rafael Rodríguez told a conference of economic planners: "We find that we harvested only 40% as much corn this year as last; only 65% of the beans; 55% of the peanuts; 37% of the soy beans." Tomato production, according to Rafael Rodríguez, showed a similar decline.

As a result, the Soviet Union allocated to Cuba $33 million of its total purchases of wheat and flour from Canada. Furthermore, it was shipped directly to Havana from Canadian ports, a slap in the face of the United States whose officials, according to an AP dispatch out of Canada on September 13, "were kept fully informed." Asked to comment on U.S.

reaction to the deal, Canadian Trade Minister Mitchell Sharp said in the same AP dispatch: "I have not been aware of any objection by Washington." With the wheat deal consummated in the face of lethargic U.S. policy, the number of free world ships arriving in Cuba's ports again rose in the ensuing months. The only action taken by the Kennedy Administration was to bar individual ships—not the ship companies themselves —trading with Cuba from trading with the United States. Even this was watered down to almost nothing when the State Department announced that those foreign ships blacklisted for trading with Cuba could still carry cargoes to and from the United States so long as those cargoes—such as potatoes, corn, wheat—where not subsidized by the Federal government.

And, in June 1963, 59 U.S. "students" broke laws and travelled to Cuba illegally. Their travels inside Cuba were kept under a strict control of Cuban Communist officials that precluded any opportunity of obtaining a true picture of Cuba. The fact is that the "students" were willing pawns in Castro's rule of terror and repression. On July 5, the 59 young Americans "celebrated" U.S. Independence Day under the auspices of a Communist front, the Association of North American Friends of Cuba, by attending a forum billed "as a fight of the Negroes for their civil rights in the United States." It was this forum which developed plans to penetrate the Negro communities in the United States to urge them to indulge in acts of sabotage, incendiarism, and violence. The chief participant was Robert Williams, the Negro who had fled to Cuba from the United States to escape criminal charge. One of the visitors addressed his Communist hosts and lauded nonexistent "new factories, homes, and newly built schools." The true political coloration of the "students" was exposed by the Cuban Communist regime itself, primarily through its radio organs which could be monitored in Miami.

One U.S. student, identified as Victoria Ortiz, said in a Havana interview that she hoped for a "Socialist [i.e. Communist] Latin America because it would make it easier to make a revolution in the United States." Miss Ortiz's comments were broadcast over Radio Rebelde the end of July, following Castro's 26th of July address, prompting President Kennedy to say at an August 1 press conference that among the students who travelled to Cuba "are a few who are not students, but Communists." Nevertheless, nothing concrete was done by the Administration to prosecute the visiting youths for their illegal trip where they gave aid and comfort to the enemy. They returned to the United States after having established the Communist Progressive Labor Party in Havana, made connections with Negro leaders in Puerto Rico and the United States, and, according to F.B.I. reports, were responsible in considerable measure for the bloody Harlem riots which took place in the summer of 1964.

The subversive activities of Robert Williams and the Progressive Labor Party are described in detail in the following chapter.

While the visit of the young Americans to Cuba was prominently carried in our press, the visits of other groups from Latin America and elsewhere were not. From January through August 1963, Cuba hosted 21 conferences, ranging from the World Conference of Women, to a "Solidarity Conference with the People of Venezuela." Vilma Espín de Castro urged the women: "Return to your countries and carry out the same battle that you have seen here." Her husband, Armed Forces Minister Raúl Castro, addressed a group of Latin Americans and urged them to "fight for unity with Cuba and the plan announced by Fidel Castro . . . towards Socialism, towards Communism!" Meanwhile, the Union of Young Communists of Cuba played host to "children of other lands," including 1,000 Algerians and 3,000 Latin Americans.

The surge of activity in Cuba was remarkable in that it gave the lie to the fatuous statements coming out of Washington to the effect that Fidel Castro had had his wings clipped by the October nuclear "confrontation" and that his revolutionary energy was flagging. Teodoro Moscoso, head of the Alliance for Progress, was irked that the matter of Cuba kept creeping into print and said on several occasions that reporters ought not to be so concerned with Cuba, but should turn their hands to reporting the "positive" benefits of the Alliance.

Behind Mr. Moscoso's statements were those made earlier by President Kennedy in San José, Costa Rica, where he pulled the rug out from under a Central American effort to eradicate Communism in Cuba. The week of March 18, 1963, the Central American Presidents hosted President Kennedy in the expectation that the meeting would result in tightening the noose around Castro's neck.

President Francisco J. Orlich of Costa Rica put it this way: "Communist infiltration is spreading throughout the Caribbean as a result of Castro's treason. I expect that during the meeting with the Chief Executive of the United States benefits will be derived for all of the continent." That the Costa Rican President fully expected President Kennedy to throw U.S. support behind Central American countries in their struggle against Castroite guerrillas is apparent in his next statement: "I am in favor of fighting in the streets of Havana . . . whatever course the United States, as the policy-maker of this hemisphere, takes against Communism, it will have the full support of my government."[1] These words were echoed by Ramón Villeda Morales, President of Honduras. "It is absolutely essential to win the battle of Cuba . . . that battle cannot be considered ended with the mere withdrawal of Russian missiles . . . it must end by returning millions of Cubans to liberty."[2]

But President Kennedy turned the question of Cuba aside with the comment that the Organization of American States was the proper forum in which to debate the case of Cuba. His address spoke of building "a wall of free men" around Cuba, a remark that reportedly nearly cauterized the gastric glands of Guatemala's gutty President Miguel Ydígoras Fuentes. What came out of the Costa Rican conference was a series of parades, excellent publicity for President Kennedy in the United States, and an eight-page document. Six and one-half pages dealt with the economics of the Alliance for Progress; political considerations were squeezed into one and one-half pages.

Upon his return from Costa Rica, President Kennedy was asked by reporters what had happened to the strong anti-Castro stand expected of him when he departed. Ignoring the public utterances of the leaders of Central America, he blandly stated that no anti-Castro views had been expressed to him. He observed that responsibility for a blockade or other meaningful action taken against Cuba would have to be borne by the United States, not by Central America, and spoke of other "commitments," among them West Berlin, and, of all things, South Korea. President Kennedy simply was not disposed to deal with the beachhead of Soviet power in the Caribbean.

The Cubans were disposed to deal with it, however, and they fought through the balance of 1963 and well into 1964—against the militia, even against Russian troops which President Kennedy was saying at the time were leaving Cuba in response to his repeated requests to Premier Khrushchev. The President's weak stand was directly at odds with the sentiments of the American people. On September 23, 1963, the *Washington Post* published a survey conducted by public opinion pollster Louis Harris in which it was revealed that "77% of the American people think the President should insist that Russian troops evacuate Cuba," and "67% would support U.S. re-imposition of the October 1962 blockade if Russia fails to remove the troops." The report concluded: "The American people would like to see a more decisive stand taken against Russian troops remaining in Cuba. The vast majority of the American people believes Mr. Kennedy should be more insistent that the last vestige of armed forces be removed."

Cuban freedom fighters were in tune with the attitude of their American brethren, if for no other reason than that they were now fighting the Russians. President Kennedy's assertions that the Russians were withdrawing from Cuba were met with open-mouthed wonder by Cuba's escaping refugees. To the contrary. Reports coming out of the island indicated that the Russians were building permanent camps, bringing in their families, and had even expropriated farms in Las Villas, Camaguey, and Oriente Provinces where Soviet menials were put to work to produce food especially for Russian troops.

By the summer of 1963, stories of conflicts between anti-Castro resistance forces and elements of the Soviet military based in Cuba could no longer be ignored. Miguel Velasquez, one such freedom fighter, told me the following story upon his arrival in Miami:

"We operated in the hills of Oriente Province. The morning of March 26, a band of us attacked the garrison guarding the Nicaro mines. Our assault surprised the garrison, and we succeeded in wounding six and killing two others. As we withdrew we were attacked by a group of Russian soldiers dressed in Cuban Army uniforms. They overpowered our smaller group, capturing twelve, and shooting our commander Armando Govea." The captured anti-Castro patriots were subsequently tried at Mayarí, Oriente Province. "A Russian officer took part in the drumhead court which summarily condemned the twelve to death," said Velasquez. Velasquez was a courier for guerrilla groups operating in the area. When Govea's guerrilla band was captured, Velasquez's name became known to Castro's counter-insurgency forces, and he was ordered by his resistance chief to get out of the country.

That the Russians were indeed wearing Cuban Army uniforms came to light from other sources. Exhaustive interviews with escapees to Miami turned up significant information as to the numbers of Soviet troops in Cuba. Through a stroke of sheer luck I came upon the head seamstress of the San Ambrosio uniform factory who had just managed to get out of Cuba with the help of fishermen (all flights between Cuba and the United States were cancelled during the missile crisis and not resumed for three years). Here is what Señora Pérez Cabrera told me:

"For three years, until I escaped from Cuba last month, I was the head seamstress at the San Ambrosio military post where most of the military uniforms are made. Just two months before I escaped, the supply officer of the Cuban General Staff issued an urgent order for us to manufacture 1,000 Cuban Army uniforms *daily*. Great speed was demanded, and we worked overtime. The average size of the uniforms struck me as very peculiar. Cubans are relatively small people, but the order was largely in the 44 and 46 sizes. I thought it was a mistake, and examined the order again. The order stated clearly that the uniforms were for Soviet troops who are awaiting delivery."

Upon further questioning regarding the number of days spent in manufacturing, it turned out that at least 40,000 uniforms had been delivered, just from the San Ambrosio factory alone. Señora Pérez Cabrera could not hazard a guess as to how many oversized uniforms were turned out, if any, by Cuba's other three uniform factories.

Señora Pérez Cabrera's estimates of the number of Russian soldiers in Cuba in 1963 found an echo from unidentified official sources in the Pentagon. The *New York Times* carried a story on April 20 citing Pentagon sources as saying that Soviet armed forces in Cuba may run as high as 40,000. Claims by President Kennedy and Secretary of State Rusk that Russian military personnel were thinning out were indirectly challenged by our intelligence sources who said that the Russians most probably were rotating troops to Cuba, not withdrawing them. Hanson Baldwin, the military editor of the *New York Times*, pointed out in his article published on April 20 that it had been relatively easy to spot the numbers of Soviets leaving the island (their departure was as ostentatious as the withdrawal of the missiles in November, 1962), but not the numbers that had been brought in. Baldwin also wrote that some Pentagon officials were now calling the lodgement of Soviet power in Cuba the "Soviet expeditionary force." And just how strong those officials were in their opinions is revealed in a passage taken from the Baldwin article: "Though many intelligence experts and some Government officials say they do not know how many Russian troops are in Cuba, one said he would bet a year's pay that the number was closer to 30,000 than to 17,000, and a month's pay that it was closer to 40,000 than to 17,000."

A puzzling factor in the stationing of large numbers of Soviet troops in Cuba is that President Kennedy apparently accepted Khrushchev's claim at the time of the missile crisis that those troops were mere support forces for missiles. And, when the President accepted, as well, Khrushchev's assurances that all missiles had been withdrawn, he was forced to accept the corollary proposition that the need for Soviet personnel no longer existed. For the President to admit that Russian troops remained in Cuba in large numbers would obviously require an explanation as to just why they were there—an explanation that would have turned President Kennedy's emotional speech at the time of the missile crisis, and post-crisis claims of victory, to ashes. This was why, apparently, President Kennedy chose to make the facts fit the theory when, on April 3, he claimed that Soviet troop strength in Cuba had been reduced to 13,000.

To the serious observer, for example Hanson Baldwin, President Kennedy's claims regarding Russian troop reductions were very thin gruel to sustain his claims to victory in the missile crisis. Senator Kenneth B. Keating of New York sensed that the New Frontier was manipulating a post-crisis cover-up, just as it had manipulated a cover-up following the Bay of Pigs failure two years earlier. Saying that the continued presence of Soviet troops in Cuba posed "a very serious situation," Senator Keating badgered the President, charging that his claims were "nothing more than talk."[3] Few were aware at that time of the Kennedy-Khrushchev exchange of letters, and on each occasion that a question was asked whether a deal had been made between the two heads of state, it was heatedly denied by the New Frontier. President Kennedy was in a strait jacket of his own making, for, after having virtually invited the Russians to occupy Cuba before and during the missile crisis, he could force them out only by running the very real risk that Khrushchev would make public the very deal which the President and his New Frontier denied had ever been made.

That the Russians were in Cuba in very large numbers was a fact. Russians assumed behind-the-scenes command of the provinces of Las Villas, Camaguey, and Oriente, and stationed Karelin Romanovsky, Nicolai Stepanov, and Vilenkin Krestinsky to run operations, respectively, in those three provinces. And Russian military personnel physically took charge of all heavy construction in the country—cement plants, lumber mills, transport, and auxiliary industries. The open Russian takeover, and the conversion of much-needed housing materials by the Soviets into a war industry was largely responsible for one of the most serious anti-Communist outbreaks since Castro took power in January 1959.

At a meeting held in the National Labor Palace on September 11, 1963, the National Federation of Construction Workers rebelled against the sacrifice of housing instituted to meet Russia's military requirements. Old-line Communist labor boss Lázaro Peña was late in arriving at the meeting. When he did, he was met with demands to return the construction industry to civil needs, to pay the salaries of workers when they were laid off after the very faulty Russian equipment broke down, and to publicize their demands in the press. As Peña tried to restore order, he was drowned out by cries of "We want freedom! We are hungry! We want to be Cubans!" Failing to restore order, Peña declared the meeting to be out of order and retired from the Labor Palace, prompting the unruly delegates to smash chairs, tear out light fixtures and wreck the hall.

The next day, Radio Progreso termed the meeting "clearly counterrevolutionary" and charged that the anti-Castro forces had tried to "capitalize" on an otherwise peaceful quest for higher wages. On September 19, Peña found it necessary to summon 200 hardcore Communists from the union for the purpose of castigating those officials who had participated in the September 11 protest. They met on September 24 and were perfunctorily ordered to "reaffirm our revolutionary solidarity." To head-off inevitable mutterings against his bludgeoning the officials into submission, Peña said at the meeting: "The counterrevolutionaries will say tomorrow that this new meeting was very poorly attended, or that the heavy-equipment workers were not here, or that coercion was used."

However that may be, Cuban resistance to the Soviet takeover continued in armed insurrection. In a remarkable, unpublicized engagement between Communist forces and freedom fighters at Jatibonico, on the border between Las Villas and Camaguey, Russian troops were sent in to save the militia from defeat. At least 30 militiamen and two Russians were killed in the engagement, but the anti-Castro rebels also lost heavily. Their chieftain in the mountains of Escambray, Pedro Ramírez, was reportedly killed by a direct hit from a Soviet recoilless rifle. Observers recalled a June 19 statement by State Department spokesman Richard Phillips that the United States "would not stand idly by" if Soviet troops were used to suppress internal revolt, as it did in Hungary in 1956. Yet, another resistance group was tracked down by joint Soviet-Cuban forces and its leader, Pedro Sánchez Rodríguez, alias "Perico," was shot. And despite announcements over Radio Progreso that this was indeed so, the State Department remained mum. And as other resistance leaders —Thondike, Machetero, Arnaldo, Cara Linda, for example—were systematically tracked down and crushed, the State Department said less and less about its pledge not to permit "another Hungary." In time, this pledge, like so many others made by the New Frontier, became a dead letter.

Urban resistance was generally much less spectacular than the burning of cane fields, guerrilla bands racing through the hills, and the like. But it was there. Ibrahim Quintana, a mortician of the Rivero Funeral Home in Havana, provided first-hand testimony to the constant slaughter of Cubans by the Castro regime, saying that the shooting of anti-Castro Cubans reached the point where the government was forced to resort to the falsification of death certificates. The 28-year-old mortician said that "street murders are commonplace, and occur whenever the victims indicate the slightest disrespect for the regime." How the government handles such embarrassments was also revealed by Quintana: "The victim is sent to a government first-aid station, and a mortuary is telephoned to come and remove the body. The reason why government aid stations are used as the intermediary is that the government attendant makes out a death certificate which states that the dead person was killed by means other than shooting—for example; it will state that he was run over by a truck, fell and was mortally hurt, or some such explanation." The give-away is when the government orders the mortuary not to permit the family to see the body. "In 80% of the cases in which the death certificate gives reasons other than shooting as the cause of death, we find that the person died of gunshot wounds."

As a mortician, Quintana was able to learn what was going on in most of Havana's cemeteries, and of the deaths by execution of prisoners in Cuba's jails. "In La Cabaña Fortress alone," said Quintana, "more than 30 Cubans are shot each month. A functionary of the city morgue, a Señor Menéndez, has the job of accompanying the bodies to Colón cemetery. He delivers the bodies to us at the Rivero Funeral Home during the night. Then, almost daily at 6 a.m. cars move out from our mortuary, with the bodies on the floors of passenger cars so as to not attract notice, and go to Colón cemetery preceded by other passenger cars filled with secret police. The dead have a small piece of paper bearing their names tied to their wrists. The papers are removed by the cemetery attendant. He has strict instructions to wait three days following burial and then to send a telegram to the next of kin to report to the cemetery where the attendant indicates where the dead person is buried—almost invariably in an unmarked grave."

There is one detail that precedes the executions in La Cabaña fortress. Prior to the victim's execution by firing squad, the regime ghoulishly removes blood from each victim. Dr. Virginia de Mirabal Quesada, an escapee from Cuba through Mexico answered a query by me regarding numerous reports of blood being drained from the victims of Communist firing squads in Cuba: "It is absolutely true. Before being shot by firing squad, Cuban patriots are first taken to a small first-aid room at La Cabaña where the Communists extract blood, between a quart and a quart-and-a-half, from each victim. It is then placed in a blood bank. Some of the plasma is shipped to North Vietnam." The Cuban doctor added: "Sometimes the victims are so weak that they have to be carried to the execution wall. Other times, some with bad hearts die right in the first-aid room."

For all of these reasons, and many more, the Communist regime of Fidel Castro met with a spiralling resistance that seemed almost without end. Over and above the uniform pay scales decreed for the lower categories in the system of production, the Communist elite of Cuba got what they wanted while the people suffered from inflation, criminal shortages of food, high prices, and arbitrary deductions from their wages. As the work quotas increased and the pay decreased, the living standard of the average Cuban sank to the level of austerity or worse. Added to the problems was yet another. Soviet economic policy toward Cuba was one of plunder and graft on a grand scale. One result was sporadic and unequal distribution of goods, with shortages everywhere in the economy. Another more dangerous result to the regime was that the gap between the living standard of the "new class" and the ordinary people of Cuba was a hundred times greater with regard to food and clothing than it ever was in that country during capitalism. There was, however, one significant difference. In earlier days the poor were a minority and most of those were rural, with gardens and orchards which helped to provide the tropically located Cubans with a fair diet. With the advent of Communism, the fruit of Cuba's trees and gardens became state property. The result of Communist government planning was that the poor were many and the privileged new class were few. There was no middle class.

In the period 1963-1967 virtually every single item of food in Cuba was rationed, even sugar and coffee in that sugar and coffee producing country. Each Cuban could buy only one and one-quarter ounces of coffee each week, hardly enough to wet the palate, while rations for the starchy *boniato* and potatoes were set, respectively, at one pound per month, and one pound per week. And in a country where bananas were a major staple, none were available. Another staple, rice, was rationed at three pounds per person per month. All sorts of fruit—oranges, grapefruit, and the like—so abundant in pre-Castro Cuba, could not be purchased except through the prescription of a medical doctor. Milk was available only to children, and then only in sparse quantities, as were eggs which were rationed at five per month for each child under six years of age. The meat-consuming Cuban was restricted to three-quarters of a pound of meat each week, but this commodity like so many others, was rarely available. Two pairs of shoes of very poor quality, mostly canvas, could be purchased each year. Used shoes brought up to $40 and $50 on the black market. Men and women were limited to six pairs of socks or stockings each year, usually of bad quality, and men were permitted to buy one suit and three pairs of trousers yearly. Not only were the clothes poor, they were difficult to mend when torn. Cuba got most of its needles and thread from Communist countries, and the supply was sporadic. Zippers were virtually unobtainable. The houses generally were dark at night because of the shortage of electric power. There was a complete absence of 100-watt bulbs and even 40-to-60 watt bulbs were seldom to be found.

The Cuban people knew that their miseries stemmed from the political alliance between Castro and the Soviet Union. They knew that Cuba's incompetent economic planners and its Communist bureaucrats were responsible for that alliance which had brought such misery to the country. Cuba's produce went to Russia while the Cubans virtually starved in a land of plenty. Even the $60 million in food and medicines which had been paid by the New Frontier to ransom the Bay of Pigs prisoners had been shipped off to Russia. In many instances, the packages containing U.S. medicines were emptied of their contents and replaced by crude Soviet manufactured substitutes. And, following the damaging hurricane which hit Cuba the fall of 1963, Americans, Europeans, and international relief organizations sent packages for the relief of victims which became the property of the state. When the packages, addressed to individuals, arrived in Cuba, they were confiscated at the Central Post Office and their contents marked for distribution to loyal Communist followers. And they paid for them while hundreds of thousands of Cuban *guajiros* were punished for their resistance by being denied shoes.

What happened to shoes which were shipped to Cuba by philanthropic individuals and organizations is told by Fides Martin, a laborer in the former Nestle condensed milk plant in Sancti-Spiritus, Las Villas Province: "When two or three pair of shoes sent from abroad trickle down to a local union, a Communist supply delegate calls a meeting, makes a speech that imperialism is to blame for our underdeveloped state, and says that the Revolution is working to overcome the situation. He then asks who wants to buy the shoes. Everyone, of course, raises their hands. He then makes another little speech, saying that those dedicated to the 'peoples revolution' are the most deserving, and hands the shoes over to known Communist militants who then pay for them."

Grumbling and passive work resistance became commonplace in Cuba's cities. The sabotaging of rolling stock in the sugar producing countryside was matched by sabotage of urban transportation in the cities. Speaking at a National Congress of Taxi Drivers, Transport Minister Omar Fernández criticized Cuba's taxi drivers because they often refused to pick up passengers. And when the Ministry of Interior tried to incorporate the drivers into its spy system, it met with considerable resistance from the free-spirited taxi drivers. In March 1963, nine of them were put on trial, in the words of the Communist prosecutor, "for displaying an uncooperative attitude, and failure to maintain revolutionary vigilance during the night hours." The charge arose out of refusal to become night-time informers for the government.

Cuba's bus drivers were excoriated in a May 18, 1963, editorial in the Communist newspaper *Hoy*, which said: "Bus drivers run their busses up onto curbs without regard for the fact that this practice ruins the tires," adding: "How can we permit such irresponsibility with the riches that belong to the people?" The May 18 wail in *Hoy* about Cuba's bus drivers was an echo of Transport Minister Fernández's charges made in February, when he said : "The most counterrevolutionary element in our country is Cuba's bus drivers." They, together with the taxi drivers were, in Fernández's words: "negative elements, *lumpen proletarians*, and delinquents, who refuse to do their work properly." He accused them of creating a state of "pure anarchy" in Cuba's urban transportation system, said that they "drove crazily, without regard for their equipment." He had to assign one militiaman to each eight transport workers "to observe their attitudes."

From that moment forward, Cuba's bus drivers were the object of almost daily attack in *Revolución* and *Hoy*, which published accounts of drivers missing bus stops and permitting passengers to ride free. More important, two occasions were reported where busses were driven into crowds of Communist demonstrators, their drivers pleading that the brakes had given out, a maddening excuse in parts-sparse Cuba, because it had the ring of truth. The situation got so bad that on August 27, 1963, the government established "popular tribunals" which, in the wording of the decree, judged "those workers in the field of public transportation for their infractions against the people and the state." The government had good reason to be alarmed. The effect of sabotage was felt in industry where the decay in public transportation made it easier for Cuba's sullen workers to come up with excuses for being late to work or for failing to show up at all. In a final, desperate, move to get the labor force to work on time, the government commandeered automobiles and trained domestic servants to drive them on bus routes. Within a week, the accident rate reduced the number of available cars to less than 50%, and this Communist experiment in public transportation was dropped without fanfare.

The reason for the sabotage of public transportation by Cuba's drivers is revealed in statistics. In 1958, a majority of Cuba's 4,459 busses were owned by their drivers. Most of the vehicles were modern General Motors products, many of them air-conditioned, with automatic transmissions. Owner-drivers developed highly efficient cooperatives, and worked with national and municipal transport authorities in developing 303 urban, inter-urban, and provincial bus lines which brought public transportation to the smallest towns and villages in the country. The Communist government did not laud this achievement; it destroyed it. The busses were confiscated, and the driver-owners impressed into service at a salary of 85 cents an hour, thereby setting off the struggle between a genuine democratic cooperative effort and the Communist state.

As the number of General Motor busses in Havana dwindled spectacularly from 1,600 to less than 800 through sabotage and the lack of spare parts, the Communist regime imported Czech-made replacements. The bulk of them had manual transmissions and easily shattered glass. None were air-conditioned, and few were equipped with storage for baggage. Ill-adapted to Cuba's terrain and climate, the Czech busses broke down and were easy targets for the sabotage visited on them by their drivers, maintenance crews, and conductors. Passengers slashed the seats, broke the doors, and, in moving bulky objects around inside the busses, managed to shatter the brittle glass windows. Within three months of operation of the Czech busses, according to hundreds of Cuban escapees interviewed in Miami, the public transportation system had reached the point where the Castro regime put into use Soviet military trucks, equipped with makeshift wooden benches and a small ladder extending down from the tail gate.

On January 2, 1964, Fidel Castro revealed the depth of his desperation. Speaking at an enormous military parade in Havana he shouted that he was determined to buy locomotives, planes, taxis, and other items of equipment which "are urgently needed by the Revolution," and excoriated the people of Cuba for creating the drain on scarce dollars. Following the Castro speech, on January 8, Radio Progreso reported that severe measures were being taken to curb Cuba's fractious elements in public transportation, following an "important" meeting between government heads and the Communist-controlled Railway Workers Union. "With respect to train wrecks," Radio Progreso reported, "it was agreed to ask the State Railway Enterprise and the Ministry of Transport to punish those responsible. They should be punished uniformly and inflexibly, with one year's suspension of work without pay or benefit [meaning the withdrawal of ration cards]." The meeting, said Radio Progreso, pinpointed the cause of the train wrecks and spoke of sabotage in the following terms: "Those implicated in a train wreck must be taken before the State Railway Enterprise, the labor union, and before the courts. To combat theft, the State Railway Enterprise and the union will take joint action against the thief, including his final and complete punishment and indictment before the courts."

To squeeze the vise of the totalitarian Communist state more tightly against the people of Cuba, Armed Forces Minister Raúl Castro announced the military conscription of all males between the ages of 17 and 45. Commencing on January 1, 1964, no one of draft age was permitted to leave the country through the sparse means available to them—a few flights each week to Mexico and Spain. And while the date for the call-up of conscripts was set by decree as March 1, the regime immediately put its apparatus of intimidation into high gear. The neighborhood committees of informers went from house to house, demanding immediate registration, warning that the last to register would be the first called up to work as forced labor. In other words, military conscription provided the gimmick behind which the regime recruited a slave labor force. In announcing military conscription, Raúl Castro made it clear that he had in mind another important purpose, that of curbing anti-Communist sentiments when he said that the conscription law would apply "unrelentingly to bums and loafers."

As a result of the conscription measure, the straits of Florida became jammed with Cubans fleeing to the United States by boat. In one day alone, 167 Cubans arrived in Florida in seven crowded boats, and Castro put his Russian MIGs, and patrol boats to work shooting them out of the water. One boat, the "Ballerina," was strafed and sunk by MIGs in international waters and its eight occupants were killed or drowned. Another boat was intercepted by a Russian patrol boat near Faro Lobo, a British possession, and its seven occupants, including three children, were lost. The panic created by the conscription was general. Men took tubes of truck tires and built rafts of them; four youths fled Cuba in a 17-foot rowboat and were rescued by an American merchant ship several days later while drifting in the gulf stream. Truly, Castro and his Russian masters had turned the Straits of Florida into the Berlin wall of the Western Hemisphere. And there was no counter-action ordered by President Kennedy's New Frontier or President Johnson's Great Society to protect the fleeing Cubans from MIG and patrol boat attacks on the high seas. Worse, there were no protests made from official Washington to the slaughter of Cubans on our very doorstep.

The Human Rights Commission of the Organization of American States has documented the barbarities committed against the Cuban people, stating: "In Cuba there is organized political terror of an unimagined extent. The reality of Castroist political prisons is more cruel and extensive than what one can imagine. . . . In some districts, 'executions' are staged, using salute or blank cartridge which cause many Cubans to go insane as a result of such mental tortures."[4] By early 1964, 57 prisons and 18 concentration camps dotted Cuba, holding an estimated 100,000 political prisoners in a state of servitude to the regime.

Perhaps because of the lack of a sustained public stance by the United States against those barbarities (and certainly not encouraged to help us) the British and French punched holes in the U.S. boycott by extending credit arrangements to Castro for the purchase of busses and locomotives, thus undercutting the magnificent resistance of the Cuban people to their oppressors. British cynicism regarding President Kennedy's policy to isolate Cuba economically was underscored in an editorial in the English paper, *The Guardian*. It concluded that economic sanctions alone would not drive Castro and the Communists from power, and that therefore British trade with Cuba was both logical and necessary to both parties. Contrary to the fact, *The Guardian* also said that it was the unfriendly policy of the United States that had driven Castro into the hands of the Russians in the first place. However, the British certainly had a point when, in the House of Commons, members scored President Kennedy for selling wheat to Russia in 1963, saying that the wheat would nourish, not only the Soviet Army, but Communist guerrillas throughout the world.

British members of Parliament were, of course, as correct in scoring the double standard of the New Frontier as they were incorrect in rationalizing their own economic interest because of the errors of that same New Frontier. The facts were these: In their rush to develop heavy industry and to try to catch up with the United States in missile development, the Soviets had over-reached themselves. Collective farms in Russia were beset with the same problems as were the collective farms in Cuba, and, in purchasing grain from Canada and elsewhere, the Soviet gold reserve was being depleted faster than their mines could replace it.

Yet, President Kennedy chose to help the Russians to close the gap in their own economy and that of their satellites, such as Cuba, because, in the words of Theodore Sorensen: "He welcomed the opportunity to demonstrate to the Soviet leaders that the improved climate of agreement [following the missile crisis] could serve the interests of both nations."[5] However, the President found that the Agricultural Act of 1961 contained an amendment which forbade the sale of subsidized agricultural commodities to unfriendly nations, and the Congress clearly believed that the Soviet Union was unfriendly. President Kennedy's zeal in providing the Soviets with wheat made some of the keenest observers in Washington wonder if the blackmail inherent in the Soviet missile agreement had not been carried over to include financial support, as well, to the Soviet Union.

The President armed friendly members of Congress with speeches and statistics; he went to work in persuading Polish-language newspapers in Chicago and New York to support him; arm-twisted the longshoreman to call off an announced boycott of ships taking wheat to Russia; overcame an almost solid phalanx of opposition to him by the State, Agriculture, Labor, and Commerce Departments; yielded even to the impudent Soviet haggling about freight rates to be charged the Russians for shipping on Free World bottoms. Finally, President Kennedy delivered to Russia (and to Cuba) the wheat needed by both Communist countries to survive. Thus, it was little wonder that France, Great Britain, and Canada saw in President Kennedy's moves an abdication of the U.S. role as leader of the anti-Communist world, and chose not to be left out in the cold while the two supermen, Kennedy and Khrushchev, decided what was best for them.

And what was best for K-K combine most certainly was not what was best for the youth of Cuba where Communist repression was particularly strong. As in other Communist states, the children of Cuba are a particular target of the police state. Those whose parents are known to be anti-Communist, or even backsliders of the regime, are promptly separated from their families, packed off to "scholarship schools," and made wards of the state. Houses in Havana, abandoned by Cubans who fled into exile, have been converted into barracks and youngsters moved into them with precious little regard for the most elementary need for privacy as between sexes. To the contrary.

One purpose of what amounts to state-encouraged promiscuity, apart from that of breaking down traditional Spanish morality, is to create conditions for blackmail, a common Communist practice. Should a "student" in one of the schools later decide to defect from the Party, or to refuse to carry out a distasteful task, a written or perhaps photographic record of promiscuous behavior during his years of puberty provides an inducement to think twice. Basically, however, the idea is to break down the traditional, tightly knit, family life of the Cubans. The rebellious *guajiros* and their families come in for special attention. What happened to one is related in the story told to me by a 15-year-old country girl, Migdalia Gómez:[6]

"A meeting was held December 28, 1962 in Palique de Yateras which the Communists said everyone in the area must attend. My father, Fernando Gómez, refused to go because he said that he had to earn money to buy food for the family and had no time for the bombast. My brother and I went so that our family would not be pointed out as not having attended. During the meeting, the Communist Director of Palique called me over and said that he had gotten me a *beca* (fellowship) so I could study in Havana.

"I was terrified, and said that I did not want to go, but wanted to stay with my parents. He looked at me and told me that the political reliability of my parents was suspect, and that everyone would be paid off as they deserved. There were some who were with the revolution and some who were not, and that the regime knew who they were. Then he told me, gritting his teeth, that he was disgusted with my attitude. I was frightened, because everyone knows what the Communists do when you go against their wishes. So I told him that I would accept the fellowship. He smiled then, and said that I would be educated and learn how to make dresses."

On January 2, 1963, Migdalia was summoned to Havana. It was eight kilometers from her house to the railway station. She made the trip on foot, carrying her belongings in a rucksack. "Upon arriving at the station," said Migdalia, "we were taken to a railway car used to haul sugar cane to the sugar mills. The trip took four days, and we slept on the floor of the car like animals. There were 57 other girls who had been 'recruited' in a similar fashion, and upon arrival in Havana we were taken to a house in the Miramar section.

"They taught us nothing but how to love Fidel Castro and Communism. Indoctrination classes began at 6:00 a.m. and ended at 12:00 noon. They resumed again at 1:00 and ended at 10:00 p.m. with a break for two hours between 5:00 and 7:00 in the evening. They talked a great deal about Russia in the classes, told us that religion was a lie and that God did not exist. Our only father was Fidel Castro, because we had only been born from a bout of pleasure between our parents. Those whom we believed to be our parents took care of us only because they felt obliged to do so out of a guilty conscience. Castro was the father of all, because as we could see, he took care of us and fended for us. Our 'mother' was the secretary to President Osvaldo Dorticós, Elena Gil. She was in charge of the fellowship students.

"Many times they asked us if we would like to visit the socialist countries. The question was always asked in a loud voice, and we were afraid not to say yes. But then came the selections. As the date neared to leave Cuba and go to Russia, Czechoslovakia, Poland, Bulgaria, or heaven knows where, many girls committed suicide by jumping off the balconies. Finally, students were prohibited from going onto the balconies, and they were all fenced off. We were totally fenced in for four months, yet some of the girls managed to jump and crippled themselves.

"When we wanted our family to visit us we had a bad time. We had to request permission. When we did so we would be asked if something was wrong, if we were unhappy, and so on. Sometimes we would cry when they asked us, and we were told that if we continued to cry, we would never see our families. We learned very soon not to cry, because we were locked into dark closets and not permitted to come out until we promised not to cry.

"They were particularly on guard at night. Woe be unto any girl who tried to pray. They said that our parents soon would be made to feel the wrath of the regime if we did not shut up. Then they said that it was our parents who really were to blame, because they had fooled us into thinking that religion was a good thing. Actually, they said, religion was responsible for only bad things."

Visits were regulated. One relative to each "student" was permitted each week, on a Saturday. The relative had to obtain an identification card in advance, and no one else in the family was permitted to use it.

"Even when our relatives visited," said Migdalia, "there was someone always listening to our conversation. We were always supervised." One day Migdalia talked about her "sick sister" at such length that her uncle understood what she was trying to say. He came back the following Saturday, and said that Migdalia's sister was very ill and that Migdalia ought to come home and see her. The uncle had arranged the deception in advance. Migdalia's sister was confined to bed for three weeks with the cooperation of a friendly doctor who prescribed medicines and reported her illness to the local neighborhood committees of informers.

Finally, Migdalia was permitted to visit her alleged sick sister. Instead of going to her home in Oriente Province, however, Migdalia and her uncle escaped from the Province of Pinar del Río by a fishing boat commanded by a friend. She found her brother on the boat. It had been arranged that he also escape from Cuba.

At no time did Migdalia learn dressmaking as the regime had advertised. "Some of the fellowship students," said Migdalia, "thought they were going to be educated in the law profession. They were in the fellowship centers for a few months, then sent off to the camp at Minas del Frío in Oriente to learn guerrilla training, followed by another six months of Communist indoctrination." It appears that some children received very limited vocational training, but this is incidental to the larger political design of the regime.

Migdalia Gómez concluded her interview by saying: "The young people who have been impressed into the scholarship centers are the saddest youngsters in the world."

And Jose León Fuentes, a 20-year-old, relates his experience with the fellowship program:

"The committees for the defense of the revolution [packs of neighborhood informers] in Puerto Esperanza offered me a fellowship so I could study. 'When you have received an education,' they told me, 'you will then have a world of opportunity!' I told them I wanted to be educated because I had only gone through the third grade in school. However, I also told them I wanted to learn carpentry or masonry because these are trades which are always in demand in Cuba. They agreed, and I was enrolled in the Casa Blanca school in Havana. First they said that I was to have general education, to which I agreed.

"However, from the very first day they commenced teaching Communism. The teachings began and ended with unceasing attacks upon the United States, and the fiction that we had always been exploited by American imperialism. Every Cuban knows that American investments and technical advances were respected in Cuba for having created jobs, more opportunities to learn, and contributed to our standard of living. Therefore, the Communist teachings were quite a shock. I don't think that any of my classmates believed this.

"Months went by and we learned nothing. They never again spoke to me of classes of carpentry or masonry. When I asked about them, they evaded the questions. Finally, I realized that they had no intention of doing anything other than making us conform to the Communist police state. We all resented this bitterly. We knew perfectly well that prior to Castro we at least had our individual freedoms! The smallest children went to school, even under Batista, and we could always buy clothing and shoes, and had plenty to eat. Under Communism, the only way to get the things they said were the result of capitalist exploitation was to become a Communist! *Bueno,* I prefer to be free.

"I soon learned that the Casa Blanca school was a navy school. I also discovered together with my other fellowhship students, that it was a school for war. We were taught how to handle arms, to attack and defend ourselves, and to march in military exercises. None of us liked it, and all of us resented the way we were used by the regime. The instructors were Spanish Communists.

"Many times we were sent into combat against the Cuban patriots in the Organos and Escambray mountains who were fighting against Castro's militia. This was to give us experience in actual combat. We didn't want to fight fellow Cubans, and finally they took us away. There is one thing that I learned. Indoctrination is a double-edged sword, because instead of making us hate the 'imperialists,' we soon came to appreciate what so-called imperialism had done for Cuba, for its economy, and for democracy."

León Fuentes, graduated, then joined the Cuban MRR (Movement for the Recovery of the Revolution) underground resistance group and was later exfiltrated from Cuba to Miami.

Testimony regarding officially sponsored sexual license and attendant brutality and blackmail in Cuba is heavily documented in several sections of the 65-page report issued by the OAS Human Rights Commission, supplemented by my own interviews with refugees over a period of five years in Miami. Between the two sources, a picture of deliberate moral debasement emerges, as, for example, the testimony given me by a former clerk who knows the situation through having worked in one of the "scholarship schools." A typist, Señora Concepción Toledo, was repulsed by the sight of the deliberate corruption of Cuba's youth, defected, and managed together with nine others to come to Miami clandestinely by small boat. She had this to say: "This may sound like an exaggeration to those who knew pre-Communist Cuba, but the fact is that today free love is encouraged on the grounds that it 'liberates' youngsters from their 'bourgeois' ties to the past." Those who refuse to go along, said Señora Toledo, are sent to work on state farms, known as Military Units to Aid in Production, a euphemism for slave labor camps. Some of the moral debasement visited on Cuba's youth comes through in her next remark: "Many of the teen-agers are pregnant, and the government has set aside a special ward in Calixto García Hospital, known as 'the hall of abortions,' where the operations take place at no cost to the individual."

Disillusionment was everywhere, and burst into the open with the trial in Cuba of a Communist informer, Marcos Rodríguez Alfonso. During the trial, lasting from March 14 to March 20, 1964, old-line Communists and members of Castro's 26th of July movement, paraded to the witness stand where they unravelled a story of deceit and intrigue that exposed the Cuban Communist Party as wanton murderers, and splattered filth over the entire structure of the Castro government.

The story began back in 1956, when Marcos Rodríguez Alfonso, a member of the Socialist (i. e. Communist) Youth in Cuba, was a familiar figure on the campus of the University of Havana. He dressed in a Bohemian manner, wearing sandals with pennies wedged between their straps. Marcos Rodríguez Alfonso was seldom seem without a book beneath his arm. A promising intellectual at the age of 19, Rodríguez Alfonso sought the company of those student groups which showed the most promise of elevating him to a position of power. As a Communist, however, he upheld the doctrine of "mass resistance" to Batista, and criticized what he called the "aggressive methods of fighting" the dictatorship, acts carried on outside the framework of the Party. He was thus somewhat less than successful in gaining the confidence of the Student Directorate (DRE), but was accepted by some of their members because of his known hatred for the Batista regime.

On March 13, 1957, members of the DRE made their brave and futile attack on the Presidential Palace and attempted to assassinate President Fulgencio Batista. They were beaten back by Batista forces and most of them were killed. Four managed to escape, however, and for a month they moved from hiding place to hiding place as Batista's police tried to track down and destroy all remnants of the revolutionary group. On April 19, 1957, three (Fructuoso Rodríguez, Pedro Carbó Servia, and José Machado) were taken to an apartment at No. 7 Humboldt Street in Havana that was occupied by a fourth DRE member, Joe Westbrook. When they arrived, about midnight, a friend of Westbrook's, Marcos Rodríguez Alfonso, was there.

During the early morning hours, Rodríguez Alfonso argued bitterly with the DRE members over their tactics which, he told them, not only had ended in failure, but also had placed the lives of many anti-Batista actionists in jeopardy. The DRE countered by scoring the lack of action on the part of the Communist Party, saying further that Rodríguez Alfonso and the Party were cowards. Humiliated and angry, early the next morning the young Communist telephoned Colonel Esteban Ventura, the most feared officer of Batista's repressive police apparatus, and made an appointment to see him that afternoon. At the afternoon meeting, Rodríguez Alfonso told Ventura where the four DRE fugitives were hiding. Ventura's men promptly surrounded the block, broke into the apartment at No. 7 Humboldt Street and, with no effort made to take prisoners, riddled the four DRE men with machine gun fire.

Pretending to be a fugitive from Ventura, Rodríguez Alfonso obtained asylum in the Embassy of Brazil in Havana. Given a safe conduct by the Batista police, who knew that he had been an informer for them, Rodríguez Alfonso went first to Costa Rica and then to Mexico. When Batista fell on January 1, 1959, the young Communist informer went back to Cuba where he promptly obtained a job in the Rebel Army, first in its cultural section and then as chief of the Department of Instruction. It was when he was in the latter position that two members of the DRE and the wife of one of the murdered students recognized him and, becoming suspicious, appealed to Comandante Camilo Cienfuegos, who had him arrested and held for investigation. But Marcos Rodríguez Alfonso was set free very quickly on the grounds that evidence of his complicity in the killings was lacking. He was permitted to leave the country on a Czech scholarship and later became an intelligence officer in the Cuban Embassy in Prague.

In January 1961, Rodríguez Alfonso was extradited from Czechoslovakia to Havana by the Cuban government on grounds that he had become an agent for a foreign power. He languished in jail for more than three years. At some point in the course of time he was cleared of suspicion of espionage against the Cuban government, but the charge of complicity in the murder of the DRE students was again raised. On March 14, Rodríguez Alfonso's trial opened with the presentation of his confession of guilt. The trial continued for six days and attracted public attention because of its length in a country where swift and summary "revolutionary justice" was the rule, and because of public interest in solving the Humboldt street murders. Mentioned in the news media was the fact that Faure Chomon, former DRE chief, and several ex-DRE members had testified at the trial. And suddenly, all of Cuba was talking about it.

Evident attempts to keep secret the revelations made at the trial were shattered, and Castro himself ordered full coverage of the proceedings, saying that "certain elements" were trying to discredit his regime. But he failed to say exactly who those elements wishing to harm his regime might be. In a letter published in the communist newspaper, *Hoy*, Castro left no doubt of his conviction that Rodríguez was guilty. What he apparently wanted to do was to squelch mutterings that he and members of his 26th of July had encouraged Rodríguez Alfonso to inform on the DRE.

While it was discovered at the trial that old-line Communist Joaquín Ordoqui and his wife, Edith García Buchaca, had encouraged Rodríguez Alfonso to inform on the DRE, there also were indications that Castro and his followers might be implicated. Faure Chomon, now Minister of Transportation in the Castro government, testified that Rodríguez Alfonso had been arrested by order of Army Chief Camilo Cienfuegos, and Chomón then pondered the question as to just who in the Castro government had freed him and then permitted him to leave for Prague. Alfredo Guevara also was brought to the stand, and said that Rodríguez Alfonso was known to him. But the prosecution did not press him for information regarding his own involvement in what now was known as "the Humboldt affair." This may have been because Alfredo Guevara (no relative of "Che") is considered to be one of Fidel Castro's closest friends, was with Castro at the "bogotazo," and has been with him ever since. He testified that the accused was a troublemaker and was speedily dismissed as a witness.

"Che" Guevara was in Geneva, Switzerland, attending a UN conference on trade, and no effort was made to bring this blunt-talking Communist back to Cuba to testify. Several witnesses did testify, however, that the only Batista official who could identify Rodríguez Alfonso positively as a police informer was, conveniently, executed in La Cabaña fortress by "Che" Guevara despite an official order to keep him alive. It also came out at the trial that, while in Mexico, Rodríguez Alfonso not only hobnobbed with old-line Communist, such as Ordoqui and his wife, Edith García Buchaca, but with prominent members of Castro's revolutionaries, as well. Among those *Fidelistas* were José Abrahantes, Emilio Aragonés, and Osmani Cienfuegos, who shortly were to become members of the Central Committee of the Cuban Communist Party. It is certain that Castro knew about Rodríguez Alfonso's betrayal of the DRE.

Up to this point it was the Cuban Communist Party that was on trial, and Castro put himself in the witness stand saying that this was so. Addressing the Supreme Court, which was "reviewing the proceedings" at Castro's order, the Cuban Prime Minister spoke for four hours and 35 minutes. He said that the Communist Party, not Rodríguez Alfonso, was on trial, adding that this could have no effect other than to split the unity of the ruling forces. He spoke of "sectarian cross-currents," and of intrigues, lies and rumors spreading widely among the usually political perspicacious Cubans. The net result of his "defense" of the Communists was to saddle the Communist Party more firmly with blame for the "Humboldt affair," and to direct public attention away from him and his followers. And he assumed the role of the just and impartial lord, looking down from above on the factionalism of his subjects. He gave sweeping exoneration to Edith García Buchaca and her accomplices.

Castro wondered aloud at the "incredible naivete" of the old-line Communists who put Rodríguez Alfonso forward for the diplomatic-intelligence post in Prague, but made no attempt to explain a much more important mission that he personally gave to Marcos Rodríguez Alfonso. Castro himself entrusted a personal message to Premier Khrushchev in Moscow to the young Communist informer, and mentioned his having talked to Rodríguez Alfonso alone while the trial was still in progress. Castro said that Rodríguez Alfonso told him he believed that by denouncing the DRE leaders to Batista's police the DRE would be out of the way, and therefore would not create so much friction at the University of Havana. However, it was much more important to Castro and his small band of men struggling in the Sierra Maestra back in early 1957 to have the DRE "out of the way." And Castro strongly attacked testimony that "Che" Guevara had sentenced the only man capable of identifying Rodríguez Alfonso as an informer, calling them "rumors, intrigues, and lies." But the haunting question remains: Did Guevara liquidate the witness because Castro and his followers were also involved in he conspiracy against the DRE?

What happened was that a legal trial had been turned into a political trial which challenged the Castro regime as it had never before been challenged. The trial of Rodríguez Alfonso became not only a political process which completely overshadowed his question of the guilt or innocence, but also became a moral scandal of major magnitude, with unsavory details that reached throughout the Castro hierarchy and touched the "Maximum leader" himself. Castro was enraged that CMQ radio had given the trial publicity. And he was right when he said: "Our enemies want to take advantage of the trial to sow confusion and doubt." By attacking the Communist Party for causing the death of the four DRE youths, Faure Chomón had, probably unwittingly, also implicated the Castro regime. And Fidel Castro lost what respect he still commanded from the Cuban people. They suspected that he, as well as the Communist Party, was responsible in some measure at least, for the murder of the four DRE leaders. The evidence pointed to in this direction.

With a large dose of political propaganda warfare, our State Department and the U.S. Information Agency might well have turned the situation to advantage. But they remained silent on an important propaganda weapon which Castro had gratuitously placed in their hands. And the Russians continued to move into Cuba in a massive military buildup.

CHAPTER 15

•

The Communist Offensive

•

THERE IS NO DOUBT that President Kennedy and his brother, the Attorney General, consciously set about the business of stopping all efforts to unhorse Fidel Castro—from outside exile attacks, and from Cuba's internal resistance movement. On March 18, 1963, the Cuban exile organization Alpha-66 raided the Cuban port of Isabela de Sagua in a flotilla of small, speedy, boats. The attack was coordinated with internal resistance groups, and resulted in killing a number of Soviet troops and Cuban militia. The operation was carefully planned in conjunction with internal resistance forces. I monitored Castro's internal official radio net and found that government radio operators in the area cooperated by maintaining a radio silence for 20 minutes during the initial phases of the attack. They were taken out and shot the very next day when combined Russian and Cuban units moved into the area to break the hold which the resistance forces had momentarily exerted over all access roads to the port town. The regime claimed that resistance forces had been operating from three sugar mills in the area and identified those mills as Antonio Pinalet, Hector Rodríguez,Mariana Grajales. The Armed Forces Ministry also issued a statement which said that the resistance forces were supplied by a militantly anti-Castro religious sect, the Jehovah's Witnesses.

Then in the early morning hours of March 27, another group of Cuban actionists, Commandos L, made an attack from the sea on the Russian freighter *Baku*, in the Cuban port of Caibarien. The Russian vessel was nearly sunk and several of its crew were wounded in the lightning-like assault. Nikita Khrushchev immediately demanded restitution from the United States for damages to the ship, and threatened to assign Soviet Navy units to patrol the Straits of Florida, thus publicly asserting Russian suzereignty over the vassal state. And the Russian-Cuban combine retaliated that same day with a MIG attack on the U.S. motorship *Floridian*. And though the *Floridian* was flying a 5 x 7 foot U.S. flag, and was in international waters at the time of the attack, President Kennedy played down the incident as possibly a case of mistaken identity.

More important was the President's reaction upon first hearing of the Cuban exile attack on Caibarien. Early that morning, a desk officer of the State Department was startled to receive a call directly from President Kennedy. The President asked two questions: "Is the report true?" and "How did they get away with it?" Two days later, Attorney General Robert Kennedy dispatched 600 Federal agents to Miami to prevent any more attacks from being made against the Castro regime. All anti-Castro leaders in the Miami area were placed under virtual house arrest, and forbidden to leave Dade country without Federal approval. The Seventh Coast Guard had its personnel complement increased by 20 percent, and was ordered to stop all "suspicious" boats on the high seas or in national waters and return them to Florida.

This was not all. The Presidential letter to Khrushchev not only advanced U.S. "assurances against an invasion of Cuba," but said that "other nations of the Western Hemisphere would be prepared to do likewise." With this apparently in mind, the President called upon British naval units in the Bahamas to assist the United States in tracking down and capturing Cuban exile actionists in what amounted to official piracy on the high seas. And, completely outside the law, Attorney General Robert Kennedy acceded to Castro's demand and ordered the release of Francisco Molina, the Castroite who had murdered a young Venezuelan girl in New York city, and, also outside the law, set free Roberto Santiesteban Casanova and two companions who had been convicted for sabotage activities during the missile crisis.

This very messy side of the aftermath of the missile crisis pricked the conscience of Dr. José Miró Cardona, President of the U.S.-sponsored Cuban Revolutionary Council. In particular he was appalled at President Kennedy's crack-down against Cuban exile actionists, and concerned that the President should actually appeal to the British to commit piracy on the high seas. He of course realized that the crack-down would prevent Cuban exiles from attempting to liberate their homeland. More important, the crack-down would cut off both hope and supplies for the Cuban underground resistance movement. In April, Miró left Miami for Washington to seek clarification of the policies of the New Frontier. President Kennedy refused to see him, and Miró was sent to Robert Kennedy instead. Miró told me that previously smooth relations with the younger Kennedy were now abrasive, indeed. In talking to the Attorney General, the Cuban exile leader found, he said, that the pragmatic approach to politics by the New Frontier had dictated a change in attitude. "No longer were we Cubans 'their guys,' " said Miró, adding: "Apparently the deal with Khrushchev made him 'their guy,' and we were 'them guys.' "*

The Cuban leader asked the Attorney General for help, something, Miró recounted to me, "along the order of what the Soviets are giving Castro." Bobby Kennedy became ironic, Miró continued, and asked: "Just how much do you think that would be?" Miró answered: "I don't know," adding that what he had come to Washington to obtain was not a specific amount of money or arms, but assurances that Cuba would not be abandoned to the Russians. Once that assurance had been given, he reasoned, the military and intelligence experts were competent to come up with specifics. Miró was given no encouragement by Attorney General Kennedy, and was passed on to Robert Hurwitch a State Department functionary operating at a medium level in the bureaucracy.

Hurwitch began to play the numbers game with the President of the Cuban Revolutionary Council, asking: "How much money do you think it would take to overthrow Castro?" Again Miró said that he did not know; that he was in Washington to obtain assurances that Cuba would not be abandoned. Pushed by Hurwitch to at least come up with some kind of figure, Miró thought for a moment. "Fifty million dollars?" he asked meditatively. Hurwitch scoffed at the figure, saying it was absurdly low. The Cuban said: "Look Mr. Hurwitch, the amount required may be fifty million or one hundred and fifty million. I don't know. I am neither an accountant or a graduate of West Point. Why should we sit here discussing figures which only a military expert can supply?" He made one more effort to obtain a pledge of support from Hurwitch, failed to obtain it, and then spoke to Richard Goodwin at the White House.

Of his three meetings in Washington, Dr. Miró found the one with Goodwin the most distasteful. A man of maturity and wisdom, a former professor at Havana University, and a lawyer of considerable reputation throughout Latin America, Dr. Miró Cardona was quizzed and grilled about his political philosophy by a 31-year-old novice. Miró brought up the matter of U.S. policy toward Cuba, and Goodwin answered by questioning the Cuban exile leader about his political philosophy. Startled, Miró replied that quite obviously he was a democrat, and turned again to the matter of U.S. policy. Goodwin, Miró told me, insisted on probing

*That our previous Cuban allies, whom the New Frontier had repeatedly promised to help recover their homeland, had indeed become "the other guys," is apparent in Sorensen's writings. Although it is doubtful that Sorensen could name 20 Cuban exile organizations he rages at "more than three hundred competing, bickering Cuban exile organizations," calls them "publicity seeking," and scores them for embarrassing the New Frontier by asking the President to live up to his promises. And Sorensen scoffed at Republican complaints that a crack-down on the exiles "amounted to a guarantee of Castro." What, one may ask, did it amount to, based as it was on the very letter which he and Bobby Kennedy drafted? (P. 347).

further. "Are you," Goodwin asked Miró, "a left-wing democrat?" thus alluding to Goodwin's own alignment with the Left. "Or," Goodwin continued, "are you more to the right?" The questioning continued. Finally, Dr. Miró told me, "I exploded. I told him that I was to the left of Hitler and to the right of Khrushchev, and got up and left the office."

Before leaving Washington for Miami, Miró told Hurwitch that he could not in conscience remain as President of the Cuban Revolutionary Council, because he was now certain that an agreement had been made between President Kennedy and Premier Khrushchev in which Cuba had been sacrificed for a U.S. *rapprochement* with Russia (denied, incidentally, by Hurwitch), and that he would submit his resignation. Hurwitch elicted from Dr. Miró a promise not to resign until the Administration had been given time to mull over his position. No sooner had the Cuban leader reached Miami, however, than the *New York Times* published a story that Dr. Miró had demanded $50 million and might resign if the money was not forthcoming. Seeing in this news leak an attempt to destroy his credibility in advance of his resignation, Miró telephoned his strong objections to such cavalier treatment to Hurwitch at the State Department in Washington.*

Hurwitch was immediately dispatched to Miami for a confrontation with Dr. Miró. The Cuban leader carefully documented for Hurwitch his support for U.S. policy following the Bay of Pigs at a time when most Cubans were bitterly disillusioned with that policy. Miró, too, had reason to be disillusioned and bitter. His son had fought with Brigade 2506 at the Bay of Pigs, and was one of the 1,113 captured and imprisoned by Castro. Nevertheless, the Cuban leader continued to support the United States, he told Hurwitch, "Because I have always had faith in the United States, its great history, and its institutions." Now, however, Dr. Miró emphasized, he was being lied to, as, for example, being told that no agreements existed between Kennedy and Khruschchev, when in fact he knew that they did exist. The Cuban leader pointed to the Administration crack-down on Cuban freedom fighters as conclusive evidence that the United States had guaranteed the regime of Fidel Castro. He also cited the President's appeal to the British to help police international waters and prevent exile attacks on the Castro regime as further proof that the United States and Russia were *de facto* allies in keeping Castro in power.

In view of Hurwitch's assertion that no deals existed between the President and Khrushchev, Dr. Miró asked the State Department functionary to explain to him the reason for what amounted to a conscious

*For some inexplicable reason, the USIA office in Miami kept on its payroll a stringer for the *New York Times* despite pressures from the State Department to have him removed because of an obvious conflict of interest.

effort by the Administration to crush resistance to Castro and Communism. Hurwitch replied lamely that the United States could not permit exile groups to dictate its foreign policy, an answer that was at once offensive and obtuse. Dr. Miró then stated that he had no choice other than to tender his resignation. Hurwitch, according to Miró, resorted to blackmail, saying: "If you resign, and make public your reasons for resigning, no Cuban exile leader will ever again be permitted inside the doors of the State Department," because, "your actions would be traitorous." Dr. Miró exploded: "Traitorous to what? To whom? To the Democratic Party?" The interview ended on that note. Miró resigned, stated his reasons for doing so, and was answered by a release from the State Department which called his reasons "highly inaccurate and distorted." The New Frontier refused to accept a successor to Dr. Miró and immediately dissolved the Cuban Revolutionary Council, thus ridding itself of the embarrassment caused by its very existence.

Castro quickly grasped at the opportunity afforded to crush the spirit of the Cuban resistance movement. Almost as a footnote to the resignation of Dr. José Miró Cardona, for several days the Cuban radios bulletined the following news to the Cuban public:

> A message was intercepted in Havana, sent by the Chief of Coast Guard District Number Seven of the United States to all units under his command. It follows: "The position of the United States Government with regard to attacks by Cuban refugee groups against Soviet ships and Cuba itself, although none have been supported by the United States, is that the U.S. Government will take all action necessary to see that there is no repetition of those acts. The policy is applicable to the Coast Guard and we will take all means necessary to intensify our patrols to search out, especially, those boats which carry arms and armaments." The Message went on to say: "The search will also include those boats which carry more gasoline and food than is considered necessary, or who have more than the normal complement of persons aboard."[1]

This message was the epitaph to Cuban hopes for liberation from their Communist masters. It was a particularly bitter epitaph, for of all the ethnic groups which have come to the United States in the 186 years of this country's existence as a nation, among them only the 250,000 or more Cubans were given official promises that they would be returned to a liberated homeland. What they received instead were empty promises, outright lies, and the distortion of the rule of law to suit the whims and political aspirations of a family of political opportunists. Patriots inside and outside the island prison came gradually, almost unbelievingly, to the conclusion that there was nothing in the record of the previous two years to indicate that the Kennedy Administration seriously entertained the slightest notion of freeing the Cubans from Communist tyranny, or of assisting them in any meaningful way to free themselves.

Far from retiring their troops from Cuba, as was being claimed in Washington by the New Frontier, the Soviets were using them to burrow the length and breadth of the island. And information conveyed by Pentagon sources to Hanson Baldwin, military editor of the *New York Times,* that the Russians were rotating their troops and using all manner of subterfuge to maintain the strength of their forces in Cuba, was buttressed by a story told to me in Miami by recently arrived Cuban refugees. In one instance, they said, Russian personnel embarked, supposedly for the Soviet Union, from the north coast port of Isabela de Sagua but turned up two weeks later at the southeast port of Santiago en route to Banes Bay in Oriente Province. The information was revealed in letters which some of the Soviet troops wrote from Santiago to girl friends they had left behind in Isabela de Sagua.

The area around Banes Bay indeed was filled with Russian soldiers. Throughout 1963 and well into 1964, the Russians fortified a twelve-mile stretch of beach between Cabo Lucrecia and Morales. And though Cuba's commercial fishermen were kept at a distance of several miles offshore by Russian patrol boats, still they were able to observe a constant stream of Soviet and Cuban cargo vessels entering Banes Bay. They learned from the crews of passing Cuban ships that major military construction was going on at the small port of Embarcadero where, Secretary McNamara indicated in his February 6 press conference, the Soviets had a base for Komar guided-missile ships. More information was provided by Cuban truck drivers who had defected and made their way to Miami by boat. Not only were the Russians constructing more bases in Banes Bay, the truck drivers told me, they also were enlarging and reinforcing the nearby Cuatrocientas Rozas caves. They knew this to be true, the truck drivers said, because they had for months transported cement, sand, rocks, and iron reinforcement rods to the cave entrance. From there, Russians took over and drove the trucks into the caves.

Four truck drivers said they watched as huge air conditioning units were unloaded from Soviet ships and taken to the caves where, they were told by a Cuban engineer working on the project, the machinery was to be installed. The engineer assumed from this and from the fact that Soviet military officers were in charge, that delicate instruments of war were being installed underground, an assumption that was heightened considerably when the area around the caves sprouted electronic devices, antennae, and radar, thus suggesting strongly that guided missiles were on subterranean pads. The same telltale evidence marked Soviet construction in El Pepu and La Violeta caves. And shortly thereafter it was learned that the Russians had brought in special equipment for the Cuban Nitro plant, which gave them the capability of manufacturing liquid oxygen, a propellant used in missiles.

Evidence that the Soviets were involved in massive underground military construction throughout the island was provided by that ready source of information, streams of Cuban refugees. Cancellation of the several daily air flights from Havana to Miami following the missile crisis virtually stranded more than 300,000 Cubans who had made applications to leave the country. Surprisingly, however, the inhabitants of El Chico, Wajay, Calvario, El Sitio, and other small towns on the outskirts of Havana were suddenly notified by the government that their exit visas had been approved and that they could leave immediately on one or another of the twice weekly flights to Madrid and to Mexico City. The surprise was even greater, considering that many had only recently applied for permission to leave the country, and were not due to be called up for a year or more. The mass evacuation of these towns by the government was made at the request of the Soviet commander in Cuba. And, within months of the evacuation, the Russians had connected their headquarters at Managua, through tunnels, to outer perimeter bases which they then constructed at El Sitio, El Chico, Wajay, Calvario, and even El Cano, the town crushed by Fidel Castro only a few months earlier. Hundreds of Russians walked the streets of these small villages, trading cigarettes for every alcoholic beverage they could lay their hands on. Indeed the drunkenness of the Russians was soon dubbed the "socialist soporific" by the quick-minded Cubans.

Hills behind the Soviet headquarters at Managua are honeycombed with tunnels in which staggering amounts of food, water, arms and ammunition are stored. For two weeks in February 1963, convoys of Soviet trucks transported those supplies from warehouses in the port city of Mariel, some 20 miles north of Havana. One subterranean storage dump at Guatao is so large that it is equipped with elevators capable of handling several tons of materials at a time. These dumps, together with others constructed throughout the country and on the 40-square mile Isle of Pines, contain the supplies that are shipped to guerrillas after they graduate from Cuba's training camps and have been sent back to their countries to wage "wars of national liberation."

Then there was the arrival in Cuba in 1962 and early 1963 of Soviet nurses and hospital orderlies, and of large numbers of what appeared to be Russian menials, adding to the mystery surrounding Soviet intentions in Cuba. It was cleared up, for me at least, when a Cuban refugee doctor told me in Miami that he was ordered by the Soviet military commander in Oriente Province to install an X-ray machine of U.S. make in a hospital. The doctor was blindfolded and taken away. When the blindfold was removed, he was astounded to find himself in a 200-bed hospital located underground. Russian nurses and orderlies were on hand, and took great pride in showing him, he said, not only the x-ray machine which he subsequently installed over a period of several days, but large stocks of U.S. medicines and modern surgical equipment. The day on which the doctor was first taken to the underground hospital was December 18, 1962, indicating that the Russians must have commenced constructing it several months—perhaps a year or more—before the missile crisis. The revelations of the doctor galvanized our intelligence services into action, and within a very short time anti-Castro Cuban groups inside the country located the hospital near the city of Holguín. They also located two more, one in the city of Santa Clara and another in Camagüey, and, along with these discoveries, made still another. The Camagüey installation was camouflaged above by a Russian-operated chicken farm, tended by Soviet menials, presumably because they could be trusted over the Cubans to maintain silence. The Santa Clara installation is covered by a soil-grabbing grass called "americano." The Camagüey hospital is camouflaged further by eucalyptus trees which cast long, irregular shadows. These discoveries alone might have suggested to the New Frontier that the Russians fully intended to stay in Cuba.

And indeed they were. Multiple reports by refugees told of MIG fighters popping into the air near Managua, seemingly from out of nowhere, indicating that the Russians had constructed underground plane hangars. This base was tracked down for our intelligence services by anti-Castro Cubans inside the country. They reported that there was another underground airport at Santa Clara, with ramps permitting the planes to pop into the air. All Cubans, even Cuban Air Force Chief Juan Almeida, were barred from the premises. They also reported that the Pinar del Río airbase at San Antonio de los Baños, had been equipped with underground hangars. These reports were not definitive, however, and were marked by our intelligence services as probably true, pending substantiating information. It was not long in coming. In the fall of 1963, there turned up in Miami an escapee from Cuba who actually had worked on an underground hangar. José Dans Reyes told me* he had worked for two years on one in Oriente Province.

Here is what he had to say:

"From October 1961 I worked as a mason's helper on underground hangars for Soviet military planes near the city of Holguín. Those of us

*in my capacity as Editor of *Latin America Report*

who were 'slave laborers' [Cubans] worked on the upper levels, because only the Russians were permitted to construct the deeper levels where machinery for airplane elevators was housed. When the underground hangars were completed, Russian planes, including bombers, were moved into various levels of the installation."

Dans Reyes said that the hangars were protected "by 80 inches of reinforced concrete, and camouflaged with several feet of earth, grass, and palm trees." He surmised that the construction was not visible to over-flying U.S. reconnaissance planes because, he said, the underground installation was first hollowed out from the side of a chalk cliff, then built up inside.

The revelations of this Cuban stonemason are interesting in that they show that the Russians began construction on the air base in the fall of 1961, and that bombers were in subterranean hangars at the time of the missile crisis. Certainly, his comments bolstered the arguments of those who maintained that the Soviets were well prepared underground before they revealed anything (missile sites) above ground. Taken together with other evidence of underground construction, there is considerable reason to believe that today the Russians may well have missiles siloed underground in Cuba.*

There is evidence that Soviet Colonel Alexander Ruminazev, a missile expert, and his aide Colonel Paul Saken, visited underground military construction sites throughout the island during 1963, spending considerable time in Pinar del Río where tunneling had proceeded at a rapid pace in the mountains there from the fall of 1960. A Soviet command post by that time had already been carved out of the hills of La Gobernadora, along with lateral tunnels, four of which are so large that they accommodate two-way truck traffic. Scores of Cuban refugees have told me that prior to the missile crisis they saw Russian military trucks entering those tunnels, along with 26-wheeled truck-trailers bearing long cylindrical objects covered with tarpaulins. Today, tunnels from sea ports on the north coast of Pinar del Río Province connect with the Soviet command post, and extend from there to a cave complex in the larger El Rosario mountains located further inland. The result is that the Russians have provided themselves with underground transit for armaments unloaded at north coast ports, whose nomenclature they apparently want to keep secret, all the way to the southern foothills of the El Rosario mountain range in the interior of the island, a distance of approximately 30 miles.

As these excavations continued, before and after the missile crisis, the Russians busied themselves working in the Los Portales caves, also

---

*On January 3, 1963, Soviet Marshal Nikolai Krilov took the salute of Cuban Military forces on parage in Havana. Krilov was at the time commander of Soviet strategic missile forces (see p. 411).

located in Pinar del Río Province. Tunnels from the north coast exit nearby, and a former Castro army engineer who worked on the project during its initial stages told me not only that the tunnels run in all directions for many kilometers, but are connected with other huge natural caverns, thus giving the Russians yet another underground network throughout a large portion of the province by which armaments may be moved unseen. Evidence that this particular network may house missiles may be found in the quantity and variety of electronic gear located in nearby Meseta de Anafe. Such expensive and elaborate tunneling, taken together with Soviet security measures which bar the Cuban civilians and military personnel from areas around the tunnels, make it highly unlikely that conventional weapons are to be found there.

In this connection, it may be worth repeating that President Kennedy acknowledged rather uncertainly at a press conference that he was not at all sure that long-range missiles might not still remain in Cuba, saying: "We cannot prove that there is not a missile in a cave or that the Soviet Union is not going to ship next week."[2]

The San Cristobal missile site was located very close to the Los Portales caves, and to areas in the mountains where the Russians are known to have been tunneling for at least a year and a half. Caves and tunnels in the mountains afford excellent bomb-proof hiding places. If the missiles were stored in those caves (with some even siloed underground as Bell Huertas suggests), it would have been a simple matter to transfer mobile missiles from the caves to the sites nearby under the cover of darkness. In the absence of photographic evidence, the burden of proof that no missiles were in Cuba's caves, a predominant claim of the New Frontier, would seem to fall on the Kennedy Administration. The assumption that missiles indeed were in caves at the time, poses yet another —that missiles of unknown range may still be there. And New Frontier assertions that they are not there rest on the thoroughly questionable acceptance of Soviet assurances that all missiles had been withdrawn. Was this, then evidence of U.S.-U.S.S.R. *rapprochement* on the missile question?

Powerful Russian radar installations have since sprung up around the island by which the Soviets now scan the Straits of Florida, the Yucatan Channel between Mexico and Cuba, and the Windward Passage between Cuba and Haiti. What this means is that ships passing from the ocean to our ports on the Gulf of Mexico are monitored by the Soviets from their base in Cuba. They supplement this surveillance through the activities of a fishing fleet which, although flying the Cuban flag, is under the command of Russians. One of those ships, the "Bocamoa," put in at the Colombian port of Santa Marta seeking hospitalization for a man who turned out to be a Russian crew member by the name of Leonti Kurilovich.[3] And Colombian officials found that of the 38 men aboard, ten were Russians, including the captain. Two other Cuban "fishing vessels," the "Manjuarí" and "Biajaiba," were identified by Radio Havana as being captained, respectively, by Russians Ivan Kzainiukov and Sergei Karakanov (phonetic spelling).[4] The ships are fitted with sophisticated electronic gear which is totally unrelated to fishing.

The spying activities of the high seas fishing fleet is complemented by those carried out by vessels of the Lambda class. The birth of these two fleets was provided for in the Soviet agreement at the time of the missile crisis not only to provide Cuba with a fishing fleet, but to send Castro a fleet of Soviet "fishing" vessels, as well. The follow-up to this agreement came with the arrival in Cuba of Soviet Marshal Nicolai Krilov where, on January 2, 1963, he took the salute of Russian-trained and Russian-equipped Cuban troops. Marshal Krilov and his aide, Alexei Dementiev, conferred with Raúl Castro regarding the construction of Lambda, Eta, Sigma and RP-60 vessels. The 75-foot Lambda was given priority, and within a span of six months, 81 of these vessels had been constructed at a cost of $175,000 each. Testifying before a Senate Subcommittee in January 1964, State Department aide William C. Herrington admitted that many of Castro's fishing craft are thought to be spy vessels, and said that their numbers had increased substantially during 1962 and 1963.

There was further evidence that the Russians used their ships for purposes other than fishing. One, the "Osegsk," patrolled the Straits of Florida, scanning the horizon with powerful radar. When a boat carrying escapees from Cuba was spotted, the "Osegsk" alerted MIGs and Russian patrol boats lying in nearby waters, which then pursued the refugee craft, machine-gunning the occupants and leaving the boats to drift on the ocean. The slaughter of Cuban escapees during 1963 and 1964 was great, prompting the two exile organizations, The Cuban Association of Judges and Law Clerks and the Association of Professionals, to propose three measures to halt murder on the high seas. Claiming that for every four persons to escape to freedom, three others are gunned-down, the exile groups called for 1) the International Red Cross and the American Red Cross to station picket ships in international waters, just outside Cuban jurisdiction, to rescue escapees in small boats; 2) merchant vessels plying the waters of the Florida straits and the Caribbean sea to sail close to Cuban waters, and be on the alert to carry out rescue operations, and; 3) passenger and transport airlines flying Caribbean routes to scan the ocean for boats adrift in international waters, plot their positions, and report them to Red Cross picket ships. Neither the State Department nor the American Red Cross lent their support to the pleas of the Cubans, and the Florida straits became known as "machine guns alley," while, at the same time, the Cuban military buildup continued at a feverish pace.

Decree 998 of January 5, 1962, had set aside $247 million for military expenditures in Cuba for that year. The same decree established a "central military reserve" of an unknown amount for what it termed "non-budgeted expenditures" above and beyond the $247 million. In 1963, Cuba's known military budget was $214 million. These two figures did not include the outright gift of Soviet military equipment, estimated for the two-year period at $450 million. The enormous expenditures for military hardware (by a Communist government widely hailed by the "losers" as interested in the welfare of its people) contrasts sharply with the mere $55 million spent annually on the military by pre-Castro governments. The result was inevitable, and the living standard of the Cubans continued its downward march. In 1961, the annual per capita income of the Cubans had dropped to $245 from the 1959 average of $356. By 1964 it had plummeted to approximately $177.

Indeed, even the health of the Cubans, especially the children, was sacrificed for the political and military objectives of the Castro regime, as epidemics were added to the many other problems of the people. Cement that ordinarily would have been used to repair and maintain Cuba's reservoirs and its public water systems went, instead, to the military. By 1963, water trucks and fire hydrants spewed out streams of contaminated water, caught in unsanitary buckets by unsanitary Cubans, bereft of the soap needed to cleanse themselves and their utensils. For lack of repair, sewage systems broke down, adding to the health problems of the Cuban people. Using figures supplied by the Cuban Medical Association in Exile, former Supreme Court Justice Julio Garcerán forwarded a complaint to the OAS, charging that the health of the Cuban people was being sacrificed for the onward rush of Communism. His report said that 169,546 Cubans contracted gastroenteritis between January and October, 1963, and that another 3,037 had died from the malady, a conservative estimate as it turned out. In sum, these figures are surprising in that gastroenteritis was virtually unknown in pre-Castro Cuba; it is a disease that serves as an index to the efficiency of the public health system. As a result of the breakdown in public health, Cuba's mortality rate jumped from 5.8, the lowest in Latin America in 1958, to 6.5 in 1962. By 1966, it had climbed to 6.8.

The poor state of Cuban health was attested at the time by any number of Castro's officials, including Vilma Espín de Castro, who, on June 8, 1963, convened an "Infants Week" in Havana where she said: "Cases of gastroenteritis have increased . . . we must carry out a successful campaign . . . you know that notices are being published in the newspapers explaining the measures to be taken." Cynically, she blamed the breakdown in sanitation to "the shortage of rain this year," when, in fact, Cuba's rainfall was above normal. The seriousness of the health situation was elaborated by Vice Minister of Public Health, Heliodoro Martínez Junco, when he announced at a seminar on gastroenteritis in the city of Santa Clara that the disease "constitutes the principal public health problem of the nation." His observations were followed on June 18, 1963, by an announcement from the Public Health Ministry over CMQ radio: "In the last fourteen days 212 children have died of gastroenteritis." The following month, Dr. Eduardo Garriga of Santa Clara said that in one day fifteen children had succumbed to the disease. And, in a rare burst of honesty, on November 11, 1963, the Communist newspaper *Hoy* revealed: "Between May 1962 and June 1963 528,460 cases of gastroenteritis were reported at our first-aid centers just in the rural area of Cuba alone." The number of *guajiros* who did not report the disease at government centers probably swelled the total number of cases considerably.

The government finally was forced to admit that the epidemic was due to its substandard water system, and promised that repairs on reservoirs and water mains would be undertaken immediately. Until they were effected, the Public Health Ministry urged, people were to burn their sewage and garbage. Subterranean springs which, prior to Castro, provided clean, clear water at a low price, were left in disrepair by the Communist regime. Instead, water from the sewage-ridden Almendares river was sold to the populace at $1 a bucket, thus adding typhoid to the many diseases afflicting the Cuban people.

On May 14, 1965, Major Faustino Pérez, President of the National Institute of Water Resources, admitted on a program over CMQ radio that Havana was receiving less than one-fourth of the water provided prior to Castro, but, true to the Communist code, Pérez blandly covered up, saying: "However, the water shortage is a heritage of past evils, and the revolution is trying to solve it with every means at its command." He blamed the Cubans for "indiscriminate use of water" when in fact few houses had any running water at all. Major Pérez also blamed pre-revolution regimes for "the insufficient size of the distribution network of water mains," despite the knowledge that pre-Castro Cuba had all the water its population could use. Everyone was blamed but the Communists themselves.

After attending a Latin American medical conference in Cuba, convened by the Cuban regime to get doctors of other nations to help bail it out of its predicament, Brazilian Dr. Joao B. Aguiar told Rio de Janeiro's *El Globo* newspaper in the fall of 1963 that as many as 200 out of every 100,000 Cubans were dying from gastroenteritis. Dr. Aguiar found that gastroenteritis was not the only disease plaguing the Communist-ridden people of Cuba, noting that one in three Cuban families suffered infectious hepatitis or other forms of communicable diseases, and that the lack of shoes contributed to the already high incidence of intestinal parasites. He was particularly depressed to find that the directors of

Cuba's hospitals worked under the orders of Communist Party managers, that their skills as doctors were subordinated to their political reliability. He also found government-encouraged promiscuity among Cuban youths to be responsible for a marked increase in syphilis and other venereal diseases.

And, in contrast to the well-stocked and well-equipped Soviet underground hospitals, Cuba's network of private clinics and state hospitals had decayed spectacularly following their takeover by the Communists. Dr. José Delgado, who managed to avoid Soviet picket ships, MIG fighters, and torpedo boats and made it to Key West in a small boat, told something of that decay. "We cannot prescribe drugs for our patients because the simplest medicines—iodine, laxatives, even aspirin—are not to be found," said Dr. Delgado, adding: "Sheets are changed only once a week in the hospitals, despite the amount of blood, vomit, and excrement on them." The doctor spoke about the situation in his own field, gynecology, in these terms: "The number of premature births is beyond count, due to the weakness of mothers who do not have proper food and must work for the Communist regime to within a few months of birth." Prior to the Communist takeover, pregnant women had an average of 80 percent hemoglobin, with a red corpuscle count of 4,200,000. By 1963, hemoglobin had dropped to 69 percent, with a red corpuscle count of 3,900,000. And in 1958, the percentage of premature births stood at 8 percent, but in 1963 it had risen to 14%. There is another factor regarding still-born children, and that has to do with the mental state of the mother. Babies are taken away from the mother by the state when they are 45 days old, and reared, during the work day, in Communist indoctrination centers. About 30,000 children between the ages of eleven and twenty have been taken from their families and now live under strict state discipline on the isolated Isle of Pines. Pregnant women are aware of what lies ahead for their unborn babies, and the number of natural abortions and still-births increased six times over the 1958 figure.

Dr. Rogelio García Oramas, former consulting physician in the Los Angeles Polyclinic in Pinar del Río until he opted for the United States in June 1963, said that gastroenteritis deaths totalled 36 per day in Pinar del Río for a period of well over two months, adding that hepatitis and uremia ran a close second. "Nearly all of our patients suffered from avitaminosis because of the lack of nourishing food," said Dr. García," and "when surgery is needed, the patient is at the mercy of chance. Time after time, surgery has had to be abandoned because of the lack of anesthetics. In extreme cases, internal surgery is performed under conditions for the patient that are very much like the Dark Ages." The shortage of water is also blamed for a widespread inability of doctors to perform even minor surgery.

Certainly, these facts, many of them made known by official Communist Cuban sources, gave the lie to assertions made by attorney James B. Donovan in a speech to the 83rd Ohio State Bar Association meeting in May 1963, when he said that the sending of medicines to Cuba in return for the Bay of Pigs prisoners was well worth the cost because: "For four years the Cuban people have been taught to hate Americans. But now in their drugstores there are millions of medicines labelled 'Made in U.S.A.' " Donovan said further: "The propaganda value is worth fifty Voice of America broadcasts a day." He attempted to justify his role in the ransom negotiations by adding: "It was far less expensive and achieved superior results than the so-called tractors for freedom plan would have achieved."[5] Yet, the tractors for freedom plan would have offered Castro a value of $26 million, while the plan which Donovan carried through for President Kennedy not only cost $53 million in food and medicines, which, despite Donovan's assertions, did not reach the Cuban people in any significant amount, but another $6 million in cash. Two-and-a-half million dollars were paid in April 1962 for the return of wounded prisoners, and three-and-a-half million more on December 24, 1962, when the last planeload of prisoners landed in Miami.

Donovan was taken to task for playing fast and loose with the facts. Dr. Enrique Huertas, President of the Cuban Medical Association in Exile, wrote Donovan: "The medicines received by the Castro regime in exchange for members of Brigade 2506 have not reached the Cuban people, except for a small amount of Alka-Seltzers and aspirins that are sold to the public at a very high price." Members of the faculty of the School of Medicine of Havana University exile in Miami told Donovan in a letter: "Not even the most elementary medicines can be obtained by the sick in Cuba." Certainly, these professionals kept more closely in touch with the medical situation in Cuba than Mr. Donovan, through correspondence with doctors of other nations who travelled to Cuba, through contacts within Cuba, and through very thorough questioning of doctors who fled Cuba and came to the United States.

Time after time, Fidel Castro and his Communist functionaries railed at the "imperialist blockade" of Cuba, saying that it was responsible for the lack of medicines and food. The fact is, however, that the U.S. embargo on shipments to Cuba specifically excluded medicines and food, and by selling Russia wheat in 1963 President Kennedy had actually provided wheat for Cuba, since a large amount of the Russian purchase was sent there.

However, Fidel Castro had learned that the only absolute in the conduct of foreign affairs is the premium which is placed on initiative. He took the initiative to drive the United States out of Cuba in 1959 and 1960, and in the absence of U.S. efforts to stop it much earlier, he was able from 1963 to 1967 to replace much of the vital U.S. trade with trade from our own allies, the Western bloc of nations. By 1964 forty Cuban vessels of various tonnage were under construction in Spain's shipyards, while two others had been delivered earlier—the "Clodomiro" and the "El Jigue," each weighing 13,000 tons. And British ships, among them the freighter "Barrister," transported to Cuba from Mexican ports vast amounts of spare parts, electric motors, and other made-in-U.S.A. products which were vitally needed by Castro to keep his economy from breaking down completely. Old guard Communist Blas Roca mocked the so-called U.S. blockade, saying on July 18, 1965: "The U.S. blockade has failed because we receive busses from Britain, and products from other countries—Spain, Italy, France, and Japan." Obviously, the greater the commerce with Western countries, the less need for the Russians to shore up Castro's shaky economy.

Not only that, but England, France, Italy, and Spain extended credits to Castro amounting to several hundred millions of dollars. State Department "de Gaulle-watchers" clucked disapprovingly when France sent Paul Pierre Richards to Havana, where he signed a $35 million trade pact and even vowed that France would defend Cuba against any outside attack. Britain followed by sending Leyland busses to replace those which had been sabotaged by the rebellious Cubans and by selling Castro a $45-million fertilizer plant, while Spain's financial stake in Cuba in 1965 amounted to around $60 million. And, in 1966, Canada sold Russia $40 million worth of wheat and delivered it directly to Cuba. What this amounted to, of course, is that allies of the United States that have been beneficiaries of billions of dollars in American aid, and although looking to this country for protection in the event of a nuclear war, supported a Cuba whose subversives were at work attacking the free world.

By the end of 1966, Cuba's trade with our partners in the free world accounted for about $400 million of Cuba's total export trade of $1.4 billion. More important, most of that trade was in critical items which Cuba could not get from Communist countries. In the cases of Spain, Japan, and Morocco, Cuba had cumulative trade credits for the years 1963, 1964, and 1965. It was little wonder that, on October 14, 1966, Radio Havana crowed: "The U.S. government reaps new failures in its criminal intent to impose a total blockade against Cuba." That de Gaulle's overtures to the Soviet Union benefitted Cuba is apparent in another Radio Havana comment: "The latest blow against this indescribable imperialist policy occurred at the port of Marseilles. Last Wednesday the Cuban merchant ship 'Uvero' . . . loaded the first consignment of tractors and bulldozers which are a part of a contract of $35 million." And a news dispatch out of Havana told of the help being given Cuba by nine European countries—among them England, France, and Italy—to build up the Cuban sugar industry.

Despite criticism from the State Department, which amounted to a slap on the wrist, Britain said that it was free to deal in anything not considered to be strategic goods, and specifically defended the sale of 750 Leyland buses as being of no military value to the Cubans. The statement was made in the face of an announcement out of Havana that all vehicles, including British buses, were part of a military transport pool held in reserve. And in February 1966, American molasses interests revealed that British purchases of Cuban molasses were supplying Castro annually with $15 million in desperately needed foreign exchange. Democratic Florida Congressman Dante Fascell took up the matter in a speech on the floor of Congress March 16, 1966, saying: "The British have been buying virtually the entire Cuban molasses crop each year, thereby sweetening the Castro Communist war chest from $10 to $25 million a year."[6] But that was not all, said Congressman Fascell. The British bought their molasses at half the cost in non-Cuban markets and then dumped it in the United States, thus hurting U.S. domestic producers to the tune of $40 million a year. Fascell also pointed out that, at the request of the British government, the United States immediately joined in an oil embargo against the African state of Rhodesia for its internal policies, but made no evident effort to get the British to reciprocate by honoring our embargo of Cuba. It is perhaps unnecessary to point out that Rhodesia threatens no one, while the Soviet base in Cuba threatens the security of every democratic nation in the world.

Secretary of State Dean Rusk turned aside criticism of his policies by suggesting that the American people might react to Britain's trade with Cuba by refusing to purchase British products. Congressman Fascell said as much in his House speech: "Our own Secretary of State has pointed out that if practices such as I have outlined continue, there very well could be in the United States an immediate and strong consumer reaction." But considerably more was required from our diplomatic establishment to enforce its embargo of a predatory Communist Cuba than Rusk's off-hand comment regarding what Congressman Fascell termed "strong consumer reaction." Indeed, President Kennedy's policies in 1961 which permitted this country virtually to subsidize our enemy, Cuba, through the United Nations Technical Assistance Fund, continued under the administration of President Johnson.

At the very moment when Russia was sponsoring its January 1966 Tricontinental Conference on subversion in Havana, the United States was agreeing at the United Nations in New York to provide Cuba with money through the United Nations Development Fund—$1,240,000, representing 40% of the $3,100,000 total allocated. This initial grant to Cuba was to be followed by a total of $25,000,000, with the United States scheduled to contribute 40% of that larger amount. As Edward W. O'-

Brien of the *St. Louis Globe Democrat* put it in a front-page story on January 24: "An ultimate total of $25,000,000 in UN aid to Cuba is being discussed. Whether it materializes will probably depend largely on congressional and public reaction to the first portion." Mr. O'Brien also noted that Brazil and Paraguay "strongly objected to helping Castro through the UN," and pointed out: "Both countries are among the principle targets of Communist subversion directed from Cuba."

Ambassador James Roosevelt, son of Franklin Delano Roosevelt, represented the United States at the UN Development Program, where, he said, he would neither object to the project as a whole, nor recommend that U.S. money be withheld. He would, he said, merely place on public record our government's objection in principle and then contribute $1,240,000 to the fund. In doing so, Ambassador Roosevelt referred to previous objections by Congress which resulted in blocking U.S. aid to Cuba in 1961 and 1963, calling them "gimmicks, that didn't mean a thing in the whole concept of the fund."[7] In taking this stand, Roosevelt was supported by aid chief Paul Hoffman who maintained that United States support to the fund "must be kept free of ideological and political considerations."

The Citizens Committee for a Free Cuba, composed of leading Americans from virtually every walk of life, took note of how the fund's money was to be spent in Cuba—to strengthen the University of Havana's technological faculty—and issued a statement which said: "Cuban technology is specifically oriented toward training in computers, electronics, and other areas of endeavor which Fidel Castro has stated are related to the military potential of Cuba, and particularly to radar and military communications." The Committee also pointed out that the faculty at Havana University was made up of Russians, Czechs, and professors from other East European Communist nations. Committee President, former Assistant Secretary of State Spruille Braden, fired off letters to senators and congressmen, taking issue with Ambassador Roosevelt's position, stating: "I am sure you will agree that it is inconceivable that this country voluntarily give funds to an international base of subversion which is located only 90 miles from our shores." Senate Minority Leader Everett Dirksen queried the State Department about its inexplicable stand, and received a letter from Douglas MacArthur III, Assistant Secretary for Congressional Relations, which Dirksen forwarded to Mr. Braden, adding: "I know you will read this with interest."

The letter from Assistant Secretary MacArthur contained virtually the same arguments for helping Cuba in 1966 that were advanced by Deputy Assistant Secretary Richard Gardner back in 1961. "The UN Special Fund has approved, since 1959, a total of 604 Special Fund projects in 92 nations," wrote MacArthur, who then complained: "Of this total, only two projects have been approved for Cuba. . . ." The United States had to go along in support of Cuba, MacArthur argued, so as not to "jeopardize other projects of special interest to friendly countries such as Viet Nam, the Republic of China and Korea." As a result of Spruille Braden's letters, however, congressmen in Washington got their backs up and bombarded the State Department with demands for a better explanation than that contained in Assistant Secretary MacArthur's letter. Newspapers also asked questions, and one typical example was the *Miami Herald* which asked in an editorial on May 19: "Our Dollars To Fidel's Army?" The *Herald* scored Ambassador Roosevelt, calling his position "incredible," concluding: "It is bad enough to do nothing while Castro builds power to cause trouble in this hemisphere. It is much worse to help finance the military education of those who would destroy the inter-American system." The State Department backed off, and, in a mid-summer press release, defended in principle the position it had taken, but altered it to say: "No part of our contribution to the Special Fund will be used to pay for projects in Cuba. They will be financed entirely from the contributions of other countries." The press release took the steam out of the story, but considerable suspicion remained that the State Department had merely juggled the books and had found a way to get around public objections to its policies.

While the State Department occupied itself with sterile maneuvers to defend its policies, the Soviets continued to build their apparatus of subversion and sabotage in Cuba. Evidence that the Cubans were following a master plan to sabotage and terrorize this country was provided as early as November 17, 1962. On that date, three Cubans were arrested and charged with attempted sabotage of oil refineries in New Jersey and retail stores in New York City. The head conspirator was Roberto Santiesteban Casanova, and his two accomplices were José Gómez Abad and his wife. All were cloaked with diplomatic immunity by virtue of their assignment to the Cuban mission at the United Nations. Under this cloak, they recruited three others, including an American woman, and attempted the sabotage that was described by the Attorney General of New York as aimed at the heart of the internal security of the nation. UN Secretary General U Thant intervened on their behalf, and, pleading diplomatic immunity, arranged the release of the trio of Cubans. They were then permitted by Attorney General Robert Kennedy to return to Cuba without having been brought to justice. Santiesteban Casanova was revealed to have been a member of Castro's overseas spy apparatus, the DGI, and later turned out to have been involved in the April 1965 Communist uprising in Santo Domingo.

Then there was the startling case in which three American Negroes and a Canadian woman, all travelers to Communist Cuba, were seized on February 16, 1965, as they attempted to blow up cherished symbols of American heritage—the Statue of Liberty, the Washington Monument, and the Liberty Bell. Ringleader Robert Collier, an advocate of "black power," traveled to Cuba in the summer of 1964, along with 84 U.S. and 46 Canadian "students." While there, Collier received instructions in terrorist tactics from a major in the North Vietnamese army. Walter A. Bowe, another of the plotters, was revealed to be a member of the Castro-financed Fair Play for Cuba Committee. Both Negroes contacted Robert Williams, another advocate of "black power," in Havana and were present at a meeting on July 13 when Williams addressed the 130 "student" visitors in the following terms: "Some overzealous cats have started to sing a little song about Jim Crow being dead. It's a dream, man, it's a dream. Non-violence is what is dead!" Referring to the white population of the United States as "Mr. Charlie," Williams continued: "Mr. Charlie is a savage, and no amount of begging, pleading to conscience, praying, and flashing teeth will curb his evil wrath. Cats, the word is go for broke! Wheel out the old lye can or the old shooting irons, and organize and give Mr. Charlie one whale of a tail beating!" This was not the first instance in which Williams consorted with Communists, neo-Communists, and dupes from the United States. He had done so a year earlier with the visit to Havana of the first group of 59 so-called U.S. students.

Phillip Abbott Luce, one of the "students" who went to Cuba in 1963, defected from the group, and has since published his account of the link between Communist Cuba and Negro violence in this country. In this book, *Road to Revolution*, Luce writes: "When I was in Cuba, I met with Communist guerrillas from all over the world and saw a number of people being trained by the Cubans for guerrilla warfare upon their return to their homelands." Robert Williams was in the forefront of that training. Luce puts it this way: "Robert Williams has conducted classes in Cuba for Americans on the use of bombs and firearms." And while the Canadian and U.S. "students" were consorting with Williams in Havana in 1964, the group of visitors to Cuba in 1963 were on the move in New York. Luce writes that, in the early summer of 1964, Milton Rosen, the head of Progressive Labor (PL), met in New York's Central Park with five members of the PL, and told them "to consider going underground and to start guerrilla operations similar to that used in Cuba by the Communist to destroy the government."

Luce tells how Progressive Labor worked to promote and inflame the week of bloody riots in Harlem the summer of 1964: "Progressive Labor was in the center of these riots and did everything possible to expand and extend riot conditions."[8] This first major experiment in promoting Negro riots was taken, according to Luce, because the Communists in

Cuba believe that the Negro in the United States holds the key to their dreams of revolution and the destruction of our democratic heritage. Here is how Luce interpreted the failure of the Kennedy administration to deal with subversives who returned from Cuba: "The government did not crack down on Progressive Labor, and so this initial underground operation was put into effect."

And, it may be surmised, that it was because the Kennedy administration did not crack down on illegal travel to Cuba that Collier, Bowe, and others were encouraged to go there in 1964 and learn the tactics of urban guerrilla warfare. Negro police lieutenant Raymond Wood testified at the Bowe and Collier hearings in New York that he had penetrated Collier's "Black Liberation Front" and turned up enough information to justify the arrest of the group. He said that Collier met with Cuba's guerrilla chief, Major Ernesto "Che" Guevara, at the Cuban mission to the United Nations and received instructions from him to carry out the sabotage described in Collier's indictment. In addition to blowing up our national monuments, detective Wood said, the "Black Liberation Front" intended to spearhead a Negro uprising in the United States, along with air attacks against the Capitol building and the White House. Destruction from the air was to have been accomplished by Negro military pilots, who, Collier apparently believed, could be persuaded to turn against their own country. The plan called, as well, for creating chaos within the armed forces by means of false communication, and terror in the cities à la Vietcong through mortar and machine-gun fire directed against police and street crowds, and the bombing of the homes of federal authorities.

Indeed, it was in the summer of 1964 that Cuba emerged openly as the North Vietnam of the Western Hemisphere. On July 10, Havana's Radio Progreso announced: "Delegations of the National Liberation Fronts of Venezuela and South Vietnam, the Viet Cong, located in Cuba, approved a joint declaration in which the status of both movements were analyzed and found to be very much the same."

The announcement revealed, perhaps for the first time, that a Viet Cong mission was operating in Havana, and it seemed clear from the radio broadcast that the type of war unfolding in Latin America, and perhaps even the United States, was being patterned closely on the terroristic tactics of the Viet Cong. The next day, Manuel Galich, Foreign Minister under overthrown President Jacobo Arbenz of Guatemala, and, like Arbenz, an exile in Cuba, broadcast a message to Latin America in language that linked the war in Vietnam to the battles being waged in Latin America. Said Galich over Radio Havana: "Guerrilla warfare is spreading, and as we see by the Yankee army's failure in Vietnam to stop it, will succeed."

Earlier, on June 25, Radio Progreso announced that U.S. citizens

Collier, Bowe, and the balance of the "student" visitors to Cuba in 1964 were to be shown the link between the tactics of the Viet Cong in Asia and the guerrilla wars developing in Latin America, saying: "The North American students who are visiting Cuba in defiance of threats and restrictions of the Yankee Department of State will meet tomorrow, June 26, with the permanent mission of the National Liberation Front of South Vietnam, and Saturday, June 27, will meet with members of the National Liberation Front of Venezuela." On June 29, Radio Progreso followed up with a report that the visits had been extremely successful. "The students conversed extensively with the Vietnamese," said Radio Progreso, reporting: "They saw documentary movies of the fighting of the South Vietnamese guerrillas." Another broadcast said that some of the movie scenes "showed U.S. Army helicopters knocked out of the air by the Viet Cong, and our foreign visitors from North America applauded the actions."

According to a Radio Progreso broadcast on July 9, Comrade Ngo of the so-called Popular Army of the Democratic Republic of Vietnam, arrived in Havana, where he was feted. His arrival statement threatened the United States with "extinction" should any moves be made against Cuba. It was during this period of Castro's open identification with North Vietnam that Cuban underground leaders reported that Viet Cong cadres and Red Chinese instructors now had joined Russians and Czechs in Cuba's growing complex of guerrilla training camps. The introduction of battle-hardened Viet Cong guerrillas into Cuba was perfectly consistent with the announcements and pronouncements being made in Havana as, for example, the July 26, 1964 celebration where again the war in Vietnam was linked with guerrilla depredations being committed by Communists in Venezuela. Indeed, the two slogans of the celebration were: "Imperialist Hands Off of South Vietnam!" and "Long Live The Heroic Fight of the Venezuelan People!"

The Cuba-Vietnam parallel was unmistakeably evident in the kidnapping of U.S. Lieutenant Colonel Michael Smolen by Venezuelan terrorists. Colonel Smolen, attached to the U.S. Embassy in Caracas as a member of the U.S. Military Mission to Venezuela, was kidnapped by Castroites on October 9, 1964, the date set for the execution of a Viet Cong terrorist in Saigon. The terrorist, Nguyen Van Troi, had attempted to assassinate Secretary of Defense Robert McNamara on one of his many trips to Saigon. The Venezuelan kidnappers, the so-called Armed Forces for National Liberation (FALN), offered to spare Smolen's life if the South Vietnamese government would release Van Troi. Fortunately, the Venezuelan police were hot on the trail of the Castroites, who then set Colonel Smolen free. The New York Times put a strange cast on the event, claiming in an October 13 editorial that the daring exploit showed that the Communists were weak, not strong. Shunning the word Communist, the editorial referred to "the extreme left wing," and remarked on its "feebleness." And ignoring the connection between the tactics of Cuban-supported terrorists in Latin America and those of the Viet Cong in Asia, the editorial writer lectured the "left wing" FALN in the manner of a school teacher, saying that by resorting to kidnapping "The FALN only enhances its association with the moral squalor of terrorism." More arresting was the comment that the kidnappings might "goad a democratic government into repressive measures," apparently the real concern of the lecturer.

In December of the same year CMQ radio announced that the Viet Cong and Communist Venezuelan missions to Havana had signed "a mutual aid pact." And it was but shortly after this that elements of the 56th Division of China's Red Army were located in the environs of Tacajo sugar mill in Cuba's Oriente Province. A purser on Castro's *Cubana* airlines told how they got there. The purser, Salvador del Pino Díaz, had been making the Prague-Havana and the Mexico City-Havana flights for a period of four years. He defected and subsequently told me in Washington: "Of those coming to Cuba from Prague, 90% are military men from North Vietnam and Red China." He knew, he said, because he cleared the flight manifests. Within a few months of my interview with him, the Russians supplied Red China with transport in the form of 18 four-engined Ilyushin turboprop aircraft for the stated purpose of transporting cargo and passengers between China and Cuba, thus making highly suspect the claims coming out of Washington that the Russians and Chinese were at odds over Communist policy toward Cuba. Actually, Russia shares Cuba's 43 guerrilla camps with the Red Chinese, the better to advance the subversion of Africa.

The guerrilla training program in Havana for Africans began in the latter part of 1961 when trouble-shooting Cuban Ambassador Pablo Ribalta established a political and propaganda office in Havana for rebels from the African island nation, Zanzibar. This event was followed by the introduction of hundreds of black Africans into guerrilla training camps, especially the camp named after Patrice Lumumba, the murdered Congolese Communist leader. Located on Cuba's Isle of Pines, Patrice Lumumba camp is staffed with Viet Cong guerrilla instructors, while political indoctrination and overall direction is supplied by the Red Chinese. Still another guerrilla camp for African Negroes is located in Oriente Province. Together, they turn out more than 1,000 guerrilla trainees a year, with some estimates placing the number as high as 2,000. Cuban Negroes are trained alongside their African brethren, and many are shipped to Africa to fight. One identified by former Congolese President Moise Tshombe as Sadez Gómez García was killed while operating with guerrillas in the eastern district of Maniema in the Congo. A diary found on his body indicated that he had arrived in the Congo via Moscow, Prague, and Dar-es-Salaam, the capital of neighboring Tanzania. John Okello, the Zanzibari who maneuvered the overthrow of the government of Zanzibar on January 12, 1964 in which 30,000 people were slaughtered, was identified as having been trained in Cuba, along with 100 other Zanzibari. When mainland Tanganyika and the off-shore island of Zanzibar joined to form the Leftist nation of Tanzania, Cuban Negroes established guerrilla training camps on Zanzibar while Tanzania's President Julius Nyerere joined visiting Red Chinese Premier Chou En-lai in vicious attacks against the United States and opened diplomatic relations with Red China.

Gaston Soumialot, Communist leader in the former Belgian Congo, came to Cuba on August 31, 1964, and, in the company of high-level Soviet and Chinese embassy officials, toured guerrilla camps training hundreds of Tanzanians, Senegalese, and Congolese. On five occasions during his visit, Soumialot was closeted with Fidel Castro, the Soviet and Red Chinese Ambassadors, and Nguyen Van Tien, the Permanent Representative to Havana of the Communist government of North Vietnam. On September 12, Soumialot was seen off at the airport personally by Fidel Castro, something the Cuban dictator reserves only for high-ranking guests. Defectors from Castro's army told me that at least 200 Africans who received "leadership training" at the Patrice Lumumba and Minas del Frio camps, were then sent back to Tanzania, a story that was confirmed when, on September 17, Congolese government forces intercepted and sank a troop and supply boat, the "Ajax." This boat had been running Cuban-trained guerrillas from Tanzania over Lake Tanganyika into the eastern Congo, thus suggesting a high degree of coordination in efforts to subvert the nations of Africa. The previous June, twenty-seven Senegalese were arrested and tried by a court in Dakar and found guilty of subversion. All twenty-seven, it was brought out at the trial, had spent eight months in Cuba's guerrilla camps where they were trained by Red Chinese and Viet Cong instructors. This again strongly suggests that Cuba was the fulcrum of subversion in Africa.

In December 1964, Alphonse Massamba-Debat, for all practical purposes a Communist, and President of the French Congo, was promised by the Communist combine in Havana that he could expect to be supplied with hundreds of Cuban Negro soldiers to prop up his shaky regime. Between January and May 1963, seven hundred were sent to the capital city, Brazzaville, and there broken up into units and sent to encampments around the city. In late June a group of young army officers attempted to oust Massamba-Debat from power because, as reported in the June 29 issue of the New York Times: "Many top officers have long been known to resent Mr. Massamba-Debat's decision to form a private presidential army of around 100 Cuban Negroes dispatched from Havana." The army, it seemed, resisted government decrees establishing a special political department for Marxist indoctrination of the troops. That Cubans indeed formed a presidential force was also reported in the *Times* dispatch, which said: "Leaders of the Left-wing government of the former French Congo were reported to have taken refuge in a Brazzaville stadium, protected against the insurgent Army forces by Cuban soldiers of the Presidential Guard." Cuba's official newspaper *Granma* admitted its role in the French Congo, saying in its June 29 issue: "The Cuban Revolutionary Government sent arms and instructors to assist the military capability of the people of the Congo." It clouded up the admission by asserting that its intervention was a duty undertaken because of its "international obligations," apparently referring to the December 1964 decision taken in Havana to do so. And wire service dispatches out of Brazzaville reported that the Cubans were led by Red Chinese military personnel who, it seems highly probable, accompanied their Cuban charges to the Congo.

Cuban roving Ambassador Pablo Ribalta was highly successful in his mischief-making maneuvers in Africa. A graduate of Marxist schools and guerrilla camps in Russia and Red China, he was the ideal person to carry out the Cuban part of Red Chinese ventures in Africa. And it was because of Ribalta's activities that mention could be made of subversion on the continents of Asia, Africa, and Latin America. Ribalta was complimented by Ahmed Ben Barka, a Moroccan and one of the intellectual authors of Havana's up-coming tricontinental conference, in a telegram sent to Fidel Castro and published in *Granma* on September 19. Cuba's Radio Rebelde followed with an announcement the following day, which said, in part: "Ambassador Pablo Ribalta is building ties of the three continents—Asia, Africa, and Latin America."

That the Soviet Union is as responsible for the advance of guerrilla wars in Latin America as is Red China in Africa, is shown by a Tass announcement out of Moscow on January 18, 1965. Apparently satisfied with the success of Cuban-exported terrorism over the previous four years, the communique told the Communist parties of the Western Hemisphere to support Fidel Castro, thus giving the Cuban dictator the coordinated support of the Soviet-controlled apparatus in Latin America. It was "mandatory," the communique said, "for local organizations, leaders, and Parties" to line up behind Cuba's terroristic wars. More immediately important to an assessment of Russian policy was that the Moscow communique openly told terrorists in Latin America that they could expect to receive "active aid" in the overthrow of six Latin American governments, and named them—Venezuela, Colombia, Honduras, Paraguay, Haiti and Guatemala.

Less than a month following the Moscow communique, 88 Cuban-trained Guatemalans were infiltrated into the mountains of Guatemala, forcing the government to declare martial law. According to Colonel Enrique Peralta, who then ruled the country at the head of a military junta, the increasing assaults by Castroites were designed to frustrate democratic elections which were scheduled to select a civilian president to succeed the military. In declaring martial law, Colonel Peralta made a dramatic about-face, for only a month earlier he had dismissed guerrilla activities as of little importance. Now, he said that the situation had changed radically, as indeed it had. Guerrilla leaders Marco Antonio Yon Sosa and Luis Turcio Lima commanded respectable numbers of men in the mountains. The two were former officers in the Guatemalan army, and, incidentally, had received training at Fort Benning, Georgia, prior to their defections. As Castro insurgents, they now were being supplied with men and equipment through the Guatemalan border with Mexico, made possible by the cooperation of Lázaro Cárdenas, a Socialist and former President of Mexico. Cárdenas owns large chicle plantations in the Yucatán Península, and assigns guides to take the Cuban-trained guerrillas, who are landed by Lambda vessels, through the Quintana Roo jungles and across the Mexican border into Guatemala.

Colombia, third in size of all the countries on the South American continent, had felt the sting of Cuban-Russian penetration and guerrilla wars for years prior to the Moscow communique openly supporting those wars. With the explosion of 41 bombs in five Colombian cities, President Guillermo León Valencia addressed the nation on July 12, 1963 in these terms: "We now are faced with a vast terrorist plan," he said, adding: "This is the start of a struggle between constitutional government and terrorists." He accused the Castroites of attempting to take advantage of Colombia's political unrest which, from 1948 to 1958, took the lives of an estimated 200,000 people in a vast civil war known as *La Violencia*. While *La Violencia* had diminished considerably following an agreement in 1958 between Liberal Party chief Alberto Lleras Restrepo and Conservative leader Laureano Gómez to share power between the two parties in four-year cycles for a period of sixteen years, it also had produced a sturdy off-shoot—Castroite guerrillas.

Indeed, Fidel Castro was involved in person in the event which set off *La Violencia* when, in April 1948, he took part in an attempt to assassinate the President and take over the government by force. Known as the *Bogotazo*, violence spread to the countryside where for the following ten years Liberal and Conservative party fanatics killed each other off in the bloodiest civil war in the history of Latin America. And it was because of his knowledge of this internal strife, and of the strength of partisan bands which roamed Colombia's back country and its towering Andes mountains, that Castro, as mentioned in an earlier Chapter, had sent his guerrilla leader Adolfo Rodríguez de la Vega as his first Ambassador to Colombia where he built Castroite groups on the natural guerrilla structure provided by Colombia's armed gangs, and recruited "Tiro Fijo" as one of the Castroite leaders. And it was because of President León Valencia's knowledge of Castro's activities that he said: "Arms and money have been sent from Cuba to the gangs, and Colombian students have been offered scholarships in Cuba to study guerrilla warfare and urban terrorist tactics." One incident among many, supports President Valencia's charges.

In October 1963 a group of Colombian guerrillas captured attorney German Mejia Duque and held him for five days. The army pursued the kidnappers, defeated them in a skirmish, and rescued Duque. The attorney was able to provide a wealth of information regarding Castro's support to the guerrillas, including the revelation that a high Cuban official was personally sending both instructions and money to guerrilla forces. Duque led army officers to the place where he had been held captive. Apparently fearing this, the guerrillas did not return to their base, and the army found a letter written to the guerrillas by Cuban Major Manuel Piñero, head of Cuba's DGI (Directorate General of Intelligence), threatening to reduce or even suspend a 20,000 peso monthly payment to them unless they carried out Cuban instructions to the letter.

Another document gave full details of several shipments of arms and clothes to the guerrillas, and revealed that they were sent to Colombia's guerrillas from Santiago de Cuba by planes which landed at Colombia's Guajira Peninsula. This information, published in Bogota's newspapers on October 17, 1963, was officially confirmed on November 13 when President Leon Valencia notified all diplomatic missions in Bogota that he held Cuba responsible for trying to overthrow his government.

The seriousness with which President León Valencia viewed guerrilla assaults from Cuba may be seen in a January 3, 1964 broadcast to the nation. In it he said that the Number One task facing the nation was the eradication of Castroite guerrillas. On January 31, 1965, it became clear why the President considered it important to do so. On that day, the government disclosed that guerrilla gangs operating in Colombia's mountains were receiving instructions from Havana through the efforts of a Colombian by the name of Castulo Heli Barba. A raid on Barba's home turned up a clandestine radio transmitter and receiver, together with evidence that Barba had been to Cuba where he personally had talked with Fidel Castro.

More important, the security police found a list of Colombian army messages which Barba had intercepted and relayed to the guerrillas. The army messages were directives to army units telling them where to deploy their forces in pursuit of Castroite guerrillas. Barba relayed these messages to the Castroites, who then knew in advance every move the army was to make. The messages not only enabled the guerrillas to elude their pursuers, but also made it possible for them to attack villages which had been left unguarded by military forces.

On February 26, a Communist plot to assassinate President León Valencia was uncovered by the police in Cali. León Valencia was scheduled to visit that city just two days after the plot was discovered. Judge Gonzalo Arévalo tried eleven persons involved, and the army seized 18,000 rifles and 10,000 rounds of ammunition from the house of the ringleader, identified as Alfonso Zuluaga García. The disclosure was important for a number of reasons, among them that the Communists now were placing increasing emphasis on urban terrorism as a complement to guerrilla activities in the mountains. Among the Communist instructions disclosed at the hearing in Cali were those urging wanton murder as a means of terrorizing the population into supporting the Castroites. Indeed, these tactics had proved so successful that guerrilla leaders were able to claim that they had created "five independent republics" within the boundaries of Colombia. The five were identified as Sumapaz, Marquetalia, Rio Chiquito, El Pato and Guayabero, representing 15% of the riches of the nation. Rómulo González Trujillo, Governor of the state of Huila, acknowledged shortly thereafter that those areas "are partially or totally under the control of guerrillas."

Other startling events took place in late 1964 and early 1965 which added to the already considerable alarm over terrorism and proved that Soviet Agents were actively involved in Colombia. On November 17, 1964, President León Valencia ordered the expulsion of two Russians, identified as Opekemod Alexandre and Mikhail Kalenikov, for intervening in the internal affairs of Colombia. The Russians were officials of Soviet labor organizations and were in Colombia to attend a labor conference. Colombia's security agency, the Department of Administrative Security (DAS), found the two Russians to be subversives, and said that they had met with Castroite terrorists in Cali where they helped plot a course of guerrilla warfare in the countryside and terrorism in the cities.

On March 19, 1965, President León Valencia addressed the nation in a special radio and television appearance occasioned by a wave of kidnappings and killings which were traced to instructions from Cuba to Colombian guerrillas to increase terror through wanton murder. The specific event that caused the President to take to the air waves was the assault by "Tiro Fijo" (Sure Shot) on the small town of Inza in southeastern Colombia and the cold-blooded murder by him and his guerrilla accomplices of seventeen occupants of a bus. Among those murdered were two Catholic nuns. And the very day that "Tiro Fijo" committed his wholesale murder, Radio Moscow broadcast a message in Spanish to Latin America which said: "The guerrilla fight in Colombia will not end, and the government cannot stop it with dollars or with repression." The timing of the two events, wholesale murder by "Tiro Fijo" and Soviet support for that murder, was not lost on the Colombian President.

Indeed, President León Valencia's dramatic address to the nation had been preceded four days earlier by action taken by civilians to protect themselves from Castroite guerrillas. On March 15, the National Cattlemen's Association took the unprecedented step of setting up a tax of five percent of each member's total yearly income and turning the funds over to the government to step up the fight against guerrilla forces who were attacking ranches in the back country. Bogota's *El Tiempo* editorialized about the state of affairs in the back country on March 18 in the following terms: "The gangs headed by 'Tiro Fijo' are organized by the Communists and directed from outside by agents of Castroism."

These events were followed by Communist-inspired rioting at the University of Antioquia in the city of Medellin which resulted in the death of one student and injury to hundreds of others. Damage to the buildings was placed at a value of nearly half a million pesos. So severe was the rioting that for the first time in the history of Colombia the Rector of the university allowed police to enter university grounds to restore order. His actions may be taken as a measure of the seriousness of the situation, since traditionally students attending universities in Latin America enjoy immunity from government authority while they are on campus.

Colombia's neighbor, oil-rich Venezuela, was also staving off attacks by Castroite guerrillas. The great beginnings of 1959, when Rómulo Betancourt was inaugurated President after nearly a decade of military rule, soon were placed in doubt as, first, Right-wing dictator Rafael Trujillo of the Dominican Republic, then, Communist dictator Fidel Castro of Cuba, loosed their minions to undercut the weak beginnings of Venezuelan democracy. In July 1960, Trujillo money and arms backed a military rebellion in San Cristobal in the west near the Venezuelan border with Colombia. President Betancourt took his case against the Dominican dictator to the Organization of American States, and Trujillo responded with an attempt to assassinate Betancourt. The bombing incident left Venezuela's President with both hands badly burned, his left ear drum damaged, and his vision severely impaired. And Raúl Castro and "Che" Guevara tried to come to Caracas to celebrate the anniversary of the Russian Revolution, sponsored by the Venezuelan Communist Party, but were prevented from entering the country. Indeed, President Betancourt writes that as early as January 1960 he had classified Cuba "as just one more satellite in the Soviet constellation," and in doing so demonstrates that he was considerably advanced over the thinking at the

U.S. Embassy in Havana which pursued a course of accommodation with Castro. He also writes: "Castro became the chief supplier of money, arms, and instructions to the enemies of Venezuelan democracy," and adds: "Havana became the conspiratorial and supply center of the Venezuelan Communist Party, its allies, and its accomplices. Activists specializing in sabotage, bank holdups, and assassination were trained in Cuba."[9]

At the time, Venezuela was producing more than three million barrels of oil a day, and the country represented a rich prize for the Communists. As bombs exploded in Venezuela's major cities and policemen were shot in the back, the population reacted in stunned surprise that produced a kind of paralysis. But the government fought back against the guerrillas lodged in the mountains and the terrorists in the streets and, during the October 1962 missile crisis, considered itself strong enough to be among the first to mobilize its armed forces, and was one of two governments to send warships and planes to take part in the blockade of Cuba. (The other was the Dominican Republic, now ruled by a civilian junta following the May 1961 assassination of Trujillo). President Betancourt earned the undying hatred of Fidel Castro for his support of the United States and at a meeting of Latin American Communists in Havana on January 24, 1963, old-line Party leader Blas Roca spelled out Communist policy toward Venezuela in these terms:

> When the people of Venezuela are victorious, when they get their total independence from imperialism, then all of America will be aflame, all of America will push forward, all of America will be liberated once and for all from the ominous yoke of American imperialism. Their fight helps us today, and their victory will mean a tremendous boost for us. We no longer will be a solitary island of the Caribbean facing the Yankee imperialists, for we will have land support on the continent.[10]

And in December 1963, the Cuban cache of arms was discovered on a beach in Venezuela, the same arms that Ricardo Lorié had purchased for Fidel Castro back in 1959. Another discovery was that Cuban operations against Venezuela were carried out through the Poultry Section of the Cuban Institute of Agrarian Reform. This latter revelation supports the memorandum written by Manuel Artime in 1959 in which he contended that the Agrarian Reform Institute indeed was a cover for its many other activities, and denies the contentions of professor Samuel Shapiro, Arnold Toynbee and other Castro apologists that the Institute was devoted to raising the standard of living of Cuba's *guajiros*. Certainly, the Poultry Section of the Institute cannot be concentrating too much of its efforts on raising chickens if it is busy smuggling arms into Latin America.

In the summer of 1964, William Benton, publisher and former U.S. Ambassador to the UNESCO, met in Moscow with Premier Nikita Khrushchev where the two discussed Venezuela. During their conversations, Khrushchev at first insisted that neither the Soviet government nor its Communist Party appendages abroad took any part in revolutionary activities abroad. Then, according to Betancourt who was provided with an account of the conversations, Benton asked Khrushchev about the Venezuelan case and said it was his understanding that Cuba most certainly was guilty of attempts to subvert Latin America. Then, according to Benton's letter to Rómulo Betancourt: "The Chairman did not let me continue. He waved his hand at me and said emphatically, 'Who placed the arms in Venezuela? Was it Castro? Was it the CIA?' " Benton then said he laughed, and that Khrushchev laughed a long time. Benton remarked of the Soviet dictator: "He has a very good sense of humor. And he added with another laugh, 'Both things could have happened!' " Betancourt found the laughter of the two men to be in enormous bad taste, commenting: "There would have been very little laughter in my country if these arms had reached the Venezuelan agents of Castro."[11]

The arms were not destined for the bands of guerrillas holed up in Venezuela's mountains. They were for a surprise massacre of the population, to be carried out through urban terrorism, the new tactics being taught in Cuba's guerrilla camps staffed, it may be added, with Soviet instructors, thus making Benton's merriment even more inexplicable and of Khrushchev's joking a monstrous thing. Several days after the discovery of the cache of Cuban arms, the Venezuelan police apprehended Luis E. Sánchez Madera, a leader of the *Armed Forces of National Liberation* (FALN), and found that he had travelled to Cuba many times. He, like thousands of other subversives, was able to travel back and forth to Cuba via Mexico because the Mexican government maintained both diplomatic and trade relations with Castro at that time, and continues to do so today when all other nations of the hemisphere have broken with Cuba. More than that, the Mexican government goes along with the Cuban government in its efforts to prevent any official record of travel to Cuba from appearing in passports of the subversives. When the guerrilla recruit, courier, or Communist leader arrives in Mexico City, he reports to the Cuban Embassy where a visa is affixed to a slip of paper and inserted in his passport. Mexican immigration officials collect the slip of paper when the subversive returns from Cuba on his way home, thus leaving no evidence of travel which his government could use to take legal action against him.

In any event, Sánchez Madera returned to Caracas from Havana with a detailed description of strategic areas where weapons of great fire power, included among the Cuban arms cached in Venezuela, were to be placed on D-Day. The criminal mentality of the Castroites is revealed in the discovery that among the strategic areas was a maternity hospital in Caracas where mortars and machine guns were to be placed in the halls, in the apparent belief that counterfire would be withheld so as to save the lives of the more than 300 women and babies in the hospital. Other weapons, including large caliber mortars, were to have been unleashed against people in the crowded streets, so as to create the greatest amount of confusion and terror among the population and to intimidate them from supporting the Venezuelan police action against the terrorists. This terrorist plan failed in Caracas in 1963, just as the Negro plot failed in New York City in 1965, merely because of the chance discovery of arms and plans by the authorities.

For a period, it appeared that Venezuela had weathered the guerrilla assaults of the Cuba-Russia combine in Havana. But this was not the case. Time after time, President Betancourt and his successor President Raúl Leoni declared that assaults from Cuba had abated, even claiming that guerrillas in the mountains had been liquidated for all time. But also time after time the guerrilla movement exploded in size and intensity, in response to the thrust of men, money and arms from Cuba, as 1965 blossomed into a year of Communist experimentation and advance throughout Latin America. For Venezuela, the conflicts in 1965 were set off with a broadcast on January 19 over Havana's CMQ radio by Eduardo Gallegos Mancera, Secretary for International Relations of the Venezuelan Communist Party (another traveller to Cuba via Mexico), who told Venezuelan guerrillas: "The anti-imperialist fight in Venezuela will be intensified on all fronts during the course of this year," and laid out the plans for doing so, saying: "We must keep the ruling clique in Caracas in a state of permanent crisis." What he meant was an intensification of urban guerrilla warfare which already had caused Raúl Azparren, President of the Chamber of Commerce in the State of Lara, to complain on January 15 that the government was unable to provide adequate protection against urban guerrillas. He said, also, that banks and businesses were plagued with holdups by Castroite terrorists which enabled them to finance some of their activities. Señor Azparren's complaints were triggered by two lightning-fast guerrilla raids on the town of Baquero and the sacking of businesses which he identified as belonging to Juis Hung and Leoncio Ruíz García.

As the Venezuelan police and army tried to track down the attackers of Baquero, the guerrillas struck again, this time against a cattle ranch in the neighboring state of Barina. Owner Francisco Morales was slain, and leaflets left on his body by Castroite guerrillas headed by Fabricio Ojeda warned that other cattlemen in Venezuela's back country could expect a similar fate if they refused to supply them with food, money, and arms. Then at 2:00 a.m. on March 16, a group of 18 Castroite guerrillas attacked the village of Masparrito, also in the State of Barinas, killed a school teacher, and fled with money and arms. The attack was coordinated with another, simultaneously against the village of Villanueva. And on May 10, terrorists blew up an oil pipe line belonging to the Venezuelan government, and the same day attached 36 sticks of dynamite to an oil pipe line belonging to the Mene Grande Oil Company, a subsidiary of Texaco, in the State of Anzoategui. Fortunately, the charge was discovered and dismantled.

Further evidence that terrorizing the civilian population was a major tactic of the Communist guerrillas in 1965 was revealed on August 23, when a peasant woman in Lara State who had refused to collaborate with terrorists, together with her six-year-old child, was rescued from guerrillas by a military helicopter. The little girl was wounded by a grenade thrown at her and at her mother when the 12-man guerrilla group fled as the helicopter arrived. And in Valencia, southwest of Caracas, Luis Cisnero Groquer, a legislator belonging to the Democratic Action Party of President Raúl Leoni, barely escaped a murder attempt when the engine of his car was fitted with a bomb, designed to blow up when he turned on his ignition.

This brief outline of Castroite activities in Venezuela provides a negative answer to assertions of the New Frontiersmen Rostow, Schlesinger and Goodwin at the Punta del Este conference in January 1962, that the bettering of living conditions through cooperation with the Alliance for Progress would undercut the Communists by depriving them of the support of the people. Indeed, many of the terroristic assaults occurred just as President Leoni was presenting a rosy picture of the economy at the opening of the 1965 session of the Venezuelan congress, including a sizable seven percent rise in gross national product. And, pressed in Caracas by newsmen to square the high point in Venezuelan economic growth with a high point in terror, Defense Minister Ramón Florencio Gómez said that he had never promised the total extermination of the guerrillas. He had been concentrating on defensive tactics to neutralize their activities. Interior Minister Gonzalo Barrios told newsmen that the precarious security situation prevailing in Venezuela was caused by Cuba-trained guerrillas.

Evidence that the Dominican Republic could expect an onslaught by guerrillas was provided in late 1962 when 25 Dominican Communists were recruited to undergo training in Cuba by Roberto Santiesteban Casanova, while he was assigned to the Cuban mission to the United

Nations. Santiesteban Casanova was the Cuban UN official found guilty of attempted sabotage in New York City and New Jersey in November 1962, and released through the joint efforts of U Thant and Robert Kennedy. His subversive activities while in the United Nations related to his position as an officer of the Cuban General Directorate of Intelligence—in other words a spy and *agent provocateur*. The twenty-five Dominicans were dispatched to Cuba in early 1963 where they received six months training. The names of some are listed here because of the role they played in the Dominican uprising in April 1965. Among the most important of the twenty-five were Fidelio Despradel Roque, Manuel Tavarez Justo, Juan Mejía Gómez, and Juan Matos Rivera, all prominent members of the Castroite June 14 Movement (1J4), the paramilitary organization that took its name from the date in 1959 when Castro launched his abortive assault on the Dominican Republic. Other Communist groups were represented among the twenty-five trained in Cuba in 1963, including Diomedes Mercedes Batista, Pedro Mir Valentine, Antonio E. Isa Conde, and Milvio Pérez Pérez, all members of the Russian-line Dominican Peoples Socialist Party (PSPD); and Luis Felipe Giro Alacatara, Silvano Lora Vicente, and Cayetano Rodríguez del Prado, members of the Chinese-line Popular Dominican Movement (MPD).

Back in Cuba, in 1963, Santiesteban Casanova mounted a special DGI operation in support of the now trained band of Dominican guerrillas. The operation, known as "Flora," (named, incidentally, after the hurricane that devastated Cuba in 1963) was to transfer a huge arms shipment at sea from a Cuban Navy ship to a Dominican vessel which was then to run the arms ashore. Bad weather in late October prevented the operation from being completed on schedule, and it was not until early December that it was carried out, this time with the arms transferred from a Cuban Lambda fishing vessel to the Dominican fishing vessel "Scarlet Woman." The shipment was intercepted on December 6 by Dominican authorities, and the guerrilla movement fizzled and died as the Dominican Army moved in, killing some and capturing most of the others. An intriguing point to be made here is that the "Scarlet Woman" was built in Cuba, registered there as "Sigma Three" and brought to Miami in 1962 by Francisco Pérez Rojas, a Cuban fisherman who fled to the United States in the boat. Sold to an unidentified American in 1963, the boat went to Santo Domingo the same year. When seized, authorities found that PSPD member Facundo Gómez Pérez was a part owner.

The Liberal Establishment was outraged by the crushing of the guerrillas, and on December 29 the *Washington Post* editorialized over the resignation of Dr. Emilio de los Santos, no apparent friend of the *Post* up to this time, saying: "Dr. Emilio de los Santos, head of the civilian triumvirate that nominally rules the country, has resigned in protest over the apparent massacre of 16 pro-Castro guerrillas. The killings occurred on December 21, and the toll included the young leader of the Fidelista June 14 movement, Manuel Tavares Justo, and six of his top lieutenants." Like the *New York Times* in its comments on the FALN terrorists in Venezuela, the *Post* seemed more concerned over measures taken by Dominican authorities to defend their country than in the events which showed the need for that defense, pegging that concern on de los Santos by saying: "Dr. de los Santos has been concerned for some weeks by the ruthlessness of repressive measures aimed at leftist groups." Yet the band of Dominicans had received training in Cuba, were avowed members of three Communist groups, deserved to be called Communists, and had themselves precipitated the guerrilla wars in which many were killed and others captured. In fact, those captured were not tried and sentenced for treason, as their activities may well have deserved, but were merely deported from the Dominican Republic, an extraordinary act of kindness on the part of what the *Post* considered to be a ruthless and repressive government. Indeed, the deportation of Communists to Lisbon turned out to be as foolish as it was magnanimous, for some of the Communists made their way to Red China and Russia, while most spent their exile time in Cuba receiving additional training in guerrilla warfare techniques, particularly in those techniques related to urban uprisings. More important, by April 1965, forty-five of the exiled Castroites had made their way back to the Dominican Republic, some of them clandestinely, to rejoin their organizations. That they were there for a purpose became clear when, on April 24, a revolt exploded in Santo Domingo which forced President Johnson to intervene with U.S. troops.

CHAPTER 16

Santo Domingo—A Case Study

AT EIGHT O'CLOCK sharp on the morning of April 24, 1965, Captain José Rebellón walked out of the cabin of his ship "Venus," docked on the Ozama river in downtown Santo Domingo, and decided to go into the heart of the old city, called Ciudad Nueva, located but a few blocks away. Before stepping onto the gangway of the ship, Captain Rebellón looked briefly at the flag of Panama hanging limply at the stern of his ship, and wondered if foreign registry would provide protection in the event of trouble. The captain was disturbed, for only the night before, as he walked through the park near the old cathedral on his way to visit a friend, he noticed *turbas*, street gangs of toughs, surging along El Conde street and talking in loud voices about an imminent coup to topple President Donald Reid Cabral from office.

The talk was in itself not surprising. For weeks *El Caribe* newspaper had been publishing front-page stories about a conspiracy in the making. And just two days earlier, on April 22, Donald Reid Cabral, who ruled the country in a triumvirate arrangement with two other civilians, sacked seven Air Force officers apparently involved in that conspiracy. Yet Captain Rebellón had noticed an air of expectancy among the *turbas* and had noticed, as well, that the police on duty seemed nervous. So the morning of April 24, he decided to visit the hospital where one of his crew was recovering from dysentery brought on by drinking contaminated water and, at the same time, to judge the temper of the *turbas*.

The Captain had a car at his disposal and, together with First Mate Adolis Cobos, drove to the hospital where he learned that his crew member, Máximo Delgado Pérez, was going to be all right. As the two drove away from the hospital and approached Independence Park, they saw that it was filling up with people, and learned that this was in response to a rumor that Reid Cabral had already been overthrown.

Rebellón drove back to his ship to be ready to leave port if the mobs turned ugly, and sent Cobos to the house of a friend, Antonio Aguirre, to ascertain if the rumor was true. The time was about 10:30, and the crowds were in a happy mood. Reid Cabral was unpopular because he had instituted an austerity program to pull the country out of debt. Cobos learned nothing from Señor Aguirre and returned to the ship. At 2:30 in the afternoon, the ship's radio crackled out the following announcement: "Return to Constitutionality with Juan Bosch as President!" The shout was repeated several times, then came a rush of information by rebels who had seized the station, saying that the Triumvirate had indeed been overthrown. Captain Rebellón again drove into Ciudad Nueva to judge for himself what was happening.

According to the official log of the "Venus," which Captain Rebellón permitted me to copy when I arrived in Santo Domingo on April 29: "The *turbas* ran through the streets, many of them armed, shooting bullets in the air. They made an attack on police stations at this time, apparently in the hope that the police would side with the mobs." By 4:30 in the afternoon, according to the ship's log, loyalist forces had regained control of Santo Domingo Radio, and an unidentified police colonel broadcast that the coup had failed, and urged the people to return to their homes. "It was too late," according to the log, "because some organizers saw a crack in the solidity of the regime, and began to move." Captain Rebellón was in his car at the scene when the *Cascos Blancos*, the riot police, many of them mounted on horses, broke up the mobs around the radio station. Throughout the night, crew members of the "Venus" listened from their vantage point of 300 yards away as tanks from the Armed Forces Training Center at San Isidro Air Base rumbled over the Duarte bridge on the Ozama river and took up positions at the entrance to Ciudad Nueva, now under control of the mobs. They saw the rebels burning cars and turning over trucks and placing them as barricades against the tanks. At 3:00 in the morning, a bazooka was fired from the barricades at one of the tanks, bringing a point-blank return which tore down a high tension wire and set fire to a house.

At six o'clock on the morning of April 25, three radio stations in rebel hands began broadcasting prepared messages, including repeated requests to the armed forces, demanding to know: "Are you with the people, or are you against the people?" The log book then reads: "All the symptons of Communist management are here, though it is difficult to pin it down at present." The captain was sufficiently disturbed at the ugly turn of events to order the engines started on the ship and then to drive to the house of his friend Aguirre, again to check on the situation to determine if he should leave the harbor. After considerable trouble getting through the mobs, Captain Rebellón arrived at the house, and found there Señora Ligia Fernández, the sister-in-law of Donald Reid Cabral. The report on that meeting is contained in the log, with the time given as 7:00 A.M.: "Señora Ligia Fernández left the house of Antonio Aguirre after a few moments, saying that all was lost, and that they would have to leave the country."

When the Captain returned to his ship, he found several hundred civilians and a score or more of military men aboard

An officer who identified himself as Lieutenant Reyes announced that the ship was being taken over "because this is a revolution of the people." Rebellón had feared such an event, for as he passed through the mobs in Ciudad Nueva, he noticed that well-armed civilian organizers were haranguing the crowds in Independence Park to support the revolt. He also noticed a white Volkswagen stationwagon fitted with loud speakers cruising through the downtown area, urging the people to join in the revolt against Reid Cabral. Then he saw another mobile unit, and another. He was astonished to see Army officers handing out hundreds of arms from trucks to the *turbas*. A little further on, he saw civilians handing out arms from busses to other civilians, while small groups formed themselves into squads and trotted away in semi-military formation. "This," he commented in the log book of the "Venus" "is not a spontaneous uprising—it is organized." It was with this knowledge that Captain Rebellón proceeded with all haste to his ship and found it under the command of the rebels. Such was the confusion among the military, however, that Rebellón was to note: "At this moment, the Navy had taken no decision as to which side it was on." This was clearly the case when, within a few moments of being confronted with the demand by Lieutenant Reyes to turn over the ship to him, an officer and another fifty Navy men arrived. The Commander, who outranked Lieutenant Reyes, rescinded Reyes' orders and kicked the civilians off the ship, advising Captain Rebellón that he would be wise to sail.

The Captain was prevented from steaming away when police opened fire against mobs on the docks (who were shooting at them), striking and killing five persons and wounding in the leg one crew member of the ship. Still in rebel hands, Radio Santo Domingo was the only station on the air; nothing was heard from loyalist Commanders at San Isidro, to the east of the Ozama River. Rebels used the radio skillfully in propaganda warfare, shouting over the airwaves that the entire military establishment had sided with them against Reid Cabral. The answer was given negatively when military planes from the San Isidro Air Base began to attack positions of the now organized mobs. Rebel radio announcers responded by claiming that Cuban exile pilots were flying the planes. In the words of the ship's log: "At 9:00 p.m., Radio Santo Domingo commenced to say that responsibility for the bombings lay with Cuban exiles, claiming that they were mercenaries hired by General Elías Wessin y Wessin." Captain Rebellón had little more to do than to listen to the radio and move around the center of the city for, as the log states: "Port Commander Bordas turned down my request to leave the docks, saying he had no authority to permit me to do so until he was sure where he stood," meaning until he found out which side the Navy was on.

Some of what the captain of the "Venus" found during the several days he was immobilized is highly important to an understanding of what went on during this critical period, for the only other sources were the U.S. Embassy in Santo Domingo, foreign diplomats, most of whom did not leave their chanceries, and the rebels. The first 36 hours of the revolt found the military almost totally confused, as the following notation made in the ship's log at 2:30 p.m., Sunday, April 25, indicates: "The headquarters of the Port Authority, containing 150 sailors has not been occupied as yet, but neither is there any unity among the sailors. The indecision is fantastic, due to a lack of communications everywhere among the armed forces." The log book goes on: "The National Police freed all the political prisoners, and they were rushed by trucks to Radio Santo Domingo where they claimed that the armed forces are with the people." Other passages in the ship's log were to take on considerable importance in later debates among the U.S. press regarding the truth or falsehood of an off-the-record briefing given by U.S. Ambassador Tapley Bennett the night of April 29. For example, one notation in the log, dated Sunday, April 25, at 2:30 p.m. tells of rebel excesses in the city in these terms: "During my drive around the center of the city, I saw the rebels organizing quickly to repel the forces of General Wessin y Wessin. Armed mobs flood the whole area, the sacking, the robbings, the killings are uncontrollable because, lacking any leadership whatsoever as to what to do, the police have withdrawn into their headquarters in the Ozama Fortress, leaving the streets in the hands of the *turbas*. Under the able direction of the Communist cadres, they are occupying the center of the city, street by street." And at 6:00 p.m., the log book reads: "A policeman was killed, his head put on a long stick, and it is being paraded around the neighborhood to incite the mobs."

Radio Santo Domingo continued sending optimistic bulletins, among them that "Provisional President" Juan Francisco Molina Ureña had been installed at the Presidential Palace and was passing decrees. This propaganda was an evident attempt to give the impression that the country now was being governed by a rebel "constitutional" President.

Behind the first few hours so graphically portrayed in the log book of the Panamanian vessel were 30 years of rule by dictator Rafael Trujillo and the seven-month reign of Juan Bosch, virtually the first elected

President in the history of the country. Señor Bosch was for 24 years more or less a professional exile. He was befriended and given a position in Cuba by President Carlos Prío Socarrás, taught at a labor school in Costa Rica, was the friend of Venezuela's President Rómulo Betancourt, Costa Rica's President Pepe Figueres, and, at the time of the Santo Domingo revolt, was living on a $10,000-a-year salary, as a sometime lecturer at the University of Puerto Rico, provided by another friend, governor of the U.S. island, Luis Muñóz Marín.

Bosch returned to the Dominican Republic following the assassination of Trujillo on May 30, 1961, ran for President and was elected in 1962 with 62 percent of the vote. His campaign speeches were not without a touch a demagogy, as he attacked the moneyed class and promised the people that sweeping social and economic advantages would flow from his new regime. However, one view is that Bosch's rival National Civic Union party lost the election—not that Bosch and his Revolutionary Dominican Party won—because the leadership of the Civic Union said that it would punish all former collaborators of dictator Trujillo. This policy alienated many in the electorate since, after 30 years of dictatorship, virtually everyone was tainted to a degree. But, following his election, Bosch and his party asked that stiff confiscatory measures be taken against all who might have benefited—even indirectly—under the fallen tyrant. Many alleged to see in Bosch's double dealing a trace of Fidel Castro, a view that was supported when the Dominican President set about creating a "popular militia," reportedly consisting of about 17,000 youths.

President Bosch repeatedly refused to crack down on the Communists, alleging that all parties in a democracy had the right to grow. He repeated the line of the Schlesingers and the Goodwins that the only way to combat the appeal of Communism was to provide materially for the people. All three gentlemen apparently had profited little from the lesson learned by President Rómulo Betancourt, who commenced his reign in Venezuela with much the same philosophy only to find that it got him into more trouble. The fact was that from the moment of Bosch's inauguration in February 1963, the country's Communist parties* began openly agitating for the overthrow of the very democratic government that defended their right to conspire. They were better organized and financed than any of the democratic parties that sprang up following Trujillo's assassination. At least four Communist publications were put into circulation—*Libertad, Popular, June 14,* and *Fragua*—while the Communists actively organized their ranks and built their strength. They were strong in the cities of Santiago de los Caballeros, Mao, San Francisco de Macoris, and Monte Cristo. In Mao alone, a town with about

*There were two Communist Parties, the Chinese-line MPD and the Moscow-line PSP.

17,000 inhabitants, the Castroite 1J4 had six subcommittees, and the Red campaign included radio shows, weekly meetings in various neighborhoods, and the distribution of enormous amounts of literature, some of which was printed in Cuba.

To impress upon Bosch the need for a militant anti-Communist posture, an organization called the Manifestation of Christian Reaffirmation called two public meetings in Santo Domingo and neighboring La Vega which attracted thousands of sympathizers who had begun to feel the bullying tactics of the Communists. It seemed very clear within months of Bosch's taking power that he would have to change his pacifist tune or be forced out of office, either by the Communists or by the military. Disillusionment with Bosch was to be heard on all sides, even among Bosch's supporters. Germán Ornes, publisher of *El Caribe* told Dom Bonafede of *The Miami Herald* to quote him as follows: "All the elements of an explosive situation are here. We cannot any longer ignore the Communist problem in this country."[1] Communists had infiltrated all but key positions in the government, and in the summer of 1963 three lieutenants were cashiered for being involved in Communist activities, only one indication that the Communists were making inroads among junior officers of the army.

Bosch moved from disaster to disaster. He was receiving approximately $4.5 million per month in Alliance for Progress funds and he took office at a time when extremely high prices were being paid for sugar; yet he could not make the economy work. Sugar prices in 1962, the year before he came to power, were 2.98 cents a pound. When he took office in February 1963, the price had gone up to 6.06 cents, and by May it was 10.36 cents a pound. Nevertheless, reliable estimates placed the number of jobless at about 280,000 out of a total labor force of about 800,000. Labor unrest, complicated by open Communist agitation, was viewed serenely by the President who told visiting newsmen that this problem, like most of the others, would disappear in time. But time was a major factor for the success of untried or nonexistent democratic institutions, and the frail structure of government was being assaulted on every side.

Though knowing full well that foreign investment was needed to build the country, President Bosch by word and deed drove away foreign investors and even placed the future of $100 million in U.S. investments in jeopardy when he falsely accused the United States-owned South Puerto Rico Sugar Company of conspiring against him. In a speech he told the Dominicans never to do business with U.S. oil companies and accused a Roman Catholic chaplain of being the mastermind of an armed forces' plot against him. And very soon after taking office, Bosch nearly plunged the Caribbean into war when he sent the Dominican Army to the border of Haiti in an attempt to force Haitian President Francois Duvalier to grant safe conduct to 22 political refugees who had taken asylum in the Dominican Embassy in Port-au-Prince. Bosch thought nothing at the time of asking the Organization of American States to discard the principle of non-intervention and, in effect, to back him in an attack on Haiti. It now seems probable that Bosch's military moves in May 1963 were designed to distract attention from his shortcomings in ruling the country. Bosch was opposed by the military in this mad adventure, and finally a combination of domestic pressures and diplomatic moves forced him to back down.

Congressmen Armistead Selden of the House Foreign Affairs Subcommittee had been receiving reports of Bosch's apparent inability to rule, together with information regarding the growing Communist menace. A government that cannot rule obviously cannot protect itself from Communist subversion. On May 31, 1963, Selden warned that Communists were moving into the Dominican Republic from exile in Soviet Russia, China, and Cuba, and stated that the situation was serious enough for the State Department to tell President Bosch of U.S. concern. President Bosch replied with an attack on Selden, accusing him of trying to run Dominican affairs from Washington, an attack which only increased Representative Selden's concern. The Congressman replied that it was not encouraging to see that Bosch "chooses to attack United States friends of Dominican freedom while he apparently ignores threats to that freedom by Communists operating within his own borders."[2] Indeed, President Bosch proved extraordinarily sensitive to opinions that differed from his own, saying on May 27: "I consider very dangerous to the democratic future of the Dominican Republic the fact that some American newspapermen attribute to themselves the power to show how the problems of this country should be handled." He went on to defend his soft policy regarding the Communists, saying: "The only way to face Communist propaganda is with deeds that show the efficiency of democracy to resolve the social and economic problems that all our countries have."[3]

Behind Bosch was Sascha Volman, a naturalized U.S. citizen of Rumanian birth, one of the shadow cabinet of a select group of foreigners who acted as sort of gray eminences behind the President. Volman knew Bosch when both were instructors at Costa Rica's Institute of Social and Political Democracy, a pet project of former Costa Rican President José Figueres. Volman opened a similar school in Santo Domingo which, like its parent in Costa Rica, was more anti-American than not. And when Bosch was overthrown, Volman succeeded in eluding the police who wanted mightily to question him about his activities, and left the country. A member of the so-called democratic left, Volman had been given a clean bill of health by the White House, an unsurprising revelation in view of the fact that those dealing in Latin American affairs in the White House also were identifiable with that same democratic left. President Kennedy availed himself of the opportunity to issue a formal statement on the occasion of receiving the credentials of Bosch's first Ambassador to Washington. Ignoring reports of Communist infiltration in the Dominican Republic, President Kennedy said that the similar aims of the United States and the Dominican governments were evident, and he found that Bosch's progress was excellent "in so remarkably short a time."[4]

Nevertheless, the Dominican President was faced with a major internal crisis when, in the middle of July 1963, a group of military officers told him to get tough with the Communists, and said they would back him in any measures he put into effect to deal with them. Bosch reportedly told them that cracking down on the Communists would deal a death blow to democracy since, he maintained, a government cannot be tyrannical toward one group and democratic to another. Taking to the airwaves in a report to the people, the President admitted that the military asked him to take action. And shunning the word, "Communist," Bosch referred to a "certain political sector" as the object of the concern of the military and in something of a non-sequitur said: "I am not willing to head a dictatorship—neither a complete one or a partial one—in the Dominican Republic."[5] By misinterpreting the intent of the military to mean that cracking down on Communist subversion meant a return to tyranny, President Bosch most probably at that moment set in motion the forces which were to oust him from office in September.

The military had good reason to confront the President. They had learned that Bosch had agreed to permit 30 Dominican Communists to go to Cuba to attend the July 26th Celebration there. This Bosch permitted despite the fact that Dominican passports prohibit travel to Russia, Red China, and their satellites. In effect, Bosch broke the law of the country in order to accommodate the enemies of democracy. Furthermore, nineteen of the Communists made their way to Havana aboard a chartered aircraft of *Aerovias Quisqueyanas*, an airline owned by Diego Bordas, Minister of Industry and Commerce under Bosch. The plane flew the Cuba-bound passengers to Panama where they then boarded flight 420 of Guest Airlines to Mexico City and proceeded on to Havana. An American, William Hartshorn, piloted the *Quisqueyanas* plane that took the Dominican Communists to Panama, among them Cayetano Rodríguez del Prado and Diomedes Mercedes Batista. He later told U.S. Senate investigators that at the last minute a group of priests was put aboard the plane at Caucedo airport in Santo Domingo "in order to disguise the true nature of the trip."[6] Thus, the Dominican military had good reason to believe that collusion existed between President Bosch, his Minister of Industry and Commerce, and the Dominican Communists.

Then there was the matter of Bosch's new Constitution. Rammed through a Congress swept into office with Bosch, the 1963 Constitution was so vague that a President could do most anything he wanted under it. All subsoil wealth, oil, and minerals were declared to be the property of the state, while Section Four permitted expropriation when it is "in the general interest," and Article 28 restricts land ownership to Dominican citizens, but permits Congress to approve the acquisition of land in urban areas by foreigners, again if such acquisition is considered to be "in the national interest." And "excessive" holding of land is not permitted, but the Constitution did not define what is excessive, and left it up to the Congress to make the determination. The Bosch Congress itself was really of "the people"—bootblacks and day laborers, many of them illiterate—and, in response to Bosch's wishes, it eliminated any reference to God in the Constitution. Little was done even to organize the legislature and to run it efficiently. Indeed, Bosch finally became alarmed, sending a message to a Congress which he had publicly described as "my steamroller," telling Congressional leaders that unless they took their jobs seriously they could get him toppled from office.

It is not accurate for Tad Szulc to claim as he does in his book, *Dominican Diary,* that it was only "right wingers" who accused Bosch of being soft on Communism and that they alone "began a powerful and well-financed campaign that Dr. Bosch was at best a dupe of the Communists."[7] (Szulc argued that no evidence of Communist infiltration was ever proved.) Indeed, in September, a commercial strike was launched protesting Bosch's refusal to crack down on the Communists. Stores and businesses in Santo Domingo were closed down as employees joined employers in the protest. And Bosch, who had refused to so much as enforce the laws against travel by Communists to Cuba because it might make him a dictatorial figure, used dictatorial powers in ordering the electricity shut off to the capital's three major radio stations because of their support of the strike and arrested fourteen employees of the La Voz del Tropico radio station. Yet, when Communist travelers to Cuba returned they were unmolested by Dominican authorities, and the *Washington Post* was to note in an editorial: "Let it be noted that few claimed that the President was dictatorial."[8] The question, rather, was dictatorial against whom?

It was in this atmosphere of crisis piled upon crisis that silver-thatched Bosch, on September 25, was ousted from power by a combination of military officers and prominent civilian chiefs, this bringing about the thoroughly false claim by resigning Dominican Ambassador to the

United States Enriquillo del Rosario that the overthrow was due to "some of the newly rich businessmen who were happy at making a profit under the Trujillo dictatorship, and have been fighting the democratic government from the start."[9] Del Rosario, who had done nothing to oust Trujillo, was aiming his darts at General Antonio Imbert Barrera and Luis Amiama Tio, who assassinated the dictator in a daring night attack on his car. Both helped rule the country until elections, and turned over their positions on the Council of State to Juan Bosch when he was elected.

Senator Wayne Morse, chairman of the Latin American Affairs Subcommittee of the Senate Foreign Relations Committee, apparently took del Rosario's charges seriously and headed an investigation to determine whether any U.S. business interests were involved in Bosch's overthrow. Morse repeated on the floor of the Senate that it had been charged in some unidentified quarters that powerful U.S. interests indeed had supported the military in their overthrow of President Bosch, and said that CIA Director John McCone should be questioned regarding the whole affair. Meanwhile, statements from the White House and the State Department insisted on a rapid return to constitutional government and gave the clear impression that this meant the return of Juan Bosch. Ambassador John Bartlow Martin was jerked out of the Embassy, all aid programs were stopped, and United States representation in Santo Domingo was turned over to Chargé d'Affairs Spencer King. Mr. King then infuriated the ruling civilian junta by suggesting that Senate President Juan Casanovas Garrido be installed, despite the fact that the military had evidence that Casanovas was linked to the Communists. This was the price asked by the New Frontier in return for a return to full diplomatic relations and a resumption of economic aid to the country.

A junta member, Yale-educated Manuel Tavares, saw in the U.S. proposal total ignorance of the New Frontier to understand why the coup had taken place in the first place. And while the junta was preparing a polite rejection of the U.S. proposal, the story of the State Department's demands was leaked to the Associated Press by someone in the State Department in what Sr. Tavares and his two ruling companions considered to be an effort to force them to accept the U.S. position. The leak merely forced them into a public position of denouncing crude American intervention in the internal affairs of the Dominican Republic. No government could long stand without such a public denunciation in the face of a news leak that was bound to rile the Dominicans. In making the denunciation, Sr. Tavares said: "I'm no one's stooge. Our friends pushed us into this role."[10]

Charges made in Washington that the three-man civilian junta acted as mere puppets of the military did not hold up to serious scrutiny. An interview with members of the junta by the *New York Herald Tribune*'s William Haddad is revealing as to the relationship between the military and civilian leaders in the Dominican Republic. "When the military took over," Sr. Tavares told Haddad, "they called in the six opposition parties and told them to pick a government." The parties chose Manuel Tavares, Emilio de los Santos, and Ramón Tapia Espinal. Indeed, the means by which cabinet posts were allotted showed an extraordinary amount of democratic choice and rejection. The six political parties submitted names for cabinet positions, but the three-man civilian junta rejected six names in arriving at a group to help rule the country. The military made no recommendations. And Sr. Tavares said that Bosch himself was responsible for the coup, remarking: "No one liked constitutional government to end . . . but Bosch was not equipped to run the government. Nothing moved, he just kept everything to himself." Sr. Tavares said that he had just reviewed a $150 million loan agreement contracted by Bosch and said of it: "It is the most preposterous contract I ever saw," and then got to the heart of the matter: "He, one by one, alienated the businessmen, the farmers, the church, and the military. In three more months, the country would have been beyond salvation."[11] What Tavares was saying, of course, was that Bosch had dissipated his initial popularity and that by the time he was overthrown he commanded little respect anywhere in the country, a fact that "losers" later were to ignore altogether in reporting their version of the Dominican uprising. Indeed, Peace Corps Volunteers in the interior of the country reported that they had witnessed celebrations by Dominican *guajiros* as a result of the overthrow of Bosch.

Chief of Staff General Victor Elby Viñas Román shed some light on the views of the military toward Bosch and toward the new civilian junta. He told the *Herald Tribune:* "I am not one of those who said Bosch was a Communist. I just felt he didn't understand the dangers of allowing the Communists to get control of key positions," and gave an instance: "In one position there was a man who could bring arms into the country. There were the Communist schools. And Bosch was organizing a militia." The man referred to was Diego Bordas. As we shall see later, he, and apparently Bosch himself, were involved in bringing arms into the country. General Viñas Román said: "Cuba is too vivid for us here. And we don't want a Venezuela where the Communists engage in indiscriminate bombing." And after arresting about 500 Communists, said Viñas Román, "we turned them over to the junta, and they let them out of jail."[12] The military abided by the decision of the junta, thus helping convince the civilian leadership that the military would not dictate policy. They said that many of their difficulties arose from the inflexible position taken by the United States which seemed to want to preserve constitutional succession by insisting that the Presidency be turned over to Sr. Casanovas. More interesting is that the U.S. policy of trying to divide the military and civilian leadership had, instead, united them, and the pressures which were supposed to have come from businessmen to the junta as a result of the cut-off of economic aid was not forthcoming. Except of course for Bosch, his PRD, and the Communists, there was remarkable unanimity in the country to reject U.S. pressures and to continue with the civilian junta until new elections could be held.

Yet, the *New York Times* came to the defense of Bosch, finding for some unassignable reason that the overthrow of Juan Bosch would cause "Castroite Cuba to rejoice," adding that the reasons for the coup "have a stale sound—the usual accusations of pro-Communism, Socialism, and mismanagement." It said of the overthrown President merely that he was a "left-of-center intellectual in line with the democratic left represented by such leaders as President Betancourt of Venezuela and Governor Muñóz Marín of Puerto Rico."[13] One would imagine that the liberals would have been angry at Bosch for having muffed the opportunity of a lifetime to develop a democratic society in his country. But no, he was found largely to be blameless despite his weakness of character and a vanity that would permit no views to prevail over his own. The *New York Times* emotionalized about Bosch in its September 29 editorial: "In the Dominican Republic President Juan Bosch, a high-minded, high-principled intellectual, tried to run a weak, divided, half-illiterate society . . . The United States helped to create a police force whose leaders were badly chosen and turned against Juan Bosch."[14] As erroneous as it was emotional, the editorial claimed that military officers were in power, and said of the non-existent military government that it ought not be condoned. In its zeal to arouse the U.S. government to take action, the editorialist completely vandalized the truth. The fact was, the Secretariat of State of the Dominican Armed Forces, announcing the overthrow of President Bosch, stipulated at the outset that it had called upon the six major political parties to choose civilians to run the government until elections could be held, and then supported their choice.

And Tad Szulc was no more accurate than the editorialist when, on September 28, his version of what had happened was published in the *Times.* He said that the death of the Bosch regime came "when a group of Dominican generals and colonels acting as the battering ram for a motley collection of ambitions Rightist politicians and disgruntled businessmen, ousted President Juan Bosch after seven months in his elective office." Despite the announcement by the military that it was turning over the country to six political parties to choose a civilian government Szulc found that this merely represented a return to the dictatorship of Rafael Trujillo. (An interesting comment came out of Havana, by the way, which was largely ignored. On September 27, Fidel Castro gave a 95-minute speech in which he said that Bosch was overthrown by elements in the United States because he would not follow "a policy of hate toward Cuba."[15]) The *Washington Post* editorialized on September 29 that economic aid should be withheld from the Dominican Republic, and warned that the Dominican coup would result in a wave of military dictatorships throughout the hemisphere (something that didn't happen). Curiously, the *Post* said in the same editorial: "In Nicaragua, the Somoza oligarchy is sponsoring the training of rightist Cuban exiles, allegedly as an anti-Castro force," and then made the preposterous charge that this "rightist" force was to be used to overthrow governments in Latin America, "with the aim of creating a holy alliance of military dictatorships in the region." This gratuitous defense of Fidel Castro through such twisted logic, equating anti-Communism with "rightism," may be taken as a measure of the panic which hit the Liberal Establishment over the downfall of President Bosch. It most surely brought joy in Communist Cuba, which at that very moment was struggling with a popular rebellion.

Republican Congressman William Cramer seethed over suggestions coming from many quarters "to restore Bosch to power," describing them as "the height of idiocy." Mr. Cramer said that several "far leftists in Latin America are calling for U.S. action to reinstate Communist-sympathizer Bosch." The Florida Congressman said: "They are being joined by leftist supporters in this country, including Teodoro Moscoso who is in charge of our Alliance for Progress, Gonzalo Fascio, President of the Organization of American States, an Ambassador from Costa Rica, and the Ambassadors of other far-left countries." Cramer added, perhaps for the benefit of the *Washington Post:* "It is interesting that these same people are the ones who vociferously object when someone suggests stronger measures—short of war—to oust Communist Castro from Cuba because they object to the usage of 'the big stick' by the United States, how swiftly they turn and ask for intervention when one of their far-left rulers is being deposed."[16] It seems certain that Cramer was answering Democratic Senator Ernest Gruening of Alaska who demanded that "the United States send a destroyer" to intercept the vessel carrying Bosch to Puerto Rico. Bosch should be "taken from it," said Senator Gruening, "and returned under United States protection to the Dominican Republic."[17] Liberals jumped on the bandwagon. But the *Washington Daily News* asked of Gruening's proposal: "Does he think the United States is more justified in intervening in the Dominican Republic than in Cuba?" and joked: "It all adds up to Bosch, we think."[18].

And as soon as Juan Bosch landed on U.S. soil in Puerto Rico he violated his political exile by broadcasting to the Dominican Republic from the city of Mayaguez, located across the channel from Santo

Domingo, to urge the Dominicans "to take to the streets and revive liberty." He muddied up the waters by claiming that the military had acted when the political foes whom Bosch had defeated for election telephoned Army leaders and told them that they would be assassinated unless they got rid of the President. He also said that he had failed to act against the Communists for fear of triggering what he called Batista-type terrorism, again equating anti-Communism with "rightism." He did not say that certain members of his cabinet and Congress were ardently pro-Castro or that in their hatred of the Trujillo image they might be driven into the hands of the Communists. Nor did Bosch admit that he was surrounded by powerful pro-Castro advisers, notably Attorney General Luis Moreno Martínez, a self-proclaimed admirer of the Cuban dictator.

The story was not told by Bosch for the simple reason that some of it he did not know, and what he did know could be revealed only at the risk of justifying his own overthrow. A key man in the story was Colonel Raphael Morel Tineo, chief of the secret police, and clearly unsympathetic to a resurgence of a right-wing dictatorship which he had personally helped bring to an end. Morel had been watching the Communist activities, particularly those of the Castroite 1J4, and on several occasions had tried to persuade President Bosch to investigate the pro-Castro members of the Cabinet and Congress, but in each instance Bosch said no. Colonel Morel decided to investigate on his own, slipped undercover agents into the insurgent groups and began watching and recording the conduct of suspected leaders. He found that a Communist, pro-Castro plot coup was planned for December and he had tape recordings of secret meetings in which the December plot was discussed. The discussions revealed among other things the Communist belief that Bosch's incompetence would by that time have pretty well wrecked the economy. Bosch, of course, did not know about this plot.

The President did know about another matter, however, and this tells something about the character of the man and suggests why he was overthrown. Despite the knowledge that Diego Bordas had made a questionable fortune by working with Trujillo, Bosch had made him his Minister of Industry and Commerce. Bordas got his hands on the Colt Firearms Company's new AR-15 machine gun which had been sold to the Dominican government for tests. The gun is small and deadly, causing as much damage as a dum-dum, and had just been accepted by the U.S. Army. Bordas realized that a number of AR-15s could equip a group with enough fire-power to match a small army, and got Miguel Angel Dominguez Guerrera, Secretary of State, Interior, and the Police, to sign a requisition for an order of the AR-15, along with an order for 50 of the 75-millimeter anti-tank grenades and tear gas bombs that can be fired from the AR-15. It is significant that, like Attorney General Luis Moreno Martínez, Dominguez Guerrera was known to be pro-Castro, and that the only tanks in the country against which AR-15 grenades could be fired belonged to the army. This plot-within-a-plot indicates that the arms were to be used against the country's military forces. Colonel Morel of course learned of the Bordas-Guerrera plot, and also discovered that Bosch was aware of it. Bosch found out that the military knew about the impending purchase of the AR-15s and postponed the requisitions, but advised Colt to keep the orders pending and took no action against either Bordas or Guerrera. The important point, of course, was that the President of the country knew what was going on, and there is evidence that at some point along the way he may actively have joined in the plot. One suspicion is that Bosch planned to arm the 1J4 or his newly created militia, and to use them as a force to play off against the Army. The evidence was overwhelming, either that Bosch was playing directly into the hands of the Communists or, in his many frustrations, had decided to join them in destroying the power of the military. The military officers (there were five altogether), after debating whether or not they should approach the American Embassy, decided that the New Frontier not only would not be convinced by the evidence but might even tell Bosch about the impending coup, a decision that shows how little trusted the United States had become. The decision then became simple. Either they took over, or the Communists would. So they moved on September 25 in a bloodless coup that found few Dominicans rallying to the defense of President Juan Bosch.

Bosch vowed that he would return to the Dominican Republic "within 90 days." Meanwhile, Senator Wayne Morse witchhunted in the Senate Foreign Relations Committee, trying, and failing, to connect Texaco's Dominican representative, Duane D. Luther, with the overthrow of Bosch.[19] And while Foreign Minister Donald Reid Cabral was in the United States asking for a resumption of full diplomatic relations and a continuation of U.S. aid programs started under Bosch but cancelled with his overthrow, U.S. aid officials were packing and leaving Santo Domingo. Reid Cabral pointed out to unhearing Washington officials that the civilian junta had inherited a chaotic economic situation from the Bosch government which meant national bankruptcy unless the aid programs were reinstituted. He said of the New Frontiersmen: "They simply do not know Dominican reality."[20] And, in San Juan, Bosch was making semi-Marxist statements, as, for example, that Latin America was standing on the brink of a social revolution that "will once and for all do away with the power of the minority of large land owners, businessmen and the upper-middle class of our hemisphere, and dispose of the military cliques which serve them."[21] He claimed in an article in the *New*

Leader that his popular support was as great when he was overthrown as when he was elected.

It is significant to note here that the leftist Social Christian Revolutionary party went into opposition to the civilian junta's plans for an election, and later joined rebel forces in April 1965. Those plans now had jelled, calling for the election of a constituent assembly on December 14, 1964 and Presidential elections in mid-1965. And they received the support of *El Caribe*, which called the junta's proposition a "positive step" toward the restoration of democracy in the country. Bosch's now defunct Congress refused to go along, met, and "elected" Senate President Juan Casanovas Garrido as national President, then asked the State Department to recognize him as such. The State Department blundered into another sharp rebuke from the civilian junta when U.S. Chargé d'Affaires Spencer King asked what their plans were for returning the country to democratic government in view of the fact that Casanovas Garrido had been designated President by the "Congress." The junta promptly rejected what it considered to be a "suggestion" by the United States to turn the country back to a member of the ousted Bosch regime. Political leader Viriato Fiallo, a long-time friend of the United States called the U.S. move "unwise, even stupid," and accused the New Frontier of "seeking to establish another Cuba" in the Dominican Republic. The junta characterized Spencer's undertaking as "unprecedented interference" in Dominican affairs. A spokesman for the military, when advised of the U.S. action, asked: "Are they crazy?" then added: "If they want a military government here that is just what they will get by following this course,"[22] meaning that U.S. diplomatic intervention might well precipitate a civil war by encouraging left-wing and Communist elements in their efforts to force the civilian junta to step down.

The attitude of the New Frontier in support of Bosch became even more inscrutable when, in a notarized statement, Inocencio Marrero, contact secretary for Bosch's PRD, said that he had been given $40,000 to organize a "Force of Revolutionary Ethics," and described that force as a Bosch goon squad. This revelation recalled to the military Bosch's complicity in the AR-15 Colt contract, and their suspicions regarding the President's motives were heightened when Marrero said that the purpose of the Force of Revolutionary Ethics was to maintain vigilance over the armed forces, national police and government civil servants, and "to substitute for them when it became necessary." In fact, Sr. Marrero said that on one occasion he had been told by Jose Francisco Peña Gómez, an officer in Bosch's PRD, to send a group of about 500 dedicated members of the Force to break up an anti-Bosch political rally. For lack of written orders, Sr. Marrero said that he instructed the group to go to the rally, but to do nothing more than jeer the speakers. He was dressed-down at PRD headquarters, Marrero said, "because I had failed President Bosch by not carrying out his orders."[23] Taken together with Bosch's crackdown on radio stations and announcers who favored an anti-Bosch strike, it appeared to observers in the Dominican Republic that the President was not above strongarm tactics when used on his behalf.

The governing triumvirate also revealed, following Boschs' ouster, that the former President had been diverting at least $22,000 a month from the coffers of the PRD to unknown use elsewhere. This discovery took on some added significance when the national police raided leftist, Communist, and PRD headquarters and turned up enough armaments to equip the country's 3,500-man air force, all of the 3,000-man navy, and a third of the army or half the police force. In the face of these discoveries, Bosch woodenly postulated in an article published in the October issue of the liberal bi-weekly magazine *New Leader* that it was an over-armed and ambitious military establishment that caused his downfall. There was no hint that he might, even in the tiniest measure, have been somehow responsible for triggering that armed might against him. Professor John Roche, President of the left-wing Americans for Democratic Action, endorsed Bosch's position in the same issue, adopting the by-now-familiar liberal line: "Unfriendly newspaper accounts have attributed the coup d'état to Bosch's incompetence, his intellectualism, his blindness to the threat of communism, his vindictiveness against the Dominican upper class—indeed, they have assigned blame to every consideration except the correct one; that from the day he took authority he was powerless to cope with his oversized armed forces." Bosch, he added, was "destroyed by United States policy."[24] Bosch himself, of course, was held utterly blameless.

Some of the underlying reasons behind Bosch's ouster came out in a letter to the editor, published in the *New York Times* on October 27. The writer was Thomas F. Reilly, Bishop of San Juan de la Maguana in the Dominican Republic. Writing from Rome, Bishop Reilly took issue with the misleading pro-Bosch editorial published in the September 29 issue of the *Times*. Said Bishop Reilly: "Dr. Bosch, a most astute campaigner, proved himself as President to be hypersensitive, doctrinaire, contemptuous of the many elements devoted to democracy and strangely out of touch with the traditions of his country." According to Bishop Reilly, Bosch had lost much of his popular support: "The Apostolic Nuncio Emmanuele Clarizio and other Bishops in friendly talks with Dr. Bosch and members of his Government indicated what must be done to regain in some measure his lost popular support." They did so, wrote Bishop Reilly, because "it is undeniable that responsible civilian groups were disturbed by the open smuggling of small arms to the little Communist groups, the bland tolerance of Communism, the formation of a Bosch-directed militia ostensibly to protect the cane cutters. There was widespread determination that the Dominican Republic would not permit itself to become another Cuba. Dr. Bosch obstinately refused any gesture to the nation that he shared this determination." Bishop Reilly then pointed out: "After the coup, the army and the police retired swiftly to their barracks." He concluded that the civilian junta, "representative of five parties, are likely to be in closer touch with the tradition of the nation, more competent in administration and more effective in carrying through socially progressive plans."

Apparently encouraged by statements coming from the liberal U.S. press, and by the State Department's pro-Bosch maneuverings, pro-Bosch elements began to plot against the Triumvirate. On October 31, authorities arrested two high officers in the air force, and, of all things, an "industrialist," for plotting the overthrow of the civilian junta. Arrested and charged with plotting to install Juan Casanovas Garrido as President were Colonel Guarien Cabrera Ariza and Lt. Colonel Danilo Simo, along with Bosch-man Dr. Ambrorix Díaz Estrella, former Attorney General of the Province of Santiago. Colonel Simo told authorities that he had in turn been told by General Pedro Rodríguez Echavarría that the United States had been "exerting pressure" on him to stage the coup.[25] When successful, the general reportedly told his subordinate officer, the United States would immediately recognize Sr. Casanovas as President of the Republic. This suggested that perhaps the New Frontier was not above using U.S. intelligence (CIA) for left-wing purposes.

Also apparently encouraged by the pro-Bosch attitude of the United States, the Communists openly hitched their wagon to the Bosch star, calling on students and *turbas* to destroy private and public property, under the slogan: "Return to Constitutionality with Juan Bosch as President." On November 21 (all of this happened in 1963) the authorities cracked down, and in doing so found a subversive terrorist plan drawn up by the Communists in collaboration with extreme left parties and organizations, including Bosch's PRD. A communique issued by the Press Office of the National Palace said that the plan called for "the paralysis of activities in shops and businesses, and the propagation of false information within government offices to create general panic, and the fomenting of discontent until the outbreak of civil war." Quoting from the plan, Radio Santo Domingo said: "Groups are to be given specific instructions to stone the vehicles of the rich in the streets so they will speak ill of the government because they are not allowed to enjoy the comforts of life, and others will stone the homes of the supporters of the Triumvirate. They must set fires. They must spread false rumors unfavorable to the ruling class. Groups must be organized to destroy the public lighting system and to sabotage electric and telephone lines."[26]

These events were aided and abetted by Juan Bosch who, from political exile in San Juan, Puerto Rico, kept erecting road-blocks to the efforts of the Dominican Triumvirate to return their country to constitutional order. On December 10, the *San Juan Star* published a 2,000-word document signed by Juan Bosch and nine of the principal PRD leaders formally appealing to the PRD inside the Dominican Republic to rise in armed rebellion against the government, and to abandon any election activities, (such activities might lead to a democratic solution to the problem of the people and, incidentally, show that Juan Bosch's popularity had indeed evaporated.) The Bosch document effectively aligned his PRD with the leftists and the Communists. Rather than formally stepping down from power and permitting the country to settle its problems without his unsettling influence, Bosch chose to accept violence as the means to impose his will.

It was against this background that a handful of American reporters, including myself, made their way on April 28, 1965 to the city of Santo Domingo aboard the maddeningly slow Navy vessel, Landing Ship Tank (LST), the "Wood County." I had flown to Puerto Rico the day before where I joined Howard Handleman of *U.S. News and World Report.* I was asked to handle the Dominican story for *Hearst Headline Service* until such time as they could get a man into Santo Domingo, and for the Mutual Broadcasting Company. Twenty-two of us boarded the "Wood County" at the invitation of the U.S. Navy, specifically at the invitation of Russell Bufkins, the Public Information Officer of the Caribbean Sea Frontier in San Juan. We were about an hour-and-a-half out of the port of San Juan the evening of April 28 when commanding officer Lieutenant Commander James R. Allington received a Presidential Flash ordering the landing of several hundred Marines aboard the vessel.

About 11 a.m. April 29, the "Wood County" came alongside the aircraft carrier *Boxer,* and the reporters were transferred aboard it on a highline via a bosun's chair which slid along the cable. We were then transported by helicopter from the *Boxer* to the Embajador Hotel, located on the outskirts of Santo Domingo. A company of Marines had landed and proceeded to the U.S. Embassy the night before, and more Marines were dispatched to the Embassy as we landed. The Marines had been fired upon immediately by rebels and in counter-fire killed seven of them. U.S. military forces could fire only after they had first been fired upon.

We trooped into the lobby of the hotel, carrying our portable typewriters. Tad Szulc spotted someone whom he called "the best informed diplomat in Santo Domingo," and, as always very generous with his contacts, Tad set-up an informal briefing for five or six reporters on the terrace of the hotel. The diplomat was Benno Varon, the Israeli Ambassador. In his book, *Dominican Diary*, Tad says of the interview: "I still believe that this was the most coherent and complete briefing I received at any time during my stay in the Dominican capital,"[27] but he does not say what the briefing was all about. My notes reveal that Ambassador Varon told us that he was at Independence Park where, in his words: "Arms were being handed out to the mobs by Moscow-line Communists, Peking-line Communists, and Castro-Communists." Indeed, Ambassador Varon gave a complete briefing, the substance of which is at odds with what Tad Szulc and Barnard Collier subsequently wrote regarding the revolt. In the opinion of the Ambassador the Communists were in on the revolt at the very beginning, and he said that the "street celebrations" (reported in the log of the *"Venus"*) though Communist-organized at the outset, gave to the military the impression that they were spontaneous. Ambassador Varon told us that in his opinion the almost fatal hesitancy of the military chiefs to move against the mobs derived from their conclusion that a regime as apparently unpopular as the Triumvirate could be maintained in power only by force of arms, and this they were unwilling to do.

Also important to the decision of the military not to back Reid Cabral, the president of the ruling civilian junta, was that they felt their own positions to be threatened. What had precipitated the revolt itself was a move on April 24 by Reid Cabral to dismiss two officers. He sent the army chief of staff, Brigadier General Marco Rivero Cuesta, and his deputy, Colonel Maximiliano Américo Ruiz Batista, to the 27th of February Barracks to do this, and it did not sit well with the military. The general and his deputy were taken prisoner by junior officers at the encampment, and news of the event spread like wildfire throughout the city, causing the 16th of August Barracks to join the insurgents. (Both camps are named after famous dates in Dominican history.) It is important to note that as of this moment the majority of the military insurgents apparently had no intention of expanding their pocket rebellion into open civil war. They merely wanted to get rid of Reid Cabral, a view shared by the military hierarchy of the country. When Reid Cabral had gotten rid of National Police Chief General Belisario Peguero Guerrero, Air Force General Miguel Atila Luna, and other high-ranking members of the military establishment, officers of rank lower than general approved of his decision to do so since it permitted them the opportunity of moving up. But when Reid Cabral had reached down to fire officers of the rank of Lieutenant Colonel, as was the case on April 24, those same junior officers turned against him.

At the outset of the revolt it appears that the military were solidly opposed to Reid Cabral continuing in power, but Reid Cabral apparently was unaware of the unanimity of his opposition. General Eliás Wessin y Wessin, commander of the Military Training Center (CEFA), and San Isidro Air Base with its armored force, paratroops and counter-insurgency teams, was a powerful man. He also was a friend of Donald Reid Cabral, but, in the belief that there was little public support for the Triumvirate and even less support for Reid Cabral within the military, the General stepped in and tried to mediate the dispute, suggesting the formation of a joint loyalist-rebel junta with elections to be called within 90 days. General Wessin y Wessin tried to reason with Reid Cabral and to get him to step down: "I would rather that you resign than see the country plunged into chaos, and bloodshed."

Nevertheless, Reid Cabral made an attempt to stay in power. Overriding the advice of his General, on the evening of April 24 he broadcast an ultimatum to the rebels that they were to surrender by 5:00 a.m., or be attacked by loyalist forces. But the fact was that the forces he counted on no longer were loyal to him. When General Wessin y Wessin refused to back him, Reid Cabral was through. And he was through because he had done all of the things that Juan Bosch in his seven month-reign had failed to do. Reid Cabral had clipped the wings of the military, had withstood seven major labor strikes brought about by PRD and Communist agitators, and valiantly tried to shore up an economy that had been left in chaos by Juan Bosch. Unlike the period when Bosch was in power, Reid Cabral endured poor sugar prices in 1964 and 1965. In 1964, prices averaged 5.87 cents a pound, compared to the average of 8.5 cents enjoyed by the deposed President. And for the first four months leading up to the uprising in April 1965, sugar prices averaged a disastrously low 2.4 cents a pound.

Contrary to assertions made by Theodore Draper in his far-fetched defense of Juan Bosch, the Johnson administration did not do more for Reid Cabral "than the Kennedy Administration had ever done for Bosch."[28] The Draper article, published in the December 1965 issue of *Commentary*, sums up the case of the liberals against the Johnson Administration for not supporting Bosch. For example, he charges that "the money lavished on bolstering his (Reid Cabral's) regime was being largely wasted, the Dominican foreign debt was reaching alarming proportions, that the balance of trade was becoming more and more unfavorable [and] that a contraband operation run mainly by the military was milking the entire economy. . . ."[29]

The fact is, the massive U.S. economic support which Draper alleges was given Reid Cabral from January 1964 to April 1965, averaged $3.8 million a month compared to an average of $4.5 million given to Juan Bosch when he was President. And it was during the regime of President

Juan Bosch that the military chiefs, among them National Police Chief General Belisario Peguero Guerrero, made their biggest haul in running contraband goods into the country. President Bosch did nothing about it. Reid Cabral fired General Peguero, along with three other Dominican generals, and brought an end to illegal trafficking in everything from nylons to dope. While Draper's allegation that the Dominican foreign debt was much too high is true, it is not true that the Triumvirate was responsible for this indebtedness. The fact is that, as President, Juan Bosch maintained no rational budgetary procedures and permitted military contractors to make deals that gave them graft on contracts amounting to 20 per cent of the total amount of money expended on purchases. They signed agreements that committed the Bosch budget for five, even ten, years ahead. It was Reid Cabral and the Triumvirate who founded a budget commission to correct these ills, who cancelled Bosch-made contracts in excess of $150 million, and instituted fiscal controls that eliminated the opportunities for graft. And while Bosch himself apparently did not share in the ill-gotten gains of civilian and military contractors, it is fair to say that his was a graft-ridden administration.

Clearly, by the time Reid Cabral was in a position to control the economy, there was little economy left to control. It is also clear that Reid Cabral had had the courage that Juan Bosch lacked, to buck the vested interests in the military and elsewhere in order to advance necessary social reforms. And he might have succeeded, with more political acumen and the absence of Bosch's conspiracy against him, in bringing about a much-needed social change in the country. However, Reid Cabral had alienated the three pillars needed for support—the military, labor, and business—and in each instance anti-Reid Bosch forces were there, preying upon weak institutions in order to return Juan Bosch to power. The facts suggest that the doughty Scotch-Dominican came on the scene too late. Badly needed in 1962 and 1963, his administrative skills and democratic principles were largely wasted in 1964 and 1965.

The rebel officers had set off the revolt, the Communists were prepared for it and joined, and both incited the mobs to join them. When, in the confused situation, it appeared that only the military rebels were involved, the so-called military loyalists were inclined to go along with them. It was only after Wessin y Wessin and the loyalists perceived the Communist involvement that they decided to fight and to seek a military junta to rule until elections. By this time Reid Cabral had resigned and was out of the picture. The loyalists expected that the military rebels would join them, and some did. But Francisco Caamaño changed all of that.

Opposition to Reid Cabral had initially cemented the loyalists and rebels, but this alliance soon came unstuck when the rebel leadership refused to join in a military junta and, came out, instead, for the return of Juan Bosch to the presidency. This indicated not only that Bosch's subversive tactics had been successful, but that the uprising had been *planned* by Bosch. Indeed, Theodore Draper writes: "It was to have been launched, I have been informed by Juan Bosch, on Monday, April 26."[30] Somehow he does not seem to find anything unwholesome about Bosch plotting a rebellion while in political exile on U.S. soil, even though the Triumvirate was guiding the country toward a more democratic system of government. Apparently the revolt was triggered two days earlier than planned because Reid Cabral had learned of the conspiracy and acted to prevent it from succeeding. The dispatch of General Marcos Rivera Cuesta to fire two lower ranking officer set off the revolt, whose leaders, Colonel Miguel Hernando Ramírez, Colonel Rafael Fernández Domínguez, Lt. Colonel Manuel Ramón Montes Arache, and Captain Mario Peña Tavares, had been plotting with Juan Bosch for some time.

Acting under Bosch's orders, or at least with Bosch's agrement, it was this small group of officers who took up the slogan: "Return to constitutionality with Juan Bosch as President." Captain Peña Tavares played a key role in the initial stages of the revolt, kept in contact with Juan Bosch by telephone in Puerto Rico, and with José Francisco Peña Gómez, the PRD's chief official in Santo Domingo. Most liberal writers advance the fiction that the military rebels were firmly in control of the revolt. Draper, for example, writes: "In these approximately thirty-six hours, no one raised the question of a Communist threat or Communist domination."[31] That depends, of course, on what Draper means. Perhaps he means that, since no question was raised publicly about it, Communist domination did not exist. But this most certainly is open to refutation.

When Colonel Miguel Hernando Ramírez triggered the revolt, he had perhaps 2,000 military officers and men with him. Then Captain Peña Tavares telephoned PRD chief Francisco Peña Gómez, told him to raise the cry of "constitutionality," and also asked him to rally the men of an organization of ex-military people, a sort of American Legion, and to send them to Colonel Hernando Ramírez at the 27th of February Barracks. It is important to consider the background of these men, about 200 to 300 of whom showed up at the Barracks. Many had been sacked from the military by Reid Cabral for politicking, for indulging in graft, and for plain insubordination. If they took up arms for Bosch, Peña Gómez told them, they would be given back their lost positions in the military. There is circumstantial confirmation for this. In September the rebels demanded re-integration of about 300 officers and men who, they claimed, had been re-commissioned into the rebel forces.

About half of the 2,000 military officers who joined the rebel forces fell away from the revolt when it was declared that the revolution was to return Juan Bosch to power, leaving about 1,200 in the rebel forces, including the 200 to 300 who had been cashiered by Reid Cabral. Some joined because they believed that the purpose of the revolt was to get rid of corrupt military leaders; others joined in the hope that they could profit somehow; still others did so because they wanted a military junta to take power and rule until elections could be held. Some wanted Bosch; and others weren't so sure that they wanted Bosch. The point is that far from being a unified force as journalists Draper, Szulc, Dan Kurzman, and others would have us believe, the rebel military was divided as to purpose. On the other hand, among the armed civilians were 1,500 who were Communists united as to purpose, or Communist sympathizers under Communist command, and about 3,000 other armed civilians, most of them *turbas* over whom Communists had control. And while most of the 3,000 to 3,500 civilians very probably never came under Communist discipline, they were dependent upon the Communist leadership for arms, ammunition, and direction. The Communists moved swiftly on April 24 to exert control, and by April 25 and 26 they had achieved it. Indeed, the defection of military men from rebel ranks showed that the military element of the revolt was outnumbered. This prompted Captain Peña Tavares to call for trucks, cars, and busses to come to the 27th of February and the 16th of August Barracks to pick up arms and to take them to Ciudad Nueva for distribution to civilians.

On Sunday, April 25, the day that the rebels installed Señor Molina Ureña as provisional "President," the Communists were to all intents and purposes in control of the uprising. When the trucks and busses arrived in Independence Park, the PSP and 1J4 leadership were in a position to take the weapons and set up their own arms depots, many of them in the private homes of party members. Diómedes Mercedes Batista had sequestered the white Volkswagen sound truck seen by Captain José Rebellón and, the very day the revolt broke out, was driving it around exhorting the mobs to join in the revolt. Narciso Isa Conde, PSP Central Committee member, was already armed with a machine-gun, along with Asdrúbal Domínguez Guerrero, a PSP propagandist. Communist leaders said by Israeli Ambassador Benno Varon to have handed out guns in the park included Hugo Tolentino Dipp, Fidelio Despradel Roque, Felix Servio Ducoudray Mansfield, Eduardo Houellemont Roque, Daniel Ozuna Hernández, and many others, representing all the Communist elements in the country. Weapons depots and distribution points were immediately established. A building on Arzobispo Portes Avenue was a PSP stronghold, and Diómedes Mercedes Batista and José Rodríguez Acosta were seen there, leading a paramilitary force of civilians armed with submachine guns, rifles, and hand grenades. Another paramilitary center was established for the PSP in the home of PSP member Buenaventura Johnson Pimentel on Espaillat Street, while a 1J4 stronghold was set up on José Gabriel Street in Ciudad Nueva, and a heavily armed force of Castroites were using it as a base of operations. Still another "commando" was established on the corner of El Conde and Hostos Streets, and was commanded by Manuel González González, Communist veteran of the Spanish civil war, a PSP Central Committee member and Cuban intelligence agent.

This was the situation prevailing when members of Bosch's PRD arrived at the National Palace with the intention of installing Sr. Molina Ureña as "President" (Bosch had agreed to this by telephone from Puerto Rico). And at this point, some of the rebel officers began to object, supporting the idea of a military junta to call for new elections. After heated discussions, the PRD leaders, rebel Army officers and Communists prevailed, and Molina Ureña was designated Provisional President. As a result, more military officers defected from the movement, thus leaving power more firmly in the hands of civilian leadership. More important, among those taking part in the discussions with Molina Ureña were Facundo Gómez, the PSP member who was found to have owned the gun-running ship "Scarlet Woman." Altogether, sixteen powerful Communist leaders were at the National Palace, took part in the discussions, and were instrumental in installing Molina Ureña as Provisional President. And they exacted their pound of flesh for the favor. "President" Molina Ureña appointed Alejandro Lajara González to the position of Deputy Director of the Security Service. Lajara González was one of the Communist leaders in the 1J4 who had been identified as having passed out arms and ammunition to other members of the 1J4 in Independence Park. Yet, Tad Szulc dismisses Communist influence in the investiture of Molina Ureña: "The young military commanders who had set off the revolt the day before took control of the Presidential Palace and announced that, instead of a military junta, they were now pressing for the restoration of constitutional government ... and installed before noon Sunday José Rafael Molina Ureña to serve as Provisional President."[32] Neither Szulc nor Draper looked behind the facade to see who was pulling the strings. It wasn't just a handful of extremists who attached themselves to a preponderantly military-led revolt, but quite the reverse. Power clearly had passed into the hands of the Communists at the time of the Molina Ureña investiture, and they exerted it at once to place one of their men in a sensitive security post.

To those acquainted with the background of Juan Bosch's collaboration with leftists and even the Communists themselves, the events that took place at the National Palace on April 25 were not surprising. The history of his complex dealings with the Communists and extremists goes back to what is known as the Pact of Rio Piedras, named after the residential section in which Bosch lived in San Juan, Puerto Rico during the exile. In December 1964, Bosch conferred there with leaders of his own party and with those of the Social Christian Revolutionary Party (PRSC). The purpose of that conference was to work out definitive plans for the overthrow of the civilian junta under Donald Reid Cabral, reestablish "constitutional" government, and reinstate Juan Bosch in the presidency. The pact was signed, either in late January or early February 1965, two months before the revolt. Leaders of the Castroite 1J4 demanded partnership in the pact but were turned down by Bosch as being too closely identified with the Communists, with the clear implication that the refusal was for reasons which might unbutton Bosch's claims that he had nothing to do with the Communists.

It was agreed, however, that the 1J4 leaders would be kept advised of developments and serve as the informal link between the pact signatories and the two Dominican Communist Parties—Peking-line and Moscow-line. Bosch, of course, was the architect of that agreement. In return, Bosch was told he could count on the militant youth of the 1J4 to join in the overthrow of the Reid Cabral government, and this indeed happened. What other commitments were made by Bosch to the Communists at that time is not fully known. However, it is known that two members of the 1J4 Movement travelled to San Juan in early March 1965 and met with Juan Bosch. The two Communists taped a Bosch message to the public, took it back to Santo Domingo and delivered it to José Brea, Secretary of Finance of Bosch's PRD. Prevented from airing the tape by a Reid Cabral law, a transcript of the tape was read over the air. The program, called "Here is Santo Domingo," was sponsored by the June 14th Movement. I reported this in the February 8, 1966 issue of *National Review*, and brought down upon me the wrath of Mr. Draper, who contacted Juan Bosch to see if he had met with the two Communists from the 1J4 Movement—Victoriano Félix and Rafael "Fafa" Tavares. Bosch replied, according to Draper, that he had "heard the name of Rafael 'Fafa' Tavares for the first time on June 14, 1965,"[33] which is on the order of claiming that President Lyndon Johnson had never heard the name of U.S. Communist leader Gus Hall. Draper then substitutes other points in support of Bosch, for example that the radio program was sponsored by something called the Dominican News Agency, not by the 1J4, and bases his claim on a newspaper account which said that Félix was a "special representative" of the Dominican News Agency. Yet, there was no indication whatsoever that the Dominican News Agency "sponsored" the program. And, after noting that none of the Dominican newspapers even subscribed to a Dominican News Agency, I inquired about it and found that it was a small agency specializing in the import of film clips. Thus, the Communists did not interview

Bosch as legitimate reporters. And Draper neglected to inform his readers that Félix was a member of the 1J4 and overlooks completely the "special representative" nature of his affiliation with a "news agency." This probably was a cover, since there is no other ready explanation. Finally, immigration authorities in San Juan recorded that Félix and Tavares had entered the country together, in March, making even more suspect Bosch's claim that he had not seen Tavares.

That the Bosch-PRSC-Communist combine accommodated one another is to be seen elsewhere. The Social Christian Revolutionary Party played a key role in liaison between Bosch and the Communists. According to some observers the PRSC, and in particular its labor arm, CASC, is closely associated with and influenced by the Communists. Others go no further than to say that the PRSC is no friend of the United States. This is certainly true of CASC, an affiliate of CLASC, the Latin American Confederation of Christian Unions. Just a month before the revolt, the national committee of the Bosch-aligned PRSC joined the 1J4 and the Communist Dominican Students Federation (FED) in staging a wildcat strike at the privately owned La Romana sugar mill, the most efficient in the vital sugar economy of the nation. CASC slogans during the strike were heavily larded with Marxist charges of "reactionary plots by imperialists." Thus it came as no surprise when, following the revolt, Henry Molina, Secretary General of the CASC, attacked the "traitors to the fatherland" and declared that "Even when the modern automatic weapons of Yankee imperialism are used to destroy our citizens, we will die with honor. . . ."[34] The easy accommodation of apparently conflicting principles among the members of the leftist coalition may be summed up this way: In exile, Bosch allied himself with the Communists in return for their support, and lent his name and reputation to the revolt at a time when the Communists clearly were in charge.

U.S. Ambassador W. Tapley Bennett had surmised as much when he met with us reporters at the Embassy the night of April 29. I was present when he said he had a report that a man had been killed, and his head stuck atop a pole, and said he was checking on it. He also told us of a report that Colonel Juan Calderón, former aide-de-camp of Reid Cabral had been shot, reportedly by rebel leader Francisco Caamaño, and said that he was checking this story. The Ambassador emphasized that no organized units of the Army were with the rebels and accurately described the defection of military officers when extremists among them raised the cry: "Return to constitutionality with Juan Bosch as President." Mr. Bennett also said that cries of *Paredón* were heard as twenty defecting Navy personnel were lined up and shot because they had turned against the rebels and wanted to defect. Following this, he said, military defectors, many of whom spoke to Embassy personnel about their experiences, donned civilian dress to facilitate their slipping away from what had now become their captors in the rebel forces. The Ambassador also told us that for weeks the Embassy had known that Communist leaders in Ciudad Nueva had been teaching the *turbas* how to make home-made bombs and how to carry out paramilitary missions.

More important, Ambassador Bennett recounted almost word for word the essential parts of the briefing given to some of us reporters by Israeli Ambassador Varon—that the Communists had gained control of arms and arms distribution and had effectively taken charge of the revolt. In this connection, Ambassador Bennett said that about 50 known Communists were involved in the revolt, and, in response to a request by Howard Handleman of *U.S. News and World Report*, had his CIA staff type a list of 53, carbon copies of which were given to each of us. He did not, as some have asserted, force the list of Communists upon us. I was surprised to read Tad Szulc's reaction to that list. He writes that "a number" had been allowed to travel freely between the Dominican Republic and Communist countries, but found that they had been permitted to travel, not by Juan Bosch (as was indeed the case) but by "The Council of State Government in 1962 and then by the government of Reid Cabral."[35] the debunking by liberal reporters of the list of Communists active in the revolt reached truly heroic proportions, with Draper writing: "Of all the controversial issues that have arisen in the course of the Dominican crisis, the least necessary to dispute is President Johnson's pronouncement that there was a Communist takeover of the revolt," adding scornfully: "One school of U.S. officials . . . inspired stories to the effect that Bosch had sold out to the Communists before the revolt."[36] Is Mr. Draper unaware of the so-called Pact of Rio Piedras, of the AR-15 deal, of the pro-Castro sympathies of two high-level members of Bosch's administration, of the conscious collaboration of then President Bosch in the 1963 trip to Cuba by 30 Dominican Communists?

Draper writes of the list of 53 that it "was apparently made possible by ransacking old, pre-revolt lists. . . ."[37] But the fact is that of the 53 given out by Ambassador Bennett, most had been trained in Cuba, and many, as we have already seen, were active in Ciudad Nueva and elsewhere, with sixteen taking part, as we also have seen, in the investiture of Rafael Molina Ureña. What was said, and amply proved, was that Communists or Communist sympathizers, including Lajara González, were in the Molina Ureña "government" at the time of his investiture. Yet, Draper quotes James Nelson Goodsell of the *Christian Science Monitor* as writing: "A good degree of sloppy intelligence work went into the preparation of the lists" of Communists, and adds: "Goodsell found two in prison; six not in the country; four jailed within two days of the outbreak and, therefore, *hors de combat* when the Communist takeover supposedly took place; at least three others released from jail before the list was promulgated; four and possibly six not in Santo Domingo at the time."[38] In going over a later list of 58 Communists in which the 53 were incorporated, I found four names repeated and eliminated them; found two in jail and eliminated them; four who may or may not have been Communists and eliminated them. Each of the remaining 48 names was active in the revolt almost from the hour that it started; many of them have been identified as to what they were doing and where they were doing it earlier in this chapter.

Further efforts are made by some reporters to prove that Ambassador Bennett and his Embassy staff issued the list of Communists to make the facts fit their will to intervene on behalf of the Dominican loyalists. Writes Draper of the lists of Communists: "They were all *ex post facto* jobs, hastily put together to justify an already adopted policy . . . they were not available to President Johnson and his small circle of advisers when they had to make up their minds to send the marines to frustrate a reported Communist takeover." If they were *ex post facto* jobs, then Mr. Draper must admit by the record that the Embassy had extraordinary perception, and apparently does when, curiously, he writes: "it is possible to argue that the President was later proven right by the information which the intelligence services subsequently gathered."[39] This is very neat juggling of words, but does little to bear out Draper's contention that insufficient knowledge on Communist activities was available when the crucial decisions were made. And what intelligence services "subsequently" gathered proved that the Communists were where they said they were in the first place, an extraordinary coincidence which apparently doesn't faze Mr. Draper.

Then there was the famous meeting at the Embassy between the chief participants—Molina Ureña, Colonel Francisco Caamaño and Ambassador Tapley Bennett. Mr. Bennett told us correspondents crouching in his candle-lit office the night of April 29 that Molina Ureña had come to see him, a thoroughly dejected man. The "President" was accompanied by Colonel Francisco Caamaño and a group of fifteen others whom he described to the Ambassador as his principal political and military advisers. One of the prime reasons why Molina Ureña came, first to the U.S. Embassy and later into political asylum in the Colombian Embassy, was his realization that the PRD had been devoured politically by the Communist coalition. The Papal Nuncio, Emanuele Clarizio, revealed to his diplomatic colleagues that several of his PRD friends had told him that they had lost power to the Communists. Power among the rebels was based on control of the arms, and that control now was in the hands of the Communists. Furthermore, the Communists remained the only cohesive fighting force because the PRD rebels, as we have seen, were split as to purpose. PRD leader Maximo Lovaton, the rebel "Foreign Minister," and PRD leader Jose Francisco Peña Gómez had taken asylum in foreign embassies that day. And they did so a good number of hours before Molina Ureña and Francisco Caamaño met with the American Ambassador.

However that may be, pro-Bosch supporters claim that at the meeting between Caamaño, Molina Ureña and Ambassador Bennett, Mr. Bennett insulted Colonel Caamaño in a manner that prompted him to head the revolt and continue fighting. Therefore, this argument runs, the blood of the revolt was on Ambassador Bennett's hands. The fact is that Caamaño was infuriated because the U.S. Ambasssador would not do what he wanted—interpose U.S. power and influence on the PRD side and thus give them the victory. Ambassador Bennett's recollection is that the meeting was polite and that indeed one of the PRD officials suggested that Bennett get together after the revolt had fizzled and carry on a philosophical discourse on the nature of Dominican society.

The Ambassador recalls why he was unable to mediate the dispute the evening of April 27. While Molina Ureña did indeed want the U.S. Embassy to mediate, the rebel leader said he would meet with the military leaders from the San Isidro base only if they acknowledged his legitimacy as Provisional President and *came to him* for the talks. Obviously, this made mediation efforts impossible, for the very issue of Molina Ureña's right to the presidency was at the bottom of this phase of the conflict. Ambassador Bennett also told Molina Ureña that the Embassy had arranged cease fires on four previous occasions over the preceding three days, and in each instance the rebels had violated them. What the rebel leader apparently indicated was that he was not about to compromise, but, instead, wanted San Isidro forces to capitulate through what would have amounted to U.S. intervention on his side. And the belief that the Communists had made significant inroads in the Molina Ureña government prompted Ambassador Bennett not to accede to rebel wishes. Certainly, the rebellion had been politically identified at that moment as one potentially dangerous to the security of the hemisphere.

Yet, despite the long history of Communist infiltration and activities in the Dominican Republic, Draper and his informants (including Senator J. William Fulbright) incorrectly claim that the Embassy turned swiftly and erroneously between Saturday and Sunday April 24 and 25, to an assessment that Communism now was a force to be dealt with. Draper quotes Senator Fulbright: "The essential point, however, is that the United States, on the basis of ambiguous evidence, assumed almost from the beginning, that the revolution was Communist dominated, or would certainly become so."[40] But the fact is that the meeting at the

National Palace on Sunday in which the Communist leadership exerted considerable influence on the decisions taken there forced the Embassy drastically to revise Saturday's erroneous estimate that the coup would not alter the U.S. relationship with the Dominican Republic. Indeed, if the Embassy was at fault for anything, it was at fault for not supporting Donald Reid Cabral and helping him over his difficult moments. He was the most effective Dominican chief of state since the assassination of Rafael Trujillo, and support for him at the proper time might have avoided all that came after.

However that may be, as soon as the American Embassy learned the details of the meeting at the National Palace, and when its political officer Ben Ruyle found "President" Molina Ureña sitting dejectedly in the Palace, surrounded by both Communists and military rebels, previous indications of PRD and Communist involvement in the coup fell into place, and the Embassy ceased being neutral. The PRD-Communist alignment could no longer be ignored, and the Embassy concluded that the split within the military leadership of the revolt would benefit only the Communists through a long, drawn-out civil war.

At the very moment when Molina Ureña was sitting so dejectedly at the National Palace, the 1J4 established another "commando" on Juan de Morpha Street and placed in command Jaime Durán Hernando, a Cuban-trained guerrilla warfare expert, and still another "commando" on Caracas Street under the command of Fidelio Despradel Roque, also Cuban-trained. And Gustavo Ricart, member of the Central Committee of the Chinese-line MPD, was identified as the commander of yet another rebel stronghold, along with Ramón Pineda Mejía, also an MPD member. Both had seen trained in urban guerrilla warfare in Cuba. The manufacture of "Molotov Cocktails" was under the supervision of three PSP members, Ignacio Pérez Mencia, Carlos Dore Cabral, and Porfirio García. It was little wonder, then, that rebel forces became easy prey for trained and disciplined Communist leadership.

Indeed, armed groups over which Molina Ureña had no control violated an agreement made between the U.S. Embassy and the rebels to permit the orderly evacuation of U.S. nationals. A group of about 100 armed civilians went to the Embajador Hotel and there terrorized several hundred U.S. citizens awaiting transportation out of the country, thus adding some urgency to Ambassador Bennett's plea for Marines to protect American lives. That is why the Ambassador told us the night of April 29 that the situation was now completely out of hand, and that no group existed which could claim ability to rule the country.

It is important to return again to the briefing given us by Ambassador Bennett the night of April 29 because Mr. Draper calls it "The classic case of contaminated news," apparently forgetting that his own Bosch sources might well fit that category. Here is what Draper says about the briefing, much of which I have already described above: "The Ambassador devoted most of the meeting to the 'Communist takeover' and rebel atrocities. The first list of 53 Dominican Communists was passed out. The Ambassador horrified the assembled correspondents with some of the reports he had received: rebels shooting people against walls to the accompaniment of the Castroite cry, *"Paredon!"* (To the wall!); they had severed heads and paraded them on spikes; Colonel Caamaño had machine-gunned Colonel Calderón. . . ."[41] One report by Ambassador Bennett of a severed head being passed around became, for Draper, "severed heads paraded on spikes." On my own, I had stumbled onto the story of the head on a pole, finding it in the log book of the "Venus" on April 30, thus confirming Ambassador Bennett's story. It is therefore a distortion for Draper to contend: "No one had ever seen heads on spikes," and to exult that Colonel Calderón was later found with a gunshot wound alive in a hospital, without saying why he was hospitalized. And while no Embassies were sacked and burned, as Draper was quick to say, the fact is that the Embassies of El Salvador, Mexico, Peru, and Guatemala had been violated in other ways by rebel forces.

Mr. Draper's article in *Commentary* reveals an excellent synchronization of views of liberal reporters and liberal Senators since he did not journey to Santo Domingo, and draws upon their views to support his own. Thus, the phrase "contaminated news" is more applicable to his article than to Ambassador Bennett's briefing. The Ambassador did indeed tell us of reports of looting and sacking in the rebel zone, reports that again were contained, quite independent of any briefing by him, in the log book of the "Venus." And these are again found by Draper to be false. "Ambassador Bennett never expressed regret for his horror stories of April 29."[42] It is appropriate, concerning Draper's denial that atrocities took place, to recall the words entered in the log book of the ship: "Armed mobs flood the whole area, the sackings, the robbings, the killings are uncontrollable because, lacking any leadership whatsoever as to what to do, the police have withdrawn into their headquarters in Ozama Fortress, leaving the streets in the hands of the *turbas*. Under the able direction of the Communist cadres, they are occupying the center of the city, street by street."

Struck by Ambassador Bennett's briefing on reports of the breakdown in law and order which, in the first instance, led to the landing of Marines to protect U.S. citizens, and by the log book of the "Venus" which I was able to copy the day following the briefing, I decided to dig into the matter. Draper says: "When the correspondents were able to see for themselves and talk to Dominicans in the street, they quickly learned that the mass executions and cries of *Paredón*, had never taken place."[43]

Draper's source for this statement is Barnard Collier, reporter for the *New York Herald Tribune*, who found, according to Draper, "no more than six to ten bodies in the streets at one time." Yet, a Scottish photographer who landed with us on April 29 went immediately into the city and returned, incidentally after being held by rebels as a "Yankee spy," sickened by what he had seen. He had counted 90 bodies in just one block, he told us. And there were opportunities aplenty to check Ambassador Bennett's stories—right in the hotel where the correspondents were staying. Literally thousands of people fled the rebel zone during the first days of the revolt and came to the hotel to be evacuated from the country. I spoke to several, and here is what Ina French, a Negro domestic servant, had to say:

> I saw them (*turbas*) kill a Chinese merchant who lived above his store. He heard the *turbas* coming Saturday night, ran down to close his shutters and was shot through the stomach and died right there. The *turbas* attacked homes, killed people, and broke down the steel doors of a department store. When they were finished with the store you couldn't find one pin left.
>
> Bodies of people killed by the *turbas* were all over the streets. Some of the bodies had stomachs higher than their faces. They had been lying there in the sun for three whole days.

A Peace Corps volunteer who worked at a downtown hospital told me that the wounded and dead came in at such a rate that "they were stacked up like cordwood." A similar story of terror was told me by a Puerto Rican woman, Maria de los Santos. She fled the rebel zone, she said, "because the rebels and the Communists knew that I was an American citizen and anti-Communist." Her home was broken into, her car stolen, and her three children badly beaten with rungs taken out of chairs and wielded by the *turbas*. I myself saw them huddled in the lobby of the hotel, bearing lumps and bruises from those beatings, administered, said the mother, "because we are Yankees."

And Francisco Aybar, told me the horrifying story of Julio Pérez Sánchez who was literally torn apart at the entrance to the Duarte bridge because his brother was in the Dominican Air Force. Scores of witnesses have testified that families of Dominican military men were set upon by the mobs, taken to the television station and forced to plead with the pilots to stop bombing rebel concentrations in the city. In some cases, witnesses have testified, rifles aimed at the victims were clearly visible to the viewers. And when the televised appearances did not stop the planes from bombing and strafing, families of the pilots were herded into military target areas to be among the first to die when the planes strafed. The planes came anyway.

The Organization of American States rushed a fact-finding mission to Santo Domingo, and here is what one of the members, Colombian Ambassador Alfredo Vasquez Carrizosa, had to say:

> What were we to do when blood was running in the streets —What happened when a state in this condition is so close to Cuba? Are we to sit silently on balconies and watch the end of the tragedy as if we were watching some sort of bull fight?[44]

Brazilian Ambassador Ilmar Penna Marinho also had something to say regarding the absence of law and order:

> It was a no-man's land. There had been a complete collapse of public authority. The Dominican Republic had disappeared as a legal and political entity—arms had been given to a disorganized nation of fanatics and adolescents who were in a frenzied state egged on by subversive broadcasts—anarchy reigned—and any organized group that made a landing in the Dominican Republic could have dominated the situation.[45]

Certainly, as Draper, Szulc, Kurzman, and Collier allege, many people were killed by the strafing planes. More than that, the military had inadvertently handed the rebels an excellent propaganda weapon and may indeed have stiffened the spine of the mobs operating in the center of Ciudad Nueva. But this does not take away from the breakdown of law and order in an area which Draper and his sources claim were under the control of military rebels. The fact is that Communist propagandists urged the people to go to target areas which had been designated as such by the military who warned them to stay away, and said that they could get food, shelter, and water at the Quisqueya baseball stadium, the Perla Antillana Hipodromo and the Embajador Hotel. Indeed, among the pro-Bosch writers Mr. Draper is almost alone in trying to prove inferentially at least, that there was no breakdown of order. He places the blame for the deaths in Ciudad Nueva exclusively in the laps of the loyalists and their strafing planes. He does so, presumably, because for him to admit that there was little law and order in the first several days of the revolt would mean that the military rebels were not in charge, leaving the clear implication that the Communists were.

Szulc reports that U.S. military attaches were sent to the San Isidro base where they relayed back to the Embassy requests for assistance.[46]

Draper goes one step further, actually accusing the American military attaches of triggering the bombings and strafings and therefore to be held responsible for some of the civilian lives lost during these attacks. This is an outrageous charge, and that Draper has made no evident attempt to contact the attaches themselves on this vital point is a reflection of his pro-Bosch bias. Indeed, Draper bases his charges on his stretching the findings of one U.S. reporter, and on a *New York Times* interview with Juan Bosch. To the careless reader, Draper's account appears to be based on the findings of the *New York Times*. He writes: "Bosch's information was made known in part by Homer Bigart in the *New York Times* of May 7, 1965." Draper then goes on to make it clear that, as in many instances of his reporting, Bosch is the only source. What Juan Bosch has to say is outrageous, yet Draper endorses it root and branch: "On the evening of Saturday, April 24, the first day of the revolt, when the military leaders were still immobilized, *Bosch said*, the U.S. air attache had called the San Isidro Air Force Base to talk to General de los Santos Céspedes. The attache ordered the Dominican general to have two air squadrons ready to bomb the city early Sunday morning." (Italics added.) Bosch then followed up with a letter to Draper: "Bosch has added that both the U.S. air and naval attaches began on Saturday evening to 'order' the Dominican air force, navy, and General Wessin to attack the Boschist forces, and that another demand for an air attack on the National Palace was made on Sunday afternoon."[47] And what was the source of Bosch's information? The source was Bosch's informants in the Dominican Republic, which is to say that the information came from the rebels themselves. Having accepted this "contaminated news," Draper elaborates on it, saying: "It is unclear from this account whether the attache's persuasion as well as the embassy's concern should be dated Sunday or Monday." He adds: "If the intervention of the U.S. military attaches should prove to have been the determining, or even a major, factor in the Dominican air force and navy decision to launch attacks on Sunday and the following days, the verdict of history will be that U.S. pressure contributed to the prevention of an early Boschist victory and helped plunge the country into a bloody civil war."[48] That all of these accusations, in the final analysis, are based on statements by Juan Bosch or come from rebel sources, reflects seriously on the adequacy of Mr. Draper as a reliable observer.

On May 4, Colonel Francisco Caamaño was "elected" to head the rebel forces as "Constitutional President." He was "elected," as was Juan Casanova Garrido two years earlier, by Bosch's defunct and now scattered "Congress." I was present in Independence Park when Caamaño took the oath of office, noting to myself that Bosch's 1963 Constitution under which Caamaño was sworn in specifically forbids any military

officer from holding office. This did not prevent Juan Bosch from violating the terms of his own Constitution, however, and by telephone from Puerto Rico he agreed to Caamaño's investiture. Present were cheering crowds of armed *turbas* and uniformed military rebels. In the section into which I was squeezed, they were passing aroud bottles of whisky, which, loudly and laughingly, they said had been provided through looting.

It was far from clear where the "Congress" had met and what procedures had been used in selecting Caamaño. I also noticed that at the side of Caamaño was Hector Aristy, with whom I had spoken by telephone on April 30. A man of an impressive opportunistic background, Aristy had tried every angle in Dominican politics, having worked with the post-Trujillo Council of State and then as Secretary General of a political party headed by one of Trujillo's assassins, Luis Amiama Tio. When the revolt broke out, he appeared magically on the side of Bosch and reportedly helped burn down the headquarters of his own party, the Liberal Evolutionists. More important, Aristy was a friend of Diego Bordas and with his financial help was involved in a number of enterprises. As for Colonel Caamaño, he was the son of General Fausto Caamaño, one of Trujillo's most brutal aides. Brought up in the Trujillo tradition, Caamaño was himself tainted with the brutality and opportunism which characterized the late dictator's regime. Serving in the *Cascos Blancos*, he commanded a detachment at Palma Sola that slaughtered hundreds of members of a dissident religious sect. He participated in the military movement that overthrew Bosch, and when in the National Police Force, plotted to overthrow his immediate superior. Caamaño's erratic behaviour was accompanied by fits of melancholy, and he had been treated for mental fatigue at least twice, possibly more often. Among the first to join the rebels, Caamaño also was among the first to take asylum in a foreign embassy, doing so on Sunday, April 25. The shame in having done so may account for some of Caamaño's later actions as when he came out of asylum the next day and proceeded to head the rebellion. One theory is that having acted the coward on Sunday, he had to show that he had "macho" (manliness) on Tuesday.

With rivulets of sweat pouring down his face, chainsmoking U.S. cigarettes, and guarded by foreigners composing an elite force of Navy frog men, "President" Caamaño conducted a conference in which he accused the United States forces of making new penetrations into the rebel zone of the city, saying he would not tolerate "a dictatorship of the right or of the left." But in general he seemed conciliatory. The reasons have to do with a change in tactics which we shall come to later. Caamaño announced his cabinet. Hector Aristy was made "Minister of the Presidency," Jottin Curi was made "Foreign Minister," and Lieutenant Colonel Montes Arache, the commander of an elite military force of frog men,

which included many professional fighting men, was made "Secretary of Defense." Reports of Montes Arache's brutality, his drinking and wenching in at least three different houses and apartments in the rebel zone caused U.S. Ambassador to the OAS Ellsworth Bunker later to comment to me: "Constitutionalists, my foot!"

The following day, May 5, a group of civilians called on Colonel Caamaño, saying that they wanted to submit a statement of support for him to the OAS commission that was at that moment consulting with the rebel leadership, trying to persuade them to sign a cease-fire agreement. It was finally signed by Caamaño, and was followed by a little ceremony in which the Colombian, Ricardo Colombo, made a short speech and Caamaño replied, heaping praise upon the OAS delegates for their help in bringing about the ceasefire. Then the civilians dutifully stepped forward and called for an end to "North American intervention." The group said that they represented professionals—doctors, dentists, merchants, and lawyers. One of the group was indeed a lawyer and his name is Guido Gil. This same Guido Gil represented the *Sindicato Unido* of the Romana Sugar Mill, a group of extreme leftist and Communist labor leaders who comprised only about 2,000 out of the total labor force of 17,000. With the help of lawyer Gil they had tried to get the government to endorse their claims as spokesmen for the entire force. Failing to do so, they set about creating a reign of terror among the other workers. During the revolt *Sindicato Unido* officials and Guido Gil moved in and out of rebel territory.

More important, Guido Gil, lawyer and supporter of Francisco Caamaño, headed a three-man delegation of Communists from the Dominican Republic to Havana's Tricontinental Conference in January 1966. Clearly a Communist, Gil was interviewed over Radio Havana on January 9 where he made the eyebrow-lifting comment: "President Caamaño's democratic and popular government was created by mobilizing the workers, students, and professional classes." Though the "democratic revolution of the people" had failed, said Gil, valuable lessons had been learned in the conduct of urban guerrilla warfare, among them that other Communist countries must be prepared to send aid to those carrying out a revolution. Earlier, on January 5, Gil spoke at the plenary session of the Havana Conference, endorsing the view that a central headquarters for coordinating and supplying revolts such as the one in the Dominican Republic, should be created in Havana. (This was done.) In proposing the central headquarters, Gil said that another benefit could be expected by providing a place where Communist leaders could gather, exchange experiences, and "correct our deficiencies," among them the very embarrassing one to Dominican Communists that outside of Ciudad Nueva the rest of the country refused to throw in with the rebels. This would be corrected in the future, said Gil, by having the "peasants occupy the land."

Indeed, pro-Bosch reporters also must share in the embarrassment of Guido Gil. The countryside remained pointedly on the side of the "imperialists," making nonsense of Draper's cry: "For perhaps the second time in their entire history, they have fought for something worth believing in. Lawyers and peasants have been stirred by the same common aspirations and ideals."[49] This was not so, and I knew it was not so. On May 1, I drove through the Cibao valley and up to Santiago de los Caballeros. In every small town and village I found business being conducted, albeit with a sense of nervousness. Each roadside *bohio* serving food had its radio on, and this serves to demonstrate a point. The rebels controlled the only nation-wide radio network, spewed out their hatred of the United States by the minute, called upon the Dominicans to rise and overthrow the "oligarchs," and said the United States was supporting the "gorillas" of General Wessin y Wessin. Yet, outside the Ciudad Nueva section of the capital of Santo Domingo, it was hard to believe that a war was going on.

In a sense, the policies being pursued by the United States represented a triumph in intelligence. Spanish-speaking members of the Special Forces (Green Berets) among them Cuban veterans of the Bay of Pigs, were dressed in civilian clothing and sent into the countryside at the outset of the revolt. Their mission: "What is the temper of the people?" Mexican- and Cuban-Americans explained away their non-Dominican accent by saying they had gone to university in Caracas, Mexico City, or even Peru. Thoroughly briefed on their mission, they found this: The idea was rapidly getting around that ours was not old-fashioned gunboat diplomacy, as the rebels were charging. Having watched for years the turmoil in the country, the Dominican citizen still free of rebel domination knew that being pulled into the streets to demonstrate did nothing to put more food on his table or to assure him of steady employment. The idea dawned very early that the presence of U.S. troops might turn out to be something entirely new—that it would give the Dominicans another chance to put their own house in order. And while they did not want again to turn to the military to provide peace and stability, neither did they feel that the chauvinistic slogans coming from the pro-Bosch mobs in Ciudad Nueva offered much promise for a democratic future. More to the point, the majority of the people who, back in 1963, were plainly worried at Bosch's inability to keep the Communists in line, found even less indication in 1965 that Bosch could handle the pro-Communist mobs.

I spoke to several members of the Special Forces who had been given this important and taxing job. They emphasized that their intelligence was not conclusive, that it was one of many sources being considered by our military and diplomatic representatives, but they were proud of their efforts. And it lies within the context of the work that these Army personnel performed for their country that Draper's slurs against our intelligence community may be assessed. He writes: "When something goes wrong, we hear about the diplomats but not about the CIA agents or the military attaches."[50] It is perhaps unnecessary to point out that when something goes right, as with the work of our Special Forces, we generally do not hear about it, either. They don't usually talk. I suppose that I am the first to write about this important and critical work performed by our men in the Dominican Republic. I am able to do so only because several were personally known to me, and I hope that I am not out of line in making their contribution public. I believe that it is safe to do so, since the Dominican revolt is now well behind us.

This phase of the revolt is, of course, of extreme importance. Pro-Bosch reporters were insisting that the United States should have backed the Bosch forces because, in their opinion, Bosch enjoyed overwhelming popular support in the country. Again we turn to Draper, the chief proponent of this view: "There is every reason to believe that U.S. backing of Molina Ureña on Sunday would have given the Bosch forces a quick, easy, almost bloodless victory." Yet in a letter to the editor, published in the August 23, 1966, *National Review,* in answer to articles I had written in *National Review* and *The Reporter* Draper denies that he had ever suggested intervention: "It is grotesquely unfair and wildly untruthful to say that I have ever exhorted the United States to intervene again in behalf of Juan Bosch or anyone else." What, one may ask, does Mr. Draper's "backing of Molina Ureña" mean if it is not intervention? The demands made on U.S. Ambassador Bennett by the rebel leader amounted to the very intervention which Mr. Draper allegedly abhors.

However, reporters do have a legitimate complaint, which arises from repeated U.S. professions of neutrality long after neutrality had been abandoned as our national course in the Dominican Republic. Reporters' questions to the U.S. Embassy and to military briefers more often than not were met with restatements of Washington press releases. But the fact seems to be that this situation is a reflection of the political reflexes of President Lyndon Johnson, who, knowing that intervention is never popular, tried to hide or obscure it. Indeed, President Johnson kept abreast of the events unfolding in the Dominican Republic and must be held responsible for the bungling that helped to alienate the press. Pro-Bosch reporters thus found it easier to move Senators Proxmire, Fulbright, Church, and Clark, for example, into denouncing the whole of the U.S. operation. While the juxtaposition of U.S. forces between rebel and loyalist forces was a neutral action, the initial landing of those forces was not. The United States became neutral between the two sides after its landing of troops.

A landing was soon made by elements of the 82nd, increasing U.S. military forces greatly, and changing radically the extent of the U.S. involvement in the country. A tall, lanky red-head, Ambassador Bennett did not shrink from the hard decisions when he returned to Santo Domingo following consultation in Washington. He was in the United States when the revolt occurred, and returned to his post immediately where he made the recommendations that led to U.S. intervention in that strife-torn land. He told us reporters that the U.S. troops were coming "to do whatever may be necessary to achieve our objective."

Yet, while the character of the U.S. commitment to the Dominican Republic had taken a hard turn, it did not merit the assessment made by Tad Szulc: "Playing on a sensitive chord in the Dominican psychology, the charge that Washington is leading the Dominican Republic back into a military dictatorship like that of the Trujillo era is being increasingly heard."[51] Heard from whom? Certainly such accusations were heard every day from rebel chieftains in Ciudad Nueva, but not from the balance of the country not under their command. Szulc arrives at his conclusion largely because by Sunday, May 2, the U.S. forces in the Dominican Republic numbered 14,000 men, who the day following, forged a security corridor which separated the rebels in Ciudad Nueva from loyalist forces at San Isidro and in the northern part of Santo Domingo. He writes: "Now Caamaño's main stronghold, in Ciudad Nueva and the capital's business district, was in effect surrounded by American forces,"[52] but does not point out that loyalist forces which had now regained their momentum were prevented by U.S. troops from attacking the rebels. I was at the headquarters of General Jacinto Martínez Arana when he met with other members of the General Staff, and heard them explode with indignation upon being warned by the United States not to attempt to cross U.S. lines into Ciudad Nueva. Hundreds of soldiers were being transported from Santiago de los Caballeros and elsewhere in the country to bolster the loyalist forces in Santo Domingo, indicating that the loyalists believed that the population outside of Ciudad Nueva was sufficiently anti-rebel to permit them to reduce their forces there and bring them into Santo Domingo.

Together with Mitchell Wer Bell, I covered the fight in which loyalist troops cleaned out the rebels in the northern section of the city. Wer Bell was a banana planter in the Dominican Republic and a former Captain in the OSS in World War II. He went with the lead tank as loyalist forces fought their way across the northern part of the city in four hours, arriving at the Ozama river, to the north of Ciudad Nueva at 12:00 noon. I accompanied the lead formation for about a mile, recording some of the noise of battle, then went back to the hotel to broadcast for Mutual News what I had seen and heard. The troops did well in the difficult business of flushing out snipers, taking their guns and sending them to the rear in trucks, thus returning the greater part of the city to normalcy. Suspected snipers in each of the houses searched over a vast area had their shoulders examined for bruises from rifle and automatic weapons recoil. Their pants were rolled up above their knees for signs of extended kneeling in sniper nests. Telltale evidence sent the suspect to the rear for interrogation. Other suspects were let go. Arms caches were transported out of the area in trucks and armored vehicles. One thing struck me. Ambulances operated right along with the lead tanks. When a rebel or a loyalist was struck down, he was immediately carried to one of the ambulances and cared for.

One vignette of the war tells something about the character of the people involved in it. A group of rebels firing a 50 caliber machine-gun sandbagged atop a British Land Rover were cut down as they came around a corner and blundered, firing, into loyalist lines. An Army ambulance arrived almost immediately and took away the bodies. People in the houses nearby began to emerge as the loyalists moved on up the street. One said: "When the tanks are in the next block, we can dismantle it." He meant the vehicle. I was sickened and shocked by what I had seen, and the remark made no impression on me at the time. But when I returned about an hour later to the scene of battle following my broadcast for Mutual, the car was stripped. Gone were its headlights, steering wheel, tires, much of the engine, and even the brake drums. I looked at it uncomprehendingly for a moment, then asked one of the men who was busy prying off a hub cap why he was doing so. He turned to me and said with a shrug: "We have to live don't we?" I drove on in my Opel Rekord, loaned to me by Amadeo Barletta, Jr. (former owner of Cuba's *El Mundo*); and talked to people along the streets. Almost as soon as the loyalists had passed, housewives began to sluice down the steps of their houses, removing the dust and grime of battle. Asked in which direction Martínez Arana's troops had gone, one woman told me, referring to them as "our troops." I asked why they were now "our troops," when only a few hours before, the section had been used by snipers. She said that the residents had no means to get them out of their houses. She paused, and leaning reflectively on her *trapeador* (mop) added: "I think Caamaño is going to lose."

One particular shading of the truth was to backfire against the Johnson administration, and it involved General Antonio Imbert, one of Trujillo's assassins. Imbert is a political general and that is all. With no military background, Imbert was made a Brigadier General by Juan Bosch himself for having freed the Dominican people from the clutches of Trujillo, guaranteeing him, incidentally, a bodyguard for the rest of his life to protect him from being assassinated by Trujillistas. It was either just before or just following our briefing by the Israeli Ambassador that a few of us noticed that a black station wagon bearing the insignia of the U.S. Government drove up to the helicopter pad at the Embajador hotel, discharging Catholic Apostolic Nuncio Msgr. Emannuele Clarizio and a plump man in khaki slacks with a 45 caliber pistol slung at his waist. Tad Szulc immediately recognized him as Antonio Imbert and correctly surmised that he would be used in some capacity by the U.S. government. He questioned Ambassador Bennett the same night and received a non-committal reply, for the simple reason that the Ambassador was unaware of the role Imbert was to play. Mr. Bennett also said, accurately as it turned out, that the bogeyman of the rebels, General Elías Wessin y Wessin, was just that and little more. He said that exaggerated attention had been given to the general by the rebels. This was true. General Martínez Arana was in charge of the fighting elements of the Army, with Comodore Francisco Rivero Caminero commanding the Navy and General Juan de los Santos Céspedes in charge of the Air Force.

Ambassador Bennett also told us that he had received a request for U.S. intervention from Air Force Colonel Pedro Benoit who, not Wessin y Wessin or Antonio Imbert, was calling the shots from San Isidro. A Negro, Benoit shared his power with two others—Army Colonel Enrique Apolinario Casado Saladin, and Navy Captain Olgo Manuel Santana Carrasco. Pro-Bosch reporters claim that the military junta was a crea-ture of the United States and came into being at the summons of Ambas-sador W. Tapley Bennett for the purpose of requesting U.S. military intervention which Mr. Bennett had been wanting all along. The argu-ment of the pro-Bosch political critics goes something like this: The CIA, the military attaches, or some U.S. intelligence group, established the junta, and elicited from it the request to Ambassador Bennett for inter-vention "to prevent another Cuba," and put down a Communist-led revolt. But, the critics claim, it was believed in Washington that it would put a better face on it if the U.S. authorities merely said that Marines were needed to protect American lives. Therefore, the State Department instructed Ambassador Bennett to tell Colonel Benoit to change his message, emphasizing, instead, the need to protect U.S. citizens. Once this new message was received, President Johnson gleefully ordered in the Marines. Senator Fulbright in particular is a spokesman for this view.

What actually happened was this: Before 9:00 A.M., on the morning of April 28, Ambassador Bennett sent his military attaches to San Isidro base by helicopter to find out what was happening. They were surprised to find that everyone was reporting to Colonel Pedro Benoit, who at that moment was heading a three-man junta which nobody knew about for

the simple reason that there were no communications. Thus, the Junta
was already in existence the morning of April 28. Next, Colonel Benoit
told the U.S. attaches that his own military forces could not enter Santo
Domingo and that another group headed by General Augusto Montas
Guerrero had bogged down enroute from the other side of the city.
Therefore, he could not guarantee the lives of American civilians. This
statement regarding the inability of the junta to protect U.S. citizens was
relayed orally to Ambassador Bennett. Mr. Bennett telephoned to Washington the substance of Benoit's statement that morning. At noon, San
Isidro got a radio in operation and broadcast the formation of the already
existent three-man junta. It was in the *afternoon* that Ambassador Bennett received another message from Benoit, this time stating that the
junta forces lacked arms and ammunition, and requesting help from the
United States "to prevent another Cuba." Benoit sent that message *in
writing* via helicopter. Mr. Bennett relayed the new Benoit message to
Washington, actually recommending *against* giving support to the junta.
This message was received in the State Department at exactly 3:16 p.m.
on April 28, it having taken two hours in transmission, drafting, coding
and de-coding.

But just as that message was being received in Washington, Bennett
had reassessed the situation and sent off another, saying that the situation
had changed, that it was critical, and that the landing of Marines definitely seemed justified. Marines were in the area, and at 7:00 p.m. the
first contingent landed at the Embajador in response to his last message
which had been sent priority-urgent and took exactly fourteen minutes
in transit. Having received the written message from Benoit which spoke
of "another Cuba" but none regarding his inability to guarantee the lives
of U.S. citizens, the State Department then requested Ambassador Bennett to send along this statement in writing. The White House also told
Mr. Bennett that the Marines were landing in response to his previous
telephoned statements carring the oral message from Benoit, and added
that the written request from Colonel Benoit was needed "for the record." The military attaches relayed Bennett's request to Benoit, who
received it late that night of April 28, and it was cabled on to Washington
about mid-night—after the Marines had begun to land in considerable
force.

Thus Tad Szulc is in error when he writes that the United States had
already intervened in the Dominican Republic even before it had been
requested by the junta to do so. According to Szulc, it was when the later,
formal, request was received in Washington that "Ambassador Bennett
telephoned the White House and told President Johnson that the situation was getting out of hand . . . and that he personally favored a landing
by the Marines."[53] Szulc got his information by reading the exchange

of cables (probably provided by Senator J. William Fulbright), and did not take into account the existence of previous telephoned messages, the lag time in drafting, coding and sending messages, or the fact that a priority-urgent message might be received before one not so marked. Another point. Szulc writes that the junta was a government on paper only, since it had no control over Ciudad Nueva. However, that burden seemed to fall on the insurgents—to prove that *they* were more than a government on paper. They controlled only about an 80-block area in the capital city and absolutely nothing in the balance of the country.

What this all proves, it seems to me, is that what happened in the Dominican Republic was not a straight line of history as Senator Fulbright has sought to depict it. Each new act in the drama required a different response by the United States. Many critics refuse to recognize this. They mix things up by applying one U.S. response in one situation to the realities of another. For example, from May 1 on, the top leadership of the three Communist parties met together to plan joint tactics and strategy. They decided to have false papers prepared for the key men in all the parties. By May 5, Milvio Pérez Pérez was preparing these papers. A rank and file member of the Moscow-line PSP, Pérez Pérez's importance in this work derives from the fact that he owns a book and photography shop. Known Communists who had been much in evidence everywhere, at "commandos," in the streets, at rallies, suddenly disappeared from view. They did so because U.S. intervention had spoiled their bid for a direct military takeover. It was about this time that first reports were received of smuggling arms outside Ciudad Nueva, in a hearse, in trucks, and in gasoline tank trucks. The two Communist Parties, MPD and PSP, also issued orders to some members and followers to return their arms so they could be hidden in secret depots. More important, U.S. intelligence reported that the Communist parties decided at a leadership meeting to give full support to the Caamaño government, the night before he was sworn in, and to subordinate themselves to it. There is adequate proof that this is so, and we shall come to the Bosch-Communist alliance a little later on.

So again we find that at each change in the situation, the U.S. response changed. After Caamaño took power, Secretary of State Dean Rusk softpedalled charges of Communist control. This does not mean that he backed down from earlier findings of Communist control, but, in my opinion, was wrongly trying to use words as a weapon, probing to see if Colonel Caamaño would make some kind of peace that would keep the Communists out of power. This later led to the McGeorge Bundy-Cyrus Vance mission to Santo Domingo which resulted in what White House strategists called a "consensus government," but did not eradicate the Communists.

Critics also said that the Johnson-Thomas Mann line had reversed President Kennedy's policies by recognizing the Reid Cabral government after Bosch had been deposed. Yet, Mr. Kennedy seemed to have been quite pragmatic in recognizing governments established by coups. A military coup in Peru on July 18, 1962, following considerable bluster from the New Frontier, was recognized on August 17; still another in Ecuador on July 11, 1963, was given recognition on July 31. If anything, President Johnson and Thomas Mann took longer periods to recognize coup governments—from September 23, 1963 to December 14, 1963 for the Dominican Republic, and from October 3, 1963 to December 14, 1963 for Honduras. So the rage exhibited by pro-Bosch reporters and sympathizers on this point is quite unfounded.

There is the case of Thomas Mann, the hard-lining, pro-free enterprise former Assistant Secretary of State who, as Undersecretary of State, took charge of the Dominican crisis and was maligned for it by the liberals. Hacking through the jungle of Draper's comments on Thomas Mann one comes upon this one: "Should the United States show a special affinity for a regime that owed its existence to a military coup?"[54] Judging from the length of time it took for Mann to recognize a successor to Juan Bosch after he was overthrown, the Mann answer is no. An evident supporter of the "non Communist" Jacobo Arbenz regime in Guatemala, Draper is outraged that Mann finds that all things in democracies are not perfect, particularly the elections that placed Arbenz in power. Though Arbenz got into power constitutionally, this did not mean said Mann in an address at Notre Dame University, that he should remain in power once the people found that he was not a democrat, but a Marxist-Leninist. Says Draper in excoriating Mr. Mann: "The real question raised by the Guatemalan coup was not whether the United States should have restored Arbenz to power but whether it should have conspired to overthrow him."[55] But he does not seem to think it a bad thing at all that Juan Bosch should take U.S. money, and, from the safety of U.S. soil with help from U.S. citizens, including Puerto Rico's Governor Luis Muñoz Marín and Chancellor of the University of Puerto Rico Jaime Benítez, conspire against a friendly country.

We come now to the role played by General Antonio Imbert. As we have seen, the Caamaño-led rebels changed their tactics from trying to gain power by force alone to one of reaching power through the addition of diplomacy and propaganda. In maintaining their positions in Ciudad Nueva by shooting U.S. soldiers who blundered by mistake into their zone, the rebels had gained their point, and hoped that this *de facto* recognition of their status would eventually lead to even greater concessions by a United States which now was playing down the Communist menace. To counter the real gains made by the rebels, the United States gave birth to its own junta, with former U.S. Ambassador, pro-Bosch John Bartlow Martin, acting as the mid-wife. The junta consisted of Imbert, Colonel Pedro Benoit, and three civilian members, Carlos Grisolia Poloney, Alejandro Zeller Cocco, and Julio D. Postigo. Postigo, by the way, had been a supporter of Juan Bosch, but was not now. The government was known as the "Government of National Reconstruction." Sworn in on May 8, it was destined to be nothing more than a bridge to a new "consensus government" proposed by McGeorge Bundy and Undersecretary of Defense Cyrus Vance.

It can hardly be denied that the Johnson administration's press policies gratuitously brought upon it the criticism of the *New York Times* which editorialized the day before the swearing-in ceremonies, surprisingly: "The practical reasons for intervening against a genuine threat of a Communist takeover would also have been understood." This followed an earlier phrase that "no one questioned the need to protect American lives in Santo Domingo when law and order broke down." Then, typically, the editorialist overstepped himself, writing: "United States policy since World War II has been based on anti-Communism, accompanied by efforts to achieve a detente with the Soviet bloc." This was fine, according the editorialist, except that "the Johnson Doctrine means that the emphasis is now going to be on resisting the advance of Communism anywhere in the world with military force rather than on differentiating between various kinds of Communism or trying to co-exist with any of them."[56] The *Times* overlooked the kind of "coexistence" the rebels were trying to achieve by force of arms. No one in possession of his faculties could imagine that the expressions of anti-Americanism which developed into regularly scheduled rebel radio programs of vilification and falsehoods, the calculated murder of U.S. soldiers, and a regime based on mob violence could possibly represent the critical differentiation called for in the *Times* editorial. And to be fair, Walter Lippmann, a "loser" on Cuba, professed for at least a moment or two to be a winner on the Dominican Republic, and by doing so caught himself in a contradiction. He took the view on May 5 that it is normal, not abnormal, for a great power like the United States to insist that within its sphere of influence no other power shall hold sway over a military and political force, but he remained silent on the arsonist in Cuba who had set and fanned the flames that were enveloping Santo Domingo.[57]

Finally, the "consensus government" wished for by the White House in Washington was worked out, and a Provisional President, Héctor García Godoy, was approved by the Caamaño forces and the "Government of National Reconstruction" set up to bridge the gap until elections could be held on June 1, 1966. However, one important piece of information came to light which more than anything else proves collaboration in the revolt existed between the Communists, Bosch's PRD and the left-wing Christian Socialist Revolutionary Party. On July 8, 1965, a group of Caamaño supporters met in Santo Domingo to discuss whether to accept or reject Héctor García Godoy as Provisional President. Those who met, and what they said are revealing as to the strategy followed by the Communists. A copy of the minutes of the meeting constitutes a formal indictment of the group in their own language. Among those attending the 9:00 a.m. session, the minutes reveal, "held on the third floor of the Copello Building at number 79 corner of El Conde and Sánchez streets, seat of the Constitutional Government of the Dominican Republic," were the following: "Citizen Colonel Francisco Caamaño Deno; Sr. Hector Aristy, Minister of the Presidency; Dr. Salvador Jorge Blanco, Attorney General of the Republic; Andrés Lockward for the Christian Socialist Revolutionary Party Commission; Dr. Juan B. Mejía for the 14th of June Revolutionary Movement (1J4); Sr. José Francisco Peña Gómez for the Dominican Revolutionary Party (PRD)" and four others of less importance. The point is that the Castroites and the Christian socialists met together with PRD chief Peña Gómez and Colonel Caamaño. The counsel of the Communists and the extreme left-wing was sought at the highest levels of rebel leadership.

The minutes record Castroite Mejía as follows:

> American intervention . . . has created new conditions for us. I believe now that there are two ways to achieve our goals— through negotiations or through open warfare. If it now is not possible to achieve our goals through open war, then negotiations must be established at once. . . .[58]

What Mejía is saying, of course, is that U.S. intervention did, indeed, frustrate a Communist, and more particularly a Castroite, takeover of the country.* For this reason, Mejía recommended the classic Communist one-step-backward. Said Mejía: "The national and international situation now favors the constitutionalist movement because of the positions being taken by other powers." The 1J4 leader wanted no part of the Organization of American States because it might "impose strong control." Mejía recommended to Caamaño and PRD chief Peña Gómez that negotiations be pursued through the United Nations because, "We can be assured that there will be no attack while those negotiations are being conducted." Then he told the assembled group to use the time

*This view was effectively confirmed by Leftist U.S. publications, some of which have extensive contacts with the Castroite and revolutionary elements in Latin America. A common—and candid—theme in these papers was the rebel lament that, had the U.S. delayed just 24 hours before intervening, the "popular democratic forces" (read: Communists) would have won.

spent in delaying negotiations to prepare for guerrilla war: "We must call upon the people, explain the situation, and arm everybody for popular defense. Then we will say to the entire world that we do so in defense of the impositions being placed upon us by the OAS."

Castroite Mejía's tactics are understandable. He would count on the Communist bloc in the United Nations to tie the United States in knots while the Communist-led rebels in the Dominican Republic would tie up the country. Note that, predictably, UN Secretary General U Thant gave up an important mission in Geneva to return to New York and hear the Russians accuse the United States of aggression. And let it also be noted that U Thant's special emissary to the Dominican Republic was Juan Mayobre, not only a holder of the Lenin Peace Prize, but also a "former Communist." The combination of the extreme left, the "Constitutionalist," and the Communists, had joined in common cause in a manner which more than suggests that they had been joined long before the revolt had broken out.

José Francisco Peña Gómez had emerged from asylum and was again spokesman for Bosch's PRD. He spoke of his party's policy that "mass demonstrations and public protests" were now endorsed as a means to regain power. The PRD had, in effect, thrown in with the mobs and, more important, with the mobs' leaders in the Communist camp. He flattered the 1J4, saying "they are more or less immaculate, having been purified in the torture chamber," outlined a program which included a refusal to deport Communists, and called for the reinstatement of military men (who had been called to join in the insurrection by Captain Peña Tavares on April 24). A vote was taken among the leaders to determine whether or not to accept Héctor García Godoy as Provisional President. He was accepted.

Thus, as the Dominican Republic moved toward presidential elections on June 1, 1966, the changes wrought by revolution and U.S. intervention became more sharply defined. Some of them—the change of leadership to Héctor García Godoy and the beginnings of reforms in the Army —were all to the good. But, predictably, others, and especially the increasingly effective organization of the Communists, the Autonomous Confederation of Social Christian Workers (PRSC) and Bosch's Dominican Revolutionary Party (PRD) were bad. And the assessment by the Special Forces that the U.S. occupation was not as bad as it seemed, or as Communist slogans would have the people believe, was true. One frequently saw beneath the omnipresent "Yankee Go Home" signs a painted postcript: "If you Go, Take Me With You."

As Provisional President García Godoy put it to me in an interview in the Palace: "Maybe history will say that this interlude helped us break with the past and start with a new future for the Dominican nation." He

believed that his countrymen were experiencing "a great mental change
. . . the realization that social, economic, and institutional change is
attainable."[59] As for his own role, he told me that he was brought in to
bridge the gap "between the old way and the new future." He also said
that whoever won the elections will have to deal not only with the
staggering economic and social problems that have always beset the
country but also with the changes that had occurred in government, and
even more important, in the labor unions, the army, and the police, the
sectors that provided the most powerful leverage for action and control.

The two main candidates were Juan Bosch, who finally returned to the
Dominican Republic in September, saying he would demand a billion
dollars from the United States in indemnity, and Joaquín Balaguer, a
mild-mannered man who returned from exile in New York as candidate
of the Reformist Party. Although he was made puppet President by
dictator Rafael Trujillo in 1960, Balaguer cooperated in the expulsion
of the Trujillos after the Generalisimo had been assassinated, and is not
considered to have shared in the brutalities of the Trujillo era. Quietly
confident, the Reformist candidate went everywhere in the country,
talking to the people and shaking hands. In favor of taking labor out of
politics and government out of state-run enterprises, Sr. Balaguer was
diametrically opposed to Bosch who based much of his strength on a
politically motivated labor force. Bosch seldom left his house during the
campaign, apparently afraid of being assassinated, and as the race grew
hot he threatened to withdraw himself and his party unless guaranteed
protection against the possibility of harassment and intimidation from
his many foes. His was a pitiable performance, and his cowardice soon
was to label him "Juan, the Cave Man" after the known fact that he taped
radio broadcasts in the basement of his house and, afraid to emerge
himself, had them played over the radio stations of the country.

Bosch's greatest support in the 1966 elections, as it was when he won
a sweeping victory in 1962, lay among the workers of the cities and the
state-owned sugar mills. But, he no longer was certain of being able to
control his allies on the Left. In his campaign he went to great pains to
disassociate himself publicly from his extreme Left supporters with
whom, as we have seen from the minutes of the July 8 meeting, he was
privately cooperating. What worried foreign diplomats, as well as many
knowledgeable Dominicans, were the compromises Bosch made with the
Communists and extremists to assure himself of the labor vote. The
intricate and ambiguous relations with Dominican labor and the extreme
Left came to a test in the general strike which Bosch called in early
February 1966 and which lasted for eight days. Contributing to the
immediate impetus of the strike was a struggle for control of the University of Santo Domingo, which served to reinforce a widespread demand

from the Left for the expulsion of military generals from the country. Led by 1J4 militants, including members of the general secretariat of the Student Federation, pro-Communist students and professors seized control of the University just before its scheduled opening in the fall of 1965. Rector José Ramón Baez López Penha and the university's governing council were physically ousted, and a 1J4 member, Andrés Aybar Nicolas, was installed as acting rector along with four student representatives, a professor, and two vice rectors—all pro-Communist.

When Provisional President Héctor García Godoy refused to recognize the Communist coup and the government subsidy continued to be paid to the legitimate rector, an impasse developed at the university that continued from October until February. On February 9, Student Federation members, 800-strong, marched in a body to the Palace, shouting anti-American slogans and falsely accusing the army of having seized university funds. Following a melee in which five persons were killed by police and a policeman was clubbed by the mob and then covered with gasoline and burned to death, tensions in the city reached the breaking point. By this time, Bosch and his PRD had decided to call a strike aimed at forcing the government to dismiss three generals (incidentally, eight had already left the country) and send them out of the country. According to diplomatic sources, Bosch already knew that Commodore Francisco Rivera Caminero, now the Armed Forces Minister, had agreed to leave, and was hoping to win credit for his departure.

What was important about the strike is that Bosch's strike committee contained no labor-union members, but did contain leftist politicians. Labor support was essential, however, and once again Bosch turned to the extreme Left for help—to the anti-American CASC and to the leaders of FOUPSA, a union once controlled by his party but now dominated by the Communists. Once again, as at the Pact of Rio Piedras, he suggested that the PRD should take sole leadership in order to avoid the taint of Communist influence.

There was no question that FOUPSA was being run by the Communists. Bosch knew it, and solicited their cooperation. On August 28, 1965, when the rebels were still in command of their sector of downtown Santo Domingo, the Communists succeeded in ousting the PRD leaders of the union and captured eight of twelve positions on its executive board. The president of FOUPSA at the time, a faithful Bosch man named Miguel Soto, was isolated by the Communist coup and responded by publicly accusing the secretary general of the union, Julio de Peña Valdez, who is a member of the 1J4, of having made a trip behind the Iron Curtain. Soto followed up his counteroffensive in a paid advertisement that appeared in the Dominican press in September, charging that control of FOUPSA had passed into the hands "of those who take their orders from Moscow." On December 17 Soto, together with the vice president of FOUPSA, Marcos de Vargas, also a PRD man, was kicked out of the union or, as other reports at the time had it, was ordered out by Bosch. All this led to the curious situation that when Peña Valdez, in February, agreed to call out the FOUPSA in response to Bosch's general strike, he was taking orders from Miguel Soto, whom Bosch had named president of his strike committee, and who had been kicked out of the FOUPSA by that same de la Vega.

One aspect of the strike, which lends support to the view that the PRSC is increasingly dominated by the extremists, was the role played by the Labor Ministry and in particular by Vice Minister Herardio Paniagua, a leading member of the "democratic Left" Christian Socialists. Shortly before the strike was called, Paniagua in a conversation at the Ministry with a western diplomat declared that he was in favor of the strike. With apparent knowledge of what was to come, he said the strike "would be successful because the government employees would join." Fifteen minutes after the conversation, this diplomat told me, all employees at the Ministry of Labor itself had vacated their posts, and as the strike spread through the city of Santo Domingo, other government departments shut down. So Sr. Bosch gave a performance which again emphasized the easy accommodation of apparently conflicting principles among Bosch and members of the Leftist coalition. And it may be summed up this way: Bosch called the strike, the leftist Minister of Labor gave his tacit approval, Communist 1J4 leader de Peña Gómez provided bone and muscle through the full support of FOUPSA and the federation of government employees, CASC joined in, and the strike was on. All elements who made the strike possible were those who had met at Caamaño's headquarters on July 8 and agreed to join forces. The July 8 meeting was the Santo Domingo version of the Pact of Rio Piedras. In both instances, Bosch called upon the Leftists and the Communists for support, and they gave that support.

PRSC leader Paniagua, whose labor arm, the CASC, was important in bringing off the strike, was powerful enough to arrange to pay all government employees in full for the time that they were absent on the strike despite the fact that the Labor Code forbids walkouts of government employees, as did a decree signed by the Provisional President. Thus, the "democratic Left," represented by Labor Minister Paniagua, most definitely cooperated and worked with the Communists. Further cooperation came to light when Paniagua appointed Juan Matos Rivera to the post of Director of Social and International Relations of the Labor Ministry. Matos Rivera was trained in Cuba's guerrilla camps and had taken part in the Castroite guerrilla uprisings in the Dominican mountains in the fall of 1963. Deported, he went to France, where he was met by French Communists, given money and an apartment, enrolled in courses at the Sorbonne, and sent on a free trip behind the Iron Curtain. He turned up in 1965, as we have noted earlier, in charge of a rebel "commando." Early in 1966, Matos Rivera switched from the 1J4 Movement to the PRSC, and was made secretary general of the party in Santo Domingo while still holding his post in the Ministry of Labor.

Bosch finally called off his strike on February 17, having ostensibly gained his ends. But his cooperation with the Communists had helped them achieve their ends as well. During the strike, the Inter-American Peace Force, which now was functioning in the Dominican Republic, and U.S. officials and military officers, were impressed by highly effective terrorist attacks, which suggested that the Communists had greatly improved their military organization and used the strike to test its usefulness. When violence extended from the Palace to the downtown area of Santo Domingo, riflemen and machine gunners, flanked by grenade throwers, stationed themselves on balconies overlooking the city's narrow streets. As Inter-American Peace Force vehicles passed below, grenades were thrown, thirty-second bursts of machine fire followed, and the terrorists disappeared by prearranged routes into the night. According to the best U.S. intelligence estimates, about 20 Communist action groups of between twelve and twenty men each were operating in Santo Domingo in 1966 as civilian-clad urban guerrillas, with the potential of expanding to ten times that number. This brings us to the question of what happened to the arms that had been handed out to the civilians. By conservative estimate, about 7,000 rifles and side-arms were handed out during the revolt, and Provisional President Héctor Godoy's timid policies permitted the recovery of a mere 150.

From December 1965 on, according to intelligence reports, about 50 new Communist leaders had slipped into the country from Cuba. There were Dominicans, but there also were Uruguayans, Chileans, and others well trained in Cuba's guerrilla training camps. Possibly owing to García Godoy's polite policy of having rebels integrate into the government "in order to learn a sense of participation in national affairs," a number of immigration and customs posts were immediately taken over by the rebels, and from September 1965 to July 1966, Communists had no difficulty moving in and out of the country. As a result, the United States trained the Dominican armed forces in riot control, and the hope is that eventually the Dominicans will be able to handle their own internal problems without the need for the OAS or the United States to again intervene.

With this background of Communist activities, subversion, and violence, the Dominican people went to the polls on June 1, 1966, overwhelmingly rejected Juan Bosch and his PRD, elected Joaquín Balaguer and his Reformist Party by 57 percent of the vote, and swept both houses of Congress. Surprisingly, Bosch and his party lost several precincts in Santo Domingo known to be Communist Party and 1J4 strongholds, indicating that when the people have the opportunity to opt secretly for what they want they will do so. Predictably, 1J4 leader Rafael "Fafa" Tavares, whom Bosch denied knowing earlier, said that the elections "were a gross fraud perpetrated by Yankee imperialism," a charge that was repeated by his other leftist supporters. Also predictably, Senator J. William Fulbright said that he was not moved by the election returns to change his opinion at all.

And for the most part, pro-Bosch supporters in the press and elsewhere promptly lost interest in the Dominican story. They did so, perhaps, because recalling some of the positions they had taken during and immediately following the revolt would have been excruciatingly embarrassing. Their claims that Bosch enjoyed widespread popularity throughout the country turned out to be grossly exaggerated. Yet, none of those who took that position have since recanted. Nor do they consider the seriousness of their error in suggesting that the United States should have supported "Provisional President" PRD chief José Molina Ureña on April 25 because, in their view, the Boschistas represented the will of the people. Their error, and it is a grave one indeed, lay in equating the militancy of the Communist-dominated rebels and their mobs in Ciudad Nueva with the will of the people throughout the country. If Bosch supporters among the U.S. press had had their way they would have saddled the Dominican people with an unpopular, rather than a popular, government. What is at stake here, it seems to me, is the political judgment of those who were more interested in putting Juan Bosch back in power than they were in reporting the revolt.

Juan Bosch left the country following his defeat, first charging that the ballot boxes had been stuffed in favor of his opponent, then denying the charge. Bosch and members of his party went on a tour of Europe from where he issued pronouncements that were read over Radio Santo Domingo by his henchmen. And they were alarming. For example, on August 28, 1967, Bosch was quoted as follows: "Since April 28 I have been studying Yankee history—something which I had not done before —and I learned this: The United States uses men and then liquidates them." The following day, Bosch's PRD radio program made announcements and pronouncements that differ very little in content from those emanating from Castro's Radio Havana. The August 29, 1967, PRD broadcast excoriated the United States in guttersnipe language. Claiming that the United States was trying to deal "a death blow" to Juan Bosch and the PRD, the commentator then said of Bosch: "But the Dominican leader was not afraid to reply. His answer represents the best way to counter the exploitive system." He then quoted Bosch's answer: "I would rather die as a Communist than die pro-Yankee."

The PRD philosophy came out in the open when, on the same radio program, the commentator said: "Revolutions no longer can be democratic, for the Yankees and the local exploiters have killed the last vestiges of democracy in Latin America." Then using the Communist phrase, "Revolutionary comrades" in addressing the public, another PRD radio bulletin quoted Juan Bosch as follows: "I believe that after Santo Domingo was invaded, only a petty politician would dare talk of 'democratic revolutions' in Latin America." Bosch lined up with Fidel Castro, saying: "The Castroites are right about one thing—Latin America's revolution will be basically anti-Yankee. Why? Because the intervention in our country proved that the Latin American oligarchs have genuine, absolute support from Washington." Bosch also said that Fidel Castro was justified in turning Cuba into a Communist state, remarking: "Fidel Castro has been saying that the oligarchs have Washington's support, but we did not believe him. Events have proved Castro to be right, and a man who has shown he is right in something so fundamental to America's life must be respected. It was the Yankee democrats who fooled us, not Communist Fidel Castro." And Bosch said he had given two speeches in Europe, admitting with pride: "I concluded both speeches with the same words: 'I would rather die being a Communist than pro-Yankee!'" adding: "Anyone wishing to draw arbitrary conclusions from these words is free to do so."

On September 1, 1967, Jose Francisco Peña Gómez, Secretary General of Bosch's PRD, revealed that Juan Bosch had edged even closer to an open endorsement of the Communist system, stating over Radio Santo Domingo that Bosch proposed the creation of "popular dictatorships." The PRD chief also claimed that "Che" Guevara was right when he said back in 1959 and 1960 that it was U.S. imperialism that drove Cuba into the arms of the Communists. Moreover, Peña Gómez said that if the United States did not accept the concept of "popular dictatorships" it would have the effect of driving Bosch into accepting Communism. But a close study of Bosch's "popular dictatorships" shows that they are virtually indistinguishable from the Communist dictatorship of the proletariat, and would require very little in the way of alterations to make them so.

On October 14, 1967, Bosch bestirred himself in exile in Alicante, Spain, to remark in a taped interview played over Radio Comercial in Santo Domingo: "Spain made a second Spain in Latin America, whereas the United States needs subjugated peoples." Bosch then talked about world peace in the following terms: "The world situation has reached such a state that it rather seems that Russia is becoming the country of moderation while the United States is the one threatening the peace of the world." Bosch continued his attack on the United States by submitting a thesis called "Pentagonism—Substitute for Imperialism" to a Castroite audience attending an economic and social conference at the Autonomous University of Santo Domingo. The thesis is as inaccurate as it is anti-American, claiming that the Pentagon in Washington is holding the American people in its vise. According to Bosch, an alliance of big business and war materials manufacturers work with the Pentagon to promote a war economy to satisfy the blood-thirsty nature of the military and the insatiable longing for money of big business. But, to have a war economy, says Bosch, there has to be a war. And the military sees to that.

Bosch states that the ascendency of the military and the debasement of civil power began in 1951. From 1951 to 1960, says Bosch, the military budget of the United States jumped from thirteen billion to 27 billion dollars. But he does not point out that defense spending rose precisely because of a war in Korea which was initiated by the Communists, anymore than he mentions that this decade was marked by Communist military thrusts throughout the world. Indeed, he scores the United States for arming other countries in self-defense, saying that by doing so it is extending "Pentagonism" beyond its borders, meaning the alliance between big business and the military in foreign countries. He writes of the Russians: "The military expenditures of the Russians may be higher than the United States, but the Russian military establishment cannot ally itself with the industrial and financial sectors . . . it cannot disburse funds to subsidize industries . . . therefore, the Russian military has no means to become a pressure group, much less a power group."[60]

Juan Bosch compliments Senator J. William Fulbright for denouncing the use of military power against aggressive Communism, and probably does so because of Senator Fulbright's unlearned speech before the Senate on September 16, 1965. Said Fulbright: "If there is no democratic Left then there is no doubt of choice . . .they will choose Communism, not because they want it, but because U.S. policy will have foreclosed all other avenues of social revolution, and, indeed, all other possibilities except the perpetuation of rule by military juntas and economic oligarchies."

Apart from the factual errors which are apparent in Fulbright's speech (there are many alternatives to Communist or military rule), Fulbright's comments represent an implicit attack on anti-Communism. What he and Theodore Draper have done is to demonstrate the ideological liberal's adherence to the view that the enemy is always to the right. To them, our enemy is not the Communist, but the anti-Communist. The enemy is not Fidel Castro, whose training camps produced the guerrilla leaders that exploded the revolt in Santo Domingo; their enemy is not a Soviet Union which supports Castro in promoting guerrilla wars. No, their enemy is the General Wessin y Wessins and the President Johnsons of this world who seek in some measure to stop the Communist advance.

What Draper and Fulbright really are saying is that they dislike the free enterprise system ("economic oligarchs" to Senator Fulbright) and want the "democratic Left" to triumph. Indeed, they want the triumph so badly that they berate the military who prevented the Communists from gobbling up the "democratic Left." They wanted the United States to accept the rebels' "Constitutionalist" government and then attempt to work with the rebels to remove Communists whom those same "democratic Leftists" embraced in the first place. And the fact remains that military coups in Peru, Brazil and Argentina frustrated a threatened Communist takeover, and the military turned the government back to civilian control. Indeed, the military in Colombia and Venezuela collaborated in the overthrow of Right-wing dictatorships and then collaborated with democratic elements in restoring and protecting constitutional government.

And these facts remain: In the Dominican Republic, at least, the "democratic Left" proved itself to be politically ineffective. That Juan Bosch was a Communist himself at the outset is not supportable; that he worked with the Communists before, during and after the revolt seems clear; that today he is on the Communist side seems undeniable.

Moreover, Francisco Caamaño dropped out of sight and, in January of 1969, was reported by Venezuelan and Colombian newspapers to be leading a group of guerrillas operating along the Venezuelan-Colombian border. Venezuelan authorities also stated that Caamaño attended a meeting of 70 guerrilla chieftains from seven countries in the Colombian mountains.

CHAPTER 17

•

A Soviet Latin America

•

THE UTTER FAILURE of Juan Bosch and his "democratic Left" Revolutionary Dominican Party to cope with the Communists in Santo Domingo was dramatized by headline-grabbing accounts of U.S. "intervention." But no such fanfare has attended the weakness of the "democratic Left" in other Latin American countries, where some leaders are slowly succumbing to the Soviet Union's double-track policy. That policy, as articulated by Sharaf R. Rashidov, Soviet delegate to the Tricontinental Conference of Havana back in January 1966, is worth recalling. "We believe," the Muscovite said, "that relations among sovereign states with different public systems should be based on peaceful coexistence." He added the second track of Soviet policy, saying: "It is clear that there is not, nor can there be, any peaceful coexistence between the oppressed peoples and their oppressors."[1] Following the conference, the Soviets put their two track policy into operation—first, by pressing for diplomatic and trade relations with the countries in Latin America, and second, by giving Fidel Castro and his guerrillas operating in Latin America the guidance and support needed for them to weaken the regimes which the Soviets ultimately intend to penetrate and overthrow. The first arm of Russia's policy has been widely propagandized, giving rise to the myth that the Russians are following a dove-like course, innocently seeking no more than trade advantages and diplomatic recognition. The real villain, according to this myth, is the intractable, warlike Fidel Castro who, through his Latin American Solidarity Organization (OLAS), is upsetting Soviet plans by exporting and supporting guerrilla movements throughout the continent.

This myth was given high-level currency in a July 4, 1967 Associated Press story out of Anchorage, Alaska, quoting Vice President Hubert H. Humphrey (returning from a trip to the Far East) to the effect that at the meeting between President Johnson and Soviet Premier Alexei Kosygin in Glassboro, New Jersey, the previous month, President Johnson had remonstrated with Kosygin over Castro's export of revolutions to Latin America. Premier Kosygin then hopped on his plane and flew to Havana, according to Vice President Humphrey, where he dealt with Castro "very firmly."[2] Nothing could be further from the truth. Although OLAS is the organization through which Castro works, it is a creature of the Soviet Union, and came into being following the Soviet sponsored Tricontinental Conference. And how well OLAS is performing for the Russians is revealed in a report made by First Secretary Leonid Brezhnev to the XXIII Congress of the Soviet Communist Party. He said: "Special mention must be made of the courageous liberation struggle of the peoples of Latin America. Only recently, the United States regarded Latin America as its reliable rear guard. Today, there is not a single country in that continent where the people are not waging a struggle against United States imperialism and its accomplices."[3]

While supporting guerrilla movements (Castro could not train one guerrilla conscript nor ship a single rifle to Latin American terrorists without Soviet support and approval) behind the screen of an "intransigent" Fidel Castro, the Russians are propagandizing the alleged "peaceful" intentions of their party apparatus in Latin America. This relatively softer approach, in line with Soviet avowals of "peaceful coexistence," gave rise to an editorial in the June 27, 1967 *New York Times*, in which it was stated: "Fidel Castro's revolutionary policy is strikingly at odds with the one now being followed by the Soviet Union." However appealing this picture of Soviet policy may be for those determined to press for rapprochement with the Russians, it is a grotesque distortion of Soviet designs. For the Soviet Union is at once the greater and lesser evil. Those who recall pre-Castro Cuba also recall one important part of Communist strategy at the time. The "good guy" was Fidel Castro, holed up in the mountains of Oriente Province. The "bad buys" were members of the city-based PSP, the Cuban Communist Party, tainted because of their open collaboration with Fulgencio Batista. Eventually, both were revealed to be different branches of the same tree.

Basically, the same strategy is being followed by the Kremlin in Latin America—with one important difference. For the most part, Cubans and Americans believed at the time that Castro was a democrat. The opposite is true of opinions regarding mountain-based guerrillas in Latin America. No one can be deluded into believing that guerrilla chieftains César Montes, Lutven Petkoff, Douglas Bravo, Tiro Fijo, and so on are democrats, intent on reflecting the 1958 image of Fidel Castro. They are breast-beating Communists, openly allied with Castro and openly defended by him, an identification that is damaging to the Communist parties and, ultimately, to the Soviet Union which controls those parties. So, in a deft maneuver, the Kremlin switched signals. Openly, even ostentatiously, the Soviet Union and its allies are pretending to disengage from the mountain-based guerrillas, whose depredations have brought the full fury of the police and armed forces down on the relatively vulnerable city-based party apparatus. The Kremlin needs the parties intact, to serve as the screen of respectability behind which the Soviets seek their trade and diplomatic relations. Obviously, with their parties openly identified with the guerrillas, the Russians are no less an enemy of the state than those same guerrillas.

More important, the Kremlin fully intends to control events and not to be swept along in a guerrilla tide. The party is the ultimate political organ of the Communists, and whatever the utility of the guerrillas, it is the Kremlin, operating through its party appendages, which gives the orders, not "do-it-yourself" guerrillas. Furthermore, there is no real evidence that the guerrillas are expected to overthrow governments and take power. Their job, as the OLAS slogan states, is "to make revolution," to create political and economic instability, to force a flight of capital and eventually make it easier for a strengthened party apparatus, supported and directed by the Soviet Union, to penetrate the institutions and governments of Latin American countries, and thus take over in a two-stage, "peaceful" operation. For this reason, the outwardly onerous task of supporting the guerrillas has been given to Fidel Castro. Widely pictured as a heretic, uncompromising and erratic, Castro's portrait is very much to the liking of the Kremlin, and the task given to the Cuban dictator at the same time feeds his enormous ego.

An announcement out of Bolivia, where guerrillas headed by "Che" Guevara were operating in the summer of 1967, sketches some dimensions to the success of Russia's double-track policy as it applies to the role of guerrillas. The government announced that expenditures for internal defense had been raised from $6 million to $12 million a year. For those accustomed to reading of military budgets of $50 billion and more, Bolivia's expenditure of $12 million may seem a paltry sum. But when it is realized that the yearly national budget of that Andean nation is only $60 million, the outlay of $12 million for internal defense alone takes on alarming proportions. The U.S. taxpayers at the same time were giving Bolivia an additional $36.3 million in direct foreign aid, an amount which probably will have to be increased as guerrilla depredations, momentarily stopped by the shooting of Guevara on October 8, 1967 by Bolivian troops, resume.

Colombia's President Carlos Lleras Restrepo said of guerrilla assaults in his country: "Guarding the country against attacks is bleeding the country economically. It consumes resources which could be invested in the many needs of the Colombian people."⁴ The flight of capital occasioned by political instability in Colombia led the government to clamp down on currency exchange and, shortly thereafter, to cut back imports by an announced total of 30 per cent. Well-informed financial people told me in Bogota that the cutback was actually in the vicinity of 60 per cent.

The shading of the truth regarding Colombia's cutback in foreign purchases points up another serious problem. Many Latin American governments dare not talk too much about guerrilla depredations, for the simple reason that the more the talk about them, the greater the loss of outside capital, and the more depressed the economy. And, following President Lleras' complaints about guerrilla attacks "bleeding the country economically," the Russians came in right on cue with an offer of trade advantages to Colombia in return for diplomatic representation. Bogota's *El Siglo* was quick to judge the Russian offer as one end of its policy to promote violence, saying in an editorial on April 21, 1967: "This economic 'friendship' will give the Reds opportunities for political activism. We run the risk of seeing them open offices, ostensibly for commercial purposes, but actually for the clandestine purpose of fomenting and financing terrorism." Underscoring *El Siglo's* warning, a group of young Russian *Komsomols* visiting Colombia on a "good will tour" were interviewed by *El Espectador,* which wrote about them in its July 4 issue. Downing bottles of "imperialistic" Coca Cola, spokesman Gennary Silipotich spoke of the Russian attitude toward Colombia's guerrillas in language which is more than faintly reminiscent of that employed by Sharaf R. Rashidov and Leonid Brezhnev. He said: "We, in general, look on with sympathy, and give our support, both politically and morally, to those peoples who are fighting for their national liberation." Silipotich was in Colombia, he said, to connect the Komsomols with Colombian youth organizations.

That the Soviet Union has been successful in peddling its double track policy under the guise of peaceful intentions is evident. And it is nowhere more evident than in the United States where both the State Department and much of our press seem to have accepted Soviet avowals of "peaceful coexistence" to mean live and let live. An Associated Press dispatch out of Moscow serves as one example among many. The reporter noted that Russia's Communist Party organ, *Pravda,* carried a story condemning Castro's armed ventures in Latin America. The reporter wrote: "The Soviet Communist Party newspaper, *Pravda,* carried an article on Latin America Wednesday that condemned the export of revolutionary policy as espoused by Prime Minister Fidel Castro of Cuba." The story, written by Rodolfo Gioldi, a member of the Argentine Communist Party, was offered by *Pravda* as evidence that the Soviet-controlled parties in Latin

America shun the guerrilla movements of Fidel Castro and follow the "peaceful" line of the Soviets. Apparently, it did not occur to the AP correspondent that the publication of the article might have been a ploy, for he added his own judgment in the following terms: "The article in Pravda defended the Soviet Union's handling of affairs with Latin America, including Kremlin opposition to trying to export revolution from one country to another."[5]

In reading Gioldi's article in its entirety, however, I find the allusions to Fidel Castro and to Cuba to be only inferential. More immediately important, "Kremlin opposition" is nowhere to be found in Gioldi's piece. And the inferences drawn by AP's man in Moscow that Russia is following a respectably peaceful course in its relations with Latin American countries, are negated by the following sentences written by Gioldi: "In Argentina, conditions are developing for the formation of a broad coalition directed against the dictatorship, which has the aim of overthrowing it and replacing it with a truly popular and national [i.e. Communist] government. That is our central task."[6] These words, written by the Argentine Communist, were not mentioned in the AP story, and indeed, may have been omitted in the text published in Pravda. What they mean, of course, is that the tactics of the Soviet Union are no less violent than those of their puppet, Fidel Castro.

On August 10, 1967, the *New York Times* editorialized about the OLAS meeting just concluded in Havana in language which must have pleased the Soviet Union: "The OLAS . . . gave the already fractured Communist movement another gaping wound. This one came in a vote to condemn the Soviet Union's economic policies in the Western Hemisphere." The observation appears to have been based on an unsubstantiated *Reuters* report which was published in the *Times* the day of its editorial. It reads: "The Organization of Latin American Solidarity approved a resolution today condemning Soviet economic and technical policy in the Western Hemisphere." But what was the source of the *Reuters* dispatch? The fact is that Western reporters who went to Havana to cover the OLAS conference were not permitted to attend any of the sessions, indicating that the information contained in the *Reuters* dispatch came from a second-hand source, undoubtedly a Castro-Communist source. And that Castroite sources are spectacularly unreliable might have occurred to the *Times*, whose Herbert Matthews was conned by Fidel Castro back in February 1957 into reporting that Castro's forces were operating "in groups of 10 to 40" when in fact the total number of men with Castro at the time numbered a pitiful eighteen. Predictably, of the 20 resolutions passed at the OLAS conference, not one of them clashes with the Russians, and the resolution "condemning" Soviet policy is conspicuous by its absence.

Undaunted by its earlier failure accurately to report on Communist intentions, the *Times* carried a dispatch from Moscow on November 7, 1967 which reads: "The Soviet Union, which provides the principal economic and military support to Cuba, disapproves of Havana's insurgency in a number of Latin American countries." The *Times* the following day headlined a story: "Soviet's Jubilee Snubbed by Cuba," and said that the snub was related to Russia's failure to ink a new trade pact with Cuba. The dispatch reads, in part: "The Cuban Minister of Commerce visited Moscow early last month and was received by Premier Kosygin, but left shortly thereafter without any announcement of a new trade agreement." If the *Times* correspondent had looked a little deeper into the matter he would have found that there was no need for Cuba and Russia to sign a new trade pact. In February of that same year, they concluded a trade agreement amounting to $800 million a year. More important, the trade agreement represents an increase of 23 per cent over previous agreements and is to run until 1970. Trade pacts between all members of the Soviet bloc, and Red China, were up by a total of seventeen per cent.

Another example of uncritical acceptance by the news media of the "peaceful" intentions of the Soviet Union on the flimsiest of evidence is contained in the November 15, 1967, issue of a newsletter published by *Vision*, the respected Spanish-and-Portuguese language magazine. *Vision* told its readers that friction between Havana and Moscow is on the rise and based its conclusions on the Gioldi article in *Pravda*, on another published in the same newspaper by Luis Corvalán, Secretary General of Chile's Communist Party, and on still another written by a Venezuelan intellectual, Rodolfo Quintero, which appeared in Moscow's *Za Rubezhom*. Chile is the country in Latin America most likely to succumb to the Communists through Russia's "peaceful coexistence." Thus, Corvalán's words, so prominently featured in Pravda, should be considered in that context. *Vision* quotes him: "In these times when imperialism is improving its economic and commercial relations with the countries of Latin America to strengthen the dominion which it exercises over them, the Soviet Union seeks to foment relations which favor independent development of each nation's economy." After quoting Corvalán, *Vision*'s editors wrote their own appraisal of what this meant: "In other words, Moscow wants trade rather than revolution and Castro is prejudicing this policy."

It is obvious that Corvalán and his Russian master want to promote trade and diplomatic relations with Chile. Without such relations, "peaceful coexistence between sovereign states with different public systems," would be inoperable. But this does not mean, as the *Times*, the Associated Press, *Vision*, and Vice President Humphrey maintain, that the Soviet Union and its Communist parties oppose Fidel Castro's thesis of the armed struggle. The Kremlin has never said that Castro's guerrilla activities are prejudicial to its policies. In fact, there is adequate evidence to prove that the Soviet-controlled Communist parties support Castro's ventures. For example, Luis Corvalán has stated Communist strategy in a vein much more open than his article published in *Pravda*. Writing in the July 1967 issue of the Soviet-controlled *World Marxist Review*, Corvalán states the obvious—namely, that guerrilla movements will be accepted or rejected according to their chances of success. "Reality sometimes plays havoc with preconceived ideas," wrote Corvalán regarding guerrilla wars. "We believe, therefore," he continues, "that in some Latin American countries revolution may be sparked off by a guerrilla movement, such as was the case of Cuba. . . . It would be wrong both to reject out of hand or blindly to accept any specific form of struggle." He also writes about "the imperatives of solidarity with the other peoples of the world, particularly of Vietnam and Cuba, and with the anti-imperialist and anti-feudal movements on our own continent, *especially those forced to resort to armed struggle* [in Guatemala, Venezuela, Colombia, and Bolivia] or to function under-ground"[7] (italics added).

Perhaps the most specific formula was fashioned by Mario Soza, Central Committee member of the Communist Party of Honduras. Also writing in the *World Marxist Review*, he thus interprets Lenin: "To regard the Leninist thesis on peaceful coexistence as being contrary to the interests of the national liberation movement of our peoples not only is wrong, it is dangerous." The two must operate together, wrote Soza, adding: "In Honduras we believe that the main contradictions in our society will in all likelihood be resolved through force."[8]

That violence definitely remains the touchstone of Soviet Communist policy in Latin America was illustrated in the writings of yet another Soviet-controlled Communist leader, Gustavo Corvalán, theoretician of the Paraguayan Communist Party. Writing in the September 1967 issue of *World Marxist Review*, Corvalán parrots the Soviet Union's "peaceful coexistence" line: "The Party works to promote the mass struggle for the vital economic, political and democratic demands." He then adds the other, harder Soviet line: "The Party at the same time calls for arming the masses," and bluntly states: "The Party . . . advocates the setting up of the first armed groups of peasants with a view gradually to build a guerrilla movement on a nationwide scale."[9]

These samples of Communist policy in Latin America are not mere heady discourses written by the Party elite; they reach the level of the guerrilla actionist and Party activists. Germán Lairet, Moscow's man in Venezuela, speaks with the authority of his position as Military Secretary of the Politburo of the Venezuelan Communist Party. Sporadic halts in guerrilla operations, writes Lairet, "are in order for us to repair the damage which has seriously hindered our capacity to wage armed struggle." In Venezuela, each time there was an outbreak of guerrilla activity in the mountains, the police retaliated directly against the Party apparatus in the cities, virtually destroying it. This is evidence that Venezuelan authorities are not taken in by the double-track policy of the Russians, and consider the Party and the guerrillas to be working together. Indeed, Venezuela has refused to consider opening diplomatic and trade relations with the Soviet Union until guerrilla operations have come to a halt. Thus, Lairet was pleading for a temporary halt in guerrilla activities, writing that this was necessary "in order for us to find the conditions that will permit us to strike back later with greater advantage." Lairet's article was contained in the February 1967 issue of *Confidencial*, an intelligence digest published by Venezuela's Ministry of the Interior.

Francisco Mieres, another member of the Venezuelan Communist Party, has removed all doubt that violence is the order of the day in his country. Mieres writes in the November 1967 issue of *World Marxist Review:* "As regards the general strategic road in Latin America there exists practically complete unanimity: armed struggle here is the rule, and the peaceful way—the exception." Mieres continues: "Our Party maintains that Venezuela has been and remains within the framework of the rule. A recent meeting of our Central Committee pointed out that the 'decision to take to arms was correct,' and it also reaffirmed the general concept of the 'non-peaceful revolutionary road to national liberation and socialism' in Venezuela."[10] And when the Communist Party was outlawed in Venezuela, its Secretary General, Pompeyo Márquez, fled to Colombia where it is legal. On May 24, 1967, Bogota's *El Espectador* quoted the Venezuelan Communist leader in terms that support both ends of Russia's double-track policy. He said: "Our immediate objective is to fulfill our role through a broad popular front," meaning a conglomerate of political parties manipulated by the Communists. Márquez then added the other track of the Soviet policy when he said: "We have no intention of disbanding the guerrillas."*

The Venezuelan secret service intercepted a letter written by Teodoro

---

* The Central Committee of the Communist Party of Colombia passed a resolution in January of 1968 which exults: "The guerrilla movement is active and has successfully resisted all attempts to destroy it." An article in the June, 1968 issue of the authoritative *World Marxist Review* (p.88) spells out Communist double-track policies in unmistakeable terms. Written by Jaime Gonzalez, theoretician of the Colombian Communist Party, the article reads, in part: "There is no contradiction between armed and non-armed forms of struggle—they complement each other. *By supporting and facilitating both, our party has proved that armed struggle is harmoniously blended with other forms of struggle which, in combination, make up our strategy.*" (emphasis added).

Petkoff, a member of the Politburo of the Communist Party, to his brother Lutven, a guerrilla actionist in the hills, and published it in the May 1967 issue of *Confidencial*. Teodoro relates the "armed struggle" to the visible Soviet policy of "peaceful coexistence," writing: "The most important thing for us to do is to save the Party . . . and then work with skill and patience to revive the armed struggle." Equally important, the letter brought up the major difference between Fidel Castro and his masters in the Kremlin when he bitterly remarked in the same letter: "Fidel Castro believes that now the headquarters [Communist Party] really is in the mountains."

There is evidence that Castro wants to take leadership of the Communist Parties in Latin America away from the functionaries now holding power and to transfer it to guerrilla actionists in the hills. If Castro were to be successful, he would then control the Party apparatus, and the Kremlin could impose its views on the Party in Latin America only by directing its commands through Havana. But this difference is not related to an alleged struggle between proponents of the Soviet policy of "peace" on the one hand, and proponents of the "armed struggle" of Fidel Castro, on the other. The difference rests on who is to control Communist policy in Latin America—the Kremlin or Fidel Castro.

Evidence that Castro wants to gain control of the Communist apparatus in Latin America comes from his speeches, in which he indirectly criticizes the Soviet Union and the Communist parties in Latin America, and from the anger expressed at Russia's policies which tend to support those parties against his claims of leadership. What seems to be forgotten, however, is that the fight is carried on principally in Fidel Castro's corner. The Kremlin is in charge, knows that Castro has no other place to turn for effective military and economic support, and remains silent. Furthermore, Castro's guerrilla activities are in line with Soviet policy in that they make the ultimate task of softening up Latin American countries that much easier. True, compared to the bombast coming out of Havana and Castro's open support to the guerrillas, the Soviets indeed look like doves. There is little reason for the Kremlin to be concerned over Castro's attempts to gain control of the Communist movement in Latin America. They know he can never achieve that control through guerrilla operations alone.

Other evidence that Castro is trying to shift Communist power into the hands of his guerrilla leaders comes from a pamphlet written by French Marxist Regis Debray. The pamphlet, *Revolution In The Revolution?* says: "In the majority of Latin American countries, only the armed struggle will bring the revolution out of the ghetto of university blabber." This observation is followed by another along the same vein: "The popular army [guerrillas] will be the nucleus of the Party, and not the reverse."

Debray gets to the heart of Castro's thesis when, at the end of his pamphlet, he writes: "The guerrilla is the political vanguard, and only through his development can the true party be born. Principal emphasis must be placed on developing guerrilla warfare, and not in strengthening the existing parties or in creating new ones. For this reason, the insurrectional task is today the number one political task."[11]

There is little doubt that Debray is the megaphone of Fidel Castro. *Revolution In the Revolution?* was published in Cuba by the government's Casa de las Américas, and a foreword by its director, Roberto Fernández Retamar, demonstrates that Fidel Castro went to considerable lengths to accommodate Debray. Fernández Retamar writes of Debray and his work: "Throughout the year 1966 he had the opportunity to talk directly with numerous participants of our revolutionary phase; among others with the one who conceived and directed the revolution, Comandante Fidel Castro, with whom he made long trips to listen to the vivid stories of his experience." The "vivid stories" of Fidel Castro apparently were not unlike the lies which Castro told Herbert Matthews nine years earlier, stories which were accepted in the main by Messrs. Huberman and Sweezy, Jean Paul Sartre, and a number of other Castro apologists. The English translation of the pamphlet carries a foreword written by Leo Huberman and Paul Sweezy in which they say: "We have here for the first time . . . the revolutionary thought of Fidel Castro and Che Guevara." And in the end, Debray was no less a victim of Castro's lies than Huberman and Sweezy, for his myth emphasizes that Fidel Castro came to power through a peasant-supported guerrilla operation. Debray writes that other guerrilla operations like it will sweep Latin America.

In fact, Debray went to Bolivia where he joined the guerrilla forces of Ernesto "Che" Guevara in order to see his prophecy fulfilled. But the Debray history of Cuba could not be duplicated in Bolivia for the simple reason that, like their counterparts in Cuba nine years earlier, Bolivian *guajiros* and *campesinos* refused to support a guerrilla movement. Something of that refusal comes through in Guevara's diary, captured when he was shot to death on October 8 at Valle Grande in a remote area of Bolivia. He wrote: "The inhabitants of this region are as impenetrable as rocks. You speak to them, but in the deepness of their eyes you note that they do not believe you." The importance of "Che's" failure is that it destroys the theories of Regis Debray and those of a considerable portion of the U.S. intellectual community concerning peasant support of guerrilla warfare.

Guevara disappeared from public view in Cuba in March 1965, among rumors that he had been shot by Castro for an anti-Soviet attitude, or that he had succumbed while fighting with the rebels in Santo Domingo.

His reappearance in Bolivia, leading a rag-tail band of between 60 and 100 guerrillas, spurred the imagination of the "losers." Rheumatic and constantly ill with asthma, at times "Che" had to be carried about on a makeshift litter by his guerrilla companions, thus hardly projecting the picture of the dashing, clear-eyed humanitarian revolutionary drawn by so many "losers," some of whom enshrined him in the pantheon of heroes reserved for George Washington and Simón Bolivar. Reportedly, he was captured, screaming: "I am 'Che' Guevara. I'm worth more to you alive than dead."

It is too often unnoticed in the flurry of publicity surrounding Guevara's death that at least fifteen Cuban Army officers were with Guevara, providing almost ostentatious proof of Cuban intervention. Among the Cubans were the following Majors: Juan Vitalio Acuña and Antonio Sánchez, both members of the Central Committee of Cuba's Communist Party. Among the Captains were: Orlando Pantoja and Eliseo Reyes, also members of the Central Committee; Jesús Suárez, a former vice minister of Cuba's sugar industry; and Alberto Fernández, Director of Mines.

More immediately important is the part played in the drama by the Soviet Union and its Communist Party in Bolivia. The group of guerrillas reached Bolivia through Leningrad, Moscow, and Prague. The red leather-bound diary of a Cuban medical doctor, Carlos Luna Martínez, tells about it. Found after the doctor had been killed, portions of the diary were read at the trial of Regis Debray by a military court in La Paz. The court found Debray to be a member of the guerrilla forces and sentenced him to 30 years in prison. Dr. Luna Martínez commenced his diary in November, 1966, when he wrote:[12] "November 20, left Havana. November 21, arrived in Leningrad, and on the 22 left Leningrad for Moscow by train. November 25, Prague, where it is a white inferno of snow, and I learned to play chess. December 3, we departed for Buenos Aires, and arrived there on December 4. On December 5 and 6 we went to the movies, and then bought books and medicines. December 7 and following, we arrived at the Hotel Copacabana in La Paz. Arturo couldn't stand the altitude and he fainted. We helped him and he responded. We then made some purchases in the name of a fictitious company, 'Malmist, Inc.'
"

The doctor wrote that the group then went to Cochabamba by car, "crossing a 'Siberia' at an altitude of over 13,000 feet." When they arrived at the camp, the doctor recalled in his diary that Castro had personally talked to the group of guerrillas before they left Cuba for Leningrad, writing: "Castro told us before leaving: 'If you arrive, then triumph.' " The diary continues: "On December 12 we caught up with 'Ramón' ["Che" Guevara] who proceeded to name men to command. 'Marcos' is the chief of the vanguard, 'Joaquín' chief of the rear guard,

'Alejandro' operations, and 'Pompo' services. 'Ramón' then explained to us his plan for guerrilla operations."

A few days later, the diary indicates, the guerrillas changed to another camp for security reasons. But an arresting part of the Cuban doctor's comments at this state of the operations came in an entry dated December 31, 1966: "The Secretary General of the Communist Party of Bolivia, which follows the Soviet line," said the diary, "arrived at our camp." The purpose of his visit was to join the guerrillas, but only, the diary recounts, on three conditions, listing them: "He would give up his present duties with the Party if he was assured that we followed 'a line parallel to that of the Party'; that he would be named political and military chief of the guerrillas; and that he was free to seek the support of other parties. 'Ramón' rejected the second condition, and said: 'I am the chief.' " Upon receiving Guevara's negative response, the Communist official left. The balance of the diary tells the story of privation, of living off monkey meat and putrid fish, and of encounters with the Bolivian armed forces which tracked them down. The diary ends on April 12, 1967, when the doctor presumably was killed.

The diary, whose authenticity has since been vouched for by Bolivian and U.S. officials,* contains two important revelations. The first is that the Cubans went to Bolivia via the Soviet Union and Czechoslovakia. Officials of both Communist countries had to be aware of the purpose as well as the ultimate destination of the Cuban guerrillas—people don't just move in and out of a Communist country without an approved purpose. It is entirely possible that the Russians provided the guerrillas with false passports which enabled them to enter Argentina and Bolivia. The second point of major importance is that the Communist Party of Bolivia, described by doctor Luna Martínez himself as following the Soviet line, knew where to find the guerrillas in their secret camp and offered secretly to cooperate in guerrilla activities. That the Party Secretary General did not do so rested on Guevara's refusal to turn political and military direction over to him. Guevara did not object to following "a line parallel to that of the Party," and presumably was already on that course. Nor did Guevara demur at the suggestion by the Communist Party official that he obtain the support of other parties. In fact, the Bolivian Communists did recruit guerrillas from among Bolivia's tin miners, one of whom was captured and confirmed that Cubans were leading the operations.

An important point is this: The Russians know perfectly well that Castro's claims to guerrilla victory in Cuba are overstated, and in that knowledge prove themselves to be more flexible in their judgements than Matthews, Huberman, Sweezy, and Debray, who appear to rigidly com-

*And also by "Che" Guevara's own diary.

mitted to the Castro myth. The Soviets know the truth—namely, that it was the Cuban middle class, operating through urban civic action, that brought Fulgencio Batista to his knees and eventually forced him to leave the country.* For this reason, the Kremlin does not place primary emphasis on guerrilla operations in Latin America. While Castro maintains that guerrilla warfare is the *only* way to propel a Communist government into power, the Soviets accept guerrilla operations *as one of several methods* to be employed. This fact explains the contradictions in some writings of Latin American Communists leaders as they try to straddle the ideological fence. On the one hand, they are compelled to reject Castro's claims that Communist power be taken from them and placed in the hands of the guerrillas, if for no other reason than to protect themselves. On the other hand, the Communist leaders support guerrilla operations, since they are an integral part of Soviet strategy.

Soviet success in the first arm of its double-track policy—infiltration and control through "peaceful coexistence between sovereign states"— is bearing fruit in at least two Latin American countries. Chile is the outstanding example of the failure of the "democratic Left" to cope with Communism, and is the number one danger spot of Latin America. The course taken by Colombia, another danger spot, is unsettling, at best. Though it would be unfair to judge the course that will emerge on the basis of less than two years operation of the administration of President Carlos Lleras Restrepo (Liberal Party), it is well to point to an anti-business, even anti-American and pro-Soviet, attitude.

In population, (18 million), Colombia ranks third among the nations of South America, but in the number and variety of economic and political problems it must be ranked even higher. President Carlos Lleras Restrepo has been struggling with those problems since his inauguration in August 1966, but his methods have been watched in diplomatic and business circles in Bogota with lively interest and sharply rising concern. And that concern was reflected in Washington where the General Accounting Office (GAO) issued a report to Congress charging that millions of U.S. aid dollars had been squandered by President Lleras' economic planners. The report, issued to the press on September 26, 1967 found that in examining the books of the Colombian Fund For Private Investment, to which the United States contributed $37.8 million, at least $24 million had been used for programs "contrary to U.S. objectives or of doubtful necessity and priority."[13] The GAO found officials of the Alliance For Progress to be much too casual in disbursing U.S. tax dollars on dubious projects.

Only two weeks prior to the GAO release, Alliance For Progress

*We can anticipate greater emphasis by the Communists in student disorders and urban guerrilla warfare.

officials in Washington claimed that Colombia was at the forefront of Latin American nations offering the best opportunities for private investment. Yet, during a trip to Colombia about the same time, I was told by business leaders there—U.S. and Colombian—that Colombia was at the bottom of the list of countries to attract foreign investments. More than that, many of them felt that current cuts by Congress in the U.S. foreign aid program might force Lleras to cooperate with the business sector. They believe that Alliance For Progress funds have permitted the "democratic Left" administration of President Lleras to pursue anti-business, even anti-American, policies while opening trade and diplomatic relations with Russia and its bloc of satellites.

Whatever the truth may be concerning these charges, President Lleras has felt the need to control absolutely the money economy of Colombia. There is by now a general belief among Western embassies in Bogota that President Lleras prefers government-to-government loans to private capital investment, the better to control the nation's economy. For example, in 1967 his Bank of the Republic issued its semi-annual report, claiming a favorable balance of trade amounting to $48 million. And on July 20 the same year, President Lleras announced to incredulous foreign investors that Colombia's economic recession was at an end, and that he was quite certain that the World Bank and other international financial institutions would make loans of several millions of dollars to his administration.

However, while President Lleras may have been accurate in stating that he could obtain loans from international financial institutions (international bureaucrats have an affinity for each other), he did not explain that the need for loans was made more urgent because his decrees were discouraging private capital investments, or that government loans are very thin gruel on which to build and sustain a robust economy. Nor did the president mention that income from major exports (coffee, oil, minerals) for the first six months of 1967 had diminished by 20 per cent over a similar period of 1966, or that the $48 million favorable balance reported by his Bank of the Republic for the first six months of 1967 was made possible only by cutting imports. Nor did he mention that loans have to be repaid while foreign investments tend to stay in the country and build upon themselves. More important, loans made to Colombia through the Alliance For Progress and other international agencies cannot possibly replace the shortage of capital caused by the suspension of private investments in the country.

Why capital investments came to a standstill in 1967 is revealed in just a few of the many Presidential Decrees promulgated since Lleras came to power. For example, Article 116 of Decree 444[14] placed an arbitrary restriction on the profits in foreign investment. These may not "exceed 10% per year, calculated on the net value of foreign currency of the respective investments." The alleged purpose of Article 116, a Colombian government official told me, is to encourage, even force, foreign corporations to reinvest profits made in Colombia back into their businesses so as to expand the country's industries. This purpose is negated, however, because according to Article 116, the businesses can send back to their stockholders in the United States only 10% of the "foreign currency" invested. In other words, the profits obtained from expansion of a business by investment in Colombian pesos brings no reward to the investor. One need not possess a degree in economics to grasp the effect which Article 116 has had on outside foreign investments. Nor is that all. The foreign investor must always have an eye cocked on the value of the Colombian peso in relation to the U.S. dollar. Pegged at 8 (9 on the open market) to the U.S. dollar in 1962, by 1967 the peso was worth only 16.25 to the dollar. What devaluation means, then, is that the U.S. corporation must exchange more than twice the number of pesos (16.25 instead of 8) for each dollar its sends home to its stockholders. Thus, the profit margin on an investment, say, of $10 million becomes not 10 per cent ($1 million), but only 5 per cent ($500 thousand). Few investors have been interested in such restricted profits when they can get between 12 and 15 per cent in less unstable Latin markets.

Still another restriction was placed on foreign firms operating in Colombia by President Lleras' economic planners. This is exercised through government control over the price of imports. In one instance, which is by no means rare, a U.S. manufacturer importing raw material for manufacture and export found his prices artificially jacked-up by the Colombian government from whom, under Article 172 of Decree 444, the importer must contract for his imports. The actual price for this particular import was 9 pesos a pound, but the government claimed that U.S. dollars were in short supply and charged the company 13.50 pesos, thus arbitrarily raising the cost to the manufacturer. And when the manufacturer applied to the government for a raise in domestic prices to compensate for his considerable loss, he was turned down on the grounds that price rises were inflationary. As it stood at the end of 1967, the U.S. firm was losing an average of 100 pesos on each unit manufactured and might have to close down, an event which, the president of the firm told me, was met with indifference by the government.

A glaring case, either of the ignorance of President Lleras' economic planners or their anti-Americanism, or both, involves the U.S. drug company, Pfizer. Taking into account that drugs have a tendency to lose their value as new products come on the market, Pfizer made a drastic cut in the price of tetracyclin. To the surprise and dismay of the firm, the

Colombian government charged Pfizer with double invoicing, and based its charge on the assumption that the reduction in price simply meant that the firm had been overcharging and exploiting the Colombian people all along. The readiness with which the charge was made indicated to many, including some members of the U.S. embassy, that the government was almost eager to indict an American firm, a belief that was given even greater currency when a Minister of the Lleras administration told a member of our embassy in Bogota that the Pfizer case was representative of the "crookedness" of U.S. business. When Bogota's *El Tiempo* had a field day running the story, foreign residents recalled that President Lleras was at one time editor of the newspaper, and surmised that the story had been given official encouragement. And *El Tiempo's* headlines summing up President Lleras' address to Colombia's *guajiros* that "Only Selfish Interests Oppose Change," with a sub-head reading: "They Try to Persuade The Masses To Oppose Our Reforms,"[15] was not without a trace of demagoguery.

President Lleras' attitude toward business and professions took an ugly turn when, on July 20, 1967, he promulgated Tax Decree 1366. Articles 77 and 78 can have no effect other than to create, or fan, class hatreds. Article 77 stipulates that the names of all taxpayers "shall be posted on the inner walls of the local National Tax Offices, where they may be easily accessible to the public for reference purposes."[16] The list of names will disclose the individual's earnings, his employer, and the amount of personal taxes assessed. Article 78 removes the need even to walk to the tax offices for "reference purposes," since it provides that the government shall also publish a directory containing the information posted in the tax offices. The tax decree came as a multiple shock to Colombia's productive sector, who had expected that the tax decree would bring in a large number of new taxpayers and thus broaden and strengthen the tax structure of the government. Instead, Decree 1366 raised the ante on those already paying taxes by an average of 10 per cent, thus providing more onerous taxation on those who had been meeting their obligations.

A hue and cry was raised over the discrimination inherent in Articles 77 and 78 of the decree. Opponents of the articles claimed with justification that the first and most obvious argument was that they intrude upon the privacy of the individual in a manner akin to blackmail. Second, they said, by posting the information the government was providing a ready reference to urban terrorists and Castroite guerrillas to determine who should be kidnapped and how much ransom to demand for the release of their victims, a principal means by which these groups finance their operations. In both instances, U.S. residents shared the alarm of their Colombian colleagues, suffering the additional fear that the government, by posting the names of foreigners, was raising the banner of anti-Americanism.

The Colombian economy stagnated during much of 1967, because a number of outside projects planned for the country were cancelled. One export industry being planned by W. R. Grace and Co. would have brought Colombia desperately needed dollars amounting to $6 million the first year of operation, and increasing amounts in succeeding years. Another important feature of the project (which was to grow and export pineapples) was that the industry was to have been located in Colombia's back country where it would have given employment to hundreds of poverty stricken peasants and stimulated auxiliary businesses. W. R. Grace's president in Colombia found that the 10 per cent limitation on profits, the discrimination against remitting profits from the reinvestment of pesos, created too great a risk, and shelved the project. His hope, and that of a number of outside investors, is that the Colombian government will see its mistake and permit free capital movement.

Some fear was expressed within responsible business circles in Bogota that the tax decree may not only play into the hands of the Castroite guerrilla bands, but may deal a severe blow to collective bargaining, as well. As one U.S. business executive told me: "With the salaries of management made a matter of public knowledge, what is to prevent union leaders from trying to force through unrealistic labor demands on the grounds that our Colombian and American executives are overpaid?" With unemployment estimated conservatively at 15 per cent of the total labor force in Colombia, genuine fear was expressed that the legal Communist Party of Colombia would make the most of the Articles 77 and 78, and force democratic unions to follow their lead. Indeed, by appealing to class consciousness, its labor arm, the Colombian Socialist Workers Confederation (CSTC), has successfully raided the Colombian Federation of Labor (CTC) and the Union of Colombian Workers (UTC), capturing six important unions in two years time. Although not large (75,000 compared to the CTCs 200,000 and the UTCs 350,000), the CSTC has concentrated on gaining control of unions in strategic sectors of the economy—banks, textiles, metals, and oil. In fact, it is believed that a July 5, 1967, raid on the Andean Oil Company by Castroite guerrillas headed by Fabio Vázquez, was successful because of intelligence supplied to the guerrillas by Communists in the oil and bank unions.

Colombia's democratic unions have shown some uneasiness over President Lleras' attitude toward the Communists specifically, and toward labor generally. The President has placed his Cabinet Ministers largely above the task of representing the various segments of Colombian life—commerce, labor, etc. For instance, the Minister of Labor made it clear to the unions that his task is not so much to represent labor's views at the cabinet level, as it is to consider labor's role in the totality of President Lleras' national aims. Thus, organized labor feels that it has no strong advocate for its cause within the government, and many union officials feel that labor's force and power is being dissipated in the grand designs of President Lleras. As a private citizen, Lleras helped form the CTC in the 1930s, and, in 1955, rescued it from Communist domination. As President, however, he has not given his support to measures which would strengthen the national federations, which receive only about 5 per cent of union dues paid into their locals, nor has he looked with sympathy on outlawing the Communist Party and its labor arm, the CSTC. As a result, the CTC and UTC express fear privately that Communist raids on the conglomerate of semi-independent unions will intensify in the coming years.

Labor is also deeply concerned over President Lleras' having opened trade missions with six Soviet-bloc countries and the Soviet Union itself. CTC President José Mercado, a Negro and former Communist, expressed his displeasure in the presence of President Lleras, remarking that it would be difficult for the labor confederations to fight Communist inroads now that the President, inferentially at least, has cloaked them with respectability by accepting trade missions and diplomats from their Communist masters. Businessmen, Colombian and American, see an unwholesome contrast between the evident anti-business attitude of the Lleras administration on the one hand, and the opening of trade relations with Communist countries on the other. Leaders in labor and business believe that President Lleras will use his relations with the Soviet bloc as a lever to extract more money from the Alliance for Progress.

The Russian trade offer began early in 1967, prompting the *El Siglo* editorial referred to earlier in this chapter to warn that the Soviets were up to no good. Nevertheless, President Lleras ordered trade talks to continue and based his actions on the grounds that Colombia's precarious economic situation justified trading with all countries. In July the talks culminated in a vaguely worded agreement by which Colombia agreed to barter its surplus coffee in return for Russian machinery and goods. One phrase in the agreement, concerning Russia's supplying "technical services" raised a considerable number of eyebrows in Bogota's diplomatic community, where it was interpreted as meaning the arrival of numbers of Soviet military and secret service personnel in the guise of "technicians." As for the trade agreement itself, it did not escape notice that that Russians are tea drinkers and that there is a good possibility that the Soviets may sell Colombia's coffee in Colombia's natural markets, as they did with Cuba's surplus sugar in 1960.

Nevertheless, President Lleras is bitterly opposed to Castroism and to the declarations which came out of the OLAS conference in Havana in August 1967. On the other hand, as the Soviet trade deal seems to indicate, the President apparently believes that Soviet avowals of "peace" are genuine. In this belief, the Colombia President is sharply at odds with his Venezuelan neighbors, as mentioned earlier, who have correctly analyzed Soviet policy. Perhaps the most striking facet of President Lleras' trade deals with the Soviet-bloc of nations is his rationale that barter deals are needed in order to better Colombia's economic position. But the facts seem to indicate that the benefits which he expects to derive from the Communist nations are nothing when compared to what would be gained if only he would create a sensible climate for foreign investment. And the President's agreements with the Soviets seem all the more inexplicable in the light of the vocal support given to Colombia's guerrillas by Soviet Sharaf R. Rashidov, and later by Leonid Brezhnev himself when he claimed at the XXIII Party Congress that the Communist maneuvers in Latin America "are headed by the working class and by the Communist parties."[17] What this means, of course, is that the Colombian Communist Party and its Socialist Workers Federation are the chosen instruments of Soviet subversion.

Yet, it is virtually impossible for the United States to take exception to President Lleras' policies, for the simple reason that the State Department either is unaware of the double-track policy of the Soviet Union or, aware of it, has refused to challenge the Kremlin. The State Department authorized the Consular Treaty with the Soviet Union and is constantly paring down the list of items which are forbidden to be shipped to Russia. There is some feeling in Latin America that the United States is a weak ally in helping the nations there to challenge Communit subversion. This was dramatized in August, 1967, when Venezuela's Senate Majority Leader Carlos Andrés Pérez said he viewed as hopeless the upcoming OAS meeting in Washington, called to take action against another Cuban-led guerrilla expedition on the shores of Venezuela, because: "The problem begins and ends with the United States, whose interest in maintaining relations with the Soviet Union inhibits the position it takes in the OAS."[18]

Senator Andrés Pérez was right. The September 1967 session of the OAS turned out like all the others which have been convened over the years to deal with Russian-Cuban subversion. It did not deal with it. It merely talked about it. And while Secretary of State Dean Rusk did call Fidel Castro's regime "neighborhood delinquents and violence peddlers," his recommendations to deal with it fell far short of what is needed. In fact, Mr. Rusk seemed to put the problem of Cuba in a minor category, saying that Castro would not "distract us from our major task in the hemisphere," meaning U.S. economic programs. This was a flight from leadership. The purpose of the meeting was further lost through the lack of resolve of liberal regimes in Latin America, particularly Chile, and the behind-the-scenes maneuvering of "neutralist" Mexico. Indeed, Mexico was taken to task by the Caracas newspaper, *La Republica*, which charged in its June 21 issue that Mexico tried to persuade Venezuela to tone down its charges against Cuba, even to drop the word "grave" in describing Cuban subversion.

The United States was taken to task in many quarters for its weakness in dealing with Castro. The influential Argentine daily, *Clarin*, editorialized in its September 19 issue: "It is obvious that the Cuba problem pertains exclusively and bilaterally to the United States and Russia," adding: "Since the missile crisis, Cuba has ceased to be a priority matter in the U.S. State Department," a sentiment echoed a few days later in the editorial columns of Ecuador's *El Telegrafo*. In Washington, Ecuador's Foreign Minister, Julio Prado Vallejo, pointed out that time after time, the OAS has merely "denounced and criticized Castro, and has spoken of its principles." He asked: "Haven't we made any progress at all along this road?"[19] Bolivia's President René Barrientos, at the moment beating off guerrilla attacks led by "Che" Guevara, was blunt. He told a reporter for Brazil's *O Globo:* "If the guerrillas manage to lodge themselves in Bolivia, the neighboring countries of Argentina and Brazil will be the new object of Castro-Communism."[20] He called for "continental action against Castro," and said that his government would fully support it.

Nevertheless, Secretary Rusk limited the U.S. proposal to minor action, chiefly the suggestion that the nations of the Free World stop trading with Castro. But in making the proposal, Mr. Rusk couched it in language that revealed extraordinary care lest any feelings be hurt. He merely asked Free World nations "to consider whether such assistance" to Cuba is the proper thing for them to be doing. He did not explain why the United States failed to react when Great Britain, a few months earlier, installed a fertilizer plant in Cuba on a government credit of $45 million. Nor did he explain to the OAS why, back in January 1965, the United States promptly joined in an oil embargo of Rhodesia because of that country's racial policies, without insisting in return that the British honor our embargo of Cuba.

The *New York Times* chastised the Venezuelan government in a September 26, 1967 editorial, following the OAS meeting, saying: "At one point, Caracas, seemed bent on pushing for strong actions that would have split the OAS and possibly done more harm to friendly governments than to Cuba." The *Times* was pleased that the OAS, supported by the U.S. State Department, rejected the only meaningful sanction put forward—to blacklist all firms trading with Cuba, saying: "That kind of sanction could lead to all manner of trouble, not least in Congress, where it would encourage the sort of restriction on foreign aid and food aid which has only exacerbated American relations with countries in other parts of the world." That sanctions on trade with Cuba have nothing to do with foreign aid seems obvious, and the linking of the two could have no effect other than to bring joy to Moscow and Havana. A perceptive Argentinian editorial writer in *Clarin* thus summed up the OAS meeting: "It would have been better not to have called it." In advance of the meeting, *Clarin* also remarked that the OAS session should be avoided, "unless one wants to put on a show to amuse the Russians."[21]

For all of these reasons, Colombia's President Lleras' inner circle of advisers are quick to point to evidence that U.S. editorial opinion and U.S. State Department policy are not hostile to the Communists, and continued to press for diplomatic ties with the Soviet Union. And with the economy brought under tight regulation through a complicated system of licensing, restrictions on profits, limitations on business profits and the like, all supervised through a cumbersome array of government departments and agencies, President Lleras has more power in his hands than any other President since dictator Gustavo Rojas Pinilla was overthrown in May 1957. He governed by Presidential Decree for two years and derived his authority for doing so from a State of Seige declared in May 1965 by his predecessor, President León Valencia. More important to the people of Colombia, and eventually to the U.S. taxpayer whose dollars support the Alliance for Progress, is the effect which the foreign and domestic policies followed by President Lleras' government planners will have on Colombia's destitute population. Statistics in Latin America are always tricky, but one accepted statistic places the average annual wage of Colombia's destitute *guajiro* about one-third the national average of only $250 per capita. And it is this situation which the Alliance for Progress, together with private capital investors, are trying to improve in order to undercut any appeal which Castroite guerrillas may have for Colombia's restive peasants. But private investors have learned that more often than not cooperation from the Lleras administration is lacking.

Many patriotic and intelligent Colombians believe that the inhibitions which characterize present government policy should be replaced by bold and daring appeals for foreign capital investment, and by an aggressive policy to encourage immigration by sturdy European stock. One of the problems of Colombia is its Indian population, and those of Indian blood, who live on pocket-like farms and concern themselves chiefly with producing just enough to sustain themselves. Inefficient farming methods contribute to keeping the crop yield low. Neither the backward Indian population nor large farmers have the incentive or the capital to break through to modern methods of production. In addition, government price controls on many food crops lessen the incentives to increase production, while government restrictions placed on the import of agricultural machinery have further lessened the ability of even the large farmers to produce anywhere near capacity. There is a great body of opinion in Colombia which believes that the removal of the many restrictions on economic growth is the surest road to opening up the vast riches of a nation over twice the size of France.

There are signs that President Lleras may modify his economic philosophy. But whether his attention will be diverted from the Soviet bloc, and, more important, whether his government will in the end prove strong enough to withstand Soviet subversion remains to be seen.

Chile is quite another matter. The stringbean-shaped country, dangling down the Pacific coast of South America from the desert country of Peru to the icebound straits of Tierra del Fuego, where it borders Argentina, is in deep trouble. This is so, because promises made by its Christian Democratic President, Eduardo Frei, that his party of the "democratic Left" would prevent a Communist takeover of his country, are today little more than ashes in the mouth.

The tactics which have been subsequently employed by the surging Christian Democratic Party were revealed back in 1963 when Renán Fuentealba, the CD party president, replied to a report in the *New York Times* predicting that the then weak Christian Democrats might join forces with the ruling Democratic Front. This would have been a logical move to increase CD strength. And by entering some its members into a coalition cabinet, it was thought in political circles in Chile, the CD would gain experience which was notably absent among its leadership. Fuentealba's letter denying any such notion was published in the April 17, 1963 issue of the *Times*. Fuentealba said that the CD would not collaborate with the government of President Jorge Alessandri because the Democratic Front "favored the interests of the few instead of the many." The Fuentealba letter was greeted with some surprise and consternation in political circles in Santiago because the coalition of the Socialists, led by Senator Salvador Allende, and the Communists, headed by Luis Corvalán, known as the Revolutionary Popular Action Front (FRAP), were considered to be strong contenders for the presidential elections, scheduled to be held in 1964. Democratic Front President Alessandri could not succeed himself, and there was a serious need to overcome an evident lack of a strong candidate through a coalition of forces among the non-Communist parties. The Fuentealba letter suggested that for the CD the enemy was on the Right, a point of view that was to lead the CD, first into a position of peaceful competition with the Communist-Socialist coalition, and eventually to chart a political course virtually indistinguishable from that of the Communists.

Renán Fuentealba's letter was written after the municipal elections, in which the ruling Democratic Front showed that they had a considerable following among the Chilean people. The Democratic Front polled 46.1 per cent of the vote, taking 2.7 per cent away from the FRAP. The biggest gain, however, was made by the Christian Democrats, who rose from 14.6 per cent of the vote in 1960 to 22.9 per cent in 1963. The CD then began showing its political muscle, claiming, as the Fuentealba letter indicated, that it was a magnet capable of attracting to it enough voters to assure its success in the presidential elections.

The strength of the Communists served to fan public interest in the coming presidential elections. Signs of increasing popularity among Chileans for the Christian Democrats was evident when the Student Federation of the University of Chile elected a Christian Democrat as president, and the anti-Communists among Chile's voters breathed more easily. The 12,000 students of the Central University of Chile, located in Santiago, also gave the CD a majority in the governing university student council. In Chile, as in most Latin nations, university students are politically active, and the election of a national party's candidate to the presidency of the student council is considered a sensitive barometer of the nation's electoral trends.

The rise to popularity of the Christian Democrats, and particularly its candidate Eduardo Frei, brought a landslide of criticism from their political opponents. The FRAP considered Frei to be a weak liberal who was ideologically adrift, and claimed, with some justification, that he was little more than an opportunist intent on stealing Communist economic policies and playing on a popular desire for reforms. Conservatives were no less alarmed than the FRAP over candidate Frei's tactics. They pointed out that the Christian Democratic leader had journeyed to Moscow, and claimed, in an overstatement, that he was a Communist garbed as a Christian.

On December 11, 1963, the FRAP-controlled labor organization, the Single Center of Chilean Workers (CUTCH), ended a conference in Santiago by calling on Latin American nations to support Fidel Castro and his Communist regime. CUTCH also adopted a resolution supporting a doctrine of non-interference in the affairs of other countries. This doctrine was pushed by pro-Castro groups in Latin America as a means by which to prevent any meaningful action from being taken against Cuba. More important, Presidential candidate Frei embraced non-interference as a fundamental tenet of CD foreign policy. With the two major opposition parties so aligned, the Democratic Front government of Jorge Alessandri announced that it would not support Venezuela wholeheartedly in the charges levelled against Castro by President Rómulo Betancourt. The decision was taken most probably because the Democratic Front did not control the majority of seats in the Chilean Congress. The charges involved the cache to Cuban arms that had been found on a Venezuelan beach in December 1963. Betancourt asked the Organization of American States to take action against Cuba under the Defense Pact of Rio de Janeiro. This pact permits armed action to be taken against any country which commits acts of aggression against a member state of the OAS. Chile said it would abstain from taking a stand until all the facts had been made available. Yet, Chile itself was a major target of Communist subversion from Cuba.

On January 30, 1964, the Preparatory Committee to the Second Latin American Youth Congress opened in Havana, where Chilean delegate Rosendo Rojas was a featured speaker. He said over Havana's Radio Progreso on that date: "The Chilean National Committee has begun a campaign to collect 200,000 signatures in support of this preparatory conference. The petition will be delivered to the Minister of the Interior in Chile as proof that the Chilean people support the conference, and we will request the government to permit us to hold our main conference in Santiago, Chile."

The government did not oppose the meeting, and the conference opened in Santiago on March 9, 1964. The conference slogan, "For the Liberation of Latin America," unbuttoned the purpose of the meeting for what it was—an effort to promote Castro-type guerrilla wars throughout Latin America.

José Antonio de Oliveira, leader of the Democratic Youth of Sao Paulo, Brazil, created a sensation by revealing that the official list of delegates from his country was comprised of known Communist leaders and leftist extremists. Vicente Goulart, son of the leftist President of Brazil, was one of them. He had been in Cuba, along with his mother and two sisters, and Oliveira said of him: "This person does not belong to any youth movement whatsoever in my country; neither is he a student. We know him only as a member of an extremist group, trained in terrorist tactics."[22] The members of the conference were shocked further to learn from Bolivar Ruíz of Ecuador that two delegates from his country, named by him as Milton Reyes and Alfonso Reyes, had received guerrilla training in Cuba, and said that after returning home the two had proceeded to compile impressive records as terrorists. Both had served terms in the García Moreno state penitentiary for their activities.

As a result of these charges, the conference fell apart. Many of the youths came to Chile expecting to discuss matters of concern to all youth groups in Latin America. The slogan of the conference was revealed on the day of the opening, shaking some. But revelations regarding the Cuban ties of some of the delegates caused the conference to break up completely. Even though the meeting was unmasked as a Communist undertaking, designed to propagandize the Communist cause and to endorse the guerrilla wars of a Russian-propelled Fidel Castro, the organizers did not appear displeased with the results. The Communist labor organization, CUTCH, had played a prominent role in the conference, and its leaders believed that in the end the conference had helped them to achieve some standing as a political force to be reckoned with in the presidential elections. More important, as Santiago's La Voz de Chile radio station reported on March 12, the meeting brought together groups of subversives from all over Latin America where they were able to meet and to coordinate plans for street demonstrations, sabotage, and guerrilla activities without having to journey to Havana and thus be labelled as Communists.

In this atmosphere of tension, amid rising alarm at the strength being shown by the Communists, all of Chile watched intently for the results of an election, held on March 15, 1964, in the small Province of Curico. Although the election could not logically be considered of any importance in revealing a trend in national thought, the Chileans traditionally watched it anyway, much as Americans used to watch the state of Maine for evidence of a national trend among U.S. voters. But this particular election in Curico took on more than its usual importance because it was the last provincial test of party strength before the presidential elections, only six months away. Senator Julio Durán, chosen to head the Democratic Front in the next presidential elections, made the mistake of claiming that the results of Curico would determine which of the parties would win the presidential elections, and, of course, predicted a resounding victory for his Democratic Front. What Durán and the Chilean electorate overlooked was that the FRAP had chosen as its candidate Oscar Naranjo, an enormously popular local medical doctor with a long record of attending the poor without charging them for his services. The result was a resounding victory for FRAP. Second place went to the Christian Democrats, and the government candidate, a lackluster figure, came in a poor third.

Panic hit Chile as the result of the election was interpreted to mean that conservative government was doomed and that the Communists stood a good chance of winning the presidency in the national elections. Durán was the victim of his earlier boast of victory and could do no better than to remark that Chile's peculiar democracy permitted, even encouraged, the Communists to infiltrate Chile's institutions. Nevertheless, the election results were widely accepted as meaning that the Christian Democrats, a party with only a few years of political experience, remained the only hope of preventing the Communist-Socialist coalition from taking power. Eduardo Frei was quick to take advantage of this mood, claiming: "Ours is the only road for the country to take and not fall to the Communists." [23] The Christian Democratic candidate said that radical reform was needed, and that if his party did not supply it, the Communists surely would.

Largely unnoticed in the general excitement which followed the election in Curico, the Christian Democratic Youth allied themselves with the Communists. On March 18, 1964 the CD Youth joined with the Czechoslovak Youth Union in issuing a joint statement in Santiago expressing the "need for consolidation of peaceful coexistence among all countries with different social systems."

The Czech Communists and the young Christian Democrats said jointly: "The search for peace which is the basis for justice, the Common welfare, and understanding is our principal task."[24] And in the same joint communique, the two groups called for cultural exchange between Chile and Communist nations. The significance of this alliance between the young Christian Democrats and the Czech youth group was not lost on the Communists, causing Radio Progreso in Havana to remark in some surprise that a declaration of such importance could not have been made without the prior knowledge and approval of the national executive committee of the parent Christian Democratic Party.

However that may be, another statement, issued on March 24 by the National Council of the Christian Democratic Youth praised both Frei and his political enemies, the FRAP for having jointly knocked the conservatives out of the political ring. The first paragraph of the statement reads: "By means of their support to the Christian Democratic Party (CD) and to the Popular Action Front (FRAP), the people of Curico expressed their repudiation of the existing system of government and their irrevocable desire for social change." The CD Youth exulted in the defeat of the conservative, but democratic, Democratic Front, and made it clear that the enemy of Chile was not the Communists, but the conservatives, saying: "The Democratic Front suffered an historic defeat." They placed the cloak of respectability around the Communists, by adding: "Today, only two presidential candidates exist to vie for the support of the electorate—that of FRAP, and that of the national and popular movement headed by Senator Eduardo Frei!"[25]

Senator Julio Durán paid for his election boast by resigning as leader of the Democratic Front. He did so at a meeting with leaders of the three parties which made up the Front. But after several hours discussion, leaders of Durán's party, the once powerful Radical Party (which in Chile was not "radical" at all), decided to support Durán and to go it alone. Radical Party leaders were shocked and outraged by the alliance forged between the Christian Democratic Youth and Communist youth leaders in Czechoslovakia, and rejected Frei's claims that his was the only party capable of saving the country from Communism. Many Radicals were convinced that the CD was not the alternative to Communism, but was merely a sugar-coated version of it. Perhaps reassured by alleged Catholic influence within the Christian Democratic Party which, they believed, would in the last analysis put a brake on neo-Communist elements within the party, the two other members of the conservative coalition—the Liberal Party (which is on the conservative side) and the Conservative Party—pulled out of the coalition. However, they were to find that elements in the Catholic Church in Chile were only slightly less radical than the CD Youth and, indeed, supported it in many radical statements.

On April 7, 1964, Senator Durán held a press conference in which he admitted that the conservative forces were in a state of disarray. His comments on this fact were underlined when the Liberal Party announced that it actually would support the candidacy of Eduardo Frei. This came in press conference held by Jorge Prat, an independent presidential candidate who had considerable backing from members of the Liberal Party. Prat said that the Curico elections had removed all possibilities for the conservatives to win the presidential elections, and threw his support to Frei in negative fashion, saying of Senator Allende and FRAP: "If they win, it cannot be written in Chilean history that I was the one who facilitated a Communist victory."[26] That Prat's negative endorsement of Frei was symptomatic of the thinking of the Chilean voter was speculated upon by Julio Durán. Addressing a group of 100 Radical Party leaders, Durán said: "Many people are trying to determine which party [FRAP or CD] is the lesser evil" and claimed that votes cast for Frei in the presidential elections would in fact be votes cast against the FRAP.

Frei and the Christian Democrats were benefitting, as well, from the mistakes made by FRAP. University professor Enrique Paris, a member of the Central Committee of the Communist Party, did nothing to help his cause when he announced: "Those participating in our campaign are willing to give everything that they have in order to make our country into the second Free Territory of the Americas."[27] His comment was made in specific reference to Cuba. The excesses of the Castro regime were known in Chile, and Professor Paris was much too open in identifying FRAP with those excesses.

By contrast, the program of Eduardo Frei and the Christian Democrats was vague. Yet, U.S. government officials in Washington openly supported Frei, and theirs was not a negative endorsement prompted by the fear of a Communist victory. It was quite positive. Reporter Jerry O'-Leary of the *Washington Star* explained why this was so. After interviewing someone in the White House or State Department, O'Leary wrote of U.S. government opinion: "The Christian Democrats represent to the United States . . . an acceptable alternative for either the parties of the right or those of the extreme left in Latin America." And, quoting the official, the article continued: "They [Christian Democrats] also represent the emergence of a third force to which Latin Americans can turn from the former poles of Communism on the one hand and ultra-conservatism on the other."[28] By this interpretation, Chile's Radical, Liberal, and Conservative parties were considered in Washington to be ultra-conservative. They did not fit this category at all, and the U.S. official's remarks tell us more about the political orientation of the official than about those parties. Yet, it is fair to say that the spokesman's comments accurately reflected U.S. policy, and to say also that the New Frontier embraced the Christian Democrats and that President Johnson's Great Society continued to do so.

However, the program of the Christian Democrats was assessed quite differently by the managing editor of Santiago's Socialist daily, *Las Noticias de Ultima Hora*. He couched his assessment in words that should have brushed the stars from the eyes of Washington officials. The editor assured his readers that differences between candidates Frei and Allende were a mere matter of degree, and wrote: "Electorally, the Marxists may suffer a defeat [in the presidential elections], but politically they have already scored a victory." He meant by this that the conservatives had virtually been eliminated by the CD, and that in eliminating them, the CD had adopted a stance that differed but little from that of the Marxists themselves. This point was made by Milan J. Kubic in a Sunday feature article that appeared in the *Washington Post.* He said: "Both Frei and Allende promise numerous drastic reforms, all frankly designed to soak the rich." Kubic then commented on the views of the two candidates as they were expressed by the editor of *Las Noticias de Ultima Hora*, writing: "There are important differences, but their ends are similar enough to justify the editors' observations about Marxism."[29] And Peter Weaver of the *Miami Herald* also observed: "CD candidate Frei promises sweeping social reforms in language that the Marxists often use."[30] For example, Frei agreed with Allende when he said that the Alliance for Progress was "inoperable," and did so in the face of the knowledge that Chile was receiving more aid ($132 million in 1962) from the Alliance than any other country in Latin America.

On September 4, 1964, three million Chileans went to the polls. Catholic women and Catholic action groups turned out the voters, warning that unless Frei was elected the Communists would take over the country and destroy democracy. Indeed, Chile's women must be credited with having played a major role in Frei's victory. When the votes were counted, Senator Eduardo Frei emerged the winner, accumulating 56 per cent of the vote and beating Senator Salvador Allende by a margin of more than 400,000 votes. Queried about the philosophy of his party, President-elect Frei told a news conference following the election: "The Chilean people want a government capable of making rapid reforms and of pushing economic development and social justice. That is the essence of our movement."[31] Frei won the election because of a number of factors—the mistakes of his political opponents; support of the Catholic Church; support of the unaffiliated voter. But most of all, Eduardo Frei became Chile's 28th President because the Chileans voted as much against the FRAP as they did for the CD.

One week before his inauguration, the President-elect said that he would seek trade relations with Red China. Señor Frei also said that he was "determined" to reopen diplomatic relations with the Soviet Union and with a few Iron Curtain countries, thus justifying in some measure the doubts expressed earlier by members of the Radical Party regarding Frei's anti-Communist posture. Concern over the direction being taken by the Christian Democrats in foreign affairs was heightened when, on November 27, just three weeks following Frei's inauguration, Foreign Minister Gabriel Valdés announced that Chile would establish diplomatic relations with Poland, Hungary, and Czechoslovakia. On January 4, 1965, the Christian Democratic administration of President Frei, not only recognized those three Communist countries, but extended recognition to two others—Rumania and Bulgaria. By this time, relations had already been established with the Soviet Union.

Despite the concern being expressed in many quarters over President Frei's haste in recognizing so many Communist countries, the new President was enormously popular with the bulk of the Chileans. The lean and ascetic looking Frei stumped the country on behalf of his party, pleading for the electorate to give him a Christian Democratic legislative body which, he told the people, he had to have in order to carry out his election promises. On March 7, 1965, President Frei was given one of the biggest victories in the history of Chile. For the first time in this century, a Chilean President was given an absolute majority of his party in the Chamber of Deputies (corresponding to our House of Representatives). President Frei did well in the Senate, where his party jumped from just two seats to eleven. The Christian Democrats were jubilant. A review of the election results, however, carried grave warnings. The gain of the Christian Democrats were made at the expense of other democratic parties. FRAP remained as strong as ever. Yet, the CD saw nothing unwholesome about this event, chortling in an announcement released by its Political Committee: "The parties of the right have been historically liquidated."[32]

Following the election victory, Rafael Moreno, President of President Frei's Agrarian Reform Corporation, announced that the agrarian reform which had been hammered out by the Democratic Front in 1964 had been radically revised, adding that President Frei was bending his attention to a new reform measure which he was soon to sign. In announcing details of the plan, Sr. Moreno indicated that the Christian Democrats were attempting to out-reform the FRAP. He said that the property of large landowners would be expropriated, and that peasants and small farmers would immediately be settled on the land. While digesting this gloomy announcement, landowners were then told that they would receive only ten per cent in cash when the expropriations took place, and that they would have the balance liquidated over a span of 25 years. The Christian Democrats also announced that their goal was to settle 100,000 peasants on expropriated land before President Frei stepped down from office in 1970. Christian Democrat Justice Minister Pedro Rodríguez said of the confiscation of property that it was the proper thing to do, since "the right of private property must be subordinated to the social interests of the community."[33]

The Frei administration said that it proposed to give land to those who work with it. Actually, however, the reform program gave land to no one. Property was confiscated from large landholders and divided into parcels called "asentamientos," and settlers were placed on them. Settlers are required to sell their crops to the government Agrarian Reform Corporation, and billed for financial assistance received at the end of each crop year. What happened, very much as in Cuba, is that the property passed from the hands of private owners into the hands of the state, and the settlers in effect work for the government which controls markets and denies the small farmer even a modicum of independence. Worse, the government maintains that it has created new property owners and refuses to extend the state's social security coverage to include the settlers, on the fiction that they are employers of labor and therefore not entitled to it.*

There is one peculiarity that is shared in common among parties of the "democratic Left" in Latin America. They are anti-American. And Foreign Minister Gabriel Valdés proved the CD in Chile to be no exception when he tried to blackmail the United States, saying that Chile would lead the countries of Latin America in demanding that the United States pay economic compensation in return for their political support. "Loans or aid are given to the nations which the United States believes are democratic. This intolerable discrimination cannot continue."[34] Chile's Foreign Minister said that demands made by the United States upon the countries of Latin America were accomplished through a pliant Organization of American States, and suggested that the United States was the puppeteer and the OAS the puppet. The attack by Señor Valdés came

---

*This is not surprising. Jacques Chonchol, architect of Chile's "agrarian reform," worked for two years in Cuba as a paid planner of Fidel Castro's Communist "agrarian reform."

the day following a most unusual move made by President Frei. Frei turned over a copy of Alliance for Progress plans for Chilean development to Czechoslovakia, and then invited the Czechs to participate in a program that was being funded by U.S. taxpayers. This astonishing turn of events left official Washington unruffled. Asked by a reporter to comment on Chile's actions, a State Department spokesman replied that the plan was at the disposal of whatever nation President Frei chose to invite to participate in it.

As these developments took place, Communist students burned a U.S. flag. A factory manufacturing Chilean Army uniforms was sabotaged and burned to the ground. A Red Chinese mission chose this moment to arrive in Santiago, where it concluded the purchase of 30,000 tons of saltpeter worth two million dollars. Foreign Minister Valdés said of U.S.-Chile policy in Latin America: "Each time we meet, it is to come up with some kind of announcement of solidarity with the Colossus of the North or to adopt political sanctions against some country." By "some country" he meant Cuba. And three Cuban officials arrived in Santiago, including the government managers of the confiscated Cuban Telephone Company and the Cuban Electric Company. Their purpose was to consult with Chilean government officials regarding their problems and successes in running state enterprises. A vastly more important visitor at this time was Rafael Reyes Zamora, an official of the Cuban Union of Young Communists. He went immediately to CD Youth headquarters where he consulted with CD Youth Leaders.

The arrival of the Cubans recalls an article published in the *New York Times* a few months earlier which reported that the Frei administration wanted to reopen relations with Cuba. The *Times* article of September 7, 1964, said of President Frei: "One proposal discussed privately by some of his foreign policy advisers in informal consultation with other Latin American governments, is for a fresh attempt to draw Cuba back into the hemispheric community." *The Times* story continued: "Mr. Frei said at a news conference yesterday that he expected 'more favorable' conditions for a peaceful solution of the Cuban problem to develop after the United States election." In this connection, the *Times* quoted Frei on the OAS in a manner quite in keeping with the denigrating remarks made by his Foreign Minister: "The OAS no longer has any vitality. The moment is approaching for a decision . . . to put it up to date." Reports that President Frei was annoyed by OAS restrictions which made it difficult for him to reopen relations with Cuba brought a vigorous negative response from Venezuela's Foreign Minister Ignacio Iribarren, who suggested that President Frei was out of touch with the realities of the Communist threat.

Continued attacks upon the United States by officials of the Frei administration seemed to ignite Communist riots. Following the scorching of the United States by Foreign Minister Valdés, Communist students at the Central University of Chile rioted for two straight days. They distributed leaflets protesting U.S. efforts to contain the Communist thrust in Vietnam, placed a time bomb which exploded in a theater showing an American film, and clashed with police in the streets of the cities of Santiago, Concepción, and Valparaiso. FRAP also contributed to the woes of President Frei by sending two of its legislators to the small village of Canate in southern Chile where they incited the Indians of the Mapuche tribe to invade private land and to claim it as theirs. The Frei administration, Socialist Deputies Fermín Fierro and Leoncio Medel told the Indians, was not living up to its promises to provide land for the people.

The Communist Party held its annual meeting, where its delegates were told to accuse the Christian Democrats of failing to adopt reforms which were radical enough to meet the needs of the country. "Push them! Push them!" CP Secretary General Luis Corvalán told a tumultous session, "until their measures are our measures." Corvalán meant by this that the Christian Democrats were competing with the Communists on the issue of "reform" and in doing so were accepting an unequal contest. The CD could never expect to appease the Communist opposition, no matter how hard it tried. Corvalán outlined the two tracks of Communist policy when, on the one hand, he said that Communist youths "are in the front line of the struggle of the students," and, on the other, cried out for more legislative reforms from the CD, saying: "The need for change is greater than ever."[35] FRAP's labor arm, the Single Central Labor Organization (CUTCH), responded by calling a nation-wide strike because, it claimed, President Eduardo Frei was not meeting Chile's need for radical reform, and indeed was backing down on his campaign promises. The situation became serious, with students rioting in the streets and labor out on strike. The Frei administration responded by organizing a peaceful demonstration by the CD Youth in support of the President's policies. Interior Minister Bernardo Leighton talked with Luis Corvalán, saying only: "We believe that both sides of the dispute should fight each other through democratic methods,"[36] a plea for the Communists to act like democrats.

This brief counter between the government and the FRAP ended when the Christian Democrats and the FRAP lined up together against U.S. intervention in the Dominican Republic. And in vying with FRAP in denouncing the United States, President Frei overlooked concrete evidence of U.S. friendship which had been extended to him and to his party. The State Department had earmarked $80 million in Alliance for Progress funds to Chile, and helped President Frei to renegotiate his foreign debt payments with countries in Europe, Asia, and with the United States, as well. While accepting United States understanding of Chile's problems, President Frei felt no corresponding obligation to understand just why the United States had intervened in the Dominican Republic.* Foreign Minister Valdés denied that the Dominican rebel movement had been infiltrated or that the country might have been taken over by the Communists without United States intervention. Scoffed Valdés: "It is dangerous to put the label of Communist on every movement. The Dominican Republic is not Vietnam." President Frei said it was "disgraceful" for the OAS to implicate itself in the Dominican Republic. The way to handle the Communists, said Chile's Foreign Minister, is "by offering the people rapid social and economic reforms." By applying this program to Chile, Valdés claimed: "We will win out over the Communists,"[37] thus placing the Christian Democrats more firmly in a posture of peaceful competition with the Communists. Santiago's *El Diario Ilustrado*, disagreed with Valdé's claims, noting sardonically: "In almost three-quarters of a year of administrative effort by the present administration, Congress has been unable to pass one single law of importance in fulfilling its so widely advertised program." And speaking in Berlin before a world conference of Christian Democrat Youth, Radomiro Tomic, Chile's Ambassador to Washington, loosed a verbal shot at the United States. He told the youths that the United States "deals with Latin America as though it is its own backyard,"[38] attacked U.S. intervention in the Dominican Republic, and said that loans for development should be given directly to governments and not to "Latin American capitalists." Government planners are more competent than the business community in curing a country's economic ills, he said.

The Communist CUTCH joined in the general attack upon the United States, announcing that it would hold a Congress of Solidarity with the Dominican Republic and Cuba, and scheduled the meeting for September, some five months following U.S. intervention in Santo Domingo. The Congress initially had been scheduled for Montevideo, but the Uruguayan government withdrew its permission following the discovery of its Communist nature, together with information that large numbers of Communist subversives from all over the world had been invited to attend. The attitude of the Uruguayan government did not affect the Chileans, however, and in granting permission for the Congress to meet in Santiago, Interior Minister Leighton said that the administration's decision was "in accord with the Chilean tradition of freedom to assem-

*Shoveling money into Latin America actually breeds both envy and contempt, for Latins have an exaggerated idea of U.S. wealth and find no sacrifices involved in our extending financial aid. "It is," a Brazilian official told me, "your easy way to solve complex social and financial problems and frankly we view this practice with contempt. You have not learned how to conduct yourselves as a 'rich relative.' "

ble." Pressure from the OAS, together with a rundown on the background of some of the participants provided to the Chilean government by the CIA, persuaded the Frei administration to change its mind and to cancel permission for world Communist leaders to participate in the congress. Abruptly and with no further comment, cancellation of the Communist meeting was announced in a most unlikely place—the Chilean Embassy in Washington—prompting diplomatic sources to speculate that Frei was intent on making it clear that United States pressure was responsible for the cancellation.

The Christian Democrats were in a muscle-flexing mood and, on July 31, 1965, said that they would eliminate Communist control of CUTCH, and would do so at the annual meeting of the labor organization on August 25. The Communists in CUTCH responded by inviting functionaries from the Soviet and Red Chinese blocs to attend the meeting. As this confrontation was developing, President Frei absented himself from Chile. During a twenty-three day tour of Europe, Frei visited the Berlin Wall, but when asked by reporters for his reaction to it, declined to comment. And Ambassador Tomic returned to what apparently was his favorite sport—belaboring the United States. Speaking at the Chilean-United States Association in New York, Tomic scored U.S. involvement in Vietnam, and did so on the grounds that it was too expensive and might unleash a nuclear war. He also said that the United States could expect, at best, only a negative victory if it succeeded at all in stemming the Communist advance in Vietnam. "By comparison," the Chilean Ambassador boasted, "Chile is showing the way positively by demonstrating to 20 Latin American countries that the democratic system can mobilize a country, overcome underdevelopment and modernize civilization."[39] Ambassador Tomic received support for his tasteless performance when an announcement out of Santiago said that his views reflected those of President Frei.

With the Chilean government's hostility toward the United States very much on record, the day arrived for the Christian Democrats to take control of CUTCH away from the Communists, thus putting into practice, in some degree at least, Ambassador Tomic's theories. However, the CD delegates did not lock horns with FRAP leaders in CUTCH, but merely offered a "unity slate" of labor candidates to the Executive Committee, apparently believing that this show of conciliation would appease the Communists. But FRAP leaders controlled the session and refused to accept what amounted to pleas by the CD to be given a greater share in labor leadership. As matters stood, FRAP controlled nine seats on the Executive Committee, while the Radicals and the Christian Democrats had the other six. And, apparently fearing that the CD would indeed make gains if it chose to carry out its earlier threats to fight, the FRAP majority arbitrarily raised the number of members on the Executive Committee from fifteen to twenty-one.

Inexplicably, the CD delegates met together and voted to withdraw their candidates altogether, thus turning all 21 seats over to FRAP without so much as a challenge. Apparently infuriated by the weakness of CD labor leaders, Andrew C. McClellan, Director of Inter-American Affairs of the AFL-CIO, said that as a result of CD weakness, the destiny of 60% of Chile's labor force had gratuitously been placed in Communist hands. And, as in Cuba in 1959, functionaries from the Soviet Union pulled the strings, supported by others from the governments of Red China, East Germany, Czechoslovakia, Yugoslavia, and Bulgaria. This amounted to direct interference in the internal affairs of Chile, but nothing was said or done about it by the Frei administration. President Frei now was at the mercy of the Communists, who were in a position to oppose his measures by strikes, or perhaps by even the mere threat of strikes.

The new power of CUTCH may have accounted for a strange television program that took place on October 6, 1965. Communist leader Luis Corvalán met on the TV program with Patricio Alwyn, President of the Christian Democrats. In the course of the discussion, Corvalán praised some of the measures sponsored by the CD, and said that in some instances the Communists were willing to support them. Alwyn responded by saying that the two parties had different philosophies, but added the important comment: "Discussion is useful in a pluralistic society which fights to achieve progress." The two party leaders agreed to establish "a certain degree of cooperation."[40]

Two days following the Alwyn-Corvalán interview, the Socialist wing of FRAP met to discuss the ramifications of the apparent togetherness of its ally, the Communist Party, with the Christian Democrats. For its part, the Communist Party saw an excellent opportunity to work with the CD and thus penetrate the government in power along the lines of the Soviet policy, "peaceful coexistence." But the Socialists, who in some ways are more militantly Communist than the Communist Party itself, refused to go along; perhaps out of fear that leadership eventually would fall to Luis Corvalán and that the Socialists would then have to accept a position subordinate to the Communist Party. The Communist Party was not strong enough to go it alone, did not want to take any action that would break up FRAP at this stage of political development, and chose not to cooperate with the CD. It was the Communist Party, not the CD, that made the decision not to cooperate. The Communist Party's position in this regard was ratified at its annual conference on April 5, 1966. Luis Corvalán was in Moscow, apparently receiving instructions following his attendance at the XXIII Congress of the Communist Party of the Soviet Union. Moscow's decision to accuse Frei of failing to enact reforms which were radical enough, and thus to push him even closer against the wall, is evident in one of the resolutions which came out of the Party meeting: "We support massive demonstrations in favor of our agrarian reform. Opposition to the reactionary government of Eduardo Frei."

Chilean congressman and senators travelled to Cuba in increasing numbers, interrupted briefly when Fidel Castro said that Frei "was a reactionary coward," and was heading Chile "not in a direction of a revolution without blood, but blood without revolution." He referred to an encounter which had developed between the police and copper miners during a strike called by CUTCH in which eight miners were killed. A curious event occurred at this time. On March 22, 1965, a Mrs. Nicolai Yurolov, wife of a Soviet petroleum engineer, surrendered to the police, saying that she had murdered her husband. The case was unusual because the Chilean government had no record of the two Russian citizens having legally entered the country. Mrs. Yurolov said that her husband held a top position in the National Petroleum Corporation (government-owned) and lived in the southern part of the country in the small town of Cerro Sombrero.

Fidel Castro turned aside a speech made by President Frei in which the Chilean leader suggested that Cuba and Chile compete to see which of the two governments—Communist or Christian Democrat—were most effective in meeting the needs of the people. Liberal reporters in the United States endorsed the idea of peaceful competition with the Communists, but Castro didn't. He had more important matters on his mind. Intent on transferring leadership from the city-based Communist parties to his guerrilla leaders in the mountains, Castro, in a July 26 speech, attacked Frei and the Chilean Communist Party, but left the Socialist Party alone. This was perfectly consistent with the double track policy of the Soviet Union. An attack by Castro on the Soviet-controlled party apparatus inferentially, at least, made the Communists out to be considerably more respectable that the militant Chilean Socialists. They were "bad guys." Socialist leader Salvador Allende attached himself to the Castro bandwagon and endorsed "armed struggle." In a speech delivered on September 9, 1965, Allende made it clear that no serious differences existed between the Communists and Socialists, saying: "We will continue to struggle to unmask Eduardo Frei's Christian Democracy. We will continue to struggle against imperialism."[41] Allende's speech was, in effect, an endorsement of the line taken by the Communist Party at its annual meeting in April. And, apparently looking toward the Tricontinental Conference which would open in Havana on January 5, 1966, in December the Socialists transferred Allende from his post as head of the

Socialist Party to the position of Secretary of International Relations of the party.

On January 6, just one day following the opening of the Tricontinental Conference in Havana, the FRAP, supported by splinter groups of Marxists, took over Congress, and in its chambers, reserved for the most solemn occasions of state, held a meeting which honored the eighth anniversary of Castro's assumption of power. And it should be pointed out that members of Chile's Communist Party sat at the speaker's table, along with Senator Allende and a representative of CUTCH. The Christian Democratic administration of President Frei did nothing.

In January 1967, President Lyndon B. Johnson invited President Eduardo Frei to come to Washington on a state visit, and in making the invitation revealed rather starkly his ignorance of what was transpiring in Chile. He called the Christian Democrats the party of "revolution with liberty." The conservatives were outraged by what amounted to blatant interference in Chile's internal affairs, and shocked to find that apparently President Frei was being rewarded by the United States not only for his leftward turn, but for his anti-American posture, as well.* The FRAP saw in President Johnson's blunder an opportunity to further embarrass its political opposition. The conservatives and the FRAP voted to refuse President Frei the permission of the Congress, required under Chile's constitution, to visit a foreign country. President Johnson thus alienated the non-radical segment of Chile's parties on the one hand, and brought joy to the Communists and Socialists on the other.

The Chilean voters did not agree with President Johnson's praise for the Christian Democrats, and registered their disagreement by handing the CD a sharp defeat in the 1967 spring municipal elections. The Radical Party made some surprising gains in the spring elections. It gained at the expense of FRAP and, more important, at the expense of the CD. This sag in the fortunes of the Christian Democrats was said by diplomatic observers in Chile to constitute public reaction against crippling government regulations and the inability of President Frei to get the economy moving. Public disenchantment with Frei was underscored when, a few months later, CD candidate Jaime Castillo, was defeated in a side election. The defeat was made all the more bitter for the CD because Castillo was the ideological leader of the party. The CD had expected to increase its share of the popular vote by three per cent, but instead, lost by more than that amount, causing Party leadership to worry considerably over its future.

President Frei's popular support was estimated to have dropped from 56 per cent at the time of his election in 1964 to somewhat less than 40

*U.S. policy, in the end, had the effect of encouraging political opportunists within Chile's parties to swing those parties to the far left.

per cent in the summer of 1967. And that "the enemy is on the Right" was apparent when the CD headquarters issued the following statement: "The big losers are nationalists who decreased in popularity considerably in provinces which were their stronghold."[42] Socialist Senator Carlos Altamirano was elated at the decline in the fortunes of the Christian Democrats, and remarked: "The conditions for guerrilla warfare, though they may not be as good as in other nations, are present in Chile."[43]

Rather than to react against the push in the Communist direction, as, for example, to make common cause with Chile's democratic political parties, the Christian Democrats seemed to be moving in a Communist direction themselves. For example, on July 12, 1967, the CD issued a statement saying that the Havana-based Tricontinental organization of subversion should not be blamed for the upsurge in guerrilla wars in Latin America. And in making the statement, the CD consciously overlooked the fact that Havana was claiming credit for the guerrilla movements in Latin America. The CD chose to cling to its theory that guerrilla wars were inspired by the failure of governments to "eliminate misery and underdevelopment." And to the profound dismay of Chile's friends, President Frei permitted the Tricontinental organization in Havana to establish an office of its Latin America branch, the Latin American Solidarity Organization (OLAS), in Santiago.

Widespread consternation in Latin America accompanied President Frei's approval to permit the OLAS to operate in Chile, for the monster of subversion had been lodged right in their midst. Rafael Caldera, the Venezuelan political leader, demanded an explanation for Frei's actions, saying that he was "shocked by the news that the Christian Democrats of Chile will permit the installation of the OLAS."[44] The Chilean CD replied lamely through party president Patricio Alwyn, saying that President Frei's permitting the OLAS office to operate in Chile, did not mean that the Christian Democrats approved of the declared purpose of the OLAS—to overthrow the government. In July, the Latin American Regional Workers Organization (ORIT) issued a statement from Mexico City bluntly accusing Chile's Christian Democrats of being allied with the Communists, couching the statement in exceptionally strong language. The ORIT took issue with statements made by Chile's CD, for example, that hunger and misery was the cause for guerrilla violence and charged that in making such statements the CD was "giving support to demagogic, terrorist Communist subversion."[45]

The weakness of President Frei ultimately lost for him the control of his own party. Radical elements within the CD demanded "reforms" that fitted the Communist mold, and supported another radical, Rafael A. Gumucio, in his successful bid for the presidency of the CD. Following Gumucio's election, CD militants announced their "ideological solidarity with the OLAS," and the Christian Democratic Youth joined with FRAP in demanding that diplomatic and commercial relations be extended to North Vietnam and Cuba. FRAP and the CD Youth also demanded that United States political and economic influence be eradicated entirely in Latin America. Senator Salvador Allende accepted a high-level position in the OLAS office in Santiago, thus giving it quasi-legal status. Press reports coming out of Chile which spoke of OLAS complicity in training Chilean students in the tactics of urban terrorism and guerrilla warfare were given credibility when General Vicente Huerta revealed that he had sent anti-riot trucks and reinforcements of Carabineros to the city of Concepción.

In the midst of these Communist advances, President Frei chose to jail his opposition—not the Communists, but leaders of the conservative Nationalist Party. A border dispute between Chile and Argentina was touched off in the Beagle Channel, and, concerned over the implications of the dispute, the Nationalist Party ventured to say that the Chilean armed forces were not equipped to defend Chile's borders. The statement issued by the Nationalist Party headquarters also noted, though somewhat obliquely, that the Frei regime had alienated both Latin America and the United States by permitting the OLAS to exist openly in Chile. The Nationalist Party demanded that the OLAS office be booted out of the country. Frei responded by jailing Nationalist Party leaders in a pre-dawn raid. The Chileans were shocked at Frei's actions and by his contention that the opinions expressed by the Nationalist Party constituted an attempt to stage a *coup d'etat*. Chile had not experienced a coup in 40 years, and the charges levelled against the opposition party were considered by most Chileans to be absurd. The Nationalists finally were released, and the Christian Democrats sought to play down the incident, attributing it to a fit of bad temper by the President.

However, the radicals in the CD exerted their new-found power by pressuring the President to be more radical in his programs. CUTCH supported CD militants when they accused the Minister of Labor and Public Health of being "much too moderate," and demanded that they be replaced with more "progressive" figures. Cuba poet Laureate, old-line Communist Nicolás Guillén, was permitted to enter Chile where he addressed a huge FRAP rally, held "in defense of Cuba." In response to mounting Communist agitation and pressures being exerted by neo-Communists in his own party, Frei attacked the Nationalists, stating bluntly of their remarks regarding the military preparedness of the country: "The Nationalist Party's declaration once again demonstrates that the campaign unleashed against this country is . . . from the extreme Right!"[46] Nothing could be more expressive of the sharp leftward turn of Chile's Christian Democrats. It was little wonder, then, that the CD

Youth found common cause with the FRAP Youth in denouncing the United States at a rally whose slogan was "Latin American Solidarity with Vietnam." CD Youth leader Antonio Cavalla spoke at that meeting and said of the slain "Che" Guevara that he was "one who knew how to be consistent in his struggle against imperialism."

While the Christian Democrats were belaboring their enemy on the Right, Emilio Oelckers, General Director of Investigations, disclosed that police had located a Communist training center for terrorists on the outskirts of the city of Concepción. He revealed that 20 university students, all members of the pro-Castro Left Revolutionary Movement (MIR), had been receiving training in detonating high explosives, and reported as well that the purpose of the training was to unleash Communist urban terrorism in Chile's cities.

In an apparent effort to meet the radical demands of his party, President Frei attempted to force the Chilean people to save money. He explained that the purpose of his compulsory savings plan was to form a "popular economy." Finance Minister Sergio Molina announced simultaneously that private enterprises in Chile also would be forced to save 66 per cent of their annual profits, thus stifling incentives of the businessmen to expand production. More important, the business sector was astonished to learn that labor was to administer the funds accumulated by the government through the compulsory savings plan. CUTCH was the most important labor organization in Chile, and it was controlled by the Communists. And when the Inter-American Society of Publishers accused the Christian Democrats of having used the resources of the *Banco de Estado*, together with political pressure, to purchase five newspapers that were editorially in opposition to the CD, President Frei had no ready answer. The leftward trend of the Christian Democrats took another sharp swing when, on December 29, 1967, President Frei espoused a law which would to all intents and purposes give FRAP youth and CD Youth control of Chile's universities. Under that law, the student groups controlled by CD and FRAP would have the authority to elect university authorities. Juan Gómez Millas, Minister of Education, opposed the law and resigned, but his resignation was not accepted by President Frei. If the law obtains, this will mean total government control, exercised through the FRAP-CD coalition of students, over the curriculum of studies. In sum, little in Chile was left untouched by the Christian Democratic administration of President Eduardo Frei except, unfortunately, the Communists.

Regimented settlers on confiscated land have failed to produce for the economy, and Chile, with 25 per cent more arable land on a per capita basis than the United States, imported $200 million worth of foodstuffs in 1967. These facts of economic life were not admitted by the Frei administration, which turned them aside and claimed that it had settled 70,000 persons on small farms. In a report prepared by the UN Food and Agricultural Organization (FAO), the Frei regime asserted that the 70,000 persons represented 12,000 families who had received land when in fact they had received no land at all. The FAO report avoided commenting on the economic and financial repercussions of Chile's agrarian "reform" and confined itself to a social survey of the program. But the fact is that the rural program of President Frei and his Christian Democrats failed utterly to increase farm production while absorbing large amounts of development capital provided by the Chilean taxpayer and the Alliance for Progress.

This state of affairs was addressed by Professor Paul Aldunate of the Santiago Catholic University faculty of economics and agronomy. He pointed out that the lack of incentive among what amounted to government serfs was largely responsible for the spectacular lag in farm production and said that, by comparison, private farms, whose labor costs are much greater than those of the asentamientos, produced profits 196 per cent higher than the asentamientos. The productivity of the settlements, Aldunate said, was so low that it did not pay for the cost of invested capital. Commenting on the FAO report, and particularly on figures in it relating to the government's investment in the asentamientos, the economist said that the capital was being used principally as a "subsidy to give the settlers an income" which was totally uneconomic, adding: "Invested capital will disappear if the economic results of the effort do not improve."[47] Failure in Chile's farm program means inflation and ruin. For though copper is Chile's main export and brings in foreign exchange, it is agriculture that must provide the real base for the country's economic growth and food for its people.

By the end of 1967, the increasingly totalitarian direction of the Christian Democrats was unmistakeably evident. Government planners themselves, CD leaders found that they had more in common with Communist government planners than they did with the other democratic parties of Chile. By putting into practice many of the methods espoused by the Communists, the Christian Democrats failed, as the Communist system has failed all over the world, to provide for the needs of the people.

Endorsed by the Democratic administrations of President John F. Kennedy and Lyndon B. Johnson, Chile has received the staggering amount of $767 million from U.S. taxpayers. Yet this endorsement has seemed to fuel the anti-American attitude of the Christian Democrats, rather than to cool it. And the Christian Democrats earned for themselves the derisive sobriquet, "little Red fishes swimming in holy water," while President Frei often was called "the Kerensky of Chile."*

The sobriquet took on concrete meaning when on February 27, 1968, President Frei permitted five members of Guevara's ill-starred guerrilla venture to enter the country from Bolivia. He refused Bolivia's request to extradite them for trial, and in fact extended to the group—three Cubans and two Bolivians—political asylum in Chile. Indeed, while under detention, the five guerrillas played football with members of Chile's police force in the town of Pascua located on a small island offshore from the Chilean mainland. President Frei described the men as "essentially kind persons." The Cuban Ambassador to France, Baudilio Castellanos, journeyed to Chile with whom Cuba had no diplomatic relations and arranged for the guerrillas to leave the country and to return to Cuba via Prague. Bolivia's indignation boiled over at the Organization of American States where its representative, Raul Diaz de Medina, pointed out that Chile's conduct not only was in violation of Inter-American Treaty of Mutual Assistance, but that by his actions President Frei had made Chile a sanctuary to which guerrillas could flee in the future.

*In March, 1969, Chileans voted in congressional elections. Final results showed that the Christian Democrats had slumped to 31.1 per cent, while the Nationalist Party headed by former President Jorge Alessandri, surged to 20.9 per cent. The Nationalists made their biggest inroads among the middle-class and lower middle-class who voted overwhelmingly for Frei in 1964 when the alternative was Communism.

Radomiro Tomic made a bid for Communist support, saying; "The battle to replace capitalism must be won . . . ." (*Clarin*, December 1, 1968). He also bragged that during his tour in Washington he "criticized the OAS, opposed the Inter-American Peace Force . . . while obtaining U.S. aid for Chile which was eight times higher per capita than any other Latin American country could obtain. . . ."

•

Winners or Losers?

•

AN IMPORTANT RESULT of Soviet moves in this hemisphere, first in Cuba and then in Latin America, is that Soviet Premier Alexei Kosygin and Party Secretary Leonid Brezhnev now act as though the United States is a coward and the battle all but won. Lenin and Stalin spoke of world Communist domination over the long term, while Soviet leaders today see the task with frightening immediacy. By pursuing their double-track policy of peaceful penetration and guerrilla wars on the one hand, while threatening the world with nuclear war on the other, the Soviets have been extraordinarily successful in making inroads against the West, always just this side of all-out war. And the sober fact is that since World War II the Russians and their stooges have gained the tacit acceptance by our political leaders that wars shall be fought in non-Communist territory—in South Vietnam and South Korea, in the vast jungles and towering Andes of Latin America. And the battle has now been extended by the Communist to America's towns and cities where it is being met with purely sociological measures.

The Soviet Union has become a party to the affairs of the Western Hemisphere as it concludes trade treaties and opens diplomatic relations with politically underdeveloped, confused, or cowed governments. A case in point is Colombia. On January 19, 1968, President Carlos Lleras Restrepo resumed full diplomatic relations with the Soviet Union for the first time in 20 years. Relations were broken on May 3, 1948, after the Communists stirred up the *bogotazo* and a Soviet flag was hoisted to the top of the City Hall in Barranquilla. The 1968 signing ceremony with the Soviet Union that took place at the United Nations in New York was far removed from the realities of jungle warfare in Colombia. There, two civilian functionaries from the Ministry of Defense were decapitated when the government refused to pay a large sum of money in ransom

for their lives. And as news of this grisly story sank into public consciousness, the government was staggered to learn that two more Cuban-
trained guerrilla groups had opened new fronts in the countryside. One
band of guerrillas landed at the peninsula of Guajira along the border
of Venezuela, and the other appeared as though by magic in the jungles
of Alto Sinu. The grim fact was that the Colombian armed forces by
January 1968 were fighting guerrillas in 13 of Colombia's 23 Departments (states) and it was kept from the public by government censorship.

The day before the formalization of full diplomatic relations between
Russia and Colombia, Bogota's *El Espectador* reported that Minister of
Communications Nelly Turbay had sent notes to radio stations telling
them not to give out "information regarding public order or anything that
might affect it," warning: "We will not hesitate to enforce legal means
to regulate the transmission of news." The warning was unusual in that
press censorship had been in effect for over two years, indicating that
the government believed that the matter of the new guerrilla fronts was
sufficiently serious to warn the press of its power and thus, perhaps, cut
off criticism of the Soviet-Colombian accord. Venezuelan newspapermen
who had managed to get into the area of military operations before the
clampdown reported that military planes were bombing the guerrillas
and that Colombian troops had been rushed to combat. The resumption
of full diplomatic relations between Colombia and the Soviet Union was
ushered in with quite a bang.

The Soviet Union assigned Nikolai Belous as its Ambassador to Colombia. Belous had been ejected from Argentina 12 years earlier for
espionage, but the Soviet Union assured an aroused Colombian press that
Russia was interested solely in trade and diplomatic relations and would
meticulously avoid interfering in Colombia's internal affairs. Then in
mid-May of 1968 news that the Soviets were doing the opposite burst
upon Colombia with the force of a bombshell.

Two Castroite couriers were apprehended at Bogota's El Dorado Airport carrying $101,000 and plans for fomenting urban guerrilla warfare
in Colombian cities. The money was to have been delivered to Castro's
guerrilla chief, Fabio Vázquez. More important, the two couriers revealed that the money and the plans had been handed over to them in
Mexico City by a Soviet diplomat. The total amount given them was
$150,000, and courier Feliciano Pachon Choconta told authorities what
had happened to the other $49,000. He gave the money to a Communist
courier, identified as Bolivian Rhea Clavijo, who purchased arms with
it and handed them over to a member of the Communist Party of Colombia, identified in the August 29, 1968 issue of *El Tiempo* as Juan de
Dios Aguilera. Five members of his group had been trained in Cuba, and
one was a Cuban military officer. Earlier, on August 4, *El Espectador*

reported that army units had killed guerrilla leader Bernardo Ferreira. Identified by Colombian authorities as "Pro-Soviet," the same authorities said he had been trained at Patrice Lumumba University in Moscow and also in Tirana, Albania.

For some inexplicable reason, President Lleras Restrepo lent the prestige of his office to the Lenin Peace Prize, and was subjected to a dose of political agitation in the guise of cultural exchange. Here is how an August 1, 1968 headline in *El Tiempo* recorded the event: "Violent Attacks Against the United States during the Presentation of the Lenin Peace Prize." The prize was presented to Jorge Zalamea, a Colombian Communist writer, by Soviet writer Boris Polevoi. President Lleras Restrepo and Soviet Ambassador Belous sat together in the presidential box of the theater. Reporter Iader Giraldo of *El Tiempo* wrote the story: "Polevoi and Zalamea were especially categorical in their denunciation of the United States for the Vietnam conflict, and for economic repression of underdeveloped countries."

Communists packed the theater and, said Giraldo, "applauded wildly the anti-American performance which was political [not cultural] in nature." The Soviet writer tried to identify President Lleras with Russia's violent attacks on the United States, saying: "It was just, very just, what your President Lleras has said about this war." He was referring to a statement made by Lleras a few days earlier when he criticized the United States for its involvement in Vietnam.

To top off the anti-American evening, Zalamea made the monstrous statement that the United States was attempting to force birth control upon the people of Colombia in return for financial aid. He also demanded that the United States stop its "aggression" in Vietnam so "those dollars may be invested in assistance programs,"* then condemned the United States in the same breath for "racial violence and economic exploitation of the underdeveloped countries."** That it is the Soviet Union that intends to "exploit" Latin America was revealed in a headline in the August 6, 1968 edition of *El Tiempo*, "Soviet Bloc Will Give Support," and the following story: "Commercial delegates to the VII International Fair of Bogota from socialist countries said that they are willing to extend economic collaboration to the plans for Andean integration, always provided [the Andean countries] are politically neutral." This was a bold attempt by the Soviet-bloc to undercut the Organization of American States by neutralizing the treaty commitments among its members—specifically those for mutual defense.

The Soviet-bloc entered Colombia's International Trade Fair with a

*Another indication of the contempt we reap by our open-handed aid programs.
**The U.S. Embassy in Bogota made no apparent effort to protest the anti-American meeting or to show our displeasure that President Lleras lent the prestige of his office to an anti-American tirade.

rush, erecting impressive expositions and propagandizing the "mutual benefits" of barter trade between Communist countries and the nations of Latin America. But Señor Jorge Sanchez, Director of Economic Integration of Costa Rica's Ministry of Commerce and Industry, warned against such barter arrangements in an interview in Miami. He said: "For example, when Latin countries sell coffee to a Communist nation, that Communist country then uses coffee as a barter tool to obtain badly needed machinery from East or West. The coffee eventually returns to the international market, but at a lower price. So, the coffee-producing countries in Latin America are forced to reduce their quota prices to compete with coffee they originally sold. The Latin economy suffers."

What Señor Sanchez was saying is that bartered coffee does not reach the Russian consumer (a passionate tea drinker in any case), but is sold on the world market to countries which otherwise would be direct markets for the coffee-producing country.* And this is exactly what happened in Cuba in 1960 with "surplus" Cuban sugar. Bartered to the Soviets, the sugar was re-sold to Algeria, Egypt and other markets, and it was none other than "Che" Guevara who discovered what was happening and admitted that Cuba had been taken for a ride. Whether or not Colombia's traditional markets will be respected by the Russians is very much open to question.

All of this brings up a comparison between Soviet moves in Cuba in 1960 and what the Russians were doing in Colombia in 1968. Back in 1960, the Soviet trade delegation purchased space in Cuba's newspapers and filled them with glowing accounts of the benefits of barter trade between Cuba and the Soviet-bloc. The August 3, 1968 edition of Bogota's *El Espectador* carried an eight-page section crammed full of Soviet propaganda, praising in particular the Soviet-Colombian barter deal. Sergei Kudriatsev was the first Soviet Ambassador to Havana, and had been ejected from Canada for espionage activities, just as Nikolai Belous, first Soviet Ambassador to Colombia, had been kicked out of Argentina.

What recent history tells us loud and clear is the single-mindedness, almost to the point of sterotype, of the Soviet Union in pushing Communist political and economic penetration of Latin America. Bogota's *El Siglo* editorialized on the Soviet invasion of Czechoslovakia on September 2, 1968 in terms that bear repeating: "The occupation of Czechoslovakia by the USSR should give us a clear idea of the danger posed by our new 'cordial friend,' with whom we have renewed diplomatic relations after 20 years' suspension precisely as the result of the events of April 9, 1948, when communism had the hammer and sickle ready to

---

*The Counselor for Economic Affairs at the U.S. Embassy in Bogota (a former professor) found barter trade between Latin America and Communist countries desirable. He told me: "this means that Soviet leaders are now forced to listen to the demands of their people for a better life. This is all to the good."

fly throughout our country," then asked: "Ambassador Nikolai Belous plans to purchase a residence to house 150 persons. What for? We do not know. We do know, however, that Colombian personnel in Moscow will number only five persons."

On December 13, 1968, Brazil's President Arthur da Costa e Silva suspended Congress and announced that he would rule by Presidential decree for an indefinite period. His actions brought sharp and immediate response from those in the U.S. news media who are usually quick to condemn military coups but slow to understand what triggered them.

The issue was simple by the *Miami Herald,* which boiled it down in a December 14 editorial: "This is military dictatorship in its most arrant form ... naked oppression in defiance of the republic's historic liberties." The *New York Times* thundered on December 17: "This right-wing move has been in preparation in Government ranks for some time." According to the *Times,* the coup was triggered by "hard-line younger officers" concerned by "the unpopularity that the Government has aroused by strong repression of student demonstrations and policies holding down wages while prices rose."

But the administration of President da Costa e Silva had other reasons for its actions. In suspending Congress, the government laid the blame directly at the feet of the Communists, saying that "through infiltration of our homes, schools, universities, the clergy and even military organizations, Communism is developing a revolutionary war in this country so as to take power by force of arms." Radical elements within the Catholic Church came in for a special rebuke, with the government noting "a contradiction, an aberration, when we see priests supporting Communism, a doctrine that is dedicated to the persecution of religion."

According to the *Times* article, the Government of Brazil describes "as subversives the politicians, intellectuals, Roman Catholic priests, newspapermen and students who protest against indifference to social problems, administrative incompetence and police brutality." The *Times* overlooked Brazil's progress since a popular rebellion (also condemned by the *Times*) forced Red-lining President Joao Goulart out of office in 1964 and substituted modified military rule for the country. The fact is that President da Costa e Silva's administration was anything but indifferent toward the country's problems. Brazil's annual rate of inflation has been cut from 140 per cent to approximately 25 per cent and the annual growth rate of its economy has risen from 1.5 per cent to more than 7 per cent. Annual exports increased by nearly $1 billion over 1964 and the government set about slashing in half an expected deficit in 1969, while the World Bank found Brazil's economy to be viable enough to qualify for loans of $1 billion over the next five years.

As proof that preconceptions sometimes take precedence over facts, a December 18 editorial in the *Times* omitted any mention that the Government of Brazil took the action that it did because, as Minister of Defense Aurelio Lira Tavares put it, of the discovery of "a vast Communist terrorist attack on a national scale." *Not one single word.* The *Times* merely asserts in its editorial that Brazil's "Military leaders have behaved like spoiled children." Rule by Presidential Decree was also condemned in companion articles.

True, press censorship was clamped on the country for a brief period, then relaxed. Alberto Dines, editor of the newspaper *Jornal do Brasil*, was detained by the police, then released without interrogation. Nevertheless, press censorship is difficult to defend, and the *Times* and the Inter-American Press Association were right in scoring it. But even here there is evidence of a double standard. It should be pointed out that Colombia's liberal President Carlos Lleras Restrepo ruled by Presidential Decree and imposed press censorship for more than two years without being taken to task by the *Times* or the press association. Indeed, President Lleras released his grip in December, 1968, only after forcing a new Congress to rubber stamp all Presidential Decrees promulgated by him since 1966. If press censorship is bad, it should be condemned wherever it appears; if rule by Presidential Decree is a sign of dictatorship, it should be so labelled regardless of the country where it is applied and the party which applies it.

Back on January 5, 1968, Russia's *Pravda* kicked off the campaign to subvert Brazil, saying that its Brazilian Communist Party would "join other anti-government forces" with the purpose of overthrowing Brazil's government. The strategy to be followed, said Pravda, "is to create a situation in which the people will be forced into an armed uprising or civil war." There is ample evidence that the Communists have managed to make common cause with radical elements in the Catholic Church, among subversive students, and people in the economically depressed areas.

Led by Archbishop Helder Camara, head of the Church in Northeastern Brazil, a group of Catholic priests and laymen issued manifestos charging that the Costa e Silva administration and "imperialism" were responsible for grinding poverty which is as traditional to that area as it has proved resistant to change. Speaking before a group at Catholic University in Belo Horizonte, Monsignor Helder Camara expanded his criticism to a direct and unprovoked attack on the United States, saying: "The moment that a struggle for real liberty starts in Brazil, it would be smashed by U.S. troops who do not want to see another Cuba in Latin America and would turn our country into another Vietnam." It needs little noting here that it was Castro's guerrilla chieftain, the late "Che" Guevara, who called for "one, two, or more Vietnams," a slogan now adopted by U.S. Negro militants.

There is circumstantial evidence that Helder Camara and the radical wing of Brazil's Church are following the Communist line, as charged by the Brazilian Government. A political resolution passed by Brazil's Communist Party reads: "We must search for ways to rapprochement with the Catholic Church [through] its progressive-minded elements, all in the interest of joint struggle." Rio de Janeiro's *O Globo* newspaper added to the evidence when it published a directive from the Communist Party which called for its cadres to "take advantage of the war in Vietnam and race discrimination in the United States to denounce publicly world-wide imperialism," a line constantly echoed by Brazil's clergy. The directive also urged an "all-out armed struggle" against the Government of Brazil.

In summing up its success in promoting student riots and the occupation by students of campus buildings in Brazil, the Communist Party said it had made "students the Vanguard of the revolution." Seizure of power, said the document, "will come through force of arms and the unity of popular forces," i.e., the Church, students and workers. Federal authorities revealed that the author of the document, a "comrade Meneses," was in fact Carlos Marighela and said he was the mastermind behind plots to overthrow the government. The Marighela document called for "firm and secret pacts between students and the progressive wing of the Catholic Church." When the government found French priests to be involved in subversion and expelled one of them, Father Pierre Vauthier, from the country, Monsignor Helder Camara led radical priests and students in denouncing the government.

Marighela was endorsed in a September 1968 editorial in *Granma*, official organ of Cuba's Communist Party. *Granma* said of the disturbances in Brazil that the strategy outlined by Marighela "demonstrates the adhesion to the line adopted here that armed struggle is the only way to spark a revolution." Two of Marighela's companions were captured by police and found to have been trained in Cuba's political indoctrination centers and guerrilla camps.

Jornal do Brasil got hold of a copy of Communist strategic plans for subverting Brazil. "The strategic objective," wrote *Jornal* of the document, "is to seize upon land reform, socialism vs capitalism, 'popular power' and Yankee imperialism to inflame the public." Communist planning had reached the point, said *Jornal*, "where the revolutionary organization is dividing the country into regions and assigning priorities to certain areas."

June 19, a bomb exploded in a Rio de Janeiro business section, setting off riots in which the American Embassy was attacked by those said by Rio's governor to consist of "about 800 professional agitators" intermixed with students. United Press International reported that though it was alleged that only students were involved, "it was obvious that Brazilians who were not students participated in the rioting." Francis B. Kent of the *Los Angeles Times* reported over a Rio dateline and said of the student demonstrators: "That they have been joined by subversive activists is obvious."

The smooth accommodation between radical elements in the Catholic Church and Communist-led students was evident when The Reverend Laercio Dias de Moyra of the Catholic University of Rio de Janeiro condemned the police and charged that students had been arrested without cause. On June 25, about 150 priests and professors picketed outside the Ministry of Education claiming, as the *Times* did in its December 17 story, that "police brutality" against students was responsible for the riots.

However, riot leader Vladimir Palmiera issued the following demands during the riot, which have an unmistakeable ideological ring: "Nationalization of all big business, banishment of all U.S. citizens from Brazil, radical distribution of land to peasants and the creation of a society in which workers, not owners, receive the profit."

The government admitted that the budget for universities in Brazil was inadequate and took steps to nearly double it. But radical student leadership refused this, and rioted when the United States offered $500,000 for a study of educational reform. This was so, perhaps, because one of the student leaders was revealed to be a representative of Fidel Castro's Latin American Students Organization (OCLAE). This group is trained in the art of street demonstrations, mob control and campus terrorism. It is not interested in increasing budgets for education but in overthrowing governments and replacing them with Communist regimes. Two Brazilian student organizations were outlawed for having received vast sums of money from Castro's OCLAE.

Brazil's newspapers came in for a share of Communist violence when *O Estado* of Sao Paulo and *O Globo* of Rio were bombed and attacked by student mobs. Democratic student groups disassociated themselves from these excesses, saying that "strange groups are manipulating students for political purposes." Engineering student Pereiroa da Silva testified that the Calabouco restaurant was in fact a "terrorism factory" from which assaults were launched against universities and other Communist objectives.

During one student demonstration, in which priests and Catholic laymen participated, demonstration leaders made the following statement: "We are against U.S. imperialism. Since the United States is the greatest imperialist nation in the world, naturally it is our main target." The Communist Party exulted at the participation of priests in the Rio demonstrations, saying that "Guanabara clerical authorities now lend us their official support and approval." A number of Brazil's leading writers demanded that the government bring the behavior of radical priests to the attention of the Vatican.

During this period of riot and unrest in Brazil, U.S. Ambassador John W. Tuthill notified President da Costa e Silva that the United States was reducing its military aid to his administration. And that was the last time that Tuthill was received by the Brazilian President. Soviet Ambassador Sergei S. Mikhailov moved quickly to take advantage of Tuthill's gaffe, offering credits to Brazil to build a subway in Rio.

In March, Ambassador Tuthill mired himself more deeply in the bad graces of the Brazilian government by meeting privately on two occasions with fiery opposition leader, Carlos Lacerda. Lacerda had said of the police during one student riot that "they are cowards protected by other cowards." He had also charged in an interview in Paris that the military in Brazil was weak and divided. *O Globo* compared the Tuthill-Lacerda meetings and the public uproar that followed with the reaction Brazilians could expect if their Ambassador in Washington met privately with Stokely Carmichael. The newspaper observed that both Carmichael and Lacerda were attempting to overthrow their respective governments.

O Estado of Sao Paulo, Brazil's largest newspaper located in Brazil's largest city, reported on June 2 that Ambassador Tuthill "continues to receive the cold shoulder from the Brazilian Government because of his association with Carlos Lacerda." "Because of the situation in which Tuthill finds himself," the newspaper continued, "he is expected to leave Brazil and go into private business with an Italian firm." Respect for the United States had dipped to the point where, in order to loan Brazil $73 million, the U.S. Ambassador signed the agreement in the low-ranking Planning Ministry instead of the Presidential Palace or Foreign Ministry. "This event," *O Estado* noted, "was unprecedented in Brazilian diplomatic history."

During this period, the Soviet bloc made great inroads in Brazil. The Russians listed only 17 "diplomats" among 49 officials known to be in the city of Rio de Janeiro alone, while other Soviet-bloc countries accounted for another 275 officials in the country, with only 75 listed as "diplomats." What they were doing there was suggested when it was revealed that Victor Mikhailovich, head of a Soviet commercial mission to Brazil, was an agent of the KGB. Another, identified only as "Mr. Ivanov," was said by *O Globo* to have operated as an undercover agent in Iraq from 1949 to 1962. His cover then, as it was in Brazil at the time, "was to pose as a commercial representative for the Soviet Union."

A Soviet "technician," identified by Brazil's security corps as Mikhail Mizimoff, also turned out to be a KGB agent. His work in Brazil, said the government, was "to carry out a complete survey of the extraction and industrialization of tin ore with a view to sabotage." Mizimoff was apprehended while in the process of contacting the Soviet ship "Krasmodok" to deliver maps and sketches of the mines.

Meanwhile, Moscow's Radio "Peace and Progress" continued to broadcast anti-government programs to Latin America in Spanish and Portuguese. One is typical and makes the Soviet Union no less an enemy of the government than the subversives that it supports within Brazil. It describes Brazil's government as "venal, anti-democratic and anti-worker," and flatly states: "In such circumstances, the primary fundamental task in Brazil, as in Argentina, is to strengthen the unity of action of all anti-imperialist forces in the struggle against the tyrannical regimes in both countries . . . to fight to liberate both from imperialist domination and landowner exploitation." In plain Portuguese, the Soviet government plans the demise of any government in Brazil that is not Communist.

Most probably as a result of overt Soviet intrigue, the Government of Brazil tersely turned down a Soviet request to expand diplomatic relations between the two countries. Russia wanted a cultural agreement, the appointment of military attaches to its Embassy in Rio and the establishment of a Soviet consular office in Sao Paulo. In refusing to consider the matter, Brazil's government blamed "international tensions" for its negative response. But one thing is certain—U.S. diplomacy can claim no credit for Brazil's wise actions.

The government pressed its investigation of foreign priests (300 of 600 in the Communist hotbed of Belo Horizonte are not Brazilians, but foreigners) and turned up evidence that three were engaged in subversive activities. The three Frenchmen (Fathers Michel Leveen, Xavier Bertoux and Herve Coongaunec) were active, indeed. Father Bertoux was found to be using the Church of the Good Jesus as a training center for Brazilian "Red Guards;" Father Coongaunec was accused of having formed a Vietnam-type "National Liberation Front;" while Father Leveen was found guilty of undercutting the government's anti-inflation measures by inciting workers to resist them, and of forming groups of armed guerrillas.

In Rio, the radical arm of the Church agitated for the release of the three priests. A manifesto issued by a number of priests said they "will fight to obtain the support of the working masses so as to make them aware of the situation" of the three French priests. Yet, General Sisento Sarmento produced what the newspapers described "as a mountain of subversive literature and plans to overthrow the government." Monsignor Helder Camara journeyed to the African city of Dakar where he scored the concept of private property, and attacked "imperialism and the established order."

The history of disturbances in Brazil is marked, if anything, by tolerance on the part of the government of President da Costa e Silva. Students and subversives were warned on scores of occasions that the government would not tolerate their actions forever. President Costa e Silva repeatedly refused the advice of his advisers to apprehend Carlos Lacerda and to crack down on students and radical priests. As early as the first week of July, following systematic terrorist attacks on Brazil's railways and railway stations, the government approved martial law which needed only the President's signature to put it into effect. But the President never signed it. Instead, to reduce tensions he ordered the release of a number of student agitators who had been jailed.

Finally, hard-liners in the government forced President da Costa e Silva to move against subversives. The "institutional act" which followed had the avowed aim of safeguarding "the higher interests of the nation" in the face of growing agitation and subversive attack. The immediate cause for the crackdown came when government deputies in Congress joined with the opposition in voting down a government request to strip congressional immunity from Deputy Marcio Moreira Alves who delivered a passionate speech against what he alleged were the excesses of the government in dealing with subversion.

What happens in the future will depend, in part, on the attitude of the United States toward military takeovers and its understanding of what happened in Brazil. It seems undeniable that the Brazilian government had good and sufficient reason to be alarmed by the deterioration of law and order in the country, a state of affairs clearly provoked and directed by Communist agitators.

Furthermore, the Soviet navy has taken an increasing interest in the South Atlantic, whose land boundaries are formed in Latin America principally by Brazil and Argentina. *Jornal do Brasil* calls attention to the fears of the Brazilian government that the United States is taking NATO affairs off the back burner, is concerned with the Soviet intrusion into the Mediterranean, but then asks: "Will the United States discover in time the strategic importance of the South Atlantic?" This question is a matter of extreme concern to Brazilian authorities who see the progressive advance of the Soviet Union as a threat to the nations of the Americas." What Brazil and Argentina want, *O Jornal* reports, "is a renewal of American naval patrols in this vital area."

In considering the problem posed by Brazil, the United States would do well not have a mirror image of itself. No democrat in his right mind likes military dictatorships, but there is no virtue in being stupid about them, either. First off, the military in government is part of the historical tradition of Latin America. Very often, and unfortunately, it is the military alone that can guarantee stability and provide sufficient time for significant social change to develop in Latin American society. Meanwhile, we should not overlook the fact that the modern young officer group in Latin America has been increasingly trained in the United States and can come forward with many progressive ideas in government.

Nor should we forget that historically the military in Latin America has been as quick to overthrow right-wing dictatorships which violate their constitution (Peru, Colombia, Venezuela, Argentina, the Dominican Republic, for example) and allow free elections to follow, as they have been in protecting their countries against the more sophisticated and thus more difficult to detect onslaught through internal subversion. In considering the alternatives, we can ask this question: How many countries subverted and taken over by Communists, have been permitted to liberalize and return to democratic traditions? And we answer: Just take a look at Czechoslovakia.

What these events in Colombia and Brazil underline is that despite the many statements to come out of the White House . . . in Washington claiming that we have gained the initiative in the not-so-cold war, the fact is that the United States has failed to make a single incursion into the Soviet-bloc of nations while the Soviets penetrate this hemisphere with ease. The debate centers around whether or not jet aircraft should be sold to Latin American governments, and, in the case of Vietnam, whether or not bombing of the North should be continued and just what the targets should *not* be. To turn the clock back to World War II, let us ask this question: If a responsible Allied leader had proposed that the Allies limit the war to bombing missions against Germany, and commit troops only to the defense of France and Russia, would he not have been carted off to an insane asylum? And if a responsible Allied official had suggested that the way to end World War II was to negotiate with Hitler's satraps in charge of Fifth Columns in Hungary, Rumania, Bulgaria and make them partners to a negotiated peace without victory would he not have lost his position? And although this analogy may be imperfect in its degree of present-day application, it will serve to illustrate a point. The National Liberation Fronts of today are the Communist equivalent of Hitler's Nazi Fifth Columns of yesterday. One was tied to Berlin, the other is tied to Moscow, Peking, or both.

What has inhibited the United States is that our officials respond to Communist-inspired hopes that the apparent end of one dispute (Cuba or North Korea, for example) means that all disputes are capable of settlement. But the fact is that the Communists do not believe in settlements that do not advance them along the road to victory. Thus, each negotiation is accompanied by steady erosion of the Free World's position. Cuba trains and then exports terrorists to Latin America; North Korea infiltrates terrorists into South Korea. Yet, time after time the United States tries to identify Communist desires with specific, concrete issues (as President Kennedy tried and failed with Khrushchev at the Vienna meeting in 1961). This is so, perhaps, because we cannot bring ourselves to believe that the Communist ideology is one of final, total victory. We act as though past agreements have settled particular issues in a definite manner, because, it may be surmised, the U.S. politician feels that he must point to a victory. And the Kremlin goes along because it induces us to forget or downgrade the importance of one danger point as the Communists force us to meet another ten thousand miles away.

An example of the State Department's naive view of Communist policy was provided by U.S. Ambassador John Crimmins during a foreign policy seminar held in Miami on January 16, 1968. In answer to a question from the audience why the United States was not meeting the threat posed by an offshore base of subversion, Cuba, Crimmins said: "The threat has been reduced to the point where it no longer threatens the security of this country nor the hemisphere."[1] According to Mr. Crimmins, Cuba no longer posed a threat because Castro had failed to make it a model of Communist economic success that would tempt other Latin countries to go and do likewise. Writing in the *Miami Herald* following the conference Edwin Lahey reported: "Some regard the conferences as brainwashing sessions, a charge that touches the Department of State officials to the quick."[2]

These conferences, held periodically by the State Department, have as a purpose the marshaling of public opinion here and abroad in support of U.S. foreign policy objectives. And they serve to illustrate a point. Resort to public relations reached a high under President Kennedy when his New Frontiersmen tried to fill policy vacuums with slogans and public relations gimmicks. The situation did not change under President Johnson, and there is today the conviction in the State Department that there is such a thing as "world public opinion," that it is an operating tenet of international power politics and must be wooed. It is believed that good will attracts good will; man is capable of rising above the totalitarian state and prepared to reform himself; truth has an inherent leavening process of its own; a participation in a UN Security Council sit-in against the racial policies of Rhodesia will appease the Communists and will move non-aligned countries to rush to endorse U.S. foreign policy. But the realities are different. Rich and powerful, the United States undercuts what essentially should be an aggressive propaganda policy offensive because it believes that it is under moral and political indictment by countries which, until recently, were under Western colonial rule and indeed Washington often appeals to those areas of the world in self-flagellating terms. But the Communists do not meet this appeal with one of their own, for their purpose is not so much to gain popularity for themselves as it is to arouse or exacerbate anti-West feelings among these people. But the United States, in turn, does not aim to arouse similar hostility against the Communists, and chooses, instead, to engage in a popularity contest in which it is the sole entry. As a result, it is always the United States and its policies that are under discussion, not Communist aggression and the brutality of Communism itself. There can be no effective propaganda if there is no vigorous policy to propagandize. A case in point is Cuba.

By 1965 Fidel Castro was experiencing deep trouble because of rising internal dissatisfaction with his regime. As mentioned earlier, all air travel between Cuba and the United States had been cut off since the missile crisis, and only a handful of Cubans were able to leave the country each week. Internal pressures mounted, prompting Castro to appear at the Sports Palace unannounced, to interrupt a sportscast and say that it was Yankee imperialism, not he, that was responsible for the cancellation of flights to the United States. On another day, he watched Havana residents as militia units forced them to dig up their flower gardens and plant vegetables and shouted that he was willing to get rid of the *gusanos* (worms, meaning anti-Castro Cubans) if only the Yankees would reopen Havana-Miami flights. Then on September 28, 1965, Castro addressed the country over radio and television, blistered the *gusanos* and said "all of those who wish, may leave."

The State Department evidently saw in the Castro announcement an opportunity to interrupt Washington's three-year silence on Cuba in a manner which would have some public relations appeal in the country. John Crimmins, then coordinator of Cuban affairs in the State Department, went to work on devising a protocol by which Cubans would be airlifted to the United States at the expense of the U.S. taxpayer, thus responding to Castro's belligerence in a contrasting, humanitarian manner. As Executive Director of the U.S. Citizens Committee for a Free Cuba I immediately went to see Congressman Paul Rogers (D., Fla.) at his office in the Sam Rayburn Building in Washington and enlisted his help in trying to get the Crimmins plan stopped. For it could have no effect other than to rid Castro of his opposition and tighten the hard core of his supporters. Failing that, I said, further talks with Castro on airlifting Cubans to this country should be made contingent on the prior release of Cuban political prisoners numbering between 60,000 and 90,000. We agreed that it would be a calamity to remove Castro's opponents by airlifting them out of Cuba until the United States first stood by those who had already proved themselves. We had to ask ourselves this question: What incentive would there be for Cubans to oppose Castro in the future if the United States turned its back against those now in prison who had already done so?*

There was an additional point. Some 3,000 U.S. citizens and their families were being held in Cuba in violation of all standards of international conduct. I argued that unless they and Castro's political prisoners were released, we should cut off all further talks with Castro. Directing me to a telephone extension in his office, Mr. Rogers called the White House and asked to speak with National Security Adviser McGeorge Bundy. He was not available. The Congressman then called the State Department and spoke to Crimmins, outlining the provisos he felt should be made in dealing with Castro, adding that the Human Rights Commission of the OAS had issued a scathing report on the status of political prisoners and their families which would most certainly back up our demands. Crimmins listened and then came up with the extraordinary argument that Cuba no longer was a member of the Organization of American States and therefore not responsive to its findings.

The State Department view prevailed, however, and President Johnson journeyed to New York, and there in a burst of publicity at the feet of the Statue of Liberty signed into law an Amendment to the immigration act whereby the United States could accept Castro's offer to let Cubans come to this country. Castro, however, immediately began to renege on his promises that "all who wish can leave." First, skilled workers had the "open door" slammed in their faces when the Cuban Communist regime made them sign five-year work contracts with the state. Those refusing to sign were fired on the spot by agents of Castro's secret police. They were labelled "enemies of the state," and had their ration books taken away, forcing them to live on food provided by their friends and relatives. Thousands are now in camps called Military Units to Aid Production (UMAP), a euphemism for concentration camps, where they are paid seven dollars a month. I interviewed scores of the first arrivals in Miami and found that hysteria literally had overcome Cuba with President Johnson's offer. Forms to be filled out by those wanting to leave quickly disappeared, along with the will of the Cubans to resist Castro any further.

Next, the Cuban regime created new categories of those forbidden to leave the country. Militiamen and youths between the ages of 14 and 27 were not permitted to leave, said the government. On December 1, Cuba's UN delegate Marta Jiménez Martínez, said that while the exodus was underway "the United Nations must assure against subversive or

*There is also the suspicion that U.S. agreement to airlift Castro dissidents out of Cuba was related to agreements made at the Missile Crisis—to help Castro by removing his opposition.

hostile acts against any member of the United Nations."[3] And our State Department remained silent as category after category of Cubans were prevented from leaving the country in direct violation of Castro's September 28 pledge. When U.S. newspapers began to ask why numbers of Castro's dissidents were yet being airlifted to the United States while U.S. citizens were being held in Cuba, the State Department smoothly replied that the release of Americans was not a part of the original protocol. Thus, American citizens were kept in Cuba as virtual hostages to ensure that the airlift of dissident, anti-Castro Cubans continued and the safety valve to internal pressure remained open. When in 1967 two Americans, Martha Sperling and William Gaines, were shot under mysterious circumstances on Cuba's Isle of Pines, the Cuban government, in an obvious attempt to distract attention from the murders, immediately arranged for a planeload of U.S. citizens to leave Cuba via Mexico.

In sum, the imagery of the moment provided the Communists with another victory, and the U.S. taxpayer paid for that victory by shelling out millions of dollars time to pay the cost of airlifting anti-Castro Cubans to this country. And some 30,000 Cubans who defied the government by applying to leave, even though they were within prohibited categories, were placed in concentration camps, as Castro tightened his hold on the country. It is as simple as that. By making his September 28 announcement, Castro had blundered into our hands. But, characteristically, we did not take advantage of the situation. If we had made U.S. agreement to air lift Castro's opposition out of Cuba contingent on the prior release of Castro's political prisoners, and had even insisted that a mixed Latin American commission go to Cuba to ascertain the conditions under which prisoners were living, the chances are that Castro would have refused. And by closing the door on his own proposals, the Cuban dictator would seriously have affected his peripheral support in some Latin American countries and added considerably to the number of his internal opponents.

News dispatches coming out of Havana on January 24, 1968, turned out to be the prelude to one of the great missed opportunities for taking advantage of Castro's weaknesses. The reported rumors were that Fidel Castro might step down as Prime Minister at a meeting of the Central Committee of the Cuban Communist Party, scheduled to be held that same night. The announcement of the meeting was unusual in itself, for though formed in the fall of 1965, the Central Committee had not been formally convened at any time since. And, of course, it was recalled in the news dispatches that back in July of 1959 Castro had resigned as Prime Minister in a successful maneuver that forced anti-Communist President Manuel Urrutia out of office. However, during a three-day marathon speech before the Central Committee, Armed Forces Minister Raul Castro furnished dramatic evidence that this time Fidel Castro was the victim of a plot hatched by what he called a "micro-faction" within the Party. More startling still, he revealed that the Soviet Union was involved in that plot.

Raúl Castro's charges, published in the January 28 and following editions of *Granma*, were sensational enough in themselves. But he also revealed that in addition to receiving his 15,000 word address, each of the 100 member Central Committee had been provided with a separately numbered secret briefing pamphlet and was ordered to read and return it. Exhibits relating to the conspiracy had also been provided in a hall located just across from the meeting place and the Committee members were herded into it, perhaps to impress upon them the efficiency of the Cuban police and intelligence apparatus. However that may be, the younger Castro brother put old-line Communist Aníbal Escalante in the role of villain with a supporting cast of 36 of the "micro-faction," and virtually the whole of the Soviet diplomatic establishment in Havana. The Armed Forces Minister began his scenario in 1966 when, he said, "we were informed of opinions criticizing the leadership of the revolution, and specifically criticism of Fidel Castro, which came from some members of the old Popular Socialist Party."* In November of 1966, Raúl Castro told his attentive audience, Soviet diplomat Rudolf P. Shliapnikov, Second Secretary in the Soviet Embassy, was accosted by members of the "micro-faction" and told that something had to be done to pressure Fidel Castro into removing his bungling hands from the machinery of government, or the country well might collapse. They spoke to him of dissension in the ranks of labor, the rapidly deteriorating economic and political situation and, in general, sketched a picture of a country in ruins.

Raúl Castro then dropped the bombshell, saying that Shliapnikov had replied: "In Cuba, conditions are present for a new Hungary . . . internal dissension is great," and, "in Hungary it was not the peasants that crushed the revolt . . . it fell upon the State Security" which, in Cuba, the diplomat warned, was filled with "petit bourgeois." His view, that Cuba's police apparatus could not deal effectively with a determined uprising, caused the Armed Forces Minister to remark drily: "As I recall, it was not precisely the State Security that crushed the counterrevolutionaries in Hungary," in obvious reference to the bloody role played by the Red Army. Shliapnikov was the top adviser to Cuba's Ministry of the Interior which functions in Cuba like the KGB in Russia, and it can be assumed that he knew what he was talking about when he assessed Cuba's explosive internal situation. Furthermore, Raúl Castro said that

*Cuban Communist Party

the Muscovite had maintained relations with one of the conspirators, Emilio Lopez Castillo, until he was returned to Russia the previous June.

It was at some point in late 1966 or early 1967 that Aníbal Escalante entered the conspiracy. The 59- year old Communist had held the powerful post of Secretary of Organization in the old Popular Socialist Party and in the Integrated Revolutionary Organizations that succeeded it. Back in 1960 and 1961, Escalante tried hard to institutionalize the revolution and went so far as to accuse Fidel Castro of fostering the cult of personality. This led to his expulsion from the country in the spring of 1962 and Castro did not permit him to return from exile in Czechoslovakia until the fall of 1964. From that date until he was arrested on December 10, 1967, Escalante held the very minor position of manager of a state farm. However, his ties with top European and Soviet Communists were close and they stretched back three decades. Competent and intelligent, Escalante commanded a following among the Party functionaries in Cuba quite out of proportion to his modest position as state farm manager. Through both Cuban and European contacts he watched as Fidel Castro reduced the Cuban economy to ruins and, in their opinion, dissipated his own popular support which had been the glue which kept the government from coming unstuck. It was in the nature of things, then, that the Russians and Escalante should make common cause.

The Raúl Castro account of Soviet dealings with Escalante and the "micro-faction" shows them meeting in cars driven around Havana for hours, at dinner in the homes of Soviet functionaries and less often in their offices. The younger Castro brother's speech to the Central Committee was confusing, perhaps deliberately so, as to dates and specific reference to Soviet officials. But the overall picture was there. Most of it was based on a document which Escalante had allegedly prepared for the Russians. It dwelt on the worsening political and economic situation inside Cuba which, Escalante is said to have told the Russians, would lead to what Shliapnikov had described as a "new Hungary." Production of ten million tons of sugar in 1970, as projected by Castro, said Escalante, was "virtually impossible," while production for domestic use "is also beneath the indices needed to provide for the people."

Apparently the Soviet Union agreed with this analysis and, according to Raúl Castro, sent a "journalist," actually a KGB agent identified as Vadim Lestov, to contact Escalante and take his written report "directly to the Central Committee of the Communist Party of the U.S.S.R." The "document" apparently had been destroyed before the Cuban secret police could get their hands on it, and its contents were made known by Octavio Fernandez Boris, through "intensive interrogation." Actually, the Escalante report was alleged to have been the work of three people—Fernandez Boris, Dr. Emilio de Quesada and, of course, Escalante. Fernandez Boris met with Lestov, said Raúl Castro, "and told him everything," while de Quesada journeyed to Prague where he met with a member of the Central Committee of the Czech Communist Party. Interestingly enough, the former head of Cuba's neighborhood spy apparatus, José Matar, had been transferred much earlier to the post of Ambassador to Hungary and was also identified as one of the "microfaction." Two groups of East Germans came to Cuba, said Castro, conjecturing that their status as "special delegations" concealed their interest and participation in the plot. The point is that a number of East European Communist governments were aware of the plot one way or another.

The Escalante "document" on which much of Raúl Castro's charges rested apparently was concerned in some small measure with differences between the old-line Communists and Fidel Castro. Castro's policies had, in the words quoted from the alleged report by Raúl Castro, "divorced us from the majority of the Communist parties," and negated what the old-liners believed was their "constructive" role in the revolution. However, these were relatively minor points, comprising no more than a few hundred words of the total of 15,000. Raúl Castro scored the old-liners because, he said, they had "weakened the thesis that the only road for the people of Latin America to take is to take up arms," which is to say that they do not endorse "armed struggle" as the only means by which Latin America may be sovietized. This point was addressed in the previous chapter, and Raúl Castro's words serve to support the analysis of differences which are made in that chapter regarding "peaceful coexistence."

What lay at the heart of the Aníbal Escalante affair is that the Soviets were worried that the economic and political base on which their military establishment rested in Cuba might explode and propel them out of their strategical and tactical position in the Caribbean. And, as Shliapnikov's words indicated, the fears of the Soviets were heightened by the possibility of a "new Hungary" which the Johnson Administration had pledged, at least, would not be tolerated in Cuba. This state of affairs they obviously placed at the feet of Fidel Castro whose dangerous policies, the Russians were beginning to feel, were not worth his value as a figurehead. Yet, on January 31, the *New York Times* persisted in preaching its old line, saying that Aníbal Escalante and his co-conspirators "will go on trial as 'traitors' essentially because they support the Soviet view . . . because Moscow has refused to accept as obligatory Castro's favored guerrilla warfare tactics," when in fact the Russians were concerned almost solely with protecting their Cuban base from which guerrilla wars are launched.

And Shliapnikov had good reason to make his analysis of a "new Hungary." With unrest in Cuba came spiralling terror. In July, 1967

Castro established "Peoples' Tribunals" in all of Cuba's six provinces. "Judges" were composed of members of the Committees for the Defense of the Revolution, and the neighbors were called in to see if they objected to those chosen. No one of course did, and *Granma* claimed that democracy had now reached the grass roots of Cuban society. But people disappeared with increasing frequency after the formation of the tribunals, with many turning up on the UMAPs, the state farms, as slave labor only slightly disguised. Hundreds of refugees arriving in Miami in November and December of 1967 spoke of anti-Castro slogans scratched on the walls in Havana and interior cities of Cuba, among them: "Fidel, You Don't Have Much Time!" and "Fidel, Your Time is Approaching!" Such indications of public protest had not been seen in such profusion since 1963, prompting many of the refugees to express their belief that they were the work of Castro's own militia who stood guard at night. They claimed that the population was so thoroughly terrorized that it was unlikely that one would risk paying for his life or a long prison term simply for the thrill of scratching his dissent on walls. The claims were given some credibility when Miami's *Diario las Americas* published on December 22, 1967, an Agence France cable from Havana, saying that "a number of officers, together with various figures of the 'old-guard' Communists have been detained." The story was essentially correct, for Aníbal Escalante had been arrested on December 10, and various members of the "micro-faction" were detained shortly thereafter. Slogans and signs began to diminish in frequency of appearance.

There was a highly interesting speech made on July 22, 1967, by Raúl Castro which, taken together with revelations later to come out at the Aníbal Escalante affair, added even more substance to Soviet fears that a "new Hungary" might erupt. The Armed Forces Minister told the graduating class of the Maximo Gomez Superior School of Military Training: "Counterrevolutionaries have cost us the lives of our youths and great amounts of money to liquidate them." He gave some dimensions to both by adding: "In order to liquidate these bands, 179 in total, it has cost Cuba precious lives and the equivalent in cost of between 500 and 800 million U.S. dollars." The address was rebroadcast over Radio Progreso on July 24, but it did not mention whether all of the bands had been liquidated or whether they had just been forced to disband, as was the known case of the band of anti-Castro guerrilla leader Yayo Estevez. But one thing seems certain. Even by halving or quartering the number of bands, latent organized anti-Communist resistance was there in considerable force.

As for the conspiracy charges themselves, another old-line Communist, Carlos Rafael Rodriguez, added his voice to those already excoriating Aníbal Escalante, and in doing so revealed that the plotters comprised considerably more than a mere "micro-faction." On February 1, Radio Progreso quoted him: "Without doubt, there will be three or four times more people involved in this affair, but 200 or 300 involved in similar activity in a nation does not mean a thing." That it meant a great deal was precisely why Raul Castro convened the Central Committee of the Cuban Communist Party and went to such lengths to reveal as much as he did. His speech, called "Report of the Armed Forces and State Security Commission of the Communist Party," is the most comprehensive listing of acts of conspiracy, and the alleged reasons therefore, in the history of Cuba. And just why so much publicity was given to it still remains open to conjecture. One view is that the dissension was so widespread that the two Castro brothers believed it wise to demonstrate to the public just how swiftly and capably they can react to threats against their power and position. Another was that if the country exploded, Fidel Castro assassinated, or both, the Russians would be held liable for it.

Nevertheless, efforts were made to keep the differences between Castro and the Kremlin at a low key. Raul Castro's report says: "Apart from the conduct of a few advisers, journalists and functionaries of foreign embassies, in our country numerous Soviet technicians and those from other Socialist countries have done their job, maintaining exemplary conduct and an absolute respect for our revolution." And he praised Soviet military forces in Cuba in an eyebrow-lifting statement to those wondering about the size of those forces, saying: "Thousands of Soviet military officers have worked with us in the Armed Forces, and there is not a single complaint we can make about them." But he was not successful in hiding the depth of disenchantment among the ordinary Cubans. Reports out of Cuba told about the firing of thousands of workers at the Agrarian Reform Institute, the Ministry of Industries, the fishing port of Havana and the Cuban Electric Company. From October, 1967 until the middle of March, 1968 the purge continued.

And we now have reason to believe that Kosygin's visit to Havana following his meeting with President Johnson at Glassboro, New Jersey, was related to the Aníbal Escalante affair. Kosygin arrived in Havana on June 26, remained there for five days and met with the top leaders of the Cuban Communist Party and not with the Revolutionary Government as such. Rudolf P. Shliapnikov was yanked out of Cuba the same month, and soon after the Soviet Premier left Havana, Soviet Ambassador Alexander I. Alexeiv also left his post. Alexeiv had been in Havana for three years yet left unannounced. The Foreign Ministry in Moscow said he had to undergo "medical treatment." It was not until January 12, 1968, that the Soviets named his replacement, Ambassador Alexander K. Soldatov. The Soviet Embassy was thus left uncovered for a period of six months, a most unusual length of time.

It is not known whether or not Premier Kosygin was present when Raúl Castro confronted the Soviet Ambassador with evidence of Russian intrigue in dealing sub rosa with Escalante and the "micro-faction." Castro's description of the event reveals that three top Soviet advisers were with the Ambassador, including Shliapnikov, and reveals as well how powerful was the Soviet hold over Cuban government ministries. Castro told Ambassador Alexeiv that Manuel Piñeiro, Vice Minister of the Interior, had found one of the Russians talking with Anibal Escalante in a car parked just in front of the Soviet Embassy, and reported this event to him. When faced with this, according to Armed Forces Minister Castro, the Soviet advisers were "bitterly offended" because they believed that Piñeiro should have reported the incident to them and not to Raúl Castro. To this the younger Castro said he replied: "You are almost telling me to put Piñeiro behind bars for having been disrespectful to you . . .", then warned the Soviet Ambassador that "it would be very painful to us to find some Soviet functionaries, diplomats or not, involved in some of our internal affairs." It was following this exchange that Premier Kosygin left Havana and Ambassador Alexeiv was removed from his post. The most that can be said for Vice President Humphrey's version—that Kosygin went to Havana to remonstrate with Fidel Castro over exporting guerrilla wars—is that it must have come off the bottom of his head.

Indeed, Vice President Humphrey's smoke-screen obscured even more clinching evidence that the Anibal Escalante affair revealed the depth of disenchantment in Cuba with Fidel Castro's Communist regime. From October to February—1967-68—more than 250,000 packages of food, medicines and clothing had piled up in Havana. The packages were sent from exiles to relatives and friends in Cuba but remained undelivered. In a very real sense these packages served as an index to just how shattered was the Cuban economy. And reports coming out of the island indicated that one of the reasons Castro forbade their delivery is that they also served as an index to the number of anti-Castro Cubans inside the island. No exile would send a package of medicines, food or clothing to a *Fidelista*, so the 250,000 packages gave evidence of great numbers of anti-Fidel Cuban families, a mute condemnation of both Castro and his regime.

This point was addressed by an arrival from Cuba at about the time that the mail situation had been brought to the attention of the Cuban public. The refugee, Armando Hernandez Hinojoso, revealed that writing paper, pencil and other school supplies were not available. And those students who came to school with these elementary materials said that they got them from friends and relatives in the United States. This went for clothing as well, and Sr. Hernandez Hinojoso was called on the carpet by his son's teacher, a militiawoman, and told that the youngster no longer was permitted to wear American-made pants and shirts because, she told him, "it makes for unrest among the other pupils." Such was the situation in a school which, ironically, included a course on "Imperialist Exploitation" in its curriculum. Cubans were questioned extensively when they appeared at their jobs dressed in U.S.-made clothing, and in many cases forbidden to wear them by political commissars at the work sites. Behind the order was the suspicion. Suspicion of one's neighbor was everywhere, present in Cuba in 1968, and this suspicion was reflected on the official level by the Anibal Escalante affair which had bared the Castro regime for what it was—a house of cards which might have been tumbled by a vigorous administration in Washington.

But Castro's many blunders have not been turned to advantage by the United States because we are never ready with a plan to capitalize on the weaknesses of our enemies. Is this because Americans lack ability or genius in the field of strategy and tactics? The answer is that we have no plans to advance at the enemy's expense. In other words, our government has limited the United States to a posture of defense simply because it is not contemplating measures which will lead to the enemy's defeat. Instead, we "prove" our peaceful intentions by helping the enemy out of his troubles—for example, by selling wheat to bolster Russia's marginal economy and by removing dissidents from Castro's Cuba. There are no such inhibitions at work among the Communists.

The conventional concept of war is obsolete in Communist doctrine. National sovereignty is a myth, while ideology, strategy and tactics are fact. Communist warfare is an incessant tactic with a revolutionary design of destruction envisaging the total dissolution of the social entities that they attack. Nothing is left untouched by the Communists, once they defeat a country. There is no idea of live and let live following a war. Nor can aggressive Communism be contained or isolated, simply because the Communists conduct war through subversion, infiltration and flanking tactics to undermine our moral, social, economic and political foundations at home and abroad.

Infiltration and subversion of the U.S. Negro population by Havana is so great as to be ostentatious, while flanking movements against Puerto Rico are very much in evidence. But this fact has yet to impress itself on Washington with a force sufficient to elicit a noticeable response. To turn to Puerto Rico briefly takes us to a consideration of Communist plans for that island as they were enunciated at Havana's 1966 Tricontinental Conference. Norman Pietri spelled out Communist strategy and tactics in terms that spoke of the retirement of U.S. military might from the Caribbean.* The Puerto Rican subversive said: "The use of Puerto

*Add to this the very palpable Communist efforts to force the United States to hand the

Rico as a military base accounts for fourteen per cent of the national territory . . . nine immense U.S. military bases, designed to strengthen Yankee domination of Puerto Rico . . . exposing the rest of Latin America to the constant threat of military aggression."[4] Pietri is trying to gain acceptance of the myth that Puerto Rico is not a part of the United States, and is saying that a U.S. military response to Communist guerrillas in Latin America constitutes "aggression."

While Pietri correctly outlined present Communist policy, he most certainly was not the first to do so. The island Commonwealth has been the subject of Communist attention almost from the very day Fidel Castro came to power. In January 1959 Castro immediately set about attacking the United States for relegating the island to the status of a "colony." I was present at one of Castro's press conferences at the Havana Riviera Hotel when he poked barbs at the Puerto Ricans for accepting what he called "a status of self-denigration." A Puerto Rican newspaperman jumped to his feet and defended Puerto Rico's Commonwealth association with the United States, an idea put forward by the Puerto Ricans themselves. Nevertheless, the Communists continued to work on undermining the U.S.-Puerto Rican affiliation, and in 1964 their mole-like patience was rewarded, first when so-called non-aligned nations met in Cairo and accepted a Cuban resolution condemning U.S. "colonial policy" toward Puerto Rico, and next on November 20, 1964, when a Committee of the United Nations agreed to debate the issue. The UN action was taken in the face of an event which cast doubts on the sanity of the international organization. For only a few weeks prior to the debate, free elections were held in Puerto Rico in which 778,000 out of a total vote of 800,000 reaffirmed their status as U.S. citizens within a Commonwealth status. The debate was followed by the appearance of the late and unlamented "Che" Guevara before the UN General Assembly where, on December 10, he attacked the United States in bitter terms, reached lyrical heights in heroicizing guerrilla terrorists in Latin America, and said that Puerto Ricans were born with hinges in their spines so they can bow to U.S. authority.

More important, Guevara met with two U.S. Negro militants, Robert Collier and Walter Bowe, at a party given in his honor by the Cuban UN Mission. Both had been recruited by Roberto Santiesteban Casanova of the Cuban UN Mission and had received training in Cuba's guerrilla camps that summer. Collier was given special instruction by a major in the North Vietnamese army. It was at this meeting, described in an earlier chapter, that Guevara gave the Negro militants the go-ahead to blow up cherished symbols of American heritage—the Liberty Bell, the Washington Monument and the Statue of Liberty. What is not generally

Panama Canal over to the small, weak and unstable Republic of Panama.

known, however, is the Cuban UN Mission's role in bringing Black Power leaders together with Puerto Rican Communists. This task was carried out by Mrs. Laura Meneses de Albizu, wife of the deceased Puerto Rican extremist Pedro Albizu, the original leader of the Puerto Rican Pro-Independence Movement (PMI) who, nearly two decades ago, was involved in the plot to assassinate President Harry S Truman in Washington.

Mrs. Meneses de Albizu and another Puerto Rican with the improbable name of Juan Juarbe y Juarbe have for years been members of the Cuban Mission to the UN, and as a consequence carry out their subversive activities cloaked with diplomatic immunity. They put the 26 year-old Stokely Carmichael of the Student Nonviolent Coordinating Committee (SNCC) in touch with Juan Mari Bras, Secretary General of the PMI, thus setting in motion a string of events that resulted in coordinating Communist flanking movements in Puerto Rico with infiltration of Negro communities in mainland United States.

Elements in this double-headed conspiracy all fell into place on January 24, 1967, when Stokely Carmichael journeyed to San Juan at the invitation of PMI and its student arm the Pro-Independence Student Federation, (FUPI), where he promptly organized a march on Fort Brooke protesting the conscription of Puerto Ricans into the armed forces. In a prepared statement, Carmichael said he supported Puerto Rico's "just struggle of independence,"[5] and protested the war in Vietnam in language used in the Tricontinental Resolution on Vietnam. PMI Secretary General Mari Bras has for years been an admirer of Fidel Castro and, in response to the Tricontinental Conference resolution on Puerto Rico, it was he who established the "Free Puerto Rico" embassy in Havana. And the PMI's student arm, FUPI, is a member of Castro's Continental Organization of Latin American Students. So the whole of the Pro-Independence Movement to which Carmichael pledged his support is little more than a puppet whose voice is in Havana.

Mari Bras and Carmichael formalized already existing ties between SNCC and the PMI on January 25, 1967, by signing a "protocol of cooperation." That same day, Cuba's *Granma* took editorial notice of the protocol and quoted Carmichael's little-known address to PMI members as follows: "There is a great connection between our fight for Negro power and your fight for independence," and revealed in unmistakeable terms that SNCC now was affiliated with Havana's Tricontinental organization of subversion, as well. *Granma* quoted Carmichael on this subject: "Brothers, we see our fight connected with the patriotic struggle of the peoples of Africa, Asia, and Latin America against foreign oppression, especially United States oppression." And again Carmichael's inspiration came from Havana in the form of the Tricontinental Organization's resolutions one year earlier. The passage reads: "Although geograph-ically Afro-Americans do not form a part of Latin America, Africa or Asia, the special circumstances . . . merit special consideration and *demands that the Tricontinental Organization create the necessary mech-anisms so that these brothers in the struggle will, in the future, be able to participate in the great battle being fought by the peoples of the three continents.*"[6] (Italics added.)

Thus it should have come as no surprise when Carmichael went to Cuba in late July, 1967 and took part in the Latin American Solidarity Organization conference (OLAS), the branch of the Tricontinental Or-ganization charged with the specific task of subverting the Western Hem-isphere. Nor should eyebrows have been lifted over the appearance in Havana of Juan Mari Bras. The two subversives had already made com-mon cause in promoting violence in Puerto Rico and in the United States. Made an "honorary delegate" among the 164 Communists from 27 countries and dependencies in the Western Hemisphere, Carmichael worked on the OLAS resolution to "free" the U.S. Negro from what he alleged was white oppression. Apart from the blunt rhetoric in which Carmichael couched his intentions to subvert the U.S. Negro com-munity, his statements are notable in that they spell out the importance which the nearness of Cuba to the United States is viewed by the Com-munists. *Granma* published an interview with Carmichael in its August 13, 1967 edition in which he said that "Fidel Castro is a source of inspiration" and that Cuban Communism is important "because it is the nearest system." When asked whether SNCC's activities were coor-dinated with the work of the OLAS, Carmichael replied: "Our very presence here indicates that." The Black Power militant wrote a letter to "Che" Guevara who at that moment was being pursued by the Bolivian army, and said: "You are an inspiration, not only to Blacks inside the United States but to the liberation struggle around the world." The letter was published in *Granma* in Carmichael's handwriting the day of his interview. More immediately important was what Carmichael said of Black Power. "We are moving toward urban guerrilla warfare within the United States," Carmichael told his Cuban hosts. He linked his Negro guerrilla movement to Communist objectives in Vietnam when he vowed: "When the United States has 50 Vietnams inside and 50 outside, this will mean the death of imperialism."

A curious and notable switch took place regarding Carmichael's itiner-ary following the end of the OLAS meeting. On August 12, an announce-ment out of Havana said that Carmichael and Julius Lester would go from Havana to Russia for a visit. Almost immediately, however, the signals were switched and Carmichael and Lester went first to Hanoi and from there on an ill-will tour of countries in Africa and Europe where they preached the doctrine of hate against the United States. The hate doctrine was often used by "Che" Guevara, and Carmichael quoted him: "Hatred is an element of the struggle, transforming [man] into an effective, violent, selective and cold-killing machine," and then added what was planned to do with that "killing machine," saying: "The next Vietnam will be on this continent, perhaps in Bolivia, Guatemala, Brazil or the Dominican Republic."[7]

In Hanoi, Carmichael told our enemies: "We are not reformers. We are revolutionaries. We do not want to be a part of the Government of the U.S.A. or the American regime."[8] And much like Chile's Socialist Senator Salvador Allende who stepped down as head of his party to assume its foreign affairs post, Carmichael shifted abruptly from his post as leader of SNCC to one of that gave him greater freedom to organize opposition to the war in Vietnam. And he did so in response to the OLAS resolution on the U.S. Negro which he helped draft. It claims that U.S. Negroes "are used as cannon fodder by the U.S. government for its imperialistic wars . . . and the peoples of OLAS urge them to answer the racist violence of the United States imperialist government with stepped-up direct revolutionary action. The organized Negro movement is in opposition to the imperialistic aggression against the heroic people of Vietnam."[9]

Radio Moscow obtruded into the internal affairs of the United States in an English-language broadcast to American troops fighting in Vietnam, telling them on August 28: "This is for Negro soldiers who have been sent to fight in Vietnam. Statistics show that proportionally there are more Negro casualties than white among American soldiers," and adding: "Although Negroes comprise only about eleven per cent of the populations, they comprise over 23 per cent of the U.S. soldiers in Vietnam." The broadcast then accused the U.S. high command of deliberate murder, claiming: "General Westmoreland does his best to see to it that Negroes are killed in battle. The grapes of wrath are slowly ripening in the hearts of Negro soldiers, and the U.S. imperialists and racists would be wise to heed the warning signals."

In Paris, Carmichael shouted to a cheering, stamping crowd of anti-war demonstrators: "We don't want peace in Vietnam. We want the Vietnamese to defeat the United States of America." He told the crowd how he would assist them in doing so: "Our aim is to disrupt the United States of America." Taking a leaf out of the Reverend Martin Luther King's book of pious reasons for opposing the war in Vietnam, Carmichael shouted: "There is a higher law than that of the United States," and added: "We are going to begin to escalate our resistance movement against the war in Vietnam." He called the murderous Viet Cong "our brothers as well as our comrades in arms," and generally endorsed all facets of violence to achieve Communist ends.[10]

H. Rap Brown, now head of SNCC, carried on a long-distance telephone call between New York and Havana with a member of the Castro government. It was rebroadcast in Spanish over Radio Havana on August 31, 1967, and is worth repeating. Said Brown: "Our rebellion has been against the power structure, against White America." He bragged that SNCC now was proficient in the terror tactics employed by the Viet Cong, and predicted: "Each city in America which has a large Negro population can predict with confidence that it will have a rebellion. America is the principal aggressor, and America and its imperialist government threatens the world with the blackmail of war." The interviewer in Havana prompted Brown to get on with a discussion of discrimination against the American Negro in the armed forces, and Brown falsely alleged: "It is no accident that 30 per cent of the casualties in Vietnam are black men and that 22 per cent of the forces there are black . . . they not only are killing us in Vietnam, but in the streets of America." Using a variation of the phrase made back in 1966 by the Puerto Rican subversive Narciso Rabel that "we live in the very heart of the monster," Brown shouted over the phone: "We live within the stomach of the monster and we can destroy him from within." His words also, of course, parallel Carmichael's call for "50 Vietnams inside the United States."

Following his January trip to Puerto Rico, Carmichael kept up a drumfire of letters in support of PMI, including one directed to the Rector of the University of Puerto Rico, Abrahan Díaz González. In his letter, Carmichael protested the expulsion from the University of 25 members of FUPI for creating a destructive riot on the campus. One portion of Carmichal's letter was translated into Spanish and distributed around the campus in the city of San Juan, in which Carmichael went right down the Communist line, saying that the United States is a "foreign power" and must get out of the island altogether. It reads: "SNCC believes that your actions indicate that the administration of the University of Puerto Rico is controlled and manipulated by foreign forces, and for us it is very clear that these forces are the government of the United States and all of its White Power, together with the Uncle Toms of Puerto Rico. And we, as Negro students in the United States, face the same oppression, exploitation, and repression from White America."

The riot was caused when about 300 FUPI members broke up a march by the University of Puerto Rico's ROTC cadets as a part of an honor guard honoring Dona Felisa Rincón de Gautier, the woman Mayor of San Juan. FUPI leaders apparently seized upon a statement made a few days earlier by professor Pedro Muñóz Amate. He said that the ROTC ought to conduct its classes outside the university campus, thus placing it in a category of a clandestine organization. Quick to seize upon any weaknesses in order to embarrass the United States and to force U.S. military power out of Puerto Rico, FUPI leaders organized a riot that caused great damage to university buildings and forced the suspension of classes. Public indignation against the FUPI vandals was swift, with the *San Juan Star, El Mundo* and *El Dia* newspapers calling upon university authorities to put an end to FUPI's stranglehold on the university. Another professor, however, made the patently false allegation that it was the ROTC, not the FUPI, that started the riot, and the campus erupted again. Rector Díaz González evidently was intimidated and refused to take a position, causing his former law partner Juan Nevares Santiago to call for his resignation and newspapers to decry his weakness.

Perhaps not so curiously, one of the anti-ROTC professors went off to Cuba. The May 21, 1967 edition of San Juan's *El Mundo* addressed this point: "Professor Manuel Maldonado Denis, a picket against the ROTC, is now in Havana." According to *El Mundo*, the professor was permitted to go to Cuba by Dean Robert Anderson of the university's Department of Social Sciences and Dr. Thomas G. Matthews, Director of the Department. *El Mundo* commented: "But more important, the cost of the trip is paid by the Ford Foundation."

All this, taken together with the other evidence of Communist-inspired violence, numerous acts of incendiarism against retail stores and the sugar cane fields, gave rise in Puerto Rico to the feeling that an onslaught was certain to follow the OLAS conference. The explosive situation was assessed by no less an authority than FBI chief J. Edgar Hoover, who told the House Appropriations Committee: "The potential for violence in Puerto Rico has changed radically in the past years" because "Fidel Castro's rise to power in Cuba has encouraged Puerto Rican revolutionaries and there has been a definite turning of these independence advocates to Cuba and international Communism for leadership and the funds and arms with which to mount an armed insurrection in Puerto Rico."[11]

Mr. Hoover's assessment of the situation was especially important because it concerned an area that he did not normally touch upon. For two decades Puerto Rico has been held up by liberal elements in this country as *the* shining example of how to undercut Communist influence through economic measures. During those two decades, favorable tax considerations and the availability of a large labor force have taken the Puerto Ricans out of grinding poverty and elevated their personal incomes spectacularly. But the facts so starkly put into relief by the FBI Director indicated that with all its new-found affluence Puerto Rico cannot depend on economic and social advancement alone to protect it from infiltration and subversion. In other words, Puerto Rico told theoreticians and Alliance for Progress officials in this country what sensible people already know—that the Communists can destroy what a free society can build.

The "Resolution on Puerto Rico" that came out of the OLAS conference addresses this point: It says: "The peoples of Puerto Rico are waging an identical battle to make it possible for the sacred territory of Puerto

Rico to be counted among the liberated peoples of the continent . . . it is being trampled by the U.S. Armed Forces that have established scores of bases and other military establishments for aggression against other Latin American nations."[12]

That the OLAS resolution was responsive to Communist efforts to envelop our military flank in the Caribbean is evident in appeals to Puerto Rico's Spanish heritage: "The Puerto Ricans are reclaiming their indisputable status as Latin Americans . . . and are prepared to play their part in the continental struggle against Yankee imperialism." The resolution speaks of internal subversion as a means of doing so: "They are carrying out within the very fortress of the empire the revolutionary struggle we have taken in order to liquidate it." The text ends on a note calling for "resolute support for the struggle being led by the patriotic Puerto Rican vanguard, the PMI, aimed at expelling U.S. imperialism from Puerto Rican territory."[13]

Juan Mari Bras returned to San Juan from Havana's OLAS conference and warned that acts of violence would increase "if Puerto Rico is not recognized as a sovereign and independent country."[14] On September 27 the FUPI responded by erupting the most destructive riot in the history of the university, and used "university autonomy" as a weapon of defense. This autonomy prevents the police from entering university grounds. The *San Juan Star* editorialized on FUPI maneuvers in its September 27, 1967, edition, saying: "University autonomy does *not* intend providing a privileged bastion from which groups of agitators can wage war with impunity and take shelter after having committed acts against society for which other citizens would be jailed," and spoke of the seriousness of the riot in somber tones: "The rioting and shooting at the University of Puerto Rico's Río Piedras campus was both frightening and degrading . . . there could easily have been a massacre." Two persons were wounded by gun fire, one killed, and 40, including 21 policemen, were wounded by hurled bottles, stones and Molotov cocktails. FUPI's goons simply took over the campus and immobilized university authorities.

There was evidence that the FUPI riots were coordinated with other acts of terrorism which broke out around the island. Saboteurs struck everywhere in a virtual reign of terror. Police superintendent Salvador Rodríguez Aponte linked the burning down of three department stores to directives issued from Havana, saying: "The riot and the fires at Bargain Town in Carolina, and Kresge's and Belk-Linday in Bayamon coincide with directives issued at the OLAS session."[15] Significantly, most of the sabotage was directed at U.S. mainland-owned stores as a gesture to the Puerto Ricans that they were to be spared, and as a threat to American investors to withdraw from the island. A quick check by police indicated that this was indeed the tactic being followed. They found two unexploded incendiary devices in the mainland-owned Grand Union supermarket and two more in the Sea-Land warehouse. National Police Headquarters then gave detailed instructions to all mainland-owned stores to inspect their premises at least twice a day.

A conscious effort has been made by the island government to underplay terrorism, presumably because of what the stories might do to Puerto Rico's enormous tourist business and to investments in general. Furthermore, the government is firmly committed to what amounts to an Alliance for Progress in Puerto Rico. However that might be, stores in just one shopping center, Bargain Town, were bombed to the tune of $5 million in damages in less than three years' time. Three time bombs went off in a dressing room at San Juan Stadium while 4,000 spectators were told by a radio announcer that the noise was caused by malfunctioning electrical transformers. The Uni-Royal tire recapping plant was burned to the ground, and dispatches coming from the interior of the island told of sugar cane being burned by live phosphorus on an unheard-of scale. Confused by the scope of the sabotage, police went to one area to investigate fire-bombings and shootings, and then had to race somewhere else to meet other terrorists activities.

Juan Mari Bras was not confused, however. He answered a statement by the Police Superintendent linking the PMI to the OLAS and the outbreak of terrorism, by saying: "We will continue to maintain that the imperialist violence which is aimed to drown out all our nationalistic sentiments and opinions will foment more violence," adding: "Violence brought up by the colonialist interventionist regime breeds more violence. To understand this is to understand a reality and we denounce it as our duty as a patriotic vanguard."[16] Fire Chief Raúl Gándara was disavowed by the island government when he said: "In Puerto Rico we are having problems, and it will not help by hiding it. We must realize that there is a small group of terrorists that under the inspiration of Cuba is trying to destroy the peace of our country."[17] He also said that most of the terrorists were not even students in the FUPI. The measure of concern with which the business community viewed these events finally erupted when Puerto Rico's Better Business Bureau took matters in its own hands and ran advertisements in the newspapers offering $12,000 in cash awards for "information leading to the arrest and conviction of arsonists and bomb terrorists."[18]*

The State Department was roundly criticized by the newspapers for its refusal to revoke the passports of Mari Bras and his lieutenants who travelled to Cuba. And Puerto Rican editorial leaders found the State

*The Puerto Rican Telephone Co., a division of IT&T, offered rewards of $10,000 for the apprehension of saboteurs to its lines and facilities.

Department's refusal all the more inexplicable in the face of the knowledge that the "Free Puerto Rico" embassy in Havana was a creature of Mari Bras and his PMI. And when a Communist cultural meeting was held in Havana in early January 1968, Puerto Rico's newspapers identified three Puerto Ricans attending it, Emilio Díaz Valcarcel, Marcos Rodríguez and Professor Maldonado Denis, and called for action against them. The State Department replied that it had to have proof that they were actually in Cuba. A State Department spokesman "explained" that Carmichael's and George Ware's passports were revoked because two U.S. newspapermen had testified to seeing them at the OLAS conference, but it would have been a simple matter to check the manifests of planes that took Mari Bras and his lieutenants to Madrid and to Prague, and from there back and forth to Cuba. The *San Juan Star* remarked with incredulity on January 14, 1968: "The State Department was unable to explain the difference in treatment accorded black power advocate Stokely Carmichael and George Ware and that of a group of Puerto Ricans—believed to be half a dozen—all of whom attended the Havana conference in August." After reporting the State Department spokesman's claims that Carmichael and Ware were singled out because they had attracted so much attention, the *Star* protested: "However, Mari Bras, head of the Pro-Independence Movement and one of those who attended the August conference, also received considerable publicity while in Cuba and his passport was never revoked."

But the issue of seditious behaviour goes far beyond the mere revoking of passports.* Both Ware and Carmichael were handled with extraordinary care by federal authorities upon their return to the United States. Despite assertions by the State Department that their subversive intentions while in Havana were very much on record, Under Secretary of State Nicholas Katzenbach waited until the very day that Carmichael returned to the United States from his ill-will tour of several months to ask Congress for authority to punish him and other travellers to Communist countries where travel is prohibited. Curiously enough, Katzenbach's request to Congress was made on December 11 as the Congress was about to adjourn, making it impossible for action to be taken until some time in 1968. And his request was modest indeed, asking merely for authority to fine Carmichael up to $1,000 and a jail term of one year.

Representative Paul Rogers, Senator Strom Thurmond and many others in Congress were outraged at the weakness of the State Department and demanded that action be taken on the basis of existing laws. Joseph O'Meara, dean of the law school at the University of Notre Dame pointed out in the December 1967 issue of the *American Bar Journal* that sedition could be punished without the request made by Katzenbach.

*Now reversed by a Supreme Court ruling.

In doing so, professor O'Meara included the Rev. Martin Luther King as well as Stokely Carmichael among those liable to prosecution for sedition. He based his findings on a Supreme Court ruling back in 1919 which upheld the conviction of Charles T. Schenk of New York for persuading youths to dodge the military draft by his calling the draft "despotism." O'Meara remarked that the statements made by Carmichael and King were much more inflammatory than those made by Schenk, and more likely to induce American youths to burn their draft cards.[19]

In August 1967, Republican Representative William C. Cramer of Florida joined other law makers in demanding that federal authorities stop Communist-led rioting in the streets of this country, and introduced a bill in Congress to this effect. Almost half of Cramer's testimony before the Senate Judiciary Committee was devoted to Stokely Carmichael and other members of SNCC and their highly publicized trips to Communist countries. He charged that rioters know how to make Molotov cocktails because they learned the art at Guerrilla camps in Cuba. Evidence that city riots are a part of a Communist conspiracy is "overwhelming," Cramer said. He scored those who objected to his bill on the grounds that it might inhibit free speech, saying: "Those objectors assume, erroneously, apparently, that inciting to riot is a form of speech protected by the Constitution." A stiff riot control bill is needed in this country, said Cramer, because social programs are not adequate to handle the criminal elements who lead the riots. Those programs, "assume falsely," said Cramer, "that individuals who make it their business to travel from state to state for the purpose of stirring up urban warfare will be persuaded to halt their nefarious activities by stepped-up antipoverty efforts or by effectuating long-range massive federal-aid efforts, which if done would take time to get results, assuming of course that they would be effective."[20]

Professor O'Meara's direct reference to Martin Luther King as a seditious person brings up the dramatic turn in King's nonviolent approach to civil rights. On March 30, 1967, King's directors of his Southern Christian Leadership Conference condemned the war in Vietnam and said that U.S. involvement there was morally and politically unjust. They went a step farther, claiming that the war was being fought by racially exclusive draft boards and pledged themselves to do everything in their power to bring the war to an end. On April 4, King rose on the speaker's stand in New York City's Riverside Church and delivered what ranks as perhaps the greatest condemnation of American policy in Vietnam ever to come from a well-known U.S. citizen. Suddenly, for King, the North Vietnamese became his allies in the civil rights movement and, ignoring totally the terrorist activities of the Viet Cong and their North

Vietnamese champions, he said that the United States is "the greatest purveyor of violence in the world today." King's followers helped form an organization calling itself the Spring Mobilization Committee and staged mass rallies to end the war. And the number one attraction at the New York meeting on April 15—billed ahead of Stokely Carmichael— was Martin Luther King.

The curious, indeed ominous, concordance between Martin Luther King's civil right movement and Communist objectives to end the war in Vietnam brings sharply to mind Havana's Tricontinental Resolution which urges U.S. Negroes to "develop in every way demonstrations, rallies of protest, boycott against the loading and transportation of arms and war materials to North American troops. . . ." There is a striking parallelism between the views of Mr. King and those expressed in the Tricontinental Conference resolutions.

> Havana, 1966: "The Afro-Americans are being shipped off to fight in Vietnam. For each white American, the imperialists send two Afro-Americans."
> King, 1967: "Twice as many Negroes as whites are in combat."
> Havana, 1966: "North American aggressors deliberately use new scientific discoveries . . . toxic gases that kill the forests."
> King, 1967: "We kill a million acres of their crops, poison their water."
> Havana, 1966: "The invading forces in Vietnam have competed—even surpassed—the barbaric actions of Hitler's hordes . . . mutilations, savage tortures, mass assassinations."
> King, 1967: "We try new weapons on them, just as the Germans tested out new medicines and new tortures in the concentration camps of Europe."

And King's "solution" to the war in Vietnam contained in his April 4 speech is virtually a carbon copy of demands made at the Tricontinental Conference one year earlier. Of course, all of this may be mere coincidence—King's militancy, the linking of civil rights with the Communist objectives to stop the war—stop the anti-Communist side, that is—in Vietnam, but there are many who apparently do not believe so. Carl T. Rowan, a Negro and former Director of the U.S. Information Agency, said that King had "created doubt about the Negro's loyalty to this country." Declaring that "talk of Communists influencing the actions and words of the young minister" had been revived, Rowan stated: "I report this not to endorse what King and many others will consider a 'guilt by association' smear, but because of the threat that these represent to the civil rights movement."[21] Rowan also pointed out that "most Negroes are proud of the integrated performance of colored G.I.s in

Vietnam." Rowan received an indirect answer from Robert Williams. Having removed his base of operations from Havana to Peking, Williams issued a magazine, *The Crusader,* which in a stroke of psychological warfare, called on Negro soldiers to kill their white comrades in arms. Thousands of copies were found by federal and local authorities throughout the United States where the section on killing white soldiers was widely read.

It reads: "They [the Negroes] must eliminate . . . as many as possible of their true enemies [the whites] so that these racists cannot return to the United States and mistreat and eliminate the Negro people there in the same way they are trying to exterminate the people of Vietnam."[22] The pamphlet also contained detailed instructions for the manufacture of Molotov cocktails and homemade weapons, enumerating some of them as "lye and acid bombs (by injecting lye or acid in the metal ends of light bulbs) . . . high-powered sniper rifles . . . armor-piercing bullets. . . ."[23] In Washington, a spokesman for President Johnson's Commission on Civil Disorder said that "outside agitators" were involved in the 1967 riots in Detroit, Newark, Milwaukee and elsewhere, but denied that they had any evidence of a national conspiracy. But in city after city where Negro outbreaks erupted officials spoke of a pattern indicating a nationwide guerrilla-warfare plot. H. Rap Brown and Stokely Carmichael were involved in rioting in Cincinnati and other cities which were hard hit by what clearly was urban guerrilla warfare.

On April 4, 1968 the Reverend Martin Luther King, Jr. was shot to death on the balcony of the Lorraine Motel in Memphis, Tennessee. Though he was an apostle of nonviolence, his mere appearance as a leader of a civil rights march often signalled the beginning of destructive and unlawful acts of violence. One such outburst attended his attempt to hold peaceful demonstrations in favor of striking garbage workers in Memphis just a few days before his death. With the outburst of violence, King sprinted down a side street to a waiting car. And he said that he would defy a Federal injunction against another march and he planned to do so when he was shot to death. There is no question that Martin Luther King was the instigator of civil disobedience just as much as he was the apostle of nonviolence. He preached civil disobedience by travelling around the country and telling people to disobey laws that they consider "immoral." What this meant, of course, is that under the King interpretation each man would be free to determine for himself which laws fitted his individual standard of conduct and were to be obeyed. It seems obvious that civil disobedience provides the philosophical basis for violence, for the failure to obey the law brings reprisals which in turn provokes the very violence that King professed to abhor.

Mr. King's rise to fame started back in 1955 when Mrs. Rosa Parks, a Negro, refused to move to the back of a bus in Montgomery, Alabama because her feet were tired. This set off a chain of events. King, a newly assigned pastor to the city, provided the voice and the leadership which resulted in the famous 12-month Montgomery boycott by Negroes of the segregated bus system and ended in breaking that segregation. Catapulted to national prominence, Martin Luther King pursued a career which was as much political as it was religious. He reached the peak of international respect in 1964 when awarded the Nobel Peace Prize for his Montgomery campaign, the youngest recipient (at age 36) ever to receive it.

King took the opportunity and the podium provided by the Nobel Institute to outline his doctrine of civil disobedience, saying that he would counsel people not to obey laws or submit to practices which he considered unjust. He subsequently included in this doctrine opposition to American attempts to stem the Communist tide in South Vietnam. He escalated civil disobedience to where it was virtually indistinguishable from a call to violence and, ironically, was struck down violently at the scene of violence of his own making.

And on June 5, 1968, a 24-year-old native of Jordon, described as unremorseful and occasionally flippant under interrogation, shot Senator Robert F. Kennedy as he was celebrating a razor-thin primary victory over Senator Eugene McCarthy. The two were vying for the Democratic bid for the presidency in 1968. Sirhan Bishara Sirhan shot Kennedy with a .22 caliber pistol in the Ambassador Hotel in Los Angeles, and the 42-year-old Senator died of his wounds about 24 hours following the shooting. Leaving the ballroom of the hotel, Kennedy had gone into a kitchen corridor. There he was felled—and five others hit—by a fusillade of eight bullets emptied from the revolver.

The tragedy brought a great out-pouring of self-flagellation from a great number of people, including comments that the United States is "a sick country" and the like. Most of that comment came from liberal-leftist elements. However, as Senator John McClellan of Arkansas correctly pointed out in a television interview the day that Senator Kennedy's death was announced, it was the failure of federal authorities to enforce the law that led to excesses of lawlessness. Kennedy was struck down precisely during a period when lawlessness in our nation's capital was at an all-time high. The Southern Christian Leadership Conference, now headed by Reverend Ralph Abernathy, led a group of Negroes, whites and Mexican-Americans into Washington, D.C. Designated by Abernathy as "The Poor Peoples' March," the group frankly said it would camp in the nation's capital to intimidate Congress into passing legislation which the SCLC wanted on the books.

Marchers first demonstrated before and then stoned the Supreme

Court building. They disported themselves in the fountain in front of it and hauled down the American flag, and tried to raise a Red banner. A bus driver was killed during this period and buses did not run at night for weeks, as fearful drivers refused to carry $100 in change which they considered was bait for bandits. And at almost the same time, hour and date that Senator Kennedy was struck down in Los Angeles, two Marine Corps officers were shot down by three Negroes at a hamburger stand in Washington, D.C. The officers, students at nearby Quantico Marine Base, had been to a formal dinner and were attired in summer white dress uniforms as they entered the Little Tavern hamburger shop for coffee. Three men entered, insulted the Marines for their military careers and made fun of the uniforms they were wearing.

Words were exchanged. The three bearded Negroes moved to leave the restaurant, then turned and drew revolvers and shot wildly at the Marines, killing Second Lieutenants William F. King Jr. and Thaddeus Lesnick and wounding two others who were with them. A police check found one of the murderers to be a "black militant" and the other two to be members of the Black Student Union. All had come to Washington to join the "Poor People's March" and were scheduled to move into "Resurrection City," a shanty town erected on the Lincoln Memorial Mall, to house the marchers.

A series of newspaper accounts in Washington turned up the information that the initial lack of support given to the marchers, particularly by the Washington's Negro community, prompted Reverend Abernathy to accept in his ranks Negro youth gangs, among them the Blackstone Rangers from Chicago and the Invaders from Memphis. The Invaders were prominent in the Memphis riots that led to the federal injunction issued to prevent Martin Luther King from holding another attempt at a non-violent march. Invaders' leader, "Sweet Willie," gathered his gang around him and went from "Resurrection City" to Anacostia, a Washington suburb, and on May 21 terrorized Ballou High School, set off firecrackers, rang the fire alarms and demanded that the school staff call an assembly. Yet, none of the gang was arrested and Ralph Abernathy said he intended to carry on with a system at "Resurrection City" under which most of the police duties were turned over to such youth gangs.

But what was at the bottom of all this trouble? Not a "sick America" nor, as Arthur Schlesinger, Jr. said following the death of Senator Kennedy, that "we are a violent people." It goes back to incidents such as the Negro march on Washington in 1963. In urging passage of civil rights legislation at that time, President John F. Kennedy said: "Wrongs are inflicted on Negro citizens for which there are no remedies at law. Unless the Congress acts, their only remedy is in the streets." Vice President Humphrey and other officials have tried to intimidate Congress (and with some success) by threatening violence should this or that social legislation not be passed. Threatened Humphrey: "We will have open violence in every major city and county in America" if new welfare programs were not passed. And Representative Emanuel Celler also made similar threats. These are totalitarian liberal minds which, failing to attain their goal through intellectual persuasion and dialogue, resort to the threat of intimidation, and strike at the very rule of law and order which, as elected representatives of the people, they have solemnly sworn to uphold.

It is little wonder, then, that the SCLC, Carmichael's Black United Front and youth gangs feel that intimidation is a modern political weapon and that violence is its night-stick to be used with impunity.

President Johnson chose to meet calculated subversive attacks on law and order largely through sociological programs. Addressing the nation from the White House on July 27, 1967, the President did say that the looting, arson and plunder which occurred during the riots were not part of any civil rights protest, and warned that "crime must be dealt with forcefully and swiftly, and certainly under law." Having said this, however, he added: "Not even the sternest police action, nor the most effective federal troops, can ever create lasting peace in our cities. The only genuine long-range solution for what has happened lies in attack—mounted at every level—upn the conditions that breed despair and violence." Laudable though his social programs might be, what the President of the United States had done in his address was to cloak Negro subversives with a mantle of righteousness, to hand them the very weapon they needed to justify their lawless actions and to downgrade evidence of subversion. Equally important, President Johnson made no effort in his speech to split off and isolate Negro militants from the masses, but instead seemed to identify them with the whole of the Negro population, when in fact the bulk of the Negroes needed and wanted protection from Black Power bullies who knocked on their doors and forced them to buy militant literature and support their aims. The President did not grapple with the problem because as a "consensus" politician he perhaps found direct reference to Black Power militants, and even to the Negroes, as the object of his speech, politically undesirable. And it is just possible that President Johnson's speech will go down in history as a missed opportunity to save this country.

U.S. News & World Report saw the matter in a different light, carrying a story headline in its August 14, 1967, issue: "Is Castro Behind Guerrilla War In U.S. Cities?" The magazine said: "Americans to date have given little heed to Fidel Castro's boast that guerrilla war would be waged in the U.S. Now this is changing. With more than 100 cities rocked by Negro riots, large areas going up in smoke, bands of snipers using guerrilla tactics in city after city, Castro's claims are taking on new dimensions."[24] Similar alarm was voiced in the Senate and the House of Representatives. Democratic Congressman Armistead I. Selden, Jr. of Alabama told Congress on July 31: "The presence of Stokely Carmichael in Havana clearly establishes the ideological link between the organized violence taking place in our major cities and Fidel Castro's plans to subvert and overthrow existing Latin American governments." Republican Senator Peter Dominick of Colorado noted Carmichael's presence in Cuba and said that "it is about time to sound the alarm bells to awaken our leaders and our people to the menace of expanding aggression in this Hemisphere."[25] Speaking at the inaugural dinner of the new Center for Inter-American Relations in New York City, Vice President Hubert H. Humphrey gratuitously pushed the Johnson administration into a corner, saying: "What concerns me is that progress may not be fast enough to sustain hopes that have been aroused."[26] Humphrey seemed oblivious to the fact that speeches such as his and the President's were made to order for exploitation in the form of insatiable demands by Negro subversives.

The connection between what radical liberals allege to be a depressed and deprived Negro community on the one hand and urban guerrilla warfare on the other is questionable. Many of the Negro looters during the summer 1967 riots were neither economically deprived nor socially maladjusted. Many in Detroit and elsewhere where the looting and burning was the most severe had jobs with medium or higher incomes. Yet, all, or nearly all, had been lumped into the "deprived" category by administration leaders. Here is what Michigan Congressman Gerald Ford had to say about the rioting in Detroit: "We had high employment, we had high median income, we had 220 million dollars in federal funds in the last 12 months in Detroit . . . and we had the worst riot in the history of the United States." *U.S. News & World Report* commented in its August 14, 1967, edition: "The Wall Street Journal quoted a Detroit police detective as making this comment: 'A good number of the guys we pulled in for looting worked steady at Ford, Chrysler and General Motors over the past three or four years. They were making $125 and $150 a week. And in some of the stores we saw looters driving off in new Cadillacs and Thunderbirds.' "[27] In the Detroit suburb of Highland Park, police said that of 111 looters arrested, 105 had jobs and late model cars.

Black Power leaders incited the most severe riots in Dayton and Cincinnati, Ohio, Nashville, Tennessee, Cambridge, Maryland and elsewhere in the country. Here is how Cincinnati Police Chief Jacob W. Schott described Brown's activities in riots there: "On June 15 H. Rap Brown came into Cincinnati from Dayton, Ohio, where he appeared the night before and started a minor race riot up there. He came to Cincinnati and he appeared at the Black Guard Society.

"They had guards on the door. They wouldn't allow any white people there, but we did get some intelligence out of there, and he stated that the city of Cincinnati had declared war on the Negro and that they would have to fight back. H. Rap Brown then presented 20 demands. . . . Some of those demands were, 'Get rid of white school administrators; get white merchants out of the black communities; release all black prisoners picked up during this crisis; there will be no charges on them and no records; all white landlords out of the black community.' "[28]

And a preview of what might happen to funds to go into President Johnson's attempts to undercut Negro subversives was provided when, at a Senate hearing investigating the riots, it was revealed that federal funds from the Office of Economic Opportunity had been earmarked for use by the North Nashville Student Summer Project. Its director, Fred Brooks, turned out to be a member of Carmichael's SNCC. One project for which Brooks intended to use the money was to help a "liberation school" teaching Negroes about their heritage and also to hate the white man. Indeed, Senate investigators discovered at the hearing that some of the Negro rioters in Nashville were teachers in the "liberation school." The Office of Economic Opportunity scurried around and replied through a Nashville official that the money had been budgeted but still awaited final approval.*

The popular image of rioters as poverty-stricken, uneducated and unemployed Negroes proved false in riots which hit Washington, D.C. in the aftermath of the shooting of Martin Luther King. *The Washington Post* reported on April 8, 1968: "The first riot suspects in court here yield a portrait of a typical suspect about 29, who attended 11 grades of school, has a job paying $85 to $95 a week, and has not been in trouble with the law before . . . the first sampling shows more than half the adult riot suspects were married." Many were carrying more than $50 in their pockets. Police withheld from an immediate crack-down and television cameras actually showed some law enforcement officers, acting under orders, helping looters away from the scene of their crimes so as not to provoke more violence. Looting and rioting hit 125 cities where 46 people died, 2,600 were injured and 21,700 arrested. Property damage was estimated at $45 million. More than 55,000 troops were called out. A young Negro girl skipped gaily past the heavily guarded White House, taunting the guards by waving a bright yellow blouse and shouting: "I stole this. Go ahead and shoot me!" Marine units were dispatched to Capitol Hill to curb violence described in the April 22, 1968 issue of *U.S. News & World Report* as "The Second Sacking of Washington" (the first was by the British in August of 1814). Yet, in line with impassioned pleas

---

*In the summer of 1968, Senate hearings turned up the fact that nearly $1 million in OEO funds were given to Chicago's Negro street gangs. Testimony revealed that the money was used to buy drugs and arms.

by Vice President Humphrey, Bobby Kennedy and others, the riots were blamed on poor economic conditions of the Negro. Under a barrage of intimidation by "liberals," shortly thereafter Congress pushed through an open-housing bill which, like other civil rights legislation before it, is hardly likely to quell riots, or address the threat posed by advocates of Black Power and their Communist mentors in Cuba.

Unmistakable evidence that Communist Cuba is deeply involved in the subversive work of the Black Power groups in this country again came to light on January 11, 1968, when H. Rap Brown took sanctuary inside the Cuban Mission to the United Nations for nearly six hours after a policeman tried to arrest him, following a shoving match on the street outside. Brown was carrying a large bundle out of the Mission when patrolman Richard Gleason spotted him and asked what was in the package. Brown refused to answer, and when officer Gleason moved to apprehend him for questioning, the Black Power leader ran quickly back into the Cuban UN Mission while an armed Cuban guard held the door open for him. The day before, Carmichael was in Washington where he organized the "Black United Front."[29]

The late Martin Luther King's Washington representative, Walter E. Fauntroy, attended that meeting, along with representatives from a number of Negro groups. Fauntroy also was vice chairman of the City Council of Washington, D.C. Details are lacking because of the secrecy in which the meeting was held. Enough leaked out, however, to reveal plans by the "Black United Front" to station militants in every Negro neighborhood in the country and organize what amounts to cells whose armed members constitute what Carmichael referred to in Havana as the "nucleus" of armed insurrection aimed at the overthrow of American society. And in view of the Cuban UN Mission's record of supporting subversion of the U.S. Negro community, there is every reason to believe that the big package which was so carefully guarded by H. Rap Brown contained large amounts of money or drugs to finance Carmichael's "Black United Front."

It is clear that Black Power militants plan to use the U.S. Negro to further Communist aims elsewhere in the world, and a clarification of this role came on December 6, 1967. On that date, Brown held a press conference in the offices of the Methodist Church, in the church center of the United Nations, and told reporters he would form an "African-American International Military Brigade" to fight within South West Africa against South African control. He announced that he planned to have American Negro guerrillas prepared to go at some indefinite time in the future, but did not say how they would be recruited or trained, and avoided any mention of how the costly operation would be funded. What cannot be avoided by both Brown and Carmichael, however, is that by their statements the "Black United Front" has removed itself from even a marginal interest in raising the economic and social status of the American Negro. They had locked their movement on a direct course of Communist conquest in an alliance with the Havana-based OLAS and guerrilla movements, specifically the murderous cutthroats in Latin America.

The suddenness with which the Communists take advantage of hesitation, confusion, and the delayed reflexes of "consensus" politicians make it entirely possible that the SNCC-backed Tricontinental Information Center will invite Latin American guerrillas to speak in New York City. And by the time they do so, it also is just possible that the initial shock of the event will have been dissipated through what now is an apparent acceptance by administration leaders (as expressed by Vice President Humphrey) that Latin guerrilla organizations are but manifestations of social unrest in their countries. Indeed, a move already has been made in that direction with no response forthcoming from federal authorities. As of this writing, the TIC already has sponsored appearances of Puerto Rican subversives in its headquarters, including Juan Angel Silen, President of the PMI Youth, who again sketched some dimensions to Communist strategy in the Caribbean, saying: "Puerto Rico . . . geographically belongs to the Great Antilles and together with Cuba and the Dominican Republic represent the first Spanish stronghold in America . . . and today is a military and economic base of aggression of North American imperialism . . . with the Vietnam war we are now exploited as cannon fodder . . ."[30] and so on. Unchecked, a steady propaganda offensive can have considerable effect on the million or more Puerto Ricans, many of them Negroes, in New York City.

Communists have been successful in forging a union of Latin American guerrillas with subversives in mainland United States and Puerto Rico in Washington because theories take precedence over facts. And this is true of more than one level of the United States Government. For example, in January 1968 the Senate Foreign Relations Committee issued a study on guerrilla movements in Latin America in terms that define the enemy as being on the right. The committee made all haste in implying that "right-wing" elements were responsible for the machine-gunning and killing of two U.S. military aides to the U.S. Embassy in Guatemala. And the committee did so in the face of the knowledge that the names of the two Americans—Colonel John D. Webber, Jr. and Lieutenant Commander Ernest A. Munro—were on a "kill" list published by the Castroite FAR, Rebel Armed Forces, and that the guerrilla group issued a communique claiming credit for the brutal assassinations. Moreover, the murders were part of a general plan to eliminate American military advisers throughout Latin America because, as Guatemalan guerrilla chieftain Marco Yon Sosa told a local television reporter, the United States is helping Latin American governments in their struggle against the guerrillas. Yet, the Senate study took some undoubted evidence of "right-wing" extremism completely out of context in what resulted in absolving the Soviet satropy in Cuba of blame.

Peter Laine of the Knight Newspapers summed up the committee report in a dispatch carried over a Washington dateline: "The tiger of terrorism stalking Guatemala has right-wing marks and was unleashed by the government, according to an analysis released here . . . at least ten anti-Communist groups have been formed—all defining communism, . . . the committee report states, 'broadly and unprecisely.' "[31] This, then, was how the Committee's views impinged themselves on the press. A reading of the report itself reveals that it is specific in its condemnation of the right-wing, but addresses Castroite terrorists in the language of the sociologist. The report was prepared by David Burks, identified as a professor at Indiana University. Professor Burks splashed his fingers over a typewriter keyboard and produced the standard cliche of the "losers":Communist tentacles cannot be pried loose from Latin America until "basic reforms" are made. And, of course, the Alliance for Progress is the answer. The danger of Castroite guerrillas is downgraded in the Committee report because they have failed to emulate Castro by seizing power.[32]

It is a fair question to ask how Mr. Burks and many, many Senate aides before him arrived at political truths from sociological premises. The idea behind the Alliance for Progress came originally from the Marshal Plan. But the Marshal Plan was based on a hard-headed decision to rebuild the bombed-out factories of Europe and to get Europe to producing again, while the Alliance for Progress has become a laboratory in which sociologists tinker and experiment with theories they stubbornly insist will produce political results that are nowhere even faintly visible. What makes this state of affairs particularly exasperating is that the fallacy of the theoreticians is glaring them right in the face in our own Commonwealth of Puerto Rico. It was no wonder, then, that the findings of Professor Burks were inked in the headlines of doom from Bogota's *El Espectador* to Buenos Aires' *Clarin:* "Guerrillas Cannot Be Eliminated, Says U.S. Expert." Many Latin politicians are opportunists. And while they pay lip service to the objectives expected of the Alliance for Progress because they want the money, they also know perfectly well that economic programs do not solve the problem of guerrilla conflicts. By carrying Burks' logic to its ultimate absurdity World War II was the consequence of President Franklin D. Roosevelt's failure to provide a truly underdeveloped Japan with an economic aid program to sap popular support for its militarists.

More than that, when their programs consistently fail to yield expected results the foreign affairs "expert" with a social worker mentality has a ready excuse—well, reforms have not come fast enough, or the "oligarchs" are obstructing progress, thus suggesting that a degree of intellectual dishonesty has been added to several degrees of ignorance of the subject he treats. Then an endorsement of the social worker concept of foreign relations is usually forthcoming from the *New York Times*. On January 27, 1968, to take one example, the *Times* editorialized on the topic, "Why the Alliance for Progress has failed by a substantial margin to meet its growth targets for Latin America for the second year in a row." Said the *Times:* "Some officials believe businessmen deliberately sabotaged the new measure by exploiting the initial confusion and by price gouging." So businessmen are to blame! It continues, "Here again is the problem of the Latin American oligarchies in micocosm . . . many of them equate Alliance for Progress goals with Communism. This leaves an enormous potential for Communist and Castroite agitation in a country where three-fourths of the people live in terrible poverty. It eventually breeds terrorism that brought on the despicable killing of the American officers." But facts are not as they are made to appear. For one thing, Guatemala had made great economic strides over the previous five years, precisely because of increased production by the business community described by the *Times* as "oligarchs." In fact, Guatemala was financially superior to the seven countries which comprise Central America countries, including the soundness of its currency, the quetzal, which was worth more than the U.S. dollar when the *Times* printed its editorial. The *Times* added another twist of left-wing accommodation to the editorial, saying: "This may explain why three other Americans—two priests and a nun from the Maryknoll Order—who went to Guatemala for educational missionary work finally joined left-wing guerrillas, despairing of accomplishing anything within Guatemala's existing social and political structure."

Two weeks later the nun married one of the priests, thus suggesting that their despair lay elsewhere.

The *real* enemy of democracy in Guatemala was identified in a January 18 *Times* editorial on the machine-gunning of the two American military officers. The *Times* conjectured that the attacks took place because "pro-Castro guerrillas, failing so far in their efforts to organize peasant revolts, have now embarked on a campaign of assassination against members of United States missions." The *Times* admits that the Castroite FAR claimed responsibility for the murders, but then spoke of "right-wing groups" in terms that leaves little doubt that to the *Times* at least *they* are the enemy. Twisting the evidence, the *Times* editorial says: "It is an ironic commentary on the Guatemalan situation that some * suspect that, irrespective of the F.A.R. claim, one of these right-wing groups may have murdered the officers in an attempt to provoke an American aided escalation against the left."**Yes, a right-wing was operating in Guatemala and has its reasons for doing so. The "losers" find it quite reasonable for guerrillas to fill a vacuum which, they allege, is created by economic want and social immobility, but find it quite unreasonable that right-wing groups should spring up to fill a vacuum caused when national authority fails to protect the nation from those same guerrillas. Neither would exist, of course, if the glowing political expectations of the Alliance for Progress had materialized over the six years of its operations in Guatemala. The major right-wing organization in Guatemala, *Mano Blanca* (White Hand), was formed for the sole purpose of eliminating Communists whom the President (a former university professor, by the way) had shown little stomach fully to confront. It is certain that the Communists do not agree with the Senate committee assessment that the *Mano Blanca* defines its enemies "broadly and unprecisely." If it did, the Communists would be more than happy to have the organization kill innocent people (as Castro was happy that Batista did) since this would turn the public against it. Instead, Havana urges its guerrilla arms—the Rebel Armed Forces and November 13 Revolutionary Movement, who have their differences, to forget them and face the *Mano Blanca* "in a united struggle." And they do.

A brief background. In the years preceding the 1966 presidential elections in Guatemala, the army had moved into the mountains where it dealt the guerrillas devastating blows. Badly hit, the guerrillas struck against the relatively vulnerable cities in a wave of kidnappings and street murders and in a four-month span of time made six major abductions, netting them ransom totalling almost half a million dollars. In the face of this, Presidential candidate Julio César Méndez Montenegro, an initial believer in the political efficacy of the Alliance for Progress, said in one

* Who? *Times* editorialists? People who read the *Times'* editorials?—but that is too ironic to contemplate.
** On August 28, 1968, U.S. Ambassador John Gordon Mein was brutally murdered by the Castroite Revolutionary Armed Forces. His car was forced to the side of the road and an attempt was made to abduct the Ambassador. He hit one of his would-be kidnappers in the face, made a run for it and was machine-gunned in the back. Mein was lying on the ground, still moving, so the terrorists shot him seven more times with pistols until he died. On August 31, Brazil's newspaper *Jornal do Brasil* said of the murder of the Ambassador that it was linked to Soviet efforts to bury its invasion of Czechoslovakia. "The method is to produce sensational news everywhere in the world to crowd out accounts of its [Russia's] acts in Central Europe. The murder of the U.S. Ambassador to Guatemala is an example. There will be many acts of this type in the future." What the paper is saying is that Latin terrorists, though allied directly with Fidel Castro, take orders from Moscow as well.

of his campaign addresses: "Faced with a regime enjoying wide popular support, the guerrillas will drop their attitude of belligerence." He then added in the voice of the social worker: "In some ways, I believe, they are operating as a gesture of rebellion against the present order of things."[33] And in an interview aired on February 4, 1966, over Miami's Television Channel Four, Méndez Montenegro was asked, "Do you think that Castro, Red China or Russia are trying to overthrow governments in Central America with the purpose of taking over?" And he replied: "I don't know. I just don't know." And when Méndez Montenegro was asked whether Cuban-supported guerrillas were strong in Guatemala, Méndez Montenegro replied: "I don't think so. No, I don't think so."

Elected President, Julio César Méndez Montenegro dedicated a portion of his July 1, 1966 inauguration speech to an offer of amnesty to the guerrillas. His answer came in another wave of bloody killings and, following three months of moves to appease the Castroite guerrillas, on November 4 the President was forced by the deteriorating military situation to declare martial law. His experiment in what amounted virtually to governing the nation through the philosophy preached by the Alliance for Progress was a bitter lesson indeed. More important is that during the three-month period many of the military advances made against the guerrillas, obtained at great sacrifice in men and treasure, had been seriously set back. But let it be clearly understood that right-wing groups, particularly the *Mano Blanca*, declared war on the Communists when Communist terrorism in many instances overwhelmed legal authority and threatened to sabotage out of existence the economic gains which had been made, due partially to the Alliance for Progress. Killings and machine-gunnings on the streets of Guatemala City by Communist gangs became virtually a spectator sport.

This catastrophe—a breakdown in law and order and the explosive emergence of the right-wing—would not have happened if, as the Senate Committee study implies, Castroite guerrilla bands had been neutralized. And it is highly unlikely that the *Mano Blanca* will disband in the foreseeable future because, in a January 16, 1968, specially prepared program, Radio Havana exhorted its puppets in Guatemala to intensify their guerrilla activities, saying: "Armed struggle is the only way . . . armed struggle must continue without cessation . . . until final victory!" And a message from the FAR, taped earlier, was broadcast in response: "The revolutionary war . . . is a continental war . . . leaping the frontiers," making it certain that the intensity of guerrilla warfare will rise, not fall, in the future. This is the atmosphere of violence in Latin American countries, to use the *Times* word, in "microcosm," which renders inoperable the sociological experiments of the American bureaucrat and professor. The only discernible effect they have had, and will continue to have under present conditions, is to add to an already intolerable bi-polarization of authority, and as a consequence to the possibility of final victory by the Communists.

It is not stretching a point out of shape to conjecture that the happenings in Latin America were watched carefully by intransigent Negro militants in the United States, themselves under close scrutiny by the Communists who planned to use them. The Tricontinental and OLAS resolutions appealing to the American Negro to riot are based on the Communist view that urban guerrilla wars can be stirred up in the United States. This is the final meaning of the union between Latin guerrillas and militant U.S. Negroes. Seen from the Communist point of view, the U.S. policy of offering economic aid and social programs to Latin America most certainly had made little headway against the guerrillas there. The Communists conjectured that the same means would be employed as the principle response to Negro violence in this country and believed that it would not work here either. And it may be surmised that the potential vote of 20 million Negroes, taken together with the power of pressure groups espousing "good causes," were counted on by our Communist enemies to stay the hand of the politician and give second thoughts to a "consensus" President.

In any event, the final truth of the Communist assessment that there would be a significant delay in federal action against Black Power leaders is embodied in President Johnson's July 27, 1967 address to the nation and underscored by Vice President Humphrey's New York speech which followed. The result is that our foreign policy chickens have come home to roost on rifle barrels in the hands of Negro militants. And the United States now finds itself besieged at home and in Latin America by an implacable enemy committed to the total destruction of the Free World.

For example, on August 15, 1968, Radio Havana's powerful 150,000 watt transmitters split the night air with this message: "Youths in the United States will force the Democratic Convention to quit the war in Vietnam." The vehicle for the broadcast was Dave Dellinger, billed as "organizer of the Committee for National Mobilization for Peace in Vietnam, and editor of 'Liberation' magazine.' " Dellinger responded to questions asked by telephone by an interviewer in Havana.

Question: "Your organization has announced a protest demonstration to be held in Chicago during the Democratic National Convention. Could you tell us the aims of such actions and just what they will consist of?"

Dellinger (in English, with simultaneous translation into Spanish): "Yes, the demonstrations will take place during a period of six days—from August 24 to August 29. We will show the people of the United

States and the Democratic Party that there cannot be peace and tranquility in the United States while the government continues its current foreign policy. [The following was emphasized in the transmission]: *Regardless of who the candidate is or what may be his platform, we will keep our active resistance in the streets until all U.S. soldiers return from Vietnam and the current policy of repression against the Negro community is halted!*"

Thus, in Dellinger's view, the demonstrations which broke out on Wednesday night, August 28, were intended to coerce the Democratic National Convention into accepting the views of the revolutionaries—or else!

Dellinger accused the United States of "a well-planned move to liquidate Negro leaders," adding: "the federal and state governments are carrying out a joint effort to eliminate, as well, many other youthful leaders." He named them as Huey Newton, sentenced in Oakland, California, on September 9 for murdering one policeman and wounding another, and Eldridge Cleaver, who served six years for attempted rape and assault to commit murder. Both are high-ranking members of the Black Panthers, an anti-social revolutionary organization.

As Dellinger prepared the Chicago demonstrations, two Black Panthers arrived in Cuba to attend a conference of "solidarity with the Afro-American people." The session was called by the Havana-based Asian-African-Latin American Solidarity Organization, the subversive movement dedicated to the overthrow of free governments everywhere. Honorary member: Stokely Charmichael.

At a press conference published in the August 22 edition of *Granma*, George Mason Murray said that Huey Newton was "being judged by the imperialist dogs of North America," and warned that a death penalty would mean that "no business, bank, industry or factory can be considered safe . . . nor the lives of senators, congressmen, presidential candidates, presidents, ex-presidents, generals, directors of banks. . . ."

Referring to Negroes, orientals and Latins living in the United States as people "colonized . . . by the capitalist beasts who control the power structure," Murray said the Black Panthers would "never put aside our rifles or cease making Molotov cocktails" until all had been freed ". . . through guerrilla warfare." The inspiration to launch guerrilla warfare, Murray said, came "from the people of Cuba and Vietnam."*

Dellinger also endorsed the Cuba-Vietnam corollary. Immediately following the August 28 riots in Chicago, he was again on the phone to Havana, and again his words were translated and broadcast throughout Latin America. He said: "When one fully comprehends the heroism and

---

*Murray was refused by San Francisco State College when he wanted to lecture upon his return from Cuba. Militants set off riots and the college President resigned.

dynamism, shared in common by Cuba and Vietnam, one has to stand up alongside these two tremendous sources of inspiration." And that Dellinger also endorses Vietnam-type wars in the United States is evidenced by his following statement: "The Americans are resolved to liberate their country in the same manner [as Cuba and the Vietcong]; and they will receive our support and solidarity in doing so."

Murray and Joudan Ford went from Havana to Guantanamo City, where they participated in seminars on political agitation and urban guerrilla warfare tactics. There, Murray addressed a gaggle of Communists from 32 countries: "Our view is that political power comes from the barrel of a revolver," adding: "We in the North look south and see the example of Cuba, the example Comandante Fidel Castro and Che Guevara has given us." He then shouted: "We agree with Guevara that it is necessary that we create two, three, or more 'Vietnams!'"

At 6:45 A.M. on September 11, Havana's Radio Progreso added Eldridge Cleaver and Bobby Seale to the growing list of American citizens crowding the Cuban air with anti-American statements. "Black Panther Minister of Education Eldridge Cleaver," said Radio Progreso, accused the United States "of liquidating Afro-American leaders, and said that the sentencing of Huey Newton was a good example." (Newton was not given capital punishment).

Like Dellinger, Cleaver and Seale were interviewed from Havana by phone and their messages broadcast in simultaneous Spanish translation. Seale, identified as "President of the Black Panther Party of the United States," told the Cubans: "Twenty thousand policemen and National Guard troops occupied the city of Oakland after the racist trial of our leader, Huey Newton." He charged that "Oakland police opened fire at the windows of Black Panther headquarters, the first of a series of provocations designed to start a new wave of repression. . . ."

Eldridge Cleaver said: "We will respond to counter-revolutionary violence with revolutionary violence." The balance of his statement, like the words of George Mason Murray, have a distinct ideological ring: "We ask peoples everywhere in the world to intensify their struggle against imperialism and colonialism. By overthrowing imperialism, we will gain our liberty and finish with the oppressive forces of the Gestapo."

Are these the words and actions of "youthful pacifists" who oppose the war in Vietnam? Or are they those of subversives who draw inspiration—and perhaps a great deal more than that—from the Vietcong and Castro's guerrillas?

The University of California announced in September of 1968 that Eldridge Cleaver would lecture a five-credit course called "Dehumanization and Regeneration of the American Social Order." The class was initiated by student members of the school's Center for Educational

Change, and approved by the faculty's Board of Education. A sample of Cleaver's English and qualifications for him to speak on "regeneration" was provided on August 2 in a speech given at the University of Southern California: "The pigs of the power structure say people are impotent . . . people get more guns than the pigs got guns. I don't say give me liberty or give me death; I say 'Give me liberty or I gonna pick up a gun.' There gonna be blood on the streets of Babylon."* These quotes were recorded in the September 21, 1968 issue of *Human Events.*

The contemporary history of the Communist advance in Latin America is, of course, but one manifestation among many of our disarray in the world. But Latin America has an added urgency by reason of geography and psychology, and Cuba has both strategic and tactical importance to our global political and military posture because it holds the key to power in the Caribbean and Central and South America. Until the aborted Bay of Pigs invasion, the chief strategic advantage held by the United States lay in it many overseas bases and in its security at home. This situation is being reversed. Today, the political arm of the Kremlin, the Communist parties, stand in the Western Hemisphere, along with Soviet and satellite embassies and trade missions whose ultimate purpose needs no further elaboration. Yet, while the Communist attack is global in scope and strong of purpose, it can be repelled if the enemy is forced to fight in his own backyard for a change.

If the United States is to reverse its string of defeats and the accompanying erosion of its position around the world it must first reverse the direction of its politicians and diplomats. In short, we must throw the old concepts of world conduct out the window and form a philosophy of ideological and physical combat which is responsive to the new world situation. For what the past eight years in particular have taught us, if they indeed have taught us anything, is that the traditional concepts of collective security, trade with the Soviet-bloc and the like, treats as though with national entities when in fact the enemy is a totalitarian subversive movement to whom national boundaries mean very little except as they are employed in some fashion toward the total destruction of all non-Communist societies—for example, as sanctuaries. What imperils the United States is a small group of Communists who have captured power in Russia and elsewhere, but whose identity with the countries in which they reside has little more than circumstantial meaning. And the blunt truth is that they will cease to menace us only as they cease to be Communists.

Our goal ought to be as total as theirs, but moral and practical consid-

---

*In November of 1968 Cleaver, under previous federal indictment, fled, possibly out of the United States.

erations rule this out. A better goal, then, is not the elimination of the Soviet Union as a national power, for example, but the elimination of Communists already in power there and elsewhere and the denial of power to those trying to achieve it. To take the first step in this direction, we must create a climate of victory and peace—victory over the Communists and peace with the people they hold captive. We must gain the confidence of the inarticulate masses by meaning and doing what we say. An indispensable first step in this direction is to stop assuring the Communist elite of our perpetual "good will." Our overseas propaganda must be unrelenting in its attacks upon the Communist doctrine and specific in bludgeoning Communist leaders for every act of political repression and religious persecution committed by them. It should be done in the forum provided by the United Nations and, to show we are in earnest, it must be done in private face-to-face conversations with diplomats of Communist countries. Let *us* walk out on a UN Security Council meeting when such a walk will dramatize a point. As a positive measure we must emphasize over and over—through all the means available to us—that the *United States is committed to the defense of free peoples* and that it does not consider Communist leaders to be the representatives of those peoples. This, then, is the attitude we should and must assume ourselves if we are to get across to those living under Communism.

There is no room for the social worker in this approach. What this strategy represents is an assessment that only by taking the offensive can we meet the Communist challenge to our own national security. The doctrine, if it can be called that, of the implacable Communist enemy hits him where he is most vulnerable because, for one thing, Communist doctrine perforce limits the numbers admitted to the club, so to speak. It has been estimated that only about 35 million Communists rule more than one billion people, and do so through second, third and fourth echelon bureaucrats who are kept in line by a combination of police-state intimidation and the promise that one day they too might be admitted to the club and climb the political ladder to position and power. What this means, of course, is that the whole power structure in a given Communist country is held together by a very thin but very powerful line of trusted Communist functionaries who live in a drab, grim atmosphere.

The Communists invariably try to make it look as though their Communism has its own distinctive national character, and evidence is produced from time to time in the form of real or contrived disputes with the Soviet Union. These disputes, rather than necessarily weakening the Communist system, may actually vitalize it because dissent sometimes shakes the bureaucrat and forces him to re-evaluate his position in more realistic terms. But there is never a dispute of sufficient magnitude to shatter the power structure, and a kind of self-governing mechanism between the Communist Parties of different countries stops the encounter safely before the catastrophe.* Members of the ruling class itself are, however, preoccupied with shoring up the failures of the system which they have created. They are always involved in a deadly fight for power and live in constant fear of assassination or replacement, terrified at the possibility of making an error, and are always ready to denounce a fellow official if it is expedient to do so.

What strikes those who are serious students of the Communist regime in Cuba is that the party functionaries are not particularly intelligent, a state of affairs that may be a reflection of the party membership elsewhere in the world. They are not expected to serve the people but are, in fact, automatoms in the machine of party discipline.

The personnel making up the Cuban Communist Party apparatus add to the weakness of the party. Those who sympathized with Batista find a natural answer to their totalitarian psychology by adhering to totalitarian Communism; the frustrated intellectual in a free society is a natural ally of an anti-capitalist doctrine; the *resentidos* and anti-social elements find the Communist power structure inviting because there is a use for their opportunistic talents somewhere in its vast organism. Those anti-Communist citizens who are already living under Communism and are important enough to snare because of their intellectual equipment, are wooed to serve the Party (but are seldom permitted to join) by a variety of inducements—money, position, diplomatic posts and the like. Persuaders are always present to induce the more reluctant to support the structure of power. One of the tragedies of life is that more often than not the opportunistic elements in the intellectual community of a Communist country have succumbed voluntarily to the system simply because they feel that they have no other place to go. And they are given certain carefully circumscribed liberties unknown to the average citizen living in a Communist society. They are the aphids to the Communist ant, and enjoy a security that their masters, always involved in life and death struggles in the party, do not. More important, however, is that in a Communist society they are not trusted, and by the very nature of their association with it, they reciprocate the distrust with a vengeance.

This, then, is the nature of the Communist "supermen" who, incredibly, have managed to capture some nations, to cow others and to make extensive inroads against a United States that is vastly superior to them in every way. And it is these Communist functionaries and the system that supports them that must be the object of our attack—never the national entities in which they reside. Our will to do so should be hard-

*Czechoslovakia, for example, where the Czechs learned to their sorrow that indigenous Communist leaders ultimately side with their bosses in the Soviet Union.

ened by the knowledge that Communists, to a man, harbor ideological obsessions that prevent them from living in peace with each other, much less with non-Communist nations. The tactics to fit the overall strategy are relatively simple, involving as they do unconventional warfare directed against the enemy by utilizing the many means available in paramilitary conflict. First, any overt provocation against the United States or even the interests of the United States must be met by a limited but sharp response. By propaganda and deed *the enemy must be conditioned to know that he can expect retaliation in one form or another for every overt act of aggression that he commits, and that the reprisals are intended not to trigger a general war.* The Communists have been successful in doing this since they came to power in Russia. As for the United States, the magnitude of a specific retaliatory measure must be made to fit the size of the deed. Once the enemy realizes that for each of his actions there will be a swift and effective counteraction, he will think much harder before committing himself to a peripheral target which often is designed to embarrass and denigrate the power and majesty of the United States.

Our strategists and tacticians must single out the danger spots of the world where Communist probes and thrusts are most likely to be made, analyze the probability of their size and purpose and be prepared to meet them unhesitatingly with a predetermined counter-thrust. Make it too risky for the aggressor to hit peripheral targets, and force him to contain his main thrust in a field of our own choosing. The situation might well have been different today if when the Communists in East Germany erected the Berlin Wall and the North Koreans captured the U.S. Navy vessel "Pueblo," we had met these incidents with a sharp counter blow against their source. We did not, and a peripheral encounter turned into a cheaply bought victory for the Communists and a sharp setback of respect for American power and will. The importance of these peripheral encounters is that our constant failure to respond to what clearly is designed as a denigrating move against us does indeed result in the attainment by the Communists of that very goal. Behind our thrusts we must always have the edge in conventional power to discourage even the thought by our enemies that they can get away with a counter-reprisal of their own without endangering their own power base.

Unconventional, or paramilitary, war does not represent a stepping down or up of basic military doctrine. What it does represent is a sharply honed military instrument which permits our tacticians to select their targets with precision and to bring out of the paramilitary arsenal whatever is needed to eliminate them. The tactics will vary with opportunity and necessity but the ultimate goal of eliminating the political base on which the Communist elite stand must be pursued with absolute tenacity, always accompanied with a barrage of propaganda enunciating that goal. And while the totalitarian bloc has its decisions placed in the hands of a few men, permitting them to respond quickly to an internal threat to their power, by relentless pressure and appeals to their subjects it is at least possible for us to widen the gulf between the Party structure and the people. The Communists themselves add to this possibility because they could increase their Party elite appreciably and broaden their base only at the risk of weakening Party discipline and facilitating infiltration by anti-Party elements.

Factional disputes within the Party are the rule rather than the exception, and one side or the other invariably is looking for adherents to bolster its bargaining position within the hierarchy. It is this constant state of jockeying, periodic purges and organizational changes that lend itself to the successful infiltration of Western-orientated and trained agents into the Party at important functional and policy making levels. One need only grasp the importance of the position held by Colonel Oleg Penkovskiy to consider what a really determined effort along this line might produce in the way of heightening disunity and suspicion among the Party elite once they know that we have taken the offensive in earnest. It is bound to increase the already intolerable control to which all Party members are subjected, to add to the enormous inefficiency of a government-planned economy, and lead eventually to a situation which can set into motion popular forces of rebellion.

What this means is that the United States must move its political and military operations out of the periphery of the Free World and into the periphery of its enemy behind the screen of unconventional forces—guerrillas, civic resistance movements, and propaganda warfare—and set them in motion in response to a set of strategic and tactical options available to it. Specifically, Cuba must be eradicated as a base of Communist subversion, with its vulnerability by reason of nearness to the United States, a huge coastline and the proved anti-Communist nature of Castro's opposition. The United States has the propaganda advantage in launching its own "war of liberation" in response to the many documented incidents of Cuban aggression against its neighbors in Latin America and the brazen attempts to subvert our own Negro population. The course of our propaganda warfare would by this time have made it perfectly clear that ours was a just cause.

Under this doctrine, small cadres recruited and trained from among the hundreds of thousands of Cuban exiles are to be introduced into the island to organize and give form to a resistance movement and a sophisticated approach to infiltrating Western sympathizers into Castro's organizations and institutions. More important, Castro's political base must be exploded so as to make Russia's Cuban military base untenable.

Enough internal pressure must be applied to force the Russians out of Cuba like a cork out of a bottle of vigorously shaken soda water. With Cuba's guerrilla training and supply bases denied to Latin subversives, one track of the Soviet Union's double-track policy will have been de-railed, forcing the Soviets either to identify with a now rootless guerrilla movement in Latin America or to disown them altogether and search for another means to recoup at a loss of valuable time and at enormous cost. In either instance, the Communist time table for erupting "50 Vietnams" in Latin America will first be set back and then destroyed by a political pursuit of the enemy. Obviously, it makes no sense to eradicate a Communist position of power in Cuba if we do not pre-empt Commu-nist attempts to gain power elsewhere in Latin America. And no area of our society must be exempt from participating in that pursuit—private overseas investments, U.S. aid programs, and even cultural and sports exchange—as the pre-emptive phase of the conflict becomes a part of the wider plan of anti-Communist strategy and tactics. And a people aroused in the United States to the external dangers to their institutions are not likely to tolerate for very long the depredations committed by indigenous enemies intent on erupting "50 Vietnams" here at home. Once we show the disposition to defend our own homes and the hemi-sphere in which we live from Communist attack, then we may expect the United States to be taken seriously in other parts of the world. A Cuba liberated from within would hardly go unnoticed by subjugated peoples elsewhere in the world and it is obvious that such an event could have no effect other than to strike fear in the hearts of our enemies from Moscow to Hanoi.

While the movement of our operations into the periphery of the enemy and the employment of unconventional means to achieve the initiative may not be viewed serenely by all political sectors in this country, few can deny that it is preferable to other harsher alternatives—massive destruction through conventional, nuclear war, or, as the situation now stands, slow retreat and surrender. And as seems only too clear as of this writing, the unique notion that we can win a "diplomatic war" of limited objectives in Vietnam must now be recognized as a complete failure. It has been necessary to commit over half a million U.S. military personnel to fight 10,000 miles away because our political leader have failed to grasp and use the tools available to them in meeting the Communist challenge where it will count—in their own cities and towns. Moreover, there is little appeal to the American people constantly to be told that the purpose of meeting the Communist challenge, always in the periph-ery of the Free World, is to force the enemy to the conference table. Americans have been to that conference table before—in Germany, Korea, Saigon and the Congo—only to find that it is a tactic which permits the enemy to strike again where he wishes and at a time of his choosing.

As for "losers" who counsel patience in the hope that the Communists will mellow and lose their revolutionary push, we reply that evil is tenacious and will not loose its grip on men without a struggle. To relieve the suffering, hopelessness and bloodshed under Communism is precisely a matter of utmost importance.

As historian and scholar Edward Gibbon wrote many years ago about the disintegration of the City State of Athens: "In the end, more than they wanted freedom, they wanted security. They wanted a comfortable life and they lost it all—security, comfort and freedom. When the Athenians finally wanted not to give to society, but for society to give to them, when freedom they wished most for was freedom from responsibility, then Athens ceased to be free and never was free again."

Footnotes

CHAPTER I

1. See Paul D. Bethel, "The Havana Conference," *The Reporter*, March 24, 1966, p. 25, and "Havana Manifesto," *Barron's*, March 21, 1966, p. 1.
2. U.S. Senate Internal Security Subcommittee (hereafter, USSISS): *Cuba as a Base for Subversion in America*, (Washington: U.S. Government Printing Office, 1963), p. 7.
3. *Diario las Americas*, October 31, 1965.
4. See "1965: Year of the Cuba-Vietnam Corollary," (Miami: *Free Cuba News*, January 8, 1965).
5. A complete translation of the Quechua Indian language broadcast from Moscow was carried in *The Vision Letter*, August 25, 1965.
6. For a listing of all the delegates to the Tricontinental Conference, the major resolutions to come out of the conference, and many other valuable materials, see USSISS, *The Tricontinental Conference of African, Asian, and Latin American Peoples*, (hereafter Tricontinental): (Washington: U.S. Government Printing Office; 1966).
7. Special Consultative Committee on Security, "The First Tricontinental Conference," *Another Threat to the Security of the Inter-American System*, (Washington: Pan American Union, April 2, 1966). See also, Report of the Special Committee, "The First Afro-Asian-Latin American Peoples' Solidarity Conference and its Projections," *New Instrument of Communist Intervention and Aggression*, (Washington: Pan American Union, November 28, 1966).

CHAPTER II

1. Leo Huberman and Paul Sweezy, *Cuba, Anatomy of a Revolution* (New York: Monthly Review Press, 1961) p. 57; Herbert Matthews, *The Cuban Story* (New York: George Braziller, 1961), pp. 92, 112.
2. Max Geltman, "The Decline of the Anti-Communist Left," *National Review*, January 24, 1967.
3. C. Wright Mills, *Listen Yankee* (New York: Ballantine Books, 1960) p. 27.
4. Matthews, *op. cit.*, p. 112.
5. *Memoria*, 1958-60 (Havana: *Banco Nacional de Cuba*, 1960) pp. 58-90.
6. See also, *Organizacion Regional Interamericana de Trabajadores*, "Quince Anos de Sindicalismo Libre Inter-Americano" (Mexico City, ORIT), 1963, pp. 18-25.
7. Cuban Economic Research Project, cited hereafter as CERP, "Labor Conditions in Communist Cuba," (University of Miami Press: 1963), pp. 93-94.
8. Much of the data on Cuba's labor laws come from CERP, chaps. III and IV. See also International Bank of Reconstruction and Development, cited hereafter as IBRD, *Report on Cuba* (Washington: U.S. Government Printing

Office, 1951), p. 365. See also, Moises Poblete Troncoso and Ben G. Burnett, *The Rise of the Latin American Labor Movement* (New York: Bookman Associates, 1960), pp. 107, 108.

9. CERP, p. 145.

10. Matthews, *op. cit.*, p. 112.

11. For example, Herbert Matthews writes (p. 114): "In revolutionary Cuba there are no color bars. The Chief of the Army, for instance, Juan Almeida (who was with Fidel when I went up the Sierra Maestra in February, 1957) is a Negro. There were no Negro high officers before under the Republic." Dr. Frank Tannenbaum is among the most knowledgeable and level-headed men in this country on Negro-White relations in Latin America. He writes in his book, *Ten Keys To Latin America* (New York: Knopf, 1963) p. 49, that too many Americans have the wrong view of race relations as they have developed in Latin America: "The question of segregation, so agonizing and so disturbing in our South, could never have arisen anywhere in Latin America."

12. *New York Times*, February 24, 1957.

13. Matthews, *op. cit.*, p. 61.

14. However, the avowed differences between Castro and the Cuban Communist Party (PSP) were tactical, not fundamental. On December 10, 1956, PSP President Juan Marinello wrote the Secretary General of the United Nations that Castro's 26th of July Movement was not connected with his Party. "Nevertheless," wrote Marinello, "though it [26th of July] fights with incorrect tactics, it is doing so for a laudable objective" [the overthrow of Batista] who, Marinello said, "is supported by the Government of the United States." Castro and the Communists had common enemies—Batista, *and* the United States. Certainly, this gratuitous letter from Marinello opened the door to future cooperation with Castro.

15. *New York Times*, February 24, 1957.

16. Theodore Draper, *Castro's Revolution* (New York; Praeger, 1962) p. 14.

CHAPTER III

1. Matthews, *op. cit.;* pp. 68, 69.

2. *Ibid*, p. 71.

3. *New York Times* Havana correspondent, R. Hart Phillips, writes about Castro's affiliation with gangsters in her book, *The Cuban Dilemma* New York: Obolensky, 1962) p. 17: "Persons who had been in the University with Castro said he belonged to one of the armed University gangs. Again and again I was told that he was connected with the killing of Manolo Castro. . . ."

4. As a *Times* correspondent in Havana for over two decades, Mrs. Phillips saw U.S. Ambassadors and their staffs come and go. She writes, (p. 22): "At the time of the revolution, one man laughingly asked me if I knew of the 'Castro cell' in the U.S. Embassy. It was no secret that several of the officials there favored the overthrow of Batista and the assumption of power by Castro." Yet, Matthews writes, (p. 20): "The last place to get the slightest inkling of what was happening had to be the American Embassy, whose Ambassador,

Arthur Gardner, was closely identified and very friendly with the dictator, President Fulgencio Batista."

5. Totally ignoring the background of State Department and Embassy sympathy with Fidel Castro during 1957 and 1958, Matthews writes, (p. 72): "Thanks to Smith and, I would say, clumsy work at the State Department, the United States started out in January, 1959, with an unnecessarily resentful and suspicious Cuban Government in power." He adds, (p. 86): "Three American military missions—Army, Navy, Air Force—went on instructing Cubans in arts that the Cubans used against their fellow Cubans."

6. *New York Times*, May 22, 1961.

7. Matthews also wrote of the kidnapping of U.S. and Canadian citizens by Castro, (p. 75): "This was typical of the romantic, youthful aura that surrounded the rebels in those months of struggle."

8. Draper, *op. cit.*, p. 35.

9. Matthews, *op. cit.*, pp. 123, 299.

10. Draper, *op. cit.*, p. 36.

11. Subcommittee to Investigate the Administration of the Internal Security Act and Other Internal Security Laws, Hearings, Part III, (cited hereafter as *Hearings*), *November 5, 1959*, p. 163.

12. Draper, *op. cit.*, p. 36.

13. Searching for a non-capitalist system that would please him, Matthews writes (pp. 108, 109): "It may be that a third road is beginning to open up (in Africa and Asia, as well as in the Western Hemisphere). In Latin America it might be hewed by the Brazil of Janio Quadros—not a free-enterprise, capitalistic system like ours, nor the totalitarian-socialistic type of the Soviet bloc, which Cuba is embracing. It would be socialistic in the sense of a very high degree of government planning and control. . . . Most important of all, it would be politically neutral and independent. It would be a social democratic (hence socialistic) welfare state with an exceptionally strong executive." It may be taken as a measure of Matthews' lack of political astuteness that almost as he wrote those lines President Janio Quadros resigned. His "exceptionally strong executive" machinery left behind an administration infiltrated by Communists and in the hands of pro-Communist Vice President Joao Goulart who, in April, 1964, was finally ousted by popular revulsion against a "welfare state" which had caused galloping inflation, and against the virtual Communist takeover of his regime.

14. *Hearings*, Part III, November 5, 1959, p. 164.

15. Earl E. T. Smith, *The Fourth Floor* (New York: Random House, 1962), p. 80.

CHAPTER IV

1. Phillips, *op. cit.*, p. 11.

2. *Hearings*, Part 10, September 2, 1960, p. 739. Pawley also said at the Senate hearings: "I was selected to go to Cuba to talk with Batista to see if I could convince him to capitulate, which I did. I spent three hours with him on the night of December 9. I was unsuccessful in my effort, but had Rubottom [Assistant Secretary of State for Latin American Affairs] permitted me to

say that 'What I am offering you has tacit approval, sufficient governmental backing,' I think Batista may have accepted it." (p. 739). Judging from Pawley's testimony, he did not mince words with the Cuban dictator, as, for example, in his telling Batista that "a caretaker government would be men who were enemies of his".

3. Smith, *op. cit.*, pp. 170-176.

4. *Ibid*, p. 202.

5. R. Hart Phillips notes that Herbert Matthews lauded Castro's promise to shun diplomatic relations with Communist nations (p. 13): "A *New York Times* editorial, written by Herbert Matthews in Havana, said that [U.S.] recognition was based on a solid foundation of the actions and pronouncements of the new regime.' The editorial went on to say that the Castro regime had 'pledged itself to honor all international obligations, to hold new elections within a maximum of two years, and to protect foreign property and investments.' Then it commented, 'Finally, refuting allegations of Communist infiltration, it proposes to shun diplomatic relations with Communist countries.' "

CHAPTER V

1. R. Hart Phillips obtained proof of the mass executions. She writes (p. 23) : "The Minister of the Interior, Luis Orlando Rodriguez, denied this mass execution, but it was undoubtedly true. Gene Carrier, my brother-in-law, who was a cameraman for NBC, flew to Santiago de Cuba and took pictures of the big grave."

2. Herbert Matthews, of course, accommodates Guevara's claims, writing, (p. 123): "The shadow of Guatemala hung over Cuba from the beginning," adding, (p. 125): "Fidel Castro and the others knew that elements in the United States would want to repeat the Guatemalan experience." In his several writings on Cuba, Samuel Shapiro goes along with the Matthews thesis.

3. Matthews, *op. cit.*, p. 119.

4. Castro's "History Will Absolve Me"—billed by most "losers" as a five-hour speech to the Santiago court—was written by him *following* sentence and while he was in jail. The court had no court reporter, so the text of what Castro said is the text that Castro wrote. While many of the points made in the document were included in his speech to the court, they were elaborated in the final text written by Castro while in jail, and issued as "History Will Absolve Me" by his 26th of July Movement.

5. *Congressional Record*, January 26, 1959, pp. 1152-55.

6. Samuel Shapiro writes in his book, *Invisible Latin America* (Boston: Beacon Press, 1963), pp. 79-80: "When I visited the city of Santa Clara in 1960, I was shown the marks of the bombardment by B-26 airplanes on December 28-31, 1958, and a bomb fragment marked with a handshake and the words: 'Mutual Defense, Made in U.S.A.' " His visit, made nearly two years following the alleged bombing, was undoubtedly a guided tour by what was by then a Cuban Communist government. Yet, he accepts the story of the bombing, and the exhibit of the bomb fragment, as completely credible.

7. Samuel Shapiro, "Cuba, a Dissenting Report," *The New Republic*, September 12, 1960, pp. 18, 19. He also writes of Cuba's publishers that they came to the United States with their ill-gotten gains. The fact is that the publisher and family of *Diario de la Marina* (the newspaper least liked by Shapiro) are in Miami, penniless, along with the equally penniless editors and publishers of *Prensa Libre, Informacion,* and other Cuban newspapers. He also writes of Cuba's editors and publishers, (p. 18): "Every one of them got away safely," adding the falsehood in his September 12, 1960, article, that the government had "only taken over one newspaper, *El Mundo,* "which, he also falsely asserts, "was owned by a Batista official." According to the Inter-American Press Association, at least ten Cuban editors, among them Alfredo Izaguirre of *El Crisol,* are rotting away in Castro's prisons. Undaunted, Shapiro insists, (pp. 18, 19): "For the first six months after Castro came to power, the Cuban press was freer than it had ever been. . . ."

CHAPTER VI

1. It was with considerable surprise that I read an article by Ambassador Bonsal, "Cuba, Castro and the United States," published in the January 1967 issue of *Foreign Affairs.* In it he gives the impression that Castro and he were on good terms. "In early 1959," writes Mr Bonsal, "I saw Castro a number of times and had contacts with all members of his cabinet." Mr. Bonsal's recollections of seeing Castro "a number of times" are sharply at odds with the recollections of his staff.

2. Rufo Lopez Fresquet writes in his book, *My Fourteen Months With Castro,* (Cleveland: The World Publishing Company, 1966): "When Castro finally told us that we were not to ask for aid, we were indeed surprised . . . I believe that it was never Castro's intention to ask for aid. If the U.S. had helped Cuba, he could never have presented the American as an enemy of the revolution." (p. 106).

3. For an account of the Castro-Betancourt meeting, see: Jay Mallin, *Fortress Cuba* (Chicago: Henry Regnery, 1965), pp. 73, 74.

4. For Vice President Richard Nixon's view of Castro early in 1959, see: "Cuba, Castro and John F. Kennedy," *Reader's Digest,* November, 1964.

5. Matthews, *op. cit.,* p. 179.

6. *Ibid,* p. 192.

7. U.S. Department of Agriculture, Economic Research Service, "Agriculture and Food Situation in Cuba," ERS-Foreign-28 (Washington, U.S. Government Printing Office, May, 1962) p. 12.

8. Tad Szulc and Karl E. Meyer, *The Cuban Invasion* (New York: Ballantine Books, 1962) p. 22.

9. Shapiro, *The New Republic,* September 12, 1960, p. 13.

CHAPTER VII

1. For Shapiro on the press, see chapter V, footnote 6.

2. Phillips, *op. cit.;* p. 84.

3. Daniel James, *Cuba, First Soviet Satellite in the Americas* (New York: Avon, 1961), pp. 157, 158.

4. Among the sensational revelations made by Diaz-Lanz before the Senate Subcommittee was his identification of several members of the Castro government as Communists—including Raúl Castro, "Che" Guevara, Vilma Espin de Castro, and Fidel Castro. Diaz Lanz accompanied Fidel Castro on his trip to Venezuela and testified that the Cuban dictator met for two hours with Venezuelan Communist leader Gustavo Machado. *Hearings, Part I,* July 14, 1959, pp. 7, 13.

5. See General Cabell's testimony, *Hearings,* Part III, November 5, 1959, p. 171. See also Mallin, pp. 32, 33.

6. When *Prensa Libre* was openly threatened with government seizure, Assistant Editor Humberto Medrano wrote its epitaph, describing the terror experienced by Cuba's free press, in a front page editorial: "We come before you to denounce an outrage, a crime against freedom and against democracy. Hidden forces, at the service of foreign masters, have joined with those who wish to destroy us and to take over the means of expression. They attack us because we think for ourselves, because we struggle against the sinister international conspiracy headed by Russia, directed against our land and against the solidarity of our continent. If this crime is perpetrated against us, against you, dear Cuba, let it be known that in each Cuban home, in each Cuban heart, that we have sacrificed everything—our property, our personal security, and the security of our children—because we have not chosen to submit to those who wish to replace the lone star flag with the red flag."

CHAPTER VIII

1. John Martino, *I was Castro's Prisoner* (New York; Deven Adair, 1963), pp. 89 *passim.*

2. Huberman and Sweezy, *op. cit.,* p. 79.

3. Under the Defense Pact of Rio de Janeiro, signed in 1947, the members of the American republics organization are pledged to "a common defense" if the "political independence of any American state" is threatened by an outside power. There also was the Bogota Resolution of 1948 (which Fidel Castro and Latin American Communists tried to sabotage) in which Latin American republics "condemn the action of international Communism or any other totalitarian doctrine."

4. Ambassador Bonsal did call on President Osvaldo Dorticos on October 27 where he dropped off what amounted to a press release. Headed merely "Ambassador Bonsal's Call on the President of Cuba," the "release" did not take direct and firm issue with Castro's lies. Bonsal, said the release, "expressed serious concern," and the U.S. government's "preoccupation" over *"what seemed"* (italics added) to be "efforts to replace good will with hostility." The burden of the note was a virtual apology for the over-flight of Diaz Lanz, and a promise that the United States would be more vigilant in patrolling airfields in the United States to prevent "incidents of this kind, which it deeply deplores." The "release" did, of course, deny any official connection with the Diaz Lanz pamphlet drop.

5. Draper takes Matthews sharply to task for saying in *The Cuban Story* (p.

155): "By the logic of the Revolution, Hubert Matos was a traitor." Draper wrote in reply in his book, (p. 192): "I gasped when I read those words," adding: "There can be only one answer. He [Matos] was a 'traitor' to the Communist 'Revolution'." Draper also neatly scores Matthews for rationalizing Castro's replacement of National Bank President Felipe Pazos with Communist "Che" Guevara.

6. James, *op. cit.*, p. 167.

CHAPTER IX

1. The January 22, 1960, editorial in *Revolucion* attacking Ambassador Bonsal, reads, in part "The Prime Minister had to make clear to the people the distorted imputations made by Artime who was helped by the Embassy of Spain, and afterwards by the American Embassy and its Diaz-Lanz followers. And who was at Franco's Embassy offering moral support to Lojendio? None other than Philip W. Bonsal, Ambassador of the so-called democratic republic of the United States! What a perfect alliance! Bonsal, Lojendio, the war criminals, the apostates, the thieves! What a distorted democracy! What an enslaved free world! What a monstrosity!"

2. Jose M. Illan, *Cuba, An Economy in Ruins* (Miami: Editorial AIP, 1964), p. 121.

3. Matthews, *op. cit.*, pp. 246-247, 250, 251.

4. This, indeed, happened. Mobile unit operators of the Embassy's USIS staff were under powerful intimidation from Castro's militia and paid government informers. In March, 1960, two USIS film operators on mobile units touring Camaguey and Pinar del Rio Provinces were pulled off their trucks by militia and cultural pamphlets they were transporting were burned. One operator was so intimidated that, following one harassing meeting with a squad of militia, he abandoned his truck in the middle of the road, telephoned his resignation to the Embassy, and told the duty officer where the truck could be located.

CHAPTER X

1. Professor Samuel Shapiro finds the stationing of FBI officers in Cuba highly suspicious. He also finds the "admittedly muzzled Cuba press" much more "accurate" than the free press of this country. He writes: "When, for example, the Cuban Government expelled two American embassy officials on the charge they were FBI agents, our papers ridiculed this as a typical propaganda fabrication. But 10 days afterward, in a front-page story in the *New York Times*, an anonymous State Department official admitted that the Cubans had been telling the truth. The men *were* FBI agents." Then Shapiro adds, suspiciously: "What they were doing was not disclosed." ("Castro and His Critics," *The New Republic*, December 5, 1960.) It is no secret that our embassies around the world have FBI personnel. And their assignment is known to, and sanctioned by, the host country, for the simple reason that they work with the police of that country. In fact, their offices have the seal of the FBI prominently displayed on the doors. I may have been the "anony-

mous State Department official" referred to by Shapiro, since I gave a full background briefing to U.S. reporters in Havana regarding the frame-up of Friedeman and Sweet. They were not expelled on the charge that they were FBI agents, as Shapiro has it, but on the false charge that they had been consorting with counterrevolutionaries. Communist propaganda made quite a to-do about their status as FBI officers, a line eagerly swallowed by Shapiro.

2. *New York Times*, July 10, 1960.

3. Draper, *op. cit.*, p. 102.

4. See Manuel Braña, *El Aparato* (Coral Gables: Service Offset Printers, 1964) pp. 411, 412, and *Hearings*, "Documentation of Communist Penetration in Latin America," Part I, October 2, 1963.

5. Draper, *op. cit.*, p. 102.

6. *Ibid.*, p. 95.

7. *Ibid.*, p. 77.

8. Victor Lasky, *JKF–The Man and the Myth* (New Rochelle: Arlington House, 1965), p. 447.

CHAPTER XI

1. Lasky, *op. cit.*, p. 454.

2. President Kubitchek's speech was made in favor of vast new economic plans for Latin America. Nevertheless, coupled with the address by President Eisenhower, the total picture of combatting Communism in Latin America which came out of that conference was one of economic advance plus military action.

3. Haynes Johnson, *The Bay of Pigs* (New York: Dell, 1964), p. 54.

4. Szulc and Meyer also wrote: "The Revolutionary Council suffered from the incurable defect of being an artificial creation which threw together representatives of the new generation and aging stalwarts of the old democratic movement in Cuba who were honorable but ineffective men." p. 107.

5. President Kennedy's statement that no American forces were to be used has appeared in most writings on the Bay of Pigs—for example, Szulc and Meyer, pp. 100, 113-114; Johnson, pp. 68, 71; also at Presidential press conference held on April 12, 1961.

6. See Mario Lazo, "Decision for Disaster: At Last—The Truth About The Bay of Pigs," *Reader's Digest*, September, 1964, p. 244; *New York Herald Tribune*, April 23, 1961; see also Lasky, *op. cit.*, pp. 526-529.

7. Szulc and Meyer, *op. cit.*, pp. 103, 104.

8. Theodore Sorensen, *Kennedy* (New York: Harper & Rowe, 1965), p. 338; Johnson, p. 67.

9. This was the second disaster to overcome the "landing party." Only a few days earlier, some of its members had been injured during training exercises at the Guantanamo Navy Base.

10. To make certain that no U.S. help would be forthcoming, a Presidential order to the Pentagon war room decreed that no member of the Joint Chiefs of staff could communicate with U.S. forces in the Caribbean unless all members were present and agreed to the communication.

11. See "The Real Story of the Bay of Pigs," *U.S. News & World Report*, January 7, 1963 p. 40.

12. Presidential aide Theodore Sorensen was personally outraged at U.S. attempts to oust the Communist regime of Fidel Castro. Perhaps this was because he was, according to Victor Lasky, a pacifist. Writes Lasky, (p. 164): "Apparently the pacifist sentiments expressed at home influenced Ted Sorensen to register with the Nebraska draft board as a conscientious objector available to noncombatant military service only." See also, Sorensen, *op. cit.*, p. 337.

13. See Lasky, *op. cit.*, pp. 527-528; see also editorial "Udall et. al.," *Baltimore Sun*, April 26, 1961.

14. Lasky, *op. cit.*, p. 526.

15. See Elie Abel, *The Missile Crisis* (New York: Lippincott, 1966), p. 158.

16. Walter Lippmann, "Post Mortem on Cuba," *New York Herald Tribune*, May 2, 1961.

17. Bobby Kennedy told reporter Paul Martin that some advisers had told the President to stop reading the newspaper, to stop being influenced by the opinions of columnists, and to do what he thought was right. Bobby said: "That would be the ideal solution, but newspapers are important in influencing public opinion." Lasky, p. 536-537.

18. Szulc and Meyer, *op. cit.*, p. 103. Sorensen also writes, (p. 332): "With heavy misgivings, (President Kennedy) . . . gave the go-ahead."

19. Sorensen quotes President Kennedy, (p. 346): "How could I have been so far off base? All my life I've known better than to depend on the experts. How could I have been so stupid, to let them go ahead?"

CHAPTER XII

1. *Palm Beach Post*, August 5, 1961.

2. Nixon on Kennedy, *The Reader's Digest*, November, 1964.

3. *Miami Herald*, May 7, 1961.

4. *Palm Beach Post*, July 16, 1961.

5. *Ibid.*

6. Keyes Beech & Clarence W. Hall, "Formosa: Asia's Heartening Success Story," *The Reader's Digest*, Februa,y 1966.

7. *Palm Beach Post*, May 21, 1961.

8. *Ibid.*, July 23, 1961

9. *Ibid.*, August 3, 1961.

10. *Palm Beach Post-Times*, July 4, 1961.

11. Statistics given the author by Dr. Felix Reiler, Vice President of the Pan American Bank of Miami. See also, Dr. Bernardo Benes, *Hearings*, Part 17, March 7 and 8, 1967, pp. 1192-1199.

12. *New York Times*, August 15, 1961.

13. Arthur Schlesinger, Jr., *The Vital Center, The Politics of Freedom*, (Cambridge: Riverside Press, 1962), p. 182.

14. Walter Trohan's article in the *Chicago Tribune*, February 4, 1962.

15. Nixon on Kennedy, *op. cit.*
16. Lasky, *JFK*, pp. 524-5.
17. *Ibid.*, p. 571.
18. *Ibid.*, p. 572.
19. Elie Abel, *The Missile Crisis* (New York: Lippincott, 1966), p. 38.

CHAPTER XIII

1. Told to the author by Dr. Emilio Núñez Portuondo on March 7, 1967, when we both testified before the Senate Subcommittee on Internal Security.
2. Theodore C. Sorensen, *Kennedy* (New York: Harper and Row, 1965), p. 673.
3. *Ibid.*, p. 675.
4. Elie Abel, *The Missile Crisis* (New York: Lippincott, 1966), p. 64.
5. Sorensen, *op. cit.*, p. 776.
6. Abel, *op. cit.*, p. 191.
7. Sorensen, *op. cit.*, p. 754.
8. Abel, *op. cit.*, p. 88.
9. Sorensen, *op. cit.*, pp. 784-785.
10. Abel, *op. cit.*, p. 120.
11. *New York Times*, October 23, 1962.
12. *New York Herald Tribune*, October 25, 1962.
13. *Bohemia* (Havana, Cuba), p. 45.
14. For full text of letter, see Abel, *op. cit.*, p. 203.
15. *Ibid.*, p. 207.
16. Sorensen, *op. cit.*, p. 807.
17. *Washington Post*, February 7, 1963.
18. From *The Penkovskiy Papers* by Oleg Penkovskiy, translated by Peter Deryabin, (New York: Doubleday, 1965), pp. 331-332.
19. *Ibid.*, p. 327.
20. *Ibid.*, p. 328.
21. *Ibid.*, p. 321.
22. All of these passages on the Castro-U Thant talks were printed in the November 9, 1962, issue of Castro's *Bohemia* magazine, pp. 30-39.
23. Abel, *op. cit.*, p. 211.
24. *Ibid.*, p. 212.
25. Sorensen, *op. cit.*, p. 811.
26. *Bohemia*, November 9, 1962, pp. 64-65.
27. *Ibid.*, p. 39.
28. The complete text of Castro's spirited defense of the Soviet Union may be found on pages 39-40 of the November 9, 1962, issue of *Bohemia*.
29. David Wise and Thomas B. Ross, *The Invisible Government* (New York: Random House, 1964), p. 292.

30. Sorensen, *op. cit.*, pp. 760-761.
31. Lee Lockwood, *Castro's Cuba, Cuba's Fidel* (New York: McMillan, 1967), p. 204.
32. Penkovskiy, *op. cit.*, p. 216.

CHAPTER XIV

1. *Miami News*, March 19, 1963.
2. *Ibid.*
3. *New York Times*, April 20, 1963.
4. Pan American Union, "Human Rights Commission of the OAS—Report on the Situation of Political Prisoners and their Relatives in Cuba," Document 4 (English), Washington, D.C., May 17, 1963, p. 46.
5. Sorensen, *Kennedy*, p. 835.
6. "Terror and Resistance in Communist Cuba," (Washington: Citizens Committee For A Free Cuba, 1964), p. 17.

CHAPTER XV

1. Havana, *Radio Progreso*, April 1 and 2, 1964.
2. David Wise and Thomas B. Ross, *The Invisible Government* (New York: Random House, 1964), p. 300.
3. *El Tiempo*, January 26, 1967.
4. *Granma*, August 25, 1966.
5. "The Cuban Report," (Miami: Cuban Revolutionary Student Directorate, DRE, 1963), June 7, 1963.
6. *The Congressional Record—House*, March 16, 1966, p. 5787.
7. *St. Louis Globe Democrat*, January 24, 1966.
8. Phillip Abbott Luce, *Road to Revolution* (San Diego: Viewpoint Books, 1967), p. 10.
9. Romulo Betancourt, "Betancourt On Castro," *The Reporter*, August 13, 1964, p. 10.
10. *Ibid.*, p. 39
11. *Ibid.*, p. 40.

CHAPTER XVI

1. *Miami Herald*, July 19, 1963.
2. *New York Times*, June 2, 1963.
3. *Miami Herald*, May 27, 1963.
4. *United Press International*, June 1, 1963.
5. *New York Times*, July 17, 1963.
6. *Hearings*, December 9 and 16, 1965 (Washington: U.S. Government Printing Office: 1965), p. 29.

7. Tad Szulc, *Dominican Diary*, (New York: Dell, 1966), p. 25.

8. *Washington Post*, October 26, 1963.

9. *Baltimore Sun*, September 25, 1963.

10. *Herald Tribune*, October 22, 1963.

11. *Ibid.*

12. *Ibid.*

13. *New York Times*, September 26, 1963.

14. *Ibid.*, September 29, 1963.

15. Radio Havana, September 28, 1963. See also, *Washington Post*, September 29, 1963.

16. *Washington Post*, October 2, 1963.

17. *Ibid.*, October 30, 1963.

18. *Washington Daily News*, October 30, 1963.

19. Drew Pearson, "Washington Merry-Go-Round," *The Washington Post*, October 8, 1963. See also, *Washington Post*, October 2, 1963.

20. *Herald Tribune*, October 22, 1963.

21. *New York Times*, October 13, 1963.

22. *Washington Daily News*, October 15, 1963.

23. *Ibid.*

24. A long article on the Bosch-Roche articles may be found in the *Christian Science Monitor*, October 16, 1963.

25. *United Press International*, November 1, 1963. An AP story published in the *Baltimore Sun* the same day does not mention U.S. involvement in the coup.

26. Radio Santo Domingo, November 21, 1963.

27. Szulc, *op. cit.*, p. 73. (see ftn. 7).

28. Theodore Draper, "The Dominican Crisis," *Commentary*, December, 1965, p. 36.

29. *Ibid.*, p. 37.

30. *Ibid.*, p. 38.

31. *Ibid.*, p. 38.

32. Szulc, *op. cit.*, p. 21.

33. Theodore Draper, "A Case of Defamation," *The New Republic*, February 26, 1966, p. 16.

34. Paul D. Bethel, "The Dominican Republic Goes to the Polls," *The Reporter*, June 2, 1966, p. 19.

35. Szulc, *op. cit.*, p. 80.

36. Draper, *commentary*, p. 38.

37. *Ibid.*, p. 54.

38. *Ibid.*, pp. 54-55.

39. *Ibid.*, p. 38.

40. *Ibid.*, p. 40.

41. *Ibid.*, p. 43.

42. *Ibid.*, p. 44.

43. *Ibid.*, p. 44.
44. *The Congressional Record—Senate*, August 23, 1965, p. 20505.
45. *Ibid.*
46. Szulc, *op. cit.*, pp. 54-55.
47. Draper, *Commentary*, p. 40.
48. *Ibid.*, p. 41.
49. *Ibid.*, p. 33.
50. *Ibid.*, p. 40.
51. Szulc, *op. cit.*, p. 100.
52. *Ibid.*, p. 122.
53. *Ibid.*, p. 55.
54. Draper, *Commentary*, p. 36.
55. *Ibid.*, p. 35.
56. *New York Times*, May 7, 1963.
57. *Miami Herald*, May 5, 1963.
58. The minutes of the July 8, 1965 meeting were given to the author by a Special Services officer. That this document is authentic has been proven by events which have subsequently taken place.
59. Paul D. Bethel, *The Reporter*, June 2, 1966, p. 18.
60. Juan Bosch, *"El Pentagonismo—Sustituto del Imperialismo,"* *Publicaciones Ahora*, Santo Domingo: November 24, 1967, p. 19.

CHAPTER XVII

1. Paul D. Bethel, "The Havana Conference," *The Reporter*, March 24, 1966, p. 26.
2. *Miami News*, July 5, 1967.
3. Pan American Union, "Report On The First Afro-Asian-Latin American Peoples' Solidarity Conference and its Projections," Volume II (English), November 28, 1966, p. 293.
4. Paul D. Bethel, "New Havana Meeting Spells Trouble For U.S.," *Human Events*, July 22, 1967, p. 457. Also, see Radio Caracol, Bogota, September 1, 1966.
5. *Miami Herald*, October 26, 1967.
6. Radio Moscow, October 25, 1967. The radio carried the full text of the Gioldi article, and it was reprinted in "Daily Report," *Foreign Broadcast Information Service*, p. BB-6, October 30, 1967.
7. Luis Corvalan, "Alliance of anti-imperialist forces in Latin America," *World Marxist Review*, July, 1967, p. 45.
8. Mario Soza, "Honduras," *World Marxist Review*, September 1967, p. 44.
9. Gustavo Corvalan, "Paraguayan Communists Prepare for Congress," *World Marxist Review*, September 1967, p. 75.
10. Francisco Mieres, "Lessons of October and Contemporary Revolutionary Movement in Latin America," *World Marxist Review*, November 1967, p. 80.

11. Regis Debray, *Revolución En La Revolución?* (Havana: Casa de las Americas, 1967), p. 99.
12. *Diario las Americas,* October 25, 1967.
13. *Miami Herald,* September 27, 1967.
14. "Decree-Law No. 444 of March 22, 1967," Unofficial Translation by the First National City Bank, Bogota, p. 36.
15. *El Tiempo,* August 2, 1967.
16. "Decree Number 1366," (translated by Alvaro Lopez and Eric W. Shaw), July 20, 1967, p. 30.
17. *Loc. cit.*
18. *El Telegrafo,* August 30, 1967.
19. *El Comercio,* September 26, 1967.
20. *Diario las Americas,* August 24, 1967.
21. *Clarin,* September 19, 1967.
22. *La Voz de Chile,* Santiago, March 12, 1964.
23. *Ibid.,* March 19, 1964.
24. Radio Havana, March 19, 1964.
25. Radio Emisoras Nuevo Mundo, Santiago, April 8, 1964.
26. *La Voz de Chile,* Santiago, April 27, 1964, and Radio Presidente Balmacedo, Santiago, April 27, 1964.
27. *Emisoras Nuevo Mundo,* Santiago, July 8, 1964.
28. *Washington Star,* September 27, 1964.
29. *Washington Post,* June 28, 1964.
30. *Miami Herald,* September 11, 1964.
31. *Washington Star,* November 12, 1964.
32. *Diario las Americas,* March 13, 1965.
33. *Diaro Las Americas,* April 15, 1965.
34. *La Tercera de la Hora,* Santiago, March 27, 1965.
35. *Diario las Americas,* June 13, 1965.
36. *Ibid.,* April 26, 1965.
37. *Latin American Times,* July 2, 1965.
38. *Diario las Americas,* June 13, 1965.
39. *Ibid.,* June 24, 1965.
40. *Latin American Times,* October 7, 1965.
41. Radio Havana, September 9, 1966.
42. *Diario las Americas,* June 13, 1967.
43. *Ibid.,* May 17, 1967.
44. *Ibid.,* July 12, 1967.
45. *Excelsior,* Mexico City, July 16, 1967.
46. Radio Santiago Chile, September 1, 1967
47. *The Times-Picayune,* April 18, 1968.

CHAPTER XVIII

1. *Miami Herald*, January 17, 1968.
2. *Ibid.*
3. *Latin America Report*, Volume 3, Number 22, December 8, 1965.
4. Subcommittee to Investigate the Administration of the Internal Security Act, of the Committee on the Judiciary of the United States Senate, "The Tricontinental Conference of African, Asian, And Latin American Peoples" (U.S. Government Printing Office, Washington, D.C., 1966), p. 29.
5. *New York Times*, January 26, 1967.
6. Pan American Union, "Report On The First Afro-Asian-Latin American Peoples' Solidarity Conference and Its Projections," Volume II (English), November 28, 1966. p. 194.
7. *New York Times*, August 3, 1967
8. *Ibid.*, September 1, 1967.
9. Pan American Union, *"Comision Especial de Consulta Sobre Seguridad,"* 1967, p. 223.
10. *Miami Herald*, December 6, 1967.
11. *Long Island Press*, July 7, 1967.
12. *Op. cit.*, Pan American Union, p. 237.
13. *Ibid.*, p. 238.
14. *San Juan Star*, October 3, 1967.
15. *Ibid.*, *Diario las Americas*, September 16, 1967.
16. *Ibid.*
17. *Ibid.*
18. *El Mundo*, January 24, 1968.
19. O'Meara, "No Man is Above the Law," *American Bar Journal*, December 1967, pp. 1107-1110.
20. *Miami News*, August 29, 1967.
21. *New York Times*, August 28, 1967.
22. *Diario las Americas*, August 24, 1967.
23. *U.S. News & World Report*, August 14, 1967, p. 24.
24. *U.S. News & World Report*, August 14, 1967, p. 23.
25. *Ibid.*
26. *New York Times*, September 19, 1967.
27. *U.S. News & World Report*, p. 27.
28. *Ibid.*, pp. 64-65.
29. *Washington Post, January 11, 1968.*
30. *Tricontinental Information Bulletin*, Volume No. 4, August, 1967.
31. *Miami Herald*, January 19, 1968.
32. "Survey of the Alliance for Progress, Insurgency in Latin America," Subcommittee on American Republics Affairs of the Committee on Foreign Relations, United States Senate, (U.S. Government Printing Office, Washington, D.C., 1968) p. 5.
33. *Diario las Americas*, March 24, 1966.

Index